MATLAB®

AND

ITS APPLICATIONS IN ENGINEERING

[Based on MATLAB 8.4 (R2014b)]

Second Edition

MATLAB®

AND

ITS APPLICATIONS IN ENGINEERING

[Based on MATLAB 8.4 (R2014b)]

Second Edition

Raj Kumar Bansal
Dean Research
Guru Kashi University
Talwandi Sabo, Bathinda, Punjab

Ashok Kumar Goel
Professor and Head
Training and Placement
Giani Zail Singh Punjab Technical University Campus
Bathinda, Punjab

Manoj Kumar Sharma
Associate Professor and Coordinator
Electrical and Electronics Engineering Department
University Institute of Engineering and Technology (UIET)
Panjab University, Chandigarh

Pearson

Associate Editor—Acquisitions: Neha Goomer
Editor—Production: M. Balakrishnan

ISBN 978-93-325-4209-9

First Impression, 2016
Eighth Impression, 2022
Ninth Impression, 2024

Published by Pearson India Education Services Pvt. Ltd, CIN: U72200TN2005PTC057128.

Head Office: 1st Floor, Berger Tower, Plot No. C-001A/2, Sector 16B, Noida - 201 301, Uttar Pradesh, India.
Registered Office: Featherlite, 'The Address' 5th Floor, Survey No 203/10B, 200 Ft MMRD Road, Zamin Pallavaram, Chennai – 600 044.

Website: in.pearson.com; Email: companysecretary.india@pearson.com
Compositor: SRS Technologies, Puducherry.
Printed in India at: Saurabh Printers Pvt. Ltd.

Dedicated to
our beloved Parents
and
family members

Brief Contents

Contents

4 Polynomials

7 Control Structures

8 Writing Programs and Functions

9 Ordinary Differential Equations and Symbolic Mathematics

10 Simulink® Basics

11 MATLAB Applications in Control Systems-I

12 MATLAB Applications in Control Systems-II

13 MATLAB Applications in Neural Networks

16 MATLAB Applications in Computational Mathematics

Preface to the Second Edition

Based on the encouragement and widespread response from teachers and students to the first edition of this book, we have thoroughly revised and updated the second. All possible efforts have been made to increase the usefulness of the book.

The book gives an overview of MATLAB from the scratch. Even a novice in the software can become proficient in using this software after going through this book. Our aim is to make learning MATLAB a pleasant experience.

MATLAB is used as a standard tool in various introductory and advanced courses of almost all streams of study for analysis, modeling, simulation, prototyping, data analysis and for high productivity research and development activities.

This book attempts to train students of different streams to use the functions and toolboxes of MATLAB and SIMULINK for the study, design and analysis of these systems.

Many changes have taken place in the industry since the first edition of this book. The second edition is based on the latest version of MATLAB, that is, R2014b, and it includes the required material which reflects these changes.

In this revised edition, a new chapter on 'MATLAB Applications in Computational Mathematics' has been added in view of the fact that these applications are very important for the students of different disciplines of engineering, education, economics, management, basic sciences, social sciences, etc., in addition to several additions/modifications in other chapters.

The other highlights of this revised edition are:

(i) The feedbacks received from different sources have been incorporated.

(ii) The subject contents have been refined and restructured at several points.

(iii) Several new examples have been added for the benefit of students.

(iv) Every page of the book has been read very carefully so as to improve its quality.

(v) In revising the edition, efforts have been made to retain a student-friendly style in writing as in the original edition.

(vi) The chapters have been presented in clear, understandable and well-organized manner.

Even a fraction of success achieved in meeting the goal will make all the pains taken to revise the book worthwhile.

We firmly believe that there is always scope for improvement, and accordingly we shall look forward to receiving constructive criticism and suggestions, for further improvement in the quality of the book.

Any suggestion and comment about the book from the faculty, students, research scholars and practicing engineers will be highly appreciated. Please contact us at Raj Kumar Bansal: bansalrajk2009@gmail.com, Ashok Kumar Goel: ashokkgoel@rediffmail.com and Manoj Kumar Sharma: mks_uiet@pu.ac.in.

ACKNOWLEDGEMENTS

Firstly, we are thankful to the Almighty for providing us the strength and intellect to develop this piece of knowledge. We are grateful to all faculty members, students and research scholars who have helped us directly or indirectly in preparing this revised edition of the book. Thanks are due to the unknown reviewers who have given their valuable suggestions for improving the book.

The technical help received from Book Program Team of The MathsWork Inc. is gratefully acknowledged. We would like to thank Pearson Education and its executives for providing us professional support in developing this book.

Last but not the least, patience and understanding shown by our family members in the process of developing this book is thankfully acknowledged.

Raj Kumar Bansal
Ashok Kumar Goel
Manoj Kumar Sharma

Preface to the First Edition

Education is a progressive discovery of our ignorance.

—Will Durant (1885–1981), US author and historian

MATLAB® is a software package which is being used by the scientific and engineering community all over the world. This is one of the most versatile and user-friendly software useful for solving large and complex problems. This book presents a comprehensive account of MATLAB basics and its implementation in design and analysis of systems in engineering and research. It is written as a text book as well as a reference book for theory and laboratory course for undergraduate and graduate engineering students and practising engineers. The book has been written by the authors based on their long teaching and research experience.

In this book, the topics are presented in simple language. Each topic is explained in brief so that the reader does not loose interest. At the same time, care is taken that the important concepts are not missed out. The solution of various problems has been explained in a lucid manner. A vast collection of MATLAB command statements and programs are included to illustrate the implementation of the theoretical concepts.

This book has a total of 15 chapters and is divided into two parts. The first nine chapters of the book are devoted to the MATLAB basics, which are very useful for those who are not conversant with it. The basic chapters on MATLAB are covered with elaborate illustrations to make it comprehensive and useful for readers interested in MATLAB fundamentals. It also contains a chapter on Simulink® basics. The last five chapters cover applications of MATLAB in fields like control systems, artificial neural networks, fuzzy logic and digital signal processing. Their implementation using MATLAB is illustrated with example programs.

In addition to these, this book contains two appendices covering graphic user interface and LTI Viewer. The chapter-wise detail of the book is as follows:

Chapter 1 relates to the introduction of MATLAB. It provides a detailed insight of MATLAB environment, illustrating its different features—starting and closing MATLAB sessions, taking help, setting path, etc.

Chapter 2 elaborates the basic features of MATLAB as a programming language. It discusses different types of MATLAB constants, variables, expressions, built-in functions and simple programs. The handling of complex numbers, complex variables and trigonometric functions has also been described.

Chapter 3 describes MATLAB operations on vectors and matrices. The basic building block of MATLAB is an array or matrix. This chapter illustrates the different mathematical operations carried out on vectors and matrices, generation of special matrices, reshaping of matrices and some useful commands related to matrices. Handling of structures and cell arrays has been explained.

Chapter 4 relates to handling of polynomials in MATLAB. It discusses the various mathematical operations performed on polynomials, polynomial evaluation, roots of a polynomial, characteristic equation, curve fitting and evaluation of polynomials with matrix arguments.

Chapter 5 illustrates the different methods of data input and output in MATLAB. The different types of data, data formats and file input–output; loading and saving files have been discussed. It also covers details of interactive input commands, low-level input–output functions and binary input–output.

Chapter 6 describes two-dimensional and three-dimensional graphics commands available in MATLAB. This chapter includes basic 2-D graphics commands in MATLAB to plot different types of graphs using different colours, line styles and markers. Specialized 2-D and 3-D graphics have also been discussed. It also explains drawing sub-plots and multiple plots on the same graph.

Chapter 7 relates to the basic program control structures, i.e., loops and branches and their implementation in MATLAB. It covers `for` and `while` loops, `if` structures, and other control statements such as `switch`, `break`, `continue`, and `try` and `catch`. Use of these control structures has been illustrated through several example programs.

Chapter 8 explains how a user can build MATLAB function sub-programs. The procedure for writing of different types of function sub-programs and how they can be referred to in other programs has been explained in this chapter. Use of MATLAB Editor and Debugger has also been explained in detail. This chapter also includes function workspaces, function handles and handling of errors.

Chapter 9 explains the use of MATLAB for the solving a set of simultaneous ordinary differential equations. The creation of symbolic mathematics functions, variables, expressions, basic calculus operations using symbolic mathematics along with simplification of functions has also been explained.

Chapter 10 provides the basics of Simulink®, a user-friendly graphical interactive tool for modelling, simulation and analysis of engineering systems. The detailed procedure for development of Simulink model of a system prototype, its simulation and visualization of results has been explained. Concepts of data import/export, handling of state space models, non-linear systems, creation of subsystems and their masking procedure have also been described.

Chapters 11 and **12** deal with MATLAB applications in control systems. Chapter 11 deals with the basic mathematical tools such as laplace transform, inverse laplace transform and partial fractions. The representation of dynamic systems in transfer function and state space form using MATLAB has been described. Time domain analysis of dynamic systems using standard input signals and MATLAB commands to obtain step response, ramp response and impulse response of a control system have been discussed. Response to arbitrary input has also been discussed. Steady-state errors, their calculation, stability evaluation of control systems using Routh-Hurwitz criteria have been explained.

Chapter 12 describes MATLAB commands and functions related to root locus plots, gain of the system at any given point on the root locus, Frequency response curves of dynamic systems, i.e., Bode plots, Polar plots and Nyquist plots, Nichols chart, etc. Commands for obtaining stability specifications such as gain margin and phase margin have also been included.

Chapter 13 covers the MATLAB applications in neural networks. It describes the basic concepts related to Artificial Neural Networks (ANNs) and their implementation in MATLAB. ANN architecture, learning, applications using Multiplayer Perceptron (MLP) have been explained with the help of an example. The MATLAB Graphical User Interface (GUI) tool for designing ANN systems has also been described in detail. An industrial process example is simulated and its ANN controller is designed to illustrate MATLAB applications. Radial basis function networks and self-organizing feature maps are also described.

Chapter 14 covers the MATLAB applications in fuzzy logic systems. Concepts of fuzzy logic, i.e., linguistic variables, membership functions, fuzzy inference system, have been described. Building fuzzy logic-based systems using GUI are explained with the help of an illustrative example. Its implementation using command line statements has also been described.

Chapter 15 covers the concepts of digital signal processing using MATLAB. This chapter covers representation of basic discrete–time signals, their operations and the different transform techniques. The designing of different types of filters and observing their response using MATLAB commands is discussed. The use of Filter Design and Analysis Tool (FDA Tool) and Filter Visualization Tool (FV Tool) of Signal Processing Toolbox™ has been elaborated in designing and viewing the response of the digital filters.

This book contains 300 solved examples to illustrate the implementation of various MATLAB statements/functions so that the reader may have a good understanding of the subject matter. A number of unsolved practice problems are given at the end of each chapter to enable the reader to have in-depth understanding of concepts. The solutions to these problems are given in the solution manual of the book available at the Web site link mentioned below:

www. pearsoned.co.in/rkbansal.

Suggestions and comments about the book from faculty, students, research scholars and practicing engineers will be highly appreciated. Please contact us at Raj Kumar Bansal rk.bansal@chitkara.edu.in, Ashok Kumar Goel ashokkgoel@rediffmail.com, and Manoj Kumar Sharma mks_uiet@pu.ac.in.

Raj Kumar Bansal
Ashok Kumar Goel
Manoj Kumar Sharma

About the Authors

Raj Kumar Bansal is presently dean research, Guru Kashi University, Talwandi Sabo, Bathinda, Punjab. He was principal of Chitkara Institute of Engineering and Technology and a senior professor at several institutes of repute, like Punjab Agricultural University Ludhiana, Chhotu Ram State College of Engineering, Murthal, GZSCET, Bathinda. He received his Ph.D. from the Indian Institute of Technology, Kanpur, and his teaching and research experience spans more than four decades. His research interests include power systems, control systems, optimization techniques, fuzzy logic systems and neural networks. He is a life member/fellow of professional bodies like Institution of Engineers (India), ISTE, SSI. He has published more than 50 research papers in national/international journals of repute. He is also guiding several Ph.D. students.

Ashok Kumar Goel is professor and head, Training and Placement at Giani Zail Singh Punjab Technical University Campus, Bathinda. He is also entrusted with the office of director, College Development of Maharaja Ranjit Singh State Technical University established by the Government of Punjab having more than 120 technical colleges affiliated to it. He is also the chairman of the institute's accreditation committee and coordinates the maintenance of quality standards and procedures for the institute. Prior to this assignment, he has served as director of Maharishi Markandeshwar University, Maharaja Agresen University and a number of institutions from 2007 to 2014. He holds a Ph.D. from Thapar University and has 30 years of teaching and research experience. He has many research papers and a patent published to his credit. His innovative methodology of teaching inculcates respect for social ethics and national values in the students. His strong commitment to quality in education builds the foundation of students and prepares them to excel in their career.

Manoj Kumar Sharma is associate professor and coordinator of Electrical and Electronics Engineering Department at University Institute of Engineering and Technology (UIET), Panjab University, Chandigarh, India, since 2011. He completed his graduation and postgraduation in electrical engineering of Punjab Technical University, Jalandhar, India. He has more than one and half decade of experience in teaching and research. He has published many research papers in national and international conferences and journals. He has filed a patent for electronics preferential voting machine. He has been granted research projects by different funding agencies (like UGC, DST) in the field of active noise control and renewable energy resources. He is a member of professional bodies including IEEE, ISTE. His interest includes neural networks, fuzzy logic, active noise control and renewable energy technologies.

About the Authors

CHAPTER 1

Introduction to MATLAB®

LEARNING OBJECTIVES

- Starting and ending a MATLAB® session.
- Learn about the major components of MATLAB environment.
  - Command Window
  - Command History
  - Workspace
  - Current Directory
  - Edit Window
  - Figure Window
- Learn to use help browser and `help` command.
- Know about different types of files used in MATLAB.
- Know the various platforms where MATLAB can be used.
- Find out how the search path of files/programs is defined.
- Some useful general commands such as `ver, editpath, whos, clc, lookfor,` etc.

1.1 INTRODUCTION

MATLAB developed by The MathWorks Inc., stands for Matrix Laboratory. It is a software package used to perform scientific computations and visualization. Its capability for analysis of various scientific problems, flexibility and powerful graphics makes it a very useful software package. It provides an integrated development environment for programming with numerous predefined functions for technical computations and visualization. In addition to available built-in functions, user-defined functions can also be included which can be used just like any other built-in function.

Figure 1.1 shows various products of The MathWorks Inc. MATLAB provides an excellent computational language, built-in state-of-the-art algorithms for mathematics and excellent visualization using ready-made functions. The features and programming constructs commonly available in a general purpose language such as C or C++ are also available in MATLAB. Built-in functions for matrix operations such as computation of singular value decomposition, Cholesky factorization, LU factorization, specialized math functions such as Airy functions, Bessel functions, beta function, gamma function, data analysis, Laplace transforms, Fourier transforms, interpolation, polynomials and ordinary differential equation solvers are included for saving the precious programming time of the user. For visualization, large collections of function programs are included for two- and three-dimensional graphics. MATLAB also contains functions for

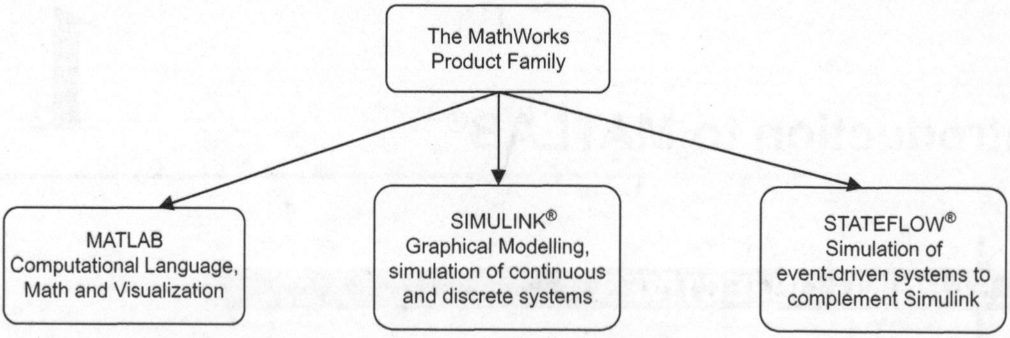

Figure 1.1 Various Products of the MathWorks Inc

specialized graphs including lighting and shading. A separate section of sub-programs is included to provide graphical user interface (GUI) tools and Handle Graphics®.

It provides collections of functions that act as tools for specific applications such as control system design, power systems, digital signal processing, neural networks, communications and image processing. Such collections of programs are called 'Toolboxes'. In MATLAB R2014a, there are more than 60 toolboxes available for a variety of special applications. The toolboxes are optional and can be purchased as per user's requirement.

MATLAB includes C and C++ Math libraries that support the development of stand-alone applications. It provides an external interface to run FORTRAN, C and C++ programs from within MATLAB programs. It also acts as the foundation for powerful simulation software such as Simulink® and Stateflow®. Moreover, more than 125 third-party software products and services have interface with MATLAB.

As the name MATLAB comes from the two words 'MAT', which stands for Matrix, and 'LAB', which stands for Laboratory, MATLAB is Matrix Laboratory, thereby implying that it deals in matrices. Hence, the basic building block in MATLAB is matrix. The basic data type, matrix, is defined as an array. The vectors, scalars, etc. are all automatically handled as matrices. The scalars are treated as a matrix (array) of a single row and single column. A single-row matrix and a single-column matrix are treated as row vector and column vector, respectively. To make things simpler for the programmer, it is not required to declare the dimensions of a matrix. There is also no need to declare any variables and their types. Variables can be simply used in the program anywhere one desires. MATLAB automatically sets the type of the variable according to the type of value assigned to that variable.

1.2 STARTING AND ENDING A MATLAB SESSION

Once the MATLAB is properly installed on the PC, it can be started in two ways, i.e., through the options in Start menu or using shortcut on the desktop of the PC. To start a MATLAB session through the Start menu, the following steps are taken:

1. Click on the 'Start' button of the PC desktop.
2. Select the option 'All Programs'. This displays some more options.
3. Select the option 'MATLAB' from the displayed options. There is a list of options displayed.
4. Click on the option 'R2014a' from these options.

MATLAB R2014a logo, a shortcut at the PC desktop, can be used to start a MATLAB session by double-clicking it. For PC using Windows8 operating system, the MATLAB session can be started by clicking on the MATLAB widget.

The MATLAB default desktop is displayed as shown in Figure 1.2.

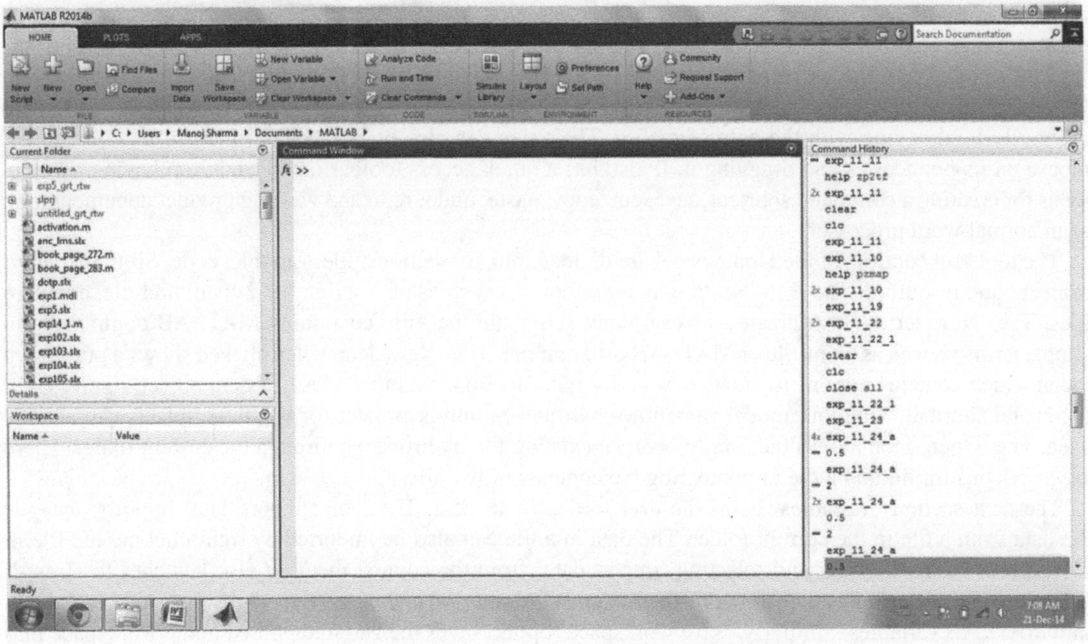

Figure 1.2 The MATLAB Default Desktop

To end the MATLAB session, click on MATLAB standard icon on the left top corner. A number of options are displayed. Click on 'close' to end the MATLAB session. Alternatively, press Alt+F4 to close the MATLAB window. The 'x' on the right top corner can also be clicked to close the MATLAB window and end the session. Another way is to type 'exit' or 'quit' at the command prompt in the command window to end or quit the MATLAB session.

> **Programming Tip 1.1:** It is possible to run a particular function such as saving the workspace or running a script/program each time the MATLAB session is started or closed.

> **Programming Tip 1.2:** It is also possible to start MATLAB by double-clicking on any MATLAB-generated file, that is, .m, .mat, .mdl or .fig file. MATLAB starts and opens the concerning tool/window depending on the type of file invoked by the user.

1.3 MATLAB ENVIRONMENT

The MATLAB desktop is shown in Figure 1.2. By default, MATLAB desktop is divided into four core components for carrying out different operations in MATLAB: the Command Window, the Workspace Browser, the Current Folder Browser and the Command History. The user can interact with MATLAB desktop using the controls in the toolstrip. The toolstrip controls are grouped into three 'Panels', denoted as Home, Plots and Apps. It contains various options or choices for carrying out various basic operations in MATLAB such as opening/closing various kinds of files, variables, importing or exporting data, variables, managing plots/

figures or various applications available. The toolstrip controls for each panel appear in the upper part of the window having light-grey background. The desktop can be configured differently by the user using the 'layout' option from the environment section of the Home panel. In this, the user can select the different windows that are desired to be displayed as part of the MATLAB desktop. The windows can be rearranged arbitrarily by dragging with the help of mouse. Their size can also be reduced or enlarged by clicking the mouse on its boundaries and dragging it. It also has a quick access toolbar on the right top having shortcut icons for creating a command shortcut, save, cut, copy, paste, undo, redo and viewing product documentation as in normal word processor.

The toolstrip controls of the Home panel are divided into six sections: file, variable, code, Simulink, environment and resources. The 'File' section includes options such as new script, new, open, find file, compare files. The 'New script' icon creates a fresh blank script file, i.e., file containing MATLAB commands, in simple terms viewed as an m-file or MATLAB program file. The 'New' icon when clicked shows a pull-down menu which contains options to create new script file, function, example, class, system object, figure, GUI, command shortcut, Simulink model, stateflow chart and Simulink project for which templates can also be used. The 'Open' icon allows the user to open an existing file by browsing through the current folder. There are also icons for finding a file or comparing the contents of two files.

The next section 'Variables' helps the user to deal with data. The icon 'import data' imports or reads the data from a file in the current folder. The data in a file can also be imported by right-clicking the file in the Current Folder browser and selecting 'import data' from the context menu. It also launches the Import Wizard, which determines the format of the file and shows a preview of the data and suggested breakdown into MATLAB variables. Similarly, 'save workspace' option saves the variables stored in the workspace into a file in the current folder. By default, the name of the file storing the workspace variables is 'matlab.mat'. The icon 'new variable' allows the user to open a new variable. It opens a new window named 'Variable' which can be better addressed as Variable Editor as it allows the user to view and edit the contents of the variables stored in the MATLAB workspace. It contains options of defining the dimensions of the new variable, creating a new variable from existing variables by editing it, taking its transpose, sorting it or even printing it. A separate variable editor window is displayed above the command window which shows the values of its elements which can be altered or added as desired by the user. The variable editor window is shown in Figure 1.3. The new variable created is untitled or un-named. Its new name can be given by right-clicking its name in the workspace window and selecting the rename option. The option 'open variable' allows the user to open an existing variable and edit it. The 'clear workspace' option clears the workspace memory from all variables stored in the workspace or all variables, functions and breakpoints stored in memory.

The next section in the Home panel is 'code'. This contains three options. First option is 'Analyse Code'. It helps the user analyse MATLAB code files in current folder for coding inefficiencies and potential bugs. The next icon is 'Run & Time'. It allows the user to run the code and measure execution time to improve the performance of the code. The next section pertains to Simulink and helps the user to open the Simulink library for designing the relevant Simulink block diagram. 'Environment' is the next section in the 'Home' panel. The 'layout' option in the 'Environment' panel allows the user to configure the layout of the MATLAB screen. The different windows can be configured and saved so that it may not be required to be configured repeatedly. It also has option 'preferences'. Clicking this option creates a fresh window which permits the user to modify the environment of MATLAB by specifying the preferences with respect to keyboard, fonts, colour, various windows and toolbars, editor, mat-files, analyser, various toolboxes and Simulink, etc. The 'Preferences' window is shown in Figure 1.4. All options and choices in Preferences window cannot be shown or discussed as their number is very large. Therefore, it is left to the reader to access MATLAB and scan through the preferences window.

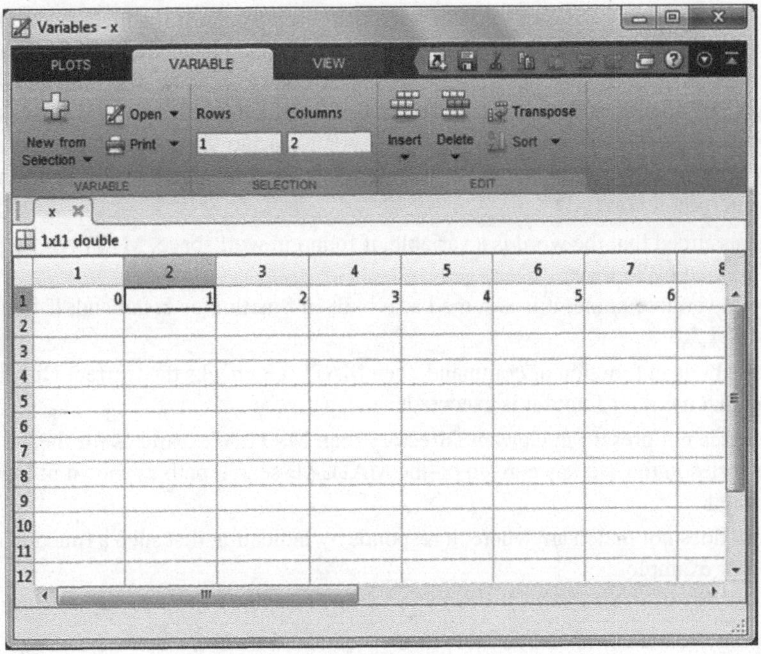

Figure 1.3 The Variable Editor Window

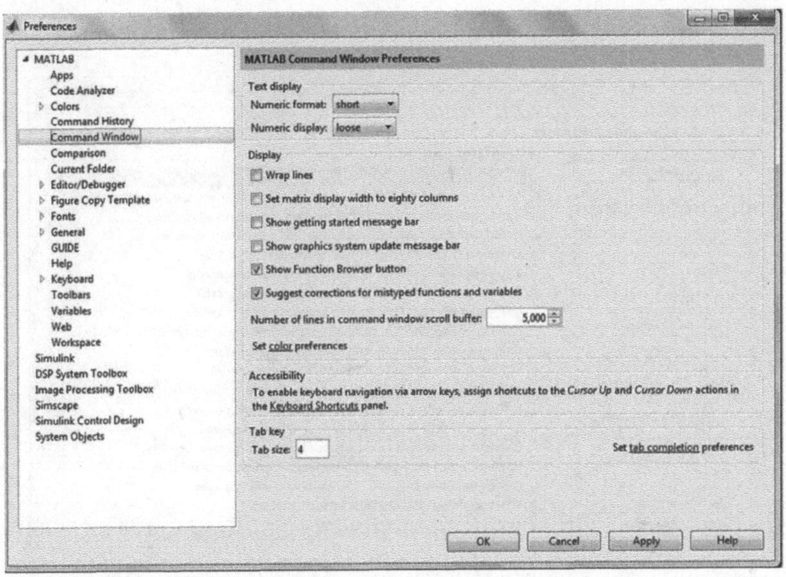

Figure 1.4 The Preferences Window

The 'Set Path' option allows the user to specify the path used by the software to search the files required for execution of any command or script, etc. Whenever any command is entered at the command prompt or a script file is executed, MATLAB searches for the appropriate code to execute the command. Many directories or folders in MATLAB contain code for various functions contained in different Toolboxes and more folders may be added by the user. The 'set path' guides MATLAB to locate the appropriate program for executing the command. Whenever a 'word' is entered at the command prompt, the MATLAB follows the following steps in order to interpret it correctly:

1. First, it is assumed that the word is a variable, if found in workspace, MATLAB displays its contents in the Command Window.
2. If it is not a variable name, it is assumed as a built-in function or command, if found, it is executed by the MATLAB.
3. If it is not a built-in function or command, then MATLAB checks the Current Directory if there is an M-file by that name. If found it is executed.
4. Finally, if it is not present in Current Directory then MATLAB searches for the M-file in all folders and directories in the sequence given on the MATLAB search path as shown in Figure 1.5. If found it is executed.
5. If the word does not match anywhere, it responds by indicating that such a function or variable is not defined. For example,

   ```
   mstep
   ```

   The response to the command/variable `mstep` obtained is shown below:

   ```
   ??? Undefined function or variable 'mstep'.
   ```

As MATLAB searches first for a variable name and then searches for functions or M-files, so a function or an M-file with the same name as a variable name is not recommended.

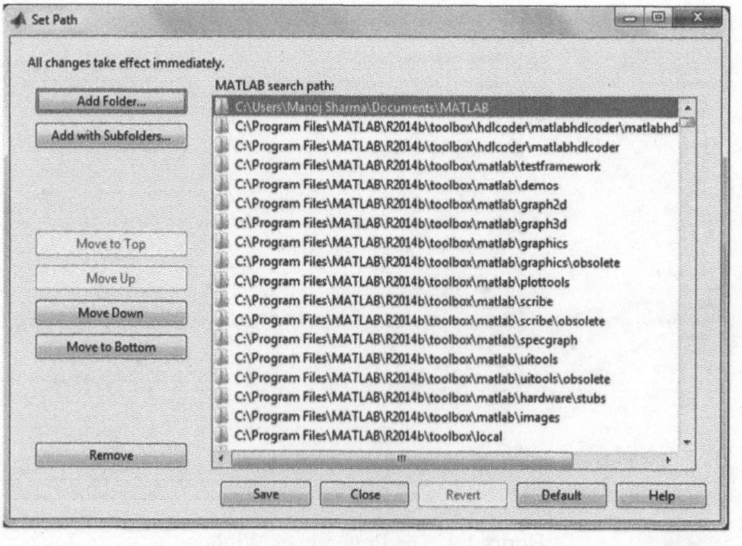

Figure 1.5 The Set Path Window

> **Programming Tip 1.3:** It is always advisable to use different names for variables, functions and files.

Sometimes, a file being executed is not present in the Current Directory and will generate an error message:

filename.m not found

This is a common problem for the beginners.

Whenever any new file is created and saved, it is saved in the default 'MATLAB' folder in the 'My Documents' folder of the user contained in 'C:/users/username' folder. It can also be stored in any other desired folder by the user. However, to execute any file, at least one of the following steps has to be followed:

- The folder, containing the file to be executed, must be the Current Directory.
- The folder can also be added to the 'search path'. The MATLAB search path can be examined and modified by selecting the 'Set Path' from the Home panel toolstrip Menu. In the Set Path Window folder, in which desired file is stored, is added.

The Set Path Window is shown in Figure 1.5. It allows a user to add, delete or change the order in which the 'search path' for an M-file is defined. If it is desired to add the selected directory and all of its subdirectories, click Add with subfolders option in the Set Path Window.

Some more path-related commands are as follows:

`addpath`	Adds directory to MATLAB search path
`path`	Displays MATLAB search path

To execute a script file, it must be included in Current Directory or search path of MATLAB.

> **Programming Tip 1.4:** To execute a script file, it must be included in Current Directory or search path of MATLAB.

The next 'Parallel' option is for using distributed computing server clusters, etc.

The last section in the 'Home' panel is 'Resources'. The '?' icon and the help option opens a help window where the user can browse through and seek help about the topic required. The help option also gives a pull-down menu where the user can seek help for MATLAB documentation, or examples, request support, access support website, seek details of terms of use, licensing, etc. The help window generated for searching documentation is shown in Figure 1.6. The next option in this section is 'Community'. Clicking it connects the user to the MATLAB community using the web. The internet site 'MATLAB Central' is opened which contains facilities for file exchange, newsgroups, blogs and interaction regarding problems faced and questions asked by the MATLAB community. The web page generated is shown in Figure 1.7. The next icon is for requesting support. The last icon 'Add-ons' facilitates the user to get more applications, updates and hardware support packages from The Mathworks Inc.

The 'PLOTS' panel allows the user to select the variables for plotting and then plot different kinds of plots using the data variable selected. The plots that can be drawn are simple plot, bar chart, area plot, pie chart, histogram, contour plot, surface, mesh plot, semi-log plot, multiple *y*-axis plots, etc. It also has option to reuse existing figure window for obtaining multiple curves on the same plot. The user can plot multiple data sets on the same figure window either overlaid on a single set of axes or by dividing the figure window into multiple axes. The variable(s) to be plotted have to first select in the Workspace browser. Then, the type of plot to be drawn is selected from the plot panel. It opens a separate figure window with the selected variable is plotted as chosen from the plot panel. The user can further format the plot obtained so that the information desired is highlighted as desired by making use of plot tools. The last icon in the toolstrip of the figure window can be clicked to activate the plotting tools in the figure window. A plot drawn with the plot tools is shown in Figure 1.8.

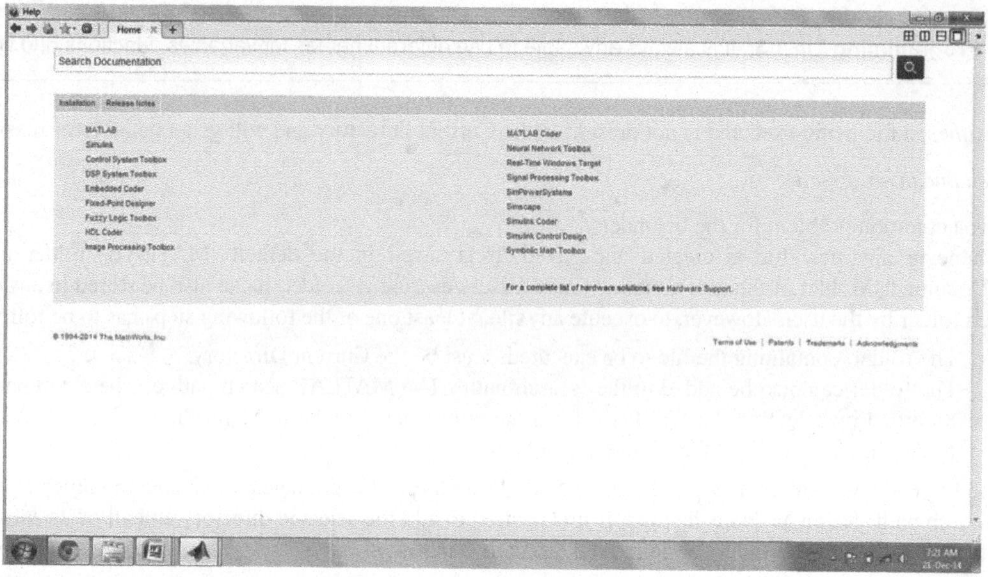

Figure 1.6 The Help Window for Searching MATLAB Documentation

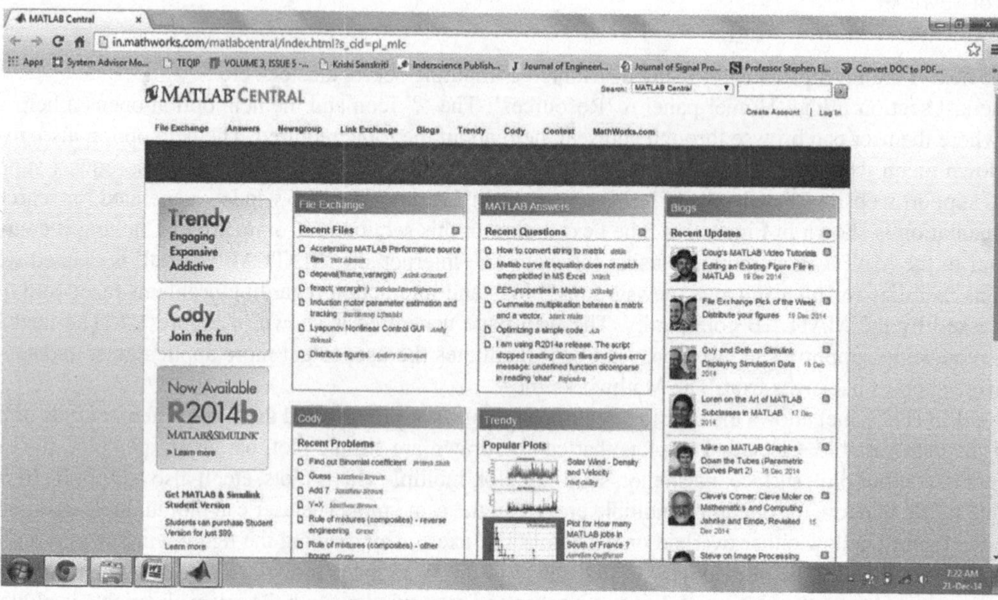

Figure 1.7 The Web Page Generated after Clicking 'Community' Icon

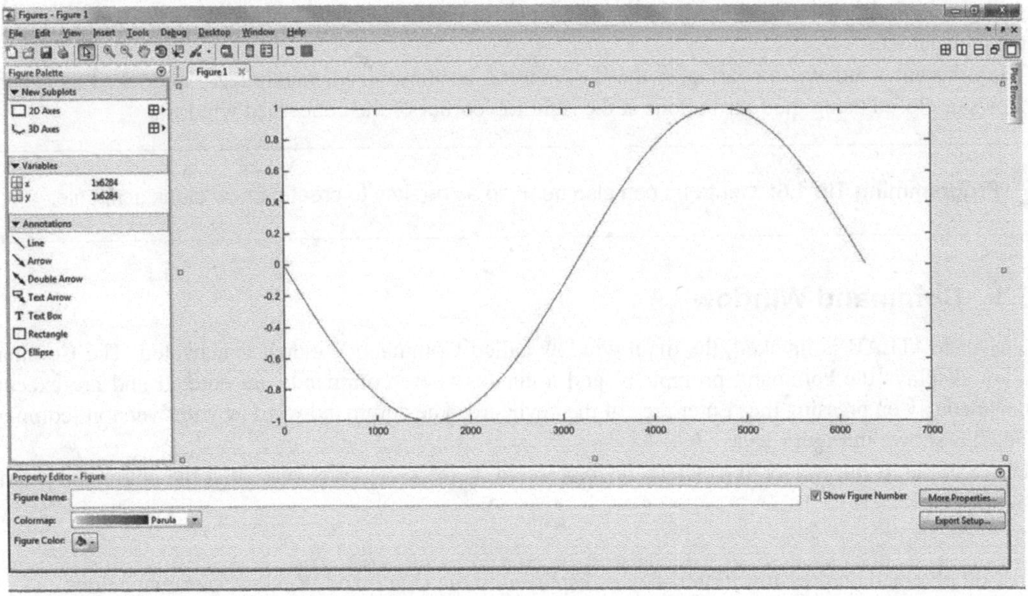

Figure 1.8 A Figure Window with Plot Tools

The part of the figure window on the left of the figure allows the user to add axes to create subplots within the figure window. In other words, the portion of figure window used to plot the figure is split into multiple plot windows, 2×1, 1×2, 2×2, 3×2, etc. as desired by the user. It also allows the user to drag and drop variables from the workspace into the axes of the plots. Further, the user can also add a variety of annotations like line, arrow, text arrow or a text box, to the plot. The plot browser is given on the right part of the figure window. It allows the user to edit the axis and the plot. The concerned property editor appears at the bottom of the window where the user can edit names of the axis, their scale, their colour, background colour, title, etc., i.e., a complete list of low-level graphic properties of the plot. The other icons in the toolstrip of the figure window help the user in zooming in/out a portion of the plot, pan along the axis of a plot, rotate a plot, add legend, use cursor to display individual data values, etc. The user can also basic fitting tool from the tool menu of the figure window to apply MATLAB functions for polynomial fitting. The Basic Fitting tool allows the user to fit polynomials of degree ≤ 10. The user can save coefficients of polynomial fits to the workspace. To add further, the user can make use of the 'save as' option by selecting 'file' from the menu bar and save the figure as binary figure (.fig) or to a graphical format suitable for other applications such as .jpg or .png or .bmp or .eps, etc.

Programming Tip 1.5: The number of Figure windows generated depends upon the system memory.

The 'APPS' panel displays the different applications of MATLAB available. The 'Get More Apps' icon results in opening the Mathworks website's discovery page where various Matlab applications are available and can be obtained using Matlab File Exchange facility. The 'install app' icon helps in installing these applications. The 'Package App' icon can be used to pack the files into an application package. The rest of the icons show various applications installed and available for use of the user. These can be invoked by clicking on the relevant icon.

The different windows appearing in the desktop can be minimized, maximized, undocked as separate windows or closed using the four buttons at the right top corner of the concerned window.

> **Programming Tip 1.6:** Control-n can also be used as hot-key to create a new blank script file.

1.3.1 Command Window

Whenever MATLAB is invoked, the main window called Command Window is activated. The Command Window displays the command prompt '»' and a cursor where commands are entered and are executed instantaneously on pressing the 'Enter' key of the keyboard. The command window with 'version' command executed is shown in Figure 1.9a.

For example, if one wants to evaluate the expression `(20*3-5)`, it is entered at the command prompt, as shown below:

```
20*3-5
```

The result obtained on pressing 'Enter' key is displayed in the Command Window as shown below:

```
ans =
          55
```

The result of the expression had not been assigned to any variable. Therefore, MATLAB stores the result in a default variable, `'ans'`. The same expression can be evaluated again by assigning the result to a variable '*x*', as given below:

```
x = 20*3-5
```

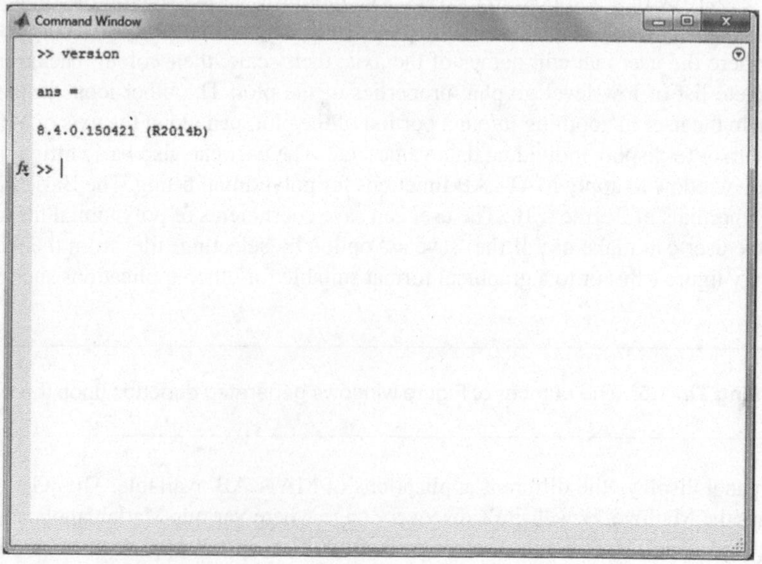

Figure 1.9a The Undocked Command Window

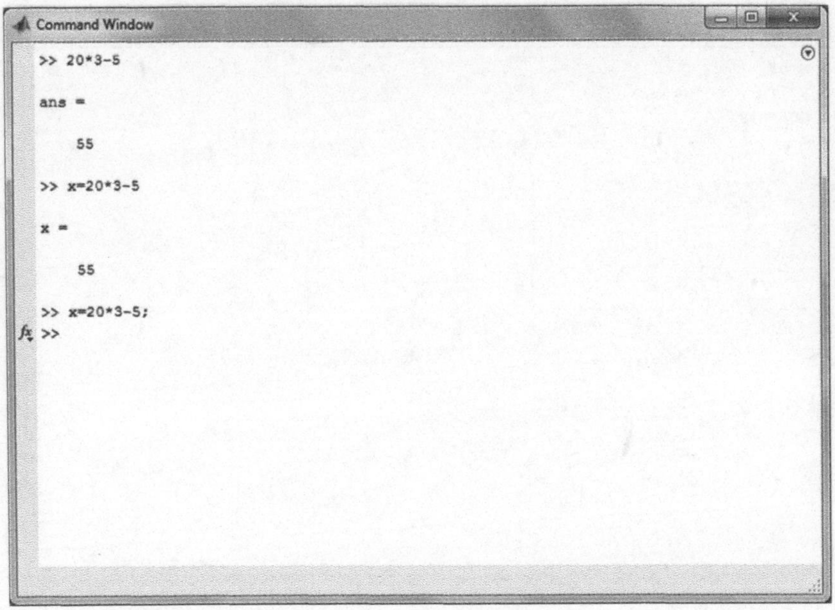

Figure 1.9b Command Window Showing Values as per Example 1.1

The result obtained in the Command Window is as shown below:

```
x =

    55
```

The output display indicates that the result is now stored in the variable 'x'. If the output of a statement is not needed to be displayed, the statement is terminated with a ';' (semicolon). For example,

```
x = 20*3-5;
```

On execution of this statement, no output is displayed in the Command Window and the result is stored in variable x.

The above-mentioned commands and the corresponding results displayed are shown in Figure 1.9b. Similarly, other commands can be run by typing them in the Command Window.

> **Programming Tip 1.7:** If the result of the MATLAB expression is not assigned to any variable, then it is stored in default variable `ans`.

Example 1.1 Find the value of z for the expression $z = 2x + y$, if $x = 5$ and $y = 7$.

Solution: The following statements are entered in the Command Window:

```
x = 5;
y = 7;
z = 2*x + y;
```

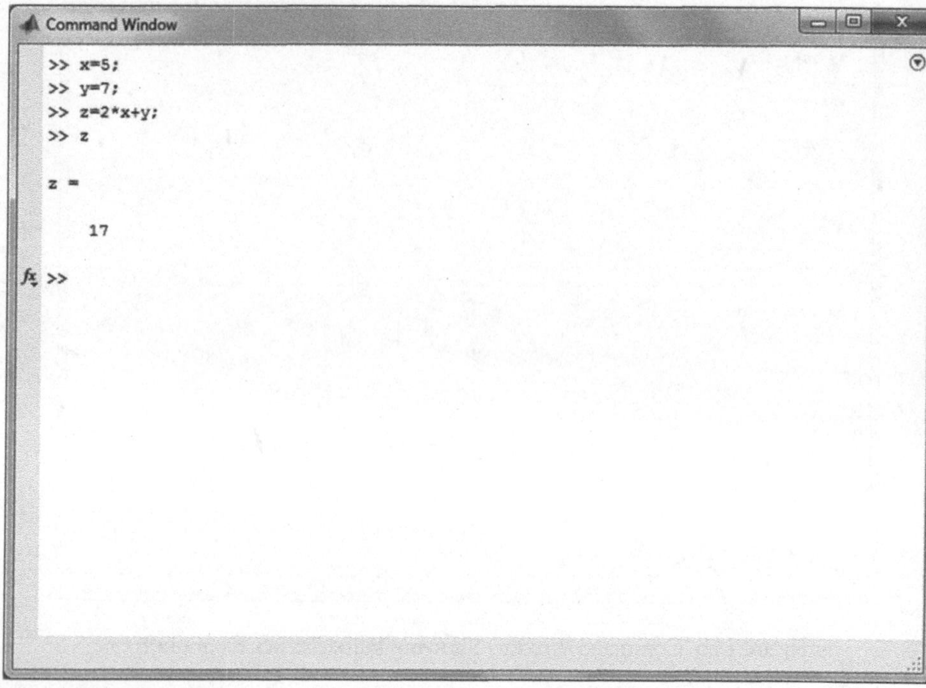

Figure 1.9c Command Window Showing Values as per Example 1.1

To display the result, type the name of variable z in the Command Window and press 'Enter' key. These commands and the result displayed are shown in Figure 1.9c.

1.3.2 Command History Window

The Command History Window consists of a list of all the commands that are entered in the Command Window. It consists of commands of previous sessions also. These commands remain in the list until they are deleted. Any command may be executed by selecting and double-clicking it with the mouse. A program file (script file) may be created by selecting a set of commands and right-clicking the mouse. On right-clicking the mouse, pop-up menu is displayed. A program file containing the selected commands can be created by choosing the 'Create script' option from the menu. Similarly, commands may be deleted by selecting the commands and right-clicking the mouse and selecting 'Delete Selection' from the pop-up menu. The Command History Window with the pop-up menu is shown in Figure 1.10.

1.3.3 Workspace

A workspace is a collection of all the variables that have been generated so far in the current MATLAB session and shows their data type and size. All the commands executed from Command Window and all the script files executed from the Command Window share common workspace, so they can share all the variables. With these variables, a number of operations can be done, such as plotting by selecting a variable and right-clicking the mouse and selecting the desired option from the pop-up menu. For example, the variables x and y can be declared as shown below:

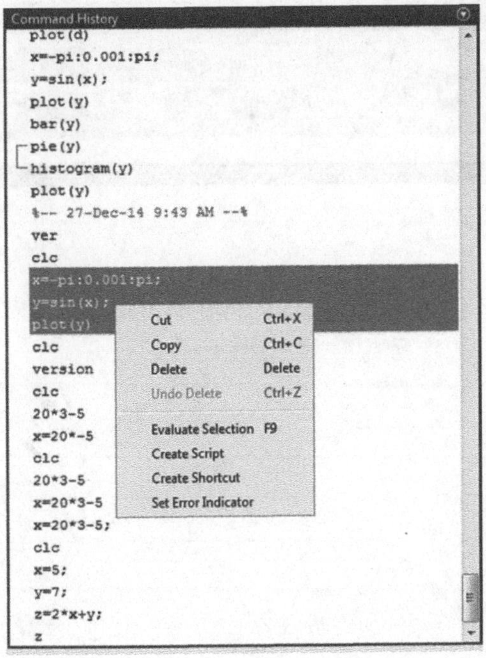

Figure 1.10 Pop-up Menu of Command History Window

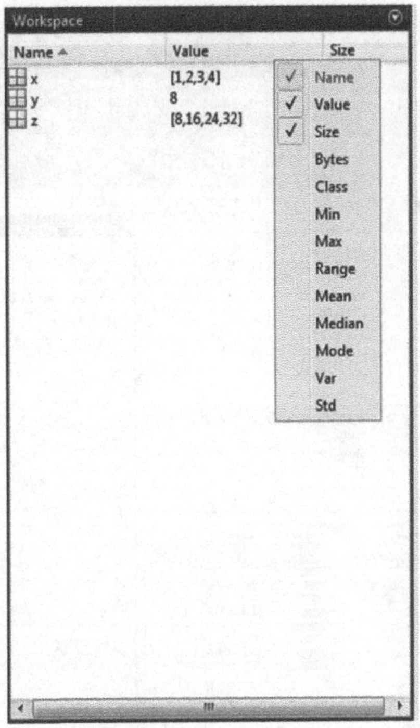

Figure 1.11 The Workspace Window with Pop up Menu

```
x = [1 2 3 4];
y = 8;
```

Compute z as shown below:

```
z = x * y;
```

The Workspace Window will contain the variables x, y and z and their details as shown in Figure 1.11. The detail of each variable that is displayed in the workspace window can be configured by right clicking on the workspace window and select 'choose columns' option from the pop-up menu. The columns that can be displayed for each variable are name, value, size, bytes, class, min, max, range, mean, median, mode, var and std. 'Var' and 'std' stand for 'variance' and 'standard deviation', respectively.

The workspace information can also be obtained by typing commands at the command prompt. The `who` command will generate list of variables currently in the workspace.

```
who
```

The response is as given below:

```
Your variables are:
x y z
```

The 'whos' command generates a list of variables currently in the workspace with their size (dimensions), number of bytes and class/type of variable. It also reports the total number of bytes used and the number of elements in the arrays.

```
whos
```

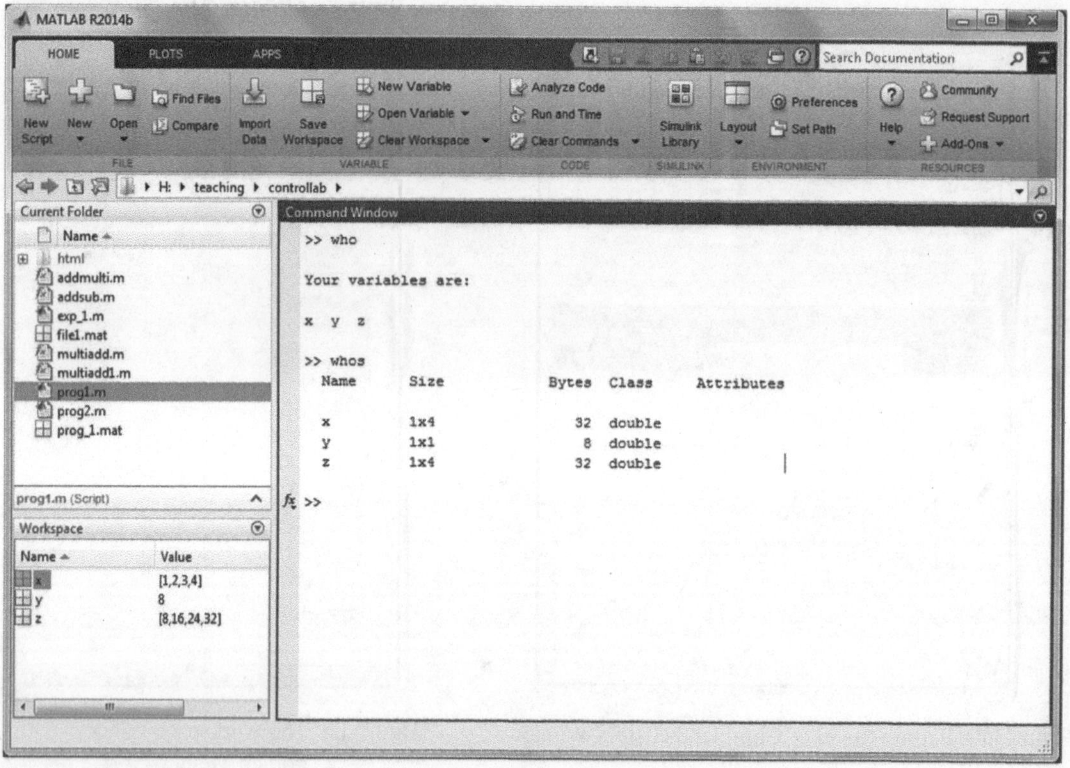

Figure 1.12 MATLAB Desktop and Command Window Illustrating WHOS Command

The response to command `whos` is as shown in Figure 1.12.

The content/value of any variable may be determined by typing its name in the Command Window as shown below:

```
x
```

The response is

```
x =
        1 2 3 4
```

`whos` command has some more forms. For example,

```
WHOS GLOBAL
```

It lists the variables in the global workspace:

```
WHOS -FILE FILENAME
```

It lists the variables in the specified .mat file:

```
WHOS VAR1 VAR2 ...
```

It restricts the display of variables to only those variables which are specified in the command.

The other commands useful for workspace information are listed at the end of this chapter.

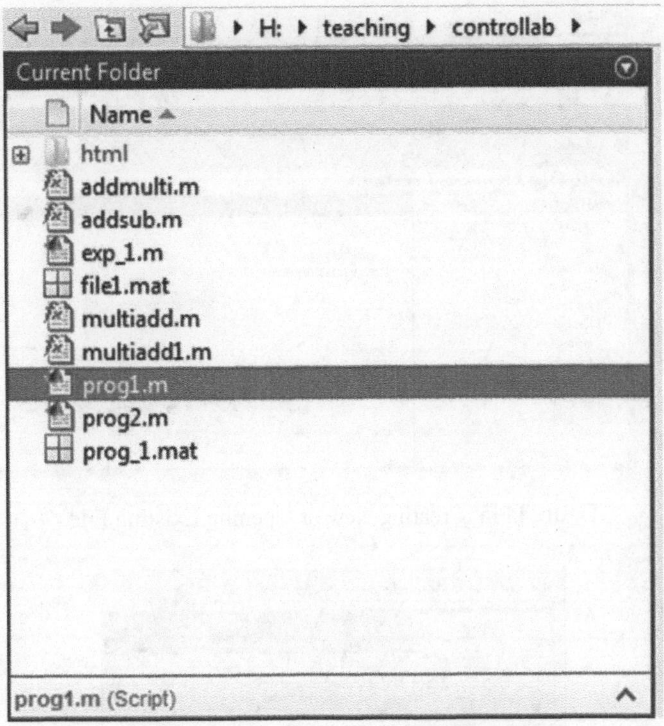

Figure 1.13 Current Directory Window

1.3.4 Current Directory

In the Current Directory Window, all the files and folders present in the Current Directory are listed as shown in Figure 1.13. To run any file, it must either be in the Current Directory or on the search path. A quick way to view or change the Current Directory or its contents is by using the Current Directory field in the MATLAB toolbar.

1.3.5 Editor Window

An Editor Window is used to create a new program file, or to modify existing files. In this window, programs can be written, edited and saved. The programs written using the MATLAB editor are automatically assigned an extension (.m) by the editor and are known as M-files.

A new M-file can be created by selecting an appropriate option from the desktop Home panel toolstrip menu, i.e., 'New Script' or 'New'. An existing M-file can be opened by clicking 'Open' option from the toolstrip menu or the relevant icon as shown in Figure 1.14. The Editor Window is opened automatically when a new M-file is created or an existing M-file is opened.

In the Editor Window, different features of the MATLAB language are shown in different colours: 'comments' in an M-file appear in green, 'variables' and 'numbers' appear in black, 'character strings' appear in 'red/purple', and 'MATLAB Keywords' appear in blue. The various features are illustrated in Figure 1.14.

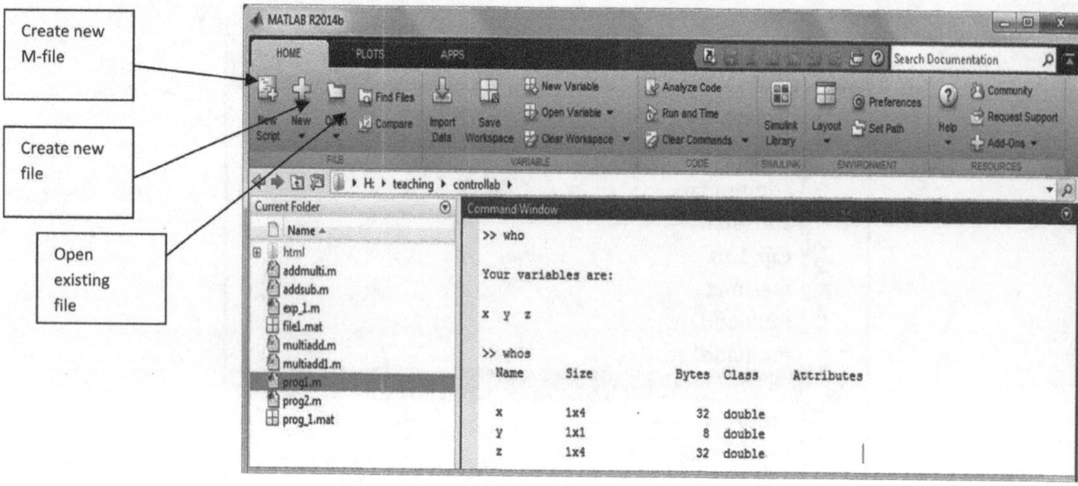

Figure 1.14a Creating New or Opening Existing File

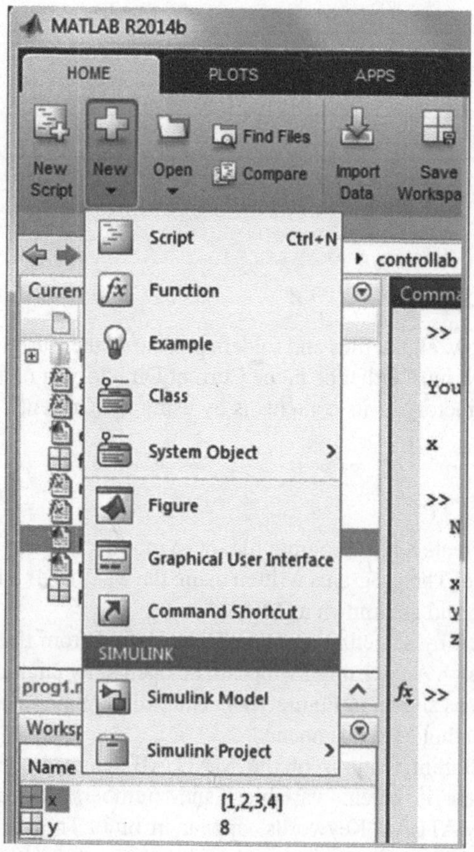

Figure 1.14b Options for Creating Type of New File

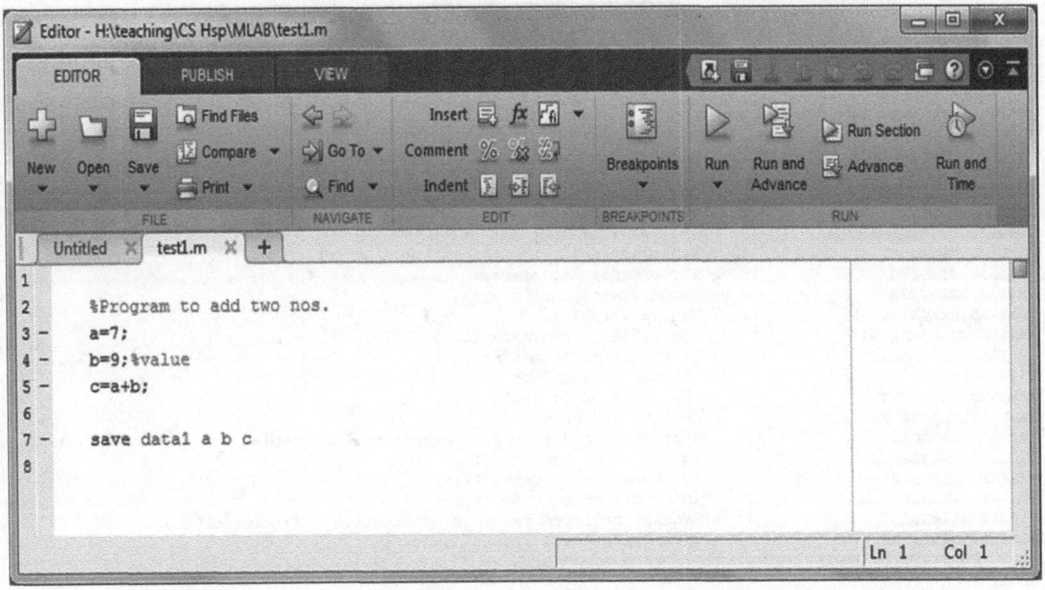

Figure 1.14c Editor Window (See Page 611 for the Colour Image)

A program written in the Editor Window can be saved by selecting File/save from the toolbar menu or by clicking the toolbar icon. All programs written in the Edit Window will automatically have (.m) extension. Once the M-file is saved, it can be executed by typing its name without the extension in the Command Window. The Edit Window can also be used as a debugger to debug programs. For debugging, 'Debug' menu is available on the toolbar.

1.4 HELP FEATURE

To get information about any function/command of MATLAB, help feature is available which has been discussed in Section 1.3. Apart from opening the Help documentation window for searching help about a particular toolbox/function/command by clicking '?' option from the Home Panel toolstrip menu, there are three more ways of getting help in MATLAB:

1. Help Browser
2. `help` Command
3. `lookfor` Command

1.4.1 Help Browser

The Help Web Browser can be opened by typing helpwin in the Command Window. The command `helpdesk` command has been removed in the new MATLAB version. Once the Help Web Browser is opened, the details of any particular command function can be obtained. Figure 1.15 shows the Help Web Browser of MATLAB. The Help navigator contains user-selectable tabs for navigating through the topics, printing and searching for seeking help about a particular command. It also provides index of default help topics for which help is available in alphabetical order for easy search.

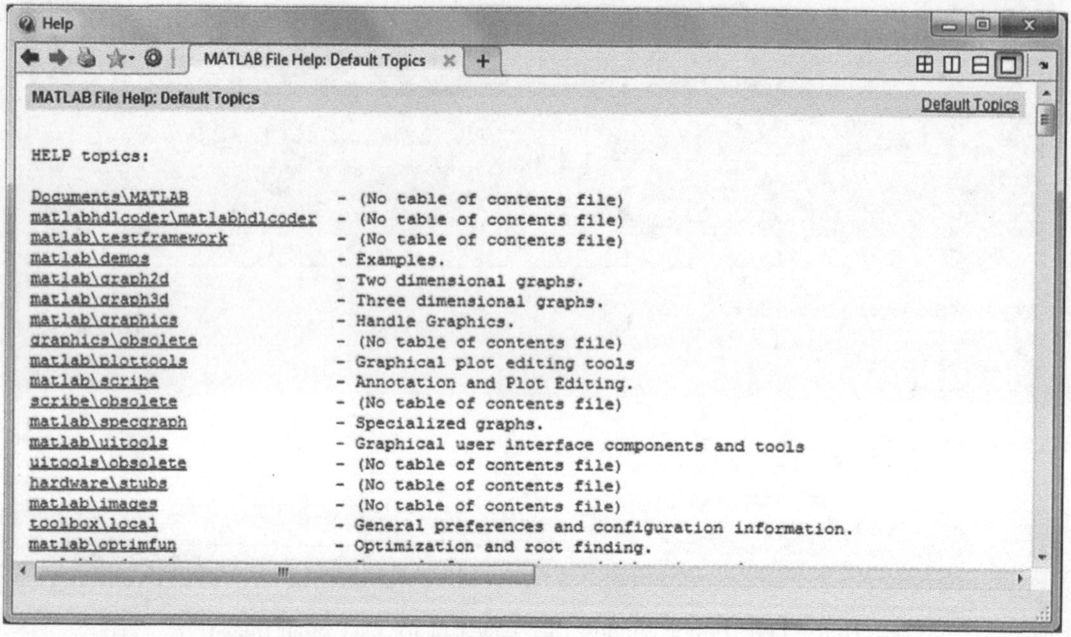

Figure 1.15 Help Window using `helpwin` Command

1.4.2 `help` Command

In this method, help for any particular command can be obtained by typing `help` followed by the function name at the command prompt. For example, type

```
help sin
```

The following help text will be displayed in the Command Window:

```
sin is Sine of argument in radians.
sin(X) is the sine of the elements of X.
See also asin, sind.
Overloaded methods:
codistributed/sin
gpuArray/sin
```

Reference page in Help browser

```
doc sin
```

This will show the text which helps in understanding the function `sin`. Help command is useful when the name of the function being used is known but its proper use is not known. If only `help` is typed on the command prompt, MATLAB will display a list of all help topics in the Command Window for MATLAB and different toolboxes installed in the system. If help is sought for commands available in a particular toolbox only, then the command `help` is followed by the name of the toolbox as shown below:

```
help control
```

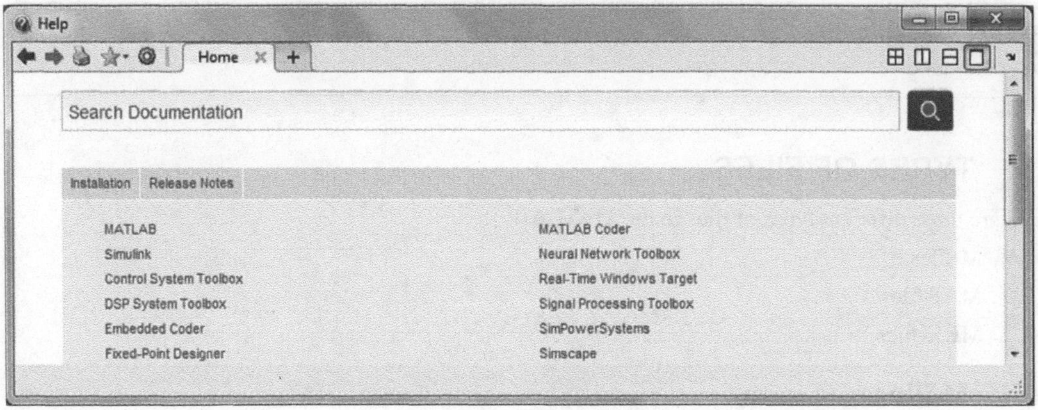

Figure 1.16 Help Documentation Window Using `doc` Command

MATLAB will list all the commands available in Control Systems Toolbox.

The doc command when given in the command window opens the reference page in Help browser and takes the user to the relevant function whose help documentation is to be searched as shown in Figure 1.16.

1.4.3 `Lookfor` Command

In this method, help can be obtained on any particular topic by typing `lookfor`, followed by function name on the command prompt. The `lookfor` command is different from the `help` command as help command searches for an exact function name match, whereas the `lookfor` command searches every function for matching the words that are being looked for. Hence, `lookfor` command is slower than the help command but it can provide useful information. For example, if help is sought for a function `inverse` and if function by the name `inverse` is not available in MATLAB, then `help` command will not provide any result. The response of `help` command will be '`inverse.m not found`'.

```
help inverse
inverse.m not found.
```

The command '`lookfor XYZ`' looks for the string `XYZ` in the first comment line of the Help text in all the M-files found on the MATLAB path. For all files in which a match occurs, '`lookfor`' command will display the entire comment line. For example, the '`lookfor`' command for the `inverse` function

```
lookfor inverse
```

will give the following results:

```
INVHILB Inverse Hilbert matrix
ACOS Inverse cosine
INV Matrix inverse
PINV Pseudoinverse
IFFT Inverse discrete Fourier transform
NCX2INV Inverse of the non-central chi-square cdf
IDCT2 Compute 2-D inverse discrete cosine transform
```

[For simplicity, all lines of the MATLAB response are not shown.]

`lookfor` command is useful when one is not sure about which function perform a particular task but one knows some keywords which are related to the function.

Programming Tip 1.8: `lookfor` command provides more detailed information than the `help` command.

1.5 TYPES OF FILES

There are three different types of files in the MATLAB:

1. M-files
2. MAT-files
3. MEX-files

1.5.1 M-files

M-files are standard ASCII text files, with a (.m) extension to the filename. Any program written in a MATLAB editor is saved as an M-file. These files are further classified as

- Script files
- Function files.

1.5.1.1 Script Files

An M-file with a set of valid MATLAB commands is called a script file. To run a script file, the filename (without the .m extension) is entered in the Command Window, just as any other MATLAB command. This is similar to executing the commands written in the script file one by one. The script files work on global variables, that is, the variables currently present in the workspace. These may have any number of commands including those which call built-in functions or functions written by the user.

1.5.1.2 Function Files

An M-file which begins with a `function` definition line is called a function file. If a file does not begin with `function` definition line, it becomes a script file. A function file is like a sub-program or sub-routine in FORTRAN, PASCAL, C, etc. The function files can be called from the script files or another function file just as a function is called from another program in C.

1.5.2 MAT-files

MAT-files are binary data-files, with an (.mat) extension to the filename. These are created by MATLAB when data is saved using `save` command. The `save` command saves data from the current MATLAB workspace into a disk file. The syntax for `save` command is

```
save <filename> <var1 var2 varf3….>
```

To load the data saved in the MAT-file, the `load` command is used and it loads data from the file into the current MATLAB workspace. The syntax for the `load` command is

```
load <filename>
```

Programming Tip 1.9: The MAT-files are in the format that cannot be read by the user directly.

1.5.3 MEX-files

MEX-file is MATLAB-callable FORTRAN and C program, with a (.mex) extension. This feature allows the user to integrate the code written in FORTRAN or C language into the programs developed using MATLAB.

1.6 PLATFORM

One of the major advantages of MATLAB is that it is platform independent. It is supported by Windows 8/7/NT and many versions of UNIX/LINUX. The MATLAB programs written on any platform will run on the other platforms as well. So, the MATLAB programs are easily portable and work in a similar manner on all computer systems, irrespective of the operating system used.

1.7 SOME USEFUL MATLAB COMMANDS

Some of the useful commands are as follows:

(a) General Commands

`clock`	Provides clock time and date as a vector
`date`	Provides date as a string
`ver`	Gives the version of MATLAB installed

(b) Directory Commands

`pwd`	Provides present working directory, same as used in Unix
`cd`	Changes present working directory, same as used in MSDOS
`dir`	Lists the files/folders in the Current Directory, same as used in MSDOS
`ls`	Lists the files/folders in the Current Directory, same as used in Unix
`path`	Displays MATLAB search path
`editpath`	Modifies MATLAB search path
`copyfile`	Copies a file
`mkdir`	Makes a directory/folder, same as used in MSDOS

(c) Workspace Commands

`who`	Lists the variables currently in the workspace/memory
`whos`	Same as `who` command but gives more information such as type and size.
`what`	Lists .m, .mat and .mex files on the disk
`clear all`	Clears the variables in the workspace
`clear xyz`	Clears the variables specified in the command
`mlock fun`	Locks function `fun` so that it cannot be deleted
`clc`	Clears screen
`clf`	Clears Figure Window

(d) Termination Commands

`Ctrl-c`	Stops execution of function/command being run currently
`quit`	Quits MATLAB
`exit`	Same as `quit` command

(e) `help` commands

`help`	Lists the topics for which help is available
`help topic`	Provides help for the topic specified in the command
`lookfor string`	Lists the comment line of all .m files containing the string specified in the command
`helpwin`	Opens the help window
`helpdesk`	Opens the web browser for online help demo Runs the demo program

SUMMARY

This chapter introduces the user to MATLAB. It can be summarized by the following points:

- The different methods of starting and ending a MATLAB session are discussed.
- The three panels and their toolstrip menu and sub-menus of the MATLAB desktop have been introduced.
- The different windows in the MATLAB environment such as Command Window, Command History, Workspace, Current Directory and Editor Window have been described.
- The Command Window displays the command prompt '»' and a cursor where commands are entered and executed instantaneously on pressing the 'Enter' key.
- The Command History Window consists of a list of all the commands that are entered at the Command Window. It consists of commands of previous sessions also. Many operations can be done by selecting a set of commands and opening the pop-up menu on right-clicking the mouse.
- Workspace is a collection of all the variables that have been generated so far in the current MATLAB session and shows their data type and size.
- Current Directory Window consists of all the files and folders present in the Current Directory Window. To run any file, it must either be in the Current Directory folder or on the search path.
- Editor Window is used to create a new program file or to modify existing files. In this window, programs can be written, edited and saved.
- Figure Window is a separate window with default white background and is used to display MATLAB graphics and contains many plot tools for formatting the figure plot.
- The different ways of seeking help about the MATLAB commands and features are described. The usefulness of lookfor command has been illustrated with the help of an example.
- Various types of files in MATLAB, i.e., script files, function files, data files and .mex files have been described so that the user is familiar with them and can easily understand the programs used to discuss various features of MATLAB in succeeding chapters.
- The concept of Current Directory and search path is introduced. This is very useful for the user to enable him/her to organize programs and data in different folders for efficient use of the software.
- In the end, some useful introductory MATLAB commands are listed.

EXERCISES

1.1 List the major components of the MATLAB environment.

1.2 What is meant by workspace? How can the information obtained regarding variables stored in the workspace?

1.3 What is the difference between `who` and `whos` commands?

1.4 How can help be sought for various commands in MATLAB? Describe various commands used for seeking help.

1.5 What is the difference between a script file and a data file? What are the other types of files in MATLAB?

1.6 What do you mean by search path? How can a new search path be added to the existing search path?

1.7 What is meant by Current Directory? How can the Current Directory be changed?

1.8 What are MEX-files? Describe the advantage of using MEX-files.

1.9 What is the difference between a script and a function file?

1.10 What do you mean by Toolbox? Why is it called so?

CHAPTER 2

Constants, Variables and Expressions

LEARNING OBJECTIVES

- Knowledge of MATLAB® character set and data types.
- Study of constants and variables and related useful functions such as `real`, `imag`, `angle`, etc.
- Study of functions used for conversion of co-ordinate systems such as `cart2pol`, `pol2cart`, etc.
- Knowledge of character constants, special constants and variables.
- Study of arithmetic, relational and logical operators.
- Knowledge of hierarchy of operations and built-in functions.
- Use of assignment statement.

2.1 INTRODUCTION

MATLAB is a powerful computing language. Programming languages process data consisting of numbers, characters and strings and provide output, known as useful information. Data processing is carried out by executing a sequence of instructions called a computer program. This group of instructions or program is written by the user, using certain symbols and words according to syntax rules of a particular language. MATLAB also has its own vocabulary and grammar. In this chapter, concepts of character set, constants, variables, data types, operators and expressions are discussed.

Any MATLAB command that can be given at the command prompt in the command window can be used in an M-file. The MATLAB has more features as compared to any other programming language. Firstly, it has incredibly powerful vector and matrix notations to make the code concise and compact. Secondly, MATLAB invisibly handles all memory allocations and supports file input/output and string manipulation. Finally, it contains an extensive collection of functions that are available in many toolboxes like numerical algebra, control systems and neural networks etc.

The commonly used `IF`, `WHILE` and `FOR` loops of any programming language such as 'C' and 'PASCAL' can also be used in M-files for control flow, although there is slight difference in the syntax of these programming constructs. Some of the most ingenious and efficient M-files instead of using explicit loops use built-in vector and matrix operations. MATLAB is also equipped with powerful debugging features to locate and remove errors in M-files. The debugger provides a variety of useful functions such as breakpoint and line-by-line execution.

2.2 CHARACTER SET

The character set is a set of characters that form a part of the statements written using the programming language. Characters can be broadly classified into four categories:

1. Alphabets
2. Numerals
3. Special characters
4. White space characters

MATLAB recognizes all 26 alphabets of the English language. Further, it is case sensitive, that is 'A' (uppercase) and 'a' (lowercase) alphabets are recognized as different characters. Numerals 0–9 also form part of its character set. The special characters including the escape sequence characters form part of the character set. White space characters like tab, blank, new line, vertical tab and line-feed are also included in the character set.

2.3 DATA TYPES

There are 14 fundamental data types (or classes) in MATLAB (Fig. 2.1). Each of these types is in the form of an array. This array is a minimum single element in size and can grow to an *n*-dimensional array of any size. Two-dimensional (2-D) versions of these arrays are called matrices.

The **char data type**, for example `hello`, is a character array. Each character is stored in Unicode (uniform code) representation and is 16 bits long. The character string is 1-by-*n* array of characters. Array of strings can be used to store number of strings, provided all of them have the same length.

Numeric data types int8 and uint8, int16 and uint16, and int32 and uint32, int64 and uint64 include signed and unsigned integer arrays that are 8, 16, 32 and 64 bits in length, respectively.

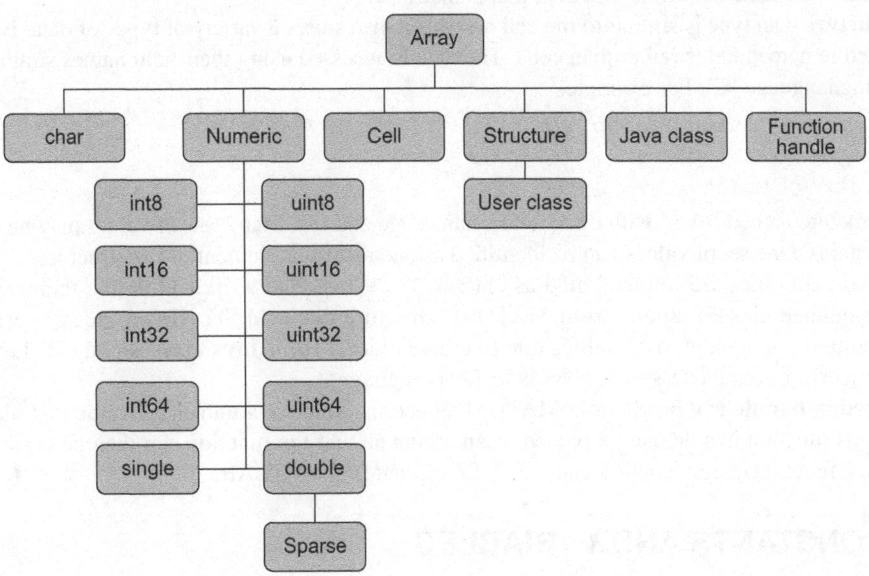

Figure 2.1 The Data Types in MATLAB

The **single data type** is a single-dimensional numeric array. It requires less storage than double precision. The data type **double** is a double precision array and is the most common data type. The data of type single have to be converted into double precision to enable them to be used in mathematical operations as all MATLAB computations are done in double precision.

> **Programming Tip 2.1:** All MATLAB computations are done in double precision.

At times, most of the elements in the array are equal to zero, that is the array contains very few non-zero elements. In that case, it is not advisable to store all the elements. To reserve memory space and increase the computation speed, only non-zero elements and their indices are stored. Such format is called **Sparse**.

A **cell array** data type is used for storing dissimilar kinds of data. One can store arrays of different types and sizes in the cells of the cell array. Cell arrays are created by enclosing the matrix variable in curly braces. For example,

```
A = [1 2 7 8];
B = [2 3 6; 6 3 8; 2 8 4];
C = zeros(2,3,3);
D_cell = {A B C};
```

Here, D_cell is a cell array having three cells, first cell contains matrix *A*, second cell stores matrix *B* and the third, matrix *C*.

The elements of the cell array can be accessed by simply giving the cell number in curly braces.

```
D_cell{1}
```

This will return the contents of the first cell, that is matrix *A*.

The **structure** data type is similar to the cell array as it also stores a variety of types of data. But, here the data is stored in named fields rather than cells. The data is accessed using their field names similar to that in programming language 'C'. For example,

```
abc.name = 'Bhanu Pratap Singh';
abc.age = 18;
abc.sex = 'Male'
```

creates a structure named '`abc`' with three fields: name, age and sex. Many sets of values may be assigned to these three fields. One set of values can be identified as one record or element of the structure.

MATLAB data types are implemented as classes. Users can also write and define their own classes. These user-defined classes inherit from MATLAB structure class. MATLAB provides interface to the Java programming language that enables one to create objects from **Java classes** and call Java methods on these objects or create one's own classes in Java language.

The **function handle** is a handle to a MATLAB function, which is a numerical value that identifies the function. This function handle can be passed as an argument and the function can then be easily evaluated using `feval` function (`f` for function and `eval` for evaluate) in MATLAB.

2.4 CONSTANTS AND VARIABLES

Constants refer to fixed values which do not change during the execution of a program. Constants can be of two types:

(i) Numeric constants
(ii) Character constants

2.4.1 Numeric Constants

Numeric constants are classified into three types, that is integer constants, real constants and complex constants. However, MATLAB does not differentiate between integer and real constants during execution.

2.4.1.1 Integer Constants/Numbers

Integer constants/numbers consist of a set of digits, 0 through 9, with an optional '–' or '+' sign. Some valid examples of integer constants are as follows:

456 –120 +34 234567

Spaces, commas and non-digit characters are not allowed between digits. Some examples of invalid integer constants are as follows:

25/670 1,500 Rs. 200

> **Programming Tip 2.2:** Spaces, commas and non-digit characters are not allowed between digits in integer constants.

2.4.1.2 Real Constants/Numbers

Scientific quantities that vary continuously, such as speed, temperature etc., cannot be represented using integer constants/numbers. Such quantities are represented by using numbers that contain fractional parts. Such numbers are called real/floating point constants. Some valid examples of real constants are given as follows:

```
0.0065      -45.67      102.345
```

A real constant/number can also be expressed in exponential (or scientific) notation. For example, the value 435.25 can be written as 4.3525e + 2 or 43525e – 2, in exponential notation, where e ± 2 means multiplication by $10^{\pm 2}$.

2.4.1.3 Complex Constant/Numbers

Complex numbers are used frequently by scientists and engineers. Very often solution of differential equations and algebraic equations gives rise to complex numbers. Complex numbers consist of two parts, i.e., a real part and an imaginary part. Imaginary parts use either '*i*' or '*j*' as a suffix.

MATLAB predefines $i = j = \sqrt{-1}$.

Therefore, a complex constant can be easily created using Cartesian coordinates. For example, the statement

```
x = -6 + j*8
```

will assign the complex constant `-6 + j8` to the variable `x`, that is

```
x = -6.0000 + 8.0000i
```

where -6.0 is the real part and 8.0 is the imaginary part of the complex number.

> **Programming Tip 2.3:** It is to note that when assigning value of complex number, the imaginary part is defined by multiplying its magnitude with *i* or *j*, such as `j*8`.

The real and imaginary components of *x* can be separated by using the `real` and `imag` functions. For example, the statements

```
x_real = real(x);
x_imag = imag(x);
```

will give the following result:

```
x_real = -6
x_imag = 8
```

The command 'conj(x)' will produce the complex conjugate of *x*, i.e.,

```
ans*=
    -6.0000 - 8.0000i
```

For example, if you give the following MATLAB statements

```
z=1 + j*3;
y=conj(z)
```

The result is given as follows:

```
y =
     1.0000 - 3.0000i
```

2.4.1.4 Magnitude and Angle of a Complex Number

There are many ways to calculate the magnitude of a complex quantity. The following commands can be used to obtain the magnitude of a complex number, $x = 6 + j * 8$.

(i) First method

```
x_mag = sqrt(x_real^2 + x_imag^2)
```

(ii) Second method

```
x_mag = sqrt(x* conj(x))
```

(iii) Third method

```
x_mag = abs(x)
```

The result obtained in all the afore mentioned methods is

```
x_mag = 10
```

In addition to magnitude, phase angle of a complex number can be obtained by using `angle` command as follows and the angle obtained is in radians:

```
x_rad= angle(x)
= 2.2143
```

Angle of complex variable *x* can also be obtained using arc-tangent function `atan2` as follows:

```
x_rad= atan2(x_imag, x_real)
```

The result obtained is given as follows:

```
x_rad = 2.2143
```

> **Programming Tip 2.4:** By default, MATLAB accepts and returns angles in radians.

2.4.1.5 Conversion of Coordinate System

In MATLAB, the coordinates of a point in space can be converted into another coordinate system using simple commands.

The command

```
[theta, r] = cart2pol(x, y),
```

converts the Cartesian coordinates *x* and *y* into Polar coordinates, i.e., angle theta and radius *r*. For example,

Let the Cartesian coordinates of a complex number be $x = 1$ and $y = 1$; then the command

```
[theta, r] = cart2pol(1, 1)
```

will produce the following result:

```
theta =
        0.7854
r =
     1.4142
```

Likewise, the command

```
[x, y] = pol2cart(theta, r)
```

will convert the Polar coordinates into the Cartesian coordinates. For example, let theta = 1 and $r = 5$, then to convert Polar to Cartesian coordinates, the following commands are used:

```
theta = 1
r = 5
[x, y] = pol2cart(theta, r)
```

The result obtained is

```
x =
     2.7015
y =
     4.2074
```

> **Programming Tip 2.5:** MATLAB supports complex arguments for any trigonometric function.

2.4.2 Character Constants

Character constants can be single character constants, string constants or escape sequence constants.

2.4.2.1 Single Character Constants

A single character constant contains a single character enclosed within a pair of single quote marks.

Some examples of valid single character constants are 'Y', 'G', ' ', '1', '_'

> **Programming Tip 2.6:** It may be noted that space is also a character.

2.4.2.2 String Constants

A string constant is a sequence of characters enclosed in pair of single quotes. The characters may be alphabets, numbers, special characters or blank space.

Examples are: 'Good' '1947' 'Best Wishes' 'G1'

Thus, a string is represented using a series of characters in single quotes.

> **Programming Tip 2.7:** A word containing a single quote (such as isn't) is specified by using two single quotes together.

For example:

say = 'isn''t'

Here, two single quotes are used and not a double quote.

2.4.2.3 Escape Sequence Constants

Escape sequence character constants are used in output functions. For example, the symbol '*b*' means back space, '*t*' implies tab, '*n*' implies new line and so on.

2.4.3 Variables

Variables and constants form an integral form of program in any language. The different types of data are identified by their names (variable names) for ease in reference. Programming languages require a programmer to declare these variables and the type of data in advance at the beginning of the program, whereas no such declaration is required in MATLAB.

> **Programming Tip 2.8:** MATLAB does **not** require any variable or constant to be declared in advance at the start of a program.

It allows the programmer to simply use the variable wherever it is required in the program. This makes programming easier in MATLAB. The following points must be kept in view while using variables in MATLAB:

1. A MATLAB variable name may consist of an alphabet used as the first character followed by a number of alphabets or numerals or an underscore. The variable name may have a maximum of 131 characters. If it exceeds the limit, the extra characters are ignored. When writing a program, it is advisable to pick meaningful names for the variables so that it is much easier to understand a program at a later stage. Unless required otherwise, it is customary to use all lowercase letters for ordinary variable names. The following are some valid variable names:

   n, nic, N, deno, f, F, P123 , r_2, polynomial_degree.
2. The variable names that contain more than one word separated by blank space are not valid. In such cases, underscore character can be used to make such variable names more explicit/meaningful. For example, the variable name 'domicile state' may be written as 'domicile_state'.

> **Programming Tip 2.9:** Blank spaces cannot be included in MATLAB variable names.

3. Variables can be defined at any step in the M-file by simply assigning values to them and the type of data assigned to the variable determines the type of variable.
4. MATLAB does not require dimension statements for subscripted variables.
5. MATLAB is case sensitive. Lower and uppercase letters represent two different variable names, for example 'GOLD' and 'gold' are different variable names.
6. Words that are reserved for the key constructs of a programming language are called 'Keywords' and cannot be used as variable names. For example, for, while, switch, and function are keywords.

> **Programming Tip 2.10:** MATLAB is case sensitive.

2.4.4 Special Constants and Variables

Some special constants and variables defined in MATLAB are listed as follows:

`pi`	3.14159
`i`	$\sqrt{-1}$
`j`	$\sqrt{-1}$
`inf`	∞

`NaN`	not a number
`eps`	number small enough equivalent to zero
`ans`	Default output variable
`nargin`	no. of input arguments of a function
`nargout`	no. of output arguments of a function
`realmax`	largest real number

2.5 OPERATORS

MATLAB operators can be classified mainly into three categories:

1. Arithmetic operators that perform arithmetic computations like addition, multiplication, etc.
2. Relational operators that compare operands quantitatively like 'less than', 'not equal to', etc.
3. Logical operators that perform logical operations like AND, OR, NOT, etc.

2.5.1 Arithmetic Operators

Let $p = 3$, $q = 2$. Arithmetic operators used in MATLAB and the result of the arithmetic expressions formed using arithmetic operators, with these p and q variables, are illustrated in Table 2.1.

2.5.2 Relational Operators

Relational operators in MATLAB are listed in Table 2.2. The result obtained from the commands, illustrating the use of relational operators, is indicated as '1' if the specified relation is true and '0' if the relation is false.

For example,

Let $p = 3$, $q = 2$;

When complex numbers are used as operands, only 'equal to' (==), and 'not equal to' (~=), operators produce correct results. For example,

Let $x = 3 + j4$, $y = 4 - j1$, $r = 1 + j2$ and $s = 1 + j2$

Table 2.1 Arithmetic Operators in MATLAB

Operator	Operation	Algebraic Form	MATLAB Form	Result of Expression
+	Addition	$p+q$	`p + q`	5
–	Subtraction	$p-q$	`p - q`	1
.*	Multiplication (Element by element)	$p \times q$	`p .* q`	6
./	Right Division (Element by element)	p/q	`p ./ q`	1.5
.\	Left Division (Element by element)	$p \times q^{-1}$	`p .\ q`	0.6667
.^	Exponentiation (Element by element)	p^q	`p .^ q`	9
+	Unary plus	$+p$	`+p`	+ 3
–	Unary minus	$+q$	`-p`	– 3

Table 2.2 Relational Operators in MATLAB

Operator	Operation	Relational Form	MATLAB® Form	Result of Relational Expression
<	Less than	$p<q$	`p < q`	0
<=	Less than or equal to	$p \leq q$	`p <= q`	0
>	Greater than	$p>q$	`p > q`	1
>=	Greater than or equal to	$p \geq q$	`p >= q`	1
==	Equal to	$p==q$	`p == q`	0
~=	Not equal to	$p \neq q$	`p ~= q`	1

The statements

`x == y` will return 0, i.e., false
`x ~= y` will return 1, i.e., true
`r == s` will return 1, i.e., true
`r ~= s` will return 0, i.e., false

Other relational operators like >, <, >= or <= when used with complex numbers act on only the real part of the complex number. For example,

`y > x` will return 1, i.e., true
`x < y` will return 1, i.e., true

> **Programming Tip 2.11:** All relational operators do not operate on complex numbers. Some operate on only real part of the complex numbers.

2.5.3 Logical Operators and Functions

The operands for the logical operators need to be logical and can assume the values TRUE expressed as '1' and FALSE expressed as '0'. If the operand has numerical values, then MATLAB takes non-zero values as TRUE. The result is expressed in terms of '1' and '0' only. Depending upon whether a certain condition is found to be true or false, MATLAB operators indicate the result as logically true or false. For example, the statement $(5+2) > 10$ will return a logical false value, that is zero.

In addition to logical operators MATLAB, provides some functions to carry out some additional logical operations.

Let $A = 2$, $B = 5$, $C = -4$ and $D = 0$. The logical expressions involving the variables defined earlier and their results are illustrated in Table 2.3.

2.6 HIERARCHY OF OPERATIONS

Generally several arithmetic operations are combined into a single expression. An expression is calculated by executing one arithmetic operation at a time. The order in which the arithmetic operations are executed in an expression is called 'hierarchy of operations' or 'operator precedence'. The rules governing the precedence of operators generally follow the normal rules of algebra. The order in which the arithmetic operations are executed are given as follows:

1. The contents of all parentheses ( ) are evaluated first, starting from the innermost parenthesis and working outwards.

Table 2.3 Logical Operators and Functions in MATLAB

<table>
<tr><th>Operator</th><th>Function</th><th>Description</th><th>Expression</th><th>Result of Expression</th></tr>
<tr><td>&</td><td>–</td><td>&(AND) returns 1 if both elements are true (non-zero)</td><td><code>A & B</code></td><td>1</td></tr>
<tr><td>|</td><td>–</td><td>| (OR) returns 1 if either one of the elements is true</td><td><code>A | D</code></td><td>1</td></tr>
<tr><td>~</td><td>–</td><td>~(NOT) complements the element ‘a’ and returns ‘−a’</td><td><code>~C</code></td><td>0</td></tr>
<tr><td>–</td><td><code>xor()</code></td><td>returns 1 if only one of the elements is true</td><td><code>xor(A, B)</code></td><td>0</td></tr>
<tr><td>–</td><td><code>any()</code></td><td>True if any element of vector is non-zero</td><td><code>any(A)</code></td><td>1</td></tr>
<tr><td>–</td><td><code>all()</code></td><td>True if all element of vector are non-zero</td><td><code>all(A)</code></td><td>1</td></tr>
</table>

2. Transpose (. ’), power (. ^), complex conjugate transpose (‘), matrix power (^)
3. Unary plus (+), unary minus (−), logical NOT (~)
4. Multiplication (.*), right division (./), left division (.\), matrix multiplication (*), matrix right division (/), matrix left division (\)
5. Addition (+) and subtraction (−)
6. Colon Operator (:)
7. Less than (<), less than or equal to (<=), greater than (>), greater than or equal to (>=), equal to (= =) and not equal to (− =)
8. Logical AND (&)
9. Logical OR (|)

Example 2.1 The variables i, j, k and l have values equal to 2, 3, 4 and 5, respectively. Evaluate the following MATLAB expressions:

(i) $i * j + k * l$
(ii) $i * (j + k) * l$
(iii) $(i * j) + (k / l)$
(iv) $(i + j) * i$^j

Solution:

(i) Working from left to right in order of appearance, multiplications are evaluated first.
$i * j = 2 \times 3 = 6$,
$k * l = 4 \times 5 = 20$
The expression reduces to 6 + 20.
The addition operation is carried out next. The result obtained is thus 26.

(ii) First expression in parenthesis is evaluated, i.e.,
$j + k = 3 + 4 = 7$
The expression reduces to $i * 7 * l$.
Now multiplication is carried out working from left to right in the order of appearance, that is first $i * 7$ is evaluated, that is $2 \times 7 = 14$. Expression reduces to `14*l`, which is then evaluated to $14 \times 5 = 70$.

(iii) The expressions in parenthesis are evaluated first, working from left to right. Then addition is done and the result obtained is 6.8.

(iv) First the expression in parenthesis is evaluated, then raised to power (^) as it has higher precedence and (*) is evaluated next. The result obtained is 40.

Example 2.2 The variables x, y, z have values equal to 2.5, 0.5 and 2, respectively. Evaluate the following MATLAB expressions:

(i) $x + y + z$
(ii) $x * y * z$
(iii) x/y
(iv) x^y
(v) x^z

Solution: MATLAB expressions and their results obtained are shown as follows:

```
(i)    x + y + z        ans = 5
(ii)   x * y * z        ans = 2.500
(iii)  x/z              ans = 1.2500
(iv)   x^y              ans = 1.5811
(v)    x^z              ans = 6.2500
```

Example 2.3 The complex variables are $x = 3 - 4i$ and $y = 1 + 2i$. Evaluate the following expressions:

(i) $x + y$
(ii) $x - y$
(iii) $x*z$
(iv) x/y
(v) x^y

Solution: MATLAB expressions and their results obtained are shown as follows:

```
(i)    x + y
       ans = 4.0000 - 2.0000i
(ii)   x - y
       ans = 2.0000 - 6.0000i
(iii)  x * y
       ans = 11.0000 + 2.0000i
(iv)   x/y
       ans = -1.0000 - 2.0000i
(v)    x^y
       ans = -21.0831 + 24.0002i
```

Programming Tip 2.12: MATLAB does not differentiate between integer and real variables and/or constants like other computer languages. Computations are made as per normal algebraic rules.

2.7 BUILT-IN FUNCTIONS

A mathematical function is an expression which has one or more input values and gives one or more values as outputs. Engineering calculations require functions which are quite complex as compared to simple arithmetic expressions. Examples of commonly used functions are trigonometric functions, logarithmic functions and input/output functions.

Besides the simple arithmetic operations, a very large number and variety of useful built-in functions for complex engineering calculations related to all disciplines are available in MATLAB. The list of built-in functions in MATLAB is very large and richer than in most of the languages like FORTRAN or C. A complete list of all MATLAB functions can be seen through help browser.

The syntax of a built-in function is

```
function_name (variable_name or expression)
```

Example 2.4 Write a MATLAB statement for the following algebraic equation, using built-in functions:

$$a = \log_e \sqrt{\frac{x}{y*z}}$$

Solution: MATLAB statement is

```
a = log(sqrt(x/(y*z)))
```

The function 'log()' computes the logarithm of the expression based to '*e*', i.e., the natural logarithm. The function 'sqrt' computes the square root. The statement could also be written as a group of two statements. First, computing the square root of the arithmetic expression, and second, computing the logarithm of the result obtained from the square root.

> **Programming Tip 2.13:** The square root or logarithm of a negative number does not give error in MATLAB. The appropriate complex result is produced automatically.

The following points may be noted while using these functions:

1. A function may be used in arithmetic expressions in a way similar to a variable name.
2. A function may be used as the argument of another function, for example if y = √x, then cos(y) may be written as cos(sqrt(x)), i.e., function sqrt(x) has been used as the argument of the cos function.
3. All functions appearing in arithmetic expression are evaluated first. Hence, the argument of a function is computed first in order to evaluate a function.
4. In trigonometric functions like sin(x) and cos(x), the argument *x* is assumed to be in radians. In case argument is in degree, then d is post fixed with trigonometric function i.e., sind, cosd, etc.

2.8 ASSIGNMENT STATEMENT

General form of an assignment statement is given as follows:

```
variable_name = expression;
```

When an assignment statement is executed, the value of the expression to the right of the equality sign is first computed and the result obtained is assigned to the variable mentioned on the left of the equality sign.

Example 2.5 Illustrate the use of an assignment statement.

Solution: Consider the following MATLAB statement:

```
y = x + 2;
```

To evaluate the expression ($x + 2$), 2 is added to the value of variable x. The result of computation is then assigned to variable y.

- The expression to the right of the assignment operator i.e., equality sign can be any valid combination of scalars, arrays, parameters and arithmetic operators.
- Parenthesis can be used to group terms whenever desired. The expressions inside the parenthesis are evaluated first.

Example 2.6 Write any five valid MATLAB assignment statements.

Solution:

```
circle_area = pi*r*r;                    %r is radius of a circle
rectangle_circum = 2*(l + b);            %l is length and b is breadth
triangle_area = 0.5*b*h;                 %h is height
triangle_speri = (a + b + c)/2.0;        %a, b and c are sides of a
triangle_area = sqrt(s*(s - a)           %triangle
                *(s - b)*(s - c));       %s is semi perimeter
```

2.9 ILLUSTRATIVE PROGRAMS

Example 2.7 Given two sides $a = 3.2$ and $b = 4.6$ of a triangle and angle theta $= 60°$ between these two sides, find the length of the third side and the area of the triangle.

Solution: The commands used are as follows:

```
a = 3.2;                                 %Input the given values
b = 4.6;
theta = 60.0;
theta = theta*pi/180.0;                  %Convert degrees to radians
c = sqrt(a^2 + b^2 - 2*a*b*cos(theta))
area = 0.5*a*b*sin(theta)                %calculate area
```

The result obtained is as follows:

```
c =
     4.0841
area =
       6.3739
```

Example 2.8 Write a program to convert temperature given in degrees Centigrade, say 35.4°C, to degrees Fahrenheit.

Solution: The commands used are as follows:

```
degcenti = 35.4;
degfah = 1.8*degcenti + 32.0         %Calculate the result
```

The result obtained is as follows:

```
degfah =
          95.7200
```

Example 2.9 Write the MATLAB statements to calculate the sum of the series:

$$s = 1 - \frac{x^2}{2!} + \frac{x^4}{4!} - \frac{x^6}{6!} + \frac{x^8}{8!} \qquad \text{for } x = 1.5$$

Solution: Here, MATLAB function `factorial` is used, whose syntax is given as

```
factorial(a)
```

which returns the factorial of the variable *a*.

The commands used to solve the given series are:

```
x = 1.5;
x2 = x*x/factorial(2);
x3 = x^4/factorial(4);
x4 = x^6/factorial(6);
x5 = x^8/factorial(8);
s = 1 - x2 + x3 - x4 + x5
```

The result obtained is as follows:

```
s =
       -0.3042
```

Example 2.10 The values of *a*, *b*, *c* and *d* are $-190.5*10^{-2}$, $14.6*10^3$, 0.00056 and 456.28, respectively. Write a program to evaluate the following statements:

$$f1 = \frac{ab}{cd} + a*b$$

$$f2 = \frac{a}{bc} - \frac{d}{a}$$

Solution: The following commands are used:

```
a = -190.5*10^-2;
b = 14.6*10^3;
c = 0.00056;
d = 456.28;
f1 = (a*b)/(c*d) + (a*b)
f2 = a/(b*c) - d/a
```

The result obtained is as follows:

```
f1 =
 -1.3666e + 005
f2 =
  239.2841
```

Example 2.11 Given the radius of a circle, r = 5 cm, find its circumference and area.

Solution: The commands used are

```
radius = 5.0;
circum = 2*pi*radius   %Calculate the circumference
area = pi*radius^2     %Calculate the area
```

The result obtained is as follows:

```
circum =
        31.4159
area =
        78.5398
```

Example 2.12 Given the base of the right angled triangle = 5 cm, and the acute angle, $\theta = 42°$, find the length of its perpendicular.

Solution: Let perpendicular, base and angle θ be denoted by p, b and theta respectively. The statements used to compute the length of perpendicular are as follows:

```
b = 5;
theta = 42;
p = b * tand(theta)
```

Please note that the angle is given in degrees, and to calculate the tangent of the angle, the function `tand` is used. The letter '*d*' post-fixed to `tan` indicates that the argument, i.e., the angle is not in radians but degrees. Likewise, if sine of an angle is to be calculated and the argument is in degrees, then the function used is `sind`.

> **Programming Tip 2.14:** To calculate trigonometric ratio of an angle given in degrees, post-fix '*d*' to the relevant trigonometric function.

SUMMARY

The first lesson of any programming language starts from its character set and the concept of constants, variables and expressions. This basic issue has been dealt with in this chapter. The types of constants and variables have been discussed at length and their use has been well illustrated using numerous examples. The different types of operators—arithmetic, relational and logical—are also given. The hierarchy of operations is described with examples. The use of functions is very important, as most of the MATLAB commands are implemented as built-in functions. The issues related to some basic functions, their arguments and their use have been discussed at length and illustrated using example programs.

List of Commands

Command/Function	Description
`abs`	Returns absolute number. In case of complex number returns magnitude
`any`	Returns True if any element of vector is non-zero
`&`	Finds logical AND

(Continued)

(Continued)

`angle`	Returns phase angle in radians
`all`	Returns True if all element of vector are non-zero
`atan2`	Gives tangent inverse
`cart2pol`	Convert Cartesian to polar coordinates
`conj`	Gives conjugate of a complex number
`factorial`	Gives factorial of a number.
`imag`	Returns imaginary part of complex number
`log`	Gives natural logarithm
`|`	Finds logical OR
`pol2cart`	Converts polar to Cartesian coordinates
`real`	Returns real part of complex number
`sqrt`	Returns square root of a number
`tand`	Returns tangent of an angle given in degrees
`xor`	Finds exclusive OR

EXERCISES

2.1 Express the following numbers in polar form:

(i) $1 + 2j$

(ii) $-2 + j1$

(iii) $(1 + 2j)(-2 + j1)$

(iv) $(1 + 2j)/(-2 + j1)$

2.2 Evaluate the following assignment statements:

(i) $p = \dfrac{cx + 2d}{cx - d'}$ for $c = 1$, $d = 2$, and $x = 4$

(ii) $I = 2\log_{10}x + \cos\pi + |y^2 - z^2| + \sqrt{5yz},$ for $x = 2, y = 4, z = 3$

(iii) $r = x^4 + 4x^3 + 3x^2 + 6x + 6,$ for $x = -3,$

(iv) $s = (4p + 5)(3p + 4q - 10)$, for $p = 3$ and $q = 4$

(v) $u = xe^{-10t}$, for $x = 0.5$ and $t = 2$

(vi) $d = a$^$(b$^$c)$, for $a = 1$, $b = 2$ and $c = 3$

(vii) $f = c$^d^e, for $c = 2$, $d = 3$ and $e = 4$

2.3 What is the value of k calculated in the following arithmetic statements?

(i) $k = I$*2/3 + J/4 − J^ 3/8 for $I = 2$ and $J = 3$

(ii) $k = x$^2 + y/2.0 + z*2 for $x = 2$, $y = 3.0$ and $z = 4.5$

(iii) $J = (I + 1)$ * (I^2) − I/2.0 for $I = 3$

2.4 What is the final value of '*A*' in the following MATLAB program:

```
A = 2.5
A = (A + 2.5) *2.5
```

$I = A*4$
$k = I$^2
$A = k/20$

2.5 Evaluate the following trigonometric functions for $\theta = 30°, 120°, 210°$ and $300°$.
(i) $\sin(\theta)$
(ii) $\cos(\theta)$
(iii) $\tan(\theta)$
(iv) $\cot(\theta)$

2.6 Evaluate the following:
(i) $\sin^{-1} 1/2$
(ii) $\cos^{-1} \frac{\sqrt{3}}{2}$
(iii) $\tan^{-1} \sqrt{3}$

2.7 Evaluate the following functions for $\theta = 3, 5$ and 8.
(i) $\sinh(\theta)$
(ii) $\cosh(\theta)$
(iii) $\tanh(\theta)$

2.8 Write assignment statements to evaluate the following equations.
(i) Volume $= \pi^2 rh$ for $r = 2, h = 3$
(ii) Power $= \dfrac{2\pi NT}{60}$ for $N = 1000, T = 10_2$
(iii) Efficiency $= \dfrac{VI\cos\theta}{VI\cos\theta + I^2R + W_c}$ for $V = 250, I = 5, R = 2, \cos\theta = 0.8, W_c = 20$

2.9 If $x = 5, y = 15$ and $z = -2$, determine the value of each of the following logical expressions. List the order of operations carried out in each expression.
(i) $x > y \,\&\, x < z$
(ii) $x < y \,\&\, x > z$
(iii) $x == y \,\|\, y > x$

2.10 For an electrical circuit with an inductance $L = 0.01$ mH and resistance $R = 100$ ohms, the damped natural frequency of oscillation is

$$\text{Frequency } f = \sqrt{\frac{1}{Lc} - \frac{R^2}{4c^2}}$$

Write a program to calculate the frequency for different values of c varying from 0.1 to 1 in steps of 0.1.

CHAPTER

3

Vectors and Matrices

LEARNING OBJECTIVES

- Knowledge of vectors and scalars and basic operations such as product, transpose, etc.
- Useful commands/functions related to vectors such as `sum`, `mean`, `length`, `max`, `min`, etc.
- Entering data to a matrix, line continuation, matrix indices, dimension statement.
- Study of different matrix operations such as `reshape`, `expand`, `append`, `concatenate`, etc.
- Knowledge of special matrices such as `zeros`, `ones`, `eyes`, etc.
- Study of different commands/functions used with matrices like `det`, `rank`, `inv`, `norm`, `find`, `eig`, etc.
- Study of arithmetic, relational, logical, operations.
- Study of structures and cells.

3.1 INTRODUCTION

The matrix notation usually simplifies the complex mathematical expressions/equations and makes solutions of problems much easier to handle and manipulate. In MATLAB, a matrix is a rectangular array of real or complex numbers. Matrices with only one row or with only one column are called row and column vectors, respectively. A matrix having one element only is called a scalar.

Although other high-level programming languages work with one number at a time, in MATLAB it is possible to work with the complete matrix simultaneously. This feature is very important as it removes the unnecessary loops and repetition of same statements. The program therefore, becomes short, concise and easily understandable. In MATLAB, matrix is chosen as a basic data element. All variables when used as a single data element are treated as single element matrix, i.e., a matrix with one row and one column.

3.2 SCALARS AND VECTORS

A scalar is a (1×1) matrix containing a single element only. A column vector is a $(m \times 1)$ matrix that has m number of rows but a single column only. A row vector is a $(1 \times n)$ matrix which has n number of columns and has only one row.

3.2.1 Assigning Data to Elements of a Vector/Scalar

All the elements of a row vector are separated by blank spaces or commas and are enclosed in square brackets.

For example, a **row vector**, $\boldsymbol{p}$ = [1 2 4] can be entered at the command window as follows:

```
p = [1 2 4];
```

or

```
p = [1,2,4];
```

All the elements of a column vector are separated by semicolons and are enclosed in square brackets. For example, a **column vector**, $\boldsymbol{q}$ is entered as shown below:

```
q = [1; 2; 4];
```

Variable q is a column vector and has only one element each in all the rows and these elements are separated by a semicolon.

A **scalar** does not need any square brackets, e.g., a scalar, $p = 10$, can be entered just as:

```
p = 10;
```

3.2.2 Vector Products

A row vector and a column vector can be multiplied with each other. However, these vectors should be of the same length. If $\boldsymbol{x}$ is a column vector and $\boldsymbol{y}$ is a row vector, then the vector products `y*x` and `x*y` are different as illustrated in the following example:

Example 3.1 Multiply the vectors $\boldsymbol{x}$, a column vector, and $\boldsymbol{y}$, a row vector, whose elements are as given below:

`x= [3 4 5]` and `y= [1 2 0]`

Solution:

```
x = [3 4 5];

y = [1 2 0];
```

The command

```
z = y * x'
```

will multiply `y` by `x'` and produce the result in `z`, a scalar and its value is given below:

```
z =11
```

The command

```
z = x' * y
```

will multiply `x` by `y` and produce the result `z`, which is a 3×3 matrix and is given below:

```
z =
```

$$\begin{pmatrix} 3 & 6 & 0 \\ 4 & 8 & 0 \\ 5 & 10 & 0 \end{pmatrix}$$

3.2.3 Vector Transpose

Transpose operation turns a row vector into a column vector and vice versa. MATLAB uses the `apostrophe` or `single quote` to denote transpose.

The command

```
xt = x'
```

will produce the following row vector ***xt*** which is the transpose of the column vector ***x***, given in Example 3.1 above, i.e.,

```
xt = [3      4      5 ]
```

The command

```
yt = y'
```

will produce the following column vector `yt`, which is the transpose of the row vector `y`.

```
yt =
     1
     2
     0
```

If a vector ***x*** is complex, its conjugate can be obtained by using `conj(x)` command and the command `x'` produces the transpose of complex conjugate of vector ***x***.

Example 3.2 Let $x = [i \quad 2 + 4i \quad -3 + 4i]$. Verify that the transpose of x actually produces the transpose of complex conjugate of x.

Solution:

```
x = [i    2+4i    -3+4i];
```

The command

```
y = conj(x)
```

will give the conjugate of vector ***x***, as shown below:

```
y = [0-1.0000i    2.0000-4.0000i    -3.0000-4.0000i]
```

To find transpose of ***x***, the command

```
xt = x',
```

gives output as shown below:

```
xt =
         0 - 1.0000i
    2.0000 - 4.0000i
   -3.0000 - 4.0000i
```

It is seen that `xt`, the transpose of `x` is nothing but the transpose of conjugate of `x`. Hence verified.

3.2.4 Creation of Evenly Spaced Row Vectors

A row vector with evenly spaced, real elements can be created by using the command as given below:

```
variable name = k : l : m,
```

where k is the initial value,
l is the step size or increment and
m is the final value.

For example, the command

```
t = 1: 2: 11
```

will create a row vector with initial element = 1, and final element = 11 with a step size of 2 as given below.

```
t = [1  3  5  7  9  11]
```

Programming Tip 3.1: In MATLAB, negative and non-integer step sizes are also allowed.

For example, the statement given below creates vector ***t*** with negative step of –2.5.

```
t = 12.5 : -2.5 :  0
```

When executed, vector ***t*** is obtained and is as given below:

```
t = [12.5000    10.0000    7.5000    5.0000    2.5000    0]
```

Programming Tip 3.2: Care should be taken that the initial and final values given must be appropriate.

For example, the statement

```
t = 11 : 1 : 5
```

will result in empty matrix, **t**, as final value is less than the initial value which is not possible when the step size is positive. Similarly, the statement

```
t = 1 : -2 : 10
```

will also produce empty matrix.

Programming Tip 3.3: If a step size is not specified, +1 is taken as default value of the step size.

For example, the statement

```
t = 0 : 6
```

will produce the row vector:

```
t =  [0  1  2  3  4  5  6]
```

Evenly spaced row vectors can also be created using the following commands:

(a) **linspace**

A row vector can also be created by using **linspace** command. The format is as given below:

```
linspace(x1, x2, n)
```

It generates a linearly spaced vector of length n, i.e., n equally spaced points between x_1 and x_2. For example, the statement:

```
a = linspace(0, 10, 5);
```

when executed, produces a vector having 5 equally spaced elements between the limits 0 and 10 as given below:

```
a = [0      2.5      5.0      7.5      10.0]
```

(b) **logspace**

Similarly the command

```
logspace(a, b, n)
```

creates a logarithmically spaced vector of length n in the interval 10^a to 10^b.

For example, the command

```
x = logspace(0, 4, 3);
```

When executed, will give the following results:

```
x = [1          100          10000]
```

i.e., three points are generated in the interval 10^0 and 10^4.

3.2.5 Some Useful Commands

Let x be a row vector, y be a column vector and z be a row vector, which are defined as follows:

```
x = [1      4       11      100];

y = [14;   200;   -100];

z = [1.4    10.7    -1.1     20.9];
```

Let two more row vectors z_1 and t_1 be defined as follows:

```
z1 = [2,    6,     5,     -7.2];

t1 = [2,    5,     3,      6.4];
```

Some useful commands/functions related to vectors, using the vectors defined above, are explained below:

1. **sum(x)**
   This command gives the sum of all the elements in a row/column vector x.
   Then command,

   ```
   a = sum(x)
   ```

   when executed gives the output as shown below.

   ```
   a = 116
   ```

   The command,

   ```
   a = sum(y),
   ```

   when executed gives the following result:

   ```
   a = 114
   ```

2. **mean(x)**
   It gives average of the elements of a row/column vector. The command

   ```
   a = mean(x)
   ```

   when executed gives the following result:

   ```
   a = 29
   ```

   Similarly, the command

   ```
   b = mean(y)
   ```

   will give:

   ```
   b = 38
   ```

3. **length(x)**
   It gives the number of elements in a row/column vector. The command

   ```
   a = length(x)
   ```

   when executed gives the following result:

```
a =  4
```

Similarly, the command

```
b = length(y)
```

will produce the output:

```
b = 3
```

4. **max(x)**
   It gives the maximum value in the row or column vector x. The command

```
a = max(x)
```

when executed gives the following result:

```
a = 100
```

Similarly, the command

```
b = max(y)
```

will give

```
b = 200
```

5. **min(x)**
   It gives the minimum value in the row or column vector x. The commands

```
a = min(x)
```

and

```
b = min(y)
```

when executed give the following result:

```
a = 1

b = -100
```

6. **prod(x)**
   It gives the product of elements of row/column vector x. The command

```
a = prod(x)
```

when executed gives the following result:

```
a = 4400
```

Similarly, the command

```
b = prod(y)
```

will produce:

```
b = -280000
```

7. **sign(x)**
   It returns 1, if the sign of an element of a vector is +ve, returns 0, if sign is 0, and returns –1, if sign is –ve. The commands,

```
a = sign(x)
```

and

```
b = sign(y)
```

when executed give the following results:

```
a = [1      1      1      1]
b = [1      1     -1]
```

8. **find(x)**
The statement

```
a = find(x)
```

returns the linear indices corresponding to the nonzero entries of the array x.

> **Programming Tip 3.4:** If no entry is found, 'find' function returns an empty array.

Linear index means the location of the value in vector. For the vector x, given above, this command when executed gives the following result:

```
a = [1      2      3      4]
```

i.e., first, second, third, fourth elements of the vector x have non-zero entries.
The command

```
a = find(y >24)
```

will return the indices of vector y, where y is greater than 24. In this case when executed the following results are obtained:

```
a = 2
```

i.e., second element of y has a value greater than 24.

9. **fix(z)**
It rounds the elements of a vector z to the nearest integers towards zero.
The command

```
a = fix(z)
```

when executed gives the following results:

```
a = [1      10      -1      20]
```

10. **floor(z)**
It rounds the elements of a vector z to the nearest integers towards $-\infty$. For the vector z,

```
a = floor(z)
```

when executed gives the following results:

```
a = [1     10      -2        20]
```

It is to note that the third element of this vector is −2 instead of −1.

11. **ceil(z)**
It rounds the elements of a vector z to nearest integers towards $+\infty$. For the vector z, given above,

```
a = ceil(z)
```

when executed gives the following results:

```
a = [2      11      -1      21]
```

It is to note that the result of this rounding command is different than the previously given commands.

12. **round(x)**

This command rounds the elements of x to the nearest integers. For the vector z, given above, the command

```
k = round (z)
```

when executed gives the following results:

```
k = [1     11     -1     21]
```

13. **sort(x)**

It lists the elements of the vector x in the ascending order.
The more refine form is

```
sort (x, 'mode')
```

where mode can be 'ascend' or 'descend' to sort in ascending and descending order, respectively.

Programming Tip 3.5: In sort command, the default mode is 'ascend, i.e., if nothing is mentioned in sort commend then values are arranged in ascending order.

If $x_1 = [5 \;\; -3 \;\; 10 \;\; -10]$, then the command

```
x1 = [5  -3  10  -10];
a = sort(x1)
```

when executed gives the following results:

```
a = [-10     -3     5     10]
```

When the command,

```
b = sort(x1, 'descend')
```

is executed, it will give the results as:

```
b = [10    5    -3     -10]
```

14. **mod(x, y)**

The general form of the 'mod' command is as given below:

```
m = mod(x, y) if y ~= 0,
```

It returns $x - n.*y$, where $n = \text{floor}(x./y)$
In present case, the command

```
mz = mod(z1, t1)
```

when executed results into another vector ***mz***, of the same size.

Each element of $\mathbf{z}_1$ is divided by the corresponding element of $\mathbf{t}_1$. The quotient is then rounded towards $-\infty$. The remainder is then calculated again using the new quotient and assigned to the resultant vector, ***mz***.

Take the fourth element of $\mathbf{z}_1$ defined at the beginning of the section = –7.2.
It is divided by fourth element of $\mathbf{t}_1$ also defined at the beginning of the section = 6.4.
The quotient obtained = –1.1250.
The quotient is rounded towards $-\infty$, and therefore becomes = –2.0.

Now taking the revised value of the quotient, i.e., –2.0, the remainder is evaluated again as shown below:

$$\text{Remainder} = (-7.2) - (+6.4) * (-2.0) = 5.6$$

which is assigned to the resultant vector ***mz*** as its fourth element. Likewise the other elements are also computed. The complete result obtained is as given below:

```
mz = [0   1.0    2.0    5.6]
```

> **Programming Tip 3.6:** In `mod(z1, t1)` statement, the resultant vector elements will have the same sign as `t1` and `mod(z1, 0) = z1`.

15. **`rem(z1, t1)`**

This function **`rem(z1, t1)`** is very similar to the **`mod`** function. But there are some noticeable differences:

The quotient obtained after dividing element of $\mathbf{z}_1$ by corresponding element of $\mathbf{t}_1$, is rounded towards zero.

Therefore, for the matrices $\mathbf{z}_1$, and $\mathbf{t}_1$ taken in the previous example, the fourth element of $\mathbf{z}_1 = -7.2$, divided by $\mathbf{t}_1 = 6.4$, quotient $= -1.1250$, is rounded towards zero, therefore revised quotient $= -1.0$.

Now taking revised quotient $= -1.0$, the remainder is evaluated again as shown below:

$$\text{Remainder} = (-7.2) - (+6.4)*(-1.0) = -0.8.$$

Therefore, the resultant matrix **rz** is given as:

```
rz = [0,    1.0,    2.0,    -0.8]
```

> **Programming Tip 3.7:** In `rem(z1, t1)` statement, the resultant vector elements will have the same sign as `z1` and `mod(z1, 0) = NaN`, i.e., not a number.

3.3 ENTERING DATA IN MATRICES

The following points are to be noted for entering an explicit list of matrix elements at the command window:

- Start with a left-handed square bracket '['.
- Type the matrix elements row wise. Each row vector should have the same length to create a valid matrix.
- Enter the elements of the first row with one or more blanks or a comma separating each element.
- Separate the different rows of the matrix by a semicolon (;) or a carriage return.
- Enclose the entire list of elements of the matrix with in square brackets, i.e., [ ].
- Elements of a matrix can be a real number, complex number or a valid MATLAB expression (provided that the values of unknown variables in the expression are supplied before the execution of the expression).

Example 3.3 Enter the matrix **A**, which has three rows and three columns and is given as follows:

$$\mathbf{A} = \begin{bmatrix} 1 & 10 & 20 \\ 2 & 5 & 6 \\ 7 & 8 & 9 \end{bmatrix}$$

Solution: The given matrix **A** can be entered as per the following in the command window:

```
A = [ 1  10  20;   2  5  6;   7  8  9 ]
```

The elements separated by space belong to the same row. The elements in different rows are separated by a semicolon. All the elements are enclosed in square brackets. The result obtained is as shown below:

```
A =

     1    10    20
     2     5     6
     7     8     9
```

Example 3.4 Enter the matrix which has two rows and two columns and whose elements are complex numbers and are given as follows:

$$\mathbf{B} = \begin{bmatrix} 1+2i & 3i \\ 4+4i & 5 \end{bmatrix}$$

Solution: Type the following in the command window to enter the matrix **B**.

```
B = [1+2i    3i;      4+4i      5]
```

The result obtained is as shown below:

```
B =

   1.0000 + 2.0000i        0 + 3.0000i
   4.0000 + 4.0000i        5.0000
```

Example 3.5 Create the matrix **C** which has 2 rows and 2 columns and whose elements may include expressions as given below.

$$\mathbf{C} = \begin{bmatrix} 1 & -2 \\ \sqrt{3} & e \end{bmatrix}$$

Solution: Type the following in the command window to enter the matrix **C**:

```
C = [1      -2;       sqrt(3)      exp(1)]
```

The result obtained is as shown below:

```
C =

    1.0000    -2.0000
    1.7321     2.7183
```

It can be seen in the examples given above, that data entry has been started with the left handed square bracket '[' and matrix elements have been entered row wise, i.e., elements of first row have been entered first and then the elements of second row have been entered and so on. The different rows have been separated by semicolon and all the elements have been enclosed within square brackets. It is important to note that the values like $\sqrt{3}$ and e have been entered using functions `sqrt` and `exp`, respectively.

3.4 LINE CONTINUATION

Sometimes, it is not possible to type the entire data input on the same line. In such case, three consecutive periods (...) are used to indicate continuation of the data to the next line. These periods are called `ellipsis`.

For example: The command:

```
A = [0.3      5.5      9.35      0.09; ...
     3        4        5.5       6.5; ...
     7.2      8.0      9.0        3]
```

when executed gives the following results, i.e., the intended 3×4 matrix **A**,

```
A =
     0.3000     5.5000     9.3500     0.0900
     3.0000     4.0000     5.5000     6.5000
     7.2000     8.0000     9.0000     3.0000
```

A matrix can also be entered across multiple lines using carriage returns at the end of the each row. In this case, the semicolons and ellipsis at the end of each row may be omitted.

Thus the following three commands are equivalent:

```
% use semicolons to separate the rows
A = [1 3 9; 5 10 15; 0 0 -5];
% use enter to separate the rows
A = [1      3      9
     5     10     15
     0      0    -5];
% use three ellipses to continue the line
A = [1     3      9;     5      10...
     15    ;0     0    -5];
```

All the above commands will generate the same matrix **A** as follows:

```
A =
     1     3     9
     5    10    15
     0     0    -5
```

3.5 MATRIX SUBSCRIPTS/INDICES

The elements of a matrix can be specified/accessed by specifying their respective row and column numbers. The first index refers to the row number and second index refers to column number. The element in *i*th row and the *j*th column of a matrix **A** is denoted by `A(i, j)`. For example, `A(2, 3)`, refers to the number in the second row and third column of the matrix **A**.

3.5.1 Sub-matrices/Sub-arrays

Subsets of arrays can be selected as if they are separate arrays. MATLAB allows portions of a matrix to be specified using colon operator. For example, statement **B**`(1:4,   2:8)` specifies rows 1 to 4 and columns 2 to 8 of the matrix **B**.

For matrix **A** defined below:

```
A = [1        3      9
     5       10     15
     0        0    -5];
A(1:2, 2:3)
```

when executed gives the following results:

```
ans =

    3     9
   10    15
```

i.e., elements of only row numbers 1 and 2 and the column numbers 2 and 3 of matrix **A** have been extracted.

The colon when mentioned alone, refers to all the elements in a row or column of a matrix.

Thus, `A (:, 2:3)` refers elements of all rows and columns 2 to 3 of the matrix **A**. When the following command is given in (refer to Example 3.3)

```
A(:, 2:3)
```

It gives the following results:

```
ans =

    3     9
   10    15
    0    -5
```

> **Programming Tip 3.8:** When all the rows (or all the columns) of a matrix are to be specified, a colon `(:)` is used as the row (or column) index.

The command `A(1:k,j)` refers to the first k elements of the jth column of the matrix **A**

If $k = 2$ and $j = 3$, then

```
A(1:2, 3)
```

gives the following result:

```
ans =

    9
   15
```

3.5.2 Array as a Single Column Vector

An array is regarded as one long column vector, which is formed from the columns of the given matrix.

The element in the ith row and jth column of $(m \times n)$ matrix **A**, may be obtained with a single index $k = (j - 1)m + i$. For example, element **A**(1, 2) of (3 × 3) matrix **A**, where $m = 3$, $n = 3$, $i = 1$ and $j = 2$, can be accessed by using the index $k = (2 - 1)*3 + 1$, i.e., $k = 4$, i.e., **A**(4) will access the same element as **A**(1, 2), i.e., = 10.

The keyword `'end'` refers to the last row or column. The command

```
A(:, end)
```

refers to all rows and last column of matrix **A** and is given as :

```
ans =

    9
   15
   -5
```

> **Programming Tip 3.9:** Matrix elements can also be accessed by means of a single index, `A(i)`.

3.6 MULTIDIMENSIONAL MATRICES AND ARRAYS

Matrix dimensions are defined automatically. However, if it is desired to know the size of an existing matrix **A**, command, `size (A)`, can be used. The format is as given below:

```
size(A)
```

The command returns the number of elements of the matrix in each dimension. These numbers returned by the size command can be assigned to variables and stored for later use in the program. For example, if the matrix is two-dimensional, the following command can be used:

```
[m, n] = size(A)
```

When executed, it will assign the number of rows of matrix A to variable *m* and number of columns to variable *n*.

Referring to matrix **A** in Example 3.3, the size can be obtained by the following command:

```
[m, n] = size(A)
```

This gives the following output **at the command window:**

```
m =
    3
n =
    3
```

> **Programming Tip 3.10:** User does not need to declare the dimension of the matrix in MATLAB as required in other high-level computer languages.

Multidimensional arrays are an extension of two-dimensional matrices described by their row and column indices. Multidimensional arrays use additional indices. A three-dimensional array, for example, uses three indices; first index refers to rows, second refers to column and third index refers to the third dimension. For example, a book can be viewed as a collection of two-dimensional pages with the page number being the third dimension. To access the element in the third row, fourth column of page 5, the indices will be (3, 4, 5). As the dimensions of an array are increased, the number of indices is also increased correspondingly. For example, a five-dimensional array will require five indices. The first two refer a row and column, the next three for third, fourth and fifth dimensions.

3.6.1 Creating Multidimensional Arrays

Multidimensional arrays can be created in a number of ways.

- Extending matrix of lower dimension
- Using MATLAB functions
- Using `cat` function

One way to create a multidimensional array is to create a two-dimensional array and extend it.

Example 3.6 The array **A** is given below. Extend the 2-D array to three dimensions by including another 2-D array as second element in its third dimension.

```
A = [1  2  3;
     5  4  3;
     1  3  6];
```

Solution: Let there be another two-dimensional matrix **B** having the same number of rows and columns as matrix **A**.

B = [2 4 6;
1 3 6;
3 6 9];

The matrix **B** can be included as second element of a three-dimensional matrix by extending the two-dimensional matrix **A**. The statements required are as shown below:

```
B = [2 4 6; 1 3 6; 3 6 9];
A(:, :, 2) = B
```

or

```
A(:, :, 2) = [2 4 6;  1 3 6; 3 6 9 ]
```

The response of the statements is as shown below:

```
A(:, :, 1) =
               [1 2 3
                5 4 3
                1 3 6]
A(:, :, 2) =
               [2 4 6
                1 3 6
                3 6 9]
```

The matrix **A** can be extended further to include more 2-D matrix elements in its third dimension or the number of dimensions can be further extended.

> **Programming Tip 3.11:** For numeric arrays, all rows must have the same number of elements and entries in its higher dimension must have the same number of rows and columns, and so on.

3.6.1.1 Using MATLAB Functions

MATLAB functions such as `randn`, `ones`, and `zeros` that are used to generate matrices can also be used to generate multidimensional arrays in the same way. For example,

```
B = randn(4, 3, 2)
```

3.6.1.2 Using `'cat'` Function

The cat function concatenates a list of arrays along a specified dimension. The syntax of `'cat'` command is as given below:

```
B = cat(dim, A1, B1…)
```

where A_1, B_1, and so on are the arrays that are concatenated along the dimension indicated by `'dim'`. For example, to create a new array with `'cat'`

```
B = cat(3, [1 3; 6 9], [3 3; 9 9])
```

The result obtained is as follows:

```
B(:,:,1) =
             1  3
             6  9
```

```
B(:,:,2) =

        3  3
        9  9
```

3.6.2 Working with Multidimensional Arrays

Most of the concepts that apply to two-dimensional matrices apply to multidimensional arrays as well. Multidimensional arrays are accessed just as 2-D matrices are done.

Many computational and mathematical functions in MATLAB accept multidimensional arrays as arguments. MATLAB functions that operate element-by-element on 2-D arrays, such as the trigonometric and exponential functions, work the same way for multidimensional arrays also. Functions that operate on simple matrices, such as the linear algebra and matrix functions, do not accept multidimensional arrays as arguments. That is, one cannot use such functions, or the array operators □, ^, \, or /, with multidimensional arguments. The multidimensional arguments or operands in these cases result in an error. But, these functions can be used with sub-arrays extracted from the multidimensional arrays.

3.7 MATRIX MANIPULATIONS

Shape and size of a matrix can be altered by using the following MATLAB commands:

3.7.1 Reshaping Matrices

Matrices can be reshaped into a vector or into any other appropriately sized matrix as described below:

3.7.1.1 Reshaping of a Matrix as a Vector

All the elements of a matrix **A** can be grouped into a single-column vector ***b*** by the command `b = A (:)`. Matrix **A** will be stored column wise in vector ***b***, i.e., first column is stored first, then second column and so on.

Example 3.7 Let matrix $\mathbf{A} = \begin{bmatrix} 1 & 10 & 20 \\ 2 & 5 & 6 \\ 7 & 8 & 9 \end{bmatrix}$. Reshape the matrix to a column vector.

Solution: The command

```
A =[1 10 20; 2 5 6 ;7 8 9]
```

The following result is displayed:

```
A =

     1    10    20
     2     5     6
     7     8     9
```

The command

```
B = A (:)
```

converts the matrix **A** to a column vector **B**. When executed the statement gives the following results:

```
B =

  1
  2
  7
 10
  5
  8
 20
  6
  9
```

i.e., matrix **A** is stored in column **B**, in column-major order, i.e., first column first, then second column and so on.

3.7.1.2 Reshaping of Matrix as a Differently Sized Matrix

If a given matrix **A** is a $(p \times q)$ matrix, it can be reshaped into a new $(m \times n)$ matrix, (as long as total elements of the two matrices are same, i.e., `p*q = m*n`. The reshaping command is as given below:

```
B = reshape(A, m, n).
```

When executed, this command will reshape matrix **A** into matrix **B** of size $(m \times n)$. The elements of matrix **B** are taken column wise from the matrix **A** as discussed in Example 3.6.

Example 3.8 Let matrix **A** of size (3×4) be defined as,

$$\mathbf{A} = \begin{bmatrix} 1 & 2 & 3 & 4 \\ 5 & 6 & 7 & 8 \\ 9 & 10 & 11 & 12 \end{bmatrix}.$$

Reshape matrix **A** into matrix **B** of the size (6×2).

Solution: The command,

```
A = [1 2 3 4; 5 6 7 8; 9 10 11 12]
```

Gives the result as shown below:

```
A =

  1     2     3     4
  5     6     7     8
  9    10    11    12
```

`To reshape the matrix as desired following command is used:`

```
B = reshape (A, 6, 2)
```

This will result into a (6×2) reshaped matrix as shown below:

```
B =

  1     3
  5     7
  9    11
  2     4
  6     8
 10    12
```

The reshaped matrix **B** has six rows and two columns.

3.7.2 Expanding the Size of a Matrix

When a single element or a few elements are entered in a matrix, MATLAB creates the matrix of proper dimensions to accommodate the entered element(s). Remaining unspecified elements are assumed to be zero. For example, suppose a matrix **C** does not exist and a statement

```
C (2, 2) = 10
```

is entered at the command window. In such a case matrix **C** of size (2 × 2) is generated with element **C**(2, 2) = 10 and all other elements are made equal to zero as shown below.

```
C =
     0     0
     0    10
```

Similarly, the command

```
D (2, 1:2) = [3    4]
```

when executed, a matrix **D** having two rows and two columns is generated. It will assign values 3 and 4 to the elements of the second row having column indices 1 and 2, respectively. Rest of the elements will be declared equal to zero. The result produced is as given below:

```
D =
     0     0
     3     4
```

> **Programming Tip 3.12:** If an attempt is made to access an element outside of the given dimension of matrix **A**, it will give an error.

For example, if matrix **A** has dimensions (3 × 3) and an attempt is made to access fourth row, e.g., `A(4, 3)`, then an error message :

```
'index exceeds matrix dimensions'
```

will be displayed.

> **Programming Tip 3.13:** If a value is to be stored in a row/column that exceeds the dimensions of the matrix, the size of the new matrix is automatically increased to accommodate the new element.

For example, Suppose,

```
A = [6 7;8 9]
```

It will give the following result:

```
A =
     6     7
     8     9
```

Now, the command

```
A(2, 3)=15
```

will result in following change in the matrix **A**:

```
A =
     6     7     0
     8     9    15
```

The dimension of the matrix is extended to (2×3), element = 15 is stored at the index, (2, 3) and remaining new elements are equal to zero.

3.7.3 Appending a Row/Column to a Matrix

Sometimes it is required that a column or a row is added to a given matrix. A column can be appended by using following command:

```
A = [A x]
```

It will append the column vector $\boldsymbol{x}$ to the columns of existing matrix **A**. To append a row to a given matrix the following command is used:

```
A = [A; y]
```

This will append the row vector $\boldsymbol{y}$ to the rows of existing matrix **A**.

Example 3.9 Let $\mathbf{A} = \begin{bmatrix} 6 & 7 \\ 8 & 9 \end{bmatrix}$ $\mathbf{x} = \begin{bmatrix} 1 \\ 2 \end{bmatrix}$ and $\mathbf{y} = \begin{bmatrix} 3 & 4 \end{bmatrix}$

Append the matrix **x** as new column of **A** and store in matrix **B**. Append the matrix **y** as new row of **A** and store in matrix **C**.

Solution:

(i) To append the matrix **x** as new column of **A** and store in matrix **B**, the MATLAB statement given below is used:

```
A = [6 7; 8 9];
x = [1; 2];
B = [A x]
```

When executed, it gives the following result:

```
B =

     6     7     1
     8     9     2
```

(ii) To append the matrix **y** as new row of **A** and store in matrix **C**, the MATLAB statement given below is used:

```
A = [6 7; 8 9];
y = [3 4];
C = [A; y]
```

When executed, it gives the following result:

```
C =
     6     7
     8     9
     3     4
```

3.7.4 Deleting a Row/Column of a Matrix

Rows and columns of a matrix can be deleted by setting the corresponding row or column to a null vector, i.e., a pair of square brackets [ ], without any element within the brackets.

Example 3.10 Given the matrices $\mathbf{F} = \begin{bmatrix} 6 & 7 \\ 8 & 9 \end{bmatrix}$ and $\mathbf{G} = \begin{bmatrix} 6 & 7 & 1 \\ 8 & 9 & 2 \end{bmatrix}$. Delete the first row from matrix **F** and first two columns from matrix **G**.

Solution: The above matrix is obtained in workspace by using following commands:

```
F = [6 7;8 9];
G = [6 7 1; 8 9 2];
```

The command

```
F (1, :) = [ ]
```

when executed, it deletes the first row of matrix **F** given above and produces new matrix **F** as given below, deleting all the columns of the first row.

```
F =
     8     9
```

The command

```
G (: , 1: 2) = [ ]
```

when executed deletes the first and second columns of all the rows of the matrix **G** and the result will be a new matrix **G**:

```
G =
     1
     2
```

Example 3.11 Let $\mathbf{A} = \begin{bmatrix} 6 & 7 \\ 8 & 9 \end{bmatrix}$. Delete the element with indices (1, 2) from matrix **A**.

Solution: The above matrix is obtained in workspace by using the following command:

```
A = [6 7; 8 9];
```

To delete the particular element as mentioned in the problem the following command is given:

```
A (1, 2) = [ ]
```

But, this will result in an error because a single element, i.e., `A(1,2)` cannot be removed from a matrix and following message will be displayed:

```
???  Indexed empty matrix assignment is not allowed.
```

> **Programming Tip 3.14:** If a single element is deleted from a matrix, the matrix does not remain a valid matrix any more. Hence, deletion of a single element is not allowed.

3.7.5 Concatenation of Matrices

Concatenation is a method of combining or connecting or joining small matrices together to make larger or bigger matrices. The pair of square brackets [ ] is the concatenation operator.

Example 3.12 Let matrix **A** be given by $\mathbf{A} = \begin{bmatrix} 1 & 2 \\ 3 & 4 \end{bmatrix}$. Compute matrix **B**, where

$\mathbf{B} = \begin{bmatrix} \mathbf{A}_1 & \mathbf{A}_2 \\ \mathbf{A}_3 & \mathbf{A}_4 \end{bmatrix}$, where the sub-matrices, $\mathbf{A}_1 = \mathbf{A}$, $\mathbf{A}_2 = \mathbf{A} + 12$, $\mathbf{A}_3 = \mathbf{A} + 24$, $\mathbf{A}_4 = \mathbf{A} + 10$.

Solution: The matrices $\mathbf{A}_1$ and $\mathbf{A}_2$ are to be concatenated column wise to form the first row of the resultant matrix **B**. Similarly, $\mathbf{A}_3$ and $\mathbf{A}_4$ are concatenated column wise to form the second row of the resultant matrix **B**. The two rows are concatenated vertically, i.e., row-wise to obtain the resultant matrix **B**. All this can be done using statements given below:

```
A = [1 2; 3 4];
B = [A   A+12;  A+24   A+10]
```

When executed, it creates a (4 × 4) matrix **B**, given below:

```
B =
     1     2     2     3
     3     4     4     5
    25    26    11    12
    27    28    13    14
```

Note: Errors will occur if the component dimensions do not sensibly match.

3.8 GENERATION OF SPECIAL MATRICES

Following **MATLAB commands/functions** which generate special matrices are often used in engineering computations involving matrices:

1. **`zeros(p, q)`**
   It returns a rectangular, $p \times q$ matrix of all zeros.
   Let $p = 2$ and $q = 3$, and execute the following commands.

   ```
   p =2;
   q =3;
   A =zeros(p, q)
   ```

   This will generate a (2 × 3) matrix with all elements equal to zero as follows:

   ```
   A =
        0     0     0
        0     0     0
   ```

2. **`ones(p, q)`**
   It returns a $p \times q$ matrix of all elements having value one.
   Let $p = 2$, $q = 3$, and execute the following commands.

   ```
   p =2;
   q =3;
   A =ones(p, q)
   ```

   It will generate a (2 × 3) matrix with all elements equal to one. The result will be as shown below:

   ```
   A =
        1     1     1
        1     1     1
   ```

3. **eye(p, q)**
It returns a $p \times q$ matrix with ones on the main diagonal and zeros elsewhere.
Let $p = 2, q = 3$, and execute the following commands.

```
p =2;
q =3;
A =eye(p, q)
```

It will generate a (2×3) matrix with all diagonal elements equal to one. The result will be as shown below:

```
A =
      1     0     0
      0     1     0
```

The three commands discussed above with a single argument p, produce corresponding square matrices of dimension $(p \times p)$, e.g. the command,

```
A =eye(3)
```

When executed, will produce a (3×3) identity matrix as shown below:

```
A =
      1     0     0
      0     1     0
      0     0     1
```

4. **rand(n)**
This command generates matrix **A** with random entries, chosen from a uniform distribution on the **interval (0, 1).**
For example, the command

```
m = rand(3)
```

when executed gives the following output:

```
m =
     0.9501    0.4860    0.4565
     0.2311    0.8913    0.0185
     0.6068    0.7621    0.8214
```

As the elements are generated at random, if executed again the command shall generate a matrix with different elements.
Another form of **'rand'** command is as given below:

5. **rand(m, n)**
It generates matrix with m number of rows and n number of columns having random entries chosen from between 0 and 1. For example:

```
d = rand(3, 2)
```

when executed gives the following output:

```
d =

     0.4447    0.9218
     0.6154    0.7382
     0.7919    0.1763
```

6. **rands(m, n)**
This command is similar to 'rand' command and generates matrix **A** with m number of rows and n number of columns having random entries, chosen from a uniform distribution on the **interval (–1, +1)**.

For example, the command

```
d = rands(3, 2)
```

when executed gives the following output:

```
d =
      -0.0871    -0.1106
      -0.9630     0.2309
       0.6428     0.5839
```

Similarly, **rands(n)** will generate a random matrix with n number of rows and n number of columns having random entries chosen from a uniform distribution on the **interval (–1, +1).**

6. **vander(V)**

It returns **VanderMonde Matrix, V,** whose columns are powers of the vector v as shown below: VanderMonde Matrix of a given vector v, which has n elements, is given by:

$$\mathbf{V} = \begin{bmatrix} v_1^2 & v_1 & 1 \\ v_2^2 & v_2 & 1 \\ v_3^2 & v_3 & 1 \end{bmatrix}$$

where v_1, v_2, v_3 are the elements of the given vector v.

Let **v** = [4 5 6]

Then, to generate a VanderMonde matrix, the following commands are used:

```
V = [1 2 3];

vander(v)
```

The result obtained is as:

```
ans =
      1     1     1
      4     2     1
      9     3     1
```

Similarly, if **a** = [1 2 4 5 2 3], i.e., $n = 6$

Then the commands are given as:

```
a = [1 2 4 5 2 3];

vander (a)
```

This will give the following result:

```
ans =

      1      1      1      1      1      1
     32     16      8      4      2      1
   1024    256     64     16      4      1
   3125    625    125     25      5      1
     32     16      8      4      2      1
    243     81     27      9      3      1
```

7. **diag(v)**

If v is a row or column vector with n elements, it returns a diagonal matrix, with vector v on the diagonal. The syntax for this command is as follows:

```
A = diag(v, k)
```

This will return a square matrix **A**, of order <u>**n + abs(k)**</u> with the elements of vector *v* on the *k*th diagonal.

$k = 0$ represents the main diagonal,
$k > 0$ represents above the main diagonal and
$k < 0$ represents below the main diagonal.

> **Programming Tip 3.15:** `A = diag(v)`, *is the same as* `A = diag(v, 0)` *and puts vector v on the main diagonal .*

Let **x** be an $m \times n$ matrix, **then the command**

```
A = diag(x)
```

will return a column vector formed from the elements on the main diagonal of matrix **x** and the command:

```
A = diag(x, k)
```

will return a column vector formed from the elements of the *k*th diagonal of matrix **x**.

Example 3.13 Let vector *v* be given as:

$$v = \begin{bmatrix} 2 & 3 & 4 & 5 \end{bmatrix}.$$

Form a diagonal matrix **A**, using the elements of *v* as the diagonal elements of **A**.

Solution: The following commands are used to get the desired output:

```
v = [2 3 4 5 ];

A = diag(v)
```

When executed, it will display the following result:

```
A =

    2     0     0     0
    0     3     0     0
    0     0     4     0
    0     0     0     5
```

It can be seen that the components of the row vector *v* have been placed on the main diagonal of matrix **A**.

Example 3.14 Let a column vector *z* be given as:

$z = [2; 3; 4; 5]$.

Form a diagonal matrix **A**, using the elements of *z* as the main diagonal elements of **A**.
Form a matrix **B**, using the elements of vector *z* as elements of first upper diagonal of **B**.
Form a matrix **C**, using the elements of vector **z** as elements of first lower diagonal of **C**.

Solution:

(i) The commands that generates matrix **A** with diagonal elements taken from vector *z* are:

```
z = [2; 3; 4; 5];

A = diag(z)
```

When executed, it will produce the following result:

```
A =

     2     0     0     0
     0     3     0     0
     0     0     4     0
     0     0     0     5
```

The elements of the column vector *z* have been placed on the main diagonal of matrix **A**

(ii) To generate matrix **B**, using the elements of vector *z* as elements of first upper diagonal of **B**, the following commands are used:

```
z = [2; 3; 4; 5];
B = diag(z, 1)
```

When executed, it will give the following result:

```
B =

     0     2     0     0     0
     0     0     3     0     0
     0     0     0     4     0
     0     0     0     0     5
     0     0     0     0     0
```

A matrix of order (4 + 1 = 5) has been displayed with the elements of the vector *z* on the first upper diagonal.

(iii) To generate matrix **C**, using the elements of vector *z* as elements of first lower diagonal of **B**, the following commands are used:

```
z = [2; 3; 4; 5];
C = diag(z, -1)
```

When executed, it will produce the following result:

```
C =

     0     0     0     0     0
     2     0     0     0     0
     0     3     0     0     0
     0     0     4     0     0
     0     0     0     5     0
```

A matrix of order (4 + 1 = 5) has been displayed with the elements of the vector *z* on the first lower diagonal.

Example 3.15 Let matrices **x** and **y** be given as:

```
x = [2  3;  4  5] and
y = [1  2  3;  4  5  6;  7  8  9]
```

Write statements to obtain

A column vector composed of diagonal elements of **x**.

A column vector composed of diagonal elements of **y**.

A matrix having first upper diagonal elements of **y**.

Solution:

(i) The commands used to obtain column vector composed of diagonal elements of **x** are:

```
x = [2    3;    4    5];
A = diag(x)
```

When executed, the result obtained is as given below:

```
A =
        2
        5
```

i.e., a column vector formed from the elements of the main diagonal of the matrix **x**, has been displayed.

(ii) The commands used to obtain column vector composed of diagonal elements of **y** are:

```
y = [1  2  3; 4  5  6 ; 7  8  9];
b = diag(y)
```

When executed, the result obtained is as given below:

```
b =
        1
        5
        9
```

(iii) The commands used to obtain column vector composed of first upper diagonal elements of **y** are:

```
y = [1  2  3; 4  5  6 ; 7  8  9];
c = diag(y, 1)
```

When executed, the result obtained is as given below:

```
c =
        2
        6
```

i.e., upper diagonal elements of the matrix **y**.

3.9 SOME USEFUL FUNCTIONS RELATED TO MATRICES

Let matrix **A** be defined as follows for the commands being discussed in this section.

```
A = [1 2; 0 4]
```

i.e., $\mathbf{A} = \begin{bmatrix} 1 & 2 \\ 0 & 4 \end{bmatrix}$

1. **det(A)**
   It returns the determinant of a given square matrix **A**.
   When executed, the result obtained is:

```
ans =
        4
```

2. **rank (A)**
   It returns the rank of a given rectangular matrix **A**.

```
rank(A)
ans =
        2
```

3. **trace (A)**
It returns the sum of the diagonal elements of a rectangular matrix **A**.

```
trace(A)

        ans =

                5
```

4. **inv(A)**
It returns the inverse of a non-singular matrix **A** (i.e., $\mathbf{A}^{-1}$).

```
inv(A)

ans =

     1.0000    -0.5000
          0     0.2500
```

5. **norm(A)**
It returns the Euclidean norm of the given rectangular matrix **A** or a given vector **A**.

```
norm(A)

ans =

     4.4954
```

6. **A′ (A transpose)**
A′, pronounced as *transpose,* returns the transpose of the specified rectangular matrix **A**.

```
A'

ans =

1      0
2      4
```

i.e., row and column elements are interchanged.

7. **x = A\b**
It returns the solution vector $\boldsymbol{x}$ of a linear system described by a set of linear algebraic equations: $Ax = b$.
Let a system of linear algebraic equations be given by:

$$\begin{bmatrix} 1 & 2 \\ 0 & 4 \end{bmatrix} \begin{bmatrix} x_1 \\ x_2 \end{bmatrix} = \begin{bmatrix} 1 \\ 2 \end{bmatrix}$$

To find the solution, the commands used are as:

```
A = [1    2;    0    4];

b = [1; 2];

x =A\b
```

This will give the result as shown below:

```
x =

0

0.5000
```

8. **poly(A)**

It returns the coefficients of the characteristic polynomial p of matrix **A**, i.e., the coefficients of determinant of matrix $[s\mathbf{I} - \mathbf{A}]$, where **I** is the identity matrix. The syntax is given as:

```
p = poly(A)
```

when executed gives the coefficients of the polynomial p in descending power of s as:

```
p =

    1    -5    4
```

This implies that the characteristic polynomial is $s^2 - 5s + 4$.

9a. **eig(A)**

It returns the Eigen values of matrix **A**.

The command

```
eig(A)
```

will give the following eigen values for matrix **A**:

```
ans =

    1

    4
```

9b. **[v, x] = eig(A)**

It returns the eigen vectors v, and eigen values shown on the main diagonal of matrix **x**.

The command

```
[v, x]= eig(A)
```

The result is as:

```
v =

    1.0000    0.5547

         0    0.8321
x =

    1    0
    0    4
```

i.e., eigen values 1 and 4 are shown on the main diagonal of matrix of **x**.

9c. **x = eigs(B)**

This function returns six largest magnitudes eigen values of matrix **B**.

10. **orth (B)**

It orthogonalizes the rectangular matrix **B**.

The command is given as:

```
c = orth (B)
```

> **Programming Tip 3.16:** The orthogonal matrix **C** has the property, i.e., $C' = C^{-1}$, provided it is a square matrix.

Example 3.16 Let matrix **B** be given by:

```
B = [1    2;    3    4]
```

Orthogonalize the matrix **B** and verify the orthogonal property of the resultant matrix.

Solution: The command used to orthogonalize the matrix **B** is:

```
B = [1   2;   3   4];
c = orth(B)
```

When executed, the result obtained is:

```
c =
    -0.4046    -0.9145
    -0.9145     0.4046
```

To obtain the transpose and inverse of **c**, the following commands are executed:

```
ct = c';          % ct is the transpose of matrix c
cin = inv(c);     % cin  is the inverse of matrix c
ct                % displays transpose obtained
cin               % displays inverse obtained
```

The transpose and inverse of matrix **c** obtained, respectively, are:

```
ct =
     -0.4046    -0.9145
     -0.9145     0.4046
cin =
     -0.4046    -0.9145
     -0.9145     0.4046
```

It can be seen that the matrices transpose of **c**, i.e., (**c′**) and inverse of **c**, i.e., ($\mathbf{c}^{-1}$) are equal. Hence it is proved that **c** is the orthogonal matrix of the given matrix **B**.

11. **find (A)**

    This function returns the row and column *indices* of the non-zero entries in matrix **A**. The syntax is given as:

    ```
    find(A)
    ```

    The command

    ```
    A = [1 2; 0 4];
    find(A)
    ```

    The following result is given

    ```
    ans =
          1
          3
          4
    ```

    i.e., it returns linear indices for the nonzero entries of **A**.
    The other form is as given below:

    ```
    [i, j] = find(A)
    ```

    In this function, ***i*** gives a vector of row indices of the nonzero entries of **A** and ***j*** gives a vector of column indices of the nonzero entries of **A**.

The result obtained is as:

```
i =
    1
    1
    2
j =
    1
    2
    2
```

12. **`sort(E)`**

The command

`sort(E)`

sorts **each column** of the matrix **E** in the ascending order.

The commands used to sort the given matrix **E** are as follows:

```
E = [2  6  -3;  8  4  10;  4  2  4]
sort(E)
```

The result obtained is as:

```
E =
    2     6    -3
    8     4    10
    4     2     4
ans =
    2     2    -3
    4     4     4
    8     6    10
```

This function is already discussed in Section 3.2.5 in detail.

3.10 MATRIX AND ARRAY OPERATIONS

MATLAB supports two types of operations between arrays, known as array operations and matrix operations.

3.10.1 Arithmetic Operations on Matrices

Matrix operations follow the rules of linear algebra in MATLAB. It allows the following **arithmetic operations** to be carried out on **matrices** provided that the operands are compatible with the operator.

+	addition
–	subtraction
*	multiplication
/	right division
^	exponentiation
\	left division

For example:

- **A** + **B** is valid if **A** and **B** are matrices of the same size.
- **A** – **B** is valid if **A** and **B** are matrices of the same size.

- **A*B** is valid if number of columns of **A** = number of rows of **B**.
- **A/B** is valid if **A** and **B** are of the same size and is equal to $\mathbf{AB}^{-1}$ for same size square matrices **A** and **B**.
- A^2 is valid if **A** is square and it equals **A*A**.
- A^*p*, effectively multiplies matrix **A** itself (*p* - 1) times.
- If a matrix equation is given by **Ax** = **b**, then the command $x = \mathbf{A}\backslash b$ will give $x = \mathbf{A}^{-1}b$.

Example 3.17 Let two matrices **A** and **B** be:

$$\mathbf{A} = \begin{bmatrix} 5 & 10 \\ 15 & 20 \end{bmatrix} \quad \text{and} \quad \mathbf{B} = \begin{bmatrix} 2 & 4 \\ 6 & 8 \end{bmatrix}$$

Illustrate the commands used for various arithmetic operations:

Solution: The two given matrices are obtained in workspace by following commands:

```
A = [ 5 10; 15 20];

B = [ 2 4 ; 6 8];
```

(i) **Addition**

The statement

```
C =A + B
```

adds the contents of matrices **A** and **B**. The result is given below:

```
C =
        7      14
       21      28
```

Same result will be obtained by using the command,

```
C = plus(A, B)
```

(ii) **Subtraction**

The statement

```
C =A - B
```

subtracts the contents of matrices **B** from **A**. The result is given below:

```
C =

        3       6
        9      12
```

Same result will be obtained by using the command,

```
C =minus (A, B)
```

(iii) **Multiplication**

The statement

```
C =A * B
```

multiplies the contents of matrices **A** and **B**. The result is given below:

```
C =
       70     100
      150     220
```

Same result will be obtained by using the command,

```
C = mtimes(A, B)
```

(iv) **Exponentiation**

The statement

```
C =A^2
```

raises contents of matrices **A** to the power 2. The result is given below:

```
C =

  175   250

  375   550
```

(v) **Right division**

The statement

```
C =A/B
```

right divides the contents of matrices **A** by **B**. The result is obtained by multiplying the matrix **A** with the inverse of matrix **B**, i.e., $\mathbf{C} = \mathbf{AB}^{-1}$. The result is given below:

```
C =

  2.5000        0

       0   2.5000
```

(vi) **Left division**

The statement

```
C =A\B
```

left divides the contents of matrices **A** by **B**. The result is obtained by multiplying the inverse of matrix **A** with the matrix **B**, i.e., $\mathbf{C} = \mathbf{A}^{-1}\mathbf{B}$. The result is given below:

```
C =

  0.4000   0.0000

       0   0.4000
```

Example 3.18 Solve the system of linear equations defined by $\mathbf{A} \cdot x = \mathbf{B}$, where matrices **A** and **B** are defined as follows:

$$\mathbf{A} = \begin{bmatrix} 2 & 4 \\ 5 & 2 \end{bmatrix} \quad \text{and} \quad \mathbf{B} = \begin{bmatrix} 6 \\ 15 \end{bmatrix}$$

Solution: The two given matrices are obtained in workspace by following commands:

```
A = [2 4; 5 2];

B = [6; 15];
```

The command,

```
x =A\B
```

can be used to solve the linear system of algebraic equations. It is same as given by $x = \mathbf{A}^{-1}\mathbf{B}$. The statement when executed, gives the following results:

```
x =

  3
  0
```

3.10.2 Arithmetic Operations on Arrays

Arithmetic operations on arrays are done on **element-by-element** basis. For these operations to work, the number of rows and columns in both arrays must be the same as the operation is performed on corresponding elements in the two arrays. This means that addition and subtraction are the same for arrays and matrices, but their multiplicative operations are different.

MATLAB uses a **period/decimal-point** on the left of the arithmetic operator as part of the notation for arithmetic operations except for addition and subtraction.

The list of arithmetic operators includes the following:

- + addition
- – subtraction
- .* element-by-element multiplication
- ./ element-by-element right division
- .^ element-by-element power
- .\ element-by-element left division

Array operations can also occur between an array and a scalar. In such cases, the value of scalar is applied to every element of the array and arithmetic operation is performed as indicated by the corresponding arithmetic operator.

e.g., if $\mathbf{A} = \begin{bmatrix} 2 & 4 \\ 4 & 5 \end{bmatrix}$ then $\mathbf{x} = \mathbf{A} - 2 = \begin{bmatrix} 0 & 2 \\ 2 & 3 \end{bmatrix}$

The commands used are:

```
A = [2 4; 4 5];
x = A-2
```

The result obtained is as:

```
x =

     0     2
     2     3
```

i.e., 2 have been subtracted from each element of the matrix **A**.

Example 3.19 Let matrices **A** and **B** be given by:

$$\mathbf{A} = \begin{bmatrix} 2 & 6 \\ 3 & 4 \end{bmatrix}, \qquad \mathbf{B} = \begin{bmatrix} 1 & 7 \\ -2 & 8 \end{bmatrix}$$

Show the use of arithmetic operators on these arrays and store the result in an array **C**.

Solution: The two given matrices are obtained in workspace by following commands:

```
A = [2 6; 3 4];

B = [1 7;-2 8];
```

(i) The command

```
C = A .* B
```

gives the following result

```
C =
      2     42
     -6     32
```

The corresponding elements of the two arrays **A** and **B** have been multiplied and the result is assigned to array **C**.

(ii) Similarly, the command

```
C = A ./ B
```

gives the following result:

```
C =
     2.0000     0.8571
    -1.5000     0.5000
```

The elements of array **A** have been divided by the corresponding elements of array **B** and the result is assigned to array **C**.

(iii) The command

```
C = A .^ 2
```

gives the following result

```
C =
      4     36
      9     16
```

Each element of the array **A** is raised to power of 2 and result is assigned to array **C**.

(iv) The command

```
C = A .\ B
```

will produce the following result

```
C =
     0.5000     1.1667
    -0.6667     2.0000
```

The elements of array **A** are left divided by the corresponding elements of array **B**, i.e., the elements of inverse of **A** are multiplied by the corresponding elements of array **B** and the result has been assigned to array **C**.

3.10.3 Relational Operators

The six relational operators which are used with arrays and matrices are

<	less than
≤	lesser than or equal to
>	greater than
≥	greater than or equal to
==	equal to
~=	not equal to.

The corresponding elements of arrays having equal dimensions are compared using relational operators. These operators always operate element by element. For vectors and matrices, the corresponding operands must be of the same size, unless one of them is a scalar.

The result of relational operation is either **`true`**, indicated by value `(1)` or is **`false`** indicated by the value **`zero`** `(0)`.

Example 3.20 Row vectors x and y are given by:
$x = [2\ \ 3\ \ 4]$ and $y = [1\ \ 0\ \ 5]$, show the use of different relational operators.

Solution: The two vectors are obtained in the workspace by using following commands:

```
x = [ 2 3 4];

y = [1 0 5];
```

(i) The command

$$k = x < y$$

gives the following result:

```
k =

     0     0     1
```

i.e., statement is true only for the third element.

(ii) Similarly, the command

```
k = x <= y
```

results in:

```
k =

     0     0     1
```

(iii) The command

```
k = x > y
```

results in:

```
k =

     1     1     0
```

i.e., statement is true for first and second elements of values x and y.

(iv) The command

```
k = x >= y
```

results in:

```
k =

     1     1     0
```

i.e., statement is true for first and second elements of values x and y.

(v) The command

```
k = x == y
```

results in:

```
k =

     0     0     0
```

statement is false for all the elements.

(vi) The command

```
k = x ~= y
```

results in:

```
k =

     1     1     1
```

statement is true for all the elements.

In all the six relational operations, the resultant vector ***k*** contains a 1 when the relation is **true** for the corresponding elements of the operand vectors ***x*** and ***y*** and 0 when the relation is **false**.

Example 3.21 Matrices **A** and **B** are given as follows:

A = [1 9 10; 2 7 8; 3 5 8]

B = [1 2 3; 4 5 6; 6 7 8]

Find the result for the relational operation: **A** is equal to **B**.

Solution: The two matrices are obtained in workspace using following commands:

```
A = [1    9    10;    2    7    8;    3    5    8];
B = [1    2     3;     4    5    6;    6    7    8];
```

To find if matrix **A** is equal to **B** or not, the command

```
A == B
```

is used. When executed, it gives the following results:

```
ans =
        1         0         0
        0         0         0
        0         0         1
```

i.e., only elements **A**(1, 1) and **A**(3, 3) are equal to **B**(1, 1)and **B**(3, 3).

3.10.4 Logical operators

Logical operators described below perform element to element logical operations on the corresponding elements of arrays having equal dimensions. These operators always operate element by element. For vectors and matrices, the corresponding operand matrices must be of the same size, unless one of them is a scalar.

There are four logical operators, described in Table 3.1 below.

Table 3.1 Logical Operators

Sr. No.	Logical Operator Symbol	Description and Syntax	Details
	`&`	`logical AND (x & y)`	Returns 1 for element locations that are non-zero in both arrays (true) and zero for all other locations.
	`|`	`logical OR (x | y)`	Returns 1 for the element location that is non-zero (true) in any one array or in both the arrays and zero for other locations.
	`~`	`logical complement (NOT) (~ x, ~ y)`	Complements every element of the given array i.e., one and zero elements are interchanged.
	`xor`	`logical exclusive-OR xor(x, y)`	Returns 1 for element locations that are non-zero in only one arrays, and returns zero for other locations.

If the condition is `true`, result is `1`, it is `zero` if condition is `false`.

Example 3.22 If vectors x and y are given by:
$x = [2\ 3\ 4]$ and $y = [2\ 5\ 1]$. Illustrate the different logical operations.

Solution: The two given vectors are obtained in the workspace using following commands:

```
X = [2 3 4];
Y = [2 5 1];
```

(i) Logical AND
The command

```
x & y
```

carries out logical AND operation between corresponding elements of vectors x and y. If both elements are **non-zero**, the result is true and returns 1, otherwise it is false and returns 0. For the two vectors x and y given above, the result obtained is as given below:

```
ans =
          1        0        1
```

(ii) Logical OR
The command

```
m = x | y
```

carries out logical OR operation between corresponding elements of matrices **x** and **y**. If any of the two elements are non-zero, the result is true and returns 1, otherwise it is false and returns 0. For the two vectors x and y given above, the result obtained is as given below:

```
m =
          1        1        1
```

(iii) Logical complement
The command

```
m = ~x
```

carries out logical complement operation on elements of matrix **x**. If the element is zero, the result returned is 1, otherwise it returns 0. For the vector x given above, the result obtained is as given below:

```
m =
          0        0        0
```

(iv) Logical Exclusive-OR
The command

```
m = xor(x, y)
```

carries out logical Exclusive-OR operation between corresponding elements of matrices **x** and **y**. If **only** one of the two elements is non-zero, the result is true and returns 1, otherwise it is false and returns 0. For the two vectors x and y given above, the result obtained is as given below:

```
m =
          0        1        0
```

3.11 FUNCTIONS WITH ARRAY INPUTS

If the MATLAB functions receive an array of input values, then the function is performed for each element of the array separately, i.e., on **element-by-element** basis.

For example, let x = [0, pi/2, pi]

The statements `y = sin(x)` and `z = cos(x)` will compute sine and cosine for each element of x to form the resultant vectors y and z. The commands used are as given below:

```
x = [0, pi/2, pi];
y = sin(x)
z = cos(x)
```

The result obtained is as:

```
y =
        0    1.0000    0.0000
```

which gives the values of `sin(0)`, `sin(pi/2)` and `sin(pi)`, respectively, and

```
z =
   1.0000    0.0000   -1.0000
```

which gives the values of `cos(0)`, `cos(pi/2)` and `cos(pi)`, respectively.

Example 3.23 Obtain the sum of the following series:

$S = 1 + r + r^2 + r^3 + \ldots + r^n$ for $r = 2, n = 4$

Solution: The following commands can be used:

```
r =2; n =4;
k =0: n;
gseries = r.^k
s =sum(gseries)
```

The response obtained is as:

```
gseries =
     1     2     4     8    16
  s =
     31
```

3.12 STRUCTURE ARRAYS

Structures are collections of different kinds of data organized by named fields. These are similar to those available in other programming languages like C. Unlike arrays which contain elements of the same data type, the fields of a structure may include data of different types. For example, one field may contain a text string; another may store a number, third may be a numeric array and so on. But, like standard arrays, structures are also array oriented. A single structure is a 1-by-1 structure array. The MATLAB commands such as `size`, `repmat`, etc. work with structure arrays just as they work with normal arrays.

3.12.1 Building Structure Arrays

A simple 1-by-1 structure array can be built by assigning data to individual fields that are accessed by structure name post-fixed by `dot` and then followed by field name as shown below:

```
student.name = 'Jasbir Singh';
student.rollno = 6502;
student.marks = [72 84 59; 76 69 77; 72 90 82];
```

Now typing the name of structure, `student`, at the command prompt, the following response is obtained:

```
student

student =

        name: 'Jasbir Singh'

        rollno: 6502

        marks: [3 x 3 double]
```

`'student'` is a 1-by-1 structure array having three fields. To increase the size of the structure array, define the second structure element of the array using index values as shown below:

```
student(2).name = 'Jarnail Singh';

student(2).rollno = 6503;

student(2).marks = [54 37 59; 18 69 59; 72 27 49];
```

The student structure array size becomes 1-by-2. It is important to note that all structures in the structure array have the same number of fields and all fields have the same field names. Now if the structure variable name `student` is entered at the command prompt, the response obtained is:

```
student =

1 x 2 struct array with fields:

     name

     rollno

     marks
```

> **Programming Tip 3.17:** Once a structure array contains multiple elements, i.e., structures, MATLAB does not display individual field contents. Instead, it displays a summary of the information about the structure.

The function `'fieldnames'` can also be used to obtain this information. It returns a cell array of strings containing field names.

The structure array can be expanded further. It is not mandatory to assign data to all fields in the structure. The unassigned fields are represented by empty matrices. For example, expanding `student` structure array as shown below:

```
student(3).name = 'Jasleen Bindra';
```

It expands the student structure array to 1-by-3 but the `student(3).rollno` and `student(3).marks` fields are empty.

> **Programming Tip 3.18:** The structure array does not require data to be assigned to all the fields in the structure. Some fields may remain empty and can be filled later.

> **Programming Tip 3.19:** In structure array it is not mandatory for a field to have the same size in each structure. For example, the name field in student structure array has different length in each structure.

One can also add a field to every structure in a structure array by adding that field to a single structure. For example, to add a field `branch_name` to the `student` structure array, the following command is given:

```
student(3).branch_name = 'mechanical';
```

This shall result in this new field to be added to all structures in the structure array, student. The field has been assigned the value `'mechanical'` for the third structure, while the same field in other structures of the structure array, student will be empty.

Similarly, a field can be removed from all structures in the array by using `rmfield` command as shown below:

```
student = rmfield(student, 'branch_name');
```

It removes the field `branch_name` from the `student` structure and assigns the resultant structure to the structure array `student` again. It should be noted that it could be stored in a structure other than `student`.

3.12.2 `struct` Function

A function `'struct'` can be used to define or build a structure array. The syntax is as shown below:

```
student = struct('field1',value1, 'field2',value2, ...)
```

where `student` is the name of the structure array,
`field1, field2` are the field names and
`value1, value2` are the data assigned to those fields.

The above MATLAB statement defines the first structure of the structure array. To define the second structure, index values may be used as illustrated below:

```
student(2) = struct('field1',value1, 'field2',value2, ...)
```

It may be noted that a structure array may contain another structure or a structure array as one of its fields. In that case, it is called nested structure array where one structure is nested within existing structure fields.

3.12.3 Obtaining Data from Structures

Like, sub-arrays in standard arrays, part of structure arrays can be accessed by using `(:)` operator. A field of a particular structure can be accessed by appending a period to the structure name followed by the field name.

```
first_studentname  = student(1).name
```

The response obtained is as:

```
first_studentname  =

Jasbir Singh
```

If part of data in a field is to be accessed, proper index may be used as shown:

```
part_marks = student(2).marks(2,2)
```

The response obtained is as:

```
part_marks =

         69
```

3.13 CELL ARRAYS

A cell array is an array of cells. Each cell stores an array. The elements of an array in a cell are all of the same type but two different cells may have different type of elements. For example, one cell of a cell array might contain array of numeric values, another cell may contain an array of text strings, and the third cell may store an array of complex values.

3.13.1 Creating Cell Arrays

The cell function creates empty cell arrays of the specified size. For example, to create an empty cell array 'sample' of size 2-by-2, the following command is used:

```
sample = cell(2,2);
```

The cell array can then be built by assigning data to individual cells, one cell at a time. Data can be assigned in two ways: cell indexing and content indexing.

3.13.2 Cell Indexing

In cell indexing the cell index values are enclosed in parenthesis using standard array notation, '()'. The cell contents are mentioned on the right side of the assignment statement in curly braces, '{}'. For example, a 2-by-2 cell array, sample is built as shown below:

```
sample(1,1) = {[54 37 59; 18 69 59; 72 27 49]};
sample(1,2) = {'Jarnail Singh'};
sample(2,1) = {[2i,  1-7i, -6};
sample(2,2) = {['abcd', 'efgh', 'ijkl']}
```

> **Programming Tip 3.20:** Just as '[]' denotes empty matrix for standard arrays, '{}' denotes empty cell array.

3.13.3 Content Indexing

In content indexing the braces are used in reverse manner. The cell indices are put in curly braces while the cell contents are mentioned on the right side of the assignment statement as done for standard arrays.

```
sample{1,1} = [54 37 59; 18 69 59; 72 27 49];
sample{1,2} = 'Jarnail Singh';
sample{2,1} = 1-7i;
sample{2,2} = ['mnop', 'qrst']
```

The two forms can be used interchangeably.

> **Programming Tip 3.21:** A numeric array and a cell array should not be created with same name. MATLAB will give an error.

MATLAB displays the cell array sample in a condensed form.

```
sample =

              [3 x 3 double]      'Jarnail Singh'
          [1.0000 - 7.0000i]      'mnopqrst'
```

To display the full cell contents, use the celldisp function.

```
celldisp(sample)
```

The response of MATLAB to the command 'celldisp' is given below:

```
sample{1,1} =
          54     37     59
          18     69     59
          72     27     49

sample{2,1} =
         1.0000 - 7.0000i
sample{1,2} =
      Jarnail Singh
sample{2,2} =
      mnopqrst
```

For a high-level graphical display of cell architecture, use `cellplot`.

```
cellplot(sample)
```

In response to the command `cellplot`, MATLAB generates Figure 3.1 as shown below:

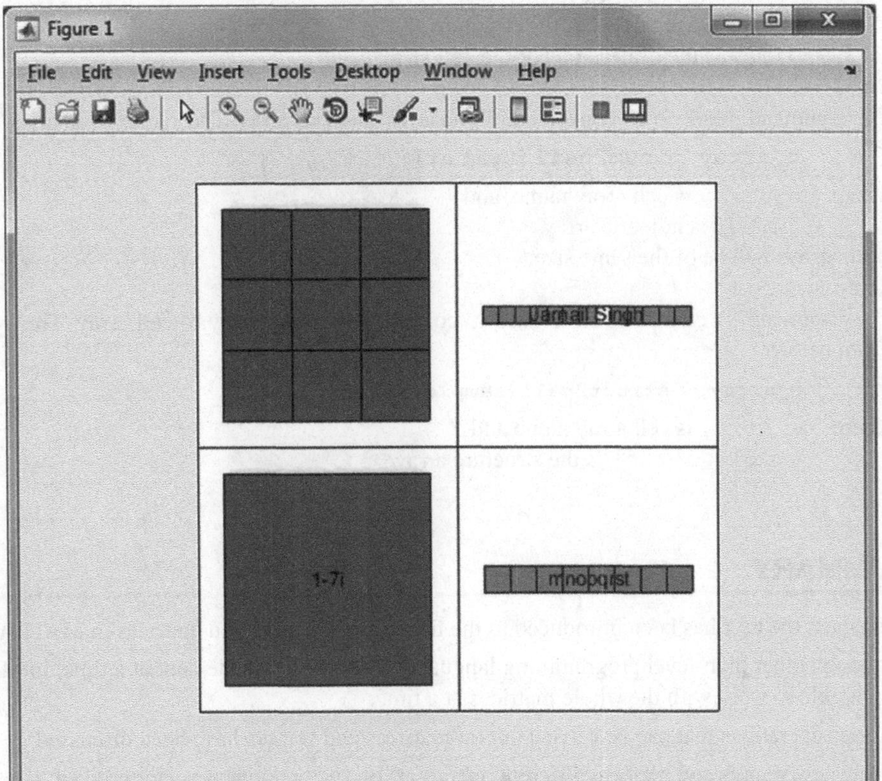

Figure 3.1 Response to `cellplot` Command

If any data is assigned to the cell array beyond its dimensions, the size of the array is expanded to accommodate the data just as in standard array. Also rows and column breaks are indicated by commas/spaces and semicolon, respectively, as in normal arrays. A cell can contain another cell array, or even an array of cell arrays. Also the commands used to access the elements of the array, sub-arrays, i.e., part of the array, deleting a cell and reshaping the array are same as used for standard arrays.

> **Programming Tip 3.22** In assignments, content indexing can be used to access only a single cell, not a subset of cells. For example, the statements `A{1,:} = value` and `B = A{1,:}` are both invalid.

3.14 SOME USEFUL COMMANDS OF STRUCTURES AND CELLS

(a) `cell2struct`

The command `cell2struct` is used to convert cell array to structure array. The syntax is as given below:

```
sample_struct = cell2struct(sample, fields, dimen)
```

where `sample_struct` is structure array,
`sample` is cell array,
`fields` are the fields of the structure and
`dimen` is the dimensions of the cell array.

(b) `num2cell`

The command `num2cell` converts numeric array into cell array. The syntax is as given below:

```
c_array = num2cell(number)
```

where `c_array` is cell array name, and
`number` is numeric array.

Both arrays will be of the same size.

(c) `struct2cell`

The command `struct2cell` is used to convert a structure array to cell array. The syntax is as given below:

```
c_array = struct2cell(sample-struct)
```

where `c_array` is cell array name and
`sample_struct` is the structure array.

SUMMARY

In this chapter, the user has been introduced to the handling of vectors and matrices in MATLAB.

- Although other high-level programming languages work with one element at a time, in MATLAB it is possible to work with the whole matrices at a time.
- Various operations that can be carried out on matrices and vectors have been discussed.
- Create new vectors and perform different operations on vectors such as vector product, `transpose`, `sum`, `mean`, `length`, `max`, `min`, `prod`, `sign`, `find`, `fix`, `floor`, `ceil`, `sort`, `mod`, and `rem`, etc. have been discussed.
- Matrix subscripts/indices, matrix dimension, matrix manipulations such as altering shape and size of a matrix have been explained using many examples.

- Operations such as appending a row/column to a matrix, deleting a row/column and concatenation of matrices are also discussed and explained in detail.
- Generation of special matrices such as matrices of all zeros, all ones, identity matrix, diagonal matrix, etc. is also described.
- Useful MATLAB commands related to matrices such as finding the `determinant, rank, trace, inverse, norm,` etc. of a matrix has also been covered in detail.
- Finding of matrix polynomial, eigen values, eigen vectors, locating indices of non-zero elements, sorting the elements in ascending or descending order are also discussed.
- Arithmetic, logical and relational operations on vectors and matrices have also been described using many examples.
- The structures and cells are discussed in the last.

List of Commands

Command	Definition
Commands related to vectors	
`x'`	Transpose of **x**
`conj`	Complex Conjugate of x, is a complex
`linspace`	Generate linearly spaced vector
`logspace`	Generate logarithmically spaced vector
`sum`	sum of all elements in row/column vector
`mean`	average of elements of row/column vector
`length`	number of elements in a row/column vector
`max`	maximum value in row/column vector
`min`	minimum value in row/column vector
`prod`	product of elements of row/column vector
`sign`	returns 1/0/−1 for positive/zero/negative value in a vector
`find`	returns indices of vector for non-zero values
`fix`	rounds to nearest integer towards zero.
`floor`	rounds to nearest integer towards $-\infty$.
`ceil`	rounds to nearest integer towards $+\infty$.
`round`	rounds towards nearest integer
`sort`	sort elements in ascending order of magnitude line continuation
Commands related to matrices	
`size`	gives no. of rows and columns of a matrix
`reshape`	reshape to new matrix (new dimensions)
`diag`	generates diagonal matrix
`det`	determinant of square matrix
`rank`	rank of matrix
`trace`	sum of diagonal elements of a matrix
`inv`	inverse of non-singular matrix

(*Continued*)

(Continued)

`norm`	Euclidean norm of matrix
`A'`	transpose of a matrix
`a\b`	division of two matrices
`poly`	coefficients of characteristic polynomial
`eig`	eigen values of matrix
`orth`	orthogonalizes the rectangular matrix
`find`	returns row and column indices of non-zero entries in a matrix
`sort`	sort each column in ascending order of magnitudes
Special matrices	
`zeros`	Create matrix with all elements as zeros
`ones`	Create matrix of ones
`eye`	Create identity matrix
`rand`	Create matrix of uniformly distributed random numbers with values in interval (0, 1)
`rands`	Create matrix of uniformly distributed random numbers with values in interval (−1, +1)
`diag`	Create diagonal matrix
`vander`	Create Vandermonde matrix

EXERCISES

3.1 Given the row vector $\boldsymbol{p} = [1 \quad -2 \quad 5]$ and a column vector $\boldsymbol{q} = \begin{bmatrix} 2 \\ 4 \\ 8 \end{bmatrix}$

Solve the following:

(i) $\boldsymbol{p}*\boldsymbol{q}$

(ii) $\boldsymbol{q}*\boldsymbol{p}$

(iii) $\boldsymbol{p}^{T}*\boldsymbol{q}^{T}$

(iv) Sum and mean of all the components of vectors **p** and **q**

(v) Number of elements in vectors **p** and **q**

(vi) Maximum and minimum values in the vectors **p** and **q**.

(vii) Product of elements of vector **p** and **q**

(viii) Arrange the elements of vectors **p** and **q** in ascending order.

3.2 Enter the following matrices at the command window:

$$\mathbf{A} = \begin{bmatrix} 1 & 10 \\ -10 & i \end{bmatrix}, \mathbf{B} = \begin{bmatrix} z & e^{x} \\ \log 100 & \sin 60 \end{bmatrix}$$

3.3 Given the matrix $\mathbf{A} = \begin{bmatrix} 2 & -4 & 6 & -8 \\ 1 & 3 & 5 & 7 \\ 2 & 12 & 30 & 56 \end{bmatrix}$

Write MATLAB statements to obtain:

(i) All the elements of all rows but first column

(ii) All the elements of first row but all columns

(iii) Element in the second row and third column.

3.4 Given the (3 × 4) matrix **Q**:

$$\mathbf{Q} = \begin{bmatrix} 2 & 3 & 4 \\ 3 & 4 & 5 \\ 4 & 5 & 6 \\ 5 & 6 & 7 \end{bmatrix}$$

Using MATLAB commands:

(i) Delete the first row of matrix **Q**

(ii) Delete the first and second columns of all the rows of matrix **Q**.

(iii) Extract the first 2 × 2 matrix sub-matrix from **Q**

(iv) Replace **Q**(2, 2) with 8

3.5 Given the matrix **P**:

$$\mathbf{P} = \begin{bmatrix} 3 & 4 & 5 & 1 \\ 5 & 6 & 7 & 2 \\ 7 & 8 & 9 & 3 \end{bmatrix}$$

(a) Reshape this matrix as a:

(i) Vector

(ii) (4 × 3) matrix

(iii) (6 × 2) matrix

(b) Given a column vector, $\boldsymbol{x} = \begin{bmatrix} 0 \\ 1 \\ 2 \end{bmatrix}$ and a row vector, $\boldsymbol{y} = [0 \;\; 2 \;\; 3 \;\; 4]$, append these column/row vectors to the matrix **P**.

3.6 Generate the following 3 × 3 matrices of common use with the help of matrix generator function.

(i) Unity or identity matrix

(ii) Null matrix

(iii) ($p \times q$) matrix with all elements equal to one.

3.7 Consider matrix as:

$$\mathbf{A} = \begin{bmatrix} 2 & 5 & 6 \\ 3 & 4 & 10 \\ 7 & 11 & 8 \end{bmatrix}$$

Show the use of following matrix commands:

(i) diag(**A**), **A** is a matrix
(ii) diag(**A**, *k*), **A** is a matrix
(iii) poly(**A**)
(iv) eig(**A**)
(v) eigs(**A**)

3.8 Create a 4 × 4 matrix of random members, multiply all the elements by 10 and then round off all the elements to integers using appropriate commands.

3.9 For the matrices given below, find:

(a) Determinants
(b) The inverse of each, if they exist and the corresponding products such as $\mathbf{AA}^{-1}$

$$\text{(i)}\ \mathbf{A} = \begin{bmatrix} 2 & 4 \\ 8 & -1 \end{bmatrix} \qquad \text{(ii)}\ \mathbf{B} = \begin{bmatrix} 3 & 0 & -2 \\ -1 & 1 & 2 \\ 0 & 1 & -2 \end{bmatrix}$$

$$\text{(iii)}\ \mathbf{C} = \begin{bmatrix} 1 & 2 & 3 \\ 0 & -1 & 1 \\ 1 & 0 & 1 \end{bmatrix} \qquad \text{(iv)}\ \mathbf{D} = \begin{bmatrix} 0 & 2 & 0 \\ 3 & -3 & 4 \\ 0 & 2 & 6 \end{bmatrix}$$

3.10 Determine the ranks of the following matrices:

$$\text{(i)}\ \mathbf{L} = \begin{bmatrix} 4 & 3 \\ 7 & 2 \\ 4 & 0 \end{bmatrix} \qquad \text{(ii)}\ \mathbf{M} = \begin{bmatrix} 3 & 5 & 0 & 9 \\ 2 & 3 & 6 & 4 \end{bmatrix}$$

$$\text{(iii)}\ \mathbf{N} = \begin{bmatrix} 2 & 0 & 0 \\ 0 & 0 & 5 \end{bmatrix} \qquad \text{(iv)}\ \mathbf{P} = \begin{bmatrix} 1 & 2 & 3 \\ 4 & 5 & 6 \\ 7 & 8 & 9 \end{bmatrix}$$

$$\text{(v)}\ \mathbf{Q} = \begin{bmatrix} 1 & 2 & 3 \\ 2 & 4 & 6 \\ 7 & 0 & 8 \end{bmatrix}$$

3.11 Obtain the following products:

(a) **AB** (b) **BA** (c) $\mathbf{A}^T\mathbf{A}$ (d) $\mathbf{B}^T\mathbf{B}$

for the matrices/vectors given below:

$$\text{(i)}\ \mathbf{A} = \begin{bmatrix} 3 \\ 2 \\ 1 \end{bmatrix} \qquad \mathbf{B} = \begin{bmatrix} 6 & 1 & 0 \end{bmatrix}$$

(ii) $\mathbf{A} = \begin{bmatrix} -1 & 2 \\ 0 & 4 \end{bmatrix}$ $\quad \mathbf{B} = \begin{bmatrix} 2 & 3 \\ -4 & 5 \end{bmatrix}$

(iii) $\mathbf{A} = \begin{bmatrix} -1 & 2 & 3 \\ 4 & 5 & 6 \end{bmatrix}$ $\quad \mathbf{B} = \begin{bmatrix} 2 & 4 \\ 6 & 8 \\ 10 & 12 \end{bmatrix}$

3.12 Evaluate:

(i) **A + B**

(ii) **A – B**

(iii) **A^3** and **B^4**

(iv) **A/B** for the matrices **A** and **B** given below:

$$\mathbf{A} = \begin{bmatrix} 5 & -8 & 10 & -2 \\ 0 & 4 & 3 & -4 \\ 2 & 4 & 6 & 8 \end{bmatrix},$$

$$\mathbf{B} = \begin{bmatrix} 3 & -3- & 6 & 5 \\ 8 & 0 & 5 & 4 \\ 0 & 4 & 3 & 2 \end{bmatrix}$$

3.13 Express the following sets of algebraic equations in matrix form, $\mathbf{A}y = b$

(i) $y_1 + y_2 - y_3 = 2$
$-y_1 + 3y_2 - y_3 = 2$
$3y_1 - 5y_2 - 2y_3 = 0$

(ii) $y_1 + y_2 + y_3 = 4$
$-y_1 + 3y_2 - y_3 = 4$
$4y_1 - 4y_2 = 0$

For the equations given above:

(a) Find the inverse of the matrix **A**, if it exists.

(b) Obtain the solution for the variables y_1, y_2 and y_3

(c) Find the Eigen values and Eigen vectors of matrix **A**.

(d) Find the rank of matrix **A**.

(e) Find the trace of matrix **A**.

(f) Find the transpose of matrix **A**.

3.14 Suppose row vectors $\boldsymbol{x}$ and $\boldsymbol{y}$ are given by:

$\boldsymbol{x} = [1 \quad 0 \quad -2]$ and $\boldsymbol{y} = [0 \quad -4 \quad 8]$, show the use of different relational operators.

If vectors $\boldsymbol{x}$ and $\boldsymbol{y}$ are given by:

$\boldsymbol{x} = [2 \quad 0 \quad 6]$ and $\boldsymbol{y} = [-2 \quad 6 \quad -4]$, show the use of different logical operators.

3.15 If $\boldsymbol{x} = [0, 2, 4]$, calculate the values of

(i) $\boldsymbol{y} = \boldsymbol{x}^2$ (ii) $\boldsymbol{z} = \boldsymbol{x}^5$

CHAPTER 4

Polynomials

LEARNING OBJECTIVES

- Knowledge and writing a polynomial in MATLAB.
- Perform different operations on polynomials which includes
  - Evaluate at a given value of the variable.
  - Find the roots.
  - Addition, subtraction, multiplication and division.
- Generate a polynomial from the given roots.
- Obtain a characteristic polynomial/equation for a given matrix.
- Compute the derivative and integration of a polynomial.
- Fit a polynomial curve for a given set of points.
- Evaluate polynomials with matrix arguments.

4.1 INTRODUCTION

A **polynomial** is an expression in which a finite number of constants and variables are combined using only addition, subtraction, multiplication, and non-negative whole number exponents (raise to power). Thus, the following expressions are all considered polynomials:

$x^2 + 2x - 7, \quad x^4 - 7x^3, \quad x$

But, $\dfrac{1}{x^2+1}$ is not a polynomial.

MATLAB provides built-in functions for standard operations on polynomials such as arithmetic operations like multiplication, division, etc. and also evaluation of roots, differentiation, integration, etc. In addition, there are functions for more advanced applications, such as curve-fitting. Polynomials have very significant role to play in engineering systems analysis. The polynomial functions are stored in a `polyfun` directory in MATLAB.

4.2 ENTERING A POLYNOMIAL

In MATLAB, a polynomial is represented by a row vector. Polynomials are entered with variable ('*s*') terms arranged in descending order of its powers. Only the coefficients of 's' terms are entered, i.e., variables *s*, s^2, etc. are not entered. Firstly, leftmost term is the highest power term of the variable ('*s*') and the last, rightmost term is the constant term with 's' raise to power zero. The total number of terms is always one more than the order of the polynomial.

> **Programming Tip 4.1:** The coefficients of a polynomial are entered as elements of a vector and can be separated from each other either by blank spaces or by commas.

Consider a polynomial, $p(s) = s^4 + 3s^3 - 15s^2 - 2s + 9$.
This can be entered as a row vector ***p*** as follows:

```
p = [1 3 -15 -2 9]
```

or

```
p = [1, 3, -15, -2, 9]
```

Here, elements of vector ***p*** are five in number with the last element being the constant term. The order of the polynomial represented by vector ***p*** is four.

MATLAB can interpret a vector of length $n + 1$ as an nth-order polynomial. Thus, if there are missing terms, zeros must be entered in the appropriate place in the vector.

Hence, the expression $y = s^3 + 1$, would be represented by the vector ***y*** as follows:

```
y = [1 0 0 1]
```

or

```
y = [1, 0, 0, 1]
```

Two zeros have been included in the vector to account for the missing powers of s, i.e., s^2 and s.

4.3 POLYNOMIAL EVALUATION

A polynomial can be evaluated for a given value of variable (say s), by using the function `polyval`. The general form of the function `polyval` is as given below:

```
polyval(c, s)
```

where ***c*** is a vector whose elements are the coefficients of a polynomial in descending order of powers of variable s, and s is the value at which the polynomial is to be evaluated.

Example 4.1 Evaluate the value of the polynomial given below at $s = 1, -3$.
$y = 2s^2 + 3s + 4$.

Solution:

(a) For $s = 1$, y is represented and evaluated as follows:

```
y = [2 3 4];
s = 1
value = polyval(y, s)
```

The result obtained is as:

```
value =
        9
```

(b) For $s = -3$, polynomial y is represented and evaluated as follows:

```
y = [2, 3, 4]
s = -3
value = polyval(y, s)
```

The result obtained is as:

```
value =

            13
```

4.4 ROOTS OF A POLYNOMIAL

The roots of a polynomial can be found using the MATLAB function:

```
roots(p)
```

or

```
r = roots(p)
```

where ***p*** is a row vector containing the coefficients of a polynomial. It returns a column vector ***r***, whose elements are the roots of the polynomial.

Example 4.2 Find the roots of polynomial $s^2 + 3s + 2 = 0$.

Solution: The given expression is represented by coefficients of its terms as given below:

```
p = [1  3  2];
```

To find the roots of *p*, the command used is as:

```
r = roots (p);
```

The value of column vector ***r*** containing the roots is returned as:

```
r =
      -2
      -1
```

i.e., $r_1 = -1$ and $r_2 = -2$, the two roots of the polynomial represented by vector ***p***.

Example 4.3 Find the roots of the polynomial $s^4 + 3s^3 - 15s^2 - 2s + 9 = 0$.

Solution: It is represented by vector ***p***, as under:

```
p = [1 3 -15 -2 9]
```

The following command is used to find the roots:

```
r = roots (p)
```

The result returned by the statement above is a column vector,

```
r =
      -5.5745
      2.5836
      -0.7951
      0.7860
```

i.e., roots are:

$r_1 = -5.5745$,

$r_2 = 2.5836$,

$r_3 = 0.7860$,

$r_4 = -0.7951$

4.5 POLYNOMIAL ADDITION AND SUBTRACTION

Two polynomials can be added by using the arithmetic operator **plus '+'**, i.e., if two polynomials x and y are to be added, following command can be used:

```
z = x + y
```

The corresponding elements of the row vectors $\boldsymbol{x}$ and $\boldsymbol{y}$ are added and resultant is $\boldsymbol{z}$ vector.

Similarly, subtraction is done by using operator minus '–' and the syntax is given as:

```
z = x - y
```

It subtracts each element of $\boldsymbol{y}$ from the corresponding element of $\boldsymbol{x}$ and resultant is stored in $\boldsymbol{z}$. In both the above operations, the dimension of both polynomial vectors must be same.

Example 4.4 Add the two polynomials, $a = (s^2 + 2s + 1)$ and $b = (s^3 + s + 5)$.

Solution: These are represented by the two vectors as shown below:

```
a = [0 1 2 1];

b = [1 0 1 5];
```

Addition is done as shown below:

```
c = a + b
```

The result obtained is as:

```
c =
     1 1 3 6
```

i.e., the resultant polynomial, $c = s^3 + s^2 + 3s + 6$.

> **Programming Tip 4.2:** For addition and subtraction, the dimensions of two polynomials should be the same. If the number of terms of the two polynomials is not equal, then zero is padded as a co-efficient to make the dimensions of the vectors same.

Example 4.5 Subtract a polynomial, $a = (3s^3 + 2)$ from $b = (s + 7)$.

Solution: The polynomials are represented by the two vectors as shown below:

```
a = [3 0 0 2];

b = [0 0 1 7];
```

Note: The leading zeros introduced in vector **b** to make the two vectors of same length.
To add the given expressions:

```
c = b - a
```

The result obtained is as shown below:

```
c =
     -3 0 1 5
```

i.e., the resultant is $c = -3s^3 + s + 5$.

4.6 POLYNOMIAL MULTIPLICATION

The product of the two polynomials is obtained by convolution operation of their coefficients using the MATLAB function `conv`. The syntax is given as:

```
conv(x, y)
```

or

```
z = conv(x,y)
```

where x and y are the vectors of coefficients of polynomials to be multiplied, and
z contains the coefficients of the resultant polynomial.

Example 4.6 Evaluate the product of two polynomials $(s + 2)$ and $(s^2 + 4s + 8)$.

Solution: The polynomials are represented by the two vectors x and y as shown below:

```
x = [1 2];
y = [1 4 8];
```

To evaluate the product, following command is used:

```
z = conv(x, y)
```

The vector z obtained is:

```
z =
 1 6 16 16
```

Therefore, the product of the two given polynomials x and y is given by the polynomial z, i.e., $z = s^3 + 6s^2 + 16s + 16$.

> **Programming Tip 4.3:** In case there are more than two polynomials, then product is obtained by performing multiplication of two of the polynomial at one time.

Example 4.7 Evaluate the product of polynomials $(s + 3)$, $(s + 6)$ and $(s + 2)$.

Solution: The given expressions are represented by the three vectors a, b and c as shown below:

```
a = [1 3];
b = [1 6];
c = [1 2];
```

Firstly, the product of two polynomials is obtained by following command:

```
z = conv(a, b)
```

The resultant value of z is as:

```
z =
 1 9 18
```

Now, the product of resultant of the product of the first two polynomials, i.e., z and the third polynomial c is obtained as given below:

```
x = conv(z, c)
```

The resultant polynomial *x* obtained is as shown below:

```
x =
     1 11 36 36
```

Hence the final result is:

x = $s^3 + 11s^2 + 36s + 36$.

4.7 POLYNOMIAL DIVISION

Generally, `deconv` function is used to deconvolve two vectors. In case vectors are coefficients of two polynomials, then function `deconv` gives polynomial division and it returns the quotient as well as remainder. The syntax is given as:

```
[x, r] = deconv(z, y)
```

where *z* is dividend vector
y is divisor vector.
x specifies vector of quotients obtained.
r specifies vector of remainders obtained.

Example 4.8 Divide the polynomial *z* by *y*, where
$z = s^3 + 6s^2 + 16s + 16$ and $y = s^2 + 4s + 8$.

Solution: The polynomials *z* and *y* are represented by the two vectors shown below:

```
z = [1 6 16 16];

y = [1 4 8];
```

The command used for division is:

```
[x, r] = deconv (z, y)
```

The resultant polynomial *x* and remainder *r* obtained are as given below:

```
x =
     1 2

r =
     0 0 0 0
```

Hence, the quotient obtained is $x = [1\ 2]$, i.e., polynomial $(s + 2)$ and the remainder is $r = [0\ 0\ 0\ 0]$, i.e., = 0.

Example 4.9 Divide the polynomial *a* by *b*.
$a = s^2 - 1$ and $b = s + 1$.

Solution: The polynomials *a* and *b* are represented by the two vectors as shown below:

```
a = [ 1 0 -1];

b = [1 1];
```

To divide the polynomial *a* by the polynomial *b*, the command used is:

```
[z, r] = deconv(a, b)
```

The quotient z and remainder r obtained are given as follows:

```
z =
    1 -1
r =
    0 0 0
```

i.e., quotient $z = s - 1$ and remainder, $r = 0$.

4.8 FORMULATION OF POLYNOMIAL EQUATION

In case the roots of a polynomial are given as a column vector, then the corresponding polynomial can be obtained by using command `poly`. The general form of the command is:

```
x = poly(r)
```

where r is a column vector containing the roots of the polynomial. It will return a row vector whose elements are the coefficients of the polynomial.

Example 4.10 Determine the polynomial with roots = –1, –2.

Solution: The roots are represented by the column vector:

```
r = [-1; -2]
```

The polynomial vector p is obtained using the command:

```
p = poly(r)
```

The resultant row vector represents the polynomial p as given below:

```
p =
    1 3 2
```

i.e., the polynomial equation is: $s^2 + 3s + 2 = 0$.

Example 4.11 Determine the polynomial with roots = –0.5 + 0.866*i* and –0.5 – 0.866*i*.

Solution: The roots are represented by the column vector:

```
r = [-0.5+0.866i; -0.5-0.866i]
```

The polynomial is obtained using the following command:

```
p = poly(r)
```

The coefficients of the polynomial equation are obtained as a row vector,

```
p =
     1.0000 1.0000 1.0000
```

i.e., the polynomial equation is: $s^2 + s + 1 = 0$.

4.9 CHARACTERISTIC POLYNOMIAL OF A MATRIX

In general, the characteristic polynomial of a matrix is obtained by solving $\det(s\mathbf{I} - \mathbf{A}) = 0$, where **A** is given matrix and **I** is identity matrix.

In MATLAB, the characteristic polynomial/equation of a matrix is obtained by using the command `poly`. The syntax is given as:

```
p = poly(A)
```

where **A** is the matrix whose characteristic equation is to be obtained, and
p is the row vector whose elements give the coefficients of the characteristic equation in descending order of powers of variable term.

Example 4.12 Determine the characteristic equation of the matrix **A** given below:

$$\mathbf{A} = \begin{bmatrix} 0 & 1 \\ 2 & 3 \end{bmatrix}$$

Solution: The MATLAB commands used to obtain the characteristic polynomial/equation of the matrix **A** are:

```
A = [0 1; 2 3]

p = poly(A)
```

The result obtained is as

```
p =
      1 -3 -2
```

the vector, $\boldsymbol{p}$ = [1 –3 –2], i.e., characteristic equation for this matrix **A** is given by;

$$s^2 - 3s - 2 = 0.$$

Example 4.13 Determine the characteristic equation of the matrix **A** given below:

$$\mathbf{A} = \begin{bmatrix} 1 & 3 & 2 \\ 0 & 1 & 5 \\ 2 & 8 & 6 \end{bmatrix}$$

Solution: The commands used to obtain the characteristic polynomial/equation of the matrix **A** are:

```
A = [1 3 2; 0 1 5; 2 8 6]

p = poly(A)
```

The result obtained is as

```
p =

   1 -8 -31 8
```

the vector, $\boldsymbol{p}$ = [1 –8 –31 8], i.e., characteristic equation for this matrix **A** is given by;

$$s^3 - 8s^2 - 31s + 8 = 0.$$

4.10 POLYNOMIAL DIFFERENTIATION

The function `polyder` is used to compute the derivative of a polynomial. The general form of this function is:

```
dydx = polyder(y)
```

where *y* represents vector of the coefficients of the polynomials whose derivative is to be obtained and
d*y*d*x* represents vector of the coefficients of the derivative obtained.

Example 4.14 Evaluate the derivative of the polynomial, $y = s^4 + 4s^3 + 8s^2 + 16$.

Solution: The following commands are used:

```
y = [1 4 8 0 16];
dydx = polyder(y)
```

The resultant vector $dydx$ obtained is as shown below:

```
dydx =
        4 12 16 0
```

i.e., $\frac{dy}{dx} = 4s^3 + 12s^2 + 16$

Example 4.15 Evaluate the derivative of the expression, $y = s^3 + 3s + 5$.

Solution: The following MATLAB commands can be used:

```
y = [1 0 3 5];
dydx = polyder(y)
```

The resultant vector $dydx$ that gives coefficients of the derivative polynomial $\frac{dy}{dx}$ is obtained as shown below:

```
dydx =

      3 0 3
```

i.e., $\frac{dy}{dx} = 3s^2 + 3$

4.11 POLYNOMIAL INTEGRATION

The function `polyint` is used to compute the integration of a polynomial. The general form of this function is:

```
polyint(y, k)
```

or

```
x = polyint(y,k)
```

where y represents vector of the coefficients of the polynomials whose integration is to be obtained, and k is scalar constant of integration and x contains the result.

> **Programming Tip 4.4:** The constant of integration k is assumed to be 0 until unless specified.

Example 4.16 Integrate the polynomial, $y = 4s^3 + 12s^2 + 16s + 1$.

Solution: The expression y is represented by the row vector given below:

```
y = [4 12 16 1];
```

To integrate the polynomial, command used is given as:

```
x = polyint(y, 3)
```

The result obtained is as:

```
x =
      1 4 8 1 3
```

The resultant vector x gives the coefficients of the polynomial representing the integral of polynomial y.

$$x = \int y = [1\ \ 4\ \ 8\ \ 1\ \ 3], \text{ i.e., } x = s^4 + 4s^3 + 8s^2 + s + 3.$$

Example 4.17 Evaluate the integration of the polynomial, $y = s^2 + s + 3$.

Solution: The expression y is represented by the row vector given below:

```
y = [1 1 3];
```

To integrate the polynomial command used is given as:

```
x = polyint(y)
```

The result obtained is:

```
x =
      0.3333 0.5000 3.0000 0
```

i.e., the resultant polynomial is $x = 0.33s^3 + 0.50s^2 + 3s$.

4.12 POLYNOMIAL CURVE-FITTING

In case, a set of points is known in terms of vectors $\boldsymbol{x}$ and $\boldsymbol{y}$, then a polynomial can be formed that fits the given points. The command used for the purpose is given as:

```
c = polyfit (x, y, k)
```

where $\boldsymbol{x}$ and $\boldsymbol{y}$ specify the vectors of the points for curve-fitting.
k specifies the order of the desired polynomial.

The command returns the coefficients of kth-order polynomial that fits the data in descending powers of $\boldsymbol{x}$, in a least square sense.

Example 4.18 Find a polynomial of degree 2 to fit the following data:

x	0	1	2	4
y	1	6	20	100

Solution: The x and y are represented by the row vectors given below:

```
x = [0   1   2   4];

y = [1   6   20   100];
```

To find a polynomial of degree 2 to fit the data given by x and y, the command is as:

```
c = polyfit (x, y, 2)
```

The result is given as:

```
c =
   7.3409 -4.8409 1.6818
```

i.e., $c = 7.3409x^2 - 4.8409x + 1.6818$

Example 4.19 Find a polynomial of degree 1 to fit the following data:

Current	10	15	20	25	30
Voltage	100	150	200	250	300

Solution: The polynomials *I* and *V* are represented by the row vectors given below:

```
Current = [10   15 20 25 30];

Voltage = [100 150 200 250 300];
```

To find a polynomial of degree 1 to fit the data given above, command to be used is as given below:

```
Res = polyfit (Current, Voltage, 1)
```

The resultant polynomial *R* obtained is given as under:

```
Res =

          10.0000 -0.0000
```

4.13 EVALUATION OF POLYNOMIALS WITH MATRIX ARGUMENTS

The polynomial can also be evaluated for a group of values of s expressed as a square matrix. In this case, the polynomial $p(s) = s^2 + 3s - 7$ becomes $p(S) = S^2 + 3S - 7\mathbf{I}$, where **I** is the identity square matrix.

The polynomials, such as $5X^2 + 4X + 20$, which have its element X as square matrix, can be evaluated by using command:

```
polyvalm(a, X)
```

where *a* is a vector of the coefficients of the matrix polynomial.
X specifies the square matrix.

Example 4.20 Evaluate the polynomial $X^2 + X + 2$, given that the square matrix **X** is:

$$\mathbf{X} = \begin{bmatrix} 2 & 3 \\ 4 & 5 \end{bmatrix}$$

Solution: The commands used are as:

```
A = [1 1 2];

X = [2 3; 4 5];

Z = polyvalm(A, X)
```

The resultant obtained is given as:

```
Z =
 20 24
 32 44
```

Example 4.21 Evaluate the value of the polynomial given below at $s = [1\ \ -3\ \ 2;\ \ 5\ \ 1\ \ 8;\ \ 6\ \ 4\ \ 3]$.
$y = 2s^2 + 3s + 4$.

Solution:

```
y = [2 3 4];
s = [1 -3 2; 5 1 8; 6 4 3];
x = polyvalm(y, s)
```

The result obtained is as:

```
x =
     3      -5     -26
   131      43     108
   106       8     119
```

SUMMARY

The chapter can be summarized in following points:

- In MATLAB, a polynomial is represented by a row vector.
- Polynomials are entered with coefficients of variable (say) *s* arranged in descending order.
- Only the coefficients of *s* terms are entered, i.e., variables s, s^2, etc. are not entered.
- MATLAB can interpret a vector of length $n + 1$ as an *n*th-order polynomial. Thus, if there are missing terms in a polynomial, zeros must be entered in the appropriate place in the vector.
- A polynomial can be evaluated for a given value of variable say *s*, by using the function `'polyval'`.
- The roots of a polynomial can be found using the MATLAB function `'roots(p)'`, where ***p*** is a row vector containing the coefficients of a polynomial.
- Two polynomials, with same dimension, can be added and subtracted by using the arithmetic operator plus '+' and minus '–', respectively.
- The product of the two polynomials is obtained by convolution operation of their coefficients using the function `'conv'`.
- The function `'deconv'` is used to divide two polynomials and it returns the quotient as well as the remainder.
- Given the roots of a polynomial, as a column vector, the corresponding polynomial can be obtained using command `'poly'`.
- The characteristic polynomial/equation of a matrix is obtained by using the command `'poly'`.
- The function `'polyder'` is used to compute the derivative of a polynomial.
- The function `'polyint'` is used to compute the integration of a polynomial.
- Given a set of points in vectors ***x*** and ***y***, a polynomial can be formed that fits the points using the command `c = polyfit(x, y, k)`.
- The polynomial such as $5X^2 + 4X + 20$ that has its elements *X* as square matrix can be evaluated by using `polyvalm(a, X)` command.

List of Commands

S. No.	Command /Function	Description
1	polyval	evaluates polynomial.
2	roots	computes the roots of the polynomial.
3	conv	convolution or polynomial multiplication.
4	deconv	deconvolution or polynomial division.
5	poly	converts roots to polynomial.
6	polyder	differentiates a polynomial.
7	polyint	integrates a polynomial analytically.
8	polyfit	fits a polynomial to given data.
9	polyvalm	evaluates a polynomial with matrix arguments.

EXERCISES

4.1 Obtain the values of the following polynomials at $s = -2$, $s = 4.5$, $s = 2 + i4$

(a) $p(s) = s^2 + 4s + 1$

(b) $p(s) = s^2 + 1$

(c) $p(s) = s^4 + 4s + 2$

4.2 Find the roots of the following polynomial equations:

(a) $s^2 + 3s + 2 = 0$

(b) $s^2 + 4s + 9 = 0$

(c) $s^2 + 1 = 0$

(d) $s^3 + 3s^2 + 4s + 1 = 0$

4.3 Add and subtract the polynomials given below:

(a) $(4s^2 + 5s + 6)$ and $(s^2 + 2s + 3)$

(b) $(s^2 + 8s + 3)$ and $(s + 2)$

(c) $(8s^3 + 6s^2 + 5s + 10)$ and $(s^2 + 2)$

4.4 Multiply the following polynomials:

(a) $(s + 1)$ and $(s + 2)$

(b) $(s^2 + 2s + 1)$ and $(s^3 + 4s^2 + 5s + 1)$

(c) $(s - 1)$ and $(s^2 + 4)$

4.5 Divide the polynomial P by polynomial Q, given below.

(a) $P = (s^2 + 4s + 4)$, $Q = (s + 1)$

(b) $P = (2s^2 + 3s + 1)$, $Q = (s - 1)$

(c) $P = (5s^2 + 8s + 2)$, $Q = (s^2 + s + 2)$

(d) $P = (s^2 + 4s + 10)$, $Q = (s^3 + 3s^2 + 4s + 2)$

4.6 The roots of polynomials are as given below. Find the corresponding polynomials.

(a) $r_1 = 2; r_2 = 4$

(b) $r_1 = -2; r_2 = -4$

(c) $r_1 = -2; r_2 = 4$

(d) $r_1 = -2; r_2 = 4; r_3 = 6$

4.7 Find the characteristic polynomials corresponding to the different matrices given below.

(a) $\mathbf{M} = \begin{bmatrix} 1 & 2 \\ 3 & 4 \end{bmatrix}$

(b) $\mathbf{B} = \begin{bmatrix} 1 & 0 \\ 0 & 2 \end{bmatrix}$

(c) $\mathbf{K} = \begin{bmatrix} 1 & 2 & 0 \\ 0 & 2 & 3 \\ 1 & 2 & 4 \end{bmatrix}$

(d) $\mathbf{X} = \begin{bmatrix} -1 & 0 \\ 2 & -3 \end{bmatrix}$

4.8 Given the data below, fit a polynomial of degree 1.

x	2	5	7
y	4	10	14

4.9 Given the data below, fit a polynomial of degree 2.

M	2	5	7
N	12	39	67

4.10 Fit the polynomial of degree 3, for the data given below.

x	2	5	7
y	24	156	384

4.11 Obtain the derivatives and integrals of the following polynomials:

(a) $p(s) = s^4 + 4s^3 + 10s^2 + 20s + 15$

(b) $q(s) = s^3 + s + 10$

(c) $r(s) = s + 5$

CHAPTER

5

Input Output Statements

LEARNING OBJECTIVES

- Data input using assignment statement
- Study different interactive input statements which include input, keyboard, menu and pause statements
- Functions for reading/storing file data such as `load`, `save`, `dlmread`, `dlmwrite`, `textscan` and `textread`
- Default format of MATLAB and how to change it
- Use of `disp` function to display formatted data
- Opening and closing of a file
- Low-level file input/output functions which include
  - Formatted input/output functions as `fprintf`, `fscanf`, `fgetl` and `fgets`
  - Binary input/output functions as `fwrite`, `fread`.

5.1 INTRODUCTION

Data processing is one of the basic functions performed by a computer. The raw information in the form of data is fed into the computer and after processing this data, meaningful information is retrieved. Data input and output, therefore, forms one of the most important functions in a computer. Consequently, a programming language is useful if it has powerful input–output statements. MATLAB too contains numerous features dedicated to data input–output. It has several commands for data input from the standard input device (keyboard) and for data output to the standard output device (monitor). In addition, it has powerful file-handling features, which makes it very adept programming language.

5.2 DATA INPUT

The fundamental data type in MATLAB is the array. It encompasses several distinct data objects – integers, doubles (real numbers), matrices, character strings, structures and cells. There is no need to declare variables as real or complex. When a real/complex number is entered as the value of a variable, MATLAB automatically sets the variable to be real/ complex. There are three common ways to input data in MATLAB:

1. Assign data to different variables through an assignment statement.
2. Input data from keyboard as per commands displayed on the monitor.
3. Read data from a file, which has been already stored in the computer's memory.

5.2.1 Assignment Statement and Variable Declaration

A value can be assigned to a variable by making use of the assignment operator '=' as follows:

```
variable name = constant value
```

In an assignment statement, value of the variable on the L.H.S. of the 'equality' sign is made equal to the value of the constant/ expression on the R.H.S.

For example:

```
index = 4;

index = index+1;
```

The above statement implies that the new value of variable 'index' is equal to the old value of variable 'index', i.e., 4 plus 1 = 5.

Programming Tip 5.1: In MATLAB, there is no separate statement required to declare a variable. Once a variable is assigned a value, it is automatically declared.

Some simple examples of assigning values to variables are given below:

1. To create a scalar variable p and to store the number 40 in it.

   ```
   p = 40;
   ```

2. To create a scalar variable i and store the value 200.567 in it.

   ```
   i = 200.567;
   ```

3. To create a char variable s and store a character string 'good' in it.

   ```
   s = 'good'
   ```

4. To create a complex variable t and store a complex number 3.0 + 4.0i in it.

   ```
   t = 3.0+4.0i
   ```

5. To create an array variable x and store (2 × 3) data in it.

   ```
   x = [4 3 1; 2 6 9]
   ```

The variable created can be seen in workspace or by running command 'whos' on the command prompt.

Programming Tip 5.2: MATLAB permits multiple assignments in one line.

Many statements separated by semicolon (;) can be written in the same line. For example, consider the following statements:

```
First number = 5;

Last_number = 500;

Increment =10;
```

These statements can be written in one line as follows:

```
First number = 5; Last_number = 500; Increment =10;
```

5.3 INTERACTIVE INPUTS

The following functions/commands can be used by the user for interactive input:

(i) input Function
(ii) keyboard Command
(iii) menu Command
(iv) pause Command

5.3.1 Input Function

A user can input data by typing it at the keyboard by using `input` built-in function. The `input` function, when invoked, displays a prompt character string in the command window waiting for the user to feed the required data. Consider the statement given below:

```
r = input ('Enter radius in meters')
```

When executed, it displays the following character string on the monitor:

```
Enter radius in meters
```

It waits for the response of the user to provide the data from the keyboard. Here, it does not force the user to enter only numeric or character string. The user may enter any type of data. The `input` function simply reads the user's response and assigns the data provided to the variable (`r` in this case) indicated on the left-hand side of the statement.

If a number, say 4.5 is entered, it is assigned to variable `r` and displayed as

```
r = 4.5
```

If the character string `'four'` (in single quotation marks) is entered, the variable `r` is assigned that value and displayed as

```
r = four
```

The input can be any MATLAB expression, which is evaluated using the variables in the current workspace, and the result is returned to the variable `r`. If the user presses the return key without entering anything, `input` function returns an empty matrix. If it is desired that the input data should be returned to the user as a character string, then the `input` function includes character `'s'`, as a second argument. For example, consider the following statement:

```
r = input('What is your father's name:', 's')
```

It displays the text string

```
'What is your father's name:'
```

on the monitor and waits for input in the form of character string.

The input entered as the user's response is not evaluated. The characters are simply returned as a MATLAB string. The argument `'s'` directs MATLAB to save the user input as a string.

If the input is entered as: Dr RKB, then this text string is assigned to the variable `r` and the output will be displayed as:

```
r =
   Dr RKB
```

Consider another statement given below:

```
test = input('Solution converged ? (Y/N)', 's');
```

When executed, it will display the message

```
Solution converged? (Y/N)
```

and wait for the user's response.

If the user enters `'Y'`, the text string entered is assigned to the variable `'test'`. The complete string including the quotation marks is treated as part of the input character string.

> **Programming Tip 5.3:** MATLAB does not restrict the user to enter only a fixed number of characters and they need not be typed within quotation marks if the second argument `'s'` is used in the input command.

For example, consider the following statement:

```
theta = input ('Enter value of theta:');
```

When this statement is executed, MATLAB will display the character string:

```
Enter value of theta:
```

and the user has to supply the proper value from the keyboard.

> **Programming Tip 5.4:** Enter key has to be pressed after typing the input value.

5.3.2 keyboard Command

The **keyboard** command when included in a script file returns control to the keyboard at the point where the command occurs. The command window prompt is prefixed by the letter `'k'`.

`keyboard` command can be used to:

- Check the intermediate results in the program
- Make changes in variable values, if required
- Add new MATLAB commands in the program

To go back to the execution of the program, `return` is typed on new command window prompt, i.e.,

k>>,

and then enter key is pressed.

Example 5.1 Write a program to illustrate the use of `keyboard` command.

Solution: The program written below illustrates the use of `keyboard` command.

```
a = eye(5);
for j = 1:5,
   disp (j);
   if j == 3
      keyboard;
   end;
end;
```

During the execution of the above program, the control is returned to the key board when the value of `j` becomes 3 and then the prompt `k>>` appears on the command window. Type `return` on this prompt and then press enter key to resume computation.

Example 5.2 Write a program to illustrate the use of `keyboard` command to check the intermediate results and to add new data.

Solution: The following program illustrates the use of `keyboard` command to check the variable calculated and add new value to the variable. The program is as given below:

```
% Program to illustrate the use of keyboard command to find variable value and
% to change it.
a =10;
b =16;
x =a + b;
y =x/2;
keyboard          % check the variable y and change its value
                  % as y=10;
ans = y - 3 + 9
```

The result obtained is as shown below:

```
ans =

    16
```

When the command `keyboard` in the program is executed, the control is returned to the keyboard and command window prompt prefixed by `'k'`, i.e., k>> appears on the screen. At this point, variables already computed can be checked, their values can be changed and new MATLAB commands can be given. The computation will be resumed by typing **`return`** at the new prompt and pressing the enter key.

5.3.3 menu Command

The **menu** command is used to give the user an option to pictorially select a particular choice from the given choices. The choice of interest when selected with mouse will return a scalar value to the program. The syntax for this command is:

```
I = menu('Desired Title', 'option1', 'option 2',......)
```

where,

I is the variable which stores the returned scalar value corresponding to the selected option.

`Title` is the title to be given at the top of the menu window to be created on the screen.

`Option 1, option 2,...` are the given choices/ options to be displayed in the menu.

When executed, it displays a menu with the title and list of the options in sequence. The user can select any of the options using the mouse or the keyboard and the number of selected menu option, a scalar value, is returned to the variable `I`. The options are numbered internally.

Example 5.3 Illustrate the use of `menu` command, to choose a particular size from three different given sizes, i.e., large, medium and small.

Solution: The command used to generate a menu to choose a size from the three given choices is:

```
I = menu ('Choose a size', 'Large', 'Medium', 'Small')
```

The above statement, when executed, will display a small menu window with the title `'choose a size'` on the screen as shown in Figure 5.1.

Suppose, `Large` is to be chosen. With the help of mouse click on the box, `Large` and the following message will be displayed:

```
I =

    1
```

Similarly, if `Small` is selected, the value of `I` returned will be 3.

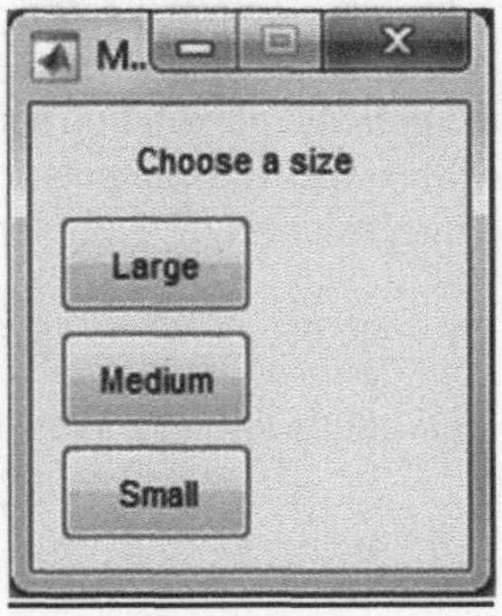

Figure 5.1 Window Generated with Example 5.3

Example 5.4 Using `menu` command, select a candidate of your choice from given choices, i.e., Kiran, Roshan, Surinder, John, Alka, Umesh, Abha and Neha.

Solution: The following command is used to display the given choices:

```
choice = menu('Select  your candidate', 'Kiran', 'Roshan', 'Surinder', 'John',
'Alka', 'Umesh','Abha', 'Neha')
```

The resulting window generated is shown in Figure 5.2, given below:

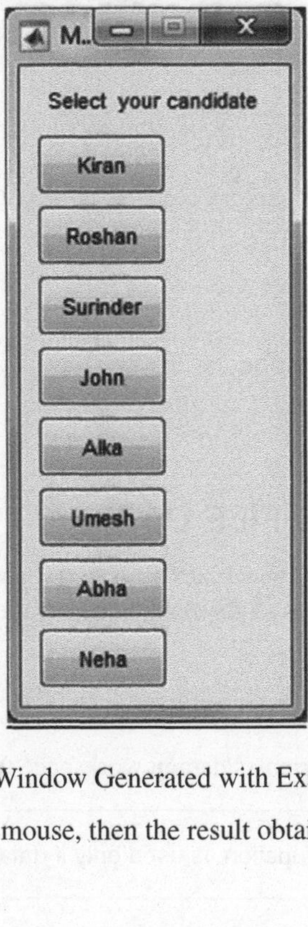

Figure 5.2 Window Generated with Example 5.4

Let, the choice `'Alka'` be selected with mouse, then the result obtained is as:

```
choice =
         5
```

5.3.4 pause Command

The **pause** command temporarily halts the current computation and waits for the user to give a command to resume the computations. Pressing any key resumes the computation. The command **pause (k)** stops the on-going computations for k seconds and then resumes the computations.

Example 5.5 Write a program to illustrate the use of pause command.

Solution: The program to illustrate pause command is as given below:

```
% Program to illustrate the use of 'pause' command
p = [1  2;  3  4];
q = [5  6;  7  8];
disp('The matrix p is given as:')
disp(p)
disp('Program is paused, please press any key to display... matrix q')
pause
disp('The matrix q is given as:')
disp(q)
z =p + q;
disp('Program is paused, please press any key to display... sum of p and q')
pause
disp(z)
```

The above program, when executed, will give the following output:

```
The matrix p is given as:
     1     2
     3     4

Program is paused, please press any key to display matrix q
The matrix q is given as:
     5     6
     7     8

Program is paused, please press any key to display sum of p and q
     6     8
    10    12
```

5.4 READING/ STORING FILE DATA

In MATLAB, there are many functions which are used to get the data from the files. These functions are categorized based on the types of format of the files. Some of the important functions are discussed in the following sections.

5.4.1 load Function

The **load** function is used to load variables/data in workspace from the disk file.

> **Programming Tip 5.5:** 'load' function is used only if data file contains numeric data.

The different syntax for `load` functions is:

```
load
load('filename')
load('filename', 'x', 'y', 'z')
load filename x, y, z
```

where filename is the name of the file which is to be loaded and `x, y, z` are the variable names. If the file name has .mat extension, the file is treated as a MAT-file by the `load` command.

The **`load('filename')`** loads all the variables from the filename given. If there is no extension with the filename, it looks for a file named filename.mat and treats it as MAT- file. If filename has extension other than (.mat), then it is treated as ASCII data file.

The **`load('filename', 'x', 'y', 'z')`** loads only the variables specified in the statement, i.e., `x, y` and `z`.

The **`load filename x, y, z`** is a command form of the syntax. It also loads the variables `x, y` and `z` from the given filename.

For example, consider that a data file abc.txt is available in the current directory which has two rows of numbers separated by space as shown below:

```
1 3 4 5 7
6 7 8 0 9
```

The following command is used to load data in workspace:

```
load abc.txt
```

To check whether this data has been loaded in the workspace, type `abc` on the command prompt and following result will be obtained:

```
abc =
    1     3     4     5     7
    6     7     8     0     9
```

The data is loaded into workspace by the same name as the name of the file, i.e., `abc` in this case. Therefore, after execution of `load` command, variable abc of size (2 × 5) will be loaded in the workspace.

In case the variable name is to be made different from the filename, the following command is used.

```
var_name = load ('abc.txt');
```

For example:

```
   test =load('abc.txt')
```

The result is stored in 'test' variable i.e.,

```
test =
        1     3     4     5     7
        6     7     8     0     9
```

5.4.2 save Function

The `save` function saves the current workspace data/variables in the disk file. It operates similar to the `load` function. The only difference is that `save` function saves data/variables from workspace to disk whereas `load` function saves variables from disk to workspace. The different forms of syntax for `save` function are as given below:

```
save
save('filename')
```

```
save('filename', 'a', 'b', 'c')
save  filename  a, b, c
```

where filename is the name of the file where the variables are saved and `a b c` are the variables to be saved in the file.

The `save` function stores all variables existing in workspace to the file named matlab.mat. The `save('filename')` statement stores all variables of workspace to the file with extension .mat, i.e., **filename.mat** in the current directory.

> **Programming Tip 5.6:** To save variables to a directory other than current directory, full pathname of the file has to be specified.

`save('filename', 'a', 'b', 'c')` statement saves the specified variables in the file named filename.mat.
`save filename a, b, c` statement is the command form of the syntax.
For example:

```
a = rand(1, 5);
b = eye(3);
save('check', 'a', 'b')
```

The variables `a` and `b` are stored in filename check.mat in the current directory.

5.4.3 dlmread Function

The `dlmread` function is used for reading numeric text data separated by character other than space. The syntax of different forms of the function is as given below:

```
data = dlmread('filename')
```

It reads numeric data from ASCII-delimited file named filename. Comma `(,)` is the default delimiter.

```
data = dlmread('filename', delimiter)
```

reads numeric data from ASCII-delimited file named `filename`, using specified delimiter.

For example, if the file abc has numeric data separated by semicolon `(;)`, then the command is as given below:

```
var_ name = dlmread ('abc'.txt', ';')
```

This will read data from file `abc.txt` till it encounters `';'` delimiter.

5.4.4 dlmwrite Function

The `dlmwrite` function is used to write a matrix to an ASCII-delimited file. The general syntax of different forms of this function is as given below:

```
dlmwrite ('filename', data)
```

It writes matrix named `'data'` into ASCII format file using the default delimiter `(,)`.

```
dlmwrite ('filename', data, 'D')
```

It writes matrix named `'data'` into ASCII format using delimiter `D` to separate matrix elements.

5.4.5 textscan and textread Functions

If the text file contains numeric as well as other characters like alphabets, etc., the method used to read the file is similar to that used in the C-programming language. The file needs to be opened for read operation using 'fopen' command and then read using 'textscan' command as illustrated below:

```
fid = fopen ('abc.dat', 'r')
var_name =   textscan(fid, '%f   % c  ........');
```

When executed, the above statements will read the data into var_name, a cell array.

The command 'textread' can be used to read the data into separate variables. The syntax of textread command is as given below:

```
[a,b,c,d] = textread ('abc.txt', 'Format specifications')
```

where a, b, c, d are variables to which data is to be read.

For example:

```
[Names, types, a, b, c] = textread('abc.txt', '%s %s %f %f %f');
```

When executed, the above statement will read first string into variable 'names', second string into variable 'types' and then the three float numeric data values into variables a, b, and c.

5.5 OUTPUT COMMANDS

In MATLAB, the output data can be displayed in a number of ways. The simplest way to print the value of the output variable is to skip the semicolon (;) at the end of the statement in the command window. The output will be displayed immediately in the command window, except for graphics and online help commands. However, there are numerous functions available in MATLAB for formatted and unformatted output statements as discussed below.

5.5.1 Default Format

The default format for representation of any non-integer value in MATLAB shows four digits after the decimal point. In case, the value is too large or too small, then it may be displayed in scientific notation with an exponent. The integer values are displayed as simple value. For example:

```
a = 7                         % integer value
b = 1.01                      % real value
c = 2100.34                   % large value
```

When the above statements are executed, values are displayed in MATLAB as shown below:

```
a =

     7
b =

     1.0100
c =

     2.1003e+003
```

5.5.2 format Command: Altering Default Format

The default format of MATLAB can be changed by using **format** command. This can be done by writing format on the command prompt followed by 'format style to be used' For example, the value of pi can be displayed in different formats as illustrated below:

To represent pi in default format, simply execute the command as:

```
x = pi
```

The result is as shown:

```
x =
      3.1416
```

Now, let's change the format to short exponential by using following command

```
format short e
```

Now, check the value of x again, which is given as:

```
x =
    3.1416e+000
```

Again, to change the format to long, the command used is as:

```
format long
```

The result obtained is as:

```
x =
     3.14159265358979
```

The different types of format in MATLAB using format command are shown in Table 5.1 given below. The table illustrates the value of '√3' that will be displayed depending upon the type of format used.

Table 5.1 Various Output Formats

Format Command	Description	Display of Value of √3
format short	4 digits after decimal (default format)	1.7321
format long	14 digits after decimal	1.73205080756888
format short e	5 digits plus exponent	1.7321 e+000
format short g	5 total digits with or without exponent	1.7321
format long e	15 digits plus exponent	1.732050807568877 e+000
format long g	total 15 digits with or without exponent	1.73205080756888
format bank	"dollars and cents" format	1.73
format hex	hexadecimal display of bits	3.ffbb67ae8584caa
format rat	approx. ratio of small integers	1351/780
format compact	suppress extra linefeeds	Not Applicable
format loose	restores extra linefeeds back	NA
format +	Format + displays a +, - and blank for positive, negative and zero numbers respectively. Imaginary parts are ignored.	NA

5.5.3 disp Function

The disp function accepts an array argument 'x' and displays the value of the array, row wise in the command window. It works the same way as skipping the semicolon after any MATLAB statement.

To illustrate the use of `disp` statement, consider the matrix 'x' given below:

$$x = \begin{bmatrix} 2 & 3 \\ 4 & 5 \end{bmatrix}$$

To display the matrix, the following commands can be used:

```
x = [2  3;  4  5];
disp(x);
```

The result obtained is as shown below:

```
2 3

4 5
```

If the array is of type `char`, then the character string contained in the array is displayed. For example:

```
disp('The largest number is:')
```

The result obtained is as:

```
The largest number is:
```

This function is often combined with the functions `num2str` (convert a number to a string) and `int2str` (convert an integer to a string) to create messages to be displayed in the command window. For example:

```
str = num2str(pi)

disp(str)
```

When the above MATLAB statements are executed, the following is displayed:

```
3.1416
```

This shows that the numeric value of `pi` has been converted into character string.

5.6 LOW-LEVEL INPUT/OUTPUT FUNCTIONS

There a number of low-level file input/output functions in MATLAB which are based on the input/output functions of ANSI Standard C Library. The functions are generally categorized as:

1. File opening and closing functions
2. Binary input/output functions.
3. Formatted input/output functions.

These can be listed as in Table 5.2.

Table 5.2 Low-level File Input/Output Functions

Type of Functions	Function Name	Description
File opening and closing functions	`fopen`	Open a file for read or write operations
	`fclose`	Close one or more opened files
Formatted input/output functions	`fscanf`	Read formatted data from file
	`fprintf`	Write formatted data to file
	`fgetl`	Return next line of file as string without line terminator
	`fgets`	Return next line of file as string with line terminator
Binary input/output functions	`fwrite`	Write data in binary form.
	`fread`	Read binary data from file

5.6.1 File Opening and Closing Functions

To read from or write to any file, it is required to select a file. In MATLAB, a file is selected by unique integral value called `file id` (also called `fid`). A `fid` is assigned to a file when it is opened and this particular `fid` is used for performing different operations on the file such as reading, writing or other control operations. The `fid` for a standard output is 1 and for standard error is 2. These are the default values thus any new file opened is allotted `fid` from 3 onwards. As more files are opened, these are allotted `fid` in continuation. As a particular file is closed, the `fid` assigned to it is released. A file is opened and closed using MATLAB functions `fopen` and `fclose` as explained below:

5.6.1.1 `fopen` Function

For performing any operation on a file, the first step is to access it and it is done by using `fopen` function. The syntax for `fopen` function is given as:

```
fid = fopen (filename, permission_code)
```

where `fid` is a file id assigned to the file and it is a positive number.
`file name` is a character string specifying the name of the file to be opened
`permission_code` is a character string specifying the mode in which the file opened

Other syntax for `fopen` function are given as:-

```
[fid,message] = fopen (filename, permission_code)

[fid,message] = fopen(filename, permission_code, format)
```

where `format` is an optional string specifying the numeric format of the data in the file
`message` is a string explaining error, in case the file open fails.

In case file opening is successful, `fid` will contain positive number and `message` will be an empty string whereas if file opening fails `fid` will contain −1 and `message` will be a string explaining the error.

The different standard values of `fid` and their meaning are illustrated in Table 5.3.

Table 5.3 Standard File Identifier Values and their Interpretation

Fid Value	Meaning
−1	fid opening fails
0	standard input (keyboard)
1	standard output (monitor screen)
2	standard error
3 onwards	assigned to files opened successfully

The `fopen` can also be used to provide file information rather than opening a file. The two ways to use `fopen` function for getting file information are as follows:

1. `fids = fopen('all')`

   This function provides a row vector of all file ids for currently open files (except for standard output and standard error). The number of elements of this vector gives the total of open files
2. `[filename, permission_code, format] = fopen(fid)`

   This function provides `filename`, `permission_code` and `format` for open file specified by `fid`.

The different permission codes with `fopen` command are shown in Table 5.4.

Table 5.4 Permission Codes with `fopen` Command

Permission Text String	Meaning
`'r'`	Open the existing file for reading. In .case file does not exist, error occurs
`'r+'`	Open the existing file for reading and writing. In case file does not exist, error occurs.
`'w'`	Open the file for writing. In case file already exists, its contents are cleared and if it does not exist, a new file is created.
`'w+'`	Open the file for reading and writing. In case file already exists, its contents are cleared and if it does not exist, a new file is created.
`'a'`	Open an existing file (or create a new file) for writing only, appending to the end of the file.
`'a+'`	Open an existing file (or create a new file) for reading and writing, appending to the end of the file.

5.6.1.2 *fclose* Function

After using a file for different operations, it should always be closed. This is done by using `fclose` function. The syntax for `fclose` function is given as

```
status = fclose (fid)
```

where `status` returns the result of the operation
fid specified file id of the file to be closed.

In case the operation is successful, `status` returns 0 and if it is successful, it returns –1. The another form of this function is given below.

```
status = fclose ('all')
```

It closes all open files except for standard output `(fid = 1)` and standard error `(fid = 2)`.

> **Programming Tip 5.7:** Standard input, output and error cannot be opened or closed with `fopen` and `fclose` functions.

5.6.2 Formatted Input/Output Functions

The different formatted input/output functions are given as:

1. `fprintf` function
2. `fscanf` function
3. `fgetl` function
4. `fgets` function

5.6.2.1 *fprintf* Function

The data can be displayed in desired format using `fprintf` function. The general syntax of this function is as shown below:

```
fprintf (fid, format, data)
```

where,

fid is the file identifier, which identifies the file to which the data is to be written and is returned by the fopen function used to open the file for write operation,

format describes the detailed format string in which data is to be printed. The format string consists of a character string containing text to be printed and the special conversion characters describing the format of the data, i.e., significant digits, field width, etc.

data represents one or more data values or the variables whose value is to be printed.

In general, format string is given as:

%-a.be\n

where

% specifies start of conversion

'-' specifies the flag used to control the alignment of the output (see Table 5.5)

'a' specifies the field width.

'b' specifies the precision, i.e., number of digits after decimal point.

'e' specifies conversion character (see Table 5.6)

'\n' specifies escape character (see Table 5.7)

For example, let us suppose a format string is given as:

% + 6.3d\n

Here,

% specifies start of conversion

'+' means always print a sign character.

'6' means that total width of the field

'3' means that there are three digits after decimal

'd' means exponential notation

'\n' means a newline character.

The various conversion characters used with fprintf are listed in Table 5.6.

Table 5.5 The Optional Flags Used Along with fprintf Function

Characters	Definition	Example
–	Left-justifies the converted argument in its field	%-6.3f
+	Always prints a sign character (+ or –)	%+6.3f
0	Pad argument with leading zeros rather than spaces	%06.3f

Table 5.6 Format Conversion Characters Used in Writing Formatted Output

Conversion Characters	Definition
%c	Single character
%d	Decimal notation (signed)
%e	Exponential notation (using a lowercase e as in 3.1415e+00)

(Continued)

Table 5.6 (*Continued*)

Conversion Characters	Definition
%E	Exponential notation (using an uppercase E as in 3.1415E+00)
%f	Fixed point notation
%g do	The more compact of %e or %f. Insignificant zeros not print.
%G	Same as %g, but using an uppercase E
%o	Octal notation (unsigned)
%s	String of characters
%u	Decimal notation (unsigned)
%x	Hexadecimal notation (using lowercase letters a–f)
%X	Hexadecimal notation (using uppercase letters A–F)

The different escape characters that are used with `fprintf` command are shown in Table 5.7.

Table 5.7 Escape Characters Used in Writing Formatted Output

Escape Sequence	Description
\n	Newline
\t	Horizontal tab
\b	Backspace
\r	Carriage return
\f	Form feed
\\	Print backslash(\)
\'	Print apostrophe or single quote
%%	Print percentage (%)

Example 5.6 Illustrate the use of `fprintf` function display the values of *x* varies from 0 to 180 with four equal intervals and also display its sine values.

Solution: The commands used are given as:

```
x = 0: 45:180;
y = [x; sind(x)];
fprintf('%6.2f  %6.4f\n', y)
% Here fid =0 i.e., output is displayed at standard
% output - monitor screen.
```

The result obtained is given as:

```
  0.00     0.0000
 45.00     0.7071
 90.00     1.0000
135.00     0.7071
180.00     0.0000
```

Example 5.7 Suppose x has five uniformly distributed values between 0 and 2. Represent the values of x in the following formats: (fid = 0, i.e., standard screen outputs)

(a) Default format
(b) Floating point format with width 6 and precision 3 and newline
(c) Floating point format with zero padding and newline
(d) Signed values and newline
(e) Exponential format and newline
(f) Compact format and newline

Solution:

(a) **Default format:** The command used and response obtained is as:

```
x =0:0.4:2
x =
     0    0.4000    0.8000    1.2000    1.6000    2.0000
```

(b) **Floating point format with width 6 and precision 3 and newline:** The command used and response obtained is as:

```
fprintf('%6.3f\n', x)
0.000
0.400
0.800
1.200
1.600
2.000
```

(c) **Floating point format with zero padding and newline:** The command used and response obtained is as:

```
fprintf('%06.3f\n', x)
00.000
00.400
00.800
01.200
01.600
02.000
```

(d) **Signed values:** The command used and response obtained is as:

```
fprintf('%+6.3f\n',x)
+0.000
+0.400
+0.800
+1.200
+1.600
+2.000
```

(e) **Exponential format:** The command used and response obtained is as:

```
fprintf('%6.3e\n', x)
0.000e+000
4.000e-001
8.000e-001
1.200e+000
1.600e+000
2.000e+000
```

(f) **Compact format:** The command used and response obtained is as:

```
fprintf('%g\n', x)
0
0.4
0.8
1.2
1.6
2
```

Programming Tip 5.8: The file identifiers for standard output (monitor screen) and standard error are not mandatory to mention and are by default to be equal to 1 and 2, respectively. Any other file opened is allocated file identifier (fid) from 3 onwards. If `fopen` cannot open the file, integer output equal to −1 is returned.

Example 5.8 Display the following statement as formatted output using `format` command: 'The largest 3 digit no. is: 999'.

Solution: The command is given as;

```
fprintf ('The largest 3 digit no. is %f \n', 999)
```

As no file identifier is given, so standard output file i.e., the monitor screen is assumed as the file to which the data is to be printed.

Therefore, the `fprintf` statement when executed will display the text string: 'The largest 3 digit no. is 999' on the monitor screen, where 999.0 is the data displayed as per the format conversion character %f, i.e., floating point format.

The escape character (\n) represents newline and thus, the cursor will be moved to the beginning of new line. The output of the above statement is shown below.

```
The largest 3 digit no. is 999.000000
```

Programming Tip 5.9: `fprintf` function displays only the real portion of a complex value.

Programming Tip 5.10: Format strings are scanned from left to right.

5.6.2.2 fscanf Function

The `fscanf` function reads formatted data in a user-specified format from a file. The syntax is given as:

```
A = fscanf( fid, format)

[A, count] = fscanf (fid, format, size)
```

where fid is file id of a file to be read

`format` specifies how data is to be read

`A` is variable to store the data

`count` returns the number of values read from the file

`size` specifies the amount of data to be read from the file.

Programming Tip 5.11: If data in the file does not match the format specified in `fscanf` statement, then `fscanf` stops immediately.

Example 5.9 Illustrate use of `fscanf` to read a file test.txt having first 10 integer numbers in:

(a) (2×5) array format
(b) One column
(c) (5×2) array format

Solution: Firstly, a file named text.txt having first 10 integers is created. The following commands are used to get the desired result:

(a) **(2×5) array format:**

% Open the file using `fopen` function

```
fid = fopen('test.txt', 'r');

[a, count1] = fscanf(fid, '%f', [2, 5])
```

The result obtained is as:

```
a =

     1     3     5     7     9
     2     4     6     8    10

count1 =

    10
```

(b) **One column:**

The statements are as:

```
fid = fopen('test.txt', 'r')
[a, count2] = fscanf(fid, '%f')
```

Here, no size is specified thus the result is obtained as in column The result obtained is as:

```
a =
     1
     2
     3
     4
     5
     6
     7
     8
     9
    10
count2 =
          10
```

(c) **(5 × 2) array format:**

```
fid = fopen('test.txt', 'r');
[a, count3] = fscanf(fid, '%f', [5, 2])
```

The result obtained is as:

```
a =
     1     6
     2     7
     3     8
     4     9
     5    10
count3 =
          10
```

5.6.2.3 `fgetl` Function

The `fgetl` function reads the next line excluding the end of line characters from a file as a character string. Its syntax is given as:

```
statement = fgetl(fid)
```

where `fid` is file id of a file to be read

`statement` is character array that receives the data.

The returned string `'statement'` does not include the line terminator with the text line. If `fgetl` encountered the end of file indicator, it returns –1.

5.6.2.4 *fgets* Function

The `fgets` function reads line from file, keeping new line character. The syntax is given as:

```
statement = fgetl(fid)
```

where `fid` is file id of a file to be read.

```
statement is character array that receives the data.
```

If `fgetl` encountered the end of file indicator, it returns –1.

5.6.3 Binary Input/output Functions

The formatted input–output functions works with human readable text in a file. This file is also called an ASCII text file. These files require more disk space as compared to binary files. In case, files are required by the computer only, than it is preferable to have data in binary files which are, though, not readable by user but will require less disk space. The different MATLAB functions are used for reading and writing binary files are as:

1. `fwrite` Function
2. `fread` Function

5.6.3.1 *fwrite* Function

This function is used for writing binary data in a user-specified format to a file. The syntax for `fwrite` function is as:

```
count = fwrite(fid, array, 'precision')
```

where `count` is number of values written to the file.
`fid` is file id of a file opened with `fopen` function.
`array` is an array of values to be written.
`precision` is used to specify the format for storing the values.

Some of the precisions used with `fwrite` Function are enlisted as in Table 5.8. In case, no precision is specified then `uchar` is used as default precision.

Table 5.8 Precisions for `fwrite` Function

Strings as Precision	Interpretation
`char`	Character; 8 bits
`uchar`	Unsigned character; 8-bits
`short`	Integer; 16 bits
`int`	Integer; 32 bits
`long`	Integer; 32 or 64 bits
`float`	Floating point; 32 bits
`double`	Floating point; 64 bits

Example 5.10 Illustrate the use of `fwrite` function for writing binary data of different formats to a file named check.txt.

Solution: The following program is written for illustration of the `fwrite` function.

```
% Program to illustrate the use of fwrite function
% Generate data of different formats
a = [2 4 6; 3 5 7];
b =105;
c = 'today is world cup final';
% open a file for writing, using fopen function
fid = fopen('check.txt', 'w')
% write an array indicated by variable a in 'double' format
x = fwrite(fid, a, 'double')
% write value of variable b in 'short' format
y = fwrite(fid, b, 'short')
% write value of variable c in 'character' format as its a %string.
z = fwrite(fid, c, 'char')
% close the file
fclose (fid)
```

The result obtained is as given below:

```
c =
   today is world cup final
fid =
     3
x =
     6
y =
     1
z =
    24
ans =
     0
```

When file is created by the above program is seen in notepad, it will display values which are not readable as it contains binary data.

Programming Tip 5.12: Binary files are not readable by text editor.

5.6.3.2 `fread` Function

The `fread` function is used to read binary data in user-specified format from a file. The general syntax is given as:

```
[variable, count] = fread (fid, size, precision)
```

where fid is file id of the file to be read and is obtained by fopen function.
size gives the dimensions of data to be read.
precision specifies format of data to be read.
variable contains the data read from the file.
count gives number of elements read successfully.

Programming Tip 5.13: To read binary data from a file correctly, it must be known how it was written.

Example 5.11 Illustrate the use of fread function to read data from a binary file created in previous example.

Solution: The program is given as:

```
% Program to illustrate the use of fread function
clear all                 % clear all variables in workspace
% open a file 'check.txt' for reading using fopen function.
fid1= fopen('check.txt', 'r')
% read variable 'x' which is 2 x 3 array of 'double' precision
[A, count1] =fread(fid1, [2, 3], 'double')
% read variable 'y' which is one element in 'short' precision
[B,count2] = fread(fid1, [1], 'short')
% read variable 'z' which is text string of 24 characters
[C,count3] = fread(fid1, [24], 'char')
% the text string will be read as ASCII codes in a column array.
% To change this into string, take transpose and then use function 'setstr'
C = C';
C = setstr(C)
% close the file after reading all variables
fclose (fid1)
```

The result obtained is given as:

```
fid1 =
     3
A =
     2     4     6
     3     5     7
count1 =
           6
B =
   105
count2 =
           1
C =
   116
   111
```

```
   100
    97
   121
    32
   105
   115
    32
   119
   111
   114
   108
   100
    32
    99
   117
   112
    32
   102
   105
   110
    97
   108
count3 =
          24
C =
    today is world cup final
ans =
     0
```

Example 5.12 Write a program to generate first five odd numbers and illustrate the use of `fopen`, `fprintf`, and `fclose` commands related to file input/output.

Solution: The program given below creates a file named `'odd.text'` and writes first five odd numbers in the file.

```
A(1) = 1;
for i = 1:4
A(i + 1) = A(i) + 2;
end;
fid = fopen('odd.txt', 'w');
fprintf(fid, 'First five odd numbers\n',);
fprintf(fid, '***********************\n');
fprintf(fid, '%3i\n', A);
fclose(fid);
```

In the program given above, the `fopen` command creates and opens a file `'odd.txt'` in write mode (specified by `'w'` in the command) and assigns a file identifier to `fid`. The `fprintf` command uses the file id `'fid'` to write to that file. The `fclose` command is used to close the file. An `odd.txt` file is created which is stored in current directory. This file can be opened through text editor and contents are checked.

The results are shown below:

```
First five odd numbers
**********************
  1
  3
  5
  7
  9
```

SUMMARY

This chapter covered different functions/commands used for data input and data output. The chapter can be summarized in following points:

- The basic method of data input through **assignment statement**, in which a value can be assigned to any variable.
- The different input/output functions such as **`load`**, **`save`**, **`dlmread`**, **`dlmwrite`**, **`textread`**, **`textwrite`** can be used to get and send the data to a file.
- The different interactive input functions which provoke user to provide input are discussed such as **`input`** function.
- Then, some special commands such as **`keyboard`**, **`pause`**, etc. are discussed which plays an important role in manipulation of program, even during its execution.
- A special command **`menu`** can be used to produce a pictorial window which consists of different options for selection.
- It also discussed the default format of MATLAB and how to change it using `format` command to represent the data in desired format.
- The function **`disp`** is discussed which are used to represent data output in different formats.
- In the last, low-level file input/output functions such as **`fopen`**, **`fclose`**, **`fprintf`**, **`fscanf`**, **`fgetl`**, **`fgets`** are discussed and illustrated with examples.
- The **`escape sequences`** used along with **`fprintf`** command is also mentioned.

List of Commands/Functions

Commands/Functions	Description
`input`	prompt user to give input from keyboard
`load`	load variables in the workspace from the disk
`save`	save variables from workspace to disk/file
`dlmread`	read ASCII-delimited file

(Continued)

(*Continued*)

`dlmwrite`	write ASCII-delimited file
`textscan`	read formatted data from text file
`textread`	read formatted data from text file
`keyboard`	transfer control to keyboard from M-file
`menu`	generate menu of options in a window for user choice
`pause`	wait for user response
`format`	change the default format
`disp`	display an array
`fprintf`	write formatted data to file

Low-level Input/Output Functions

Type of Function	Function Name	Description
File opening and closing functions	`fopen`	Open a file for read or write operations
	`fclose`	Close one or more opened files
Formatted input/ output functions	`fscanf`	Read formatted data from file
	`fprintf`	Write formatted data to file
	`fgetl`	Return next line of file as string without line terminator
	`fgets`	Return next line of file as string with line terminator
Binary input/output functions	`fwrite`	Write data in binary form
	`fread`	Read binary data from file

EXERCISES

5.1 Write a MATLAB program to generate a data file containing the names and corresponding telephone numbers of the customers.

5.2 Using the data file created in question 1, write a program in MATLAB to create a menu-driven facility to perform the given tasks

(i) Determine the telephone numbers of the specified customer.

(ii) Determine the telephone number of the specified customer

5.3 Write a MATLAB program to copy the data from one file to another file.

5.4 Write a program in MATLAB to illustrate the different format specifiers that can be used for obtaining formatted output.

5.5 Write a program to illustrate how a matrix can be processed by a single formatted output command.

5.6 Write a program to illustrate how a menu can be created using MATLAB.

5.7 What is the utility of the keyboard and pause command? How are they used?

5.8 How can data be read into a file in binary, octal and hexadecimal format? Illustrate your answer with a suitable example.

5.9 Create a text file in MATLAB. Write a program to search and report for a particular string in the text file.

5.10 How can formatted output statements in MATLAB be used to display data in tabular form? Write an example program.

5.11 Write a MATLAB program to read data from the file ab1.txt. The data stored is as given below:

```
01   anil    234   2k1   50
02   bhanu   215   2k2   54
03   charu   231   2k1   62
```

CHAPTER 6

MATLAB Graphics

LEARNING OBJECTIVES

- Study basic features of plotting a graph
  - ❒ Plot a simple graph, label its axis and give title, grid and box control.
  - ❒ Provide text at the desired location on the plot using `text` and `gtext` function.
  - ❒ Study the axis control of the plot.
- To draw multiple plots using plot, hold and line functions.
- To learn about different style options to vary colour, marker and line style
- To provide a legend on the plot.
- To study multiple sub-graph windows using `subplot` function.
- To study specialized plots such as logarithmic, polar, bar, histogram, pie, stairs, stem, etc. plots.
- To study three-dimensional plots such as `plot3, bar3, pie3, mesh, surf, contour,` etc.

6.1 INTRODUCTION

MATLAB provides very good tools for two-and three-dimensional plots, 3-D volume visualization functions, tools for interactively creating plots, and the ability to export results to many popular graphics formats. It is possible to customize plots by adding multiple axes, changing line colours and markers, adding annotations, legends and drawing shapes.

Vector data can be visualized with two-dimensional plotting functions such as line, area, bar, and pie charts, direction and velocity plots, histograms, polygons and surfaces, scatter/bubble plots, animations. MATLAB provides functions for visualizing two-dimensional matrices, three-dimensional scalar, and three-dimensional vector data. In MATLAB, one can specify plot characteristics, such as camera viewing angle, perspective, lighting effect, light source locations, and transparency. Three-dimensional plotting functions include surface, contour, mesh, image plots, cone, slice, stream, and isosurface. The graphics commands in MATLAB are very simple and easily understood. This makes graphics one of the most powerful features of MATLAB.

6.2 TWO-DIMENSIONAL PLOTS

To draw a two-dimensional plot in MATLAB, the **`plot`** command is used. The syntax is as given under:

```
plot(x, y)
```

where `x` is a vector containing the *x*-coordinates of the plot and `y` is a vector containing the *y*-coordinates of the plot.

When executed, the command will create a plot in the MATLAB figure window with data in vector x taken along *x*-axis and data in vector *y* along *y*-axis.

In case figure window already exists, it clears the current figure window and draws a new plot.

Example 6.1 Plot the curve given by equation y = x^2, where *x* varies from 0 to 10.

Solution: The program to plot the curve given by equation y = x^2 is given below:

```
x = 0 : 1 : 10;                    % Statement 1
y = x .^ 2;                        % Statement 2
plot(x, y);                        % Statement 3
```

Statement 1, creates a vector x with 11 elements = [0 1 2 3 4 5 6 7 8 9 10]. Statement 2, creates the vector y with again 11 elements each being the square of the corresponding element in x, and is = [0 1 4 9 16 25 36 49 64 81 100]. The statement 3 plots the curve using the corresponding x and y values taken from the respective vectors. The curve plotted is shown in Figure 6.1.

On executing the above three statements, the figure window will open with the desired plot. This example illustrates simplest form of two-dimensional plot without any labelling.

> **Programming Tip 6.1** The size of the vectors x and y should be same.

Let us change the size of x vector by including another element in it using the command as shown below.

```
x(12) = 11;
```

Now if `plot` command is used, it shall give error given below:

```
??? Error using ==> plot
```

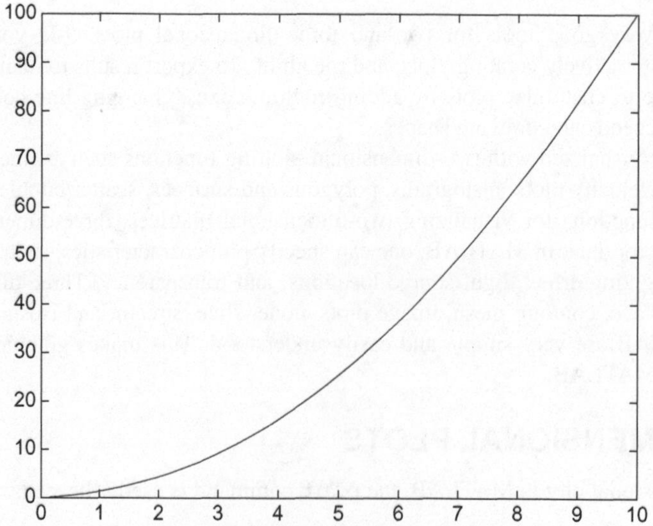

Figure 6.1 Plot for Example 6.1

Therefore, the two vectors being used to plot the two-dimensional curve, as x and y in Example 6.1 above, must be of same lengths.

When plot has only one argument, say `plot(x)`, then

- If x is real variable, the plot is drawn between x versus index of its values, i.e., `plot(x)` means

```
plot (1:length(x),x)
```

- In case of x being complex variable, then `plot (x)` gives the plot between real value of x versus `imaginary value of x`, i.e., `plot (x)` means

```
plot(real(x), imag(x))
```

Example 6.2 Plot the following variables:

(a) $a = [1\ \ 13\ \ 6\ \ 9\ \ 23\ \ 12]$

(b) $b = [1 - 2i, 3 + 4i, 5 + 6i, 3 + 8i, 4 + 9i, 23 + 12i]$

Solution: The following commands are used:

(a) $a = [1\ \ 13\ \ 6\ \ 9\ \ 23\ \ 12]$

```
% Program to illustrate plot command for single variable
a = [1 13 6 9 23 12];
plot(a)
```

The response obtained is shown in Figure 6.2.

(b) $b = [1 - 2i, 3 + 4i, 5 + 6i, 3 + 8i, 4 + 9i, 23 + 12i]$

```
% Program to illustrate plot command for single complex variable
a = [1 - 2i, 3 + 4i, 5 + 6i, 3 + 8i, 4 + 9i, 23 + 12i];
plot(a)
```

The response obtained is shown in Figure 6.3.

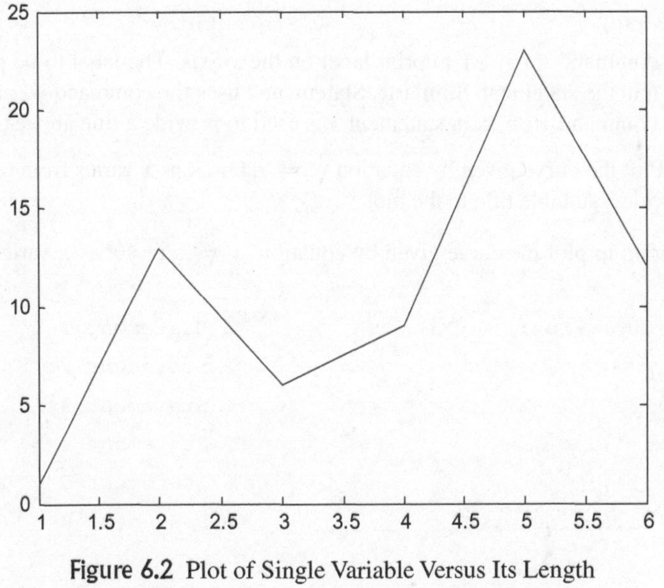

Figure 6.2 Plot of Single Variable Versus Its Length

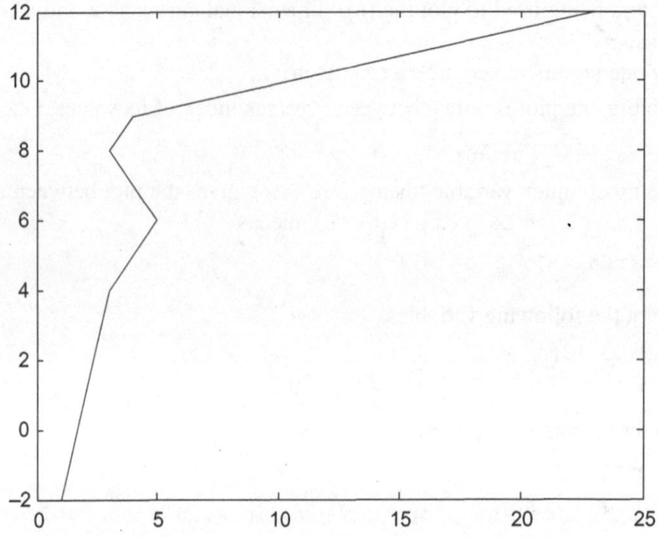

Figure 6.3 Plot of Single Variable Having Complex Values

6.2.1 Printing Labels

To make the plot more understandable, the two axes are labelled and a title is provided above the top of the plot by using the following commands:

```
xlabel('string1')                    % Statement 1
ylabel('string2')                    % Statement 2
title('string3')                     % Statement 3
```

Statement 1 uses the command `xlabel` to print label on the *x*-axis. The label to be printed is enclosed in single quotes as shown in the statement. Similarly, Statement 2 uses the command `ylabel` to print the label along the y-axis. The command `title` in statement 3 is used to provide a title above the top of the graph.

Example 6.3 Plot the curve given by equation `y = sin x` as *x* varies from 0 to 2π. Also label the *x*- and *y*-axis and provide a suitable title to the plot.

Solution: The program to plot the curve given by equation `y = sin` *x* as *x* varies from `0 to` 2π, is given below:

```
x = 0 : pi/100 : 2*pi;                  % Statement 1
y = sin(x);                             % Statement 2
plot(x, y);                             % Statement 3
xlabel('x-axis');                       % Statement 4
ylabel('y-axis');                       % Statement 5
title('Plot of a sine wave');           % Statement 6
```

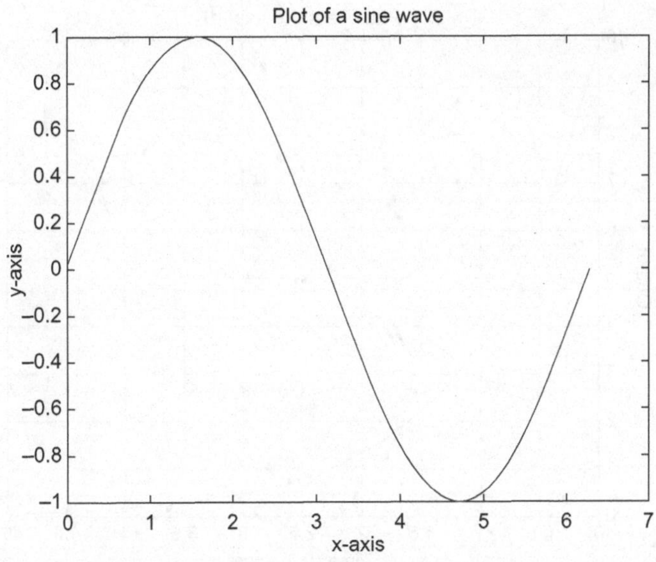

Figure 6.4 Plot of Curve Given by Equation `y = sin x` (Example 6.3)

The statement 1 generates the vector `x` with values from `0 to` 2π with interval of π`/100` between any two successive values. Statement 2 generates the vector `y` with elements equal to the sine of the angle given by the corresponding elements in vector `x`. Statement 3 plots the `x-y` graph by taking the *x*- and *y*-axis values from the vectors `x` and `y`, respectively. Statements 4–6 label the *x*-axis, *y*-axis and provide the title to the plot. The plot for this example is shown in Figure 6.4.

6.2.2 Grid and Axes Box

To give better illustration of the coordinates on the plot, a grid is used. The command **`grid`** is used to show the grid lines on the plot. The grid on the plot can be added or removed by using the argument **`on`** and **`off`** with the **`grid`** command. When command **`grid`** without any argument is used alternatively, it toggles the grid drawn. By default, MATLAB starts with **`grid off`**.

Example 6.4 Plot the curve given by equation `a = 10` e^{-t} for `t = 0 to 5`. Show the grid lines on the plot.

Solution: The program to plot the curve given by equation `a = 10` $e^{(-t)}$ as `t` varies from `0 to 5`, is given below:

```
t = 0 : 0.1 : 5;                      % Statement 1
a = 10*exp(-t);                       % Statement 2
plot(t, a);                           % Statement 3
xlabel('Time(t) in secs');            % Statement 4
ylabel('Output');                     % Statement 5
title('Plot of a = 10*exp(-t)');      % Statement 6
grid on;                              % Statement 7
```

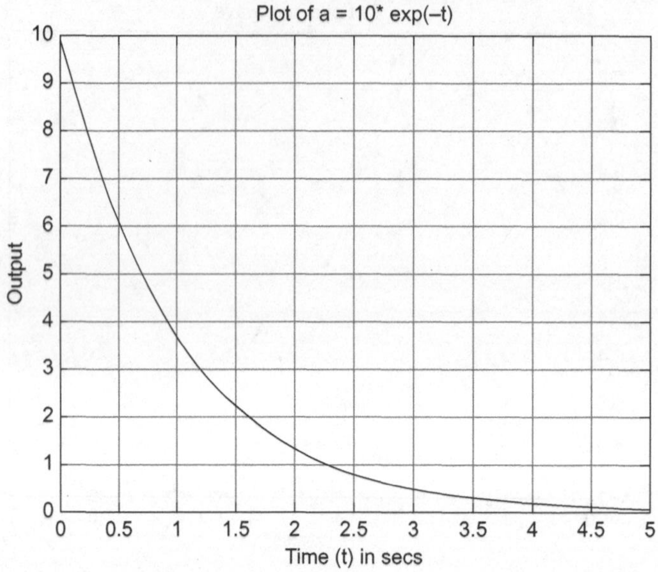

Figure 6.5 Plot of Curve Given by Equation `a = 10 e^-t` with Grid Lines

The statement 1 generates the vector ***t*** with values from 0 to 5 with interval of 0.1 between any two successive values. Statement 2 generates the vector ***a*** with elements given by the equation above by taking the corresponding elements in vector ***t***. Statement 3 plots the *x*–*y* graph by taking the *x*- and *y*-axis values from the vectors `t` and `a`, respectively. Statements 4–6 label the *x*-axis, *y*-axis and provide the title to the plot. Statement 7 plots the grid lines on the graph. The plot for this example is shown in Figure 6.5.

`Axes box`

The plot obtained in figure window is generally enclosed by solid lines called an axes box. This box can be turned off with command **`box off`** and can be turned on with command **`box on`.** When command **`box`** is used alternatively, it toggles the axes box.

Example 6.5 Plot the function $b = 4a^2$ for $0 < a < 20$ and illustrate the box command.

Solution: The following commands are used:

```
% Program to illustrate box command
a =0: 0.05:20;
b =4*a.^2;
plot(a, b)
box off
title('Plot of function b =4*a^2 to illustrate box command');
xlabel('x-axis')
ylabel('y-axis')
```

The response obtained is as shown in Figure 6.6.

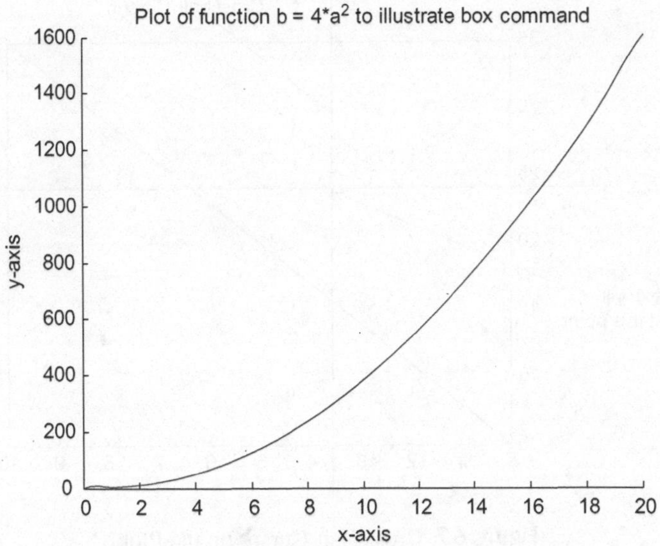

Figure 6.6 Plot of Function `b = 4a²` with Box Off

6.2.3 Entering Text in a Plot

Sometimes, it is desired to give more illustration to the plot by writing illustrative text on the plot drawn. This can be accomplished by using the command **`text`**. The syntax is as given below:

```
text(x-coordinate, y-coordinate, 'text_to_be_written')
```

where arguments in the parenthesis, i.e., `x-coordinate` and `y-coordinate` give the point on the plot from where the text has to be started and `text_to_be_written` is the character string, i.e., the text that is to be displayed or added to the graph.

The text must be a string or a vector of strings. Consider the MATLAB statement:

```
text(3, 4, 'Negative Resistance Region')
```

When executed, the text `'Negative Resistance Region'` is added to the plot at the coordinate point `(3, 4)` on the *x*–*y* graph.

To add the text in the plot at any location not mentioned by the specific coordinate position, the command **`gtext`** is used. The `gtext` command generates a cross-hair cursor, which follows the mouse to any point on the graph. The text is added to the plot at the desired location by clicking the mouse or key press. The syntax of `gtext` command is given below:

```
gtext ('string');
```

When executed, the `gtext` command shifts the control to the graphics window. The cross-hair cursor that follows the mouse and on clicking the mouse at any desired location the text `string` is added to the plot and program control shifts back to the next statement in the program.

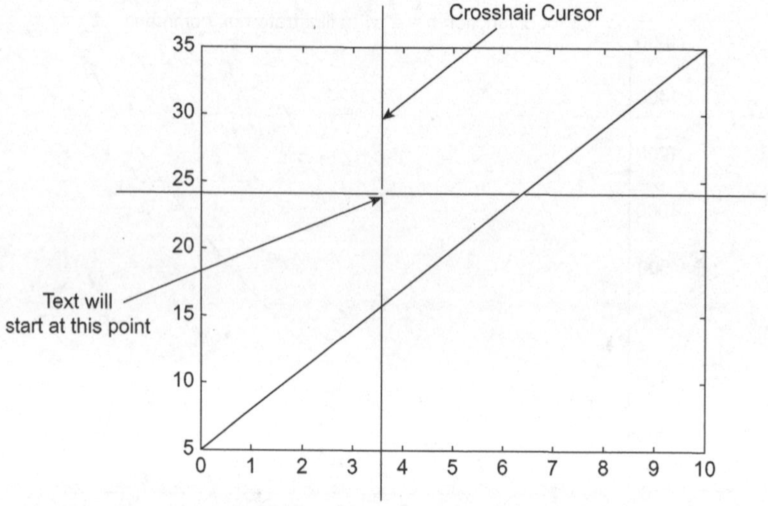

Figure 6.7 Cross Hair Cursor on the Plot

Example 6.6 Illustrate the use of `'gtext'` command on the plot of the equation `y = 3x + 5` for `x = 0 to 10`

Solution: The commands used are given as:

```
% To illustrate use of gtext command.
x = 0:0.5:10;
y = 3 * x + 5;
plot(x, y);
gtext('It's a Straight Line');
grid on;
xlabel('x-axis----->time(t)');
ylabel('y-axis----->output(y)');
title('Plot for y = 3x + 5');
```

Figure 6.7 shows the cross hair cursor on the plot whereas Figure 6.8 shows the final plot obtained.

The first two statements generate the `x`- and `y`-coordinates to plot the curve. The `plot` command plots the curve. The next `gtext` command generates a cross-hair cursor in the figure window. When clicked the text, `It's a Straight Line` is displayed on the graph. The rest of the program labels the axis and prints the title.

6.2.4 Axis Control

A numbers of options are available for setting the scaling, orientation and aspect ratio of plots, using the `axis` command. In the plots obtained in MATLAB, the default axis length depends upon the maximum and minimum values specified in ***x*** and ***y*** vectors and is selected automatically. However, the axes length can be changed as desired with the help of `axis` command. The syntax is:

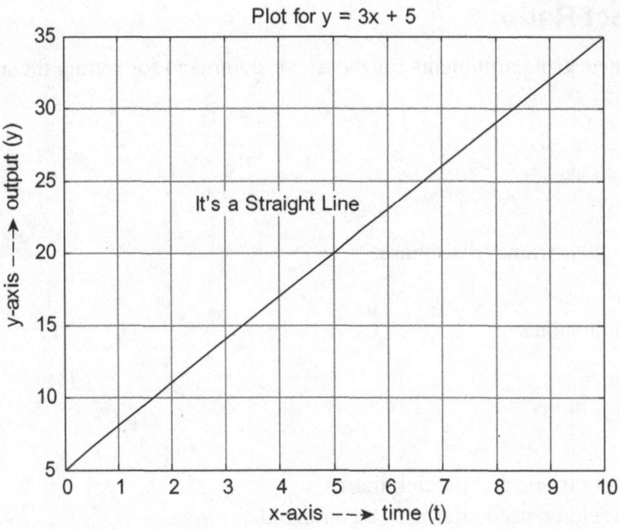

Figure 6.8 Plot to Illustrate use of `'gtext'` Command

```
axis([xmin xmax ymin ymax])
```

where `xmin` and `xmax` gives minimum and maximum limits of *x*-axis, respectively
`ymin` and `ymax` gives minimum and maximum limits of *y*-axis, respectively.

For example, the MATLAB statement:

```
axis([-3  3  0  10])
```

when executed, will set *x*-axis limits from –3 to 3 and *y*-axis limits from 0 to 10. The limits can also set by defining vectors for *x*-axis and *y*-axis and then using these vectors in `axis` command. For example:

```
a = [-3  3  0  10];
axis(a);
```

or

```
c = [-3  3];
d = [0  10];
axis([c  d]);
```

These produce same result as `axis` command containing the ***x*** and ***y*** min and max values.

The axes limit can also be allowed to set automatically partially by writing **`inf`** as the value of the limit. Consider the statement:

```
axis([-5  5  -inf  10]);
```

This command will set *x*-axis limits at –5 and 5 and lower limit of *y*-axis is set automatically based on the values of data to be plotted and upper *y*-axis limit as 10.

Similarly, consider the statement:

```
axis([-5  inf  -inf  10]);
```

This command will set lower *x*-axis limit as –5 and upper *y*-axis limit as 10 whereas upper *x*-axis and lower *y*-axis limits are allowed to be set automatically depending on the data points to be displayed in the figure.

The command `axis  auto` can be used to re-enable automatic limit selection.

6.2.5 Axis Aspect Ratio

There are some predefined string arguments for the `axis` command for setting the axis aspect ratio as given below:

```
axis('equal')
```

It sets equal scale on both axes

```
axis('square')
```

It sets the default rectangular frame to a square.

```
axis('normal')
```

It resets the axis to default values

```
axis('axis')
```

It freezes the current axes limits

```
axis('off')
```

It removes the surrounding frame and the tick marks.
The `axis` command should be used after `plot` command.

Example 6.7 Illustrate the use of `axis` command with specified limits for plot of function `y = 3x`^{2} `+ 2x + 5` for `x = -5 to 10`.

Solution: The program given below illustrates the use of `axis` command with specified limits for plot of given function.

```
% Program to illustrate the use of axis command
x = -5:0.1:10;
y =3 * x.^2 + 2 * x + 5;
plot(x, y);
axis([-5  5  0  20]);
xlabel('x-axis');
ylabel('y-axis');
title('Plot of function y = 3x^2 + 2x + 5');
grid on;
```

The response obtained is shown in Figure 6.9.

The plot can be obtained with equal *x*- and *y*-axis by replacing the existing `axis` command by the command given below:

```
axis('equal');
```

6.3 MULTIPLE PLOTS

There are three different methods of drawing multiple plots in MATLAB:

1. Using `plot` command
2. Using `hold` command
3. Using `line` command

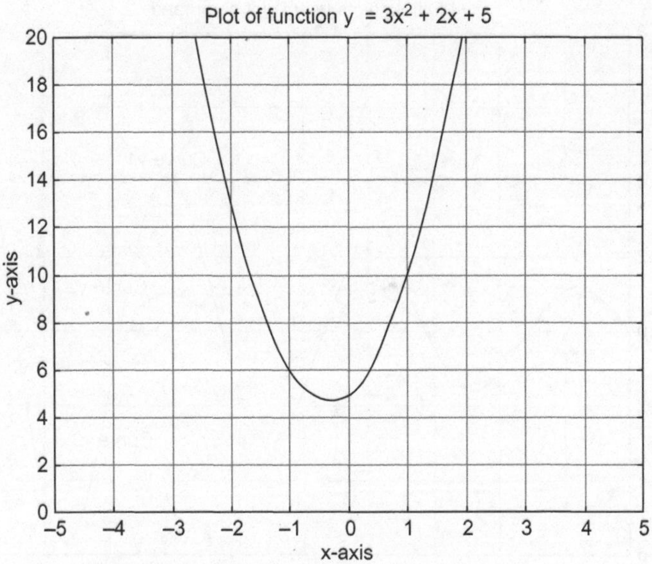

Figure 6.9 Plot to Illustrate Use of Axis Control

6.3.1 Using `plot` Command

In this method, the earlier explained `plot` command in modified by providing more arguments to generate more plots in the same graphic window.

For example, let there be three plots to be drawn for three data sets, i.e., (x_1, y_1), (x_2, y_2) and (x_3, y_3), then the `plot` command will be:

```
plot(x1, y1, x2, y2, x3, y3);
```

This will generate three graphs in same graphics window.

Example 6.8 Illustrate use of `plot` command to generating multiple plots.

Solution: The program given below illustrates use of `plot` command to generating multiple plots.

```
% Program to illustrate the use of plot command to generate multiple plots
x1 = 0:0.01:20;
y1 = exp(0.1*x1).*sin(x1);
x2 = 0:0.1:20;
y2 = sin(x2);
x3 = 0:0.1:20;
y3 = cos(x3);
plot(x1, y1, x2, y2, x3, y3);
gtext('Curve y1'); gtext('Curve y2'); gtext('Curve y3');
title('Multiple plots using plot command');
xlabel('x-axis');
ylabel('y-axis');
grid on;
```

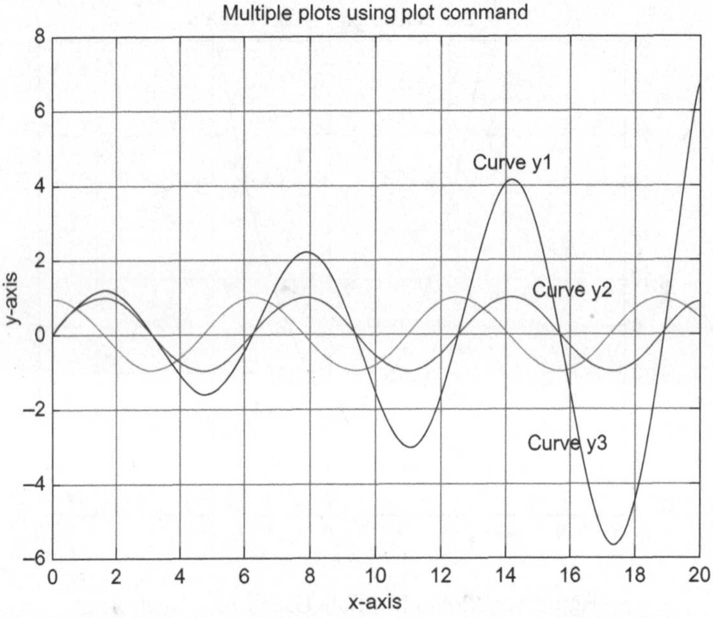

Figure 6.10 Plot to Illustrate `plot` Command for Multiple Plots (See Page 611 for the Colour Image)

The first six statements in the program generate *x*–*y* coordinates for the three curves. The `plot` command plots the three curves in single statement. In this method, vector ($\boldsymbol{x}_1$, $\boldsymbol{y}_1$) must have pair-wise same length.

The `plot` command can also be used with matrix arguments. In such a case, each column of second argument matrix is plotted against the corresponding column of first argument matrix. For example:

```
x = [x1 x2 x3];
y = [y1 y2 y3];
```

where x_1, x_2, x_3, and y_1, y_2, y_3 are column vectors of same length, then multiple plots can be generated using the command:

```
plot(x, y)
```

The graph thus generated illustrating plot command for multiple plots is shown in Figure 6.10.

6.3.2 Using `hold` Command

The `hold` command is used to freeze the current plot in the graphics window. The syntax is:

```
hold on;
```

The `hold` command holds the cursor on the current plot in the graphics window and subsequent plots generated in the program are added to the same graph.

The **`hold off`** command is used to clear the `hold` command.

Example 6.9 Illustrate use of `hold` command for generating multiple plots.

Solution: The program given below illustrates use of `hold` command for generating multiple plots. The graph thus generated illustrating use of `'hold'` command is shown in Figure 6.11.

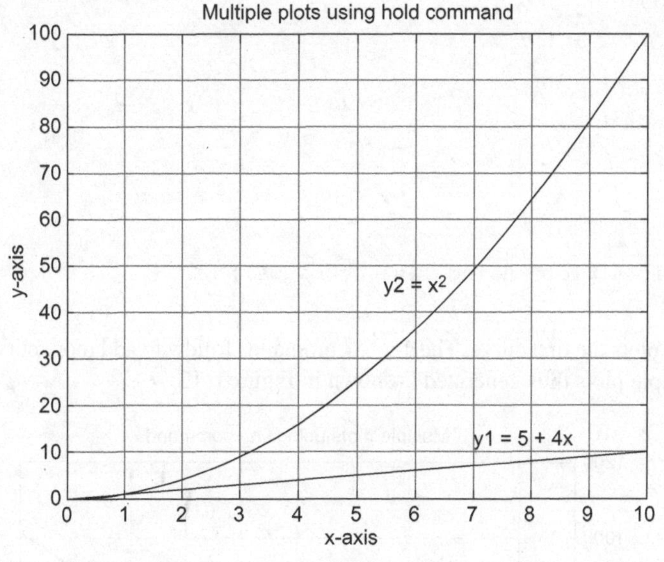

Figure 6.11 Plot to Illustrate use of `'hold'` Command (See Page 612 for the Colour Image)

```
% program to illustrate the use of hold command
x = 0:0.5:10;
y1 = x;
plot(x, y1);
hold on;
y2 = x .^ 2;
plot(x, y2);
hold off;
grid on;
title('Multiple plots using hold command');
```

6.3.3 Using `line` Command

The `line` command is used along with `plot` command to generate multiple plots. Once a plot is generated in the graphics window, more plots can be added using `line` command directly. The syntax for `line` command is:

```
line(xdata, ydata, parameter name, parameter value)
```

where `xdata` and `ydata` are vectors containing `x`- and `y`-coordinates of points on the graph and parameter name/parameter values are used to give line style options.

Example 6.10 Illustrate use of `line` command to generate multiple plots.

Solution: The program given below illustrates use of `line` command to generate multiple plots.

```
% program to illustrate the use of line command
x = 1:0.1:100;
y1 = sqrt(x .^ 2 + 1);
y2 = 5 * x + 20;
y3 = 10 * x + 3;
plot(x, y1);
line(x, y2);
line(x, y3);
title('Multiple plots using line command');
grid on;
```

The `plot` command plots the first curve. The `line` commands follow to add more curves to the current plot. The graph with multiple plots thus generated is shown in Figure 6.12.

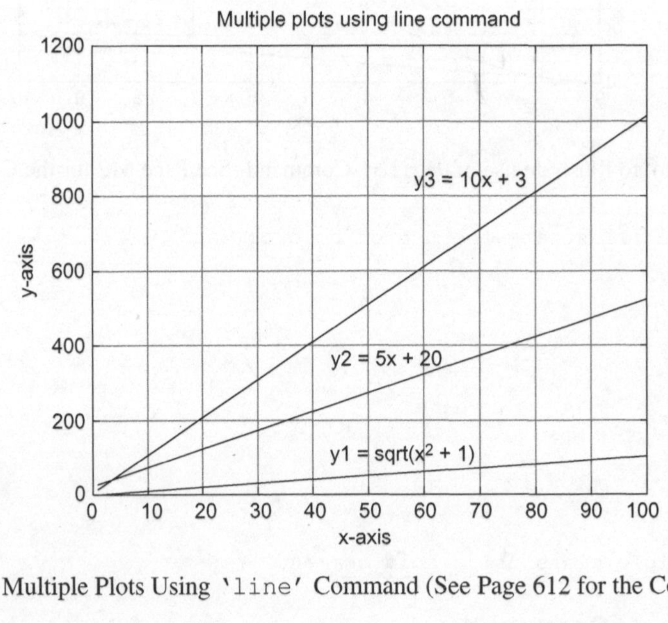

Figure 6.12 Multiple Plots Using 'line' Command (See Page 612 for the Colour Image)

6.4 STYLE OPTIONS

As seen in the previous sections, for multiple plots many plots on the same graphic window may result in confusion until or unless these are properly highlighted and labelled. Hence for better illustration and outlook of plots, different types of style options can be added. These are optional parameters that can be given in the `plot` command as shown below:

```
plot (xvalues, yvalues, 'style options');
```

where `xvalues` and `yvalues` are vectors for x- and y-coordinates, whereas `style option` is an optional argument, a string which can contain one to four characters which are enclosed in single quotation marks.

These are used to set the colour, the line style and the marker type like:

```
-colour(e.g. red, green, yellow, blue etc)
-line style (e.g. solid, dashed, dotted etc.)
-point marker style (e.g. +,*,o, ., etc)
```

The above three options in the `plot` command can be used collectively as well as singly or as a combination of the two.

For example,

```
plot(x, y)
% plot y v/s x with default solid line, blue in colour
plot(x, y, 'r')
% plot y v/s x with red coloured line
plot (x, y, 'y:')
% plot y v/s x with yellow dotted line
plot (x, y, 'g–')
% plot y v/s x with green dashed line
plot(x, y, '*')
% plot y v/s x as unconnected points marked using (*)
plot (x, y, 'ro')
% plot y v/s x as red line with circles marker style
```

The default option of MATLAB plot is a blue solid line. The different colour, line style and marker style options are given as in Table 6.1.

Table 6.1 Colours, Line Style and Marker Style of Plot Lines/Curves

Colour Style Options	Line Style Options	Marker Style Options
y yellow	. point	- solid
m magenta	o circle	: dotted
c cyan	x x-mark	-. dashdot
r red	+ plus	-- dashed
g green	* star	
b blue	s square	
w white	d diamond	
k black	v triangle(down)	
	^ triangle (up)	
	< triangle(left)	
	> triangle(right)	
	p pentagram	
	h hexagram	

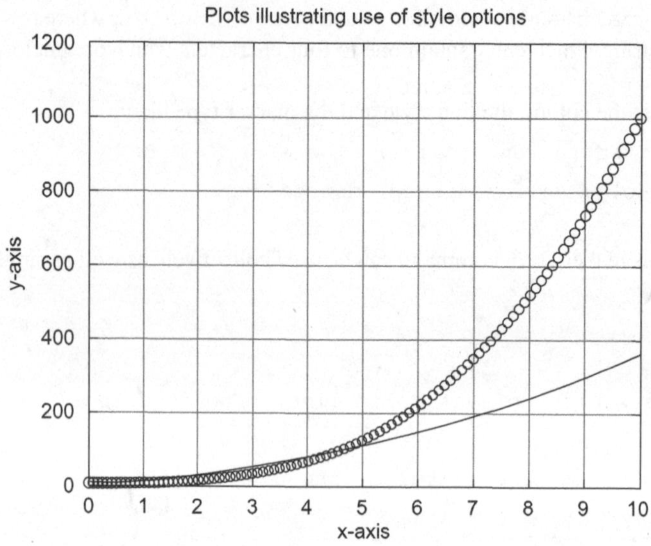

Figure 6.13 Plot Showing Use of Style Options (See Page 613 for the Colour Image)

Example 6.11 Illustrate the different `style options` as used in plots.

Solution: The program given below illustrates the different `style option` as used in plots.

```
% program to illustrate the use of style options
t =0 : 0.1 : 10;
y1 = 3* t .^ 2 + 5 * t + 6;
y2 = t .^ 3 + 4;
plot (t, y1, 'r', t, y2, 'mo');
xlabel('x-axis');
ylabel('y-axis');
title('Plots illustrating use of style options');
grid on;
```

The `plot` statement in the program above plots two curves. The style for the first curve is undefined. Therefore, solid line is plotted. The colour is however, specified as red instead of default blue. The style of second curve is using circle as marker and the colour is defined as magenta. The plots obtained are plotted in Figure 6.13 shown above.

6.5 LEGEND

As the style options are used in the `plot` command to have better outlook and illustration of the plots, there is a command `legend` to further improve the illustrations of the plot. The `legend` command produces a boxed legend on a plot, labels each curve corresponding to different styles used. It has several optional arguments as shown below:

1. `legend('string1:string2,------')`

   It produces legend using the text in string1,strings2 etc. as labels

2. `legend('linestyle, string1, linestyle, string2,-----')`
   It produces legend specifying linestyle with each label.
3. `legend('string1, string 2,------,pos')`
   It produces legend using text in string1, strings2, etc. as labels and pos specifies the location where to place legend on the plot. The different values of **pos** are as shown in Table 6.2:

Table 6.2 Different Values of `pos`

Pos	Position of Legend
0	Automatic 'best' placement (least conflict with data)
1	Upper right-hand corner (default)
2	Upper left-hand corner
3	Lower left-hand corner
4	Lower right-hand corner
5	To the right of the plot

If `'pos'` is not used, the legend can be moved with the help of mouse and placed at convenient place in the figure window.

4. `legend off`
   It removes legend from the plot.

Example 6.12 The table below gives the values of induced voltage E_1 vs. field current I_f, for a D.C. generator operating at $N = 1500$ rpm, plot the open-circuit characteristics for this generator at 1500 rpm, 1200 rpm and 1000 rpm on the same sheet (Note: $E \alpha N$). Use the proper `hold` and `legend` commands.

I_f	0	0.4	1.0	1.45	2.0	3.0	4.0	5.0	6.0
E_1	5	30	70	110	150	215	240	250	260

Solution: The program given below is used to plot induced voltage E_1 vs. field current I_f.

```
% Program to illustrate the use of legend command
If = [0.0 0.4 1.0 1.45 2.0 3.0 4.0 5.0 6.0];
% NOTE: 'If' is not same as 'if command'
E1 = [5 30 70 110 150 215 240 250 260];
plot(If, E1, '-');
hold on; % hold on current plot
E2 = (1200/1500) * E1;
plot(If, E2, ':');
E3 = (1000/1500) * E1;
plot(If, E3, '-.');
legend('1500 rpm', '1200 rpm', '1000 rpm',4);
hold off;
title('Use of legend command');
```

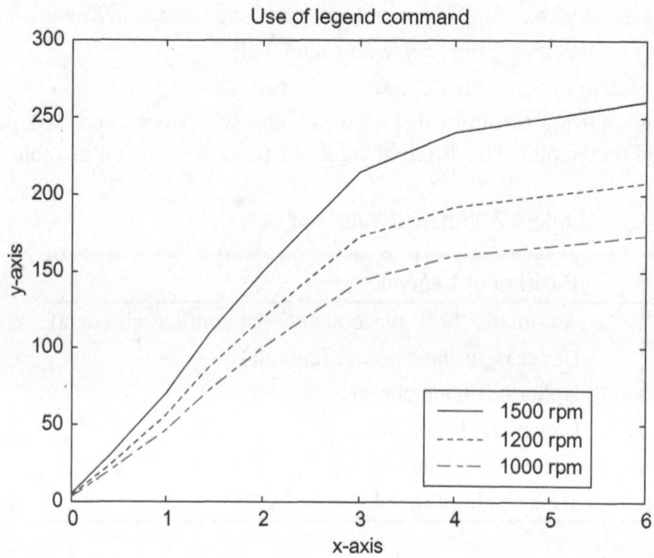

Figure 6.14 Plot Showing Use of '`legend`' Command (See Page 613 for the Colour Image)

```
xlabel('x-axis');
ylabel('y-axis');
```

The `'-'` `style` is for solid line, `':'` for the dotted line and `'-.'` for dash-dot line. The `legend` command plots the legend labelling the three curves in a rectangular window. The graph thus generated illustrating use of 'legend' command is shown in Figure 6.14.

6.6 SUBPLOTS

A graphic window can be subdivided into many sub-graphs or subplots using **`subplot`** command. The command **`subplot(i, j, k)`** splits the figure window in to ($i \times j$) parts with each treated as a subplot and selects the *k*th subplot for the current plot, e.g., The following commands:

```
subplot(2, 1, 1);
plot (profit);
subplot(2, 1, 2);
plot (loss);
```

when executed, will divide the figure window in to (2 × 1), i.e., two sub-windows horizontally and will plot profit in the top half of the window and loss on the bottom half.

The command `subplot(2, 2, 3); plot(x, y)` will divide the figure window into (2 × 2) i.e., four sub-windows and will plot *y* vs. *x* in the third sub-window ,which is the first sub-window in the second row.

Example 6.13 Divide the figure window in to four sub-windows and plot the following functions:

1. Plot *v* vs. *I*, where $v = 4 * I$ and $I = 1, 2, 3, 4$, on the upper left portion.
2. Plot *y* vs. *x*, $y = x^2$ and $x = 1, 2, 3, 4$, on the upper right portion.
   for $t = 0{:}2 * \text{pi}$ in step $t = \text{pi}/60$ plot sin(*t*) vs. *t* on the lower left portion
3. for $t = 0{:}\ \text{pi}/30{:}2 * \text{pi}$, plot cos(*t*) vs. *t* on the lower right portion.

Solution: The following program can be used to plot the four plots in one figure window by dividing the window into four subplots.

```
% Program to illustrate the use of subplot command
I = 1:4;
v = 4 * I;
subplot(2, 2, 1);
plot(I, v);
title('Voltage v/s Current');
xlabel('I-amps');
ylabel('V-volts');
x = [1 2 3 4];
y = [1 4 9 16];
subplot(2, 2, 2);
plot(x, y)
title('Parabolic plot');
xlabel('x-->');
ylabel('y-->');
t = 0:pi/60:2*pi;
subplot(2, 2, 3);
plot(t, sin(t));
xlabel('t-->');
ylabel('sin(t)');
title('Plot of sin function')
subplot(2, 2, 4);
plot(t, cos(t));
xlabel('t-->');
ylabel('cos(t)');
title('Plot of cos function')
```

The `subplot(2, 2, 1)` command splits the figure window into four subplots. The four subplots are selected one after the other and `plot` commands are used to plot the curves in the respective subplots. The other commands used for labelling the `x-` and `y`-axis or giving the title are same as illustrated in different preceding sections. The figure window with four subplots is shown in Figure 6.15.

6.7 SPECIALIZED TWO-DIMENSIONAL PLOTS

Besides drawing plots using `plot` command, there are many specialized graphics functions in MATLAB for two-dimensional plotting. Some of the specialized two-dimensional plot functions are discussed as below:

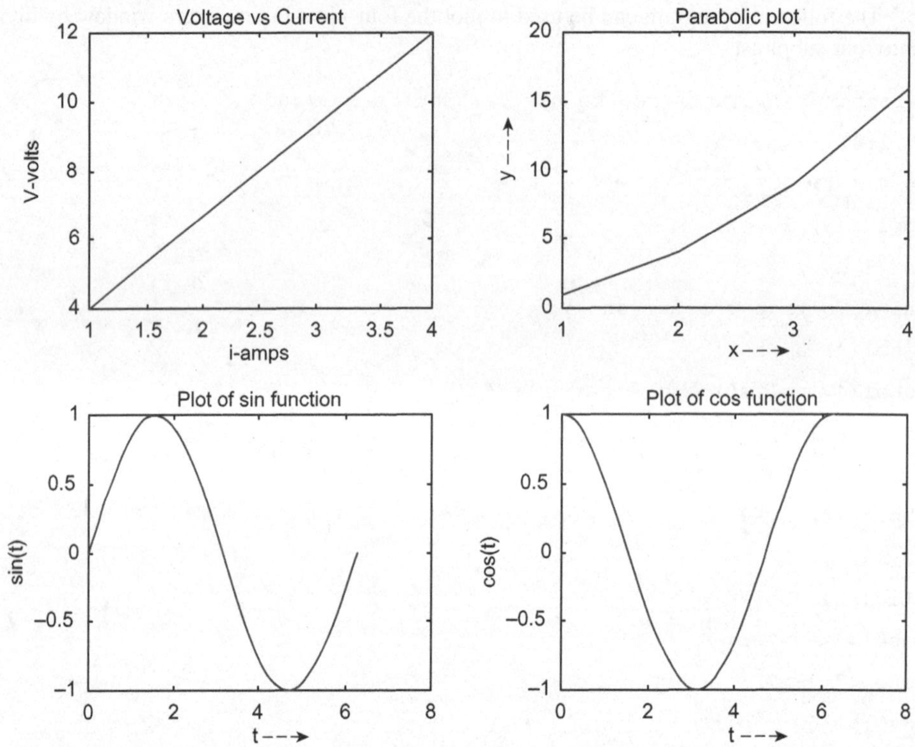

Figure 6.15 Multiple Plots Using `subplot` Command (See Page 614 for the Colour Image)

6.7.1 Logarithmic Plot Functions

These are further classified as:

(a) `semilogx`: It plots with logarithmically spaced *x*-axis.
(b) `semilogy`: It plots with logarithmically spaced *y*-axis.
(c) `loglog`: It plots with both the axes logarithmically spaced.

6.7.1.1 semilogx

In `semilogx` command, the *x*-axis is drawn on logarithmic scale and *y*-axis on linear scale. The syntax is:

```
semilogx(x, y)
```

where *x* is vector of *x*-variables
y is vector of *y*-variables

Example 6.14 Plot function $x = e^{-a}$, $y = a^2$, where `0 <= a <= 10`, using `semilogx` function.

Solution: The commands used are given as:

```
% Program to illustrate the use of 'semilogx' command
a =0:1:10;
y = a.*a;
```

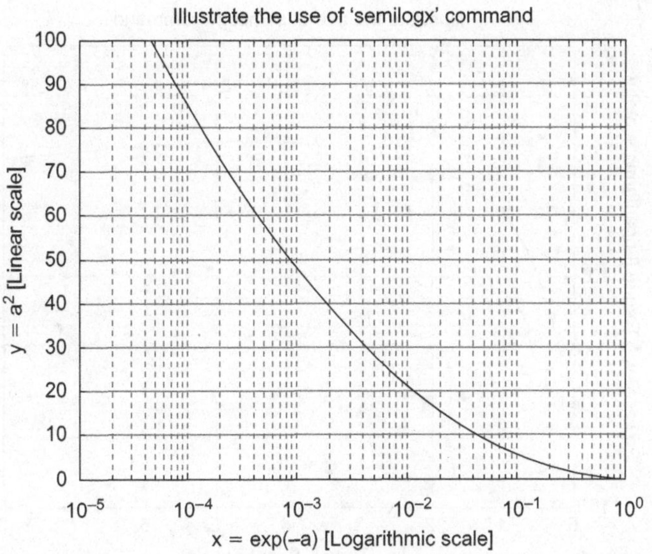

Figure 6.16 `semilogx` Plot (See Page 614 for the Colour Image)

```
x = exp(-a);
semilogx(x,y)
grid on
xlabel('x = exp(-a) [Logarithmic scale]');
ylabel('y = a^2 [Linear scale]');
title('Illustrate the use of' 'semilogx' 'command')
```

The response obtained is shown in Figure 6.16.

6.7.1.2 semilogy

In `semilogy` command, *y*-axis is drawn on logarithmic scale and *x*-axis is drawn on linear scale. The syntax is:

```
semilogy(x, y)
```

Example 6.15 Plot power vs. time for $0 < t < 8$ secs, with power on the log scale and time in the linear scale for a motor whose performance equations are as given below:

Rotational speed, $W = 190\ (1 - e^{-0.15t})$ rad/sec
Torque, $T = 8e^{-0.15t}$

Solution: The commands used are as following:

```
% Program to illustrate the use of semilogy command
% Plot semilogy graph between Power Vs Time as per the data given
time = 0:0.2:8;
```

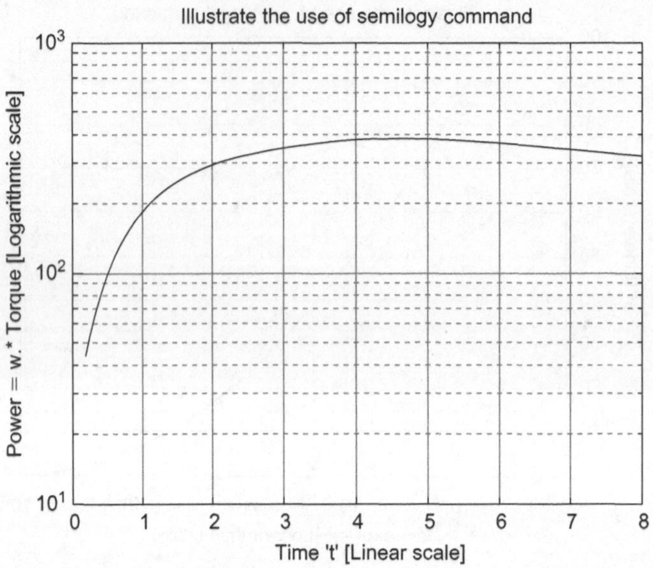

Figure 6.17 `semilogy` Plot (See Page 615 for the Colour Image)

```
w =190*(1-exp(-0.15*time));              % Calculation of angular speed
Torque = 8*exp(-0.15*time);              % Torque expression
power = w.*Torque;                       % Formula for Power
semilogy(time,power)
grid on
xlabel('Time ''t'' [Linear scale]');
ylabel('Power = w.* Torque [Logarithmic scale]');
title('Illustrate the use of semilogy command')
```

The response obtained is shown in Figure 6.17.

6.7.1.3 loglog

The `loglog` function gives plot with both *x*-axis and *y*-axis drawn on logarithmic scales. The syntax is as

```
loglog(x, y)
```

`loglog` command is the same as plot command except logarithmic scales are used for both the *x*- and *y*-axis.

Example 6.16 Plot magnitude vs. frequency on log-log scale for the transfer factor

$$G(s) = \frac{1}{1+0.02s}$$

where $g = j\omega = j2\pi f$ and f is the frequency.

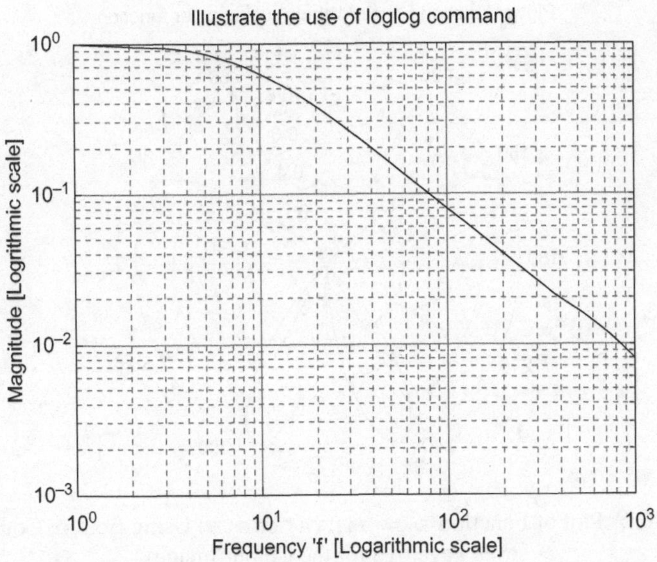

Figure 6.18 `loglog` Plot (See Page 615 for the Colour Image)

Solution: The commands used are as following:

```
% Program to illustrate the use of loglog command
% Plot loglog graph between frequency and magnitude of given function
freq = 1:2:1000;
Gs = 1./(1+j*2*pi*freq*0.02);
mag = abs(Gs);           %Calculate magnitude
loglog(freq,mag);
grid on
xlabel('Frequency "f" [Logarithmic scale]');
ylabel('Magnitude [Logarithmic scale]');
title('Illustrate the use of loglog command')
```

The response obtained is shown in Figure 6.18.

6.7.2 polar

The `polar` command draws the plot in polar coordinates. The syntax is given as:

`polar(theta, r)`

where `theta` is angle and
`r` is a distance or radius vector.

`polar (θ, r, p)`

`p` is an optional character string describing colour, line style, etc.

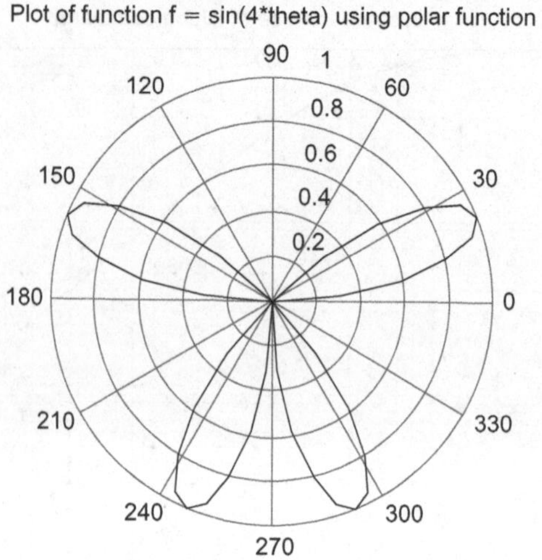

Figure 6.19 Plot of Function `f = sin(4*theta)` Using `polar` Command
(See Page 616 for the Colour Image)

> **Programming Tip 6.2:** `Polar` command is useful when data is in polar coordinates.

Example 6.17 Plot the following function on a polar plot

$$f(\theta) = \sin 4\theta \text{ for } -\frac{\pi}{2} \leq \theta \leq \frac{\pi}{2}, \text{ where } \theta \text{ is in radians.}$$

Solution: The commands used are as following:

```
% Program to illustrate the use of polar function
% Plot function f = sin(4*theta) as per the given data
theta = -pi/2:pi/40:pi/2;
f =sin(4.*theta);
polar(theta, f, 'r-')
title('Plot of function f = sin(4*theta) using polar command')
```

The response obtained is shown in Figure 6.19.

6.7.3 area

The `area` function is similar to `plot` function except that the area under plot is filled with colour. The syntax is given as

```
area(x, y)
```

Example 6.18 Plot, using `area` function, $y = \cos(x)$ for x varies from 0 to 4π.

Solution:

```
% Program to plot y = cos(x) for x varies from 0 to 4pi using area function
```

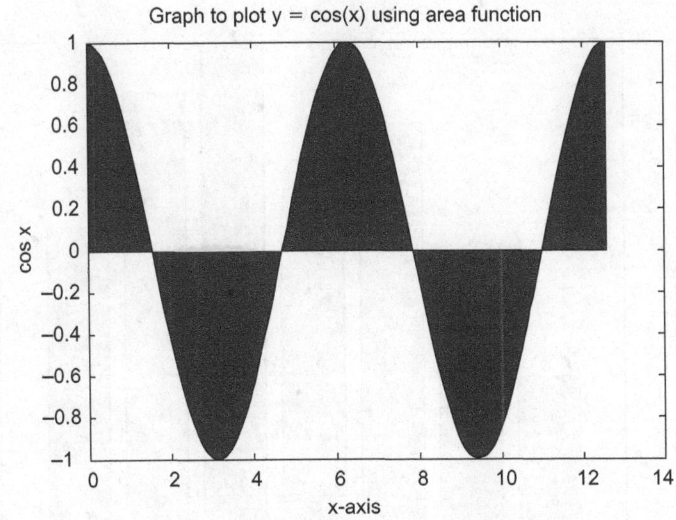

Figure 6.20 Plot of Function $y = \cos(x)$ Using `area` Function (See Page 616 for the Colour Image)

```
x =0:0.02:4*pi;
y =cos(x);
area(x,y);
xlabel('x-axis')
ylabel('cos x')
title('Graph to plot y = cos(x) using area function')
```

The response obtained is shown in Figure 6.20.

6.7.4 bar

The bar function draws vertical bar plot. The different syntaxes for bar function are as follows:

```
bar(y)
bar(x, y)
bar(x, y, 'style options')
```

The function **`bar(y)`** draws vertical bar plot using default values of $x = 1{:}\ k$, where k corresponds to number of data values in vector y and the value of y determine the height of the bar.

In case, the **y** is matrix of size $m \times n$, then the function **`bar(x, y)`** draws m groups of n vertical bars. The vector x must be monotonically increasing or decreasing. The data of matrix **y** of size $m \times n$ can be specified in a *group* or *stack* and the syntax is given as:

```
bar(x, y, 'grouped')
bar(x, y, 'stacked')
```

The function **`bar(x, y,'style options')`** uses the different style options as discussed in previous articles.

The function **`bar(x, y, width)`** or **`bar(y, width)`** specifies the width of the bars. The values of width > 1 produce overlapped bars. The default value is width = 0.8

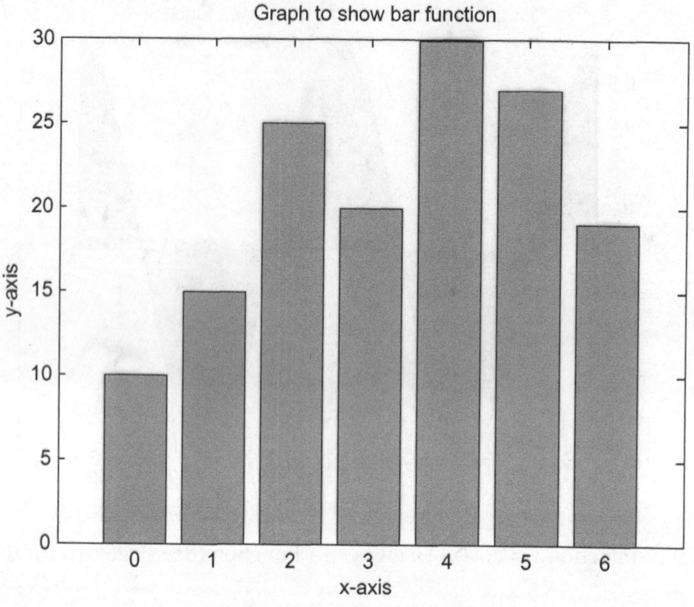

Figure 6.21 Bar Graph to Plot the given Data (See Page 617 for the Colour Image)

Example 6.19 Plot a bar graph for the data as:
$x = [0\ 1\ 2\ 3\ 4\ 5\ 6]$ and $y = [10\ 15\ 25\ 20\ 30\ 27\ 19]$

Solution: The commands used are as follows:

```
% Program to show bar function
x = [ 0 1 2 3 4 5 6];
y = [10 15 25 20 30 27 19 ];
bar(x, y, 'c')
xlabel('x-axis')
ylabel('y-axis')
title('Graph to show bar function')
```

The response obtained is as shown in Figure 6.21.

Example 6.20 Plot a bar graph to show the comparison of temperature in City A, City B and City C for the months from September to February. The data is given as:

	City A	City B	City C
September	31	28	24
October	29	26	22
November	28	25	20
December	27	24	16
January	26	22	17
February	29	25	20

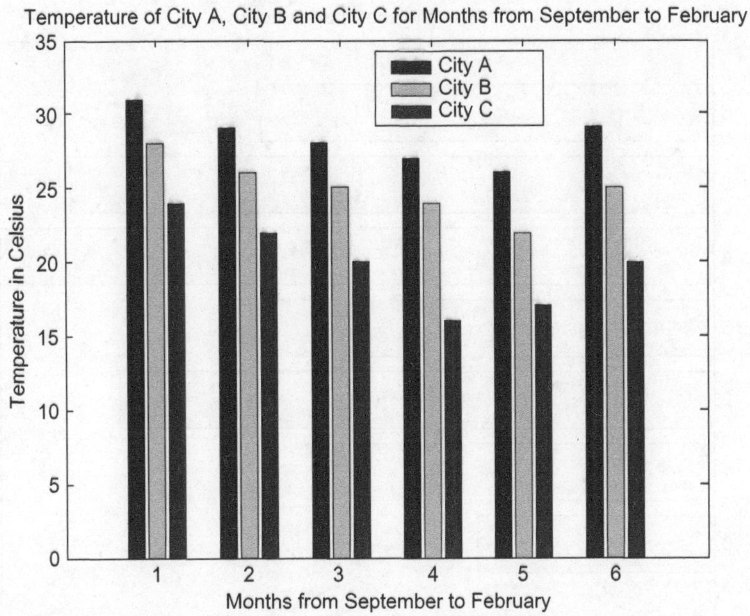

Figure 6.22 Bar Graph to Show the Comparison of Temperature in City A, City B and City C for the Months from September to February (See Page 617 for the Colour Image)

Solution: The commands used are given as:

```
% Program to Temperature of City A, City B and City C for months from Sept
% to Feb using bar graph
temp = [31,28,24; 29 26 22;28 25 20; 27 24 16; 26 22 17; 29 25 20];
bar(temp,'group')
ylabel('Temperature in Celsius')
xlabel('Months from Sept to Feb')
legend('City A', 'City B', 'City C')
title('Temperature of City A, City B and City C for months from September to
February')
```

The response obtained is as shown in Figure 6.22.

6.7.5 `barh`

The function **`barh`** creates a horizontal bar plot. It is similar to `bar` command except that it draws horizontal bars with *y*-coordinates which define the horizontal lengths of the bars.

Example 6.21 Illustrate the use of `barh` command with data given in Example 6.19.

Solution: The commands used are given as:

```
% Program to show barh function
x = [ 0 1 2 3 4 5 6];
y = [10 15 25 20 30 27 19 ];
barh(x, y, 'y')
xlabel('x-axis')
```

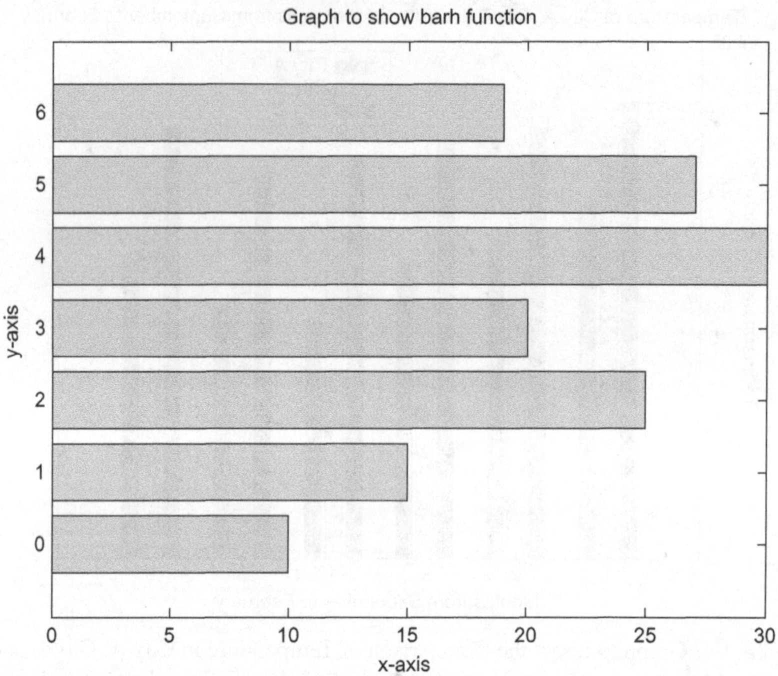

Figure 6.23 Horizontal Bar Graph Using `barh` Command (See Page 618 for the Colour Image)

```
ylabel('y-axis')
title('Graph to show barh function')
```

The response obtained is as shown in Figure 6.23.

6.7.6 hist

The function **hist** draws histogram of the given data. The different syntax forms of **hist** function are as follows:

```
hist(x)
hist(x, n)
hist(x, p)
```

The function `hist(x)` draws a 10-bin (default number) histogram for the data given in vector `x`.

The function `hist(x, n)` draws a histogram with *n* bins, where *n* is a scalar. The function `hist(x, p)` shows a histogram using the bins specified in `p`, where `p` is a vector.

Example 6.22 Illustrate the use of `hist` command.

Solution: The commands used are as:

```
% Program to illustrate the use of hist command
x =randn(100,1)*pi      % Generate 100 random data points
hist (x)                % Draw the histogram with 10 bins
title('Histogram to show 100-random values in 10-bins')
```

The response obtained is shown in Figure 6.24.

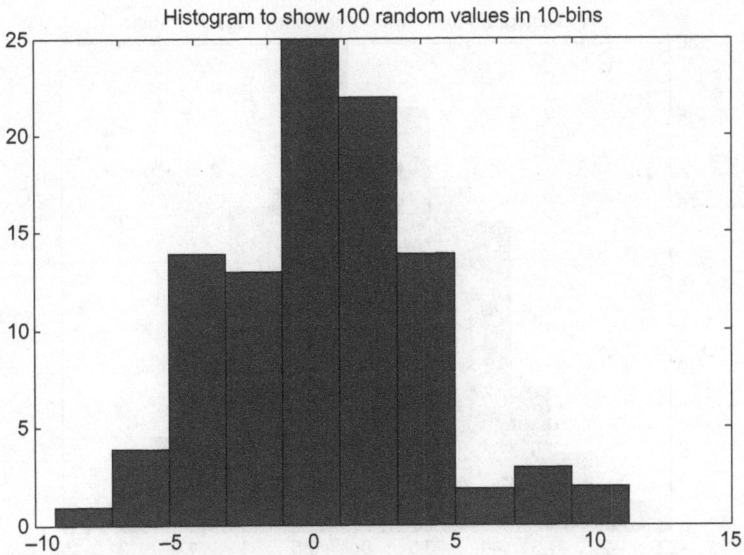

Figure 6.24 Histogram Plot (For 100 Random Values) (See Page 618 for the Colour Image)

Example 6.23 Illustrate the use of `hist` command with 15 bins.

Solution: The commands used are as:

```
% Program to illustrate the use of hist command with 15 bins
x = randn(200,1)                % Generate 200 random data points
hist (x,15)                     % Draw the histogram with 15 bins
title('Histogram to show 200 random values in 15-bins')
```

The response is shown in Figure 6.25.

Example 6.24 Illustrate the use of `hist` command with number of bins specified in a vector `p`.

Solution: The commands used are as:

```
% Program to illustrate the use of hist command with no. of
% bins specified by a vector
x = randn(300,1)        % Generate 300 random data points
p =-2:0.1:2;
hist (x,p)% Draw the histogram with no. of bins in vector p
title('Histogram to show 300 random values in no. of bins specified by a
vector')
```

The response is shown in Figure 6.26.

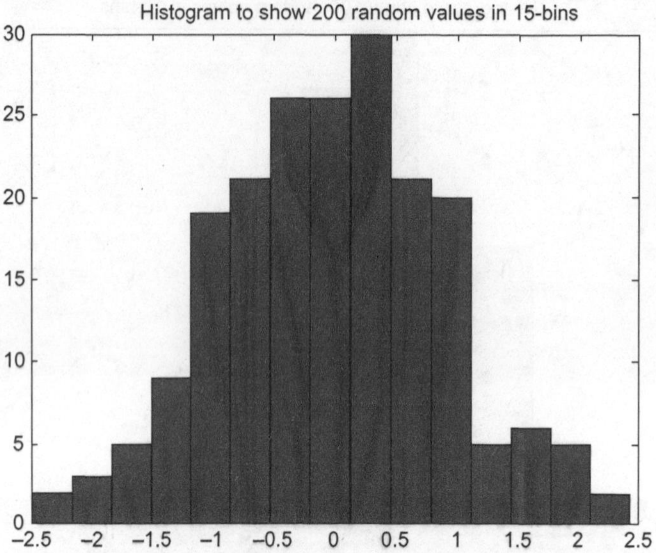

Figure 6.25 Histogram Plot (For 200 Random Values) (See Page 619 for the Colour Image)

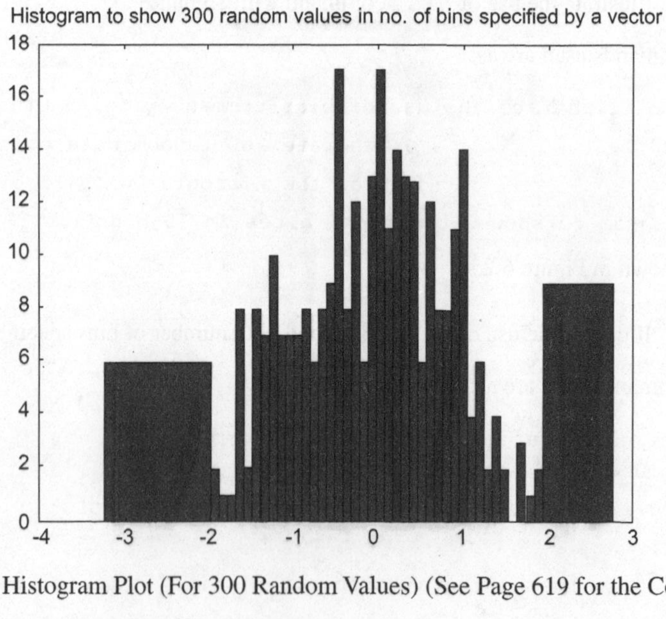

Figure 6.26 Histogram Plot (For 300 Random Values) (See Page 619 for the Colour Image)

6.7.7 rose

The `rose` function draws the angle histogram. The different syntax for this function is as:

```
rose(a)
rose(a,n)
rose(a,v)
```

where `a` is vector containing data in radians.
`n` is a scalar which specifies the number of bins.
`v` is a vector which specifies the number of bins.

The function `rose(a)` draws polar histogram for the angles given in vector `a`. The default number of bins is 20.

The function `rose(x, n)` draws polar histogram with `n` bins, where `n` is a scalar.

The function `rose(x, v)` draws a polar histogram using the bins specified in `v`, where `v` is a vector.

Example 6.25 Illustrate the use of `rose` command.

Solution: The commands used are as:

```
% Program to illustrate the use of rose command
x = randn(100,1)*pi;            % Generate 100 random data points
% Draw the histogram with no. of bins in vector p
rose(x)
title('Polar Histogram to show 100 random values using "rose" command')
```

The response is shown in Figure 6.27.

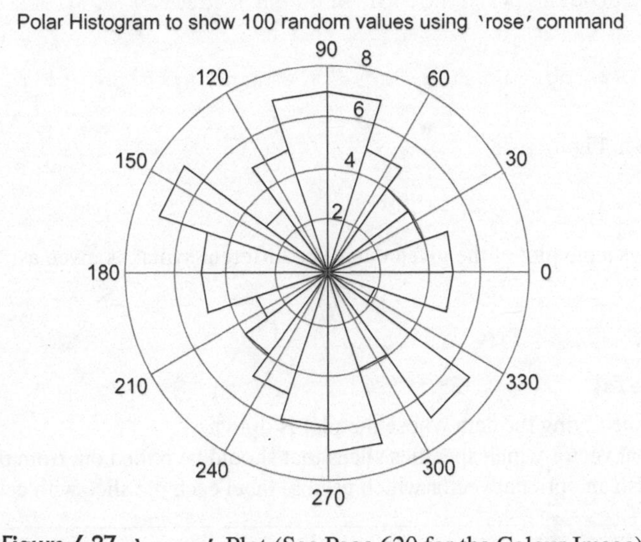

Figure 6.27 `'rose'` Plot (See Page 620 for the Colour Image)

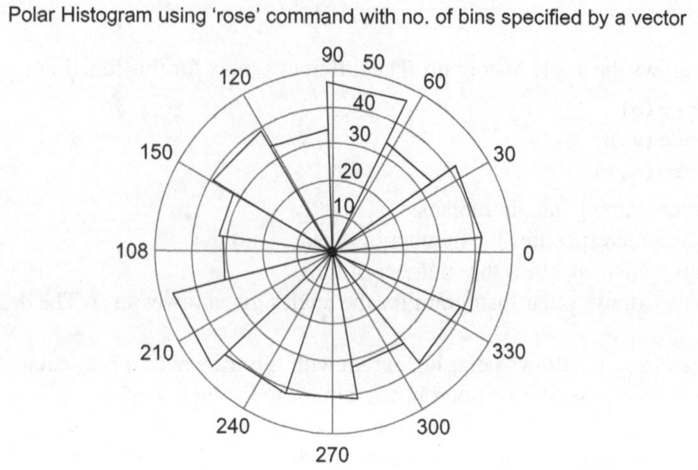

Figure 6.28 `'rose'` Plot Using Vector to Specify no. of Bins (See Page 620 for the Colour Image)

Example 6.26 Illustrate the use of `rose` command.

Solution: The commands used are as:

```
% Program to illustrate the use of rose command
x = randn(500,1)*pi;              % Generate 500 random data points
% Specifies the number of bins in a vector v
v = -pi:0.5:pi;
% Draw the histogram with no. of bins in vector v
rose (x,v)
title('Polar Histogram using "rose" command with no. of bins specified by a
vector')
```

The response is shown in Figure 6.28.

6.7.8 pie

The function **pie** draws a pie plot of the given data. The different syntax is given as:

pie(x)

pie(x,k)

pie(x,k, labels)

where x is a vector specifying the data whose pie plot is drawn.
k is an optional vector which specifies slices that should be pulled out from the pie.
`labels` is also an optional vector which used to label each pie slice with cell array labels.

> **Programming Tip 6.3:** The vector k must be of the same size as given vector containing data. The slices where k is non-zero will be pulled out.

Programming Tip 6.4: `Labels` must be of the same size as given vector containing data and can only contain strings.

The function `pie(x)` determines the percentage of each value of x and shows pie slices of that size.

Example 6.27 Illustrate the use of `pie` command to show the concentration of different industries in the region as per the following data

Name of the Industry	No. of Industrial Units
Cement	4
Textile	8
Software	20
Chemical	2
Telecom	7
Banking	10

Solution: The commands used are as:

```
% Program to draw a pie chart showing concentration of different industries
% in a region
industry = [4 8 20 2 7 10];
pie(industry);
title('Pie chart showing concentration of different industries');
```

The pie plot obtained is as shown in Figure 6.29.

For better illustration of a particular slice in the pie chart, it can be shown pulled out of the normal pie chart as shown in the following example:

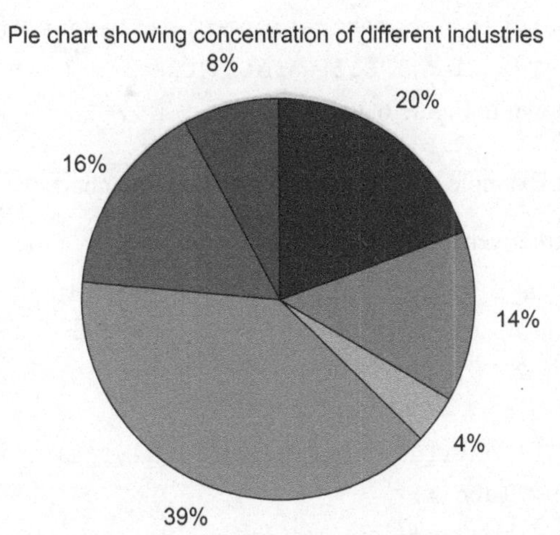

Figure 6.29 Pie Chart Showing the Concentration of Industries in a Region (See Page 621 for the Colour Image)

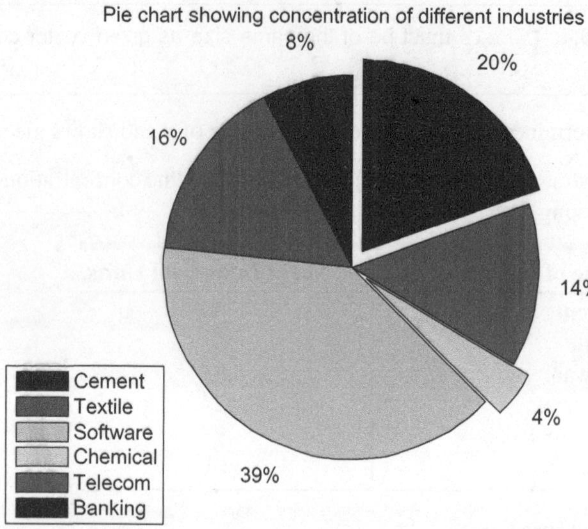

Figure 6.30 Sliced Pie Chart (See Page 621 for the Colour Image)

Example 6.28 Repeat Example 6.27 to show the sliced pie chart.

Solution: The commands are given as:

```
% Program to draw a sliced pie chart showing concentration of different
% industries in a region
industry = [4 8 20 2 7 10];
show = [0 0 0 1 0 1];
pie(industry, show)
title('Pie chart showing concentration of different industries')
legend('Cement', 'Textile', 'Software', 'Chemical', 'Telecom', 'Banking', 3)
```

The pie plot obtained is as shown in Figure 6.30.

Example 6.29 Repeat Example 6.27 to show the labelled pie chart.

Solution: The commands are given as:

```
% Program to draw a pie chart showing concentration of different industries
% in a region
industry = [4 8 20 2 7 10];
show = [0 1 0 0 1 0];
label = ({'Cement', 'Textile', 'Software', 'Chemical', 'Telecom', 'Banking'});
pie(industry, show, label);
title('Labelled and sliced Pie chart showing concentration of different
industries');
```

The pie plot obtained is as shown in Figure 6.31.

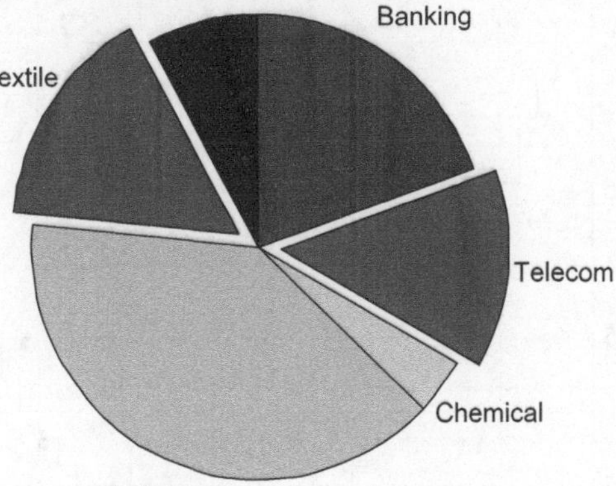

Figure 6.31 Labelled and Sliced-out Pie Chart (See Page 622 for the Colour Image)

6.7.9 stairs

This function gives a staircase graphs. The syntax is given as:

```
stairs(y)
stairs(x, y)
stairs(…,style)
```

The function `stairs(y)` draws a stairstep graph of the elements of vector ***y***.

The function `stairs(x,y)` draws a staircase graph of the elements in vector ***y*** at the locations specified in ***x***. The function `stairs(…,style)` uses the plot line style specified by the string style.

> **Programming Tip 6.5:** The values of *x*-axis vector in `stairs` function must be in ascending order and evenly spaced.

Example 6.30 Draw the stairs plot to show the function $y = x.*x$, where $-2 \le x \le 2$

Solution: The commands used are as:

```
% Program to show stairs plot to show the function y = x.*x
x = -2:0.1:2;                   % generate data for vector x
y = x.*x; % Calculate the function y
stairs(x, y, 'r')               % Create stairs plot
grid on
xlabel('x-axis')
ylabel('y = x.*x')
title('Stairs plot to show the function y = x.*x')
```

The response obtained is given in Figure 6.32.

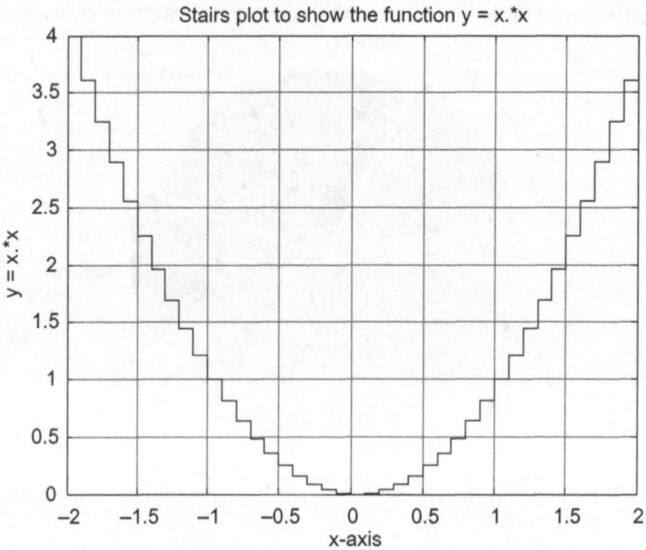

Figure 6.32 Stairs Plot to Show the Function $y = x.*x$ (See Page 622 for the Colour Image)

Example 6.31 Draw the stairs plot for the data:

$x = [0\ 2\ 3\ 4\ 5\ 7]$

$y = [5\ -1\ 8\ 4\ 7\ 3]$

Solution: The commands used are as follows:

```
% Program to illustrate the stairs command
x = [0 2 3 4 5 7];
y = [5 -1 8 4 7 3];
stairs(x, y, '*-.')
box off
title('Graph to illustrate stairs command')
xlabel('x-axis')
ylabel('y-axis')
```

The response obtained is given in Figure 6.33.

6.7.10 stem

This function gives stem plot of the given data. The syntax is given as:

```
stem(y)
stem(x, y)
stem(x, y, p)
```

The function `stem(y)` draws given data points in vector `y` as stems that extend from equally spaced and automatically generated values along the *x*-axis.

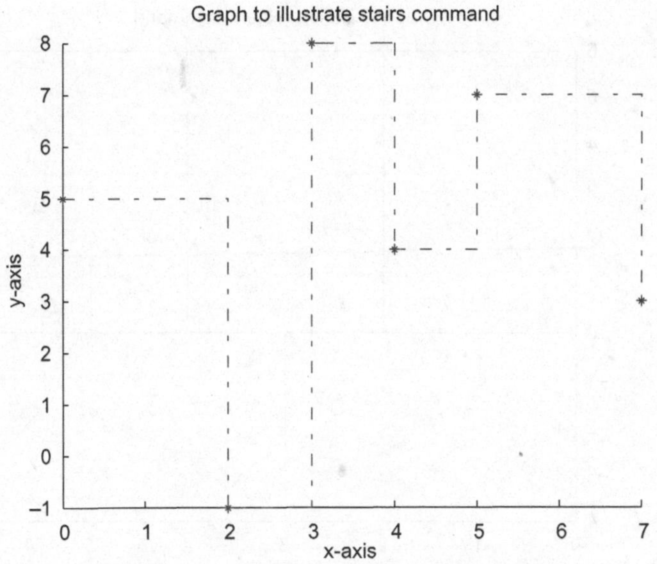

Figure 6.33 Stairs Plot for Given Data (See Page 623 for the Colour Image)

The function `stem(x, y)` plots the data points in `y` at the values specified in `x`, with a marker at each `(x, y)` point and a stem, i.e., a vertical line drawn from that point to the *x*-axis.

The function `stem(x, y, p)` plots the data sequence `y` at the values specified in `x`, where `p` is an optional character string argument to specify line style such as `stem(x, y, '- -')`

Example 6.32 Draw the stem plot for the data:

$x = [0\ 1\ 2\ 3\ 4\ 5\ 6]$

$y = [3\ -1\ 6\ -4\ 5\ 2\ 3]$

Solution: The commands used are as:

```
% Program to illustrate the stem command
x = [0 1 2 3 4 5 6 ];
y = [3 -1 6 -4 5 2 3];
stem(x, y)
title('Graph to illustrate stem command')
xlabel('x-axis')
ylabel('y-axis')
```

The response obtained is given in Figure 6.34.

6.7.11 compass

The complex data can be plotted by using function compass. The syntax is given as:

```
compass(z)
compass(x,y)
```

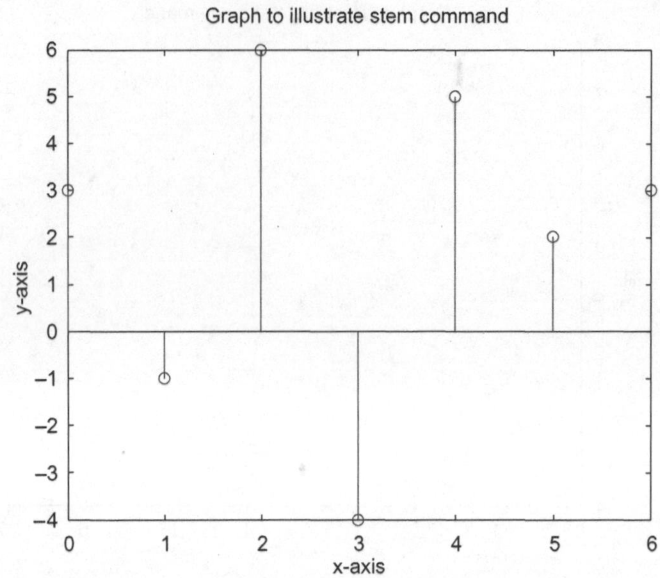

Figure 6.34 Plot to Illustrate the `stem` Command (See Page 623 for the Colour Image)

The function `compass (z)` draws a plot that displays the angle and magnitude of the complex data of vector z. The elements of `z` are in Cartesian coordinates and plotted on a circular grid. It draws n arrows, where n is number of elements of `z`. The location of the base of each arrow is the origin. The location of the tip of each arrow is relative to the base as determined by the real and imaginary components of `z`. This syntax is equivalent to `compass(real(z),imag(z))`.

The function `compass(x, y)` displays a compass graph having n arrows, where n is the number of elements in `x` or `y`. The location of the base of each arrow is the origin. The location of the tip of each arrow is a point relative to the base and determined by `[x(i), y(i)]`.

Example 6.33 Draw the `compass` plot for the data:

$z = [1 + 1i\ 4 - 8i\ 20 + 7i\ 6 + 8i\ 9 + 2i\ 12 - 4i]$;

Solution: The commands used are as:

```
% Program to illustrate the compass command
z = [1+1i 4-8i 20+7i 6+8i 9+2i 12-4i];
compass(z)
title('Graph to illustrate compass command')
```

The response obtained is given in Figure 6.35.

6.8 THREE-DIMENSIONAL PLOTS

For visualization of data in three dimensions, MATLAB provides a number of functions. Most of the functions are the extension of two-dimensional functions such as `plot3, bar3, bar3h, pie3`. The 3-D graphs are generally used to display two types of data. First, when two variables are the function of independent variable

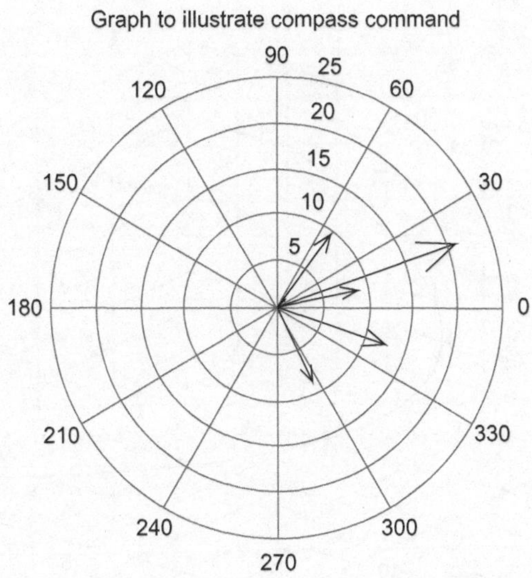

Figure 6.35 Plot to Illustrate the `compass` Command (See Page 624 for the Colour Image)

and secondly, when single variable is a function of two independent variables. To display the data which is the function of two independent variables `surface`, `mesh` and `contour` plots are used.

Some of the built-in 3-D functions are discussed as follows.

6.8.1 plot3

The **`plot3`** function is the extension of `plot` function used in two-dimensional data display. In case of plot function, two variables are used whereas in `plot3` function three variables or 3-D function of a single variable is displayed. The syntax for this function is as:

```
plot3(x, y, t, 'style_options')
```

where `x, y` and `t` are arrays specifying location of data points.
`style_options` specifies the style options as used in 2-D plot.

> **Programming Tip 6.6:** The different `style options` used in 2-D plots, specifying colour, marker symbol and linestyle, are applicable to `plot3` function.

Example 6.34 Given is $x = t^2$ and $y = 4t$ for $-4 < t < 4$. Obtain a three-dimensional plot showing the matrix in (x, y) space as a factors of time.

Solution: The commands used are as:

```
% Program to illustrate the plot3 function
t = -4:0.1:4;
x =t.^2;
y =4*t;
```

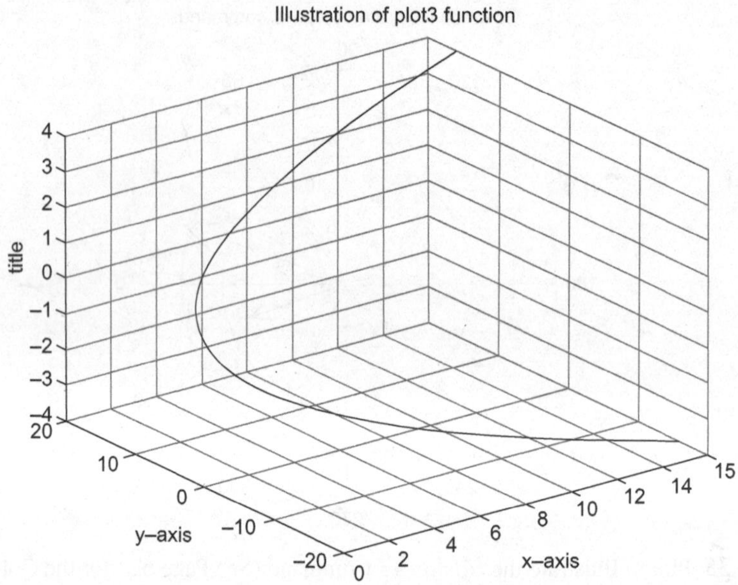

Figure 6.36 Three-dimensional Line Plot Using `plot3` Function (See Page 624 for the Colour Image)

```
plot3(x, y, t)
grid on
xlabel('x-axis')
ylabel('y-axis')
zlabel('z-axis')
title('Illustration of plot3 function')
```

The plot obtained is as shown in Figure 6.36.

6.8.2 bar3

The **bar3** function is similar to `bar` function in two-dimensional except that it gives three-dimensional plot. All features of `bar` function are applicable in `bar3` function.

Example 6.35 Draw 3D bar graph of the data:

$x = [0\ 1\ 2\ 3\ 4\ 5\ 6]$

$y = [5\ 17\ 25\ 21\ 31\ 27\ 19]$

Solution: The program is given as:

```
% Program to plot 3-D graph using bar3 function
x = [0 1 2 3 4 5 6];
y = [5 17 25 21 31 27 19];
bar3(x, y, 'g')
```

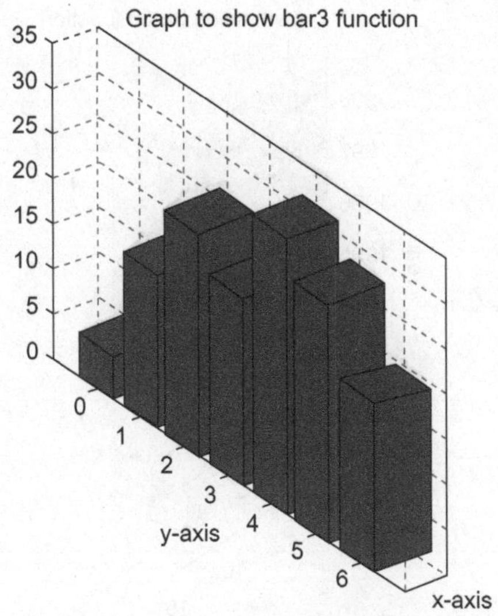

Figure 6.37 Plot to Show 3D Bar Graph of the Given Data (See Page 625 for the Colour Image)

```
xlabel('x-axis')
ylabel('y-axis')
title('Graph to show bar3 function')
```

The graph obtained is as shown in Figure 6.37.

6.8.3 bar3h

The function **bar3h** is similar to bar3 function except that it plots horizontal plot.

Example 6.36 Draw 3D horizontal bar to show the growth of a state as per following data:
Year = [1992 1993 1994 1995 1996 1997 1998]
Growth (in %age)=[12 15 10 8 6.5 9 11]

Solution: The program is given as:

```
% Program to illustrate use of bar3h function
year = [1992 1993 1994 1995 1996 1997 1998];
growth = [12 15 10 8 6.5 9 11];
bar3h(year, growth, 'c')
title('Yearly growth using bar3h function')
zlabel('Year')
ylabel('Percentage growth')
```

The response obtained is shown in Figure 6.38.

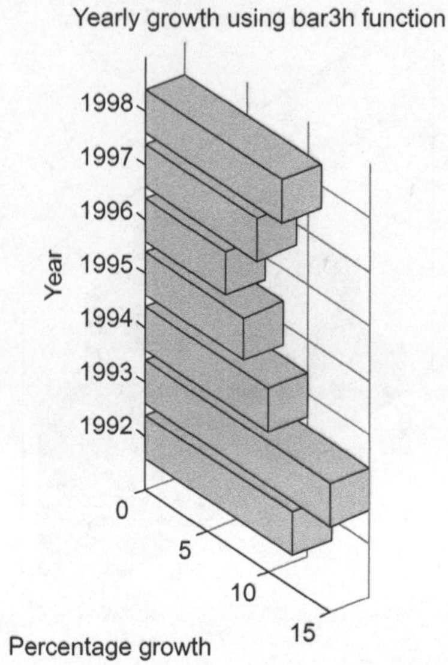

Figure 6.38 Plot to Show Growth of a State Using 3D Horizontal Bar Graph (See Page 625 for the Colour Image)

6.8.4 pie3

The **pie3** function draws a three-dimensional plot of the given data. The syntax is given as:

```
pie3(x)

pie3(x, k)

pie3(x, k, labels)
```

where `x`, `k` and `labels` have same meaning as defined in `pie` function earlier.

Example 6.37 Illustrate the use of `pie3` function to show different profession people in a group as per following data:

Profession	No. of Persons
Manager	12
Engineer	15
Professor	13
Doctor	11
Architect	6
Designer	10

Solution: The program is given as:

```
% Program to illustrate use of pie3 function
person = [{'Manager', 'Engineer', 'Professor', 'Doctor', 'Architect',
'Designer'}];
```

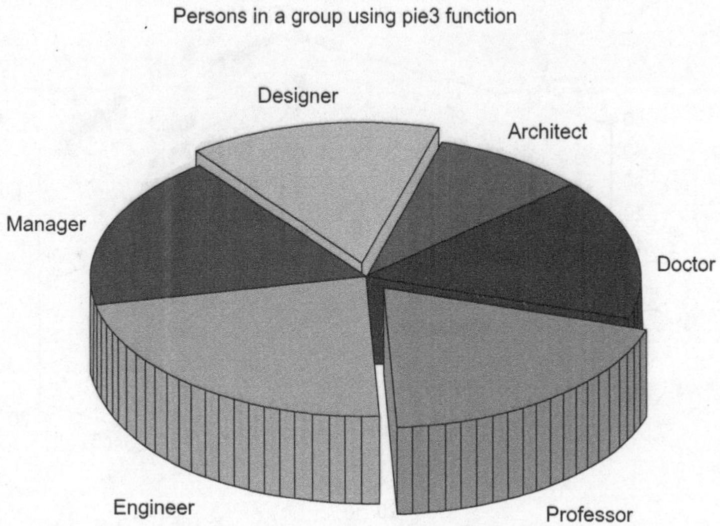

Figure 6.39 Plot to Illustrate `pie3` Function (See Page 626 for the Colour Image)

```
strength = [12 15 13 11 6 10];
explode = [0 0 1 0 0 1];
pie3(strength, explode, person);
title('Persons in a group using pie3 function')
```

The graph illustrating the use of `pie3` function is shown in Figure 6.39.

6.8.5 stem3

The syntax is given as follows:

```
stem3(a)
stem3(x, y, z)
stem3(..., 'filled')
```

The function `stem3(a)` draws the discrete surface a as stems from the *xy*-plane terminated with circles for the data value.

The function `stem3(x, y, z)` plots the surface *z* at the values specified in *x* and *y*.

The function `stem3(..., 'filled')` produces a stem plot with filled markers.

Example 6.38 Write a program to illustrate the use of `stem3` function to plot the following function:

$y = x\cos(x)$; $z = \exp(x/5)\cos(x) + 1$ for $0 \le x \le 6\pi$

Solution: The program is given as:

```
% Program to illustrate the stem3 command
x = linspace(0,6*pi,200);
y = x.*cos(x);
```

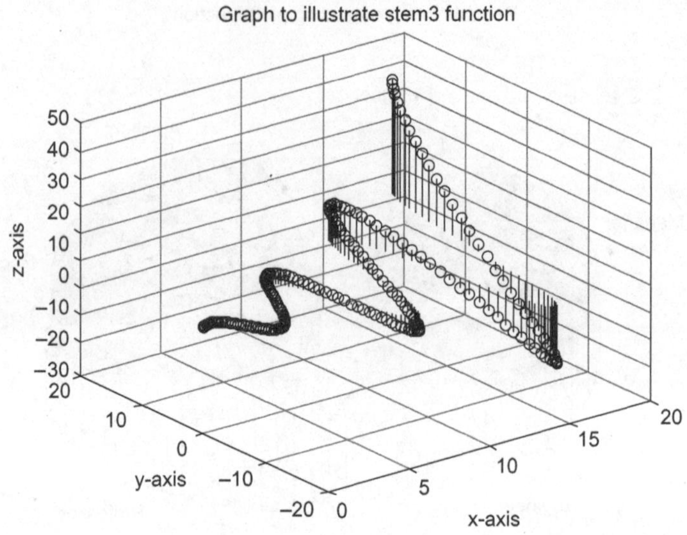

Figure 6.40 Plot to Illustrate `stem3` Function (See Page 626 for the Colour Image)

```
z =exp(x/5).*cos(x)+1;
stem3(x,y,z)
title('Graph to illustrate stem3 function')
xlabel('x-axis')
ylabel('y-axis')
zlabel('z-axis')
```

The response is given in Figure 6.40.

6.8.6 meshgrid

`meshgrid` function transforms the domain specified by vectors `x` and `y` into arrays **x** and **y** that can be used for evaluation of the functions of two variables and 3-D surface plots. The syntax is given as:

```
[x, y] = meshgrid(xbegin: xinc: xend, ybegin:yinr:yend)
```

where `xbegin` and `ybegin` are starting values of `x` and `y` variables, respectively.
`xinr` and `yinr` are increments of `x` and `y` variables, respectively.
`xend` and `yend` are final values of `x` and `y` variables, respectively.

After creating arrays of `x` and `y` values, the given function is evaluated and plotted using `mesh`, `surf` or `contour` plots.

Example 6.39 Create `meshgrid` for data: `-1 ≤ x ≤ 1` and `-2 ≤ y ≤ 2`.

Solution: The command used is as:

```
[x, y]= meshgrid(-1:0.5:1, -2:1:2)
```

This will create **x** and **y** array and the result obtained is shown as:

```
x =
    -1.0000 -0.5000 0 0.5000 1.0000
    -1.0000 -0.5000 0 0.5000 1.0000
    -1.0000 -0.5000 0 0.5000 1.0000
    -1.0000 -0.5000 0 0.5000 1.0000
    -1.0000 -0.5000 0 0.5000 1.0000
y =
    -2 -2 -2 -2 -2
    -1 -1 -1 -1 -1
    0 0 0 0 0
    1 1 1 1 1
    2 2 2 2 2
```

6.8.7 mesh

The **mesh** function draws wireframe mesh defined by the given arguments.

```
mesh (x, y, z, c)
mesh (x, y, z)
```

where **x** is an array containing x-values,
y is an array containing y-values,
z is an array containing z-values
c argument determines the colour scaling. In case, c is not mentioned it is taken equal to **z**.

Example 6.40 Create a mesh plot of the function $z = 2/(x^2 + y^2 + 1)$ over the interval $-5 \leq x \leq 5$ and $-5 \leq y \leq 5$.

Solution: The commands used are as:

```
% Program to illustrate the mesh function
[x, y] = meshgrid(-5:0.1:5);
z = 2./(x.^2+y.^2+1);          % Function to be plotted
mesh(x,y,z)
grid on
title('Program to illustrate the mesh function')
xlabel('x-axis')
ylabel('y-axis')
zlabel('z-axis')
```

The response obtained is shown in Figure 6.41.

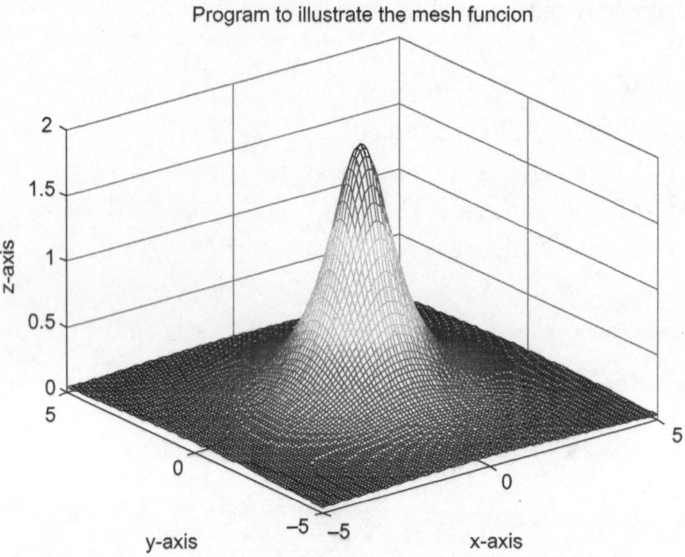

Figure 6.41 `mesh` Plot (See Page 627 for the Colour Image)

6.8.8 surf

The **surf** function is similar to **mesh** function with the difference that instead of wireframe plot it is a surface plot. The syntax is given as:

```
surf(x, y, z, c)
surf(x, y, z)
```

where **x** is an array containing x-values,
y is an array containing y-values,
z is an array containing z-values
c argument determines the colour scaling. In case, c is not mentioned it is taken equal to **z**.

Example 6.41 Create a surface plot of the function $f(x, y) = 8 - x^2 - 9y^2$ over the interval $-2 \leq x \leq 2$ and $-3 \leq y \leq 3$.

Solution:

```
% Program to illustrate the surf function
[x, y] = meshgrid(-2:0.1:2, -3:0.5:3);
z = 8-x.^2-9*y.^2;                  % Function to be plotted
surf(x,y,z)
grid on
title('Program to illustrate the surf function')
xlabel('x-axis')
ylabel('y-axis')
zlabel('z = 8-x.^2-9*y.^2')
```

The response obtained is as shown in Figure 6.42.

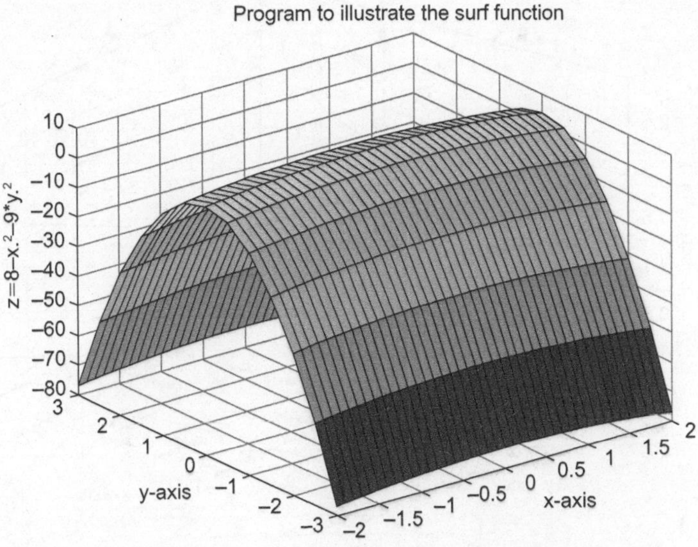

Figure 6.42 `surface` Plot (See Page 627 for the Colour Image)

6.8.9 `contour` and `contour3`

The **`contour(z)`** function gives the contour plot of the specified matrix treating the values given in the matrix as the heights above the plane.

The **`contour (x, y, z)`** is similar to **`contour (z)`** with the difference that **x** and **y** specifies **`(x, y)`** coordinates of the surface as for surf function.

The **`contour3(x, y, z)`** is the same as **`contour`** function except that the contours are drawn at their corresponding **z** level.

Example 6.42 Create a `contour` 3D plot of the function `z = sqrt(y.^2-x.^2)` over the interval $-3 \le x \le 3$ and $-3 \le y \le 3$.

Solution: The commands used are as follows:

```
% Program to illustrate the contour3 function
[x,y] = meshgrid(-3:0.5:3, -3:0.5:3);
z = sqrt(y.^2-x.^2);
contour3(x,y,z)
grid on
title('Program to illustrate the contour3 function')
xlabel('x-axis')
ylabel('y-axis')
zlabel('z=sqrt(y.^2-x.^2)'))
```

The response obtained is as shown in Figure 6.43.

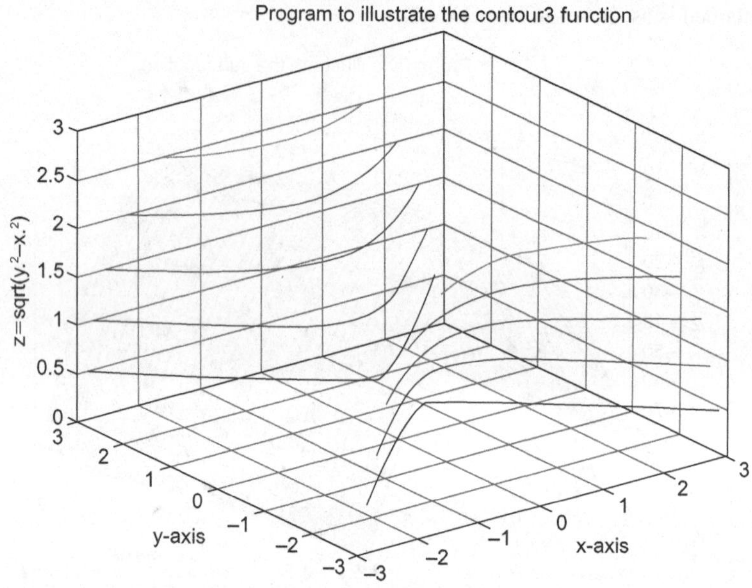

Figure 6.43 `contour3` Plot (See Page 628 for the Colour Image)

SUMMARY

In this chapter, firstly common functions used for drawing properly labelled plot are discussed. Then, specialized two- and three-dimensional plots are discussed in details. The complete chapter can be summarized in the following points:

- A simple plot can be drawn using a `plot` function and it can be further made illustrative by using `xlabel, ylabel, title, grid,` `box` and `axis` commands.
- Multiple plots can be drawn in the same graphic window by using `plot, hold` and `line` commands.
- For better illustration of multiple plots on the same window, different style options are used which specifies colour, line style and marker options.
- `legend` command is used for specified different curves on the plot
- `subplot` command divides the main graphics window into many sub graphs and is used to show many plots at the same time.
- Specialized two-dimensional plots are discussed with examples which are having many applications in representing real time data.
- Logarithmic plot consists of `semilogx, semilogy, loglog` functions.
- `Polar, area, bar, barh, hist, rose, pie, stairs, stem` and `compass` functions are discussed with illustrative examples.
- The three-dimensional plot functions mainly consist of `plot3, bar3, bar3h, pie3, stem3` are discussed which are similar to corresponding 2D plot functions except that these are plotted in three-dimensional plots.
- The other significant three-dimensional plot functions discussed are `mesh, surf` and `contour3`.

List of Commands

Function Name	Description
General Graphics Commands	
`plot`	to draw a two-dimensional plot .
`xlabel`	to label the *x*-axis
`ylabel`	to label the *y*-axis
`title`	to give a title to the figure
`grid`	show the grid lines on the plot
`text`	write illustrative text on the plot
`gtext`	place text on the plot using mouse
`axis`	to control the axis of the plot
`subplot`	subdivide graphic window into many sub-graphs
`legend`	produce a boxed legend on a plot
Two-Dimensional Plot Functions	
`semilogx`	plot with logarithmic scale *x*-axis and linear scale *y*-axis
`semilogy`	plot with linear scale *x*-axis and scale logarithmic *y*-axis
`loglog`	plot with logarithmic scale *x*-axis and *y*-axis
`polar`	draw a plot on polar coordinates
`area`	same as plot except area under plot is filled with colour
`bar`	draw vertical bar graph
`barh`	draw horizontal bar graph
`hist`	draw a histogram
`rose`	draw an angle histogram
`pie`	draw pie plot
`stairs`	give staircase plot
`stem`	give stem plot
`compass`	plot the complex data
Three-Dimensional Plot Functions	
`plot3`	plot a simple three-dimensional plot
`bar3`	plot a 3d vertical bar graph
`bar3h`	plot a 3d horizontal bar graph
`pie3`	plot 3d pie plot
`stem3`	Three-dimensional stem plot
`meshgrid`	give array for mesh grid
`mesh`	plot wireframe mesh plot
`surf`	plot surface plot
`contour`	give contour of the given matrix
`contour3`	give contour over the plane

EXERCISES

6.1 Write a program to plot the curve for a function described by the equation $y = x^3 + 2x^2 - 5$, where x varies from −10 to 10.

6.2 Write a program to plot the curve for equation $y = \sin(x) + \cos(x)$ as x varies from 0 to 2 pi. Make use of labels along x- and y-axis.

6.3 Write a program to plot the curve for equation $a = 10\ e^{-2t}$ for $t = 0$ to 500. Show the grid lines on the graph.

6.4 Use gtext command to write the equation along the curve for the function $y = x^3 + 2x^2 - 5$, where x varies from −10 to 10. Write a program.

6.5 Write a program to illustrate the use of axis command with specified limits for plot of function $y = 3x^2 + 2x + 5$ for $x = -10$ to 10.

6.6 Write a program to draw the curves for functions $y = \sin(2x)$, $y = \cos(x)$ and $y = 3x + 2$ using single plot command.

6.7 Write a program to illustrate use of different style of curves that can be drawn using `'Plot'` command.

6.8 Repeat Question no. 6.6 by using `hold` and `plot` commands. Also illustrate how `legend` command is used to indicate the different style used for the different curves plotted on the same graph.

6.9 Repeat Question no. 6.6 by dividing the graph into three subplots and plot each curve in different subplot. Label the x- and y-axis of each subplot.

6.10 Divide the graph into (3 × 2) six parts and plot a curve for linear, parabolic, exponential rise and fall and sine, cosine functions using different styles in the six subplots. Use `'gtext'` command to write the style name in each plot.

6.11 Assume suitable data and draw the following two-dimensional plots.

(i) semilog x
(ii) semilogy
(iii) loglog
(iv) bar
(v) barh
(vi) histogram
(vii) rose
(viii) pie-chart
(ix) stairs
(x) stem
(xi) compass

6.12 Draw the surface plot for the following functions:

(a) $x^2 + y^2 - 1$ for $-2 \le x \le 2$ and $-3 \le y \le 3$
(b) $y^2 - x^2$ for $-3 \le x \le 3$ and $-3 \le y \le 3$
(c) $5x/\ x^2 + y^2 + 1$ for $1 \le x \le 5$ and $1 \le y \le 5$

6.13 Draw the mesh plot for the following functions:

(a) $xe^x/2y$ for $1 \le x \le 5$ and $1 \le y \le 5$
(b) $\log(x^2 + y^2)$ for $1 \le x \le 5$ and $1 \le y \le 5$
(c) $y^2/x^2 + y^2$ for $1 \le x \le 5$ and $1 \le y \le 5$

CHAPTER 7

Control Structures

LEARNING OBJECTIVES

- Study of conditional and unconditional flow control structures
- Looping control structures
  - `for` loop and nested `for` loops
  - `while` loop
- Branching control structures
  - `If` control structure and its different forms, i.e., `if-end`, `if-else-end`, `if-elseif-else-end` and nested `if` structures.
  - `switch-case` structure
- Special MATLAB statements which control program execution sequence
  - `break` statement
  - `continue` statement
  - `error` statement
- `try-catch` structure to control the way MATLAB responds to errors.

7.1 INTRODUCTION

The instructions given in a program are executed in the sequence in which they are written in the program. But, many times program application demands that the sequence of the execution of the instructions be changed or a group of instructions be executed repeatedly depending upon some conditions. Control structures are provided in a computer language to take care of such needs of the program. Such a control structure may be used for testing a condition for true or false, repeated execution of group of statements, or the selection of a group of statements out of several different possibilities.

Like other programming languages, MATLAB also has different control structures for controlling the sequence of execution of statements of the program. Firstly, there is a conditional execution in which a condition is checked and then action is taken as per the result of the condition. In other type of control structure, instructions are executed repeatedly until some condition is met. This is called conditional looping and in this number of repetitions is not known in the beginning. Another similar type of control structure is one in which a group of instructions are executed repeatedly for specified number of times. This is called unconditional looping and in this case number of repetitions is already known. Control structure is also available for selective execution of a group of instructions from several available groups.

To solve such type of executions, MATLAB has a number of control structures. There are two broad categories of these control structures:

(i) Looping structures (Loops)
(ii) Branching structures (Branches)

(i) Looping structures cause specific group of instructions to be repeated fixed number of times or until the given condition is specified. Some of the loop structures are: `for, while, etc.`
(ii) Branching structures select the specific blocks of the program for execution depending upon the condition satisfied. Some of the branch structures are `if, if-else, switch, etc.`

Besides these, there are some commands such as `break, error and continue` to control the execution of control structures.

7.2 LOOPS

The loops are classified depending upon the manner in which the iterations are controlled. There are two forms of loops: (i) `for` (ii) `while`. In case of `for` loop, the number of repetitions is already known whereas in `while` loop, execution is repeated until the condition is specified.

7.2.1 `for` LOOP

The `for` loop control structure is used for unconditional looping. In this control structure, a group of statements, say '*n*' in number, are executed repeatedly for a fixed specified number of times, which is known before the loop starts and is decided by the `index`. The syntax of `for` statement is given as:

```
for index = initial value : increment : last value

        statement 1;

        statement 2;

        .

        .

        .

        statement n;

end;

next statement
```

The `index` is assigned `initial value` and then a group of statements is executed till `end`. After completion of one loop, the index is incremented by `increment` specified and then the group of statements is executed again, provided the new value of index does not exceed the last value. The process is repeated till the `index` attains or exceeds the `last value`. After this, `for` loop is terminated and the control is passed to the statement next to the `end` statement corresponding to `for` loop.

In more generalized form, the `for` loop syntax is expressed as given below:

```
for index = expression,

    statement 1;

    statement 2;

    :

    :

    statement n;

end;
```

where `index` is loop variable
`expression` is loop control expression .

Example 7.1 Write a MATLAB Program to obtain the sum of all even numbers from 0 to 20, using `for` loop statement.

Solution: The following commands are used:

```
sum = 0;                    % Initializing variable 'sum'
for k = 0: 2 : 20,          % start of 'for' loop, k is the index

    sum = sum + k;          % add 'sum' to 'k'

end;                        % end of 'for' loop
```

Here, index value k is incremented each time by 2 till it is equal to or exceeds 20. The value of index k is added to the variable sum in each pass. When k exceeds its last value, i.e., 20, the program control terminates `for` loop statement and exits the loop.

The result is obtained by entering the variable `sum` in the command window and is as follows:

```
sum =

    110
```

> **Programming Tip 7.1:** When the increment value of the index is not mentioned it is taken as 1 by default.

Example 7.2 Write a MATLAB program to obtain the sum of all integers from 0 to 20, using `for` loop statement, where the increment value is 1 only.

Solution: The commands used are as follows:

```
sum = 0;                    % Initializing variable 'sum'

for j = 0:20,               % start of for loop, j is index-count

        sum =  sum + j;     % add 'sum' to 'j'

end;                        % end of for loop

sum
```

This example is identical to the previous Example 7.1 except for that the increment value for index `'j'` is not given in the `'for'` statement. Here, the increment value of the index is not mentioned and thus, is taken as 1 by default.

The result is obtained by entering the variable `sum` in the command window and is as follows:

```
sum =

    210
```

Example 7.3 Program to illustrate use of `for` loop statement for discrete values of the index:

```
sum = 0;

for k = [1 5 7 6],          % The index 'k' and its values

        sum = sum + k;

end;
```

In this example, the values of the index are given as (1×4) array. As k has only four values, the loop will be executed four times only, with value of index k assigned as 1 in first pass, 5 in second pass, 7 in third pass and 6 in the last pass.

The result obtained is as:

```
sum =

      19
```

Example 7.4 Program to illustrate use of `for` loop statement that includes a decrement value:

```
for k = 10 : -2 : 0,
            result = 50 + k;
end;
```

In this example, the index-count k is initialized to 10 and decremented by 2 in each iteration till 0 is reached in the last iteration. The decrement value is indicated by the negative increment in `for` statement.

The result obtained is as:

```
result =
            50
```

> **Programming Tip 7.2:** In `for` loop, it is possible to assign negative increment i.e., decrement also. In such case, the last value becomes the minimum value for the index variable.

Example 7.5 Write a program to find average of given any 10 numbers using `for` statement.

Solution: The program is given as:

```
% This program illustrates the use of for loop for finding
% average of given 10 numbers.
% i is index value
% sum, avg. are sum and average variables respectively
sum = 0;
for i =1:10,
    n = input('Enter the value:     ');          % read the value.
    sum = sum + n;                               % Find sum
end;
avg = sum/10;                                    % Calculate average of numbers
% display the result in floating point format.
fprintf ('The average is :% f', avg);
```

On executing the above program the response obtained in the command window is as follows:

```
Enter the value:    3
Enter the value:    5
Enter the value:    24
Enter the value:    5
Enter the value:    6
```

```
Enter the value:    4
Enter the value:    10
Enter the value:    23
Enter the value:    45
Enter the value:    2
The average is: 12.700000
```

7.2.2 nested for LOOP

When one for loop is embedded in another for loop, the two loops are called nested for loops. The necessary condition is that one loop is completely nested within the other, i.e., there should not be any overlapping.

Example 7.6 Program to illustrate the use of nested for loop structure:

```
% Program to illustrate the use of nested for loops.
for a = 0 : 2 :4,                        % 'a' is index for outer loop
    b =0;
    value =0;
    for  b = 1  : 3,                     % 'b' is index for inner loop
      value = value+ a + b;              % expression in inner loop
      fprintf('Inner loop:\n')
      fprintf('a = %d \t b = %d \n', a, b)
    end;
    fprintf('The outer loop\n')
    fprintf('a = %d \t b = %d\t value = %d\n\n', a, b, value);
end;
```

The result obtained is as follows:

```
Inner loop:
   a = 0   b = 1
Inner loop:
   a = 0   b = 2
Inner loop:
   a = 0   b = 3
The outer loop
   a = 0   b = 3          value = 6
Inner loop:
   a = 2   b = 1
Inner loop:
   a = 2   b = 2
Inner loop:
   a = 2   b = 3
```

```
The outer loop
  a = 2   b = 3            value = 12
Inner loop:
  a = 4   b = 1
Inner loop:
  a = 4   b = 2
Inner loop:
  a = 4   b = 3
The outer loop
  a = 4   b = 3            value = 18
```

> **Programming Tip 7.3:** The nested `for` loops should use independent loop index variables.

7.2.3 while LOOP

A `while` loop is a used for executing a group of statements repeatedly on the basis of a condition. In this control structure, the group of statements associated with the `while` statement are executed repeatedly or indefinitely until the given condition is `true` (or non-zero). The general form of `while` loop is given as:

```
while <condition>,
  statement 1;
  statement 2;
  :
  :
  statement n;
end;
```

The group of statements may include some statements which may alter the result of the condition. When the condition becomes `false` ('0'), the program will exit from the loop and control will be transferred to the next statement after the `end` statement.

Example 7.7 Program to illustrate use of `while` loop for finding square of numbers less than 5:

Solution:

```
% Program to find square of numbers less than 5 using while loop
k = 0;                              %Initialize variable
while k < 5,
  k = k + 1;
  ksq = k^2;
  fprintf ('Square of %d is %d\n', k, ksq);
end;
```

The response obtained is as given below:

```
Square of 1 is 1
Square of 2 is 4
Square of 3 is 9
Square of 4 is 16
Square of 5 is 25
```

This example finds square of numbers less than 5. Firstly, value of variable *k* is initialized to 0. Then the condition ($k < 5$) is checked and if the condition is found `true`, the statements in the `while` loop are executed. The loop is executed again and again till condition $k < 5$ is `true`. Once it becomes `false`, the control will come out of the `while` loop.

> **Programming Tip 7.4:** Unlike `for` loop, the `while` loop statement requires that the decision variable is initialized before the loop and updated in the body of the loop.

Example 7.8 Write a program to add first 10 digits using `while` loop statement:

Solution: The program is given below:

```
% Program to add first 10 digits using while loop
   n = 0;
   sum = 0;                            % initialize the variables
   while n < 11                        % start the while loop
        sum = sum + n;                 % find sum of the numbers
        n = n + 1;
   end;
   fprintf ('The sum of first ten numbers is \t %d \n', sum);
```

The result obtained is as given below:

```
The sum of first ten numbers is 55
```

Example 7.9 Write a program to add the given numbers till the number entered is 0, using `while` loop.

Solution: The program is given as:

```
% Program to add given numbers till the number entered is 0
sum = 0;                                % Initialize the variable sum to zero
% get the first value
num = input('Enter the first number');
fprintf('Enter 0 to end the summation otherwise\n')
while (num ~= 0),
  sum = sum + num;                      % add the value
  num = input('Enter the next number');
end;
```

```
fprintf('The sum of numbers till '0' is entered is\t%d\n', sum);
```

The response obtained is as given below:

```
Enter the first number      34
Enter 0 to end the summation otherwise
Enter the next number       45
Enter the next number       6
Enter the next number       5
Enter the next number       6
Enter the next number       5
Enter the next number       60
Enter the next number       0
The sum of numbers till '0' is entered is 161
```

7.3 BRANCHES

The branches or branching control structures allow selecting and executing specific blocks of statements out of many statement blocks depending upon the condition satisfied. These include different types of `if` structures, `switch` control structure, etc. The `if` structure is a conditional control structure which allows some group of statements to be executed only if the given condition is `true`.

7.3.1 If Control Structures

In `if` control structure, a group of statements are executed only if the condition is `true`. The different forms of `if` control structures are as given below:

(a) `if` structure
(b) `if-else` structure
(c) `if-elseif` structure
(d) `Nested if` structure

7.3.1.1 *`if` Structure*

This is the simplest form of `if` control structure. It has only one group of statements which is executed if the condition is `true` otherwise the program exits the `if` control structure. The syntax of `if` is given below:

```
if    expression
statement 1     ┐
statement 2     │
.               │  group of statements
.               │
.               ┘
end
```

where expression is logical expression which gives the value `true` or `false` (non-zero or 0).

If the expression returns `true` value, then the group of statements is executed and the control goes to the next statement after the `end` statement. If the expression is `false`, then the group of statements is skipped and control goes to next statement after the `end` statement.

7.3.1.2 `if-else` Structure

In this form, `if` control structure is having two groups of statements, i.e., for `true` as well as for `false` condition. The syntax is given as follows:

```
if   expression
statement 1          ┐
statement 2          │
.                    │  group1 of statements
.                    │
.                    ┘
else
statement 1          ┐
statement 2          │
.                    │  group2 of statements
.                    │
.                    ┘
end
```

If the expression is `true`, then group 1 statements are executed and group 2 statements are skipped and the program control shifts to next executable statement after `end` statement.

If the expression is `false`, then group 1 statements are skipped and the control goes to the statements following `else` statement, i.e., group 2 statements are executed and the program control shifts to next executable statement after `end` statement.

7.3.1.3 `if-elseif-else` Structure

This is most useful form of `if` control structure. This form provides the user the option to check many conditions. The syntax is given as follows:

```
if   expression1
statement 1          ┐
statement 2          │
.                    │  group1 of statements
.                    │
.                    ┘
elseif expression2
statement 1          ┐
statement 2          │  group2 of statements
.                    ┘
else
statement 1          ┐
statement 2          │  group3 of statements
.                    │
.                    ┘
end
```

If expression 1 is `true`, the group 1 statements are executed and other group of statements are skipped and the control shifts to next executable statement after the `end` statement.

If expression1 is `false`, group1 statements are skipped and expression 2 is checked. If it is `true`, group 2 statements are executed and other statement group is skipped and program control shifts to next executable statement after the `end` statement.

In case expression 2 is `false`, then the group 3 statements are executed and control shifts to next executable statement after `if` structure.

> **Programming Tip 7.5:** There can be multiple `elseif` blocks in `if-elseif-else` structure. The `elseif` conditions are tested sequentially, and they are only tested if the previous tests are `false`. Once a `true` condition is found, then that block statements are executed and others are skipped.

7.3.1.4 Nested `if` Structure

Similar to other control structures, `if` structure can also be nested. `If` structures are called `nested`, when one of the `if` structure lies entirely within the domain of the other `if` structure. The syntax is as follows:

```
if (condition1)
   statement 1
   statement 2
   if (condition2)
      statement 1
      statement 2
   end
   statement 3
   statement 4
end
```

> **Programming Tip 7.6:** There can be any number `nested if` structures. The `end` statement is associated with the closest `if` statement. It is important to take care that for each `if` structure there should be corresponding `end` statement.

> **Programming Tip 7.7:** The multiple `elseif` control structure is preferred over `nested if` control structure to avoid syntax error.

Example 7.10 Write a program to check whether a given number is greater than or equal to another given number, using `if-end` statement:

Solution: The program is given as:

```
% Program to check whether the number is greater, equal or smaller than 50.
disp('To check whether the given number is greater, equal or smaller than
50');
a = input ('Enter a number:      ');
```

```
if a > 50,
    disp('The number is greater than 50');
elseif (a == 50)
    disp('The number is equal to 50');
else
    disp('The number is smaller than 50');
end;
```

The response obtained is as follows:

```
To check whether the given number is greater, equal or smaller than 50
Enter a number: 23
The number is smaller than 50
```

When the program is executed again, the following response is obtained:

```
To check whether the given number is greater than 50 or not
Enter a number: 50
The number is equal to 50
```

Example 7.11 Write a program to evaluate

$y = 2x + 1$, if $x < 5$

otherwise $y = 2x$. Use `if-else-end` statement

Solution: The program is given as:

```
% Program to illustrate 'if-else' structure
x = input('Enter the value of x:     ');
if x < 5,
   y = 2*x + 1;          % executed if condition is 'true'
else
   y = 2*x;              % executed if condition is 'not true'
end;
fprintf('The value of x is %d\n', x);
fprintf('The corresponding value of y is %d\n', y)
```

The response obtained is as follows:

```
Enter the value of x:     7
The value of x is 7
The corresponding value of y is 14
```

When the program is executed again, the following response is obtained:

```
Enter the value of x:     2
The value of x is 2
The corresponding value of y is 5
```

Example 7.12 Program to find smallest of the three numbers using `if-elseif-else` structure:

Solution: The program is given as:

```
% This program finds smallest of three numbers
x1 = input('Enter first number:        ');
x2 = input('Enter second number:  ');
x3 = input('Enter third number:        ');
if (x1 > x2),                                              % the outer 'if'
  if (x1 > x3),
        fprintf('The largest number is %d\n', x1);      % the inner 'if'
  end;                                            % end of inner 'if' structure
elseif (x2 > x3),
  fprintf ('The largest number is %d\n', x2);
else
  fprintf('The largest number is %d\n', x3);
end;
```

The response obtained is as:

```
Enter first number: 45
Enter second number: 98
Enter third number: 34
The largest number is 98
```

When the program is executed again, the following response is obtained:

```
Enter first number: 45
Enter second number: 34
Enter third number: 8
The largest number is 45
```

7.3.2 switch STATEMENT

The `switch-case-otherwise` structure is used for multi-way branching. It allows selection of a particular block of statements from several available blocks. A `flag` (any variable or expression) is used as a switch and based on the current value of the `flag`, particular block of statements is selected. This structure is used for logical branching. A `flag` can be a single integer, character or expression.

The general syntax of switch control structure is given as:

```
switch flag,
case value1,
      block1 statements;
-------
case value2,
```

```
        block2 statements;
    ----------
    otherwise,
        last block statements;
    end;
```

Here, depending upon the value of the flag, the particular block of statement is executed, i.e., if `flag` = `value1`, block1 is executed and the program control will exit the `switch` structure; if `flag` = `value2`, block 2 is executed and the program control will exit the `switch` structure; if the `flag` does not match any `case value`, then the last block associated with `otherwise` is executed.

The matching `end` statement indicates the end of the `switch` structure.

Programming Tip 7.8: The `otherwise` block in `switch` structure is optional. If `otherwise` block is not used and the `flag` value is out of the scope of `switch`, then no block will be executed and program control shifts to next statement after the `switch` structure.

In some cases, it is desirable to execute the same block of statements for different values of `flag` variable. Then, `switch-case` control structure is used with little modification. The syntax is given as:

```
switch flag,
    case {value1 value2 value3}
        block1      statements;
    -------
    case {value4 value5 value6}
        block2      statements;
    ----------
    otherwise,
        last block   statements;
end;
```

Programming Tip 7.9: In `switch-case` structure, case can have multiple values.

Example 7.13 Program to illustrate the use of `switch` structure involving string variables:

```
% This program tells the profession of a person using switch case structure.
Person = input ('Choose the profession code (D for... Doctor, E for Engineer,
M for Manager, P for Professor): ... \n', 's');
% Get the value of flag in a variable person
% variable name person is used as flag of switch structure
fprintf('Selected profession is :\n')
switch Person
        case 'D'
```

```
        fprintf ('Doctor \n');
       case 'E'
        fprintf ('Engineer \n');
       case 'M'
        fprintf ('Manager \n');
       case 'P'
        fprintf ('Professor \n');
otherwise
        fprintf ('Invalid choice of profession \n');
end;
```

The response obtained is given as:

```
Choose the profession code (D for Doctor,E for Engineer, M for Manager,P for
Professor):
M
Selected profession is:
Manager
```

Programming Tip 7.10: If the value of `switch` variable is character then it must be mentioned in single quote.

Example 7.14 Program to illustrate use of `switch` structure to make a choice of colour:

```
% Program to make a choice of colour.
colour = input('Select the colour code (R,Y,G,W):    ',' s');
switch  colour,
        case 'R',
        fprintf('Colour selected is Red \n');
        case 'Y',
        fprintf ('Colour selected is Yellow\n');
        case 'G',
        fprintf ('Colour selected is Green \n');
        case 'W',
        fprintf ('Colour selected is White\n');
        otherwise,
        disp('Invalid entry, select amongst the given codes');
end;
```

The response obtained is given as:

```
Select the colour code (R,Y,G,W): Y
Colour selected is Yellow
```

In case wrong entry is given the response obtained is as:

```
Select the colour code (R,Y,G,W): t
Invalid entry, select amongst the given codes
```

Example 7.15 Program to illustrate the use of `switch` structure involving numeric variables:

```
% This program tells the day of the week corresponding to given day number.
day = input('Enter the no. of the day of the week(1-7) :... , 's');
switch  day,
        case '1',                  % day is used as flag variable
                fprintf ('Day selected is Monday\n');
        case '2',
                fprintf ('Day selected is Tuesday\n');
        case '3',
                fprintf ('Day selected is Wednesday\n');
        case '4',
                fprintf ('Day selected is Thursday\n');
        case '5',
                fprintf ('Day selected is Friday\n');
        case '6',
                fprintf ('Day selected is Saturday\n');
        case '7',
                fprintf ('Day selected is Sunday\n');
        otherwise
                disp('Day  no. selected is not valid')
      end;
```

The result obtained is as follows:

```
Enter the no. of the day of the week(1-7) : 8
Day no. selected is not valid
```

Executing the program again, we get the following result:

```
Enter the no. of the day of the week(1-7) : 5
Day selected is Friday
```

Example 7.16 Program to find multiple of 2 and 3 from first 15 numbers using `switch` statement

Solution: The program is given as:

```
% Program to find multiple of 2 and 3 from first 15 numbers using switch-case
statement'
number = input('Enter a number between 1 and 15:    ', );
switch number,
```

```
    case {6 12 }
        fprintf ('The selected no. is multiple of 2 and 3\n');
    case {2 4 6 8 10 12 14},
        fprintf ('The selected no. is multiple of 2\n');
    case {3 6 9 12 15}
        fprintf ('The selected no. is multiple of 3\n')
    otherwise
        fprintf('The number selected is neither multiple of 2 nor of 3\n')
end;
```

The response obtained is as:

```
Enter a number between 1 and 15: 11
The number selected is neither multiple of 2 nor of 3
```

Executing the program again, we get the following result:

```
Enter a number between 1 and 15: 6
The selected no. is multiple of 2 and 3
```

7.4 BREAK STATEMENT

The `break` statement inside a loop is used to terminate the execution of the loop and transfer the control to the next statement after the `end` of the loop. The control is shifted even if the condition for execution of the loop is true. A program illustrating the use of `break` statement is as given below:

Example 7.17 Write a program to add first 10 numbers but stop the program when the sum exceeds 20 using `break` statement.

Solution: The program is given as:

```
% Program to illustrate the use of break statement
% Add the first 10 numbers but stop the loop when the sum exceeds 20.
sum = 0;
for k = 1 : 10,
  sum = sum + k;
  if (sum >20)
        break;        % Use the break statement to terminate the for loop.
  end;
fprintf('sum = %d\n', sum);
end;
disp('The program stops in-between as the sum becomes more than... 20');
```

The result obtained is as follows:

```
sum = 1
sum = 3
```

```
sum = 6
sum = 10
sum = 15
The program stops in between as the sum becomes more than 20
```

Here, when the program is executed, the sum is calculated till its value remains less than 20 but when it exceeds 20, `break` statement is executed and message is displayed as:

```
The program stops in between as the sum becomes more than 20
```

> **Programming Tip 7.11:** When 'break' statement is used in the nested loops then it results in program to exit from the innermost loop containing it.

Example 7.18 Program to illustrate the use of `break` statement inside the `nested for` loop:

Solution: The program is given as:

```
% Program illustrates use of break statement in the 'nested for' loop. In
% this program product and sum of two variables is done and product is shown
% if its value is less than 5.
 prod = 0;              % initialize the variables
sum = 0;
for i = 1:3
        fprintf('The first value is              %d\n', i)
       for j=1:3
           fprintf('The second value is         %d\t', j)
          prod = i*j;
          if(prod > 5)
              fprintf('Product is >5 so not displayed')
break;  % break command inside inner for loop
         end;
          fprintf ('prod = %d\n', prod)
        end;
        sum= sum+i+j;
        fprintf('\nsum=%d\t\n', sum);
end;
```

The response obtained is given below:

```
The first value is 1
The second value is 1 prod = 1
The second value is 2 prod = 2
The second value is 3 prod = 3
```

```
sum = 4
The first value is 2
The second value is 1 prod = 2
The second value is 2 prod = 4
The second value is 3 Product is >5 so not displayed
sum = 9
The first value is 3
The second value is 1 prod = 3
The second value is 2 Product is >5 so not displayed
sum = 14
```

7.5 CONTINUE STATEMENT

The `continue` command is used to skip the statements in the current pass in loop but will not exit from the loop. The remaining iterations are continued for remaining values of the index or decision variable.

> **Programming Tip 7.12:** The `continue` statement passes control to the next iteration of `for` or `while` loop enclosing it.

Example 7.19 Write a program to display the value of variable k from 1 to 10 but skip the values $2 < k < 7$ using `continue` statement.

Solution: The program is given as follows:

```
% Program to illustrate the use of continue statement
% In this program value of k is shown from 1 to 10 but skipped for 2 <k <7.
for k =1:10,
  if ((k > 2) & (k < 7 )),
         continue;
  end;
  fprintf ('k=%d\n', k);
end;
```

The result obtained is given as:

```
k =1
k =2
k =7
k =8
k =9
k =10
```

7.6 ERROR STATEMENT

Sometimes, on getting incorrect input value, the program needs to be terminated and it is desired to display a message. This can be done using `error` command.

The syntax is given as:

```
error('message to be displayed on encountering error')
```

Example 7.20 Write a program to illustrate the use of `error` statement for addition of user defined row vectors.

Solution: The program is given as follows:

```
% Program to illustrate the use of error command.
% In this program two user defined row vectors are added and error is generated
% in case of wrong entry.
fprintf('SUMMATION OF TWO ROW VECTORS\n')
a = input('Enter first row vector in square bracket    ');
b = input('Enter second row vector in square bracket   ');
if length (a) == length (b),
   sum =a + b
else
   error('Both row vectors should be of same length');
end;
```

The response obtained is given as:

```
SUMMATION OF TWO ROW VECTORS
Enter first row vector in square bracket    [2 3]
Enter second row vector in square bracket   [23 45]
sum =
     25    48
```

Again, on execution the response obtained is as:

```
SUMMATION OF TWO ROW VECTORS
Enter first row vector in square bracket    [12 37]
Enter second row vector in square bracket   [23 2 56 7]
??? Error using ==> ex721
Both row vectors should be of same length
Error in ==> ex721 at 8
   error('Both row vectors should be of same length');
```

Example 7.21 Write a program to find largest of given '*n*' numbers using `for` loop and `if` structure.

Solution: The program is given as follows:

```
% Program to find largest of n given numbers
largest =0;                          % Initialize a variable
n = input('Enter the count. of numbers   ');
for i =1: n,
  num(i) = input ('Enter the number    ');
end;
for i =1:n,
    if (largest < (num (i)))
          largest = num(i);
  end;
end;
  fprintf ('The largest number is: %d\n', largest);
```

The response obtained is given as:

```
Enter the count. of numbers 5
Enter the number 23
Enter the number 46
Enter the number 78
Enter the number 32
Enter the number 56
The largest number is: 78
```

Example 7.22 Write a program to find number of values lying between 50 and 100 from a given data of '*n*' numbers. Use `for` loop and `if` structure.

Solution: The program is given as follows:

```
% Program to illustrate the use of 'for' loop and 'if' structure
% Program to find number of values lying between 50 and 100 from a given
% n numbers,
n = input('Enter the count. of numbers   ');
for i =1: n,
  num(i) = input ('Enter the number    ');
end;
k =0;
for i =1: n,
  a = num(i);
  if (a >= 50),
```

```
        if(a < 100),
              k =k + 1;
        end;
  end;
end;
fprintf('The count of numbers >50 and <100 are %d\t\n', k);
```

The response obtained is given as:

```
Enter the count. of numbers 5
Enter the number 65
Enter the number 45
Enter the number 32
Enter the number 76
Enter the number 58
The count of numbers >50 and <100 are 3
```

Example 7.23 Write a program to find the count of even values in given '*n*' numbers. Use `for` loop and `if` structure.

Solution: The program is given as:

```
% Program to find number of even values in given n numbers
n = input ('Enter the total numbers    ');
for i = 1: n,
      num(i) = input('Enter the value    ');
end;
total =0;
for i = 1 : n,
            if(rem(num(i),2) == 0)
                  total = total + 1;
            end;
end;
fprintf('The count of even numbers in given data is %d\n',… total);
```

The response obtained is as follows:

```
Enter the total numbers 5
Enter the value 23
Enter the value 42
Enter the value 54
Enter the value 98
Enter the value 78
The count of even numbers in given data is 4
```

7.7 TRY-CATCH STRUCTURE

Generally, while executing a program if an error occurs, MATLAB aborts the program showing the error message. However, by using **try-catch** structure, errors found by MATLAB are captured, giving the user ability to control the way MATLAB responds to errors. This allows the user to handle errors within the program without stopping it. The syntax for **try-catch** structure is given below:

```
try
Statement 1  ]
Statement 2  ]     group 1
---------    ]
catch
Statement 1  ]
Statement 2  ]     group 2
---------    ]
end
```

Here, first the statements in `try` block are executed then one of the following two cases is possible:

- If no error occurs, then statements in the `catch` block are skipped and program control shifts to statement after to `try-catch` structure.
- In case an error occurs in any of the statements of `try` block, then the program stops executing the remaining statements in `try` block and executes the statements in the `catch` block and finally exits from the `try-catch` structure.

Example 7.24 Write a program to add two given row vectors. Illustrate the use of `try-catch` structure.

Solution: The program is given below:

```
% Program to add two row vectors, illustrate the use of try-catch structure
fprintf('SUMMATION OF TWO ROW VECTORS\n')
a = input('Enter first row vector in square bracket    ');
b = input('Enter second row vector in square bracket   ');
try
    sum =a + b
catch
    disp('ERROR: Both row vectors should be of same length');
end
```

The response obtained is as:

```
SUMMATION OF TWO ROW VECTORS
Enter the first row vector in square bracket    [3 6 8]
Enter the second row vector in square bracket   [12 34]
ERROR: Both row vectors should be of same length
```

When the program is executed again, the following response is obtained:

```
SUMMATION OF TWO ROW VECTORS
Enter the first row vector in square bracket    [2 4 8]
Enter the second row vector in square bracket    [5 89 34]
sum =
     7    93    42
```

SUMMARY

In this chapter, an introduction to conditional and unconditional looping is provided and this has been discussed.

- In conditional looping, the number of repetitions is not known and loop continues till the condition satisfies whereas in unconditional looping the number of repetitions is known and loop is repeated only for a fixed number of iterations.
- The control structures are classified as (i) Looping control structures—such as `for`-loop, nested `for`-loop, `while` loop, and (ii) branching control structures- `if-else` and `switch-case` structures—have been illustrated using examples.
- The special statements used to change the sequence of looping—such as `break`, `continue`, `error`—have also been discussed and illustrated using examples.
    - `break` is used to end the `for` or `while` loop
    - `continue` is used to pass the particular iteration of the `for` or `while` loop and control shifts to next iteration.
    - `error` is used to terminate the program due to incorrect input and gives the error message
- `try-catch` structure is used to catch the error generated by MATLAB and to give error message.

List of Control Structures/Commands

Control Structure/Command	Description
`for`	repeat the statements specific number of times
`while`	repeat the statements if the condition is true or non-zero
`if`	conditionally execute the statements
`switch`	switch between cases depending upon the condition
`break`	Terminate the execution of `for` or `while` loop
`continue`	Pass the control to next iteration of `for` or `while` loop
`error`	display message and abort function
`try-catch`	catch the error generated by MATLAB

EXERCISES

7.1 Examine the program given below and evaluate the values of variables *x* and *y*. Let the value of '*n*' be

(a) 1 and (b) 0 (c) –2

```
x = 2;
y = 2;
n = input('Enter the value of n:    ')
if(n > 0)
x = n*3;
y = y/3;
end;
```

7.2 Write a program to find out whether a given number is 'odd' or 'even', using 'if' structure

(a) without 'else' option (b) with 'else' option.

7.3 Write a program to find the number of integers that are greater than 50 but lesser than 250 that are divisible by 11. Also find the sum of these numbers.

7.4 Given a list of 60 students with their marks ranging from 0 to 100, write a program to compute and print the number of students who have obtained:

(a) >75 marks (b) >60 marks

(c) >50 marks (d) >35 marks

(e) <35 marks.

7.5 Admission to an engineering college is based on the following conditions:

(a) Marks in Maths ≥ 60

(b) Marks in Physics ≥ 55

(c) Marks in Chemistry ≥ 55

(d) Total marks ≥ 180

Given the marks in three subjects of 50 candidates, write a program to process the applications to list the candidates eligible for admission.

7.6 A showroom gives the following discounts on purchase of items:

Purchase Amount (in Rs)	Mill Cloths (Handloom Items)	Discount
0–200	—	5%
201–500	5%	10%
501–1000	7.5%	12.5%
Above 1000	10%	15%

Write a program to compute the net amount to be paid by a customer, if he/she makes purchases of amount varying from Rs 50 to Rs 50,000.

7.7 Write a program using `while` loop to reverse the digits of a number having minimum three digits.

7.8 Write a program to compute the sum of the digits of a given integer number.

7.9 Write a program to read the age of 50 persons and count the number of persons in the age group 40 to 50. Use `for` and `continue` statements.

7.10 Write a program to print the following output using `for` loop.

```
1
3    3
6    6    6
```

7.11 Calculate $x(t)$ from the following equation using MATLAB control structures:

$$x(t) = 2t^3 + 4 \quad \text{for} \quad t \geq 0$$
$$= -2t^3 + 10 \quad \text{for} \quad t < 0$$

for $-10 \leq t \leq 10$, in steps of 0.4.

7.12 Write a program to evaluate the function: $f(t) = 1 + e^{-2t}$, for $-5 \leq t \leq 10$, in steps of 0.2 using `for` loop.

7.13 For a given value of n, write a program to calculate the nth, Fibonacci number using `while` loop.

7.14 Determine the value of I at the end of each of the following `for` loops:

(a)
```
I = 0
for k = -5: 5
I = I + 1
end
```

(b)
```
I = 0
for k = 5: -1 : 3
I = I + 2
end
```

7.15 Determine the value of J at the end of each of the following `while` loops.

(a)
```
k = 5
I = 1
while (I × k) == 5
x = 2 (I + k)
J = x - 1
end
```

(b)
```
J = 50
while J > = 40
J = J^2
end
```

CHAPTER 8

Writing Programs and Functions

LEARNING OBJECTIVES

- Study of MATLAB Editor and different features of Editor Menu bar and Toolbar.
- Learn MATLAB programming fundamentals and types of M-files, i.e., script files and function files.
- How to write a function M-file.
- Know about the concepts of argument passing, function workspace and types of functions.
- Function Handle using `@` operator and `strfunc` function.
- Know about different types of errors encountered in programs and methods or commands to detect and correct them.
- Use the various features of MATLAB debugger for debugging run-time errors in program files.

8.1 INTRODUCTION

MATLAB is a high-level language having arrays or matrices as basic data types with control flow statements, functions, data structures, input/output, and object-oriented programming features. It contains all the features and constructs available in any other professional programming language like C or C++. It allows a user to construct small as well as large and complex applications with fair ease.

In this chapter, Editor, programs, functions and debugging tools have been discussed. The definition of functions and using them in other functions or subprograms has also been described in detail.

8.2 EDITOR

MATLAB Editor not only contains basic text editing features but also provides the user with additional facilities such as debugging tools. The Editor/Debugger has proper graphical user interface for ease in programming. It also supports automatic indenting and highlighting to indicate special parts of the program such as keywords, text strings, comments, etc. It also allows a user to observe the values of the variables/constants in the program. Features like setting/clearing breakpoints, executing programs line by line, etc. are also available to aid the programmer in effectively debugging the program.

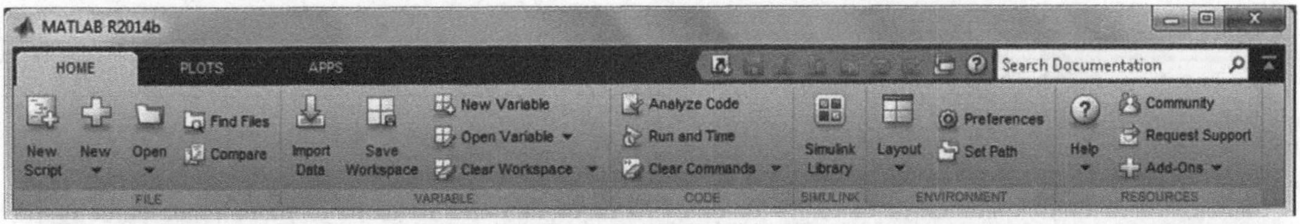

Figure 8.1 MATLAB Main Menu and Toolbar

8.2.1 Starting the Editor

Editor can be started in a number of ways given below:

1. Selecting `New` from the `File` menu in the MATLAB desktop main menu.
2. Clicking on the new file icon on the toolbar as shown in Figure 8.1.
3. Typing the command `edit` in the command window at the command prompt.

If a file that is already existing and is to be modified, editor may be started by:

1. Selecting `open` from the `File` menu in the MATLAB desktop main menu.
2. Clicking on the open file icon on the toolbar as shown in Figure 8.1.
3. Typing the command `edit` *`filename`* in the command window at the command prompt.

> **Programming Tip 8.1:** When the Editor/Debugger is used alone, i.e., without MATLAB open, it cannot be used as a debugger. It functions as plain text editor only.

8.2.2 Editor Main Menu

The appearance of the Editor window is similar to normal windows present in Windows XP operating system. It contains a Title Bar that displays the name of the file being edited. If the changes made in the file have not been saved, it is indicated by an `asterisk (*)` that appears after the name of the file in the title bar. The Editor window also contains a main menu and a toolbar. The main menu is composed of File menu, Edit menu, View menu, Debug menu and Tools menu. It also offers help menu and choice to have multiple files opened for editing simultaneously. The Editor window is shown in Figure 8.2 given below.

The **File menu** contains items to open, save and print files. It also contains choice to quit/exit from Editor/Debugger or MATLAB. File menu also has choice for importing data from outside or saving the workspace in a *.mat file

The **Edit menu** contains items that are found in normal text editor like `undo, redo, cut, copy, paste, find, replace text, select all, delete,` etc. It also has features for clearing the command window, command history and workspace.

The **Text Menu** contains item `'Evaluate Selection'` which is used to evaluate an expression and display the answer in the Command Window. There is provision for commenting or uncommenting the selected text in the program file. This is very helpful when large section of the program needs to be commented. It also contains option for decreasing or increasing the indent in the selected program text. Further, option for changing the text case is also available. Another very good feature that is included in the text menu is `Code Folding` (Figure 8.3). When large programs are to be viewed, for convenience of the programmer the functions in the program are folded, i.e., their statements are hidden and only the function definition line is displayed. This function is just like the windows explorer which hides the folder contents or displays them

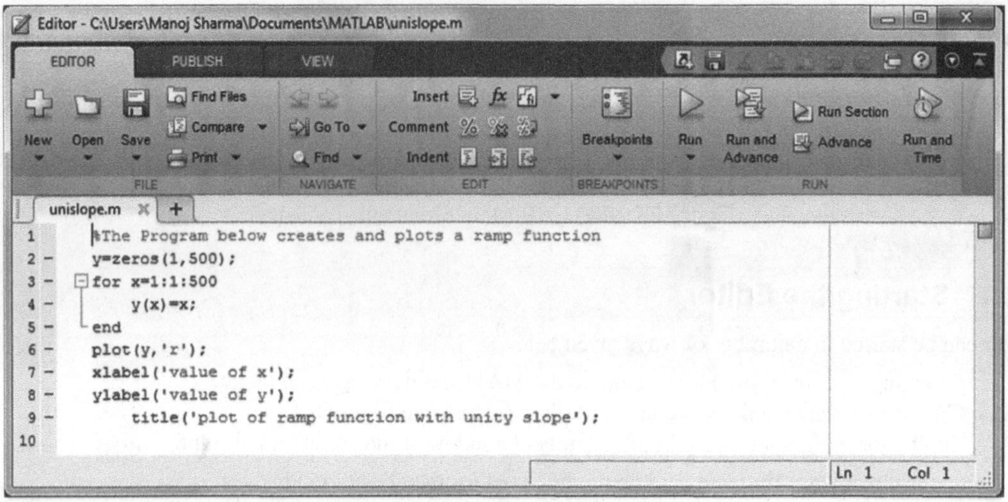

Figure 8.2 The Editor Window

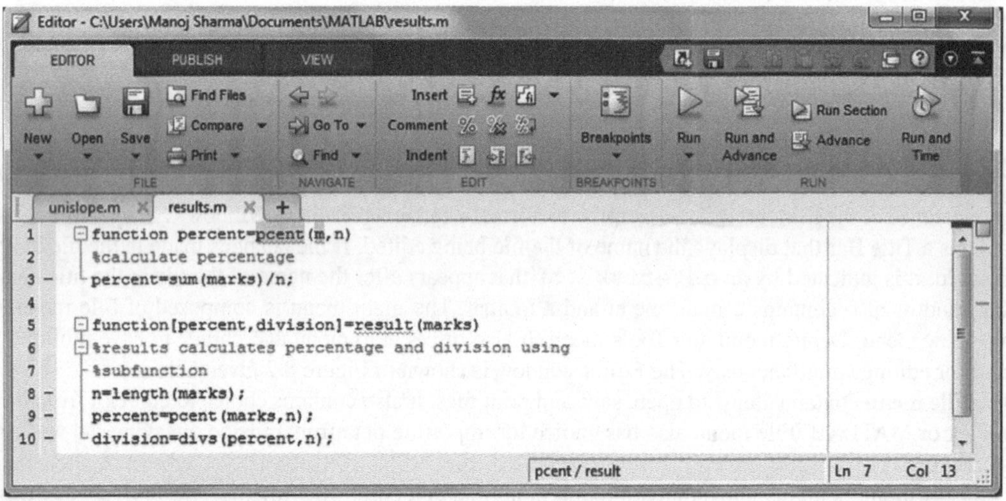

Figure 8.3 Editor Window Illustrating Code Folding

as desired by user. The editor window shown above illustrates the `Code Folding` option where the code of the function `'divs'` is folded.

The **Navigate menu** includes options for moving `'forward'` or `'backwards'` in the program text. It also includes option for moving to a particular line in the text files that are open in the editor. It opens a separate dialogue box which prompts the user to enter the line number and select the program text file from the ones that are currently opened in the editor. It also includes feature of `bookmark` to move to selected points in the program text.

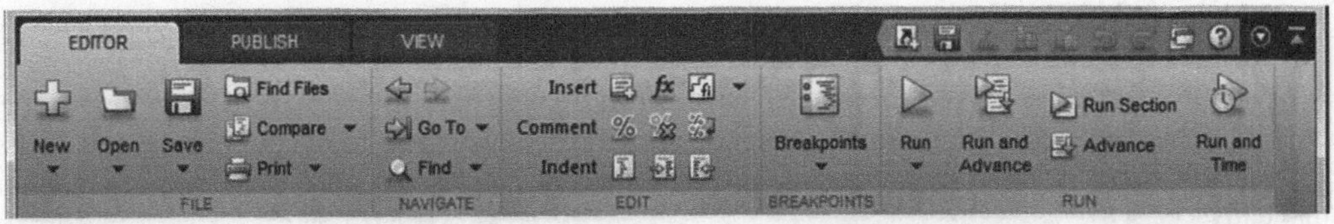

Figure 8.4 Editor Window: Toolbar

Program files are often very long and contain multiple sections. Each section of the program can be described as a single M-file cell. The **Cell menu** deals with such sections, i.e., cells of the program code.

The **Tools menu** contains option called `M-lint`. `M-lint` displays inconsistencies and suspicious constructs in program files. This menu option can be utilized by the user to find such inconsistencies. Another tool available in the editor tools menu is `'Profile'`. The Profile Report identifies where a program file spends the most time, and therefore helps the user to identify the part of the code needed to be looked into for improving the performance of the code.

The **Debug menu** contains the various features embedded in the Editor for debugging the programs. It also contains an option to run the program in the current text window.

The **Desktop menu** allows the user to dock or undock the editor window and organize the desktop to the satisfaction of the user.

The **Window menu** provides choice of how the different text files in the editor window should appear on the desktop, i.e., in a tiled manner, or two files viewed in horizontally split screen or in vertically split screen, etc. It also allows the user to move to command window, command history window, help window or workspace window directly.

The last but not the least is the **Help menu** that allows the user to seek help about various features of the editor/debugger.

8.2.3 Toolbar

The Editor Window in addition to the main menu contains a complete functional toolbar as shown in Figure 8.4. The features found in other text editors like open `new file, open existing file, save file to disk, cut, copy or paste selected text from the program, undo, redo, print` are available on the toolbar and can be invoked by simply clicking on the relevant icon on the toolbar. The toolbar also provides graphical interface for finding a particular text, moving forward or backwards in the code and another icon for listing the functions in the text file and moving to any of them by simply selecting the appropriate one from the list.

Further, the toolbar also contains icons for the complete set of debugging tools, i.e., setting or clearing breakpoints, executing programs line by line, stepping into the functions, stepping out, continuing execution after stopping at the statements indicated by the breakpoints, quitting debugging, etc. Provision for selecting the program workspace or stack is also available. The last set of icons is for viewing or editing multiple program files in tiled view, etc.

8.3 MATLAB PROGRAMMING

Programming in MATLAB is very similar to that found in C/C++. In previous chapters, it is observed that MATLAB contains most of the basic programming constructs available in other programming languages. It also has option to define classes and objects as done in other object-oriented languages. But, the most important of all is the ease of programming and the tools available in MATLAB. These enable the programmer to develop large scientific applications with shorter code and in far less time.

Program files in MATLAB are called M-files. These files contain a series of MATLAB statements along with the programming constructs or features like `for`, `while loops` or `switch`, `break` and `if` etc. Like program code files in C language have names with extension '.c', MATLAB program file are named with extension '.m'. The program files are created or edited using MATLAB Editor and saved by specifying the filename without the extension. The file extension '.m' is appended to the end of the filename automatically.

8.3.1 Creating M-files

M-files are ordinary text files and can be created using any text editor whether it is notepad, wordpad or MATLAB editor program. The editor available in MATLAB can be invoked in number of ways listed as under:

1. Choose new file or open file form the file submenu in MATLAB desktop.
2. Click on the icons for new file or open file on the toolbar available in the MATLAB desktop.
3. Enter the command `edit or edit` *`filename`* at the command prompt in the MATLAB command window.

When `edit` command is given, the editor is started with the filename `untitled` and the file can be named while storing or saving it in the appropriate folder.

The commands given from the command window are saved in the command history window. M-file can be created using these statements by selecting them in the command history window, right-clicking and selecting `Create M-File` option. The Editor opens a new file that includes these statements. The statements can also be copied and pasted into an existing M-file.

8.3.2 Types of M-files

Primarily, there are two types of M-files.

1. Script files
2. Functions

Both the type of files contains MATLAB statements, but have major differences.

- The Script files are the simplest of M-files that basically do not accept input arguments or return output arguments. Function files on the other hand accept input arguments and return output arguments. These are therefore called or contained within a Script file or another function file.
- Secondly, script files operate on data in the workspace. Any variables that scripts create remain in the workspace after the script finishes and can be used for further computations. On the other hand, function files treat the internal variables as local to that function and have their own workspace.

Example 8.1 Write a script file to plot a ramp function with unity slope.

Solution: The program to plot ramp function is given below:

```
% The program below creates and plots a ramp function
for x = 0:0.5:50
     y = x;
end;
plot(y, 'r');
xlabel('value of x');
```

```
ylabel('value of y')
title('plot of ramp function with unity slope');
```

The file can be executed from the main menu in the MATLAB desktop or by typing the name of the file at the command prompt in the command window. When execution completes, the variables (x and y) remain in the workspace. The variable list can be displayed using `whos` command at the command prompt.

8.4 FUNCTION SUBPROGRAMS

A large and complex task can be easily executed if divided into smaller sub-tasks or modules. Function subprograms are program segments that are written for implementing a sub-task or a module or a sub-module. These subprograms are developed separately and can be executed independently. These can also be used by other programs. Functions subprograms can be written for the common tasks that are frequently required by many users so that the users do not need to waste time writing code for the common tasks. All users can simply use the functions in their programs. MATLAB also has in store numerous function subprograms for common tasks related to many fields such as mathematical functions, matrices, graphs, solving differential equations, Fourier transforms, etc. Besides such predefined functions, MATLAB also contains function subprograms which may be needed frequently for solving many scientific/engineering problems.

Functions are M-files that accept input arguments and return output arguments. The structure of the function subprogram is similar to any other program, except for the function definition statement that should be included at the start of the function. The function subprogram includes commands and functions and the function file is normally named after the function name.

Example 8.2 Write a function to calculate the roots of a quadratic equation $ax^2 + bx + c = 0$, where a, b and c are constants.

Solution: A file named '`roots1.m`' containing the function roots given below is created.

```
function [r1, r2] = roots1 (a,b,c)
%This function calculates roots of a quadratic equation
%a, b and c are input arguments
%r1 and r2 are output arguments
disc = b^2-4*a*c;
disc1 = sqrt (disc);
r1 = (-b+disc1)/(2*a)
r2 = (-b-disc1)/(2*a)
```

The above function '`roots1`' can be called by giving the following command in the command window to calculate the roots of a quadratic equation, $ax^2 + bx + c = 0$.

Let $a = 1$, $b = 4$ and $c = 4$, then the command used is:

```
a = 1;
b = 4;
c = 4;
[r1, r2] = roots1 (a, b, c);
```

The following answer will be displayed which gives the two roots:

```
ans =
     r1 = -2
     r2 = -2
```

The basic parts of a function M-File are given as follows:

- A function definition line
- A H1 line
- Help text
- The function body
- Comments

8.4.1 Function Definition Line

The function definition line informs MATLAB compiler that the M-File defines a function subprogram. The general form of the function definition line is as given below:

```
function[output arguments] = function_name(input arguments)
```

where

1. '`function`' is the key word that indicates that the program following this statement is a function subprogram.
2. '`function-name`' is the name of the function and is defined just as other variable names in a program. Normally, it is chosen same as the name of the function subprogram filename.
3. The list of input arguments, if present, is enclosed in parenthesis separated by commas.
4. The function output arguments are enclosed in square brackets separated by commas as indicated in the syntax of the function definition line shown above.

> **Programming Tip 8.2:** If no output is required the square brackets as well as equality sign in the function declaration or the function call statement can be omitted or only empty square brackets can be used.

Some valid function definition lines and their corresponding file names are given below:

Function Definition Line	File Name	Remarks
function [ ] = circle_area (*r*);	circle_area.m	No output arguments
function rect_area (l, b)	Rect_area.m	No output arguments
function [*r*1, *r*2] = roots (a, b, c)	roots.m	r_1 and r_2 are output arguments

The variables that are passed to the function do not need to have the same name as those of function input arguments in the function definition line.

8.4.2 H1 Line

H1 line is the first line following the function definition line written as a comment and includes important help statements connected with the function subprogram like the details of input and output arguments and the task performed by the function. Because it consists of comment text, the H1 line begins with a per cent sign, '%.'

When the user types '`help function_filename`' at the command prompt in the command window this text HI line is displayed as the first line of help text. The `lookfor` command displays this H1 line only.

For the function given in Example 8.2 for calculating roots of a quadratic equation, H1 line is given below.

```
% This function calculates the roots of a quad. equation
```

8.4.3 Help Text

Help for M-Files can be obtained from the command line and can be created by entering help text on one or more consecutive comment lines immediately following the H1 line.

When the user types 'help function_filename' at the command prompt in the command window, these comment lines between the function definition line and the first executable statement are displayed as the help text.

> **Programming Tip 8.3:** The text that is written after the first executable statement do not form the part of the help text.

The help text for the function given in Example 8.2 for calculating roots of a quadratic equation is given below.

```
% This function calculates roots of a quad. equation
% a, b and c are input arguments
% r1 and r2 are output arguments
```

8.4.4 Function Body

The body of the function contains all the MATLAB statements that perform the required sub-task computations. These statements can consist of programming constructs, such as flow control, interactive input/output, assignment statements.

The body of the function given in Example 8.2 for calculating roots of a quadratic equation is given below.

```
disc = b^2-4*a*c;
disc1 = sqrt (disc);
r1 = (-b+disc1)/(2*a)
r2 = (-b-disc1)/(2*a)
```

8.4.5 Comments

As mentioned earlier, comment lines begin with a per cent sign (%). Comment lines can appear anywhere in an M-file, and one can append comments at the end of a line of code. For example, adding comments to the body of the function given in Example 8.2 for calculating roots of a quadratic equation is given below.

The comments are added at the end of each statement as shown below:

```
disc = b^2-4*a*c;             % calculating discriminant
disc1 = sqrt (disc);          % finds square root of discriminant
r1 = (-b+disc1)/(2*a)         % calculates the first root
r2 = (-b-disc1)/(2*a)         % calculates the second root
```

8.4.6 Function Names

The rules applied for naming the variable names in MATLAB also apply to function names. Function names must begin with a letter; the remaining characters can be any combination of letters, numbers and underscores. MATLAB uses the first 31 characters of names. The name of the function file and the function name may not be the same but in that case MATLAB ignores the function name. The function is called by the function file name.

> **Programming Tip 8.4:** While the function name and the filename can be kept different, it is strongly recommended that same name be used for both.

When a function is called, MATLAB searches for the relevant file in the order given below:

1. Finds if the name is a variable.
2. Checks to see if the name is a subfunction, a MATLAB function that resides in the same M-file as the calling function.
3. Checks to see if the name is a private function, a MATLAB function that resides in a private directory, a directory accessible only to M-files in the directory immediately above it.
4. Checks to see if the name is a function on the MATLAB search path.

MATLAB uses the first file it encounters with the specified name. If the names of variable and many functions available in different folders are same, MATLAB executes the one found first using the above rules. It is also possible to overload function names.

Function M-files can be called from either the MATLAB command line or from within other M-files. Let the function definition line of a function 'step' be given by:

```
function(y,t) = step(num,den)
```

The following are valid call/execution statements:

```
[y, t] = step(n, d)
```

The values of the input variables `'n'` and `'d'` have to be specified before calling the function. Otherwise, the statement will give error that 'the values of the input arguments are not defined'. The variables `'y'` and `'t'` are the output variables and some values (outputs) must be assigned to them in the function that is called.

> **Programming Tip 8.5:** When a function is called, all necessary arguments should be included, enclosing input arguments in parentheses and output arguments in square brackets.

Let the step function defined above be called as shown below.

```
[Df, x] = step([0,   1],[1,   1])
```

It is noted that the input variables are assigned their values directly. Also the output variables, `Df` and `x` are the output variables, have different names than defined in the function subprogram. This indicates that the names given in the function definition line are only **dummy names**. Different names can be specified at the time of call.

> **Programming Tip 8.6:** The programmer does not need to know the names of the input/output variable names given in the function definition line. It is, however, mandatory to mention the input/output variables in the same physical order as specified in the function.

8.5 PASSING FUNCTION ARGUMENTS

MATLAB appears to pass all function arguments by value. In reality, however, MATLAB passes by value only those arguments that are modified by the function. If a function does not alter the value of an argument and simply uses it in a computation, then MATLAB passes the argument by reference to optimize memory use.

MATLAB functions can be defined to use varying number of arguments. In such a case when varying number of arguments are used, MATLAB packs all of the specified input or output into a cell array.

> **Programming Tip 8.7:** Varying number of input and output arguments of the function can be passed by using `'varargin'` and `'varargout'` functions.

8.6 FUNCTION WORKSPACE

The function M-file variables take separate memory space from MATLAB base workspace. This memory space is called the **function workspace**. In fact each function has its own workspace context. Therefore, each MATLAB function has its own local variables, which are separate from those of other functions, and from those of the base workspace.

The variables that are passed to a function must be in the program workspace of the calling program. The called function returns its output arguments to the function workspace of the calling program/function. However, if several functions, and possibly the base workspace, all declare a particular variable as **global**, then they all share a single copy of that variable. Any assignment to that variable, in any function, is available to all the other functions declaring it global.

The command used to declare the variables *x*, *y* and *z* as global is given below:

```
global x y z;
```

Further, to declare and work with global variables the following rules are applicable:

- The variable must be declared as global in every function that requires to access that variable.
- If base workspace also needs to access the global variable, it should be declared as global from the command line also.
- The `global` command must appear before the first occurrence of the variable name in each function.

> **Programming Tip 8.8:** It is advised to declare the global variables at the top of the M-file to avoid any inadvertent errors.

> **Programming Tip 8.9:** It is advised to name global variables in all uppercase characters. This increases the readability of MATLAB code and reduces the chance of accidentally redefining a global variable.

Some variables are required to retain their value between calls to the function. It is possible in MATLAB by declaring them as **persistent variable**. The command used to declare variables as persistent is given as follows:

```
persistent x y z
```

The command defines `x`, `y` and `z` as persistent variables.

Persistent variables are local to the function in which they are declared and also their values are retained in memory between calls to the function. These variables are similar to global variables because MATLAB creates permanent storage for both. They differ from global variables in the sense that persistent variables are known only to the function in which they are declared. This prevents persistent variables from being changed by other functions or from the MATLAB command prompt. Persistent variable is exactly like global variable, except that the variable name is not in the global workspace, and the value is reset if the M-file is changed or cleared.

> **Programming Tip 8.10:** If a non-existent variable is declared as persistent, it will be initialized as an empty matrix.

8.7 SOME ILLUSTRATIVE EXAMPLES

Some illustrative programs are given below to help the user understand the concepts discussed above.

Example 8.3 Write a function subprogram to calculate the sum of the following series:

$S = 1 + r + r^2 + \ldots r^n$

Solution:

```
function [s]= seriessum(r, n)          % function definition line

% This function calculates the sum of a series - H1 line

% r is the common rates & n is the no. of terms - Help Text

% Function text body follows

nvector = 0:n;

series = r.^nvector;

s = sum(series)
```

The above function series can be called as follows:

(a)

```
seriessum(2, 4)
```

The function will be called and executed. Its output will not be stored. However, it is displayed in the command window as there is no semicolon at the end of the function call statement.

(b) $r = 2; n = 4;$

```
s = seriessum(r, n)
```

Here, the function will be called and executed. Its result will be stored in the variable `'s'` and will also be displayed in the command window as there is no semicolon at the end of the function call statement.

(c) $r = 2; n = 4;$

```
seriessum(r, n);
```

Here, the function will be called and executed. Its output will not be stored and will not be displayed in the command window also as the function call is terminated by a semicolon.

Example 8.4 Write a function subprogram to calculate the compound interest, given the initial amount, time period of deposit, rate of interest and time of compounding.

Solution

```
function[cap,interest] =comp(cap,yrs,rate,tcomp)-%function def.line
% This function calculates the compound interest - H1 line
% capital, no.of years, rate of interest, period of
% compounding is to be given                      - Help text
a = cap;
n = yrs;
r = rate ;
k = tcomp;
```

```
if r>1
    disp('check interest rate. For 7% enter 0.07, not 7.0')
end
cap = a*(1+r/k)^(k*n)
interest = cap-a
```

The above function named `comp` can be called by different methods given below.

(a) The function comp is called with input arguments alone:

```
comp(1000,6,0.12,1)
cap =
    1.9738e+003
interest =
    973.8227
ans =
1.9738e+003
```

(b) function `comp` is called with input and output arguments alone:

```
[capital,interest]=comp(1000,6,0.08,1)
cap =
    1.5869e+003
interest =
    586.8743
capital =
    1.5869e+003
interest =
    586.8743
```

As no semicolon is used, the values of variable `cap` and `interest` are displayed first and then as the function call is without semicolon, the values of output arguments compound and interest are also displayed.

(c) The function `comp` is called with input arguments alone but call is terminated by semicolon:

```
comp (1000,6,0.12,2);
cap =
    2.0122e+003
interest =
    1.0122e+003
```

The variables `cap` and `interest` are displayed as the statements in the function are not terminated by semicolon, but as the function call is terminated by semicolon, the result of the function call is not displayed.

Example 8.5 Write a function to check the division scored by a number of students.

Solution: The program divisioncheck finds the division scored by a number of students.

```
function divisioncheck
% The function finds out the number of students in first division among the
% given no. of total students.
```

```
n = input('Give the total number of students\n');
disp('Enter the marks of the students(out of 100)');
for i =1:n
    k(i)=input('');
end;
x =0;
for i =1:n
    if((k(i)<0)|(k(i)>100))
        fprintf('%d number is invalid \n', i);
    elseif(k(i)>60)
        x = x+1;
    end;
end;
fprintf('The no. of students securing first division ...
    is %d\n', x);
```

To execute the function, enter `divisioncheck` at the command prompt in the command window. The response of MATLAB is as given below:

```
Give the total number of students
5
Enter the marks of the students(out of 100)
23
54
75
456
76
4 number is invalid
The no. of students securing first division is 2
```

To seek help about the function `divisioncheck`, enter the command

```
help divisioncheck
```

The MATLAB displays the following help text in the command window:

```
The function finds out the number of students securing first division among the
given no. of total students.
```

Example 8.6 Write a function to ask for given number and report whether they are between 10 and 100 or not.

Solution: The `inrange` function below inputs the number and reports whether it is between 10 and 100 or not.

```
function inrange
% function finds whether the given number lies between 10
```

```
% and 100 or not.
a = input(‘Enter the number\n’);
if (( a>10) & (a<100))
    disp (‘The number lies between 10 and 100’)
else
    disp(‘The number does not lie between 10 and 100’)
end;
```

If one seeks help about the function `inrange`, the MATLAB response is:

```
function finds whether the given number lies between 10
and 100 or not.
```

8.8 TYPES OF FUNCTIONS

Functions can be classified into different categories based on their features and the manner in which they are applied. Some of them are as listed below:

- Subfunction
- Private function
- Nested function
- Inline function

8.8.1 Subfunctions

Function files can contain code for more than one function. The first function in the file is called primary function. The primary function is called by the name of the function M-file. Additional functions defined within the same file are called subfunctions. These functions are visible only to the primary function or other subfunctions defined in the same M-file. Each subfunction begins with its function definition line. These subfunctions follow each other and may occur in any order, as long as the primary function appears first.

Example 8.7 Write a function to calculate per cent and division from the marks of a student.

Solution: The function **`result`** calculates the percentage of marks and also reports if the student has scored first division.

```
function [percent,division] = result(marks)
% result calculates percentage and division using
% subfunctions.
n = length(marks);
percent = pcent(marks,n);
division = divs(percent,n);
function percent = pcent(m,n)
% Calculate percentage.
percent = sum(marks)/n;
function d = divs(p,n)
```

```
% Calculate division first or not.
If p > 60
        d = first
  else
        d = not_first
end
```

Here, `result` is the primary function which contains two subfunctions `pcent` and `divs`. The subfunction `pcent` calculates the percentage of marks and subfunction `divs` finds if the student has scored first division or not.

The following points about functions are very significant:

- Functions within the same M-file cannot access the same variables as all subfunctions have their own function workspace. The variables can be shared by declaring them as global variables or pass them as arguments.
- Further, the help command for the function file displays the help text associated with the primary function only.
- As pointed out in the previous section, when a function is called from within an M-file, MATLAB first checks the file to see if the function is a subfunction. This enables the user to supersede existing M-files using subfunctions with the same name. However, function names must be unique within an M-file.

8.8.2 Private Functions

Private functions are functions that are stored in subfolders with the special name private. These functions are visible only to the functions in their parent folder. For example, let the folder student be on the MATLAB search path. A subfolder called private can be created in the folder 'student'. The folder 'private' can contain functions that can be called only by the functions in its parent folder 'student'. Private functions are invisible outside their parent folder. Therefore, they can have the same names as functions in other folders. This is useful if a user wants to create a different version of a particular function while retaining the original in another folder.

Programming Tip 8.11: Private subfolders are not included in the search path.

8.8.3 Nested Functions

Just like a `for` loop which may be nested within another `for` loop, a function may also be nested within another function. The nested functions provide a way to pass information, without passing it through input/output arguments and without using global variables.

Basic format of a simple nested function is given below:

```
F1 = primary function (.........)
  ------------------------
  -----------------------        %Code of function F1
  -----------------------
```

```
F2 = nested function (.........)
   ---------------------
   ---------------------         %Code of nested function F2
   ---------------------
   end                           %end of nested function F2
   ----------------------
   ----------------------        %remaining code of F1
end                              %end of primary function F1
```

A primary function can contain several nested functions within itself. The `end` statements mark the end of each nested function and the primary function.

8.8.4 Inline Functions

Mathematical expressions can be evaluated by creating functions defining the expressions as shown below:

```
function y = mexp(x)
y = x^3 + 4 * x^2 + 5 * x + 6;
```

A second way to represent the mathematical function at the command prompt is to create an inline object from a string expression. For example, an inline object of the function `mexp` mentioned above can be defined as given below:

```
fx = inline ('x^3 + 4 * x^2 + 5 * x + 6', 'x')
```

General form of an inline function is:

```
Function name = inline('character.string expression', 'list of variables')
```

where character string expression and list of variables are enclosed with in single quotes.

Example 8.8 Use 'inline' function to evaluate:

$f(x) = x^3 + 4x^2 + 5x + 6$ for $x = 4$

Solution: Following MATLAB command can be used:-

```
fx = inline (x^3 + 4 * x^2 + 5 * x + 6', 'x')
```

Following statement will be displayed:

```
fx = inline function :
fx(x) = x^3 + 4 * x^2 + 5 * x + 6
```

Now type `fx(4)` in the command window, i.e., x has been given the value equal to 4. Following answer will be displayed:

```
ans
    = 154
```

Example 8.9 Obtain the value of the function given in Example 8.8 above, for `x = 2`, using the function `feval` and the `inline` function.

Solution: Following command can be used in the command window:

```
y = feval(fx, 2)
```

On pressing the enter key, following answer will be displayed:

```
y
  = 40
```

Functions having more than one argument can also be created with `inline` statement by specifying the names of the input arguments along with the string expression. For example, the following function has two input arguments *x* and *y*:

```
f = inline('y * x^2 + x * y^2', 'x', 'y')
```

To calculate the value of f at $x = 2$ and $y = 3$, the following command is used:

```
f(2,3)
```

The answer displayed is:

```
ans =

      30
```

8.9 FUNCTION HANDLES

A Function Handle stores all the information about the function which is needed for its execution later. A `function handle` can be created by any of the following two ways:

(a) Using the '`@`' operator.
(b) Using '`str2func`' function.

8.9.1 Using the '@' Operator

Suppose it is desired to create a function $f(t) = 4e^{-2t}$, for t in the range of 0 to 5. This function can be defined as follows:

```
Function timres = func(t)
timres = 4 * exp (-2 * t)
end
```

Function handle can be created by the following line:

```
handle = @ func
```

Where `handle` is the name of the `function handle` and `func` is the name of the function. The function `func(t)` can now be executed by just typing the name of the `function handle` and enclosing the arguments in the parenthesis. The following MATLAB command will evaluate the function `func(t)`.

```
handle = @ func
```

Type and save the function in the edit window and give the following command in the command window:

```
handle(0 : 5)
```

The following result will be displayed

```
ans
  = 4.000   0.5413   0.0733   0.0099   0.0013   0.002
```

which gives the value of $4e^{-2t}$, for different values of t.

Function handle created using @ can also be used to create functions called **anonymous functions**. The syntax of general statement for creation of anonymous function is as given below:

```
Function Name = @(list of variables/arguments in function) function expression
```

where @ indicates that the function name mentioned on the left-hand side is a function handle.

Example 8.10 Use anonymous function to evaluate:

$f(x) = x^3 + 4x^2 + 5x + 6$, for $x = -2, 2, 4, 6$

Solution: Let the function $f(x)$ be defined as an anonymous function as given below:

```
fx = @(x) x^3 + 4 * x^2 + 5 * x + 6
```

Table 8.1 given below provides the commands and the corresponding answer given by MATLAB for evaluating the function for different values of x.

Table 8.1 Commands and Results Obtained for Example 8.10

Command	Answer Given by MATLAB
fx(-2)	4
fx(2)	40
fx(4)	154
fx(6)	396

8.9.2 Using 'str2func' Function

Function handle can be created and used by typing the following line in the command window:

```
handle = str2func('func')
handle (0 : 1 : 5)
```

Following answer will be displayed

```
ans
  = 4.000    0.5413    0.0733    0.0099    0.0013    0.002
```

which gives the value of $4e^{-2t}$, for different values of t.

8.10 ERRORS AND WARNINGS

In many cases, it is desirable to take specific actions when different kinds of errors occur. For example, one may want to prompt the user for more input, display extended error or warning information, or repeat a calculation using default values. MATLAB's error handling capabilities let the application check for particular error conditions and execute appropriate program depending on the situation.

8.10.1 Types of Errors

There are basic two types of errors.

- Syntax errors
- Run-time errors

Syntax errors are caused by grammatical mistake in the statement included in the program, i.e., using or not using comma, semicolon, bracket, parenthesis, etc. It may be caused by misspelling a function name or using wrong array indices, etc. MATLAB detects most of the syntax errors when the program is compiled before its execution and displays a message describing the error, showing the line number of the statement where the error has occurred in the program file.

Run-time errors are errors that are caused mainly by using wrong logic by the programmer. The statements given in the program may be syntactically correct but if the logic or algorithm is erroneous, the output or result of the program that is obtained on its execution will also be erroneous. The programmer may be using a wrong variable or value of a variable or performing incorrect computations. The run-time errors become apparent when one obtains erroneous and unexpected results.

Syntax errors are easy to correct based upon the error messages displayed by the MATLAB compiler as the complier indicates the location of the error also by displaying the line number of the statement where the error has occurred. But, run-time errors are more difficult to track down because MATLAB does not report the type of error or its location. It is left completely to the programmer's skill to judge why the results obtained are unexpected. Also the function's local workspace is lost after the function has been executed and MATLAB returns back to its base workspace. There are many techniques that are useful in isolating the erroneous statements that may have caused the run-time error. Some of these techniques are listed below:

1. **Using Semicolons**: Semicolons prevent MATLAB from displaying the result of the statement executed in the program. This fact can be utilized to isolate the errors. When the semicolons are removed selectively and the program executed, MATLAB will display the result of each such statement in the program. The programmer then can easily follow the output of the program at selected points where the semicolons have been removed. This can help in detection of erroneous statement or logic.
2. **Using `Keyboard` Statement**: `Keyboard` statements stop the program file execution at the point where they appear. This allows the programmer to examine the local program or function workspace and also execute some statements from the command prompt in the command window. This mode is indicated by another special prompt, '`K>>.`' The execution of the program can be resumed by giving '`return`' command.
3. **Executing Function as Script**: If a function is being executed, the function declaration can be converted into a comment and the function can be executed as a script file. Further, the inputs can be fixed for which the results are known to find out if the output obtained is correct or not. Also the function workspace is then converted into MATLAB base workspace and can be examined even after the function has been executed (as a script file).
4. **MATLAB Debugger**: In addition to these techniques, the MATLAB Debugger is available and can be utilized in isolating the error.

8.10.2 Error Handling with Eval and Lasterr

Two functions `eval` and `lasterr` are the basic tools for error-handling in MATLAB. If an error occurs in a function, error-handling routines can be defined in another function which can invoked using `eval` tool. The `lasterr` tool can be used to return a message (string) which indicates the last error generated by MATLAB.

The syntax of `eval` function is given as follows:

```
eval('string1', 'string2')
```

where '`string1`' specifies the MATLAB expression or function that is desired to be executed or evaluated. If the expression or function is evaluated properly, `eval` simply returns to execute the next statement in the MATLAB program. If it does not execute properly and generates an error, the `eval` function evaluates the expression or function specified by the `string2`. '`String2`' is used to define the error handling routines or an alternate task that may have to be executed in case the expression or function specified by first string '`string1`' generates an error.

The `lasterr` tool is used in conjunction with the `eval` tool. When the expression or function indicated by 'string1' generates an error and the second function specified by 'string2' is executed, the `lasterr` tool can be used to report the error before the error-handling statements are executed. This can be done by including the statement given below as the first statement in the function given by 'string2'.

```
Error_reported = lasterr;
```

The error generated is stored in the character array 'Error_reported' which can be used to report the error to the user in the format desired by the user.

8.10.3 Displaying Error and Warning Messages

Error and warning messages can be displayed by including the `error` and `warning` function in the program. The error message is then displayed on the screen in the command window.

The syntax of error function is as given below:

```
error('error message')
```

If the error function is called in a program, i.e., in M-file, the error message given in quotes is displayed on the MATLAB screen in the command window and also MATLAB exits from the program being executed. For example, let the following code appear in a program M-file abcd.m.

```
if marks < 0
   error('marks cannot be negative.')
end
```

If the marks variable has value equal to –50, the following error message will appear on the screen and the program abcd will stop executing.

```
??? Error using ==> abcd
marks cannot be negative.
```

Error messages and warnings are similar. However, warning does not terminate the execution of the program. To give a warning message, the following statement is used:

```
warning('warning message')
```

Further, similar to function 'lasterr' that displays the last error reported by MATLAB, the function 'lastwarn' can be used to display the last warning message.

8.11 MATLAB DEBUGGER

The MATLAB Debugger helps in identifying programming errors in a MATLAB M-file. It allows the user to view the contents of the workspace at any time during function execution and examine or change their values. It facilitates user to view the function call stack and execute M-file statements line by line. Further, the user can define points where the program execution stops temporarily to allow user to examine the status of the program, its variables, their values, etc. to ensure that the program segment till that point is without any run-time errors. The programmer can then continue execution from that point onwards. Such points where the execution of the program stops for a while are known as Breakpoints. Debugger can be used through its graphical user interface as well as commands that can be given from the command prompt.

8.11.1 Setting Breakpoints

As mentioned above Breakpoints stop a program file execution at specified points or lines and allow the user to view or change values of variables in the function's workspace. Thereafter, the user can resume execution of the program which further stops at the next breakpoint.

A breakpoint can be set at any executable statement. If the line or statement selected for setting a breakpoint is not a valid executable statement, then the breakpoint is set at the next executable statement.

To set the breakpoint, the user can make use of the debug submenu from the main menu or select the (set/clear breakpoint) icon from the toolbar. The cursor is moved to the statement where the breakpoint is to be set and the icon is clicked or the option 'set breakpoint' is selected from the debug menu or right-click to bring up the context menu and choose set/clear breakpoint. A red stop sign (●) next to a line indicates that a breakpoint is set at that line. The editor window with a breakpoint set in the program is shown in Figure 8.5. The line number is indicated at the bottom right of the status bar in the editor window shown in Figure 8.6.

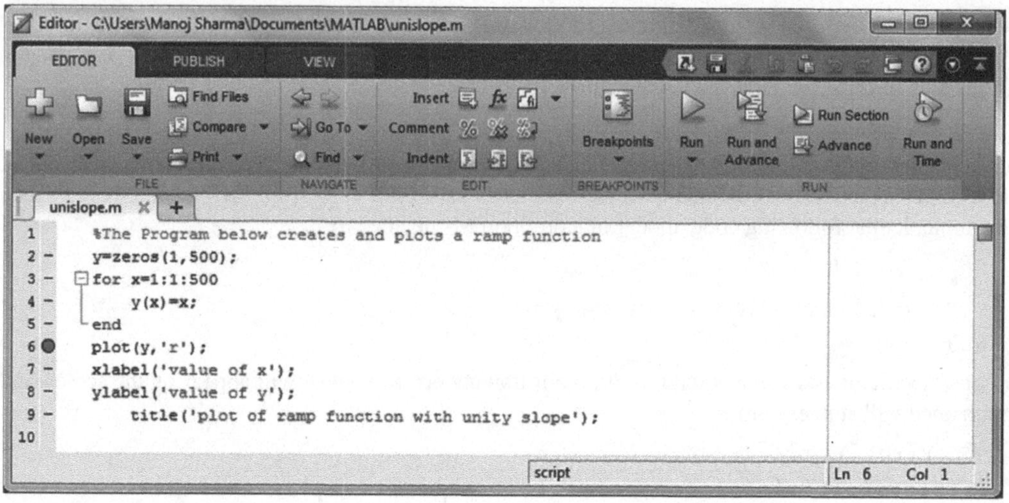

Figure 8.5 MATLAB Editor/Debugger: Setting Breakpoints

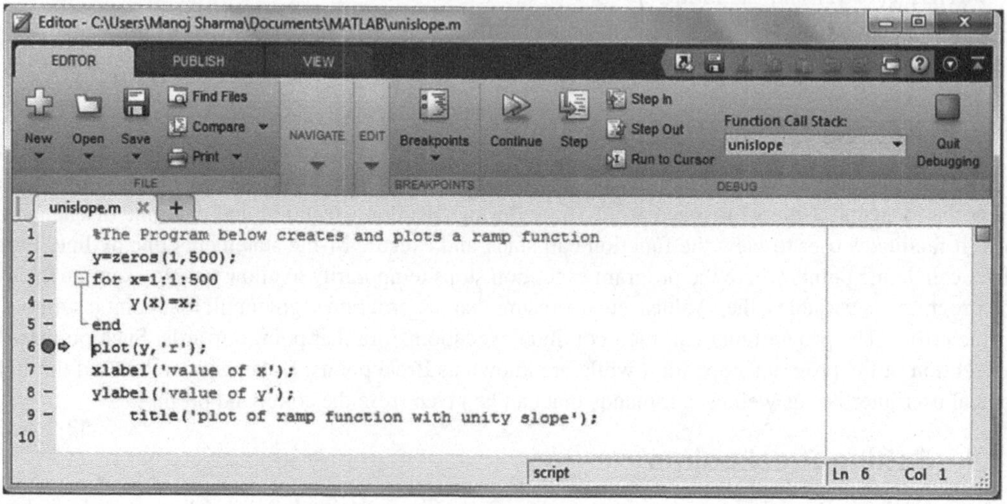

Figure 8.6 The Editor/Debugger Window: the Arrow Pointer

> **Programming Tip 8.12:** The breakpoint will not be set if there are any syntax error in the program.

The same menu option and icon in the toolbar is used for clearing the breakpoint, i.e., the icon works as a toggle switch setting and resetting the breakpoint alternatively when used at the same cursor position again. To clear all the breakpoints, the user can use the icon (clear all breakpoints) from the toolbar.

> **Programming Tip 8.13:** The Debugger's Breakpoints menu also halts the program execution if the code generates a `warning`, `error`, or `NaN` or `Inf` value.

8.11.2 Examining Variables

The values of different variables in the program or function workspace can be examined. The breakpoints are used to halt the execution of the program at the desired executable statement as discussed in the previous section. At this point, the user can examine the program workspace to know the status of the variables up to that point in the program. When execution of a program file pauses at a breakpoint, the green arrow to the left of the text shows the next line to execute as indicated in Figure 8.6. A downward green arrow appearing to the left of the text indicates a pause at the end of the script or function. This allows the user to examine variables before returning to the calling function. This is because the function workspace lasts only as long as the function is being executed. The memory space is returned to free space after MATLAB returns to the calling program. Moving the cursor to any variable in the program text also results in displaying the value of that variable or its dimensions.

MATLAB also allows the user to go to command window and execute any valid MATLAB statement/ command. Thus, the user is able to find out if the program is executed correctly up to the breakpoint or not. This helps in isolating the correct code in the M-file and therefore, effectively isolating the run-time errors.

8.11.3 Changing Workspace Context

The Stack pull-down menu in the upper-right corner of the Debugger window can be used to select the desired workspace area. The different workspace contexts are available in a pull-down menu and the relevant workspace can be selected by the user.

The editor/debugger window with the pull-down stack menu is shown in Figure 8.7.

8.11.4 Stepping Through Code and Continuing Execution

After the program pauses at the breakpoint, the execution of the program can be resumed by either stepping up to the next statement or executing the program block of statement till the next breakpoint appears in the program.

To execute the next statement in the program, user can choose single step in the debug menu or click the icon (single step) in the editor toolbar. This executes the current statement and moves the yellow arrow to the next statement in the program. If the complete block of statements appearing till the next breakpoint in the program are to be executed, then the user can choose continue from the debug menu or click the icon (continue) in the editor toolbar.

There may be many function calls appearing in a program. The user has two options: one is to execute the function as a single statement in the calling program and the other is to step into the function and execute its statements one by one or in blocks using breakpoints. The points to note are given as follows:

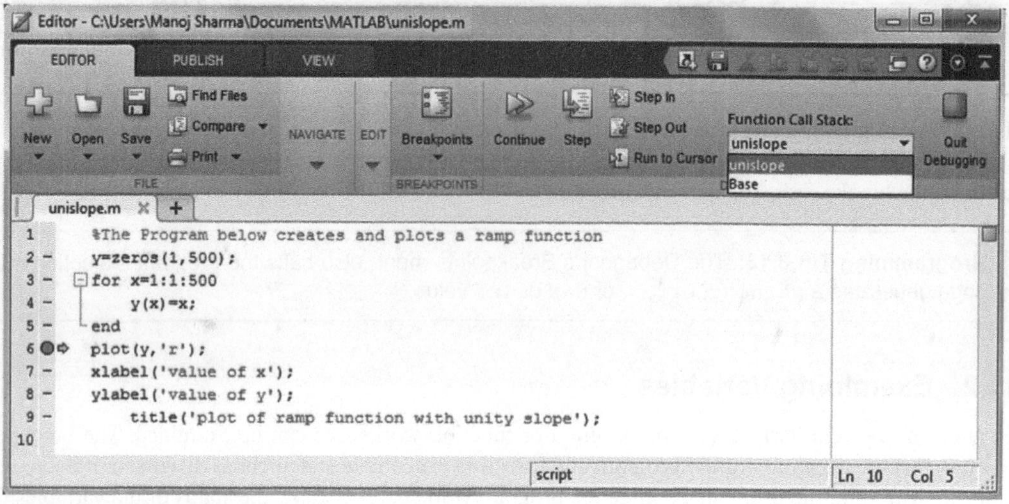

Figure 8.7 The Editor/Debugger Window: the Stack Pull-down Menu

- To execute the statements in block, the continue option is chosen from the debug menu.
- To step into the function to execute the function statements one by one, step in option is chosen from the debug menu or click the (step in) icon from the editor toolbar.
- There is also an option to step out of the function. To do so, click on the icon (step out) in the toolbar.

8.11.5 End the Debug Session

To end the Editor/Debugger choose exit from the File menu to end the debugging session or click (quit) icon from the toolbar.

8.11.6 Debugging from the Command Line

The debugging commands can also be executed from the command prompt in the command window. The different commands and their description are given in Table 8.2 shown below:

Table 8.2 Debugging Commands from Command Prompt

Debugging Command	Description	Syntax
`dbstop`	Set Breakpoint	`dbstop filename line number`
`dbclear`	Clear breakpoint	`dbclear filename line number`
`dbclear all`	Clear all breakpoints	`dbclear all`
`dbstop if error`	Stop on warning, error, or NaN/Inf generation	`dbstop if warning error naninf infnan`
`dbstep`	Single step execution	`dbstep`

(Continued)

Table 8.2 (*Continued*)

Debugging Command	Description	Syntax
`dbstep in`	Step into a function	`dbstep in`
`dbcont`	Continue execution	`dbcont`
`dbquit`	Quit debugging	`dbquit`
`dbstack`	List function call stack	`dbstack`
`dbstatus`	List all breakpoints	`dbstatus file_name`
`dbstep nlines`	Execute one or more lines	`dbstep nlines`
`dbtype`	List M-file with line numbers	`dbtype file_name`
`dbdown`	Change local workspace context (down)	`dbdown`
`dbup`	Change local workspace context (up)	`dbup`
`dbquit`	Quit debug mode.	`dbquit`

SUMMARY

This chapter covers the detailed description of MATLAB editor, MATLAB programming features, MATLAB debugger. The complete chapter can be summarized in the following points:

- MATLAB editor is discussed with detailed illustration to menu bar and toolbar.
- MATLAB programming features and types of M-files: script and function files are discussed.
- Function subprograms and their different parts such as definition line, H1 line, function text, etc. are elaborated.
- Concepts of function arguments passing, function workspace are illustrated with examples.
- The different types of functions, i.e., subfunction, private function, nested function, inline functions are described in detail.
- Creation of Function handle using `@` operator and `str2func` function is discussed.
- Types of erroneous syntax and run-time errors and concept of warnings are discussed.
- Different methods used to isolate errors are described, i.e., using semicolon, sing `keyboard` statement, executing function as a script and use of MATLAB Debugger.
- Error-handling using `eval` and `lasterr` is also illustrated.
- How to display errors and warning messages is also described.
- In the last, MATLAB debugger is explained in detail. Different features of debugger `illustrated` are as: setting breakpoints, examining variable, changing workspace context, stepping through code, ending debug session and debugging from the command line.

List of Commands

Debugging Command	Description
`error`	To display error message
`warning`	To display warning message
`lasterr`	To display last error encountered by MATLAB
`eval`	To evaluate a function
`str2func`	To convert a function string to `function handle`
`inline`	To create an inline object
`dbstop`	Set Breakpoint
`dbclear`	Clear breakpoint
`dbclear all`	Clear all breakpoints
`dbstop if error`	Stop on warning, error, or NaN/Inf generation.
`dbstep`	Single step execution
`dbstep in`	Step into a function
`dbcont`	Continue execution
`dbquit`	Quit debugging
`dbstack`	List function call stack
`dbstatus`	List all breakpoints
`dbstep nlines`	Execute one or more lines
`dbtype`	List M-file with line numbers
`dbdown`	Change local workspace context (down).
`dbup`	Change local workspace context (up).
`dbquit`	Quit debug mode.

EXERCISES

8.1 Write a function 'exchange' to interchange the values of two variables, say *p* and *q*. Illustrate the use of this function in calling program.

8.2 Write a function to evaluate:

$$f(x) = x - \frac{x^3}{3!} + \frac{x^5}{5!} - \frac{x^7}{7!} + ----$$

Illustrate its use in a calling program.

8.3 The Fibonacci numbers are defined recursively as follows:

$F_1 = 1$

$F_2 = 1$

$\vdots$

$F_n = F_{n-1} + F_{n-2}$ when $n > 2$

Write a function that will generate and print the first *n* Fibonacci numbers.

8.4 Write a function that returns 1 if its argument is a prime number and returns zero otherwise.

8.5 What is an inline function? Write an inline function to allow the user to calculate compound interest a certain sum of money *P*, at rate of interest *r*, compounded half yearly when the time is given by *t*.

8.6 Write a program to sort an array in ascending order using Bubble sort. Execute the program line by line and examine the array at each step.

8.7 What is an anonymous function? Define such a function and illustrate its usefulness.

8.8 Debug the following program to find the run-time error.

(a) using toolbar debugging icons
(b) using commands from the MATLAB prompt

```
function [per cent,division] = result(marks)
% result calculates percentage and division using
% subfunctions.
n = length(marks);
per cent = pcent(marks,n);
division = divs(per cent,n);
function per cent = pcent(m,n)
% Calculate percentage.
per cent = sum(marks)./n;
function d = divs(p,n)
% Calculate division first or not.
If p > 60
        d = first
else
        d = not_first
end
```

8.9 What are different types of functions? Give an example of each.

8.10 What is code folding? Write the procedure for code folding and illustrate its usefulness.

Ordinary Differential Equations and Symbolic Mathematics

CHAPTER 9

LEARNING OBJECTIVES

- Use of ode solvers for the solution of Ordinary Differential Equations.
- Introduction to symbolic mathematics and use of `sym` and `syms` functions.
- Evaluation of symbolic expressions using `subs` function.
- Use of `diff` and `int` functions to evaluate differentiation and integration of symbolic expressions.
- Use of `simplify, solve` functions in symbolic mathematics.
- Represent an expression in different forms using `collect, expand, horner` and `factor` functions.
- Use of `limit`, `symsum`, `taylor` functions.

9.1 INTRODUCTION

Mathematical formulation of many engineering and scientific problems yields differential equations. Only a limited number of such problems can be solved using analytical methods leading to closed form solutions. The problems which cannot be solved by analytical methods can be solved easily using computer-oriented numerical methods/techniques. Even the problems which can be solved by using analytical methods can be solved more easily by using numerical methods. In MATLAB®, there is a suite of Ordinary Differential Equation (ODE) solvers which offers eight initial value problem solvers. In symbolic mathematics, calculations are done symbolically. Use of different commands/functions of symbolic mathematics tool box has been explained.

9.2 ORDINARY DIFFERENTIAL EQUATION SOLVERS

An equation which involves an independent variable and a dependent variable with its ordinary derivatives is called an Ordinary Differential Equation (ODE), for example,

$$\frac{d^3x}{dt^3} + 4\frac{d^2x}{dt^2} + 5\frac{dx}{dt} + 6x = e^t \sin t \tag{9.1}$$

is an ODE, where t is the independent variable and x is the dependent variable.

The closed form solution of this equation means finding an explicit expression for x in terms of t. However, its numerical solution means finding the values of x at different instants of time, t. Generally many functions can satisfy a given ODE. Hence, additional information is required to obtain a specific desired solution. This additional information is provided in the form of initial values of the variables of interest and the problem is known as *initial value problem*.

There are eight initial value problem solvers available in MATLAB ODE suite which can be used to solve differential equations. Each solver has characteristics appropriate for different initial value problems. The list of solvers with their characteristics is tabulated in Table 9.1.

Table 9.1 ODE Suite Solvers

Name of Solver	Method of Solution	Description of Solver
`ode45`	Runge-Kutta	• An explicit one-step Runge-Kutta (fourth to fifth order) solver • Suitable for non-stiff problems that require moderate accuracy • **This is a first solver to be tried on any new problem**
`ode23`	Runge-Kutta	• An explicit one-step Runge-Kutta (second to third order) solver • More suitable for problems with mild stiffness and where lower accuracy is acceptable
`ode113`	Adams-Bashforth-Moulton	• A multi-step Adams solver of varying order (1st to 13th order) • Suitable for non-stiff problems that require moderate to high accuracy • Not suitable for problems where $f(t, y)$ is not smooth
`ode15s`	Numerical differentiation formulas NDFs (BDFs)	• An implicit multi-step numerical differential solver of varying order (first to fifth order) • Suitable for stiff problems that require moderate accuracy • **This solver is used if `ode45` fails or is too inefficient**
`ode23s`	Rosenbrock	• An implicit one-step solver of order two • Suitable for stiff problems where lower accuracy is acceptable or where $f(t,y)$ is discontinuous
`ode23t`	Trapezoidal rule	• An implicit, one-step trapezoidal rule using a free interpolant • Suitable for moderately stiff problems • Can be used to solve Differential Algebraic Equations (DAEs)
`ode23tb`	TR-BDF2	• An implicit trapezoidal rule followed by backward differential of order two • Similar to `ode23s`
`ode15i`	Backward differentiation formulas (BDFs)	• A solver of varying order (first to fifth order) used for solving fully implicit differential equations

> **Programming Tip 9.1:** The `ode45` and `ode15s` are the first and second solvers, respectively, to be tried on a given problem.

This MATLAB ODE suite is provided as a set of M-files that can be viewed. Also, these solvers are included internally in Simulink® for simulation of dynamic systems.

9.2.1 Syntax of ODE Solvers

Given a set of first order differential equations in vector form as follows:

$\dot{\underline{x}} = f(t, \underline{x})$

where $\underline{x}$ is a (nx1) column vector, having n components and $\dot{\underline{x}}$ is a time derivative dx/dt of vector $\underline{x}$. The function f may or may not contain t.
This set of first order differential equations can be written in expanded matrix form as follows:

$$\begin{bmatrix} \dot{x}_1 \\ \dot{x}_2 \\ \cdots\cdots \\ \dot{x}_n \end{bmatrix} = \begin{bmatrix} f_1(x_1, x_2, \ldots\ldots, x_n) \\ f_2(x_1, x_2 \ldots\ldots, x_n) \\ \cdots\cdots\cdots\cdots \\ f_n(x_1, x_2 \ldots\ldots, x_n) \end{bmatrix} \tag{9.2}$$

If this is a set of linear differential equations, it can be written in vector form as follows:

$\dot{\underline{x}} = A\,\underline{x} + B\,\underline{u}$

where $\underline{x}$ is $(n \times 1)$ state vector,
$\dot{\underline{x}}$ $(n \times 1)$ (derivative of state vector),
$\underline{u}$ $(m \times 1)$ input vector,
A $(n \times n)$ matrix of constant elements,
B $(n \times m)$ matrix of constant elements,

(I) The simple syntax for use of any one of MATLAB differential equation solvers is:

```
[t, x] = solver('fun', tspan, x0)
```

where

`solver` is the name of one of the ODE solvers as mentioned in Table 9.1,

`fun` is the name of function written by the user which evaluates the right hand side of the differential equations to be solved. It is enclosed in single quotes. This name of function can also be written as an anonymous function i.e. @ *name of function*, instead of enclosing the name of function in single quotes i.e as *@fun*.

`tspan` is a vector specifying the interval of integration, $[t_0, t_f]$, i.e., initial time t_0 to final time t_f,

To obtain solutions at specific times (all increasing or all decreasing order), use tspan = $[t_0, t_1, \ldots, t_f]$ and

`x0` is a vector of initial conditions of variable x.

The output arguments given on left hand side of the solver are defined as:

`t` is a column vector of time instants and

`x` is a solution array; each row value in x corresponds to the solution at a time which is returned in the corresponding row of t.

(II) Full syntax of ODE solvers is:

```
[t,x,pstats] = name of ODE solver(@name of function,tspan,x0,options)
```

where

(a) **pstats** vector gives six performance parameters of differential equation solvers. The different elements of this vector are:

(i) Number of successful steps
(ii) Number of failed steps
(iii) Number of function evaluations
(iv,v,vi) These parameters are related to stiff solvers only.

(b) options, is an input argument which can be created with the following 'odeset' function:

```
options = odeset('name1',value1,'name2',value2,................)
```

where 'name1', 'name2', etc. refer to the names of optional arguments that are to be specified and value1,value2 etc. refer to the corresponding values of the optional arguments.

Any unspecified properties have default values.
Names of Commonly used options arguments are:

(a) Relative error tolerance, 'RelTol' (Its default value is 1e-3) and
(b) Absolute error tolerances, 'AbsTol' (all components are 1e-6 by default).
(c) OutputFcn – This argument can be assigned any one of the following values: 'odeplot,'odephase2'etc.
It is called by the solver after each time step.
(d) Stats – Displays computational statistics [on | {off}]. When stats is specified as 'on', the performance statistics are displayed.

9.2.2 Steps to Use MATLAB ODE Solvers

The following steps are followed to use ODE solvers for the solution of ordinary differential equations:

1. Write the *n*th order differential equation as a set of `n` first-order ordinary linear or non-linear differential equations, as given in equation 9.2:
2. Write a function subprogram '*func*' to compute the derivative $\dot{\underline{x}}$ which depends on functions f_1, f_2, ---, f_n as given on the RHS of Equation 9.2. This function should return the $\dot{x}$ as a column vector. Save this function subprogram as an M-file with the *name*, *func.m.*
3. Use one of the built in MATLAB ODE solvers e.g. `ode45` or `ode23` etc. to solve the differential equations as per the syntax given above in 9.2.1.
4. Plot and interpret the results.

Example 9.1 Obtain and plot the numerical solution of the following first-order linear differential equation: `dx/dt = -2x`, with initial condition as `x(0) = 1,` for $0 < t < 10$, using `ode45` solver.

(i) Using simple syntax of ODE solver.
(ii) Using full syntax of ODE solver.

Solution:

(i) **Using simple syntax of ODE solver.**
Write a function M-file to compute the derivative $\dot{\underline{x}}$, containing following MATLAB commands, in edit window:

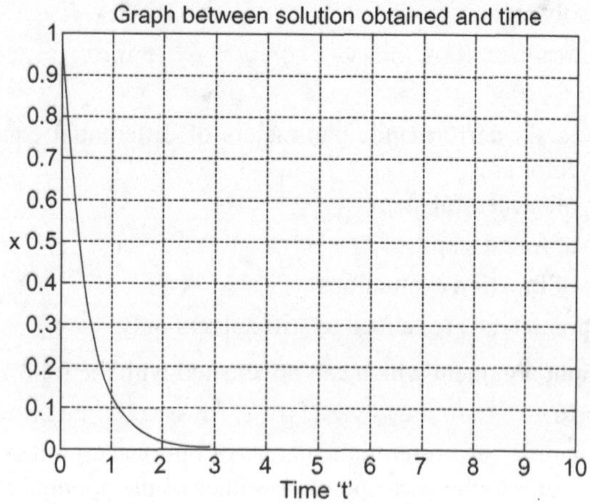

Figure 9.1 Numerical Solution of Example 9.1

```
function xdot = func1(t, x) %function will compute ẋ = -2x
xdot = -2 * x;
```

Save this function func1 as an M-file named as `func1.m`. Type and execute the following commands in the Command Window, to find the solution using `ode45` solver.

```
tspan = [0 10];      %Time span.
x0 = 1;      %Initial value of x
%Use of ode solver for solution.
[t, x] = ode45('func1', tspan, x0); %Use of ode45 solver for solution.
plot(t, x);
grid on;
xlabel('Time t');
ylabel('x');
title('Graph between solution obtained and time');
```

A plot given in Figure 9.1 will be generated, which shows the variation of x with time t.

(ii) **Using full syntax of ODE solver.**

(a) Use the same function m-file i.e. func1.m created above for this example.

(b) Type the following commands in the Command Window, to use full syntax of ode solver and to find the solution using `ode45` solver.:

```
tspan = [0 10];      %Time span.
x0 = 1;              %Initial value of x
options=odeset('reltol',1e-6,'abstol',1e-8,'stats','on','output
Fcn','odeplot')
[t, x,pstats] = ode45(@func1, tspan, x0,odeset); %Use of ode45
solver for solution.
plot(t, x);
```

```
grid on;
xlabel('Time t') ylabel('x');
title('Graph between solution obtained and time');
```

The following result is displayed in the Command Window and the plot obtained is same as already shown in Figure 9.1

Here, the first column gives the values of time instants, second column gives the values of vector x

```
ans =
         0    1.0000
    0.0251    0.9510
    0.0502    0.9044
    0.0754    0.8601
    0.1005    0.8180
    0.2032    0.6659
    0.3059    0.5421
    0.4086    0.4416
    0.5113    0.3598
    0.6093    0.2957
    0.7074    0.2430
    0.8054    0.1997
    0.9035    0.1642
    1.0018    0.1349
    1.1001    0.1108
    1.1984    0.0910
    1.2967    0.0748
    1.3950    0.0615
    1.4933    0.0505
    1.5916    0.0415
    1.6899    0.0341
    1.7882    0.0280
    1.8865    0.0230
    1.9848    0.0189
    2.0831    0.0155
    2.1814    0.0128
    2.2797    0.0105
    2.3780    0.0086
    2.4763    0.0071
    2.5746    0.0058
    2.6729    0.0048
    2.7712    0.0039
    2.8695    0.0032
    2.9678    0.0026
    3.0661    0.0022
    3.1644    0.0018
    3.2627    0.0015
    3.3610    0.0012
    3.4592    0.0010
```

```
3.5575    0.0008
3.6558    0.0007
3.7541    0.0005
3.8524    0.0005
3.9507    0.0004
4.0490    0.0003
4.1556    0.0002
4.2621    0.0002
4.3686    0.0002
4.4751    0.0001
4.5992    0.0001
4.7233    0.0001
4.8474    0.0001
4.9714    0.0000
5.1171    0.0000
5.2628    0.0000
5.4085    0.0000
5.5542    0.0000
5.7297    0.0000
5.9052    0.0000
6.0807    0.0000
6.2563    0.0000
6.4742    0.0000
6.6921    0.0000
6.9101    0.0000
7.1280    0.0000
7.3780    0.0000
7.6280    0.0000
7.8780    0.0000
8.1280    0.0000
8.3780    0.0000
8.6280    0.0000
8.8780    0.0000
9.1280    0.0000
9.3460    0.0000
9.5640    0.0000
9.7820    0.0000
10.0000    0.0000
```

Performance parameters, **pstats** of the solver are:

```
pstats =
    19 successful steps
    0 failed attempts
    115 function evaluations
    0
    0
    0
```

Example 9.2 Solve the following set of linear simultaneous differential equations, for $0 < t < 5$, using ode23 solver and plot the solution.

$$\begin{bmatrix} \dot{x}_1 \\ \dot{x}_2 \end{bmatrix} = \begin{bmatrix} 0 & 1 \\ -2 & -3 \end{bmatrix} \begin{bmatrix} x_1 \\ x_2 \end{bmatrix} + \begin{bmatrix} 0 \\ 1 \end{bmatrix} u$$

$$\underline{x}(0) = \begin{bmatrix} 1 \\ 0 \end{bmatrix} \quad \text{and} \quad u = 1$$

(i) Without using option command
(ii) With using option command

Solution:

(i) **Without using option command**

A function M-file containing following MATLAB commands is written in edit window:

```
function xdot = func2(t, x)
%Function to solve the given set of differential equations.
A = [0 1; -2 -3];
B = [0 ; 1];
u = 1;
xdot = A * x + B * u;
```

Save this function func2 as an M-file with the name func2.m. Type the following commands in the command window to find the solution using ode23 solver:

```
tspan = [0 5];        %The time span
x0 = [1; 0];          %Initial values
%solution using ode23 solver
[t, x, pstats] = ode23('func2', tspan, x0');
[t,x]
plot(t, x(:,1), t, x(:,2));
grid on;
xlabel('Time 't'');
ylabel('x1 and x2');
title('Graph between x1,x2 and time t');
gtext('x1');
gtext('x2');
```

The following result is displayed in the Command Window and its plot is shown in figure window as shown in Figure 9.2:

Here, the first column gives the values of time instants, second and third columns give the values of vectors x_1 and x_2 respectively.

```
ans =
        0    1.0000         0
   0.0001    1.0000   -0.0001
   0.0005    1.0000   -0.0005
   0.0025    1.0000   -0.0025
```

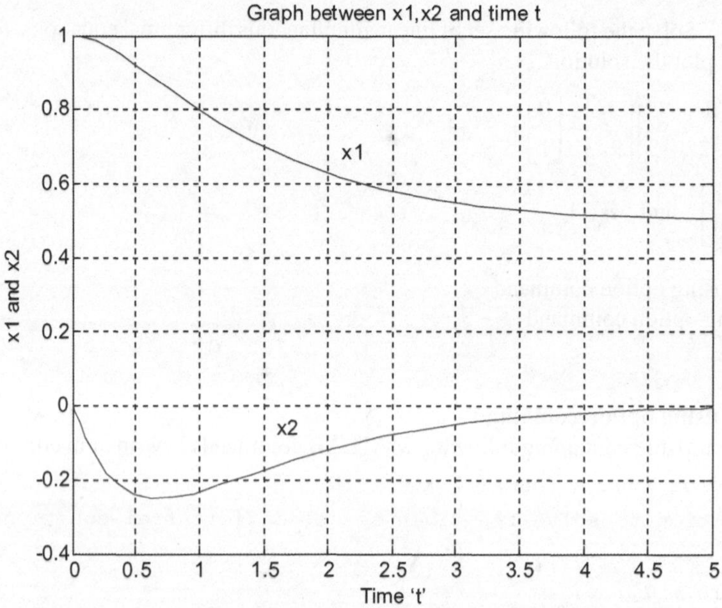

Figure 9.2 Plot of Response x1 and x2 v/s Time t

```
0.0125    0.9999    -0.0122
0.0478    0.9989    -0.0445
0.1036    0.9952    -0.0888
0.1768    0.9869    -0.1358
0.2660    0.9727    -0.1790
0.3705    0.9521    -0.2138
0.4906    0.9249    -0.2375
0.6273    0.8915    -0.2490
0.7821    0.8529    -0.2484
0.9580    0.8102    -0.2367
1.1632    0.7638    -0.2151
1.4098    0.7145    -0.1849
1.7313    0.6615    -0.1461
2.0750    0.6177    -0.1101
2.4187    0.5851    -0.0813
2.8128    0.5581    -0.0565
3.1779    0.5407    -0.0399
3.5337    0.5287    -0.0283
3.8825    0.5203    -0.0201
4.2265    0.5144    -0.0143
4.5670    0.5103    -0.0102
4.9052    0.5073    -0.0073
5.0000    0.5067    -0.0066
```

Performance parameters, pstats of the solver are:

```
pstats =
26    -    successful steps
 1     -    failed attempts
82    -    function evaluations
 0
 0
 0
```

(ii) **With using option command**

Type the following commands to find the solution using ode23 solver and using 'option' command:

```
tspan = [0 5];        %The time span x0 = [1; 0];              %Initial values
%solution using ode23 solver
options=odeset('reltol',1e-6,'abstol',1e-8,'stats','on')
[t,x,pstats]=ode23('func2',tspan,x0,odeset);
[t,x],options
plot(t, x(:,1), t, x(:,2));
grid on; xlabel('Time 't''); ylabel('x1 and x2');
title('Graph between x1,x2 and time t');
gtext('x1');
gtext('x2');
```

The same solution is obtained as shown above.

The values of various options used by the MATLAB solver are:

```
options =
          AbsTol: 1.0000e-08
          BDF: []
          Events: []
          InitialStep: []
          Jacobian: []
          JConstant: []
          JPattern: []
          Mass: []
          MassSingular: []
          MaxOrder: []
          MaxStep: []
          NonNegative: []
          NormControl: []
          OutputFcn: []
          OutputSel: []
          Refine: []
          RelTol: 1.0000e-06
          Stats: 'on'
          Vectorized: []
          MStateDependence: []
          MvPattern: []
          InitialSlope: []
```

Example 9.3 Obtain and plot the solution of the following set of differential equations for $0 \le t \le 8$:

$$\dot{\underline{x}} = \begin{bmatrix} -5 & 0 & -100 \\ 2 & -2 & 0 \\ 0 & 0.1 & -0.08 \end{bmatrix} \underline{x} + \begin{bmatrix} 0 \\ 0 \\ -0.1 \end{bmatrix} (0.2), \qquad \underline{x}(0) = \begin{bmatrix} 0 \\ 0 \\ 0 \end{bmatrix}$$

Solution:

An M-file containing following MATLAB commands is written in edit window:

```
function xdot = func3(t, x)
a = [-5 0 -100; 2 -2 0; 0 0.1 -0.08];
b = [0; 0; -0.10];
u = 0.2;
xdot = a * x + b * u;
```

Save this function func3 as an M-file with the name `func3.m`. Write and run the following program in the Command Window. The plot of solution is obtained in figure window as shown in Figure 9.3.

```
tspan = [0 8];             %Time span
x0 = [0 ; 0 ;0];           %Initial values
%Use of ode solver for solution
[t,x] = ode45('func3', tspan, x0);
plot(t, x(:, 1), t, x(:,2), t, x(:,3)) ;
grid on;
xlabel('Time 't'');
ylabel('x1, x2 and x3');
title('Graph between x1,x2,x3 and time t');
gtext('x1');
gtext('x2');
gtext('x3');
```

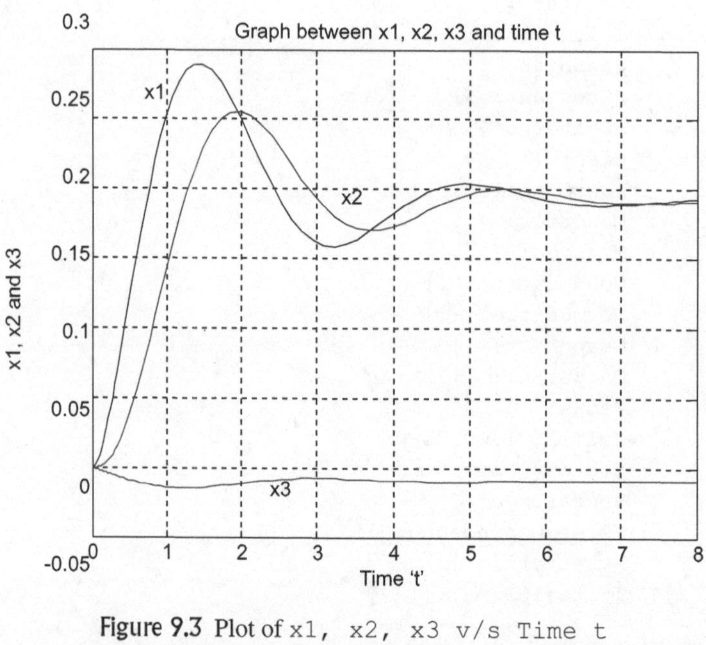

Figure 9.3 Plot of `x1, x2, x3 v/s Time t`

Example 9.4 Obtain and plot the solution of the following set of first order differential equations, which represent Vanderpol's equation:

$$\dot{x}_1 = x_2$$
$$\dot{x}_2 = \mu\,(1 - x_1^2)\,x_2 - x_1$$

For:

(i) $\mu = 1$, using ode45 solver
(ii) $\mu = 1500$, using ode15s solver

Solution

(i) **For $\mu = 1$**

Write a function M-file containing following MATLAB commands in edit window:

```
function xdot=vdpmu(t,x)
xdot=[x(2) ;(1-x(1)^2)*x(2)-x(1)];
end
```

Save this function `vdpmu` as an M-file with the name `vdpmu.m`. Write and run the following program in the Command Window.

```
[t,x]=ode45(@vdpmu,[0 25], [1.5;0]);
plot(t, x(:,1), t, x(:,2))
title('Solution of van der pol Equation, mu= 1');
xlabel('time t')
ylabel('solution,x1,x2 ')
legend('x1', 'x2')
```

The plot of solution is obtained in figure window as shown in Figure 9.4(i).

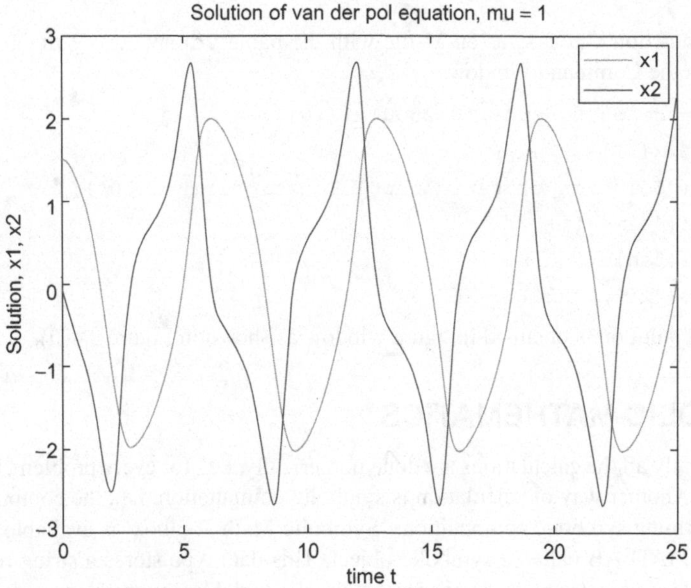

Figure 9.4(i) Plot of `x1,x2 v/s Time`

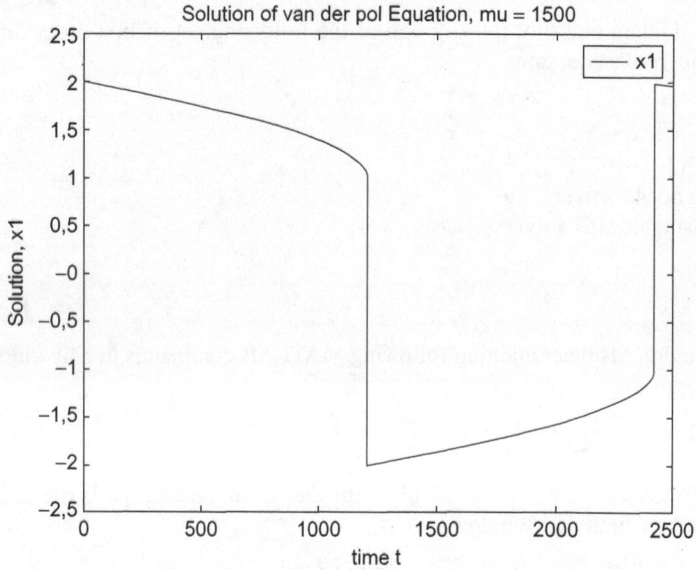

Figure 9.4(ii) Plot of `x1 v/s time`

(ii) **For μ = 1500**

Write an M-file containing following MATLAB commands in edit window:

```
function xdot=vdpmu1(t,x)
xdot=[x(2) ;1500.*(1-x(1)^2)*x(2)-x(1)];
end
```

Save this function `vdpmu1` as an M-file with the name `vdpmu1.m`. Write and run the following program in the Command Window.

```
[t,x]=ode15s(@vdpmu1,[0 2500],[2;0]);
plot(t,x(:,1))
title('Solution of van der pol Equation, mu=1500');
xlabel('time t')
ylabel('solution,x1')
legend('x1', 'x2')
```

The plot of solution is obtained in figure window as shown in Figure 9.4(ii).

9.3 SYMBOLIC MATHEMATICS

In MATLAB, generally all the calculations are done numerically, i.e., for every problem, the answer obtained is a numeric value. Another way of calculation is symbolic computation, i.e., the computation is done symbolically. For performing symbolic computation, 'Symbolic Math Toolbox' is available. This toolbox specifies a data type in MATLAB called a symbolic object. This data type stores a string representation of the symbol. The symbols as objects are used to express symbolic variables, expressions and matrices. The difference in numeric and symbolic computations is illustrated as follows:

9.3.1 Use of Symbolic Mathematics

9.3.1.1 sym and syms Functions

sym Function: `sym` function is used to create a symbolic number, variable and object. The syntax is given as

```
x = sym('x')
```

It creates the symbolic variable with name `x` and stores the result in `x`.

syms Function: `syms` function is shortcut for constructing a number of symbolic objects. The syntax is as given below:

```
syms arg1 arg2 arg3
```

For example,

```
syms a b c
```

It creates three symbolic objects `'a'`, `'b'`, `'c'`. It is similar to three `sym` functions as

```
syms a
syms b
syms c
```

Example 9.5 Find out the square root of `10` (i) when it is expressed as data type 'double' and (ii) when it is expressed as symbolic object.

Solution:

(i) **When expressed as data type double:**

```
a = sqrt(10)
```

The answer obtained is as follows:

```
a =
    3.1623
```

(ii) **When expressed as symbolic object:**

```
a = sqrt(sym(10))
```

The answer obtained is as follows:

```
a =
    10^(1/2)
```

Here, `sym` function is used to convert $\sqrt{10}$ into a symbolic object.

This shows that in case (ii) the result obtained is in symbolic notation without actually calculating the numerical value whereas, the case (i) gives the numeric solution of the problem.

Example 9.6 Find the value of square root of `101`. (i) using numerical computation and (ii) using symbolic computation.

Solution:

(i) **Using numerical computation**

```
a = sqrt(101)
```

The answer obtained is as follows:

```
a =
    10.0499
```

(ii) **When expressed as symbolic object:**

```
a = sqrt(sym(101))
```

The answer obtained is as follows:

```
a =

    101^(1/2)
```

i.e., $101^{1/2}$

Creating Fractions Using Symbolic Objects. In symbolic mathematics, the fractions are operated upon without any final numerical calculation i.e. the result obtained is also in fraction form, whereas in general computation final result is a numerical answer.

Example 9.7 Evaluate:

(i) a = 9/5
(ii) b = 6/5 + 4/3

using (a) numerical and (b) symbolic computation.

Solution:

(i) **a = 9/5**

Numerical computation:

```
a = 9/5
```

gives the following answer:

```
a =

    1.8
```

Symbolic computation:

```
a = sym(9)/ sym(5)
```

gives the answer as

```
a =
    9/5
```

(ii) **b = 6/5 + 4/3**

Numerical computation:

```
a = 6/5+4/3
```

gives the following answer:

```
a =

    2.5333
```

Symbolic computation:

```
a = sym(6)/ sym(5)+ sym(4)/sym(3)
```

gives the answer as

```
a =

    38/15
```

As shown, the evaluation of fractions is done by obtaining a common denominator and then combining the numerator as per normal procedure for rational numbers.

Example 9.8 Illustrate the use of `syms` function for an algebraic equation, x = a^3+3b+c

The commands used are as:

```
syms a b c
x = a^3+3*b+c
```

when executed gives the result as

```
x =
   a^3+3*b+c
```

Here, x is assigned a symbolic expression. If again it is defined as symbolic object using `syms` function then the previous assignment is superseded and x will behave as normal MATLAB variable i.e.

```
syms x
```

Now, x will return the output as

```
x =
   x
```

`syms` function can be used to represent a numeric value in different formats as given in Table 9.2. where x is having any numeric value.

Table 9.2 The Different Formats of `sym` Function

Format	Representation
sym(x, 'f')	Floating point
sym(x, 'r')	Rational number
sym(x, 'e')	Exponential form
sym(x, 'd')	Decimal expansion

Example 9.9 Illustrate the use of `sym` function to represent a given numeric value in different forms.

Suppose, x = 6.2. This can be represented in different formats as follows:

(i) `sym(x, 'f')`

This gives the result as

```
ans =
   '1.8cccccccccccd'*2^(2)
```

(ii) `sym(x, 'r')`

This gives the result as

```
ans =
   31/5
```

(iii) `sym(x, 'e')`

This gives the result as

```
ans =
   31/5+4*eps/5
```

(iv) `sym(x, 'd')`

This gives the result as

```
ans =
   6.20000000000000017763568394002504
```

`d` gives default number of digits after the decimal point i.e., 32.
It can be limited by using function `digits` as

```
digits(5)
```

`digits` function defines the value `d` (here `d` as 5)
Now, `sym(x, 'd')` gives answer as

```
ans =
          6.2000
```

9.3.1.2 subs Function

One of the advantages of Symbolic Mathematics is that once a symbolic expression is defined then the result for different values of variable can be obtained by substituting their values and there is no need to write the expression again and again. For substituting a numerical value in the symbolic expression `subs` function is used. The syntax of `subs` function is given as:

```
subs(x)
subs(x,a)
subs(x,a,b)
```

where x is a symbolic expression,
a is a symbolic or numeric variable or expression, and
b is a symbolic variable or a string representing a variable name.
`subs(x)` substitutes the variables in the symbolic expression x with the values obtained from the workspace.
`subs(x, a)` substitutes the default symbolic variable in x with `a`.
`subs(x,b,a)` substitutes b for a in the symbolic expression x.

Example 9.10 Evaluate the following expression for (i) $a = 2$ (ii) $a = 5$.

$$k = a^2 + 3a$$

Solution:

(i) $a = 2$

The following commands are used:

```
syms a;
k = a^2+3*a;
subs(k,2)
```

The result is as

```
ans =
        10
```

(ii) $a = 5$

The following commands are used:

```
syms a;
k = a^2+3*a;
subs(k, 5)
```

The result is as

```
ans =
        40
```

Example 9.11 Let $y = 3a^2+4b$. Evaluate y for $a = 2$.

Solution:

The commands used are given as follows:

```
syms a b
y = 3*a^2 + 4*b;
subs(y,a,2) % a = 2
```

The result obtained is as

```
ans =
     12+4*b
```

> **Programming Tip 9.2:** In case, particular variable is specified for substitution in an expression consisting of more than one variable, then the variable which is closest to x in the alphabet is substituted for the given numerical value.

Let us take the Example 9.11 with the function

```
subs(y,2)
```

Then, the result is as

```
ans =
     3*a^2+8
```

In this case, variable `b` is substituted as `b = 2` instead of variable `a`, because the letter `b` is closer to `x` than `a` in the alphabet.

9.3.1.3 findsym Function

List of symbolic variables that are present in a symbolic expression can be obtained using `findsym` function. The syntax is given as

```
findsym(s)
findsym(s,k)
```

The function `findsym(s)` gives the list of all symbolic variables in the symbolic expression *s* and the function `findsym(s, k)` gives `k` symbolic variables which are closest to the alphabetic letter `x`.

Example 9.12 To illustrate the use of `findsym` function.

Let a symbolic expression be given by:

`x = 3u + 4v² + 6a`. Obtain the list of symbolic variables in this expression.

The commands used are as

```
syms u v a;
x = 3*u+4*v^2+6*a;
findsym(x)
```

The result obtained is:

```
ans =
     a, u, v
```

`findsym(x,2)` gives the result as:

```
ans =
     v,u
```

9.3.2 Calculus Using Symbolic Mathematics

The different calculus operations, such as differentiation, integration and limits, can be performed upon the symbolic expressions and are illustrated hereafter.

9.3.2.1 Differentiation

The functions used to find differentiation of a symbolic expression say x is given as:

```
diff(x)
diff(x,n)
diff(x,n,v) or diff(x,v,n)
```

where

x is the given symbolic expression and
n is the order of the derivative.
v is a variable w.r.t. which derivative is to be evaluated

An expression is differentiated with respect to default variable in case only one variable is present in an expression. If the expression consists of more than one variable then the default variable will be the letter closest to x in the alphabet unless it is specified in the function.

Example 9.13 Let `x = sin(t)`. Illustrate the use of `diff` function.

The program is written as

```
syms t
x = sin(t)
```

(i) `diff(x)`

This command takes derivative of x with respect to variable t as there is only one variable, that is, t in the expression. This command gives the result as

```
ans =
      cos(t)
```

(ii) `diff(x,2) %2 represents the order of the derivative.`

This command takes second derivative of x with respect to t.

```
ans =
      -sin(t)
```

Example 9.14 Let `a= sin (wt)`. Differentiate 'a' using different forms of `diff` function, where w and t are symbolic variables.

Solution:

The commands used are as

```
syms w t
a = sin(w*t)
```

(i) `diff(a)`

As there are two symbolic variables w and t in the expression a and it is not specified in diff function that with respect to which variable differentiation has to be carried out. In this case, default variable is selected as per rule which states that the default variable will be one which is closest to x in the alphabet. Hence, in this case it will be variable w. So, the result will be as

```
ans =
      cos(w*t)*t
```

(ii) diff(a,2)

This gives the second derivative of expression a with respect to w

```
ans =
    -sin(w*t)*t^2
```

(iii) diff(a,t)

In this case, as specified, derivative of a is taken with respect to variable t and the result obtained is:

```
ans =
    cos(w*t)*w
```

(iv) diff(a,t,2)

This command gives the second derivative of a with respect to variable t.

```
ans =
    -sin(w*t)*w^2
```

simplify **Function.** In some cases, the expression obtained after a calculus operation, is not in the simplified form. So, to make such an expression simple, the simplify function is used. This function makes a complicated expression simple.

Example 9.15 Suppose, $a = x^n$. Differentiate 'a' with respect to 'x'.

The commands used are as:

```
syms x n;
a = x^n;
diff(a)
```

The result obtained is as given below:

```
ans =
     x^n*n/x
```

This is not a simplified term. To make it simpler, simplify function is used as follows:

```
simplify(diff(a))
```

The result obtained is as given below:

```
ans =
     x^(n-1)*n
```

Example 9.16 Differentiate expression given below with respect to t.

$A = [\cos(w*t)\ \tan(w*t);\ \sin(w*t)\ \sec(w*t)]$

Solution:

The commands used are as

```
syms w t;
A = [cos(w*t) tan(w*t); sin(w*t) sec(w*t)]
diff(A,t)
```

The result obtained is as

```
A =
     [ cos(w*t) tan(w*t)]
     [ sin(w*t) sec(w*t)]
ans =
     [ -sin(w*t)*w, (1+tan(w*t)^2)*w]
     [ cos(w*t)*w, sec(w*t)*tan(w*t)*w]
```

Example 9.17 Obtain second derivative of following expression:

$B = [\sec x \quad x; \tan x \quad x^2]$

Solution:

The commands used are as

```
syms x
B = [ sec(x) x; tan(x) x^2 ]
diff(B,2)
```

The response obtained is as

```
B =
        [ sec(x) x]
        [ tan(x) x^2]
ans =
        [ sec(x)*tan(x)^2+sec(x)*(1+tan(x)^2) 0]
        [ 2*tan(x)*(1+tan(x)^2) 2]
```

Example 9.18 Calculate dy/dx for y = sin(2x)

Solution:

The following MATLAB commands are used:

```
syms x;
y = sin(2*x);
diff(y)
```

The function **diff(y)**, will differentiate y with respect to x and the answer will be displayed:

```
ans =
        2*cos(2*x)
```

Example 9.19 Let an expression z = e^x sin x, find

(i) dz/dx
(ii) d^2z/dx^2

Solution:

(i) **The commands used are as**

```
syms x
z = exp(x) * sin(x);
diff(z)
```

The following answer is displayed:

```
ans =
        exp(x)*sin(x)+exp(x)*cos(x)
```

(ii) **To find the second derivative, the following command can be used:**

```
diff(z,2)
```

The answer obtained is as

```
ans =
        2*exp(x)*cos(x)
```

Programming Tip 9.3: To find the derivative of a constant, the constant has to be defined as a symbolic expression.

Example 9.20 To find the derivative of a constant, the constant has to be defined as a symbolic expression. Suppose, `y = 5,` find `dy/dx`.

Solution:

The commands used are as

```
y = sym('5');
diff(y)
```

The following answer will be displayed:

```
ans =
      0
```

9.3.2.2 Integration

To find the integration of symbolic expression, the following function is used:

```
int(x)
int(x,t)
```

where

x is symbolic expression whose integral is to be obtained and
t is a variable for integration.

As discussed in the previous article, if the variable with respect to which integration is to be obtained is not specified, then the default variable will be the letter closest to x in the alphabet.

Example 9.21 Find the integration for following:

(i) `a = cos(x)`
(ii) `a =` x^2
(iii) `a = 3xt +4`t^2 `(w.r.t. t)`

Solution:

The following commands are used to evaluate the above problems:

(i)
```
syms x
a = cos(x);
int(a)
```

The result obtained is as follows:

```
ans =
     sin(x)
```

(ii)
```
syms x
a = x^2;
int(a)
```

The result obtained is as follows:

```
ans =
       1/3*x^3
```

(iii)
```
syms x t
a = 3*x*t +4*t^2
int(a,t)    %Integrate w.r.t. t
```

The result obtained is as follows:

```
ans =
     3/2*x*t^2+4/3*t^3
```

9.3.2.3 Definite Integration

To perform the definite integration following function is used:

```
int(x,a,b)
int(x,t,a,b)
```

where

x is an expression to be integrated,
a and b are the lower and upper limit of integration respectively, and
t is a variable for integration.

In function **int(x,a,b)** no variable with respect to which integration is to be obtained is specified; hence, the default variable for integration will be the letter closest to x in the alphabet.

The function **int(x,t,a,b)** is used to find integration of expression x with respect to t and limits of integration are a and b.

Example 9.22 Find the integration of following expressions for given limits:

(i) A = x^3 ; limits (0,2)
(ii) A = $3x^2$+5x; limits (0,3)
(iii) A = 1/(3x); limits (1,3)

Solution:

The commands used are as

(i)
```
syms x
A = x^3;
int(A, 0,2)    %Limits are 0 and 2
```

The result obtained is as follows:

```
ans =
     4
```

(ii)
```
syms x
A = 3*x^2+5*x;
int(A, 0,3)    %Limits are 0 and 3
```

The result obtained is as follows:

```
ans =
     99/2
```

(iii)
```
syms x
A = 1/(3*x);
int(A, 1,3)    %Limits are 1 and 3
```

The result obtained is as follows:

```
ans =
     1/3*log(3)
```

Example 9.23 Evaluate the definite integrals for the following examples:

(i) $y = \int_0^1 x^5 dx$

(ii) $y = \int_0^1 e^x dx$ *dx

(iii) $y = \int_0^2 (\log x) dx$

(iv) $y = \int_0^{\pi/2} \sin(t) dt$

(v) $y = \int_0^{\pi} \sin(t) dt$

Solution:

The following MATLAB commands are used to solve the above problems:

(i)
```
syms x
y = int(x^5, 0,1)
```

The result obtained is as follows:

```
y =
     1/6
```

(ii)
```
syms x;
y = int(exp(x),0,1)
```

The result obtained is as follows:

```
y =
     e-1
```

(iii)
```
syms x;
y = int(log(x),0,2)
```

The result obtained is as follows:

```
y =
     2*log(2)-2
```

(iv)
```
syms t;
f = sin( t )
y = int(f, t, 0, pi/2)
%int(f, t, to, tf) integrates the function f(t)from t = to to t = tf.
```

```
%here to = 0 and tf = pi/2.
```

The result of these commands is as follows:

```
y =
     1
```

(v)
```
syms t;
f = sin( t )
y = int(f, t, 0, pi),
%int(f, t, to, tf) integrates the function f(t)from t = to to t = tf.
%here to = 0 and tf = pi.
```

The result of these commands is as follows:

```
y =
   2
```

9.3.2.4 `solve` Function

This function is used to find the solution of an algebraic expression or equation. The syntax for this function is given as follows:

```
solve(f)
solve(f,a)
```

where

`f` is an algebraic expression and
a is variable for which solution has to be obtained.

Example 9.24 Find the solution for following expressions:

(i) f = ax²+3xb
(ii) f = 4x²+3a+2

Solution:

The commands for the execution of given functions are

(i)
```
syms a x b;
f = a*x^2+3*x*b;
solve(f)
```

The result obtained is as

```
ans =
         0
   -3*b/a
```

Here, in this case the solution is obtained for the variable x.

(ii)
```
syms a x;
f = 4*x^2 +3*a+2;
solve (f)
```

The result obtained is as

```
ans =
      1/2*(-3*a-2)^(1/2)
     -1/2*(-3*a-2)^(1/2)
```

Here also, the solution is obtained for the variable x.

Example 9.25 Find the solution for following expressions for variable c:

(i) `f = 5x^3+4ax+3c`
(ii) `f = 12x^2 +c +1`

Solution:

The commands for the given functions are as

(i)
```
syms a x c;
f = 5*x^3+4*a*x+3*c;
solve(f,c)      %solving the expression for c
```

The result obtained is as

```
ans =
     -5/3*x^3-4/3*a*x
```

(ii)
```
syms x c;
f = 12*x^2 +c +1;
solve(f,c)      %solving the expression for c
```

The result obtained is as

```
ans =
     -12*x^2-1
```

In case, instead of expressions, the equations have to be solved using `solve` function, then these are to be enclosed in single quotes, as shown below:

```
f = solve('4x2 + 3ax = 5x + 7a')
```

To get the solution for several algebraic equations, the `solve` function is used as follows:

```
[a b] = solve(equation1, equation2)
```

Programming Tip 9.4: In case, instead of expressions, the equations have to be solved using `solve` function, then these equations are to be enclosed in single quotes.

Example 9.26 Evaluate the following equation b:

`ax^3 + bx + c = 0`

Solution:

The commands used are as follows:

```
syms a b m
solve('a*x^3 + b*x + c = 0;'b')
```

The result obtained is given below:

```
ans =
   -(a*x^ 3 + c)/x
```

9.3.3 Simplification Functions

Any function can be represented in the following different forms:

1. Polynomial form: `y = x³+ 4x² +3x+1`
2. Factored form: `y = (x+3)(x−1)(x+7)`
3. Nested or Horner form: `y = 4+(3x+6(x−1))x²`

In MATLAB, there are different functions that transform one representation of a function to another simpler representation. These functions are described as

(a) `collect`
(b) `expand`
(c) `horner`
(d) `factor`

(a) **`collect` function**

This function collects the coefficients with same power. The syntax is given as

```
collect(y)
collect(y,a)
```

where

y is the given algebraic function and
a is specified variable in the expression with respect to which operation has to be done.

Example 9.27 Illustrate the use of `collect` function for following expressions:

(i) `y = x²+5x(x+1)+x`
(ii) `y = (x²+3x+1)(x+4)`
(iii) `y = (ax²+3b)(a+1)`, for variable a

Solution:

The commands used and the results obtained for these expressions are as

(i)
```
syms x
y = x^2+5*x*(x+1)+x;
collect(y)
ans =
      6*x^2+6*x
```

(ii)
```
syms x
y = (x^2+3*x+1)*(x+4);
collect(y)
ans =
      4+x^3+7*x^2+13*x
```

(iii)
```
syms a b x
y = (a*x^2+3*b)*(a+1);
collect (y, a) %'a' as a variable for operation.
ans =
      x^2*a^2+(3*b+x^2)*a+3*b
```

(b) **expand function**

This function is used to represent or simplify the product terms in the **form of sums**. The syntax is given as

```
expand (y)
```

where y is the given expression.

Example 9.28 Illustrate the expand function for following expression:

(i) y = $(x^2+1)(x+3)$
(ii) y = (5x+1)(x-1)(3x+2)
(iii) y = exp(a+b)

Solution:

The commands used and the results obtained are as

(i)
```
syms x;
y = (x^2+1)*(x+3);
expand(y)
ans =
     x^3+3*x^2+x+3
```

(ii)
```
syms x;
y = (5*x+1)*(x-1)*(3*x+2);
expand(y)
ans =
      15*x^3-2*x^2-11*x-2
```

(iii)
```
syms a b;
y = exp(a+b);
expand(y)
ans =
      exp(a)*exp(b)
```

(c) **horner function**

This function is used to transform the given expression to a **nested form**. The syntax is as given below:

```
horner (y)
```

where y is the given expression.

Example 9.29 Illustrate the horner function for following expressions:

(i) y = $x^3 + 7x^2 + 5x + 4$
(ii) y = $x^5 + 6x^2 + 2x + 1$
(iii) y = $4x^4 + x^3 + 3x - 7$

Solution:

The commands used and the results obtained for these expressions are as follows:

(i)
```
syms x
y = x^3+7*x^2+5*x+4
```

```
horner(y)
ans =
        4 +(5+(7+x)*x)*x
```

(ii)
```
syms x
y = x^5+6*x^2+2*x+1
horner(y)
ans =
        1+(2+(6+x^3)*x)*x
```

(iii)
```
syms x;
y = 4*x^4+x^3+3*x-7;
horner(y)
ans =
   -7+(3+(1+4*x)*x^2)*x
```

(d) **`factor` function**

This function is used to make factors of polynomial with rational coefficients. If the expression cannot be factorized the result will be function itself.

Example 9.30 Illustrate the `factor` function for following expressions:

(i) $y = 4x^3+3x^2 +1$
(ii) $y = x^2+1$
(iii) $y = x^3+2x+1$

Solutions:

The commands used and the results obtained for these expressions are as:

(i)
```
syms x
y = 4*x^3+3*x^2+1;
factor (y)
ans =
        (x+1)*(4*x^2-x+1)
```

(ii)
```
syms x
y = x^2+1
factor (y)
ans =
        x^2+1
```

Note: The expression cannot be factored.

(iii)
```
syms x
y = x^3+2*x+1
factor (y)
ans =
        x^3+2*x+1
```

Note: The expression cannot be factored.

9.3.4 Limit of an Expression

`limit(F,x,a)` takes the limit of the symbolic expression `F` as `x` → `a`.
`limit(F)` evaluates the limit of symbolic expression `F` as `x` → `zero`. It uses $a = 0$, as the limit point.

Example 9.31 Evaluate the limits of following expressions:

(i) limit $\sin(x)/x$ as $x \to 0$
(ii) limit $(x + 4)$ as $x \to 0$
(iii) limit $(x + 4)$ as $x \to 1$

Solution:

(i)
```
syms x
limit(sin(x)/x)
ans =
1
```
(ii)
```
syms x
limit(x+4)
ans =
4
```
(iii)
```
syms x
limit((x+4),x,1)
ans =
5
```

9.3.5 Symbolic Summation

The command:

```
symsum(f)
```

evaluates the sum of a series, where expression *f* defines the terms of a series, with respect to the default symbolic variable. The command:

```
symsum(f,x)
```

evaluates the sum of a series, where expression *f* defines the terms of a series, with respect to the symbolic variable *x*. The value of the variable *x* changes from 0 to *x* - 1. The command:

```
symsum(f,a,b)
```

evaluates the sum of a series, where expression *f* defines the terms of a series, with respect to the default symbolic variable `defaultVar` determined by `symvar`. The value of the default variable changes from *a* to *b*.

Example 9.32

(i) The following commands:
```
syms k
symsum(k)
will  return the following answer:
ans =
      k^2/2 - k/2
```
(ii)
```
syms k, n
symsum(k,0,n)
```
will return the following answer:

```
ans =
        (n*(n + 1))/2
```

(iii)
```
syms k
symsum(k^2,0,10)
```
will return the following answer:
```
ans =
    385
```

9.3.6 Taylor Series Eaxpansion

Command: `taylor(f)` returns the fifth order Taylor polynomial approximation of f about the point $x = 0$ (also known as fifth order Maclaurin polynomial).

Example 9.33

(i) The following commands:
```
syms x
taylor(exp(-x))
```
will return the following answer:
```
ans =
        x^4/24 - x^5/120 - x^3/6 + x^2/2 - x + 1
```

(ii)
```
syms x
taylor( sin(x))
```
will return the following answer:
```
ans =
x^5/120 - x^3/6 + x
```

(iii)
```
syms x
taylor(exp(x))
```
will return the following answer:
```
ans =
         x^5/120 + x^4/24 + x^3/6 + x^2/2 + x + 1
```

SUMMARY

This chapter is divided in two parts. Firstly, the solution of a set of Ordinary Differential Equations is discussed and then symbolic mathematics is introduced and different functions used are illustrated with examples. The complete chapter can be summarized as follows:

- The available MATLAB ODE solvers are discussed. These are `ode45, ode23, ode113, ode15s, ode23s, ode23t, ode23tb` and `ode15i`.
- The steps involved for using these solvers for the solution of ordinary differential equations in MATLAB are discussed.
- The use of `sym` or `syms` functions in the symbolic mathematics has been illustrated.
- The representation of symbolic expressions has been described using illustrations.
- The `subs` function is used to evaluate the symbolic expression for given numerical values.

- The different calculus operations using symbolic mathematics are discussed. `diff` and `int` functions used to obtain differentiation and integration of symbolic expressions are discussed in detail.
- The special functions such as `simplify` and `solve` are used along with symbolic expressions to simplify and evaluate the expressions.
- Furthermore, the functions `collect, expand, horner` and `factor` are used to represent a given expression in different forms.
- The functions limit, symsum and taylor are used to evalute the limit of a symbolic expression, to obtain the sum of a series and to obtain the 5th order Taylor series expansion respectively.

List of ODE Solvers

`ode45`	An explicit one-step Runge-Kutta (fourth to fifth order) solver.
`ode23`	An explicit one-step Runge-Kutta (second to third order) solver.
`ode113`	A multi-step Adams solver of varying order (1st to 13th order).
`ode15s`	An implicit multi-step numerical differential solver of varying order (first to fifth order).
`ode23s`	An implicit one-step solver of order two.
`ode23t`	An implicit, one-step trapezoidal rule using a free interpolant.
`ode23tb`	An implicit trapezoidal rule followed by backward differential of order two.
`ode15i`	A solver of varying order (first to fifth order) used for solving fully implicit differential equations.

List of Commands

Command/Function	Description
`sym`	Construct symbolic numbers, variables and objects.
`syms`	Short-cut for constructing symbolic objects.
`subs`	Replaces variable in symbolic expression with value.
`diff`	Gives differentiation of given expression.
`simplify`	Simplifies the symbolic expression.
`int`	Gives the integration of the expression.
`solve`	Solves the given equation.
`collect`	Collect the coefficients with same powers.
`expand`	Writes each element of a symbolic expression as a product of its factors.
`horner`	Transforms each element of given expression into its nested representation.
`factor`	Returns the factorization of given expression.
`limit`	Evaluates the limit of a symbolic expression.
`symsum`	Evaluates the sum of a series.
`taylor`	Returns the fifth order Taylor series expansion.

EXERCISES

9.1 Calculate the values of `y` at all points with `step size h = 0.1` for the interval `t = 0 to 2`, if

$$\frac{dy}{dt} = 12t^2 + 8t + 4 \quad \text{and} \quad y(0) = 2$$

9.2 Obtain the solution of the following differential equation for the interval $t = 0$ to 2

$$\frac{dy}{dt} = y(e^t - 1) \qquad \text{with} \quad y(0) = 1$$

9.3 Solve the following simultaneous differential equations:

$$\frac{dx_1}{dt} = x_2 - t, \quad \frac{dx_2}{dt} = x_1 - t$$

and the initial conditions are $x_1(0) = 1, x_2(0) = 1$

9.4 Calculate `y(0.8)` for the following differential equation:

$$\frac{dy}{dt} = t - 0.1y^2$$

with $y(0) = 1$

9.5 Solve the following set of simultaneous differential equations:

$$\frac{dx_1}{dt} = -\frac{1}{2}x_2 + \frac{x_1 x_2}{20} \quad , \quad \frac{dx_2}{dt} = x_1 + \frac{x_1 x_2}{10}$$

with $x_2(0) = 5, x_1(0) = 10$

9.6 Obtain the differentiation of the following functions:

(i) $u = 2x^5 + 6x^2 - 9x$
(ii) $v = 3 \cos x + 5x$
(iii) $w = [x \cos x]$
(iv) $y = 4 \sin x + 6x \cos x$
(v) $z = x^5 + 8x^3 - 5 \cos 3x$

9.7 Obtain the integration of the following expressions:

(i) $u = 3x^3 - 5x^2 + 3$
(ii) $v = 6x^4 + 9x^3 + 4x$
(iii) $w = 4x^3 + \cos 2x + 3$
(iv) $y = 4e^{-xt} + \sin 3t$
(v) $z = 6 \cos 3x + x \sin x$

9.8 Obtain the definite integration of the following expression for given limits:

(i) $u = x^5 - 3x^2 + 5$; limits are (3, 5)
(ii) $v = 3 \cos x + \sin 2t$ w.r.t. x; limits are (0, pi)
(iii) $w = 7x^3 \sin a + 3t^2 \sin 2x$ w.r.t. x; limits are (0, 2pi)
(iv) $y = 4a^2e^{-x} - 8a^3 \sin at$ w.r.t. a; limits are (0, 3)
(v) $z = 9xe^x$; limits are (0, 5)

9.9 Obtain the solution for the following expressions:

(i) $u = 3x^2 - 4ax$
(ii) $v = 9ax^2 + 3bx + 4a$ w.r.t. a
(iii) $w = 2a^2 + 5ax^2 - 6$ w.r.t. a
(iv) $y = 4a^2e^{-x} - 8a^3$ w.r.t. a
(v) $z = 6x^4 + 5ax^3 - 3a^2 + 4x$ w.r.t. x

9.10 Using `collect` function convert the following expression into polynomial form:

(i) $y = 4x^3 + 6(x^2 + 1)(x + 4) + 6$
(ii) $y = 5(x^2 + 2x + 1)(x + 4) + 6(x - 4)$
(iii) $y = ax^2 + 4(ax + 3)(x^2 + a) + b$ w.r.t. a
(iv) $y = 5ax^3 + 6(x + 3a)(a^2 + 1) + 4x^2$ w.r.t. a

9.11 Using `expand` function convert the following expression into factored form:

(i) $y = (x^3 + 2x^2)(3x^2 - 4)$
(ii) $y = (8x^2 + 1)(x + 3)(x^2 - 1)$
(iii) $y = (ax^2 + 1)(2x^2 + 4)$
(iv) $y = (9x + 1)(3x + 1)(4x^2 - 1)$

9.12 Using `horner` function convert the following expression into nested form:

(i) $y = 5x^2 + 4x + 1$
(ii) $y = 7x^5 + 2x^4 + 3x^2 + 1$
(iii) $y = 9x^3 + 2x - 1$
(iv) $y = 4x^5 - 7x^2 + 3$

9.13 Factorize the following expressions using `factor` function:

(i) $y = 3x^3 + 13x^2 + 18x + 8$
(ii) $y = x^4 + 3x^3 - x^2 - 15x - 20$
(iii) $y = x^5 - 5x^4 + x^3 + 11x^2 + 6$
(iv) $y = x^4 + 2x^3 - 15x^2 - 68x - 160$

9.14 Evaluate the following limits:

(i) $\lim_{x \to 0} (\sin x + \cos x)$

(ii) $\lim_{x \to 0} (e^x + e^{-x})$

9.15 Obtain the Taylor series expansion of:

(i) $\cos x$
(ii) e^x

CHAPTER

10

Simulink® Basics

LEARNING OBJECTIVES

- Introduction to Simulink® environment.
- Create a model of a dynamic system in the Simulink window.
- Simulate a dynamic system represented in block diagram form and observe the results of simulation.
- Import/export data from/to Workspace and Simulink window.
- Simulate a dynamic system represented in state-space form.
- Simulate a non-linear dynamic system.
- Obtain a state-space model from Simulink model using '`linmod`' function.
- Create sub-systems of Simulink model and mask it.
- Writing S-Functions

10.1 INTRODUCTION

Simulink® is a software package and is a graphical extension of MATLAB® for modelling, simulating and analysing a variety of dynamical systems under a Graphical User Interface (GUI) environment. In Simulink, models of the systems are drawn on screen as block diagrams. It includes a comprehensive block library for creating standard components such as sinks, sources, connectors, linear and non-linear components. To make a model for any particular system, the components required for the model are selected from the Library Browser and are then dragged and dropped in the Simulink window using the mouse. It is integrated with MATLAB and data can be easily transferred between the programs.

10.2 STARTING Simulink

Simulink can be started by using any one of the following methods:

1. It can be started from the MATLAB command prompt by writing the following command in the Command Window:

   ```
   simulink and pressing 'Enter' key
   ```

2. It can also be started by clicking on the icon (Simulink Library icon) on the MATLAB desk top, as shown in Figure 10.1.

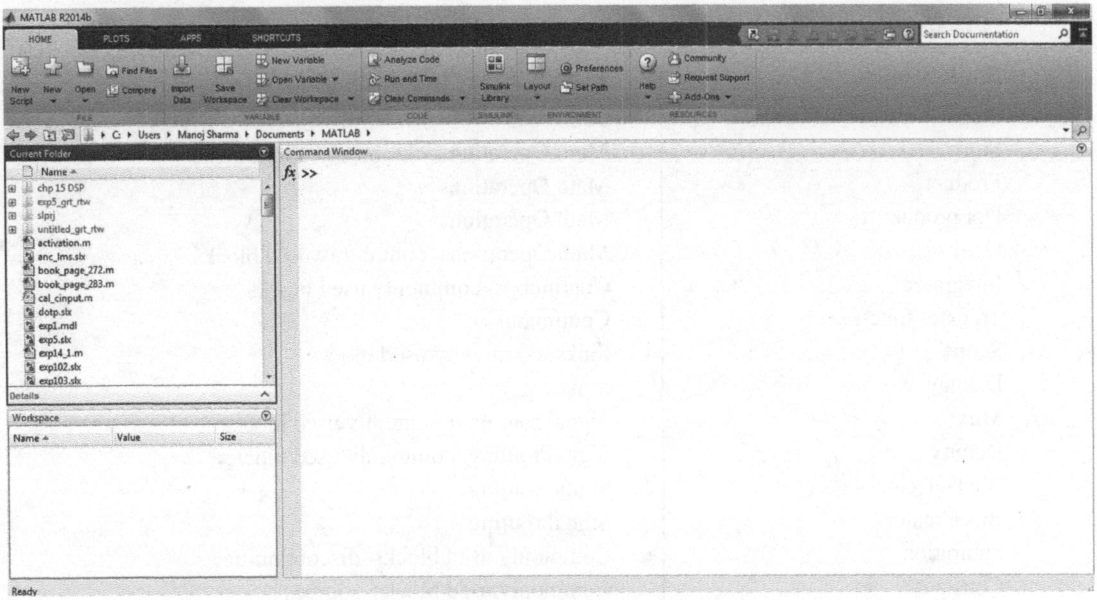

Figure 10.1 MATLAB Desktop

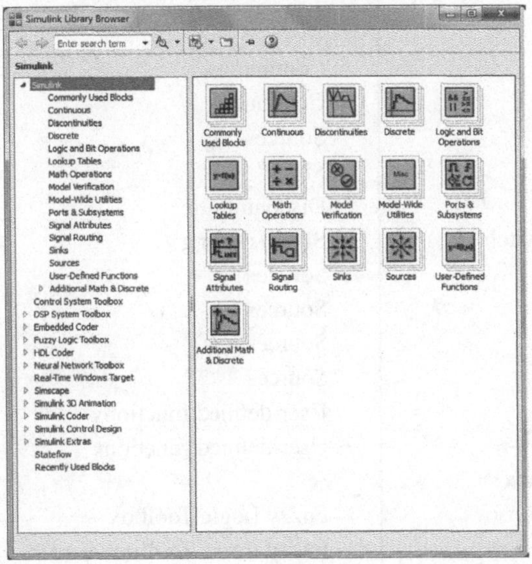

Figure 10.2 Simulink Library Browser Window

When the Simulink software starts, Simulink Library Browser window will pop up, showing different libraries as shown in Figure 10.2. Each library contains a number of blocks of a particular category. To see the different blocks that are available in any particular block library, the user has to expand it by clicking on it or by double clicking the corresponding icon.

A list of commonly used blocks is given in Table 10.1.

Table 10.1 Commonly Used Blocks and Their Location in Simulink Library Browser

Block Name	**Block Library in the Simulink Library Browser**
Step	Sources
Sum	Math Operations, commonly used blocks
Product	Math Operations
Dot product	Math Operations
Gain	Math Operations, commonly used blocks
Integrator	Continuous, commonly used blocks
Transfer function	Continuous
Scope	Sinks, commonly used blocks
Display	Sink
Mux	Signal routing, commonly used blocks
Demux	Signal routing, commonly used blocks
Bus Selector	Signal routing
Bus Creator	Signal routing
Saturation	Commonly used blocks, discontinuities
Constant	Commonly used blocks, sources
To Workspace	Sinks
X–Y graph	Sinks
LTI system	Control System Toolbox™
Derivative, $\frac{du}{dt}$	Continuous
State space	Continuous
In1	Sources
Out1	Sinks
Relay	Discontinuities
Switch, multiple switch	Signal routing
Clock	Sources
From Workspace	Sources
Sine wave input	Sources
Ramp input	Sources
S-Function	User-defined functions
S-Function Builder	User-defined functions
Fuzzy Logic Toolbox™	
Membership functions	Fuzzy Logic Toolbox
Fuzzy Logic Controller	Fuzzy Logic Toolbox
Fuzzy Logic Controller with rule viewer	Fuzzy Logic Toolbox
Neural Network Toolbox™	
Control system	Neural Network Toolbox
Net input function	Neural Network Toolbox
Processing functions	Neural Network Toolbox

(*Continued*)

Table 10.1 *Continued*

Block Name	Block Library in the Simulink Library Browser
Transfer functions	Neural Network Toolbox
Weight factors	Neural Network Toolbox
DC voltage source	sim power systems library
Series RLC branch	sim power systems
Voltage measurement	sim power systems
Current measurement	sim power systems

10.2.1 Opening Simulink Model

Depending upon whether an existing model is to be opened or a new model is to be created, following procedure can be adopted.

10.2.1.1 Opening an Existing Model

Opening a model in Simulink is similar to the standard method of opening a file in MS Windows® environment. This can be done by any one of the following methods:

1. Click on the icon on the toolbar of Simulink library browser.
2. Select Open from the File menu in the Library Browser
3. Press Ctrl+O key

'Open' dialog box will appear. Enter filename of the desired model and click the 'Open' button. Existing model will be opened.

10.2.1.2 Creating a New Model

This is also similar to the standard procedure of creating a new file in MS Windows environment. This can be done by any one of the following ways:

1. Click on the New File icon on the toolbar of Simulink Library Browser.
2. Select New Model from File menu of Simulink Library Browser
3. Press Ctrl+N key on the key board

An 'untitled' window will appear on the screen as shown in Figure 10.3.

10.3 Simulink MODELLING

This section describes how a given dynamic system can be modelled using Simulink. Once a new untitled Simulink window appears as shown in Figure 10.3, the desired model can be made by selecting the required blocks from the Simulink Library Browser window. Any block library can be detailed by clicking on it and the desired block can be selected. The block can be moved and added to the model window by clicking on it and dragging it to the desired location.

The desired block has to be selected from the particular category and then dragged and dropped into the model window.

Different blocks are then connected as per the model requirement by arranging them and drawing connecting lines from the output terminal of one block to the input terminal of the other block.

The various steps taken to make a complete model are as follows:

1. Collecting blocks to create a model
2. Modifying block parameters

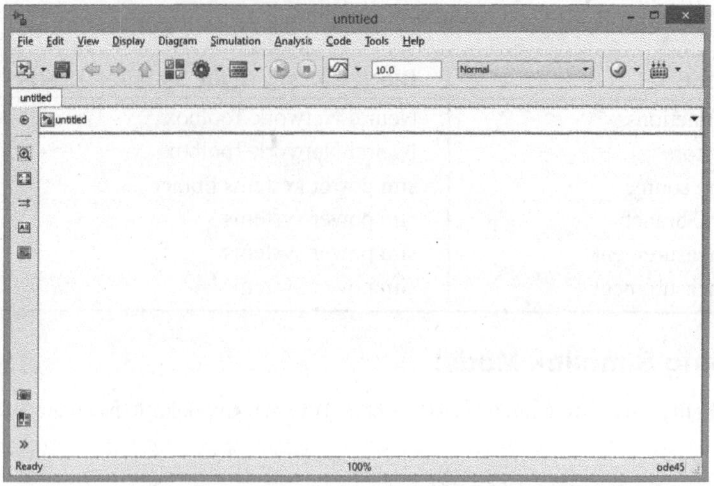

Figure 10.3 Untitled Simulink Window

3. Labelling blocks
4. Connecting blocks
5. Labelling the signal lines
6. Saving the model

The above steps are explained with the help of an example of a system model described by a transfer function. For better understanding, the complete model is shown in Figure 10.4 before developing it.

> **Programming Tip 10.1:** Some blocks are available in more than one block library.

Example 10.1 Draw a complete model of the dynamic system, whose behaviour is described by the block diagram shown in Figure 10.4.

Solution: The model shown in Figure 10.4 is an example of a simple control system, using proportional and integral controller to generate the control signal for the given plant represented by its second-order transfer function.

The different blocks required to create this model, their block libraries, and their purpose are given in Table 10.2.

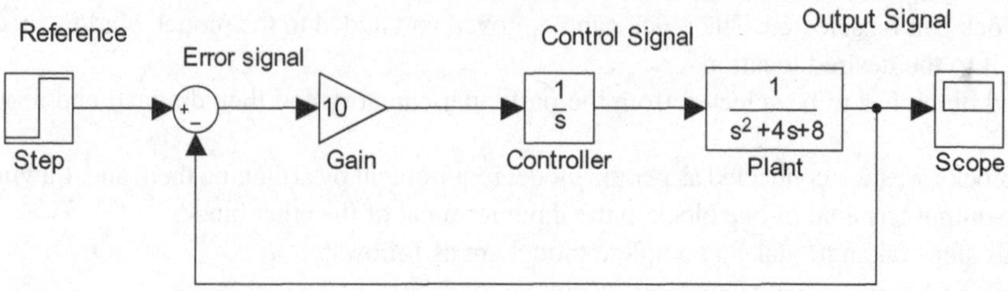

Figure 10.4 Simulink Model for Illustration

Table 10.2 Blocks Used in Example 10.1, Corresponding Block Library and Purpose

Block Name	Block Library	Purpose
Step	Sources	Input signal
Sum	Commonly used blocks, Math Operations	Addition
Gain	Commonly used blocks, Math Operations	Represents proportional controller (here)
Controller (integrator)	Commonly used blocks, Continuous	Integral control action
Scope	Commonly used blocks, sinks	Displays output
Transfer function (Plant/system)	Continuous	Transfer function of the plant/system

The input signal used is a step signal and 'Sum' block is used to add the (negative) feedback. The 'Gain' block represents the proportional controller. '1/s' in the controller block represents integral control action. The response is observed on the scope which displays the output just like an oscilloscope. The gain can be varied to obtain the desired output response.

To create a Simulink block diagram, select 'new' from the file menu. This will provide a **new untitled window** for building the model of the system. The different steps required to make the model are as follows.

10.3.1 Collecting Blocks to Create a Model

Once a new untitled Simulink model window is opened for creating a new model, the following steps are followed to obtain the blocks from the Simulink Library Browser.

- *Expand the block library*: In the Simulink Library Browser, a large number of blocks are available in the different block libraries. To view the different blocks available in block library, it is expanded by clicking over it. On clicking any block library, a complete list of blocks will be seen.
- *Selecting the desired block*: From the list of blocks displayed in a block library, the desired block is selected. In case, it is not available in a particular block library, then it is checked in other block libraries till it is found. (See Table 10.2)
- *Drag and drop block in the model window*: Once the desired block is chosen, it is dragged and dropped in new model window using the mouse or keyboard (shift+arrow keys).

The model window for the given example, with the different blocks dragged and dropped into it, is shown in Figure 10.5.

10.3.2 Modifying Block Parameters

The blocks given in the Simulink Library Browser are in their standard form. These can be modified to make them suitable for a problem under consideration. The steps followed are given as follows:

- Double click on 'step' block. Its dialog box will pop up as shown in Figure 10.6. Set step time to, say 1 and set the initial and the final values depending upon the step size—in this case, it is equal to 0 and 20, respectively and sample time to 0.5. Click **OK** button.
- Similarly, open 'Sum' block by double clicking on it. Since it is desired to subtract second input, enter '+−' into the list of sign field, click **Apply** and **OK** buttons.

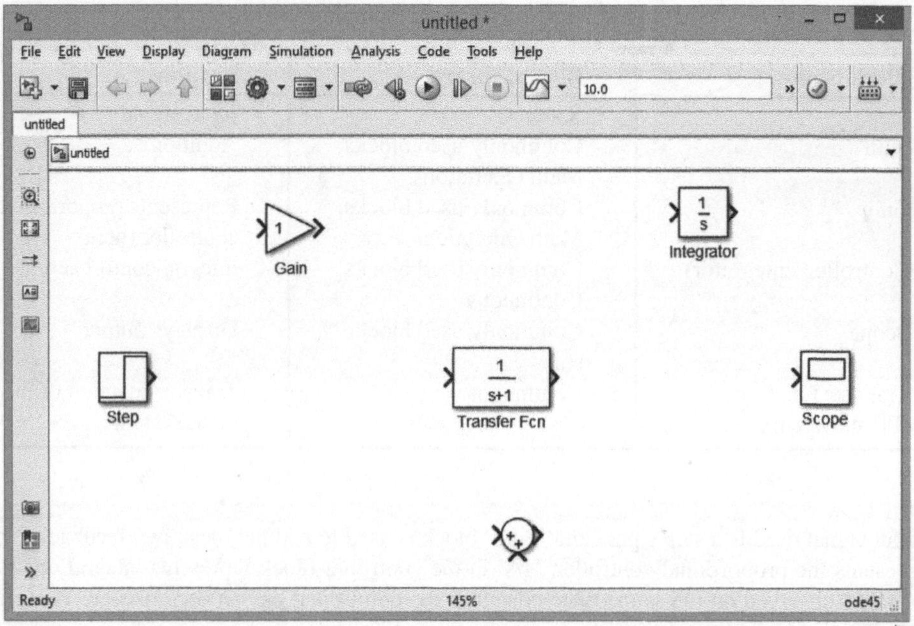

Figure 10.5 Blocks Dragged and Dropped in the Model Window

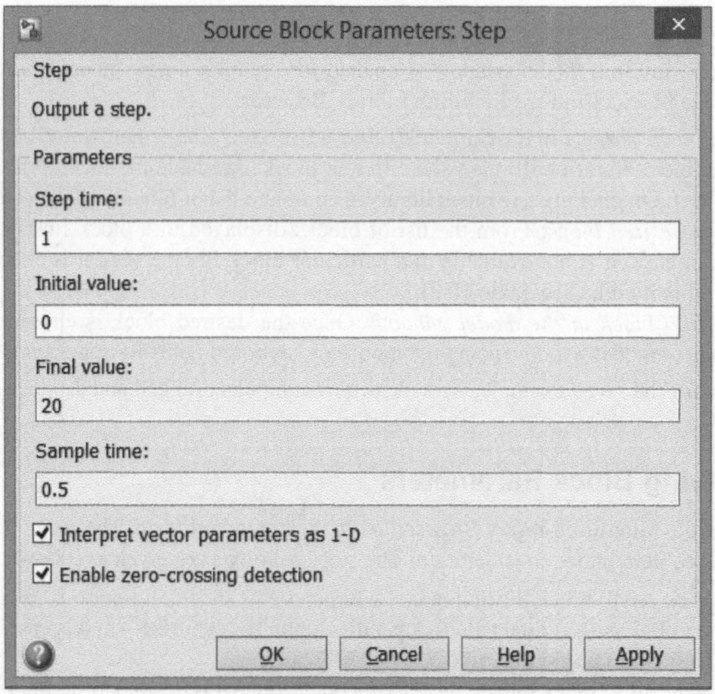

Figure 10.6 Pop-up Dialog Box of Step Block

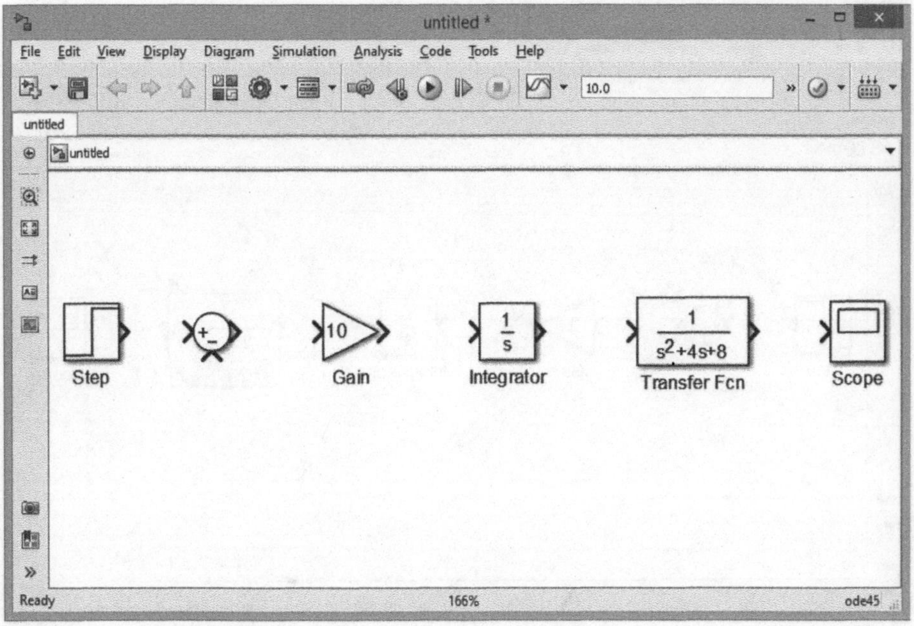

Figure 10.7 Modified Parameters of Blocks for Desired Model

- Double click on 'Gain' block. Enter the proper gain value, say, 10 in this case, and close the 'Gain' dialog box.
- Double click the 'Transfer Fcn' block. Change the denominator parameters to [1 4 8] and leave the numerator parameter as [1]. Close the dialog box.
- Leave the integrator block as such.

> **Programming Tip 10.2:** A block can be rotated by 180° by clicking on the 'Flip Block' (Ctrl+I) option and rotated by clicking 'Rotate Block' (Ctrl+R) option in 'format' menu on the menu bar.

After assigning parameters and aligning the different blocks, the model will appear as shown in Figure 10.7.

10.3.3 Labelling Blocks

The blocks are indicated by standard labels such as 'Transfer Fcn' and 'integrator'. However, in any particular model it may be desired to assign them some other label such as 'plant' and 'controller' to make them more understandable to the user. To change the label the following steps are taken:

- Click on the standard label written as 'Transfer Fcn', a box and an editing cursor will appear as shown in Figure 10.8.
- Delete the existing label and type in the new label 'Plant' in the box. Click anywhere outside the box to finish editing. Similarly, change integrator label to 'controller'. Now the model will appear as shown in Figure 10.9.

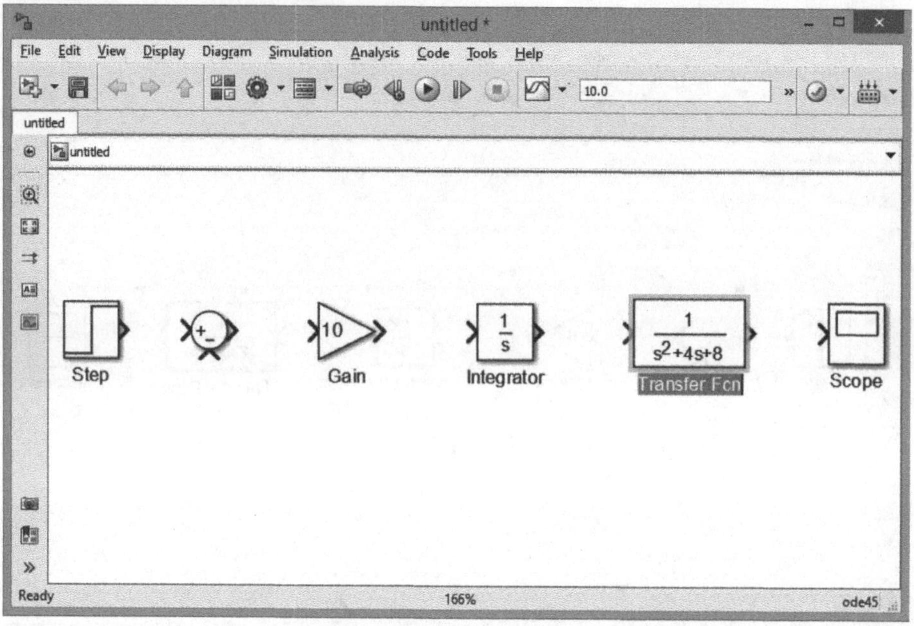

Figure 10.8 Selecting Blocks for Changing Label

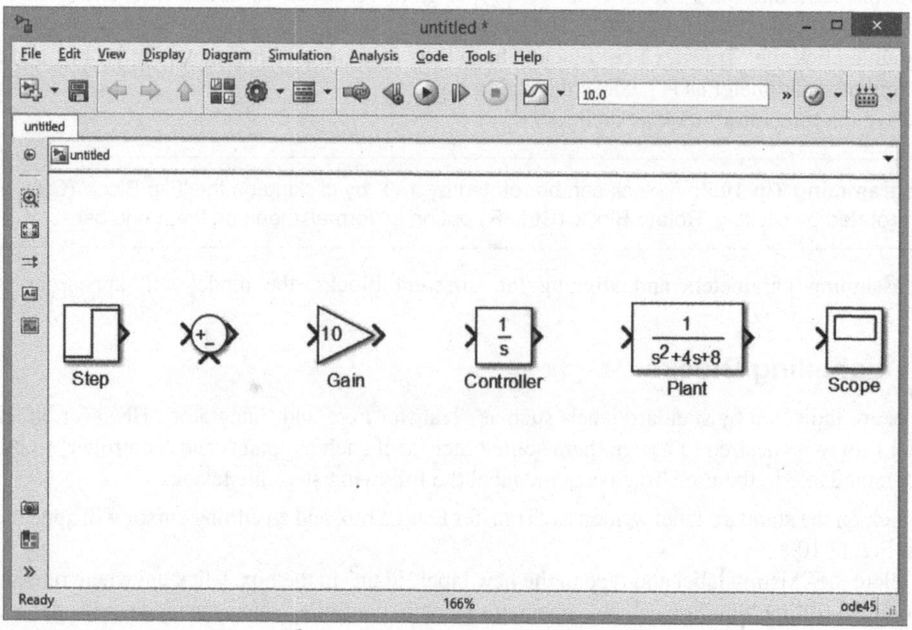

Figure 10.9 Blocks with Changed Labels

10.3.4 Connecting Blocks

After obtaining, modifying and labelling the blocks, these are connected with one another. The steps are as given below:

- Each block has input and/or output ports (as per its property) indicated by **angle brackets** on the sides.
- Drag the mouse pointer from the output port of the first block 'Step' to the input port of 'Sum' block. A dashed line will appear connecting these two blocks till the mouse button is held down and the pointer will change to double lined cross hairs as soon as it reaches the proper destination. Release the mouse button. The two blocks will get connected by a solid line with an arrow head. The arrow indicates the direction of signal flow. The resulting line should have a filled arrowhead as shown in Figure 10.10.

Programming Tip 10.3: If the arrowhead is not filled, the line is not connected to anything.

- If the arrowhead is not filled, as shown in Figure 10.11, it means it is not connected to anything.
- In case line is connected to wrong block, it can be deleted and redrawn. To delete a line (or any other object) click on it, i.e. select it and then press the delete key.
- Similarly, other connecting lines are drawn to connect different blocks as shown in Figure 10.12.

10.3.4.1 Shortcut for Connecting Two Blocks

Select the block whose output port is to be connected. Press Ctrl key and click the block whose input port is to be connected. A line connecting the two blocks will be drawn.

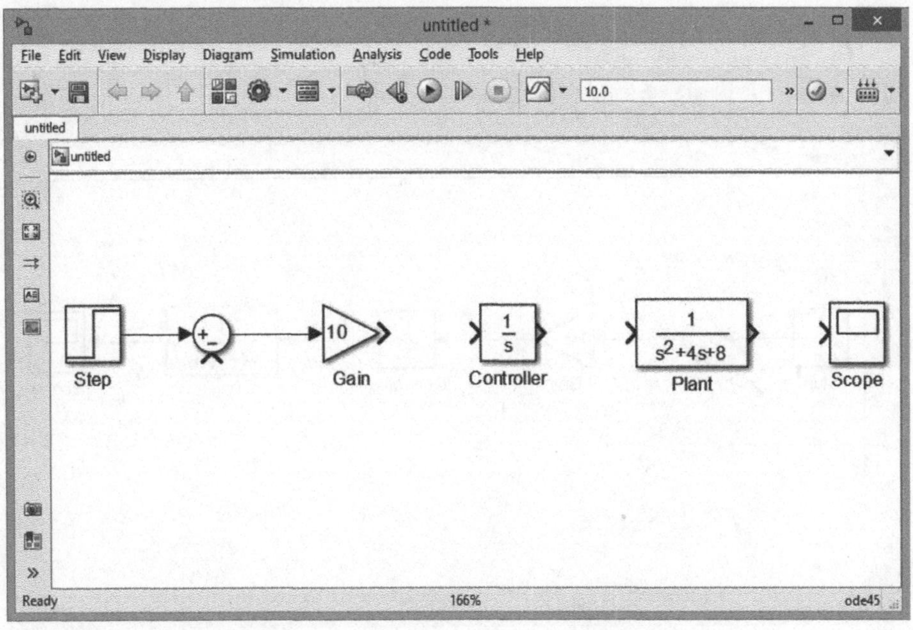

Figure 10.10 Connected Line between Two Blocks

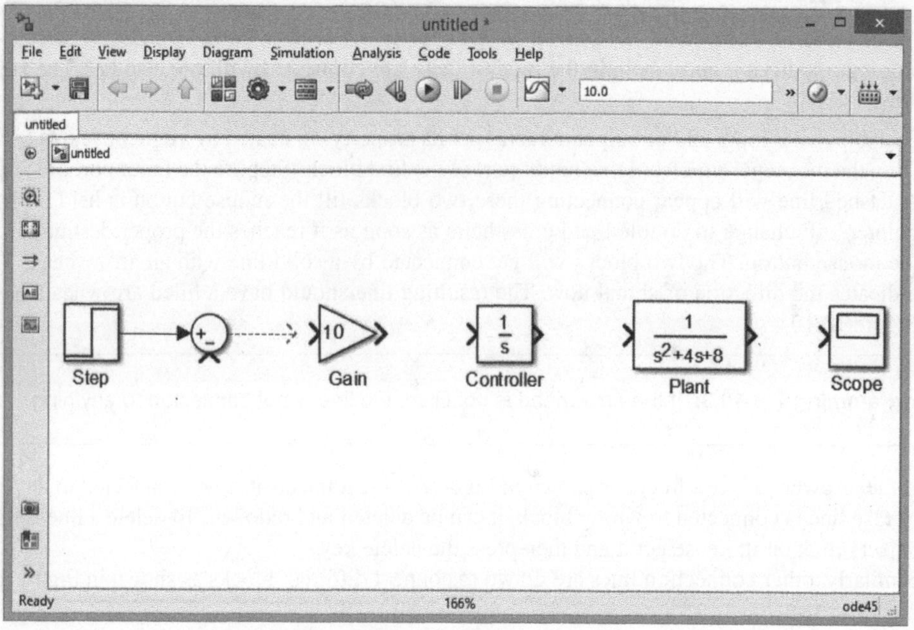

Figure 10.11 Unconnected Lines

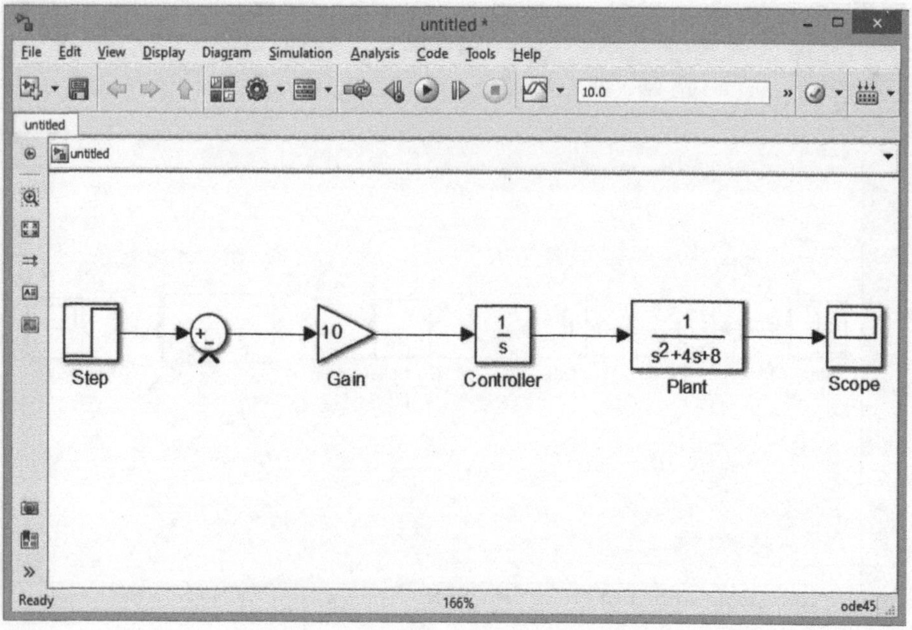

Figure 10.12 Connected Blocks of the Model

10.3.4.2 Drawing a Branching Line

- The line showing feedback signal connecting the output of the 'Plant' to the negative input of 'Sum' block is different from other lines in two ways:
  - First, this line loops around and does not follow the shortest path. So, it needs to be drawn in several stages.
  - Second, there is no output terminal to start from, so the line has to be tapped from an existing line.
- To tap the output line, position the mouse pointer on the output line at desired point, press and hold the Ctrl key and drag the mouse pointer till the destination block is reached. In this particular case, start just from right-hand side of 'Plant' block and drag a line until 'Sum' block is reached. A dashed line with an open arrowhead will appear as shown in Figure 10.13.
- The open arrowhead of this incomplete line can be treated as an output terminal. Then draw the line from this end to the input terminal of 'Sum' block as in Figure 10.14.
- Finally, the blocks are realigned to appear in proper order such that lines connecting them are straight.

10.3.5 Labelling Signal Lines

For better understanding, different labels are provided to the signals in the model. To provide label anywhere in the model, double click at the desired location. A blank textbox with a blinking cursor as shown in Figure 10.15 will appear. The desired label can be typed in the box.

Similarly, the different signal lines can be indicated by names as error signal, control signal and output signal, as shown in Figure 10.16.

A complete final model has now been created and is shown in Figure 10.16.

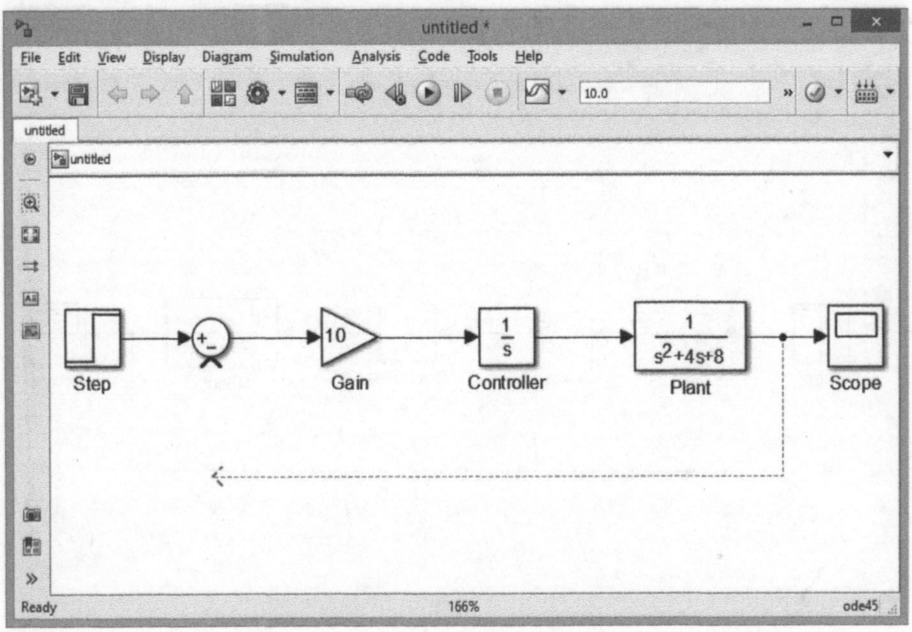

Figure 10.13 Tapping of Existing Line

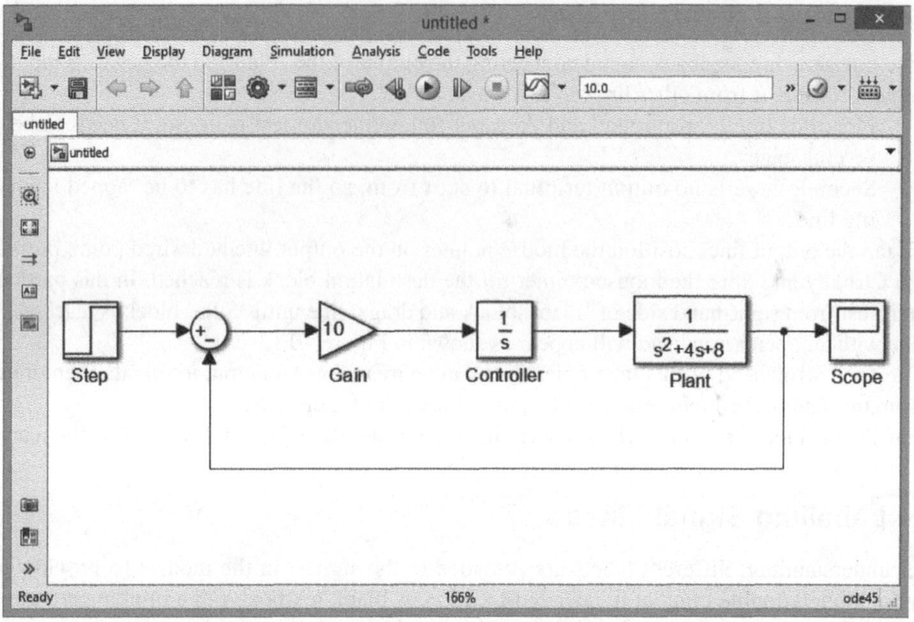

Figure 10.14 Connecting Tapped Feedback Signal Line

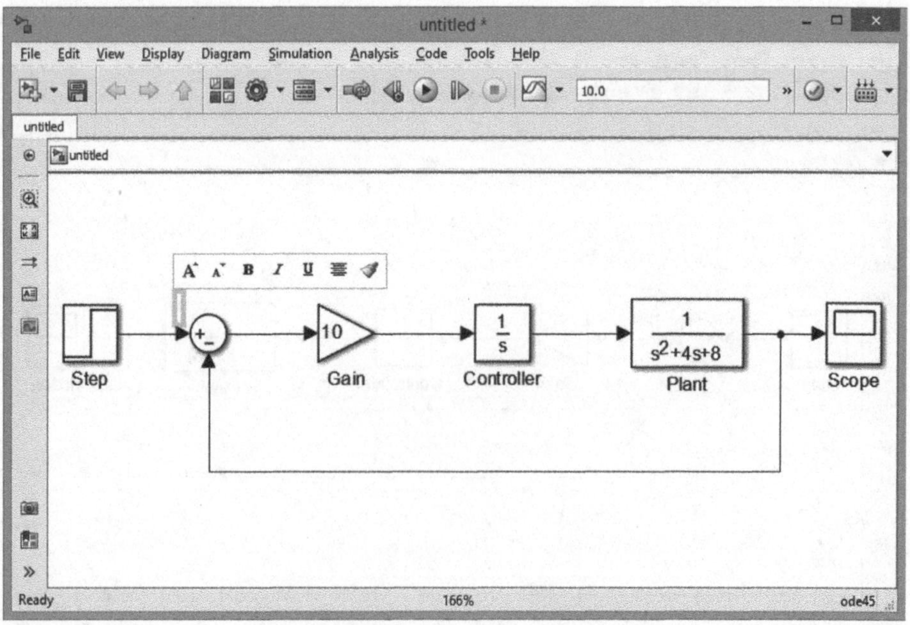

Figure 10.15 Labelling of Signal Lines

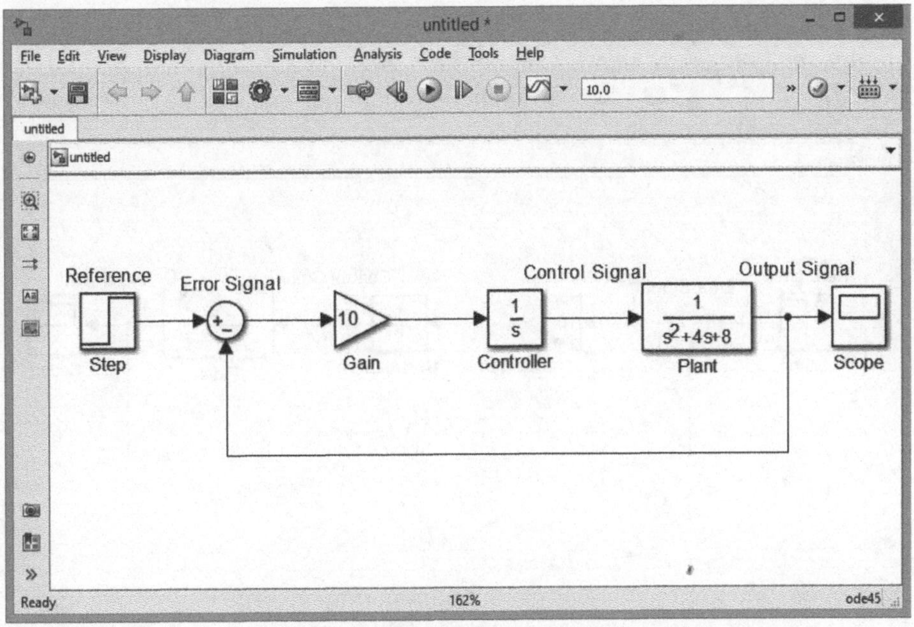

Figure 10.16 The Final Model

10.3.6 Saving the Model

To save a new model, the same procedure is used as in standard Windows desktop. Any one of the following methods can be used to save a model:

- Select 'save as' from the File menu in the model window, type the desired name of the model in the name field, and specify the location where the model is to be saved. Click **save**. The model will be saved.
- Click save icon in the toolbox for saving the model.

The saved model named as 'exp1' is shown in Figure 10.17. The name of the saved model appears on the top left hand corner of the model window.

10.4 SOLVERS

Simulink simulates a dynamic system by computing its states at successive time steps over a specified time span, using information provided by the model. The process of computing the successive states of a system from its model is known as solving the model. The different problems require different methods for solution. Simulink provides a set of programs, known as **solvers**, which can be selected from the 'solver pane' of the **Configuration Parameters Dialog Box**, each suitable for solving a specific type of problem/model.

Simulink solvers fall into following basic categories:

1. Fixed-step continuous solvers
2. Variable-step continuous solvers
3. Fixed-step discrete solvers
4. Variable-step discrete solvers

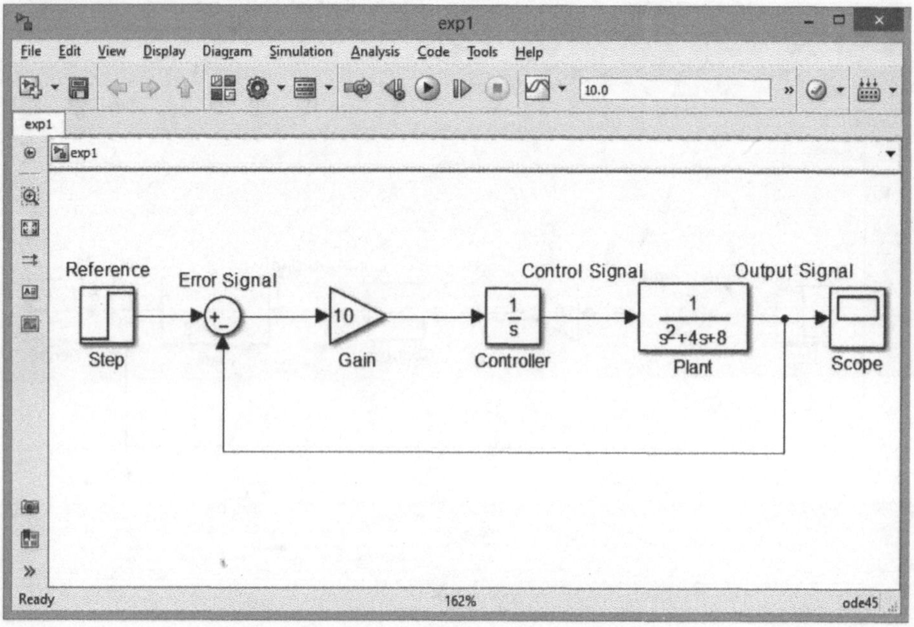

Figure 10.17 The Saved Model Named as 'exp1'

10.4.1 Fixed-Step Continuous Solvers

These solvers compute a model's continuous states at equally spaced time steps, the fixed step size remains constant throughout the solution. The solvers use numerical integration to compute the continuous states of a system from the state derivatives. Each solver uses a different integration method.

A list of options of integration methods for fixed step solver is as follows:

1. Discrete (no continuous states)
2. ode 5, the Dormant–Prince Formula
3. ode 4, the fourth-order Runge–Kutta formula
4. ode 3, the Bogacki–Shampine formula
5. ode 2, Heun's method or improved Euler formula
6. ode 1, Euler's method
7. ode 14x, extropolation

ode stands for ordinary differential equations.

10.4.2 Variable-Step Continuous Solvers

These solvers decrease or increase the simulation step size to increase accuracy depending upon whether continuous states of a system are changing rapidly or slowly. A variable step solver reduces the step size, when a model's state is changing rapidly and increases the step size, when the system states are changing slowly. The options of integration methods for variable step solver are listed below:

1. Discrete (no continuous states).
2. ode45 is based on an explicit Runge-Kutta (4,5) formula. This is a default solver used by Simulink.

3. ode23 is also based on an explicit Runge-Kutta (2,3) pair of Bogacki and Shampine.
4. ode113 is a variable-order Adams–Bashforth–Moulton solver.
5. ode15s is a variable-order solver based on the numerical differentiation formulas (NDFs).
6. ode23s is based on a modified Rosenbrock formula of order 2.
7. ode23t is an implementation of the trapezoidal rule.
8. ode23tb is an implementation of an implicit Runge-Kutta formula with a first stage i.e. a trapezoidal rule and a second stage i.e. a differentiation formula of order 2.

The other solvers are not discussed for simplicity.

10.5 SIMULATING A MODEL

After the block diagram is completed, the model can be simulated to visualize and analyse the results. Running a Simulink model is a two-step process. First, simulation parameters such as the solver options (used to solve the model), the start and stop time of simulation, and the step size etc. are specified using **Configuration Parameters** Dialog Box and then the simulation is started. The simulation can be paused or stopped while it is running.

10.5.1 Specifying Simulation Parameters

The following steps are followed for specifying or changing the simulation parameters:

- Open the model whose simulation parameters are to be specified.
- Select 'Configuration Parameters' option from the **Simulation** menu of the model window.
- The Configuration Parameters Dialog Box will pop up as shown in Figure 10.18. One of the several options such as Solver and Data Import/Export can be selected.
- If solver option is selected, this dialog box will display the current simulation settings, that is, start time, stop time and solver options, for the model as shown in Figure 10.18. These settings may be changed as per the requirements of the problem to be solved.

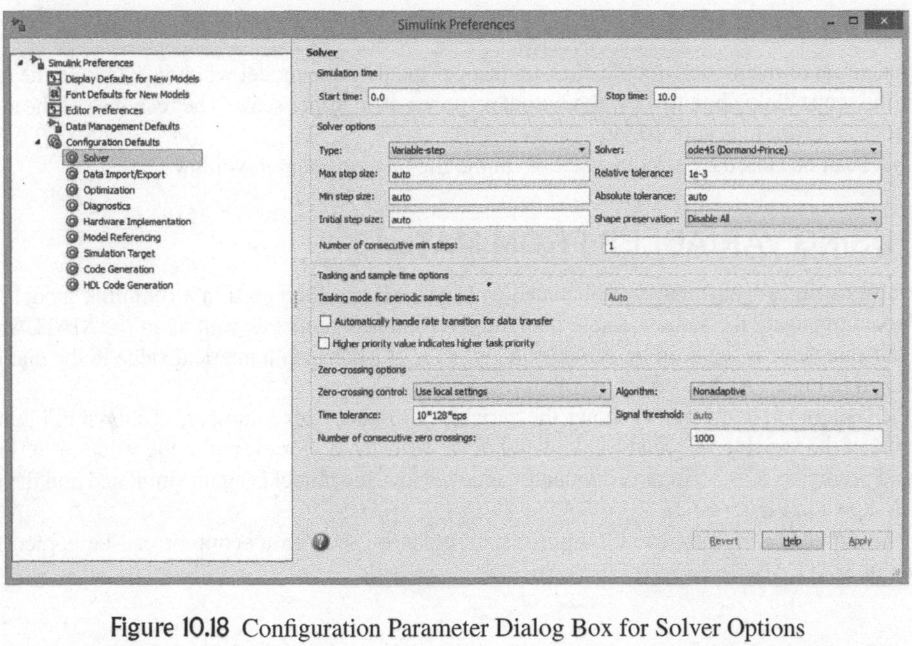

Figure 10.18 Configuration Parameter Dialog Box for Solver Options

- Click 'Apply' and 'OK' button of the dialog box to apply the changes made in the simulation parameters and close the dialog box.

10.5.2 Starting a Simulation

Once a model is completed and its parameters are configured, then the simulation can be started by any one of the following methods:

- Select 'Start simulation' option from Simulation menu on menu bar to run the simulation.
- Click run icon button on the toolbar of the model window.
- Press 'Ctrl+T' key on the keyboard.

Programming Tip 10.4: The model window must be active before starting a simulation.

Simulink starts the simulation at the start time specified and continues till the simulation reaches the final time specified in the solver option. Completion of simulation will be indicated by a beep sound. Progress of the simulation is shown at the bottom of the model window.

10.5.3 Pausing or Stopping Simulation

A simulation that is running can be paused or stopped by selecting the appropriate button from the simulation menu.

Selecting the **pause** button will stop the simulation temporarily and change the button display to 'continue'. Paused simulation can be resumed again by selecting 'continue'.

Execution can be terminated by clicking the **stop** button in the toolbar of model window. Simulation can also be started and stopped by entering Ctrl+T from the keyboard.

10.5.4 Viewing Output

To view the output of the model, double click on 'scope' block in the model window. Click on the **autoscale** icon in the scope dialog box to view the output response on a proper scale. The response of the system for Example 10.1 is shown in Figure 10.19.

The model can be closed by selecting 'close' in the file menu of model window.

10.6 USING VARIABLES FROM MATLAB

Some variables such as 'gain' may be calculated in MATLAB and then used in a Simulink model. This can be done by simply using the same variable name in the Simulink model as well as in the MATLAB. In this example, the gain value is replaced by variable '*K*' in place of a constant numerical value in the dialog box of Gain as shown in Figure 10.20.

Now, the Gain block in the model shows the variable '*K*' rather than a number, as shown in Figure 10.21.

The value of the variable '*K*' can be calculated in the MATLAB. For example, the value of '*K*' is entered at command prompt as $K = 15$ in the command window. Now, the model is again simulated and the response obtained is shown in Figure 10.22.

When the simulation is completed, output response can be seen on a **scope** or can be copied from the Workspace of MATLAB.

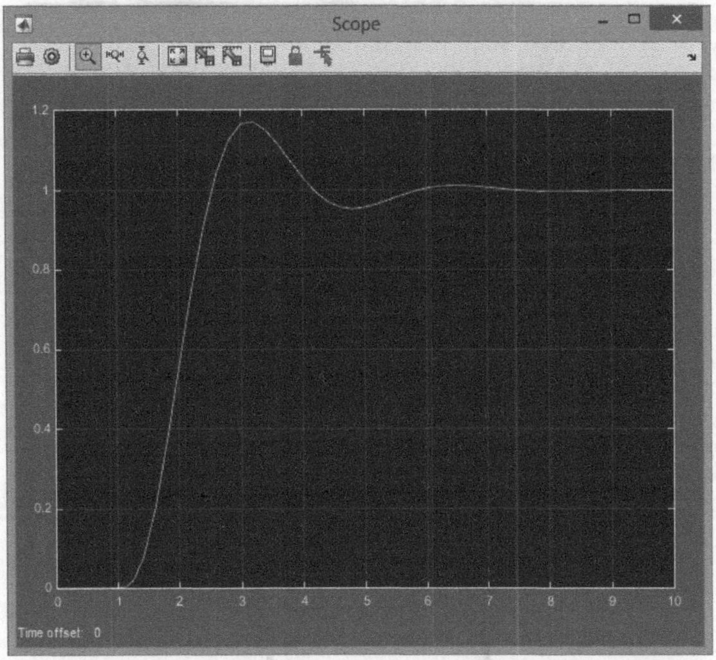

Figure 10.19 Response of the Model of Example 10.1

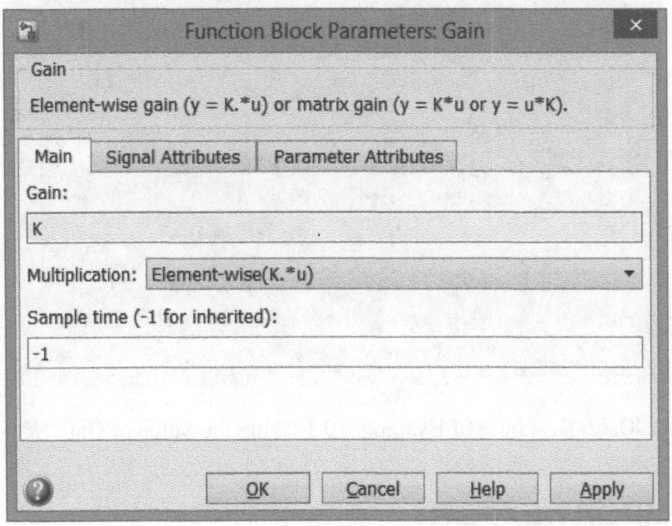

Figure 10.20 Gain Variable Defined as '*K*'

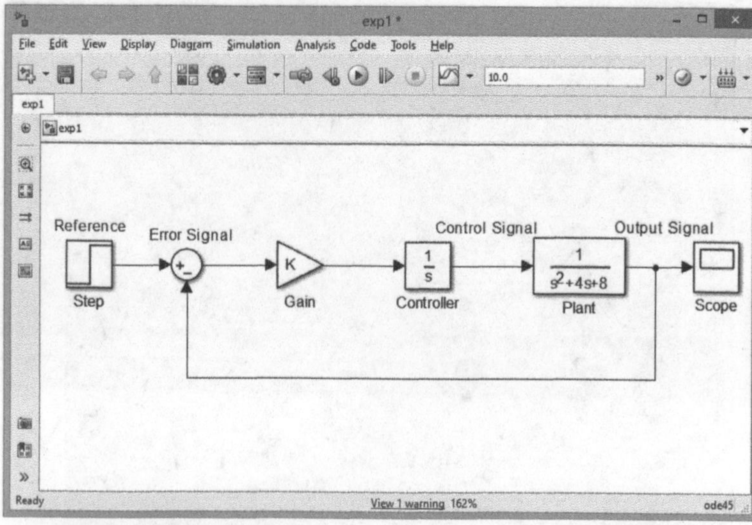

Figure 10.21 Model Showing the Variable '*K*' in Gain Block

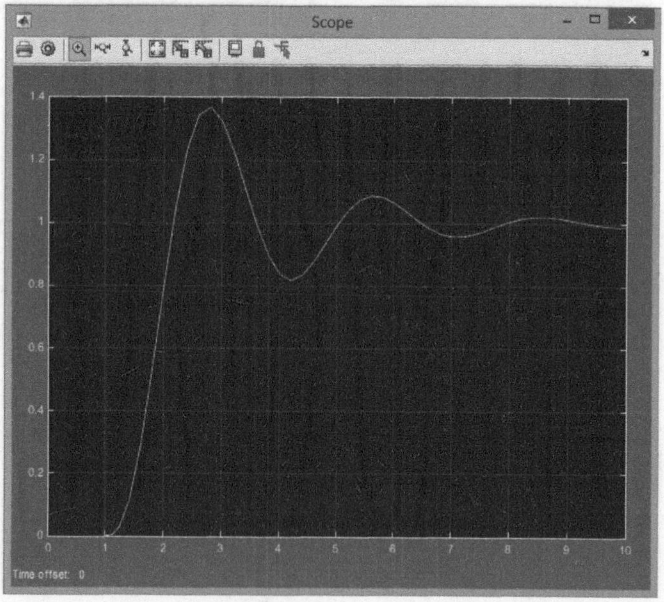

Figure 10.22 Response of Example 10.1 Using the Value of Gain '$K = 15$'

10.7 DATA IMPORT/EXPORT

The data can be loaded from or saved to Workspace by selecting the Data Import/Export option in the 'Configuration Parameters' dialog box of Simulation menu. The Workspace I/O pane is shown in Figure 10.23.

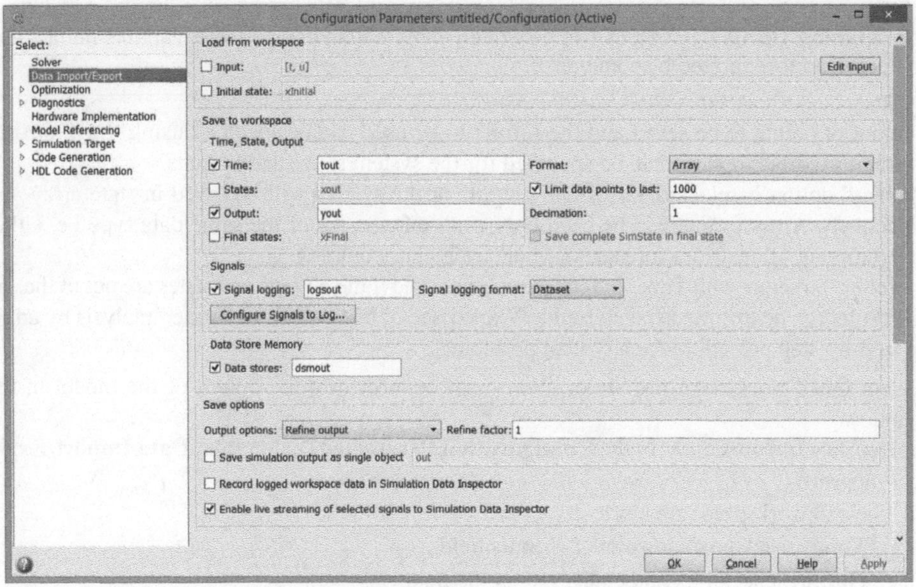

Figure 10.23 Configuration Parameters Dialog Box for Data Import/Export

10.7.1 Importing Data from the MATLAB Workspace

Actual physical data can be imported from the MATLAB Workspace to the model's input ports by adopting the following step-by-step procedure.

1. Enter the data to be imported in the Command Window.
2. Drag **In1 block** from the **sources** library and drop it in the model window.
3. Connect this block at the input of the existing Simulink diagram.
4. Select **Configuration Parameters** from the **Simulation** menu.
5. Select Data Import/Export in the configuration parameter dialog box (Figure 10.23). **Data Import/ Export pane** will appear.
6. Select **'Input'** check box in the **'Load from workspace'** area.
7. Enter the name(s) of the variable(s) (whose data is being imported) in the space provided for **input field.**
8. Click Apply and OK buttons.

Data available at the Command Window will be imported into the model.

10.7.2 Exporting Simulation Data to Workspace

The data generated during simulation of a model can be saved/exported to workspace by following procedure:

1. Select, configration parameters from simulation menu.
2. Select, 'Data Import/ Export' in the Configration parameter dialog box (Figure 10.24)
3. In the 'Save to workspace' area, return variables/results can be specified by selecting the required check boxes ie.'Time', 'States,' 'Output', etc.
4. Enter the names(s) of the variables(s) whose data is to be exported in the fields provided to the right side of the check boxes.
5. Click Apply and OK buttons.

> **Programming Tip 10.5:** If output is to be written in more than one variable, variable names are given in output option, separated by commas.

The amount of output to be saved and the format to be used can be specified using '**Save options**' area. Array or structure format options can be specified for the system states and outputs.

If an **'array'** option is selected, states and outputs of the system will be saved in state array and output array, respectively. Array format can be used only if all outputs are of the same data type i.e. either all are scalars or vectors (or all matrices for states), or all are real or complex.

'Structure' or 'Structure with Time' output formats are used if the outputs and states are not of the same type.

Output results can be exported/transferred to Workspace of MATLAB for further analysis by adopting the following step-by-step procedure for a typical problem:

1. Select **Out1** block from the **Sinks** library and connect it at the output of the model in the model window.
2. Select Data Import/Export in the **Configuration Parameter** Dialog Box. **Data Import/Export pane** will appear.
3. In 'Save to workspace' area, select.
   i. **'Time'** check box and enter 't_{out}' in its field.
   ii. **'Output'** check box and enter 'y_{out}' in the field.
4. Select '**Array**' in the drop down menu of **format** in the **Save options** area.
5. Other entries in the dialog box may be kept at default values.
6. Click Apply and OK buttons.

On completion of simulation, t_{out} and y_{out} data will be saved in the Workspace and can be observed and analysed in the Command Window.

An example illustrating the export of data to the workspace is given below:

Example 10.2 Obtain the step response of the following transfer function and save the result in the MATLAB Workspace.

$$\frac{C(s)}{R(s)} = \frac{10}{s^2 + 2s + 10}$$

Solution: The Simulink block diagram for Example 10.2 is constructed by following the procedure explained earlier and is shown in Figure 10.24.

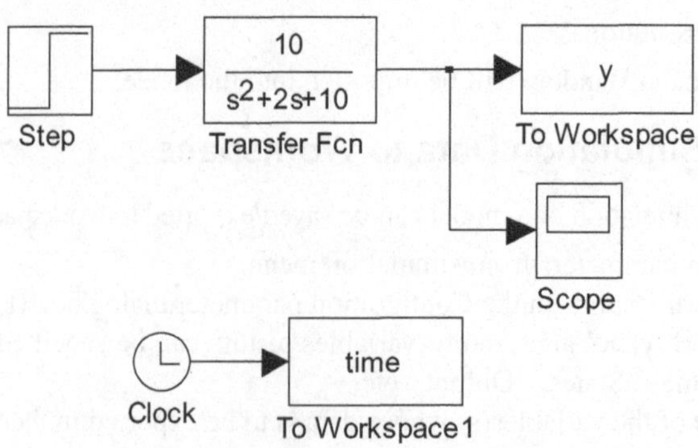

Figure 10.24 Simulink Model for Example 10.2

- 'To Workspace' block can accept a vector input, with trajectory of each input element stored as a column vector in the resulting Workspace variable.
- Double click the 'To Workspace' block to enter the variable name in the block, say **y**.
- Select 'configuration parameters' option of **Simulation** menu. Then select 'Data Import/Export' option. In 'Save to workspace' area, select 'Time' and 'Output' check boxes and enter 'tout' and 'y' in respective fields. This will export output, variable 'y' and time variable 'tout' to workspace.
- For setting block parameters, double click 'Step' block and enter the following data in respective fields:
  Step time: 1
  Initial value: 0
  Final value: 1
  Sample time: 0.2
- The time vector is stored in variable '**time**' by connecting a 'Clock' block to the 'To Workspace 1' block.
- The vectors **y, tout** and **time** are returned to MATLAB Workspace upon simulation. **tout** and **time** vectors are the same.

Note: The clock block gives the output of the current simulation time at each simulation step. This block is useful for other blocks that need the simulation time.

Start simulation and on the completion of simulation, results can be displayed by giving the following commands in the Command Window:

```
[y, tout]
```

The following output will be displayed in the Command Window:

```
ans =
          0          0
          0     0.2000
          0     0.4000
          0     0.6000
          0     0.8000
          0     1.0000
     0.1702     1.2000
     0.5488     1.4000
     0.9465     1.6000
     1.2301     1.8000
     1.3468     2.0000
     1.3145     2.2000
     1.1925     2.4000
     1.0494     2.6000
     0.9377     2.8000
     0.8827     3.0000
     0.8832     3.2000
     0.9208     3.4000
     0.9713     3.6000
     1.0142     3.8000
     1.0385     4.0000
     1.0425     4.2000
     1.0316     4.4000
     1.0143     4.6000
     0.9981     4.8000
```

```
    0.9878    5.0000
    0.9849    5.2000
    0.9877    5.4000
    0.9935    5.6000
    0.9995    5.8000
    1.0037    6.0000
    1.0053    6.2000
    1.0047    6.4000
    1.0028    6.6000
    1.0006    6.8000
    0.9990    7.0000
    0.9982    7.2000
    0.9983    7.4000
    0.9988    7.6000
    0.9996    7.8000
    1.0002    8.0000
    1.0006    8.2000
    1.0006    8.4000
    1.0005    8.6000
    1.0002    8.8000
    1.0000    9.0000
    0.9998    9.2000
    0.9998    9.4000
    0.9998    9.6000
    0.9999    9.8000
    1.0000   10.0000
```

The time response of the system for Example 10.2 can also be seen on the **scope** and is shown in Figure 10.25.

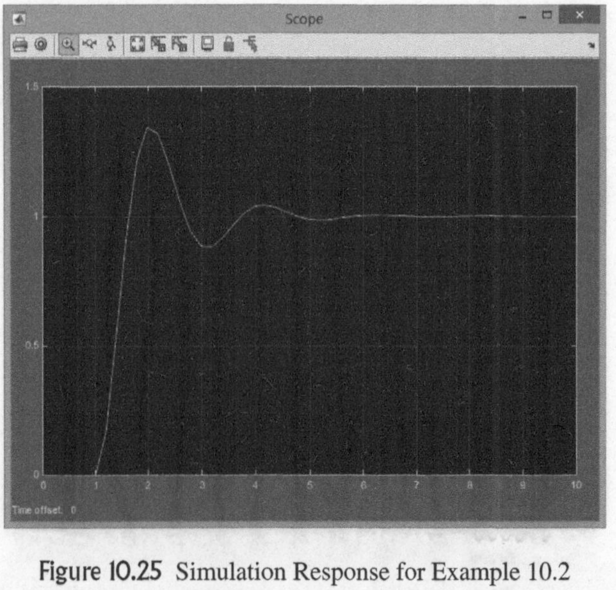

Figure 10.25 Simulation Response for Example 10.2

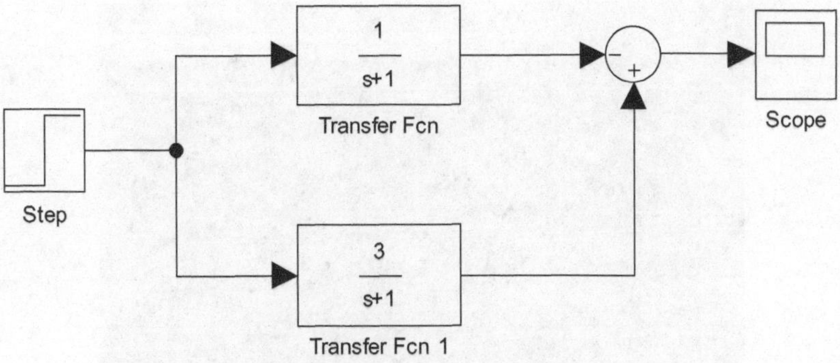

Figure 10.26 Simulink Model

Example 10.3 Obtain the step response of the model shown in Figure 10.26.

Solution:

To make the given model, the following steps are taken:

1. Drag and drop the requisite blocks from different block libraries are given below:

Block	Block library name
1. Step	Sources
2. Transfer Function	Continuous
3. Sum	Commonly Used Blocks
4. Scope	Sinks

2. Connect all the blocks as per given model.
3. Change the default specifications of the blocks as below:

Step:	Step time: 0	
	Initial value 1	
	Final value 1	
	Sample time 0.2	
Transfer Fcn	No change	
Transfer Fcn1	Numerator coefficients	[3]
	Denominator coefficients	[1 1]
Sum	−+	
Scope	No change	

4. Save and Run the Simulation
5. View the response obtained by double clicking 'Scope'.
6. The response obtained is shown in Figure 10.27.

10.8 STATE-SPACE MODELLING AND SIMULATION

The response of a dynamic system whose state-space model is described by the following matrix differential equations can also be obtained by using Simulink software,

$$\dot{\underline{x}} = A\underline{x} + B\underline{u}$$
$$y = C\underline{x} + D\underline{u} \qquad (10.1)$$

Simulink contains a block for a state-space model representation of a dynamic system, A block diagram for the equations 10.1 given above for a step input can be constructed using the Simulink Library Browser as shown in Figure 10.28.

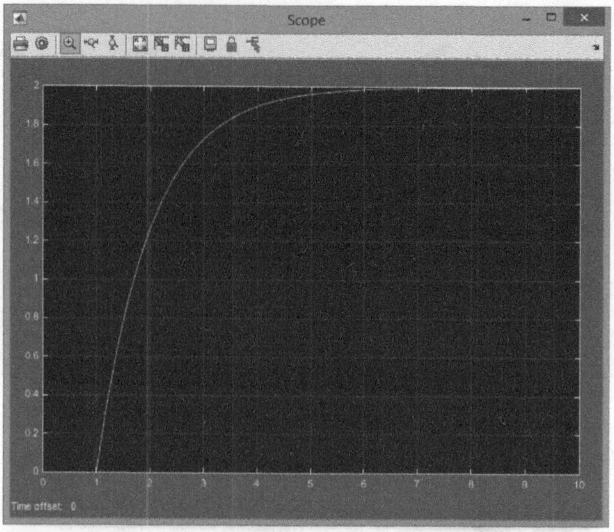

Figure 10.27 Step Response of the Model Shown in Figure 10.26

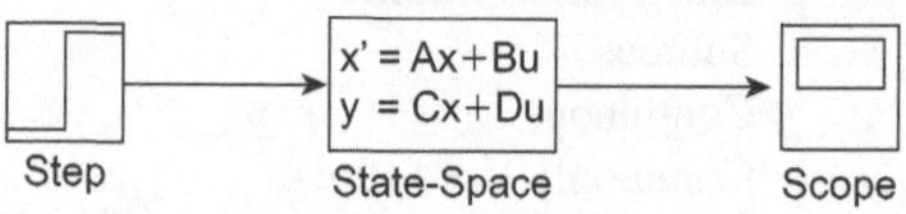

Figure 10.28 State-Space Model

State-space block is available in 'continuous' block library. Data corresponding to matrices/vectors A, B, C, D is entered in the 'block parameters dialog box' by double clicking the state-space block.

The system is then simulated as per the procedure described earlier.

Example 10.4 Obtain the unit step response of a control system described by the following state variable equations, from 0 to 10 seconds using Simulink:

$$\underline{\dot{x}} = \begin{bmatrix} 0 & 1 & 0 \\ 0 & 0 & 1 \\ -4 & -3 & -2 \end{bmatrix} \begin{bmatrix} x_1 \\ x_2 \\ x_3 \end{bmatrix} + \begin{bmatrix} 0 \\ 0 \\ 4 \end{bmatrix} u$$

$$y = \begin{bmatrix} 1 & 0 & 0 \end{bmatrix} \underline{x}$$

Assume initial conditions to be zero.

Solution:

1. *Creating a model*

   Construct the Simulink model as shown in Figure 10.28 according to the following procedure:

   (i) Open the new Simulink model window

   (ii) Drag the required blocks from the Simulink library and drop them in the model window one by one.

   - **Step** block is available in **Sources block library**
   - **State space** block is available in **Continuous block library**
   - **Scope** block is available in **Sink block library**

(iii) Connect all the blocks by connecting lines.

(iv) Open 'Function Block Parameters: State-Space' dialog box by double clicking on the 'state-space' block.

(v) Enter elements of the matrices/vectors, that is, A, B, C and D taken from the state-space equations given in this example, in the appropriate place in the dialog box, as shown in Figure 10.29

(vi) Close the box by clicking 'Apply' and 'OK' button.

2. *Simulating the model*

(i) Start the simulation by selecting 'start simulation' option from the **simulation** menu or click 'run' icon on the toolbar.

(ii) View the results by double clicking the **scope** block.

(iii) The response of the simulated system is shown in Figure 10.30.

10.9 SIMULATION OF NON-LINEAR SYSTEMS

Block diagrams representing non-linear dynamic systems consist of blocks like saturation, dead zone, back-lash, relay, etc. These non-linearities can be easily simulated using Simulink software, as the corresponding blocks are available in the **Discontinuities** block library of the Simulink Library Browser.

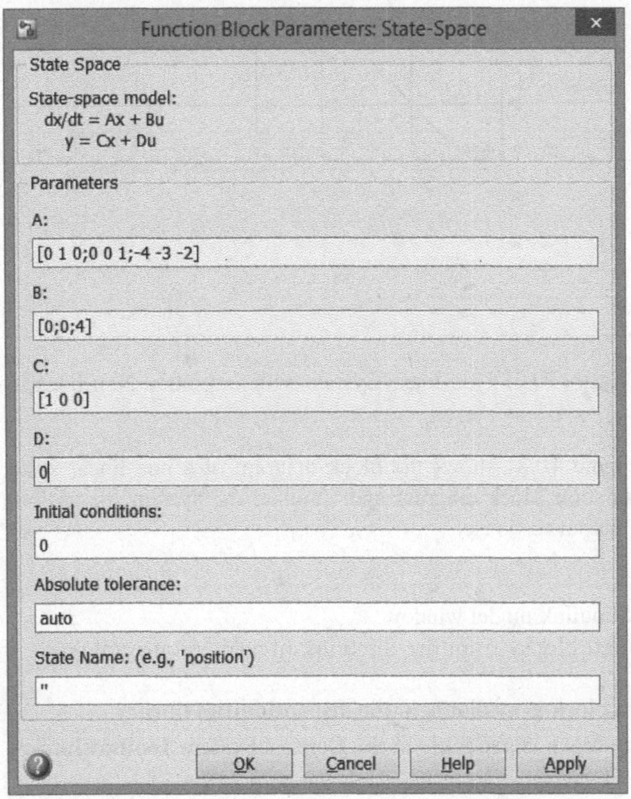

Figure 10.29 Block Parameters: State-Space Dialog Box

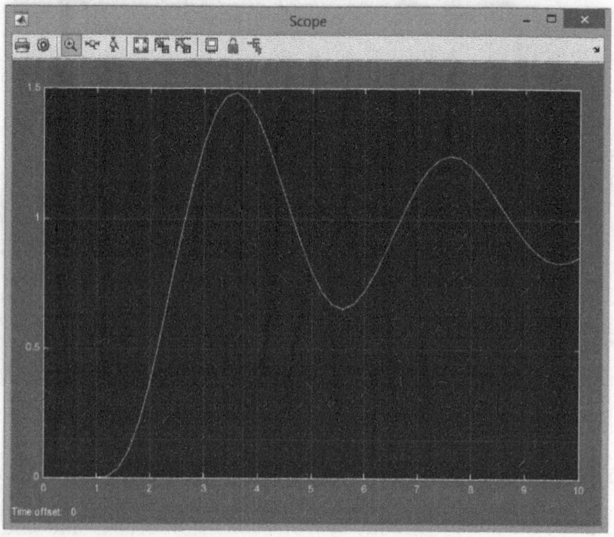

Figure 10.30 Output Response of Simulation for Example 10.4

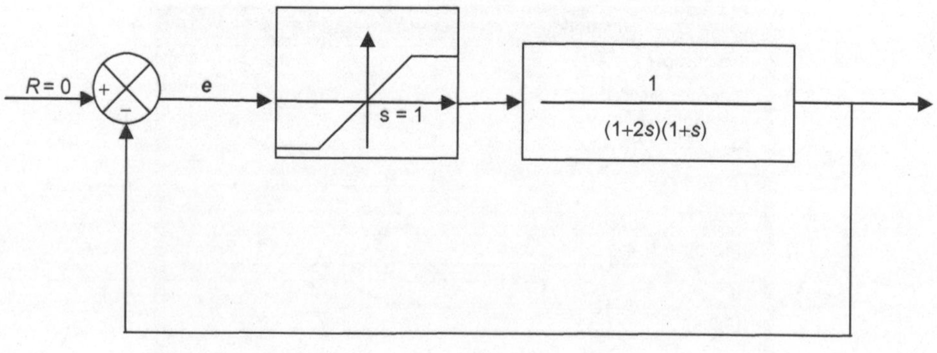

Figure 10.31 Non-linear System with Saturation Non-linearity

Example 10.5 Figure 10.31 shows the block diagram of a non-linear system with saturation non-linearity. Set up a simulation block diagram and simulate the system for an initial condition of $x(0) = [4 \quad 0 \quad 0]$ and plot the output response.

Solution:

1. Open the new Simulink model window
2. Drag the required blocks from the Simulink library and drop them in the model window one by one.
   - **Saturation block is available in the discontinuities library**
   - **LTI system block is available in the Control System Toolbox library**

   LTI system block accepts any of the three standard LTI models described in the **Control System Blockset**: transfer function, zero/pole/gain or State-space.

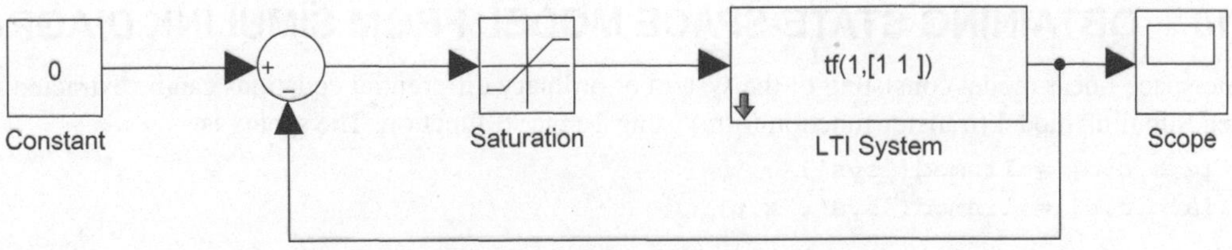

Figure 10.32 Simulink Model for Example 10.5

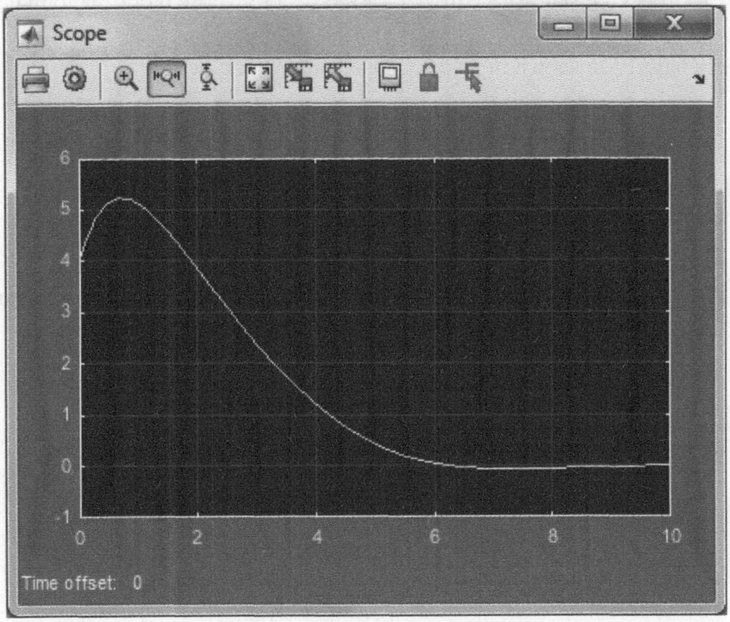

Figure 10.33 Output Response for Example 10.5

3. Connect all the blocks by connecting lines. The resultant model is as shown in Figure 10.32.
4. Set the parameters of each block as follows:

constant	0
saturation	upper limit = +1 lower limit = −1
LTI system	As per the given block diagram, i.e., *ss*(*tf*(1,[2 31])), (It converts the given transfer function model into state-space form) and initial condition = [4]

5. Set the simulation parameters in 'Configuration Parameters' option as per requirement, for example stop time = 10 sec and solver = ode45, in the Configuration Parameter Dialog Box; otherwise, the default values will be taken.
6. Simulate the model and when the simulation is complete, the output response can be observed by double clicking the 'scope' block. The response is as shown in Figure 10.33.

10.10 OBTAINING STATE-SPACE MODEL FROM SIMULINK DIAGRAM

A state-space linear model consisting of the system of ordinary differential equations can be extracted from a given Simulink model (transfer function form) using `linmod` function. The syntax is

```
[a,b,c,d] = linmod('sys')
[a,b,c,d] = linmod('sys', x,u)
```

where

`sys` is the name of the Simulink model whose state-space model is to be obtained, and

`x` and `u` are state vector and input vectors, respectively, to be specified by the user.

The following example illustrates the use of `linmod` function.

Example 10.6 Obtain the state-space model for the system whose block diagram has been shown in Figure 10.34 using `linmod` function.

In1 and Out1 blocks have been shown in place of source and sink blocks.

Solution:

1. Draw the Simulink block diagram shown in Figure 10.34 in the simulation window.
2. Save this model, say in the file named as 'exp5'.
3. Enter the following command in the MATLAB Command Window:

```
[a,b,c,d]=linmod('exp5')
```

The desired state-space model will be extracted from the Simulink diagram and is as given below:

```
a =
     -8    -22     1
      1      0     0
      0    -10     0
b =
      0
      0
      1
c =
      0     10     0
d =
      0
```

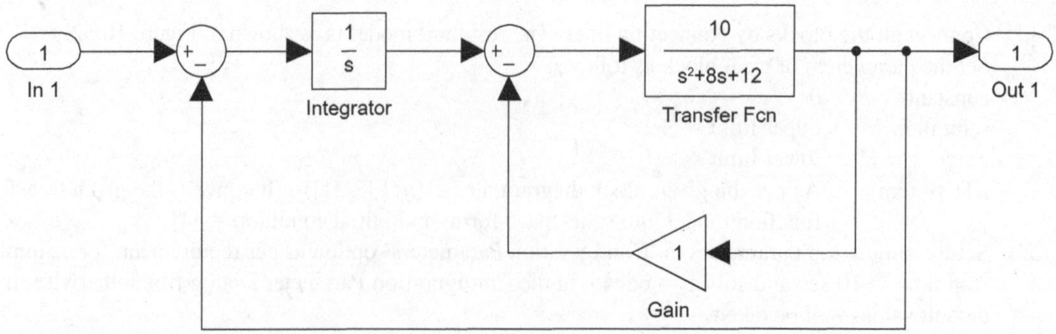

Figure 10.34 Block Diagram for Example 10.6

State-space model can be converted into transfer function form by the following command in the Command Window:

```
[n,d] =ss2tf(a,b,c,d)
```

The numerator and denominator polynomials of the transfer function obtained are as follows:

```
n =
      0 0.0000     -0.0000     10.0000
d =
      1.0000     8.0000     22.0000     10.0000
```

i.e. system transfer function can be written as

$$G(s) = \frac{10}{s^3 + 8s^2 + 22s + 10}$$

10.11 CREATING SUB-SYSTEMS

As the size of a model is increased i.e. the number of blocks in a model is increased, the complexity of the model increases, making it difficult to understand. To simplify a complex and large model, sub-systems can be created. Sub-systems can be created in two ways:

1. *By adding the sub-system block*: A sub-system can be added in a model by selecting sub-system block from **'Ports and Subsystem'** block library of Simulink Library Browser.
2. *Creating a sub-system by grouping existing blocks*: The different blocks which are to be included in a sub-system are selected using mouse. Then, select **Create Subsystem** option from the **Edit menu** of the model window or use shortcut keys Ctrl+G to create a sub-system consisting of the selected blocks. Selected portion will be replaced by a subsystem block.

Example 10.7 Consider the Simulink model shown in Figure 10.35. Encapsulate a portion of this model into a sub-system by grouping the existing blocks.

Solution:

1. Select all the blocks and signal lines (except the step block and scope) to be included in the sub-system, as shown in Figure 10.36.

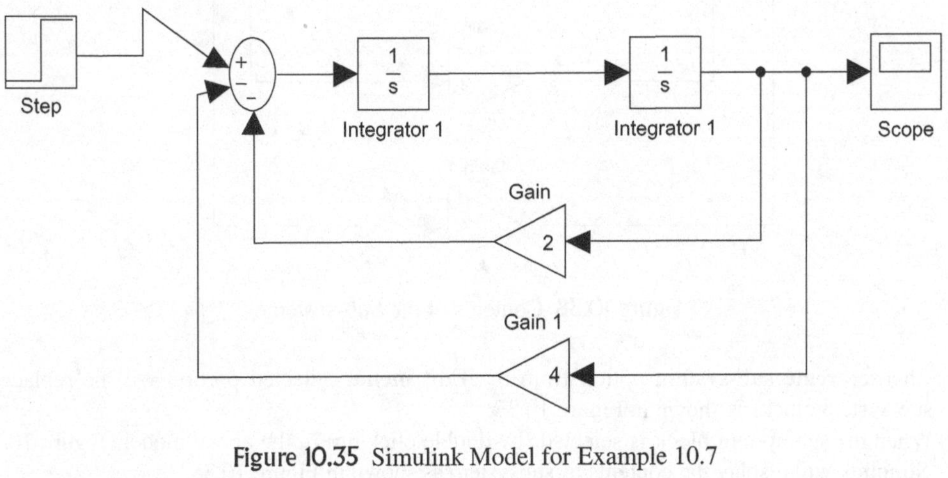

Figure 10.35 Simulink Model for Example 10.7

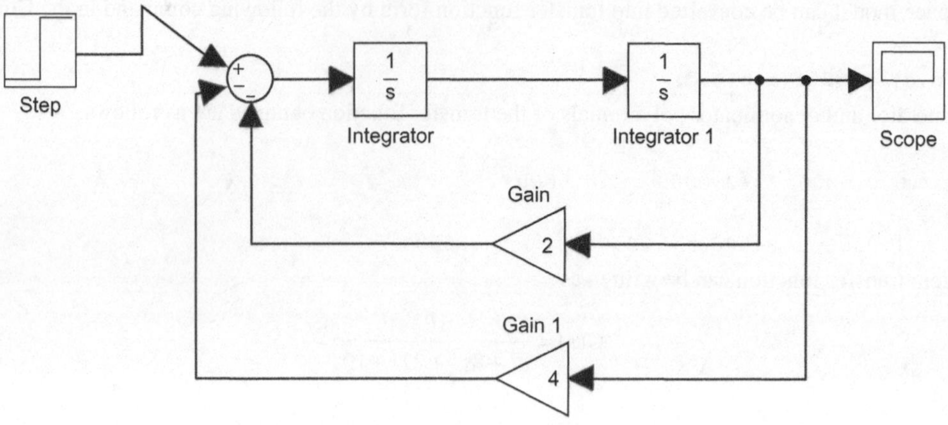

Figure 10.36 Selection for Sub-systems

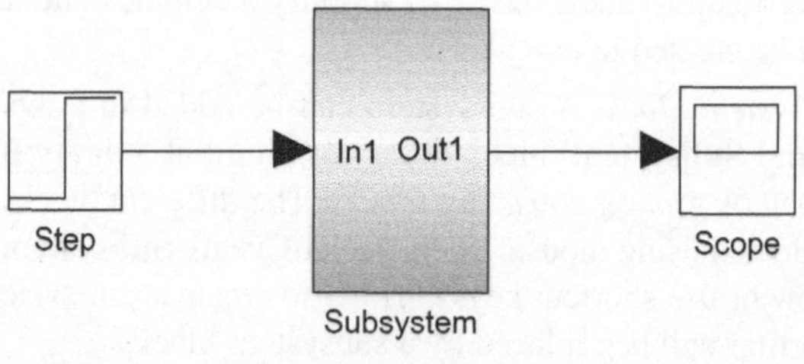

Figure 10.37 Simulink Diagram with the Created Sub-system

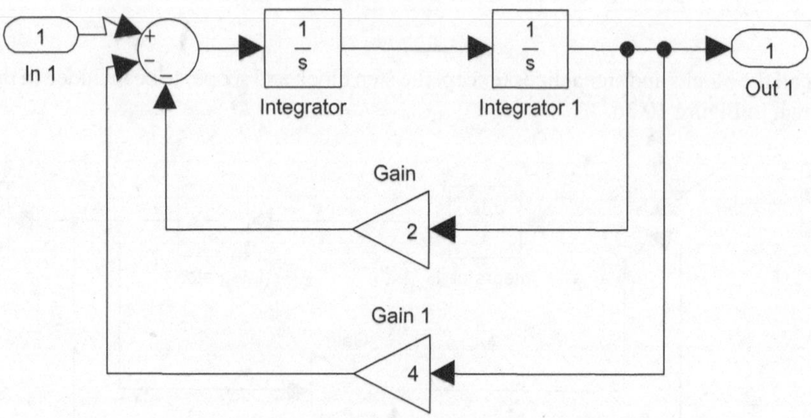

Figure 10.38 Contents of the Sub-system

2. Choose **create sub-system** option from the **Edit menu**. Selected portion will be replaced by a sub-system block, as shown in Figure 10.37.
3. When the sub-system block is selected (by double clicking) in the above model (Figure 10.37) the Simulink will display the contents of subsystem as shown in Figure 10.38.

10.12 CREATING MASKED SUB-SYSTEMS

A mask is an interface for a sub-system which hides its contents and has its own icon and dialog box defined by the user. The **Simulink Mask Editor** can be used to create the mask of a sub-system. The advantages of masking a sub-system are listed as follows:

1. It replaces the parameter dialogs of a sub-system and its contents with a single parameter dialog.
2. Prevents unintended modification of sub-systems.
3. Simplifies the use of model by replacing many dialog boxes in a sub-system with a single one.
4. It allows specifying a unique icon and a dialog box for the subsystem block.

10.12.1 Masking a Sub-system

The steps followed to mask a sub-system are given as follows:

1. Select the sub-system block to be masked.
2. Select '**mask subsystem**' option from the **Edit menu** of menu bar or use shortcut keys Ctrl+M
   Or
   Right click the sub-system block. Block's **context menu** will be displayed. Select **mask subsystem** option from this menu.
   Mask Editor will appear as shown in Figure 10.39.
3. In 'Command' field of Mask Editor, open drop down menu by clicking down arrow and then select 'disp (show text in center of block)' option.
4. In 'Drawing Commands' field, enter disp ('Example') as shown in Figure 10.40.
5. Click OK button
   Subsystem block will be masked and named 'Example'.

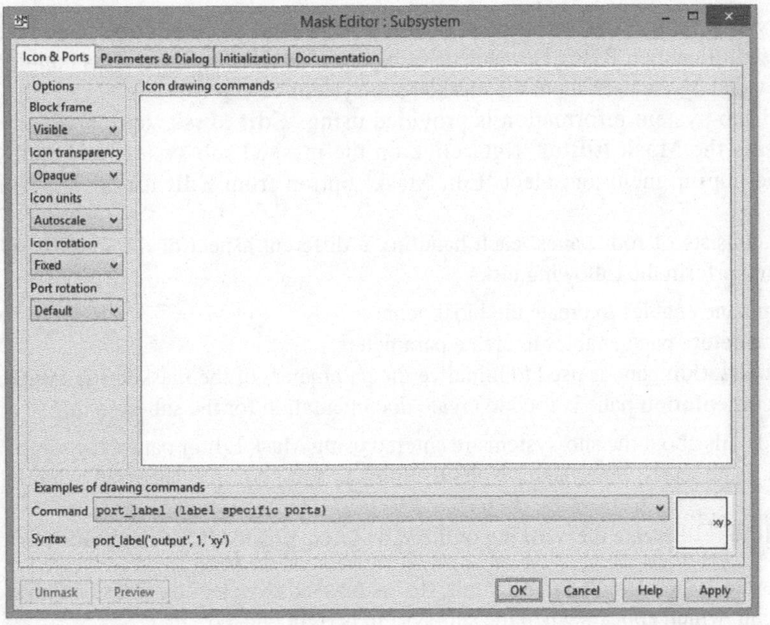

Figure 10.39 Mask Editor Window

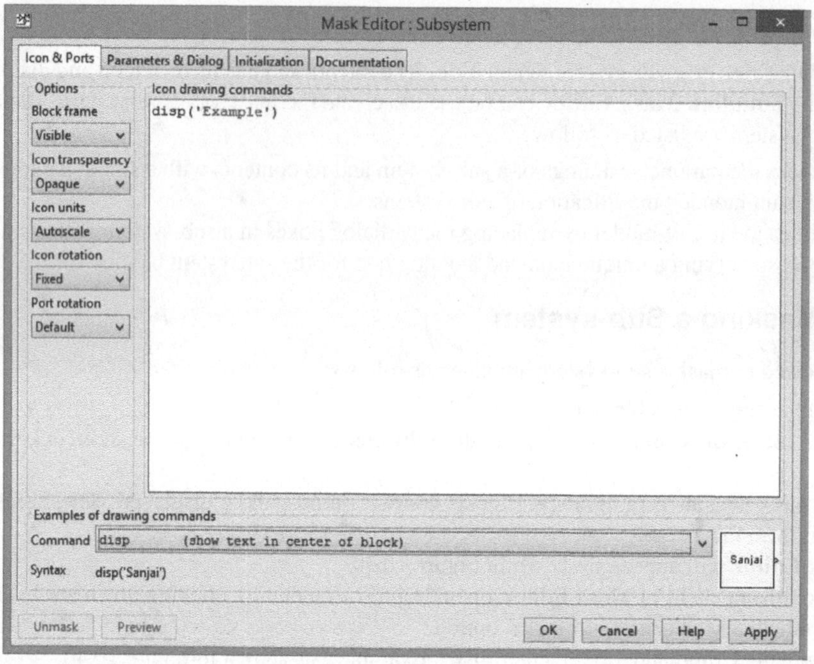

Figure 10.40 Mask Editor Showing 'Command' and 'Drawing Commands' Fields

Once a sub-system is masked, its contents will not be visible to the user. Whenever this masked sub-system is accessed, 'Function Block Parameters: Subsystem' box will pop up. This pop-up box contains all information provided by the user about the masked sub-system.

The Masked sub-system information is provided using '**Edit Mask**' option which opens up **Mask Editor**. To access the **Mask Editor**, right click on the masked sub-system and choose '**Edit Mask**' option from the pop-up menu or select 'Edit Mask' option from **Edit** menu. The **Mask Editor** will pop up.

Mask editor consists of four panes, each handling a different aspect of the masked sub-system. These panes are used to perform the following tasks:

- The **Icon** pane enables to create the block icon.
- The **Parameters** pane enables to create parameters.
- The **Initialization** pane is used to initialize the parameters of the masked sub-system.
- The **Documentation** pane is used to create documentation for the sub-system.

Once all the details about the sub-system are entered using Mask Editor panes, the same will be visible on 'Function Block Parameters: Subsystem' when the masked sub-system is accessed by double clicking on it.

Example 10.8 Illustrate the masking of the sub-system created in Example 10.7.

Solution: The sub-system created in Example 10.7 is masked by selecting '**mask subsystem**' option from pop-up menu, which appears when the sub-system is right clicked.

The 'Mask Editor', pops up when masked sub-system is double clicked and is shown in Figure 10.41 with 'documentation menu' selected.

The following statements may be entered against the various options of documentation menu in Mask Editor (Figure 10.41)

Mask type:	*Example 10.7*
Mask description:	*Example of masking a sub-system.*
Mask help:	*This is simple system to illustrate the masking concepts.*

These are then saved by clicking 'Apply' and 'OK' buttons.

Now, when the masked sub-system is selected by double clicking on it, 'Functional Block Parameters' will pop up as shown in Figure 10.42.

Similarly, the other menu options such as icon parameters and initialization can be entered and shown on 'Functional Block Parameter' dialog box.

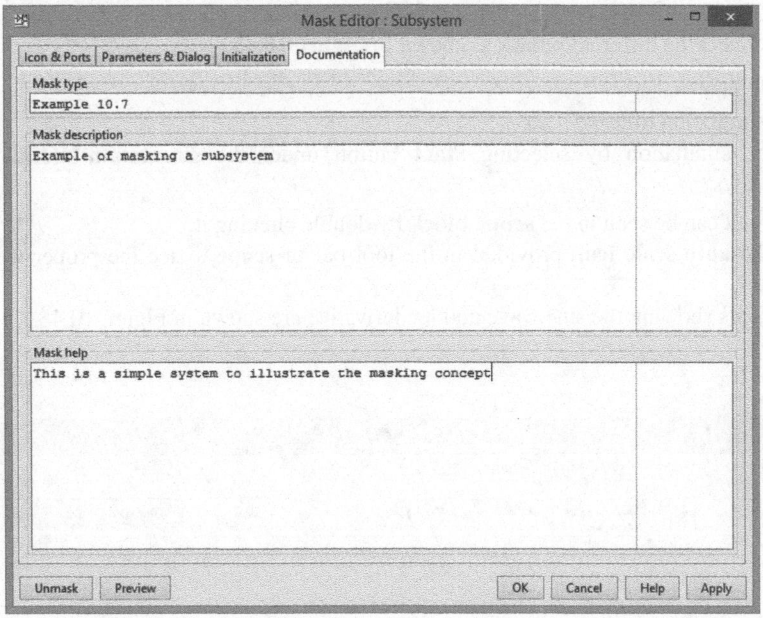

Figure 10.41 Mask Editor with Documentation Menu Selected

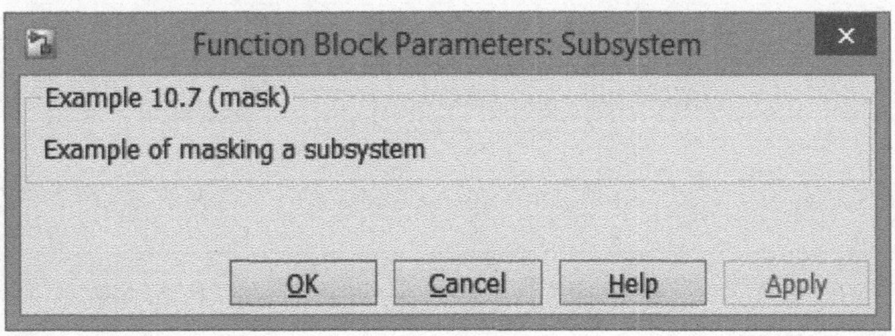

Figure 10.42 'Functional Block Parameter' Dialog Box of the Masked Sub-system

10.13 MORE EXAMPLES ON SIMULINK

Example 10.9 Obtain the derivative of a sine wave using SIMULINK

Solution:

Step 1: Open Simulink Library browser.

Step 2: Create a new model, as shown in Figure 10.43, by following the procedure given below:

(i) Select the **Source library** and drag **sine wave** block from this library and drop it in the **new model window**. Set the parameters of sine wave as shown in Figure 10.44 by double clicking the sine wave block.

(ii) Drag **derivative block** from **continuous library** and drop it in the new model window.

(iii) Select the **sink** library and drag the **scope block** from it and drop it in the model window. Double click the scope block and set its parameters as shown in Figure 10.45. Set number of axes = 2.

(iv) Connect the different blocks as shown in **Figure 10.43.**

Step 3: Save the model.

Step 4: Select simulation time = 10 sec.

Run the simulation by selecting **start** button under the **simulation menu** or by pressing Ctrl+T keys.

Step 5: The output can be seen in the **scope block** by double clicking it.

Click the **auto scale icon** provided in the tool bar of **scope** to see the proper wave shape of the signals.

The signals showing the sine wave and its derivative are shown in Figure 10.46.

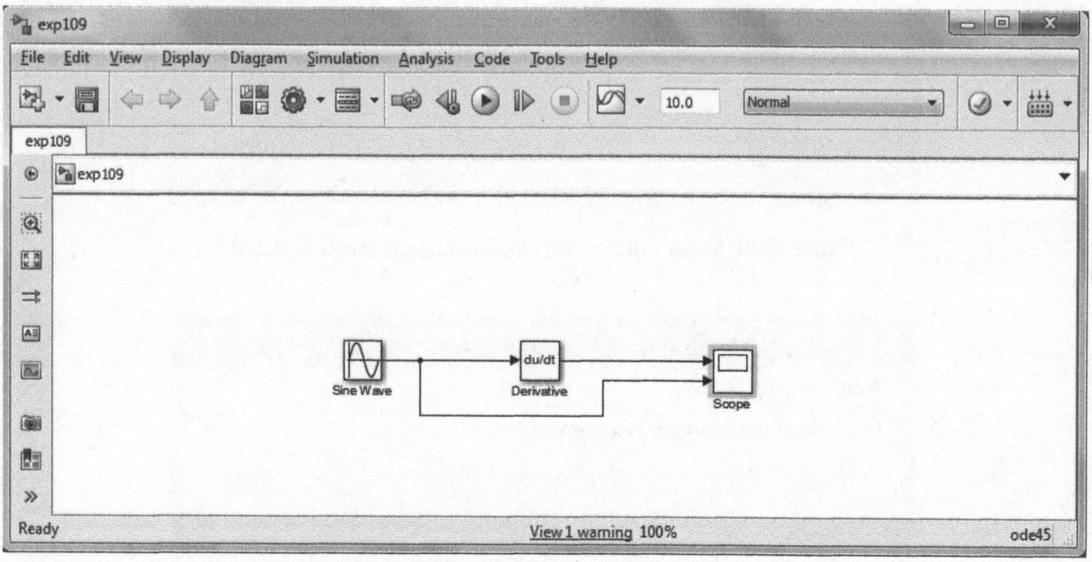

Figure 10.43 Simulink Model to Obtain the Derivative of a Sine Function

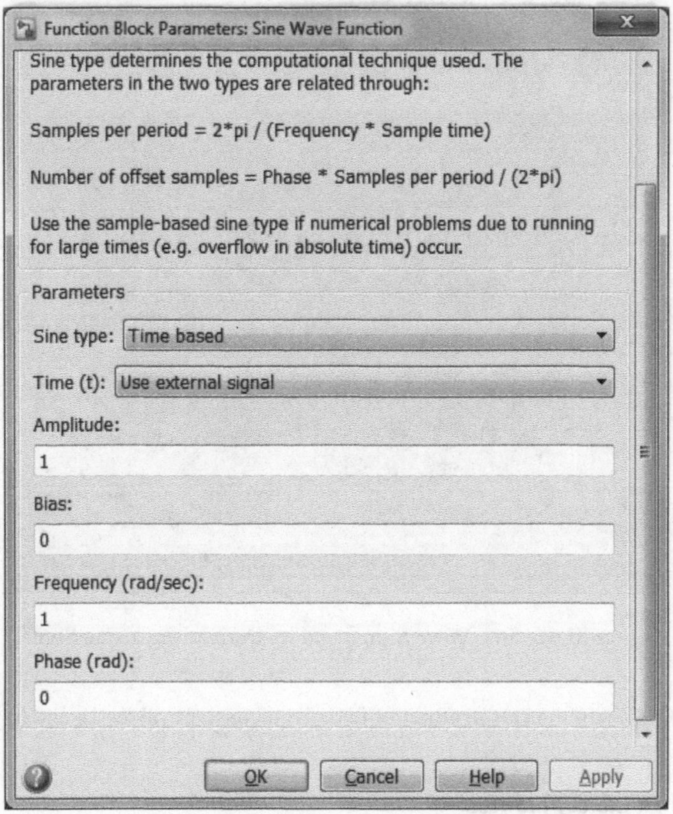

Figure 10.44 Source Block Parameters of Sine Wave

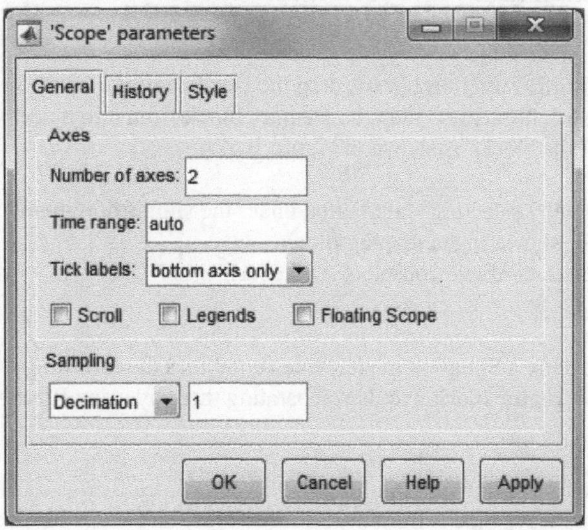

Figure 10.45 Scope Parameters

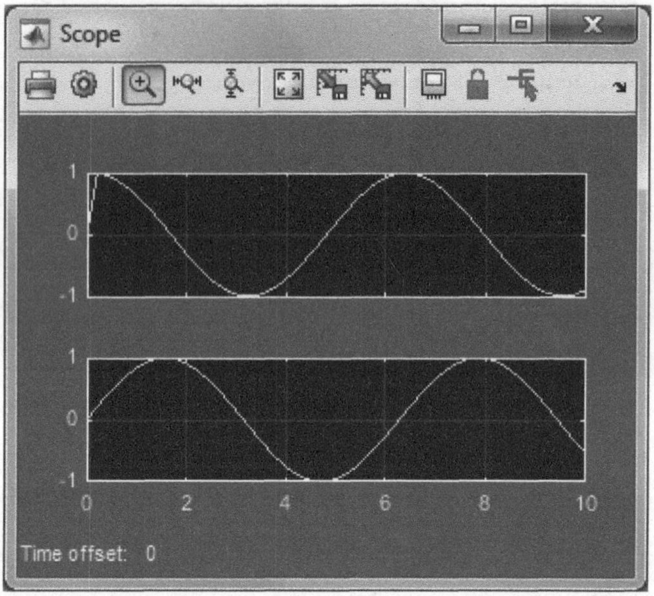

Figure 10.46 Sine Wave Signal and its Derivative Cosine Signal

Example 10.10 Obtain the **Dot product** of two given constant values 18 and 5.

Solution:

Step 1: Open Simulink Library browser.

Step 2: Create a **new model** as shown in Figure 10.47 by following the procedure given below:

(i) Select the **Source** and drag **Constant** block from it to the new model window.

(ii) Set the constant value = 18, by double clicking **Constant** block.

(iii) Drag another **Constant** block to the new model window.

(iv) Set this constant value = 5.

(v) Select the **Math Function** library, drag the **Dot Product block** from it to the model window.

(vi) Select the **sink** library and drag the **Display block** from it to model window.

(vii) Connect all the blocks as shown in Figure.10.47.

Step 3: Save the model

Step 4: Run the simulation by selecting **start** button under the **simulation menu** or pressing Ctrl+T

Step 5: The output will be shown in the **display block.**

In this case the product of two constants is given as:

= 90 (18 × 5)

Example 10.11 Develop a Simulink model which combines the following two signals (I) Step signal (II) Sine Wave using **Bus Creator block** and then separating them by using **Bus Selector block.**

Solution:

1. Open the **new model window** in Simulink.
2. Drag **step and sine wave** blocks from the **Source** library and **scope block** from the **sink** library and drop them in the model window.

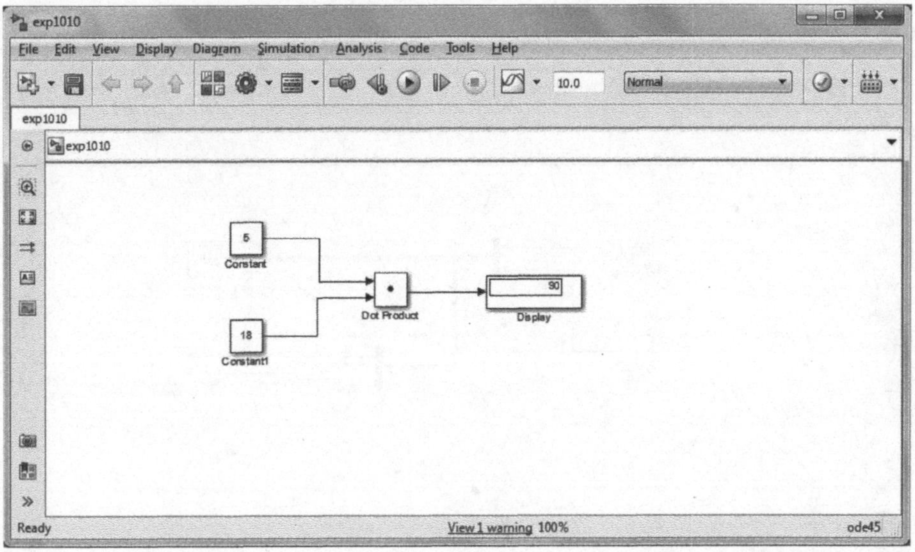

Figure 10.47 Simulink Diagram for Dot Product of Two Constants

3. Drag **Bus Creator** and **Bus Selector block** from the **Commonly used blocks** library and drop them in the model window.
   Bus creator Block is used to create signal buses. **Bus selector** block is used to access the components of a bus.
4. Connect all the blocks as shown in the Figure 10.48.
5. Set the parameters of different blocks as follows:
   (i) Double click the **step block** and set its parameters as follows:
   Step time = 0.5
   Initial value = 0
   Final Value = 10
   (ii) Now double click on the **sine wave block** and set its parameters as follows:
   Sine type: Time based
   Use: Simulation time
   Amplitude: 10
   Bias: 0
   Frequency: 1 rad/sec
   Phase: 0
   Sample time: 0
   Set simulation time = 10
6. Double click the **Bus creator block**. 'Function Block parameters' dialog box will open as shown in Figure 10.49. Select Inherit Bus signal names from input ports from the list box.
7. Double click the **Bus selector block**. 'Function Block parameters' dialog box will open as shown in Figure 10.50.
   The left list box shows the signals in the input bus
   Use the **select button** to select the **output signals**. The **right list box** shows the selections.

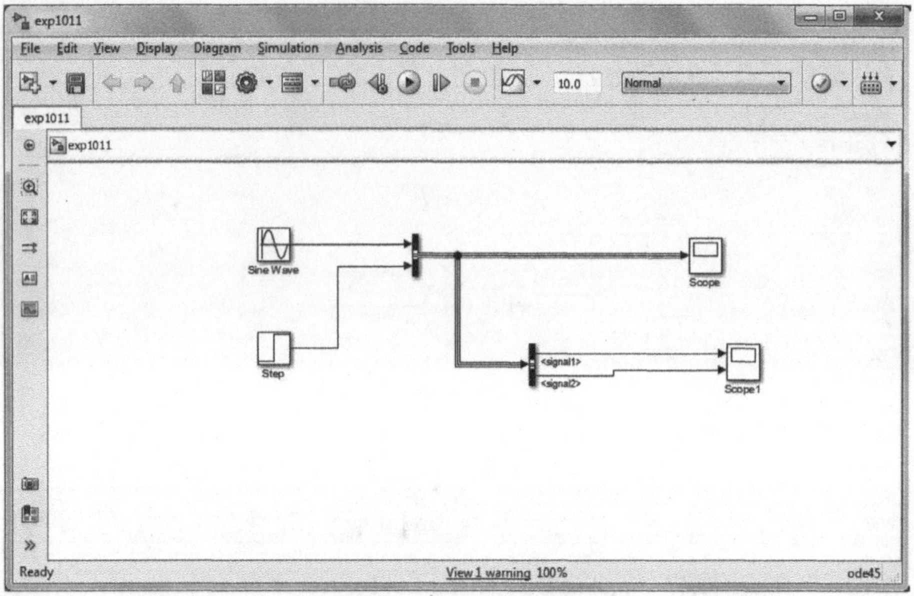

Figure 10.48 Bus Creator Block and Bus Selector Block

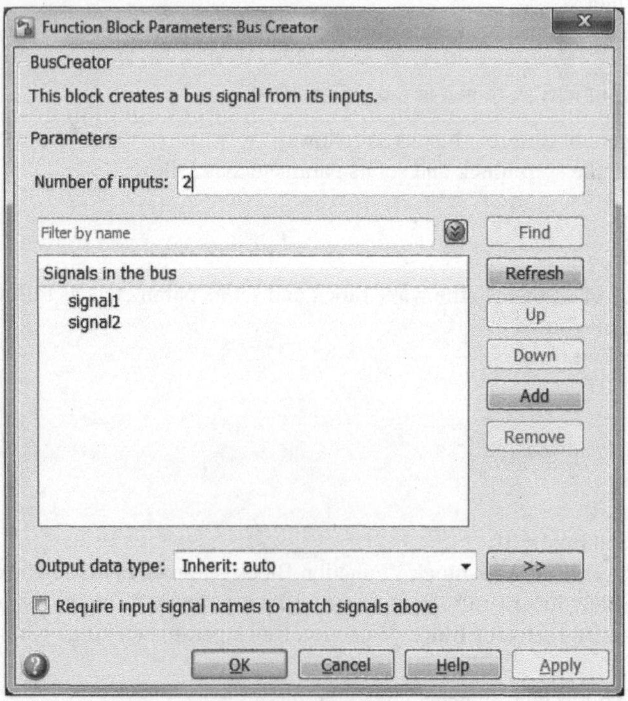

Figure 10.49 Parameters of Bus Creator Block

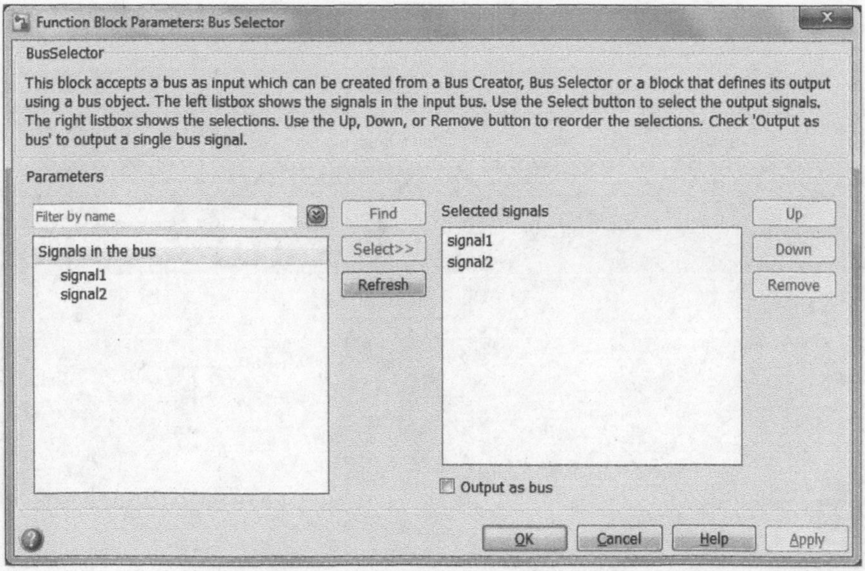

Figure 10.50 Parameters of Bus Selector Block

Two Output Signals can be seen by double clicking the **scope block** and **scope block 1** and pressing **auto scale** icon in the scope window. These are as shown in the Figure 10.51 and 10.52, given below:

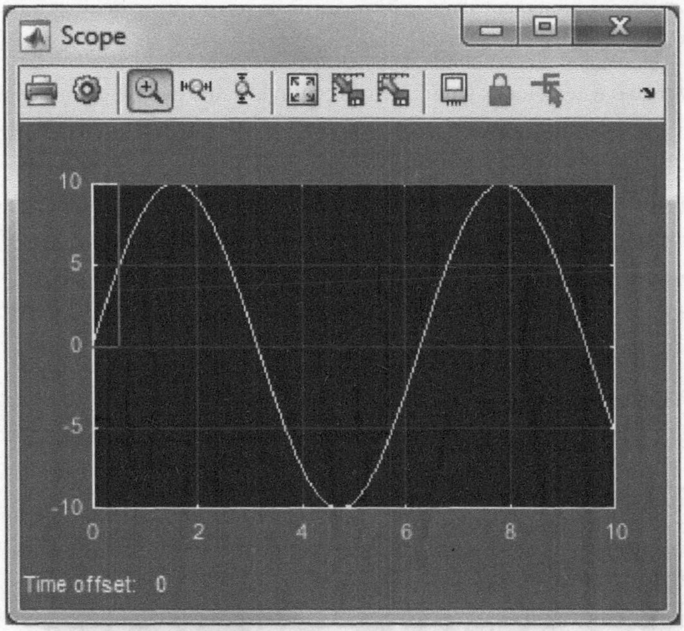

Figure 10.51 Step and Sine Wave Signals (in one figure)

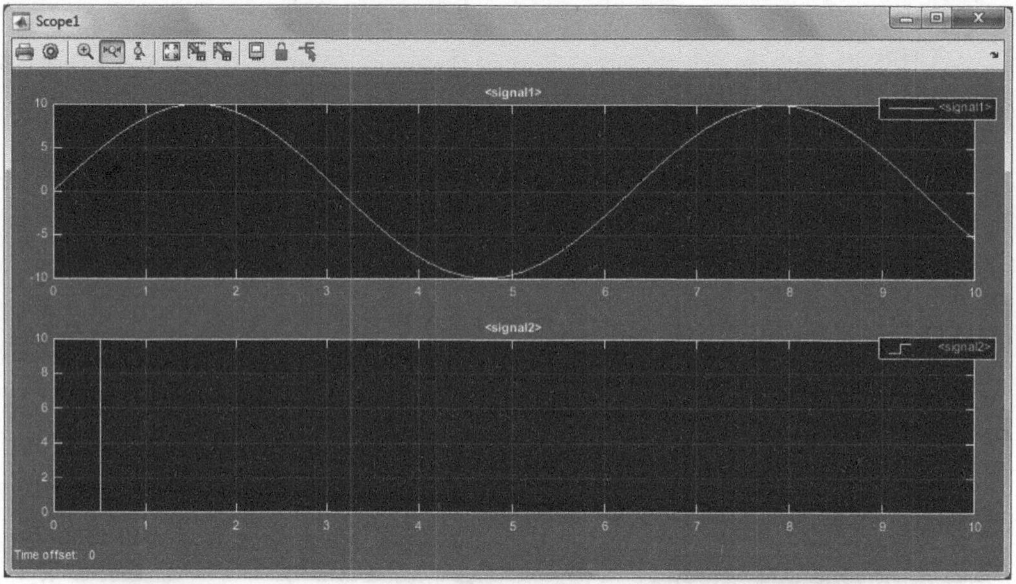

Figure 10.52 Separate Figures of Step and Sine Wave Signals

Example 10.12 Show the use of MUX and Demux blocks.

Two sine wave sources of amplitude 120 and frequency 314 rad/sec. with a phase delay of 2pi/3 are taken. These two sine waves are input to a 2 × 1 **Mux block** and then output of Mux block is fed to 1 × 2 **Demux block.**

Solution:

1. Drag the two sine wave blocks from the **source library** and drop them in the model window
2. Drag **Mux and Demux blocks** from **commonly used blocks /signals routing libraries** and drop them in the model window.
3. Drag two **scope blocks** from the **sink library** and drop them in the model window.
4. Connect all the blocks as shown in the Figure 10.53 given below:
5. Save this model.
6. Set simulation time = 50 seconds.
7. Start the simulation.
8. Run the simulation for 50 seconds.
9. The output of the **Mux** block is shown in Figure 10.54 and that of **Demux** block in Figure 10.55.

10.14 POWER SYSTEM TOOL BOX

Sim power systems tool box is used to model electrical power systems easily. The library of **sim power systems** has the following set of blocks:

1. Application libraries
2. Electrical sources

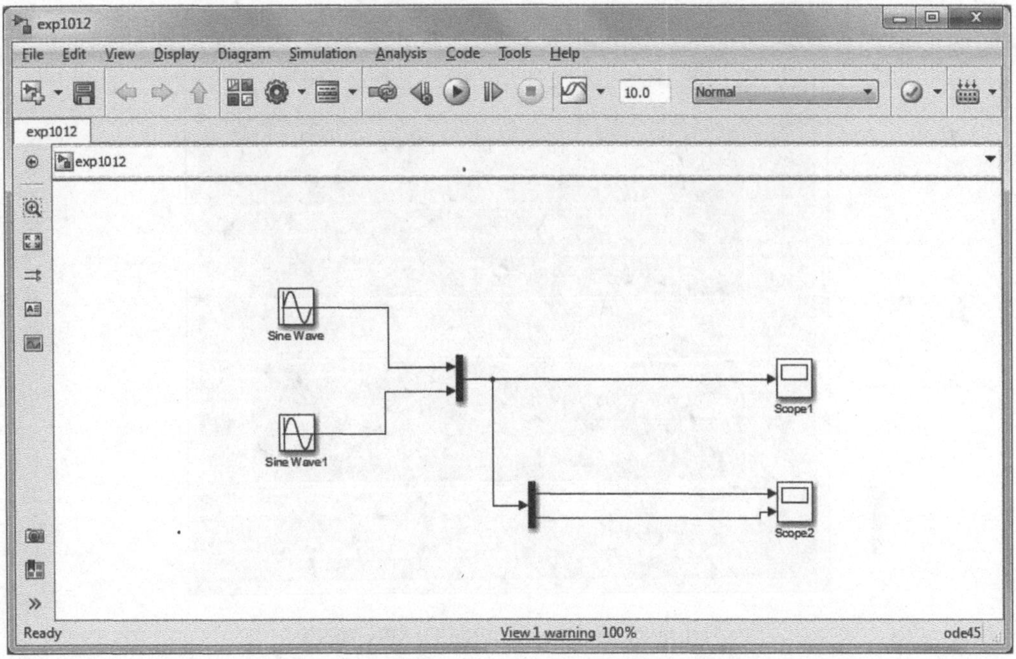

Figure 10.53 Use of MUX and DeMux Blocks

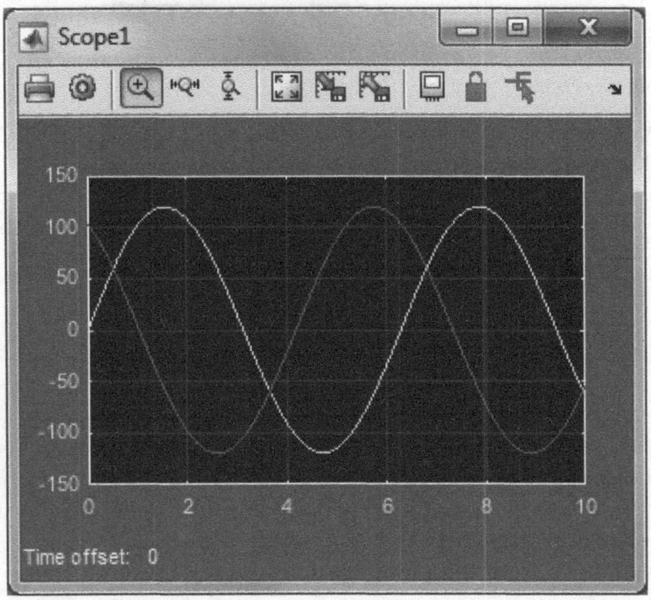

Figure 10.54 Output of the Mux Block

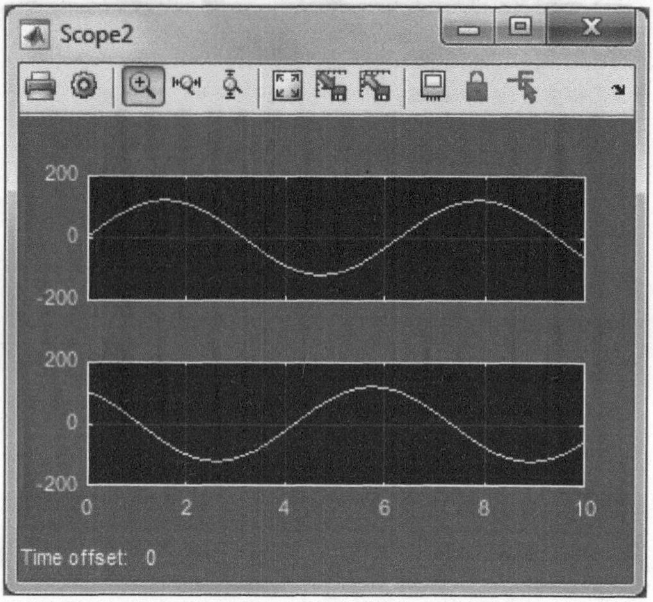

Figure 10.55 Output of the DeMux Block

3. Elements
4. Extra library
5. Machines
6. Measurements
7. Power electronics
8. Power gui

Power system/extra library/measurements dialog box is shown in Figure 10.56.

Example 10.13 Given a simple electrical circuit with a dc voltage source of 100 volts in series with a resistance of 100 ohms. Prove the **Ohm's Law** using SIMULINK model simulation i.e. $I = \frac{V}{R}$

Solution: Draw the SIMULINK block diagram as shown in Figure 10.57 by adopting the following procedure:

1. Open the new model window in **Simulink**
2. Drag **DC voltage source, series RLC branch, voltage measurement and current measurement** blocks from the **sim power systems library** and drop them in the new model window.
3. Drag **two display blocks** from **sink** block set and drop them in the model window. Connect all the blocks as shown in the Figure 10.57.
4. **Drag power gui block from sim power systems library and drop it in a corner of the model window.**
5. Run the simulation for 10 seconds.

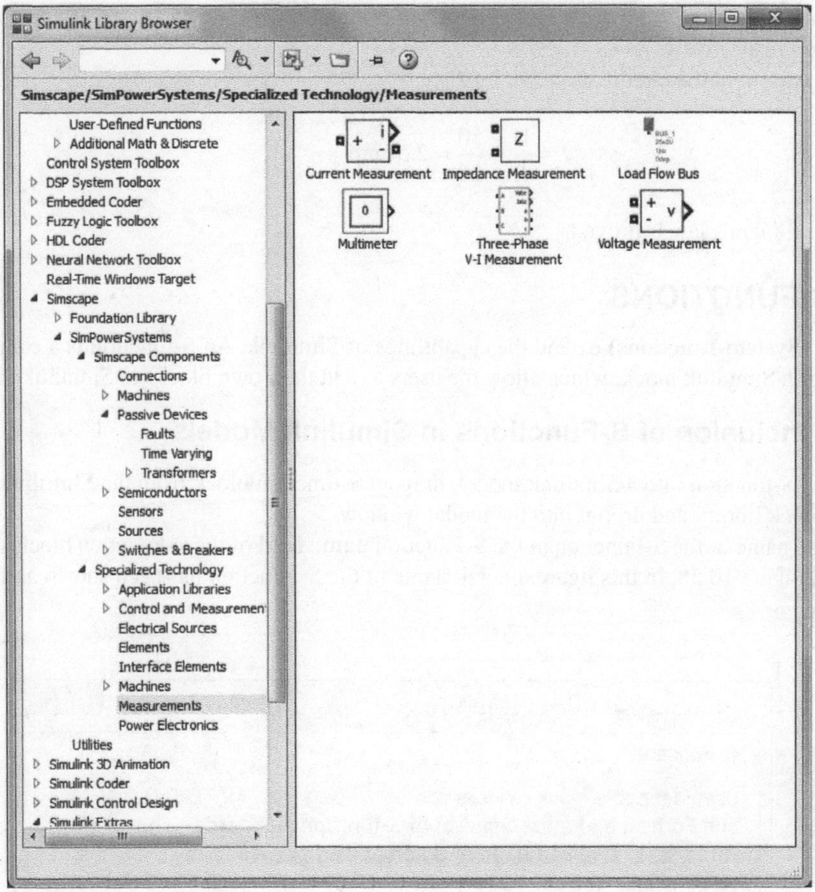

Figure 10.56 Power System/extra Library/measurements

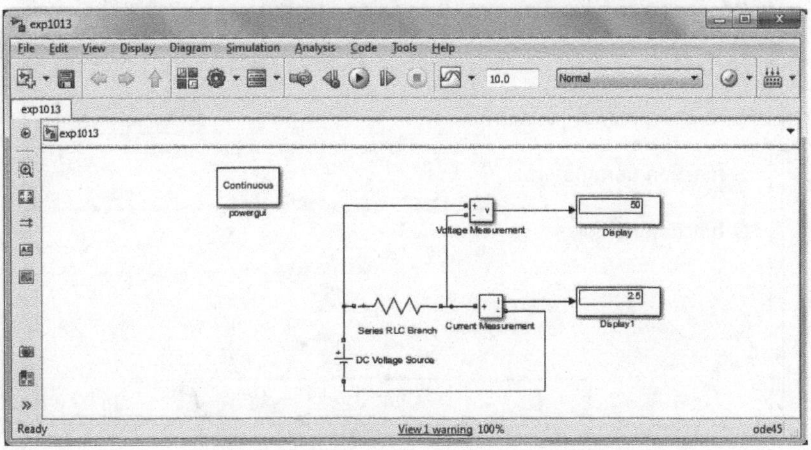

Figure 10.57 Verification of Ohm’s Law

6. Values of voltage = 50 volts and current = 2.5 amp will be shown by the **Display and Display 1** blocks respectively.
   The current in the circuit as shown by display is:

$$I = \frac{V}{R} = \frac{50}{20} = 2.5 \text{ amp}$$

   Hence, Ohm's law is proved.

10.15 S-FUNCTIONS

S-functions (System-functions) extend the capabilities of Simulink. An S-function is a computer language description of a Simulink block, which allow the users to add their own blocks to Simulink models.

10.15.1 Inclusion of S-Functions in Simulink Models

To include an S-function into a Simulink model, drag an S-function block from the **Simulink User-Defined Functions block** library and drop it into the model window.

Specify the name of the S-Function in the S-Function **name field** of the S-Function block's **dialog box**, as illustrated in Figure 10.58. In this figure, default name of the S-Function has been shown as **system**.

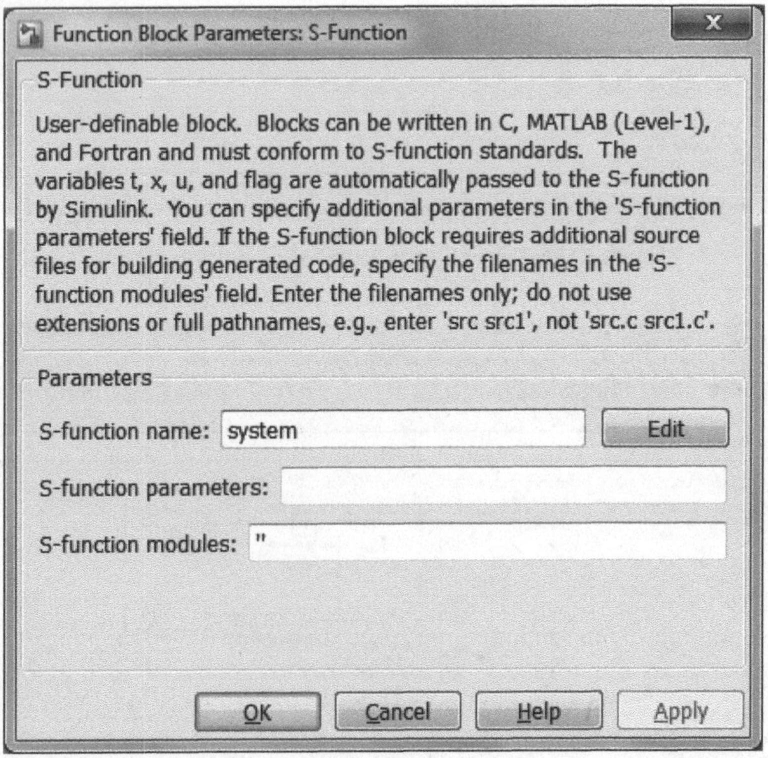

Figure 10.58 S-Function Block's Dialog Box

10.15.2 How to Write S-functions Using M-file?

Different steps involved in writing an S-function are as follows:

Step 1: Write the S-function in the MATLAB edit window according to standard MATLAB template. Save this function as an **m-file,** having the same name of the file as the name of this function. After this, follow the procedure given below:

Step 2: Open **Simulink** and open a **new model window**. In the **Simulink library browser,** Click on the **user defined function.**

Step 3: Drag the S-**function** block from the **user defined function sub library** to the new model window.

Step 4: Click on this block and **change its name** so that it is exactly the same name as declared in the M-file.

10.15.3 Method of Writing a Program for S-function in M-file

In order to write the M-file code for the S-function, adapt a standard **template** of the S-function **sfuntmpl.m** which is available under **MATLAB\Toolbox\Simulink\Blocks.**

Example 10.14 For a simple R-C series circuit shown in Figure 10.59, plot the step response of this circuit, by using S-function block of SIMULINK.

Assume Resistance, R = 10^6 Ohm, Capacitance, C = 10^{-6} Farad, Initial value = – 5. The state space equations describing the behavior of this circuit are given by:

$$\frac{dx}{dt} = -\left(\frac{1}{RC}\right)x + Vs$$

$$y = x$$

where x is state variable and y is the output.

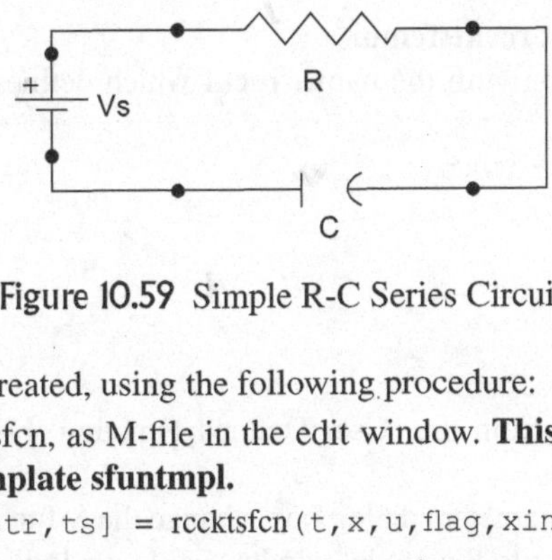

Figure 10.59 Simple R-C Series Circuit

Solution: **S-function block** is created, using the following procedure:

(i) Write the function rccktsfcn, as M-file in the edit window. **This function is written according to standard MATLAB template sfuntmpl.**

```
function[sys,x0,str,ts] = rccktsfcn(t,x,u,flag,xin)
% rccktsfcn is the name of the S-function
%sys is a return argument.The values returned depend on the value of flag.
%If flag=3, sys contains the S-function outputs.
%t is current time,x is state vector, xs is input vector, flag is an
integer %value that indicates the task to be performed by the S-function.
%x0,are initial state values
% it is set as empty matrix[].
%ts, contains sample times and offsets. For continuous sample time,
ts=[0 0]
xin=0;
```

```
switch flag,
case 0
str=[];
ts=[0 0];
x0=xin;
sizes=simsizes;
sizes.NumContStates=1; %number of continuous states
sizes.NumDiscStates=0; %number of discrete states
sizes.NumOutputs=1; %number of outputs
sizes.NumInputs=1 %number of inputs
sizes.DirFeedthrough=0; %flag for direct feedthrough
sizes.NumSampleTimes; %number of sample times
sys=simsizes(sizes);
case 1 %calculates derivatives of continuous state variables
v=u;
sys=rcckt(t,x,v); %rcckt is the name of a function which defines the
                    equation of this problem
case 3 %calculates the outputs of the S-function
sys=x;
case{2,4,9}
     sys=[];
    otherwise
error(['unhandled flag=',num2str(flag)]);
end
```

Save this S-function file as **rccktsfcn.m**

(ii) Write a MATLAB function with the name, **rcckt** which defines the equations of this problem as follows:

```
function xdot = rcckt(t,x,vs)
r = 10^6
c = 10^(-6)
xdot = -1/(r*c)*x + vs;
end
```

Save this function file as rcckt.m

(iii) Select 'S-function' block from the 'User Defined Function' blockset and drag it into the model window.

(iv) In the S-function block parameters dialog box, change the S-function name as **rccktsfcn.**

(v) Add Step and Scope blocks to the model window as shown in Figure 10.60. Set parameters of **step block** corresponding to unit step input as follows:
Step time = 1
Initial value = 0
Final value =1

(vi) Connect all the blocks as shown in Figure 10.60

(vii) Set simulation time = 10 seconds

(viii) Start simulation

(ix) On completion of simulation, double click the scope block to see the output response.

(x) Step response will be seen on the scope as shown in Figure 10.61

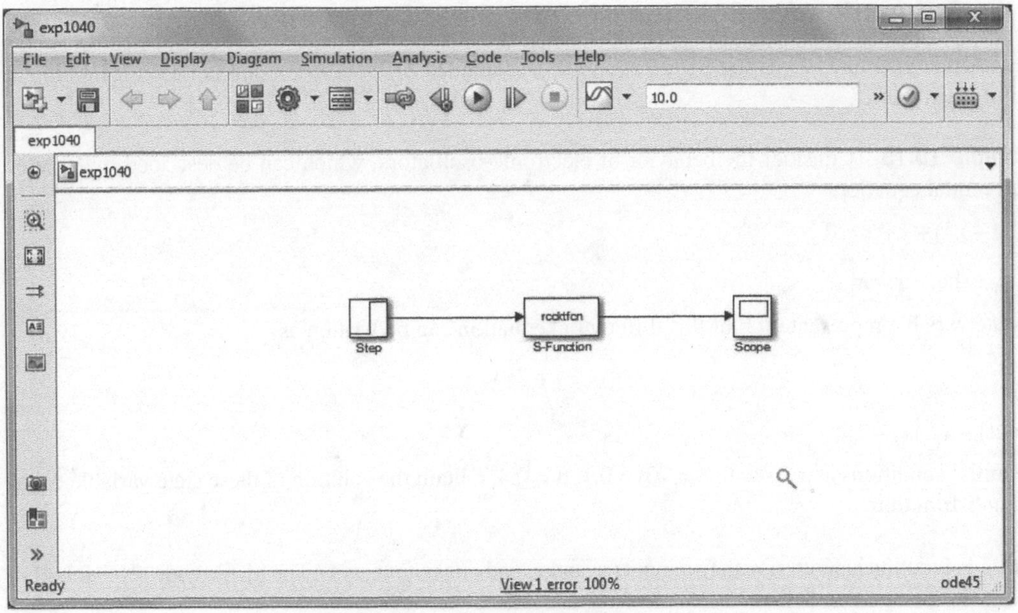

Figure 10.60 Simulink Model Using 'S' Function

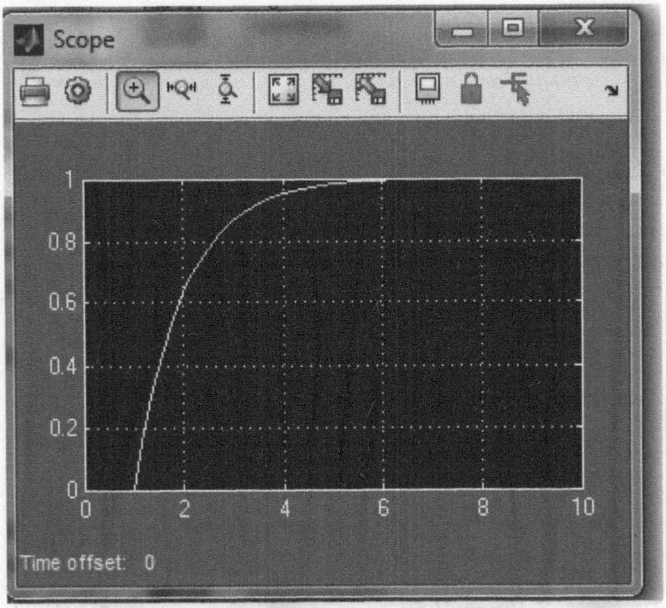

Figure 10.61 Step Response of Series RC Circuit

10.15.4 S-Function for Solution of Non Linear Differential Equations

Consider another example of writing M-file code for user-defined S-function for solving a set of nonlinear differential equations.

Example 10.15 Consider the behavior of electronic oscillators, which can be described by **Vander Pol's** differential equation,

$$\ddot{x} - \mu(1-x^2) + \dot{x} + x = 0$$

Let $x = x_1$, i.e. $\dot{x} = \dot{x}_1$

The state variable representation of this differential equation can be written as:

$$\dot{x}_1 = x_2$$

$$\dot{x}_2 = \mu(1-x_1{}^2)x_2 - x_1$$

Assume initial conditions as $x_1(0) = 0.1$, $x_2(0) = 0.1$, $\mu = 0.4$. Obtain the solution of these state variable equations using **S-function.**

Solution: S-function is written with two inputs x_1 and x_2 and one output 'sys'. The M-file code for S-function for the Vander Pol equation is listed below:

```
function[sys,x0,str,ts] = vanderpol(t,x,xs,flag)
% vanderpol is the name of the S-function
%sys is a return argument. The values returned depend on the value of flag.
%If flag=3, sys contains the S-function outputs.
%t is current time,x is state vector, xs is input vector, flag is an integer
%value that indicates the task to be performed by the S-function.
%x0,are initial state values
% it is set as empty matrix[].
%ts , contains sample times and offsets. For continuous sample time, ts=[0 0]
switch flag,
case 0
[sys,x0,str,ts]=mdlInitializeSizes;
case 3                     %calculates the outputs of the S-function
sys = mdlOutputs(t,x,xs);
case{1,2,4,9}
sys=[];
otherwise
error(['unhandled flag=',num2str(flag)]);
end
          function[sys,x0,str,ts]=mdlInitializeSizes;
sizes=simsizes;
sizes.NumContStates=0;                          %number of continuous states
sizes.NumDiscStates=0;                          %number of discrete states
```

```
sizes.NumOutputs=1;                    %number of outputs
sizes.NumInputs=2;                     %number of inputs
sizes.DirFeedthrough=1;                %flag for direct feedthrough
sizes.NumSampleTimes=1;                %number of sample times
sys=simsizes(sizes);
str=[];
x0=[];
ts=[-1 0];

        function sys = mdlOutputs(t,x,xs)
mu=0.4;
x1=xs(1);
x2=xs(2);
x2d=mu*(1-x1*x1)*x2-x1;                %system equations
sys=x2d;
 end
```

Save the function file as **vanderpol.m** file. Develop the SIMULINK model as shown in Figure 10.62 by adopting the following procedure:

1. Open **Simulink Library browser** in MATLAB and then open a **New Model window.**
2. Click **Continuous library** and with left mouse pressed, drag two integrator blocks from this library and drop them in the new model window.
   Rename the integrator blocks as Integrator and Integrator 1 as shown in Figure 10.62.
3 Similarly drag blocks of **MUX**, block of **XY Graph** and a **S-function block** and drop them in the new model window.
   Connect all the blocks as shown in Figure 10.62.

The input to the first integrator is $\dot{x}_2$ and its output is x_2, which, by the state equation, is equal to $\dot{x}_1$. $\dot{x}_1$ is the input to integrator 1 and its output is x_1.

Set initial conditions of integrators

(I) In order to run the simulation with given initial conditions, open **integrator** by double clicking it. Parameters of integrator blocks will be displayed as shown in Figure 10.63
   Set desired **initial condition,** $x_2(0) = 0.1$ for integrator.
   And initial condition for the **integrator1,** $x_1(0) = 0.1$.
   Save it by clicking **OK.**
   The variables x_2 and x_1, are respectively outputs from the first and second integrators. These are used as feedback to the input of the S-Function block through a **MUX block.**

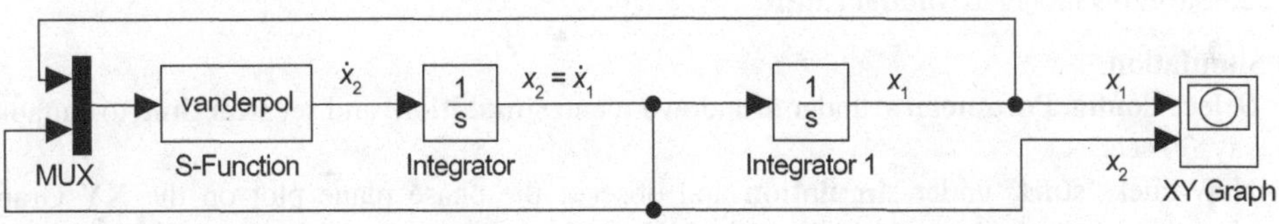

Figure 10.62 Simulink Model for the Solution of Vanderpol Equation

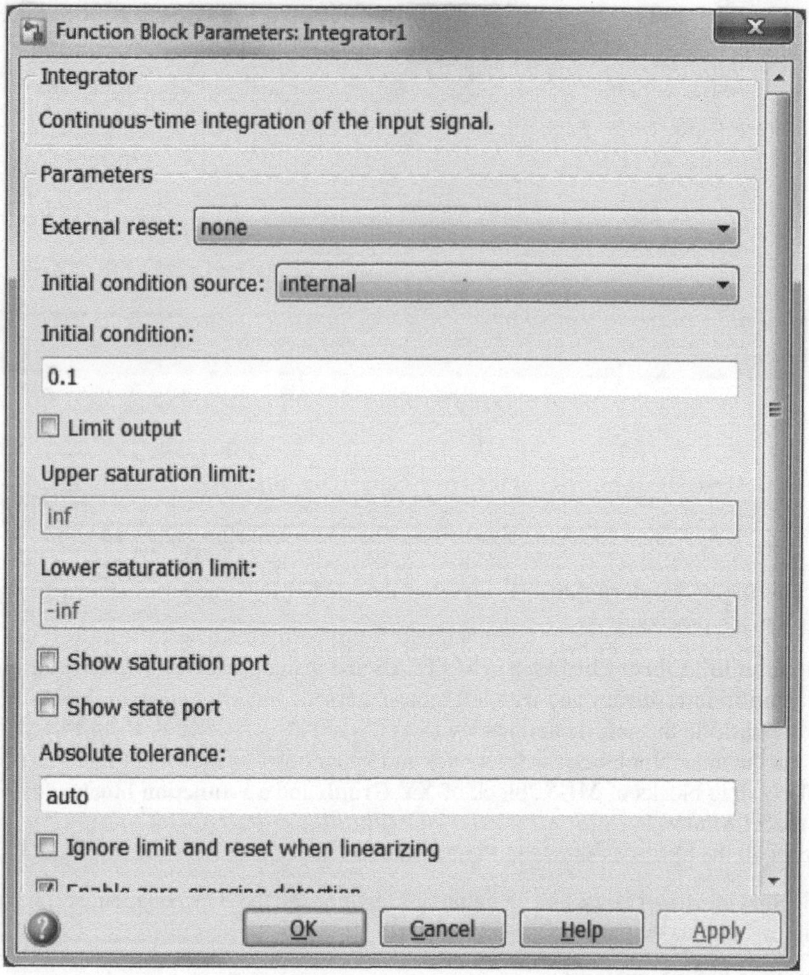

Figure 10.63 Integrator Block Parameters

These state variables are also connected to the **XY Graph** for getting the **phase plane plot**. Set the XY Graph axis values as: *x*-min = –3; *x*-max = 3; *y*-min=-3; *y*-max = 3, as shown in Figure 10.64.

1. Open the S-function block and change its name from **system to vanderpol**.
2. Save this model as **vander1.mdl**

System Simulation

(I) Select **Config. Parameters**, under dropdown menu **simulation,** and set **stop time** to suitable value, say, 30 **sec.**

(II) Now click **'start'** under **simulation** and observe the phase plane plot on the XY Graph. This phase plane plot is shown in Figure 10.65. Here X-axis represents variable x_1 and Y-axis represents variable x_2.

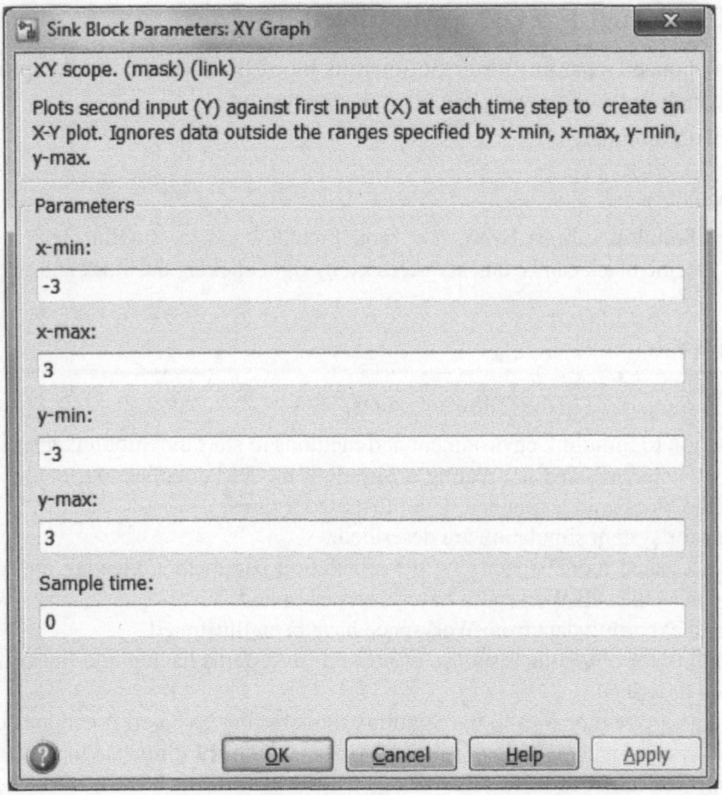

Figure 10.64 Block Parameters of XY Block

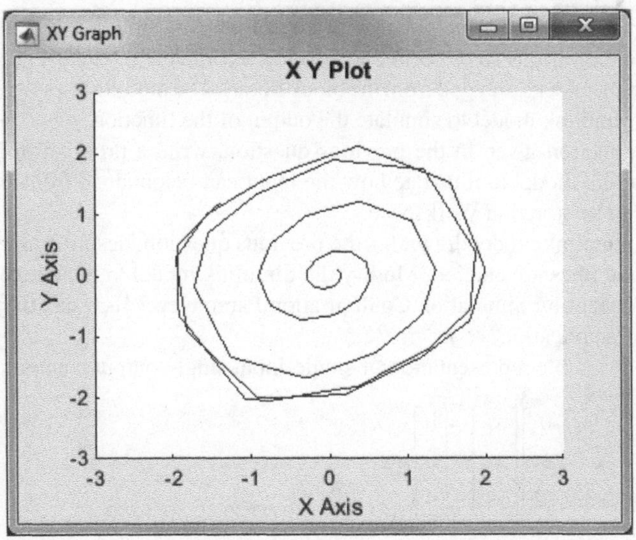

Figure 10.65 Phase Plane Plot of VanderPol Equation

10.16 GETTING HELP FOR SIMULINK

Online help can be obtained regarding different Simulink block libraries and detailed procedure for various tasks, etc. The help includes the following Simulink documentation:

Getting started with Simulink
Using Simulink
Simulink release notes, etc.

Click **Help** menu of Simulink Library Browser or model window to access online help.

Help page for a specific block can be quickly accessed by right clicking the block and selecting **Help** option.

SUMMARY

The chapter can be summarized in the following points:

- An introduction to Simulink environment and methods to start the Simulink are discussed.
- The different steps involved in creating a Simulink model i.e. collecting, modifying, labelling and connecting the blocks, are explained with illustrated figures.
- Solvers used for system simulation are described.
- Simulating a created model specifying the simulation parameters, viewing the response and using variables from MATLAB Workspace have been elaborated.
- Importing and exporting data from Workspace have been illustrated.
- Use of Simulink for obtaining response of non-linear systems having non-linearities such as saturation has been described.
- Obtaining state-space model from the Simulink model using `linmod` function is described.
- Creating sub-systems and masking of sub-systems using '**Mask Editor**' are illustrated with an example.
- Use of S-functions has been explained.

EXERCISES

10.1 List the toolboxes for which blocksets are available in Simulink Library Browser.

10.2 Describe the various steps needed to develop a complete model using Simulink.

10.3 How can the blocks dragged from the block libraries be modified to suit a particular application?

10.4 Draw a Simulink model to simulate the output of the function $y = x^2 + 3.2x - 10$, for $x = 2$

10.5 For the function given in the previous question, write a program in MATLAB and modify the Simulink model to illustrate how the input can be obtained from Workspace and how the output can be stored in Workspace.

10.6 For the Simulink model drawn for the previous question, describe how the labels for the various signal lines are entered. Modify the Simulink model to include the signal lines labels.

10.7 What is meant by Simulation Configuration Parameters? How can they be modified to suit a particular application?

10.8 The state variable representation of single-input single-output control system is given by:

$$\dot{\underline{x}} = \begin{bmatrix} 0 & 1 & 0 \\ 0 & 0 & 1 \\ -4 & -3 & -2 \end{bmatrix} \begin{bmatrix} x_1 \\ x_2 \\ x_3 \end{bmatrix} + \begin{bmatrix} 0 \\ 0 \\ 4 \end{bmatrix} \underline{u}$$

$$y = \begin{bmatrix} 1 & 1 & 0 \end{bmatrix} \underline{x}$$

Draw the Simulink model and obtain its response for $u(t) = 3.54$.

10.9 Explain the different Simulink solvers and their suitability for a particular application.

10.10 With the help of an example, illustrate how the masked sub-systems are created.

10.11 Use the Simulink software to model and simulate the step response of the system described by the following dynamic equations:

$\dot{x}_1 = \dot{x}_2$

$\dot{x}_2 = -2x_1 - x_2 + u(t)$. Assume initial conditions to be zero.

10.12 Consider a third-order system described by

$$\frac{d^3x}{dt^3} + 4\frac{d^2x}{dt^2} + \frac{dx}{dt} + 2x = u(t)$$

Draw a block diagram and obtain the system response using Simulink.

10.13 Draw the Simulink block diagram to obtain the step response of the system whose transfer function is given by:

$$G(s) = \frac{20}{s^2 + 4s + 20}$$

Store the result to MATLAB Workspace.

10.14 State-space representation of a control system is given by

$\dot{x}_1 = x_2$

$\dot{x}_2 = x_3$

$\dot{x}_3 = -4x_1 - 2x_2 - 3x_3 + u(t)$

and

$y = [1 \quad 0 \quad 0]\underline{x}$

Use the state-space model from the Simulink Library Browser and obtain the simulation results. Assume initial conditions to be zero.

10.15 Obtain the state-space model for the system represented by the block diagram, shown in the figure given below, using `linmod` function of Simulink.

10.16 Solve a simple problem using S-function.

CHAPTER 11

MATLAB Applications in Control Systems-I

LEARNING OBJECTIVES

- To obtain Laplace Transform and Inverse Laplace Transform of given functions using `laplace`, `ilaplace` functions.
- To obtain partial fractions of a given function using `residue` function.
- To represent transfer functions of dynamic systems in different forms using MATLAB functions.
- To represent dynamic systems in state variable form.
- To obtain time response of dynamic systems for different types of test inputs.
- To obtain the steady-state errors for different types of systems and different types of inputs using user defined functions `ssetf` and `ssezp`.
- To investigate stability of systems using Routh–Hurwitz criterion using user defined function `routh`.

11.1 INTRODUCTION

The study and design of a control system includes various steps such as modelling, simulation, analysis and optimization. System models are developed by applying fundamental physical laws namely Kirchhoff's current law, Kirchhoff's voltage law, Newton's Laws, laws of thermo-dynamics, etc. These laws may lead to linear, non-linear, ordinary differential, partial differential or difference equations. The response of a control system is studied by subjecting the model to standard input signals. If the response is unsatisfactory, system is improved and optimized by adjustment of system parameters or incorporating suitable compensation devices.

Mathematical equations describe the behaviour of individual components and input-output characteristics of a control system. There are two approaches for the analysis and design of control systems. The first approach is called the classical or frequency domain approach. In this approach, differential or difference equations are converted into transfer functions by relating the input and output using Laplace or z-transforms. This approach is applicable to linear time invariant systems only. The second approach is the state-variable approach or Modern control theory approach which is a time-domain approach. It is easily applicable to a wide range of control systems, such as multi input-multi output and non-linear systems etc. However, this method also requires the knowledge of Laplace Transform.

The Control System Toolbox has a large number of built in functions which can be conveniently used for analysis and design of control systems whether classical or modern control theory approach is used. The following sections describe the basics of these concepts.

11.2 LAPLACE TRANSFORM

Laplace Transform helps in converting differential equations describing the behaviour of dynamic systems into algebraic equations of a complex variable '*s*'. The operations such as differentiation and integration can be replaced by algebraic operations in the complex plane. The solution of a differential equation may thus be easily found by use of Laplace Transform. Another advantage of the Laplace Transform is that both the transient component and steady-state component of the solution can be obtained simultaneously.

Definition:

Laplace Transform can be defined as follows:

Let `f(t)` be a function of time `t` such that `f(t) = 0` for `t < 0`, and `s` be a complex variable. If `L` stands for an operation symbol indicating the Laplace Transformation of `f(t)`, and `F(s)` is the Laplace Transform of `f(t)`, then the Laplace Transform of `f(t)` is given by the following equation:

$$L[f(t)] = F(s) = \int_0^{\infty} e^{-st}[f(t)]dt \tag{11.1}$$

Laplace Transform `F(s)` of a function `f(t)`, can be obtained using Symbolic Mathematics Toolbox, and the following MATLAB commands:

```
syms t          %constructs a symbolic object for time variable 't'
ft              %defines the function f(t)
laplace(ft)     %provides the Laplace transform F(s) of the given function 'ft'
```

Example 11.1 Find the Laplace Transform of the function `f(t) =` e^{-t}`(1-sin(t))`

Solution: The following MATLAB commands are used:

```
syms t
%define the function f(t)
ft = exp(-t) * (1 - sin( t ));
fs = laplace(ft);
```

The result of the commands is as follows:

```
fs =
     1/(1+s)-1/(2+2*s+s^2)
```

i.e.,

$$F(s) = \frac{1}{(s+1)} - \frac{1}{((s+1)^2+1)}$$

11.3 INVERSE LAPLACE TRANSFORMATION

The method of finding the time function `f(t)` from its Laplace Transform, `F(s)`, is called the Inverse Laplace Transformation and is denoted as follows:

`L`$^{-1}$ `[F(s)] = f(t)` (11.2)

The standard Laplace and Inverse Laplace Transform tables are commonly used to obtain Inverse Laplace Transforms. In such cases, the Laplace Transform must be in a form which is immediately recognizable in the standard table. However, in many situations, the function in question may not be available in the desired form. Then, the function may be expanded into partial fractions, and `F(s)` can be written in terms of the sum of functions of `s` for which the Inverse Laplace Transforms are known.

> **Programming Tip 11.1:** A function `F(s)` can be expanded into partial fractions and can be written in terms of sum of functions of `s` for which the Inverse Laplace Transforms are known.

The Inverse Laplace Transform `f(t)` of a given function `F(s)` can be obtained using the following MATLAB commands:

```
syms s t;          %constructs symbolic objects for Laplace
                   Transform variable's' and time variable 't'
fs                 %expression whose ILT is to be obtained.
ilaplace (fs);     %calculates the Inverse Laplace Transform, f(t)
```

Example 11.2 Find the Inverse Laplace Transform of the function $F(s)=\dfrac{1}{s+4}$.

Solution: The following commands are used:

```
syms s t
fs = 1 / (s + 4);
ft = ilaplace(fs)
```

The result of the commands is given as follows:

```
ft =
     exp(-4*t)
```

i.e., the required Inverse Laplace Transform of $\dfrac{1}{s+4}$ is e^{-4t}

Example 11.3 Find the Inverse Laplace Transform of the function $F(s)=\dfrac{2s+1}{s(s^2+2s+4)}$.

Solution: The following commands are used:

```
syms s t;
fs = (2*s+1)/(s*(s^2+2*s+4));
ft = ilaplace(fs);
```

The result obtained is as follows:

```
ft =
     1/4+1/12*exp(-t)*(-3*cos(3^(1/2)*t)+7*3^(1/2)*sin(3^(1/2)*t))
```

11.4 PARTIAL-FRACTION EXPANSION USING MATLAB

For problems in control systems, $F(s)$, the Laplace Transform of $f(t)$, occurs as a ratio of two polynomials in 's'.

$$F(s)=Q(s)/P(s) \tag{11.3}$$

Generally, the highest power of 's' in $P(s)$ is greater than the highest power of 's' in $Q(s)$.

$F(s)$ can be conveniently expressed in terms of its partial-fraction components.

i.e.,

$$F(s)=F_1(s)+F_2(s)+\cdots+F_n(s) \tag{11.4}$$

where $F_1(s)$, $F_2(s)$, etc. are the partial fractions of $F(s)$

If $F(s)$ involves distinct poles, only then it can be expanded into simple partial fractions as follows:

$$F(s)=\frac{Q(s)}{P(s)}=\frac{a_1}{s+p_1}+\frac{a_2}{s+p_2}+\cdots+\frac{a_k}{s+p_k}+\cdots+\frac{a_n}{s+p_n} \tag{11.5}$$

where a_k ($k = 1, 2, 3,\ldots, n$) are constants and are called the residues of the poles at $s = -p_k$.

If $F(s)$ has multiple-order poles and if 'q' poles out, of the 'n' poles of $F(s)$ are same and are located at $-r$, the function $F(s)$ can be written as

$$F(s)=\frac{Q(s)}{(s+p_1)(s+p_2)\ldots(s+p_{n-q})(s+r)^q} \tag{11.6}$$

And the partial fractions of $F(s)$ can be written as

$$F(s)=\frac{k_1}{s+p_1}+\frac{k_2}{s+p_2}+\cdots+\frac{k_{n-q}}{(s+p_{n-q})}+\frac{a_1}{(s+r)}+\frac{a_2}{(s+r)^2}+\cdots+\frac{a_q}{(s+r)^q} \tag{11.7}$$

For complicated functions, obtaining partial-fraction expansion by conventional methods may be quite time consuming. However, MATLAB has commands to obtain the partial fractions of $Q(s)/P(s)$ very conveniently. Consider that a function is given by

$$F(s)=\frac{Q(s)}{P(s)}=\frac{\text{(numerator polynomial)}}{\text{(denominator polynomial)}}=\frac{a_m s^m+a_{m-1}s^{m-1}+\cdots+a_1 s+a_0}{b_k s^n+b_{k-1}s^{n-1}+\cdots+b_1 s+b_0} \tag{11.8}$$

where some of the coefficients a_i and b_i may be zero.

The numerator and the denominator polynomials $Q(s)$ and $P(s)$ are entered in MATLAB as a row vector having their coefficients in descending powers of 's', as shown below:

```
n = [a_m a_m-1 ........a_1 a_0]
d = [b_k b_k-1 ......b_1 b_0]
```

where

n represents the coefficients of numerator polynomial $Q(s)$, and
d represents the coefficients of denominator polynomial $P(s)$.

> **Programming Tip 11.2:** A polynomial is defined in MATLAB by specifying its coefficients in descending powers of 's'.

The MATLAB function **`residue`** finds the residues, poles and direct terms of a partial-fraction expansion of the function F(s), defined as the ratio of two polynomials represented by row vectors n and d respectively. The syntax is given as follows:

```
[r, p, k] = residue(n, d);
```

The residues are returned in column vector `r`, the pole locations in column vector `p` and the direct terms in row vector `k`. If the result shows that `k = [1 3 5]`, it means that the direct term is `(s² + 3s + 5)`. If the row vector `k` is shown as null, i.e., `[]`, it means that there are no direct terms.

The partial-fraction expansion of `F(s)` is thus given by

$$\frac{Q(s)}{P(s)}=\frac{r(1)}{s-p(1)}+\frac{r(2)}{s-p(2)}+\cdots+\frac{r(m)}{s-p(m)}+k(s) \tag{11.9}$$

The `residue` function can also be used to convert the partial-fraction expansion back into the polynomial ratio $Q(s)/P(s)$ by interchanging the input and output arguments as shown below:

```
[n, d] = residue(r, p, k)
```

Example 11.4 Obtain the partial fractions of the function $F(s)=\dfrac{Q(s)}{P(s)}=\dfrac{(s+1)}{(s^2+s+1)}$.

Solution: The following MATLAB commands are used:

```
n = [1 1];
d = [1 1 1];
[r, p, k] = residue(n, d)
```

The output of the commands is given as follows:

```
r =
     0.5000 - 0.2887i
     0.5000 + 0.2887i
p =
    -0.5000 + 0.8660i
    -0.5000 - 0.8660i
k =
     []
```

i.e., the required partial fractions are $\dfrac{0.5-0.2887i}{s+0.5-0.866i}+\dfrac{0.5+0.2887i}{s+0.5+0.866i}$.

It can be seen that the constant term is zero in this example.

To verify the outputs obtained above, the transfer function $Q(s)/P(s)$ can be regenerated by using the obtained values of r, p and k and using the following command:

```
[n, d] = residue(r, p, k);
```

The result obtained is

```
n =
     1 1
d =
     1.0000     1.0000     1.0000
```

i.e., the transfer function is given by $\dfrac{Q(s)}{P(s)}=\dfrac{(s+1)}{(s^2+s+1)}$.

Example 11.5 Expand the following function $F(s)$ into partial fractions:

$$F(s)=\frac{Q(s)}{P(s)}=\frac{(s+3)}{(s+2)^3}=\frac{s+3}{s^3+6s^2+12s+8}$$

Solution: The following MATLAB commands are used:

```
n = [0 0 1 3];
d = [1 6 12 8];
[r, p, k] = residue(n, d)
```

The following results are obtained:

```
r =
          0
     1.0000
     1.0000
p =
    -2.0000
    -2.0000
    -2.0000
k =
     []
```

i.e., the partial fractions are $\dfrac{0}{s+2}+\dfrac{1}{(s+2)^2}+\dfrac{1}{(s+2)^3}$.

To verify the result, the following MATLAB command can be used:

```
[n, d] = residue(r, p, k)
```

The values of n and d obtained are as follows:

```
n =
     0     1     3
d =
     1.0000    6.0000    12.0000    8.0000
```

i.e., the transfer function is $\dfrac{s+3}{s^3+6s^2+12s+8}$.

Example 11.6 Obtain the partial fractions of the following function:

$$F(s)=\frac{(s+1)}{(s+2)^2(s+3)(s)}=\frac{(s+1)}{s^4+7s^3+16s^2+12s}$$

Solution: The following MATLAB commands are used:

```
n = [1 1];
d = [1 7 16 12 0];
[r, p, k] = residue(n, d)
```

The following results are obtained:

```
r =
      0.6667
     -0.7500
      0.5000
      0.0833
p =
     -3.0000
     -2.0000
     -2.0000
           0
k =
     []
```

i.e., the partial-fraction expansion is, $G(s)=\dfrac{0.6667}{s+3}+\dfrac{-0.75}{(s+2)}+\dfrac{0.5}{(s+2)^2}+\dfrac{0.0833}{(s+0)}$.

Example 11.7 Determine the partial-fraction expansion of $F(s)=\dfrac{(s^3+9s+1)}{(s^3+s^2+2s+2)}$.

Solution: The commands used are as follows:

```
n = [1 0 9 1];
d = [1 1 2 2];
[r, p, k] = residue(n, d)
```

The following results are obtained:

```
r =
      1.0000 - 1.7678i
```

```
        1.0000 + 1.7678i
       -3.0000
p =
        0.0000 + 1.4142i
        0.0000 - 1.4142i
       -1.0000
k =
        1
```

i.e., the partial fractions are

$$1+\frac{1.000-1.7678i}{s-1.4142i}+\frac{1.000+1.7678i}{s+1.4142i}-\frac{3}{s+1}.$$

11.5 TRANSFER FUNCTION REPRESENTATION

The Transfer Function of an LTI system is defined as the ratio of the Laplace Transform of the output to the Laplace Transform of the input, assuming the initial conditions to be zero.

Let the Transfer function $G(s)$ be given as a ratio of two polynomials in `s`, i.e.,

$$G(s)=\frac{n(s)}{d(s)}$$

where `n(s)` is the numerator polynomial and `d(s)` is the denominator polynomial and the coefficients of Laplace Transform variable '`s`' in these polynomials are arranged in descending order.

The command `tf` is used to find the equivalent transfer function representation in MATLAB. The syntax of this command is

```
variable_name = tf(n, d)
```

It generates the transfer function $G(s)$ with the given numerator `n` and denominator `d` and stores it in `variable_name`, specified by the user.

For example,

```
sys = tf(n, d)
```

will generate the required transfer function and will store it in the variable `sys`.

The `tfdata` command performs exactly opposite of `tf` command and returns the `n` and `d` polynomials from the given transfer function. The syntax is

```
[n, d] = tfdata(sys, 'v')
```

The option '`v`' ensures that '`n`' and '`d`' polynomials of the transfer function are returned as row vectors and not cell arrays.

Example 11.8 Define the following transfer function $G(s)$, in MATLAB:

$$G(s)=\frac{s(s+1)(s+2)}{s(s+3)(s^2+4s+8)}=\frac{5s^2+15s+10}{s^4+7s^3+20s^2+24s}$$

Solution: The following commands are used:

```
n = [5 15 10];
d = [1 7 20 24 0];
sys = tf(n, d)
```

The following results are obtained:

```
Transfer function:
```

```
    5 s^2 + 15 s + 10
---------------------------
s^4 + 7 s^3 + 20 s^2 + 24 s
```

Example 11.9 Given below is a transfer function $G(s)$. Use the MATLAB commands poly and conv to generate the polynomials n and d and create the transfer function named as sys.

$$G(s) = \frac{5(s+1)(s+2)}{(s^2+4s+6)(s+4)}$$

Solution: The following MATLAB commands are used:

```
r = [-1; -2];
%Vector r represents the roots of num. polynomial
n = 5 * poly(r);%n defines numerator polynomial from the roots 'r'
p1 = [1 4 6];
p2 = [1 4];
%p1 and p2 are coefficients of factors of denominator polynomial
d = conv(p1, p2);
%generates the denominator polynomial by taking convolution of p1 and p2
sys = tf(n, d); %forms the transfer function 'sys'
```

The following result is obtained:

```
Transfer function:
   5 s^2 + 15 s + 10
-----------------------
s^3 + 8 s^2 + 22 s + 24
```

11.6 ZEROS, POLES AND POLE–ZERO MAP OF A TRANSFER FUNCTION

The command **tf2zp** is used to obtain the zeros z, poles p and gain k of the transfer function defined by its numerator and denominator polynomials, n and d, respectively. The syntax is given as follows:

```
[z, p, k] = tf2zp(n, d);
```

To obtain the transfer function, as a ratio of two polynomials, if the zeros z, poles p and gain k are given, any one of the following MATLAB commands can be used:

```
[n, d] = zp2tf(z, p, k);
sys = zpk(z,p.k)
```

The command **pzmap(n,d)** can be used to plot the pole–zero map of a given transfer function, and the command **printsys(n,d,'s')** prints the transfer function as a ratio of two polynomials in the variable s. The above commands are illustrated in the following examples.

Example 11.10 Find the location of zeros and poles and plot the pole–zero map of the system, whose transfer function is given by:

$$F(s) = \frac{n(s)}{d(s)} = \frac{2s^2+8s+6}{s^4+6s^3+12s^2+24s}$$

Solution: The following MATLAB commands are used:

```
n = [0 0 2 8 6];              %defines the numerator polynomial
d = [1 6 12 24 0];            %defines the denominator polynomial
[z, p, k] = tf2zp(n, d)       %generates the poles, zeroes and gain
```

The following results are obtained:

```
z =
    -3
    -1
p =
          0
    -4.5198
    -0.7401 + 2.1822i
    -0.7401 - 2.1822i
k =
     2
```

The results signify that the **zeros** are at $s = -3$ and -1, the **poles** are at $s = 0, -4.5198, -0.7401 + 2.1822i$, and $-0.7401 - 21822i$, and the **gain** is $k = 2$. Therefore, the transfer function in terms of various factors is defined as follows:

$$F(s) = \frac{n(s)}{d(s)} = \frac{2(s+3)(s+1)}{s(s+4.5198)(s+0.7401-2.182i)(s+0.7401+2.1822i)}$$

Pole–zero map for this function can be obtained by using the command

```
pzmap(n, d)
%plots the pole-zero map of the transfer function
```

and is shown in Figure 11.1.

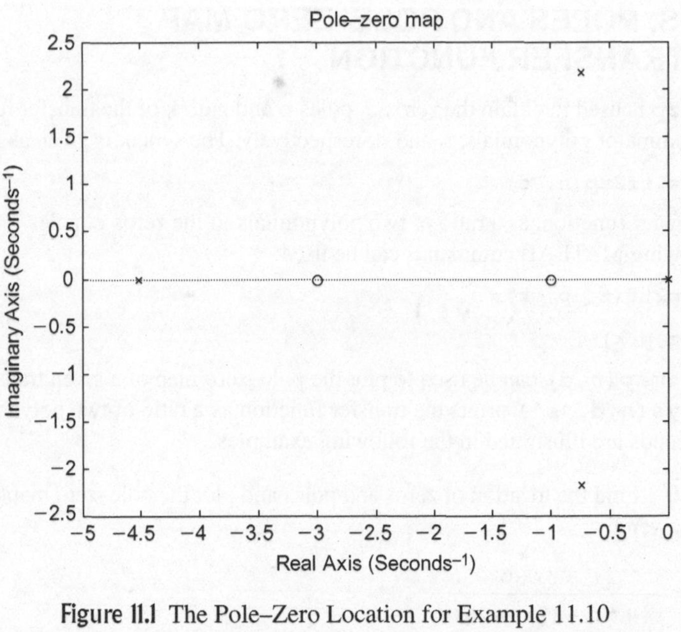

Figure 11.1 The Pole–Zero Location for Example 11.10

Example 11.11

(i) Verify the results obtained for Example 11.10 by obtaining the transfer function from the calculated values of zeros, poles and gain.

(ii) Location of the zeros and poles of a system is given as follows:
$z = -5$; $p = [0\ -1\ -2]$; $k = 1$;
Obtain the system transfer function, using the command:
sys = zpk(z,p,k)

Solution:

(i) **The following commands are used:**

```
z = [-3; -1];        %zeros and poles are in column vector form
p = [0; -4.5198; -0.7401 +2.1822i; -0.7401-2.1822i];
k = 2;
[n, d] = zp2tf(z, p, k);
printsys(n, d, 's')
%prints the transfer function as a ratio of two polynomials in the transform
%variable 's'.
```

The following results are obtained:

```
 2 s^2 + 8 s + 6
-----------------------
s^4 + 6s^3 + 12s^2 + 24s
```

(ii) **Type the following commands in the command window:**

```
 z=  -5 ;
 p = [0 -1 -2];
  k=1;
  sys=zpk(z,p,k)
```

Following transfer function will be displayed:

```
      sys =
        (s+5)
   -------------
   s (s+1) (s+2)
```

11.7 STATE-SPACE REPRESENTATION OF DYNAMIC SYSTEMS

State-space representation of multi-input multi-output dynamic systems is described by the following matrix vector differential equations:

$$\dot{\underline{x}} = A\,\underline{x} + B\,\underline{u}$$
$$y = C\,\underline{x} + D\,\underline{u} \tag{11.10}$$

where $\underline{x} = (n \times 1)$ state vector,
$\dot{\underline{x}} = (n \times 1)$ velocity vector (derivative of state vector),
$\underline{u} = (m \times 1)$ input or control signal vector
$y = (p \times 1)$ output signal vector,
$A = (n \times n)$ system matrix of constant elements,
$B = (n \times m)$ matrix of constant elements,

$C = (p \times n)$ matrix of constant elements and
$D = (p \times m)$ matrix of constant elements.

For state-space representation, model data consists of four matrices, i.e., A, B, C, and D, containing constant elements. MATLAB provides an LTI object, for state-space representation in **controllable canonical form**, which can be defined by the command **ss** as shown below:

```
syst = ss(A, B, C, D);
%'syst' is the LTI object variable name(to be specified by the user)
```

11.7.1 Phase Variable Canonical Form

Given the state model corresponding to controllable canonical form, a phase variable form can be obtained using a similarity transformation matrix 'P', such that

```
Ap = P-1 A P;
Bp = P-1 B;
Cp = C* P;
Dp = D;
```

where Ap, Bp, Cp and Dp are the system matrices/vectors in the **phase variable canonical form** corresponding to matrices/vector A, B, C, and D in **controllable canonical form.**

Example 11.12 Obtain MATLAB representation of a control system described in its state-space representation given by

$$\dot{\underline{x}} = \begin{bmatrix} 1 & 1 \\ 0 & -1 \end{bmatrix} \underline{x} + \begin{bmatrix} 1 \\ 0 \end{bmatrix} u \quad \text{and} \quad y = [1 \quad 1]\underline{x} + [0]u$$

Solution:

The following commands are used:

```
A = [1 1; 0 -1]; B = [1; 0];
C = [1 1];
D = [0];
system = ss(A, B, C, D)
```

The LTI object system is obtained as follows:

```
a =
        x1  x2
    x1   1   1
    x2   0  -1
b =
        u1
    x1   1
    x2   0
c =
        x1  x2
    y1   1   1
d =
            u1
        y1   0
Continuous-time model.
```

Example 11.13 Obtain the state model in the phase variable form for the following system:

$$\dot{\underline{x}} = \begin{bmatrix} -5 & -7 & -10 \\ 1 & 0 & 0 \\ 0 & 1 & 0 \end{bmatrix} \underline{x} + \begin{bmatrix} 1 \\ 0 \\ 0 \end{bmatrix} u \quad \text{and} \quad y = [1 \quad 1 \quad 1]\underline{x} + [0]u$$

Similarity Transformation Matrix, P is given by

$$P = \begin{bmatrix} 0 & 0 & 1 \\ 0 & 1 & 0 \\ 1 & 0 & 0 \end{bmatrix}$$

Solution: The following MATLAB commands are used:

```
%Controllable canonical form
A = [-5 -7 -10; 1 0 0; 0 1 0];
B = [1; 0; 0];
C = [1 1 1];
D = 0;
%Phase variable form
P=[0 0 1; 0 1 0; 1 0 0];
Ap = inv(P) * A * P
Bp = inv(P) * B
Cp = C * P
Dp = D
```

The state model matrices obtained in phase variable form are as given below:

```
Ap =
     0       1       0
     0       0       1
   -10      -7      -5
Bp =
     0
     0
     1
Cp =
     1       1       1
Dp =
     0
```

Example 11.14 Obtain the state model in phase variable form for the system described by the following state equations in controllable canonical form.

$$\dot{\underline{x}} = \begin{bmatrix} -1 & -2 \\ 1 & 0 \end{bmatrix} \underline{x} + \begin{bmatrix} 1 \\ 0 \end{bmatrix} u \quad \text{and} \quad y = [0 \quad 1]\underline{x} + [0]u$$

and similarity transformation matrix, $P = \begin{bmatrix} 0 & 1 \\ 1 & 0 \end{bmatrix}$

Solution: The following MATLAB commands are used:

```
A = [-1 -2; 1 0];
B = [1; 0];
C = [0 1];
D = [0];
P = [0 1; 1 0];
Ap = inv(P) * A * P
Bp = inv(P) * B
Cp = C * P
Dp = D
```

The state model matrices obtained in phase variable form are as given below:

```
Ap =
      0      1
     -2     -1
Bp =
      0
      1
Cp =
      1      0
Dp =
      0
```

11.8 TRANSFER FUNCTION TO STATE-SPACE CONVERSION

A system model which is given in the form of a transfer function can be transformed to state-space model using MATLAB. Suppose the closed-loop transfer function of a system be given by:

$$G(s) = \frac{\text{numerator polynomial in 's'}}{\text{denominator polynomial in 's'}}$$

i.e.,

$$G(s) = \frac{n}{d}$$

The command **`tf2ss`** is used to convert the transfer function model into state-space model, giving the system matrices A, B, C and D as the output. The syntax of `tf2ss` is

```
[A, B, C, D] = tf2ss(n, d)
```

It should be noted that the state-space representation for any system is not unique. The same system can be represented in many different ways in state-space form. However, using this command, only one of these representations i.e., controllable canonical form is obtained.

Example 11.15 Obtain the state-space representation for the system, whose transfer function is given by:

$$G(s) = \frac{s+2}{s^3 + 10s^2 + 15s + 150}.$$

Solution: The following commands are used:

```
n = [0 0 1 2];
d = [1 10 15 150];
[A, B, C, D] = tf2ss(n, d);
```

The following results are obtained:

```
A =

   -10   -15  -150
     1     0     0
     0     1     0

B =

     1
     0
     0

C =

     0     1     2

D =

     0
```

11.9 STATE-SPACE TO TRANSFER FUNCTION CONVERSION

To obtain the transfer function from state-space representation, the following MATLAB command can be used:

```
[n, d] = ss2tf(A, B, C, D, k)
```

where argument 'k' is required only if system has more than one input and specifies k[th] input. If the system has only one input, then it need not be mentioned, i.e., `k` may be omitted or `k = 1` may be given. The syntax is given as follows:

```
[n, d] = ss2tf(A, B, C, D)
or
[n, d]= ss2tf(A, B, C, D, 1)
```

11.9.1 State Space Representation to Zero–Pole-Gain Conversion

To obtain ZERO–POLE-GAIN representation from state-space representation, the following MATLAB command can be used:

```
[z,p,k]=ss2zp(a,b,c,d,k)
```

where argument 'k' is required only if system has more than one input and specifies kth input. If the system has only one input, then it need not be mentioned, i.e., `k` may be omitted or `k = 1`.

11.9.2 Zero–Pole-Gain Representation to State Space Conversion

To obtain state space representation from zero–pole-gain representation, the following MATLAB command can be used:

```
[a,b,c,d]=zp2ss(z,p,k)
```

Example 11.16

(i) Obtain the transfer function of the system described by the following state-space equations:

$$\begin{bmatrix} \dot{x}_1 \\ \dot{x}_2 \end{bmatrix} = \begin{bmatrix} 0 & 1 \\ -5 & -10 \end{bmatrix} \begin{bmatrix} x_1 \\ x_2 \end{bmatrix} + \begin{bmatrix} 0 \\ 15 \end{bmatrix} u$$

and $y = [1 \quad 0] \begin{bmatrix} x_1 \\ x_2 \end{bmatrix}$

(ii) Given **state space representation** of a system as in Part (I), Obtain **zero-pole-gain representation** from state space representation.

(iii) Given **zero-pole-gain representation** of a system as follows:
$z = [-3; -1]$
$p = [0; -4; -0.7 + 2.1i; -0.7 - 2.1i];$
$k = 2;$
Obtain state-space representation.

Solution:

(i) **State-space to transfer function conversion**
The following commands are used:

```
A = [0 1; -5 -10];
B = [0; 15];
C = [1 0];
D = [0];
[n, d] = ss2tf(A, B, C, D)
```

The following results are obtained:

```
n =
                  0            0        15.0000
d =
             1.0000      10.0000         5.0000
```

The required transfer function can be printed by using the following command:

```
printsys(n, d)
```

and the result obtained is

```
              15
    --------------
    s^2 + 10 s + 5
```

(ii) **Obtain zero–pole-gain representation from state space representation**
The following commands are used:

```
a=[0  1 ;-5 -10];
b=[0;15];
c=[1 0];
d=[0];
k = 1;
[z,p,k]=ss2zp(a,b,c,d,k)
```

Following zero–pole-gain representation will be displayed:

```
z = [ ]
```

i.e., Empty matrix: 0-by-1

```
p =
    -0.5279
    -9.4721
k =
     15.0000
```

(iii) **Obtain state space representation from zero-pole-gain representation**
The following commands are used:

```
z = [-3 ;-1]
```

```
p = [0;-4;-0.7+2.1i;-0.7-2.1i];
k = 2;
[a,b,c,d]=zp2ss(z,p,k)
```

Following state space representation will be displayed:

```
a =
     -1.4000    -2.2136          0         0
      2.2136          0          0         0
      2.6000    -0.8583    -4.0000         0
           0          0     1.0000         0
b =
      1
      0
      1
      0
c =   0       0       0       2
d =   0
```

11.10 SERIES/CASCADE, PARALLEL AND FEEDBACK CONNECTIONS

Let there be two transfer functions $G_1(s)$ and $G_2(s)$ interconnected either in **series (cascade), parallel** or **feedback** mode, as shown in the Figures 11.2(a)–(c).

Let $G_1(s)$ be represented by $\frac{n_1}{d_1}$ and $G_2(s)$ by $\frac{n_2}{d_2}$. Then, the following commands can be used to obtain the respective overall system transfer functions:

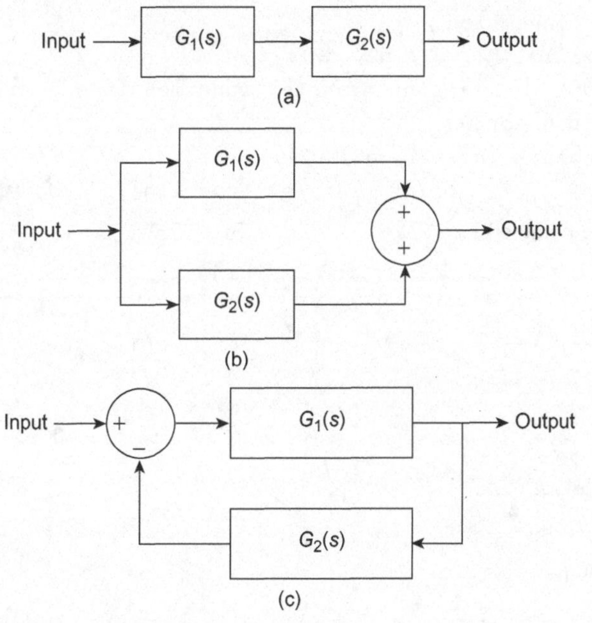

Figure 11.2 Two Transfer Functions G_1(s) and G_2(s) Connected in (a) Series, (b) Parallel and (c) Feedback Mode

For Two Systems connected in Series:

```
[ns, ds] = series(n1, d1, n2, d2);
printsys(ns, ds);
```

For Two Systems connected in Parallel:

```
[np, dp] = parallel(n1, d1, n2, d2);
printsys(np, dp);
```

For feedback (Closed loop) System:

```
[nf, df ] = feedback(n1, d1, n2, d2);
printsys(nf, df);
```

Example 11.17 Obtain the overall system transfer functions of systems composed of two sub-systems, $G_1(s)$ and $G_2(s)$, connected in (a) series, (b) parallel and (c) feedback configuration. The transfer functions of the two sub-systems are given by

$$G_1(s) = \frac{5}{s^2 + s + 5} \quad \text{and} \quad G_2(s) = \frac{2}{s+2}$$

Solution: The following MATLAB commands are used:

```
n1 = [0  0 5];
d1 = [1  1 5];
n2 = [0  2];
d2 = [1  2];
%for series connection
[ns, ds] = series(n1, d1, n2, d2);
printsys(ns, ds)        %print transfer function in s domain
%for parallel connection
[np, dp] = parallel(n1, d1, n2, d2);
printsys(np, dp)        %print transfer function in s domain
%for feedback connection
[nf, df] = feedback (n1, d1, n2, d2);
printsys(nf, df)        %print transfer function in s domain
```

The following results are obtained:

For series connection:

```
   10
----------------------
s^3 + 3 s^2 + 7 s + 10
```

For parallel connection:

```
2 s^2 + 7 s + 20
----------------------
s^3 + 3 s^2 + 7 s + 10
```

For feedback connection:

```
   5 s + 10
----------------------
s^3 + 3 s^2 + 7 s + 20
```

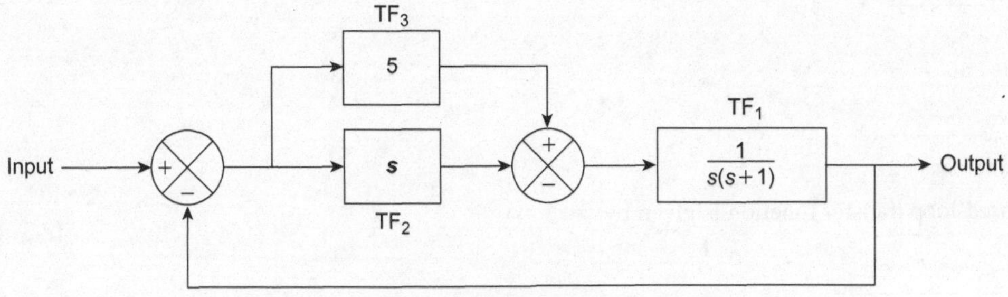

Figure 11.3 Block Diagram of a Control System

Example 11.18 Obtain closed-loop transfer function for the system whose block diagram is given in Figure 11.3. TF_1, TF_2 and TF_3 represent the transfer function of the corresponding blocks as shown in the figure.

Solution: The following MATLAB commands are used:

```
n1 = [1];
d1 = [1 1 0];
printsys(n1, d1);
n2 = [5];
d2 = 1;
printsys(n2, d2);
n3 = [1 0];
d3 = [0 1];
[n4, d4] = parallel(n2, d2, n3, d3);
printsys(n4, d4);
[n5, d5] = series(n1, d1, n4, d4);
printsys(n5,d5)
[n6, d6] = feedback(n5, d5, 1, 1);
printsys(n6, d6);
```

The following results are obtained:

```
n1/d1 =
          1
     -------
     s^2 + s
n2/d2 =
     5
     -
     1
n4/d4 =
     s + 5
     -----
       1
n5/d5 =
       s + 5
```

```
 -------
 s^2 + s
n6/d6 =
     s + 5
 ------------
 s^2 + 2s + 5
```

The closed-loop transfer function is given by

```
     s + 5
-------------
s^2 + 2 s + 5
```

11.11 TIME RESPONSE OF CONTROL SYSTEMS

To analyse the performance of a control system, its response, i.e., variation in output with respect to time, is studied, which is called time response. The output of the system with respect to time must be within the specified limits for its satisfactory performance. Thus, the time response has utmost importance for the design and analysis of a control system. The time response is divided into two parts:

1. Transient response.
2. Steady-state response.

A transient state of the system remains for a short time, while steady-state is approached as the time elapsed is quite large or it approaches infinity.
The output response $c(t)$ can be expressed as

$$c(t) = c_t(t) + c_{ss}(t) \tag{11.11}$$

where

$c(t)$ is total time response,
$c_t(t)$ is transient response, and
$c_{ss}(t)$ is steady-state response.

11.11.1 Transient Response

The response of the system before it reaches its steady state is called **transient response**. The information that can be obtained from the transient response is as follows:

(a) Time taken by the system to respond after application of input signal.
(b) Time taken by a system to achieve desired output for the first time.
(c) Whether there is an overshoot? If yes, what is its magnitude?
(d) Whether the output oscillates about its final value or not?
(e) Time taken by the system to settle down to a steady-state value?

11.11.2 Steady-State Response

The steady-state response is defined as the response of the system as time approaches to ∞. The information that can be obtained from this response is as follows:

(a) Time taken by the system to reach the steady-state value.
(b) The steady-state output error or offset.

A typical time response curve depicting the transient and steady-state components is shown in Figure 11.4.

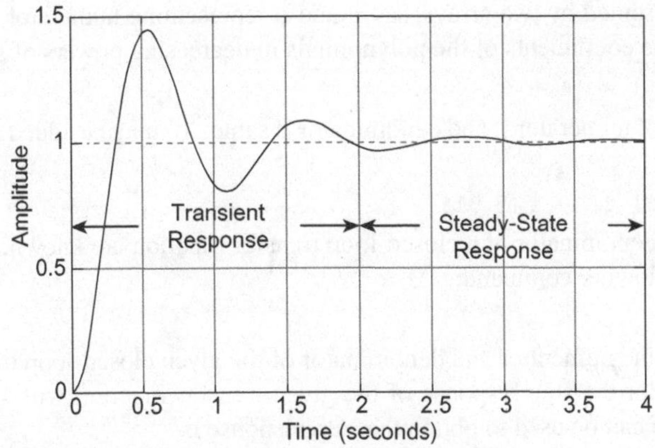

Figure 11.4 Time Response Curve Showing Transient and Steady-State Components

11.12 STANDARD INPUT TEST SIGNALS

The standard input test signals used for the analysis and design of control systems are tabulated in the Table 11.1 with their mathematical representations, Laplace Transform form and graphical representation.

Table 11.1 Standard Input Test Signals for Control Systems

Name of the Signal	Mathematical Expression	Laplace Transform Form	Graphical Representation
Step signal	$r(t) = 0; t < 0$ $= A; t > 0$	$R(s) = A/s$	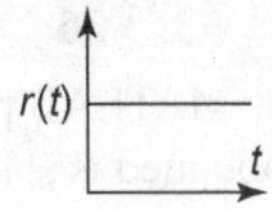
Ramp signal	$r(t) = 0; t < 0$ $= At; t > 0$	$R(s) = A/s^2$	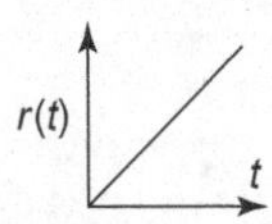
Parabolic signal	$r(t) = 0; t < 0$ $= At^2/2; t > 0$	$R(s) = A/s^3$	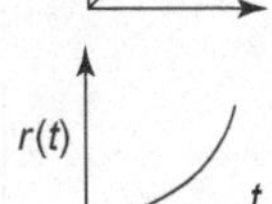

The computational approach to obtain the time response for different input signals using MATLAB is as follows.

11.13 STEP RESPONSE OF LINEAR DYNAMIC SYSTEMS

Step response of linear dynamic systems can be obtained by using either transfer function approach or by using state-space approach.

11.13.1 Transfer Function Approach

The transfer function is represented by a ratio of two polynomials. Consider a transfer function given as

$$G(s) = \frac{81s + 4}{s^2 + 6s + 81}$$

This system can be represented by two arrays, say `n` and `d` representing numerator and denominator respectively, each containing the coefficients of the polynomials in decreasing powers of s:

`n = [81 4]` and `d = [1 6 81]`

To make the dimensions of numerator `n` and denominator `d` same, '0' may be added in numerator array. Thus, the arrays become

`n = [0 81 4]` and `d = [1 6 81]`

Once the numerator and denominator of a closed-loop transfer function are known, the step response can be obtained by using the following command:

```
step(n, d)
```

where `n` and `d` represent the numerator and denominator of the given closed-loop transfer function.

This command will plot the step response of the given transfer function with default values of time `t`. Another command which can be used to obtain the step response is

```
step(n, d, t)
```

where `t` is the user-defined time vector and has to be defined prior to the use of `step` command. This command will plot the step response of the transfer function with user-defined values of time t.

Programming Tip 11.3: The user-defined time t must be defined prior to use of `step` command.

Example 11.19 Plot unit step response of the closed-loop transfer function, with default values of time `t`.

$$G(s) = \frac{36}{s^2 + 3s + 36}$$

Solution: The MATLAB program for obtaining the step response of the system is given below, and the step response obtained is shown in the Figure 11.5.

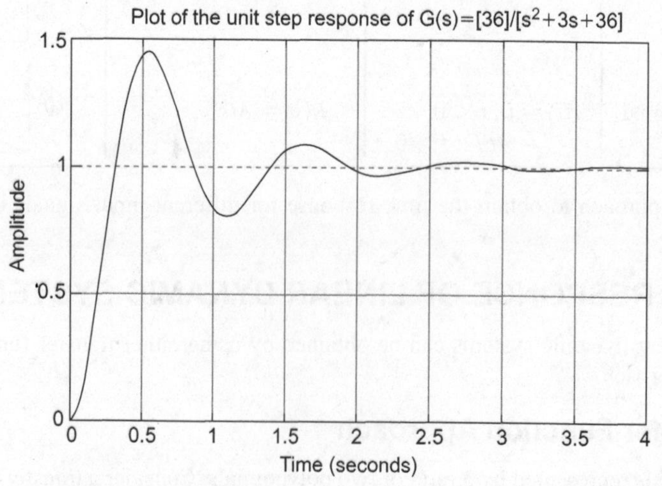

Figure 11.5 The Step Response for Function $G(s) = \dfrac{36}{s^2 + 3s + 36}$

```
%Program to get unit step response with default time values
n = [ 0 0 36];
d = [ 1 3 36];
step(n, d);
grid on;
title('Plot of the unit step response of G(s) = [36] / [s^2 + 3s + 36]')
xlabel('Time (secs)');
ylabel('Amplitude');
```

This example can also be illustrated by using a second command in which the user-defined time `t` is used in the plot.

Example 11.20 For the system given in Example 11.19, obtain unit step response of the system, for `t = 0 to 2` sec, in steps of 0.005.

Solution: The program given above is repeated with the addition of time parameter in step function, and the step response obtained is given in Figure 11.6.

```
n = [ 0 0 36];
d = [ 1 3 36];
%User defined time from 0 to 2 sec with increment of 0.005
t = 0:0.005:2;
%step command with the addition of time parameter
step(n, d, t);
grid on;
title('Plot of the unit step response of G(s)=[36]/[s^2+3s+36] with user
defined time');
xlabel('Time(sec)');
ylabel('Amplitude');
```

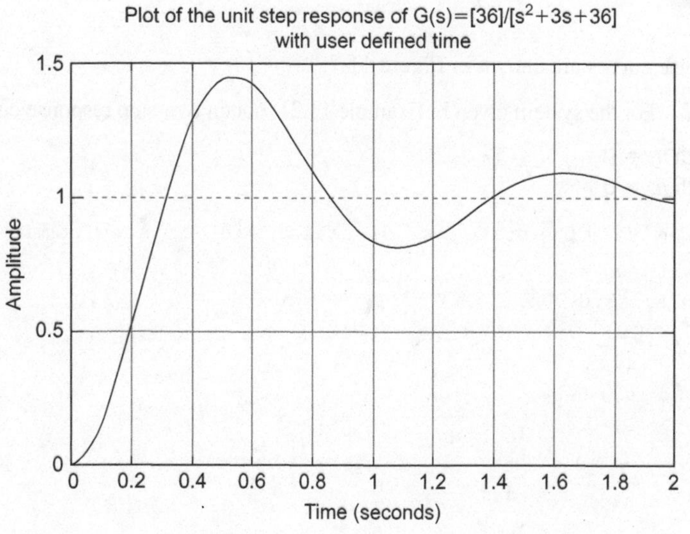

Figure 11.6 Step Response for Function $G(s) = \dfrac{36}{s^2 + 3s + 36}$ with User-Defined Time

11.13.2 State-Space Approach

The command used to plot unit step response for a system defined in state-space form is

```
step (A, B, C, D)
```

where A, B, C, D are the system matrices/vectors.
If time is defined by the user, then the command is modified as

```
step (A, B, C, D, t)
```

If a system involves multiple inputs and multiple outputs, then for obtaining step response plot for each input and output combination separately, the `step` command is modified as follows:

```
step (A, B, C, D, iu, t)
```

where `iu` is an index which specifies the input to be used for obtaining the response, if there is more than one input. If `iu=0`, four step responses will be displayed.

Example 11.21 Obtain step response of the system whose state-space representation is given as

$$\dot{x} = \begin{bmatrix} -1 & -0.5 \\ 5.0 & 0 \end{bmatrix}\begin{bmatrix} x_1 \\ x_2 \end{bmatrix} + \begin{bmatrix} 1.5 & 1 \\ 0.5 & 0 \end{bmatrix}\begin{bmatrix} u_1 \\ u_2 \end{bmatrix}$$

$$\begin{bmatrix} y_1 \\ y_2 \end{bmatrix} = \begin{bmatrix} 1 & 0 \\ 0 & 1 \end{bmatrix}\begin{bmatrix} x_1 \\ x_2 \end{bmatrix} + \begin{bmatrix} 0 & 0 \\ 0 & 0 \end{bmatrix}\begin{bmatrix} u_1 \\ u_2 \end{bmatrix}$$

Solution: The MATLAB program for the given problem is

```
%Program to obtain step response for Example 11.21
A = [-1  -0.5;  5.0  0];
B = [1.5  1;  0.5  0];
C = [1  0;  0  1];
D = [0  0;  0  0];
step(A, B, C, D);
grid;
```

The four step response curves are shown in Figure 11.7.

Example 11.22 For the system given in Example 11.21, obtain two-step response curves in one graph for

1. input u_1 with $u_2 = 0$
2. input u_2 with $u_1 = 0$

Solution:

```
%Program to illustrate use of scalar 'iu' in step command
%input u1 with u2 = 0
A = [-1  -0.5;  5.0  0];
B = [1.5  1;  0.5  0];
C = [1  0;  0  1];
D = [0  0;  0  0];
step(A, B, C, D, 1)                        %iu=1
grid on;
gtext ('y1');
gtext ('y2')
title('Step response when input is u1 and input 2,u2 =0');
```

The two-step response curves (when input $u_2 = 0$) are shown in Figure 11.8.

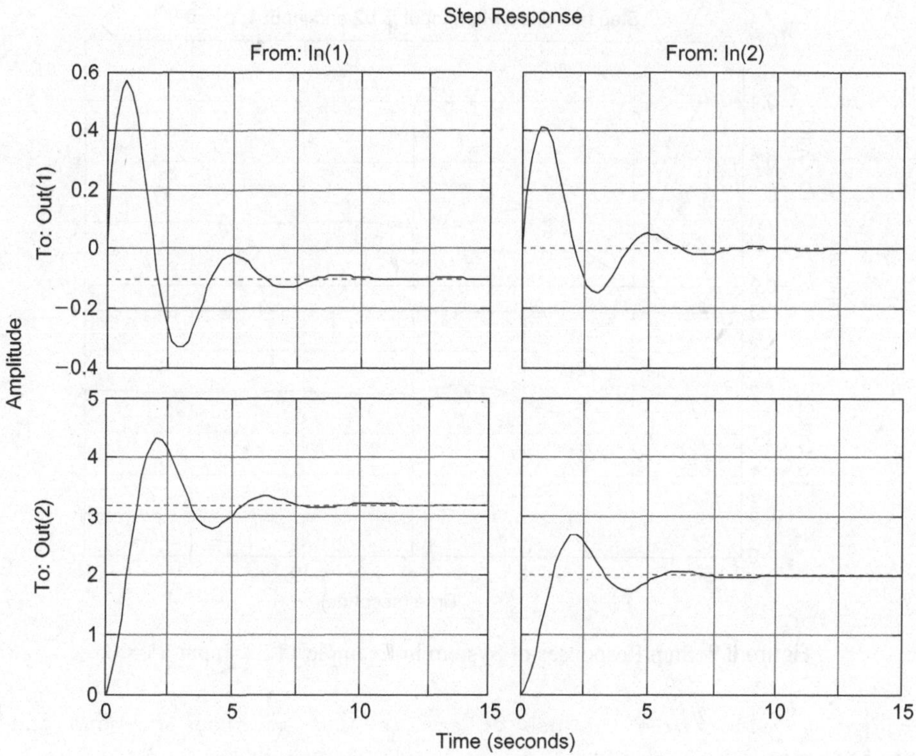

Figure 11.7 Step Responses for Example 11.21

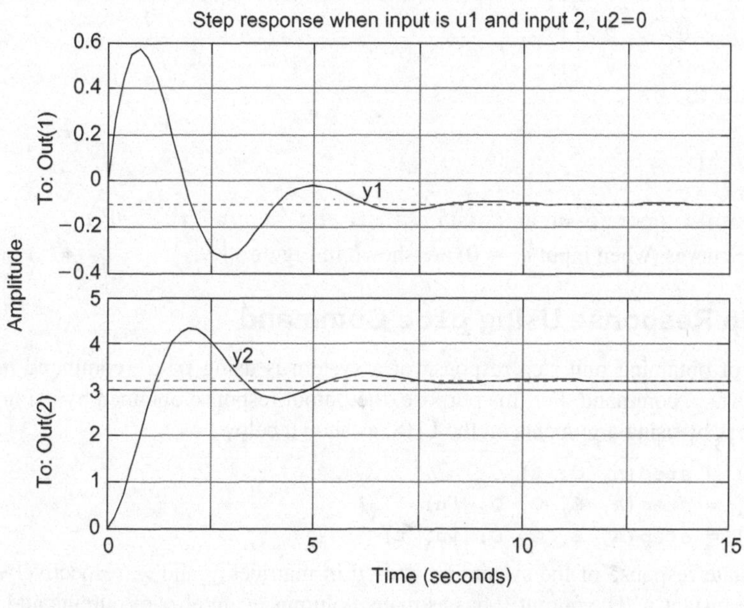

Figure 11.8 Step Responses of System in Example 11.22, Input $u_2 = 0$

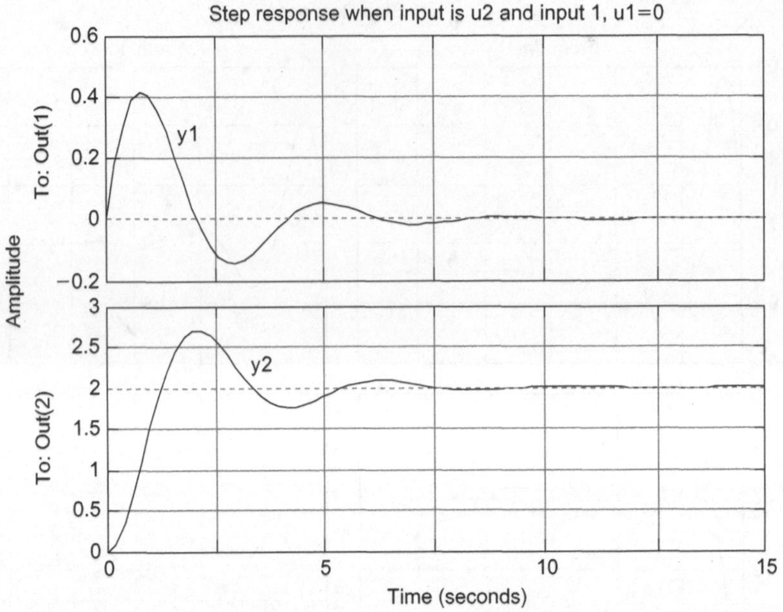

Figure 11.9 Step Responses of System in Example 11.22, Input $u_1 = 0$

```
%Program to illustrate the use of scalar 'iu' in step %command and obtain
step response
%input u2 with u1 = 0
A = [-1  -0.5;  5.0  0];
B = [1.5     1;  0.5  0];
C = [1       0;     0  1];
D = [0       0;     0  0];
step(A, B, C, D, 2);      %iu=2
grid on;
gtext ('y1');
gtext ('y2');
title('Step response when input is u2 and input 1,u1 =0')
```

The step response curves (when input $u_1 = 0$) are shown in Figure 11.9.

11.13.3 Step Response Using `plot` Command

Another method of obtaining unit step response of a system is using `plot` command instead of directly plotting through `step` command. For this purpose, the output response obtained by using `step` command is stored in a matrix by using arguments on the LHS, as shown below:

```
[y, x, t] = step(n, d, t)
[y, x, t] = step(A, B, C, D, iu)
[y, x, t] = step(A, B, C, D, iu, t)
```

The output and state response of the system are stored in matrices `y` and `x`, respectively, evaluated at the computation time instant `t`. The output `y` has as many columns as number of outputs and one row for each element in `t` vector. The state `x` has as many columns as states and one row for each element in `t`.

The command `plot(t,y)` is used to plot the output response curve of the system and is useful when the response is required at any particular time instant.

> **Programming Tip 11.4:** Obtaining step response using `plot` command is useful when the response is required at any particular time instant.

Example 11.23 Obtain the unit step response of the following system using the **`plot`** command:

$$G(s) = \frac{144}{s^2 + 12s + 144}$$

Solution: The program is given as follows:

```
%Program to obtain the unit step response of system using plot command
n = [ 0 0 144];
d = [ 1 12 144];
t = 0:0.05:2;
[y, x, t] = step(n, d, t);
plot(t, y);
grid;
title('Plot of unit step response of G(s)=[144]/[s^2+12s+144]');
xlabel('Time (sec)');
ylabel('Amplitude');
```

The step response plot is shown in Figure 11.10.

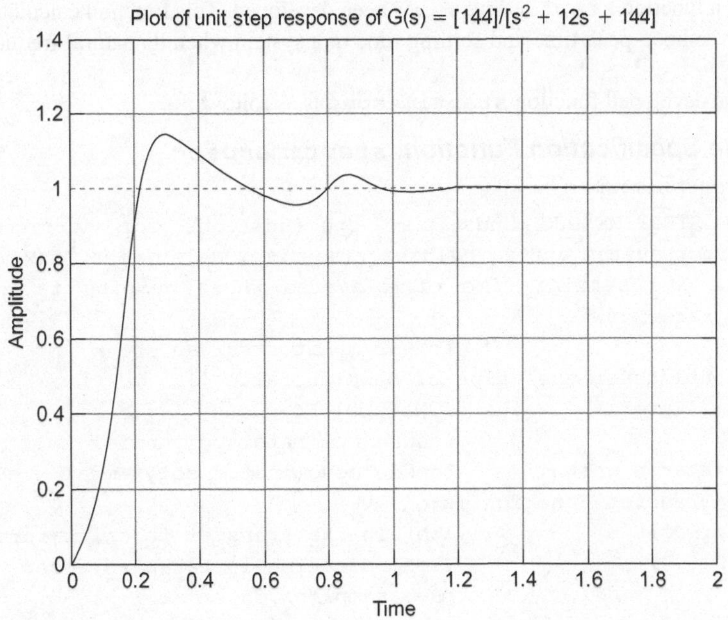

Figure 11.10 Step Response Using the `plot` Command for $G(s) = \dfrac{144}{s^2 + 12s + 144}$

11.14 PERFORMANCE INDICES

The performance indices for specifying the transient response of a second order system to a unit step input are as follows:

(i) *Delay Time, t_d*: It is the time required for the response to reach 50 per cent of the final value the very first time.

(ii) *Rise time, t_r*: It is the time required for the response to rise from 10 to 90 per cent of the final value in cases of over-damped or critically-damped second-order systems, or 0 to 100 per cent of the final value in case of the under-damped second-order system.

(iii) *Peak time, t_p*: It is the time required for the response to reach the first peak of the overshoot.

(iv) *Maximum overshoot, M_p*: It is defined as the normalized difference between the maximum value and the final steady-state output and is expressed in percent. It is given as

$$\%\text{Max Overshoot} = \frac{\text{maximum value} - \text{final value}}{\text{final value}} \times 100$$

(v) *Settling time, t_s*: It is the time required for the response to reach and stay within a specified tolerance band (usually 2–5 per cent) of its final value.

Programming Tip 11.5: Time response specifications are important for designing a system and are obtained using user-defined function **`steptimespec`** in MATLAB.

11.14.1 Development of Time Response Specifications Function

As there is no built-in function in MATLAB to find out the various specifications of a step response of a second-order system, a function `steptimespec` has been developed. This function calculates rise time, delay time, maximum overshoot, peak time and settling time of a system when its natural frequency and damping ratio are known.

The code for the developed function **`steptimespec`** is as follows:

Step Response Specification Function, `steptimespec`

```
function steptimespec
%FUNCTION STEPTIMESPEC finds time specifications for step response of a
%second order system and calculates rise time, delay time, maximum overshoot,
%peak time and setting time of a system whose damping ratio and natural
%frequency are known.
clc;                          %clear monitor screen
zeta = input('Enter the value of damping ratio ');
wn = input('Enter the value of Natural Frequency ');
n = wn*wn;                    %define numerator polynomial
d = [1 2*zeta*wn wn*wn];      %define denominator polynomial
disp('The Transfer Function is: ')
printsys(n, d);               %obtain the transfer function form.
t = 0:0.02:6.0;               %response time is taken as 6 sec. with 0.02
                              %sec sampling interval
[y, x, t] = step(n, d, t);    %obtain step response
plot(t,y);
grid on;
```

```
xlabel('Time(sec)');
ylabel('Amplitude');
title('Step Response');
%counter for sampling instants to find
%rise time i.e. time taken for output to rise from 10% to 90%
k=1;
while y(k) < 0.1,               %till output is less than 0.1 i.e. 10%
    k = k +1;
end
tenpcent = t(k);                %time at 10% output is stored
while y(k) < 0.9,               %till output is less than 0.9 i.e. 90%
    k = k + 1;
end
ninetypcent = t(k);             %time at 90% output is stored
rtime = ninetypcent - tenpcent;
%rise time is time taken from 10% to 90%
fprintf(' The rise time is: %f sec\n', ninetypcent);
format short
%to find delay time i.e. time taken to rise to 50% of step
k=1;
while y(k) < 0.5,               %till output is less than 0.5 i.e. 50%
k = k + 1;
end
dtime = t(k);                   %delaytime is time to rise 50% output
fprintf(' The delay time is: %f sec\n', dtime);
%to find maximum overshoot
for k = 2:1:300,                %for time = 0 sec to 6 sec
    if y(k) <= y(k-1),
%to find value of k till response keeps rising
        break,
    end;
end;
%maximum overshoot is the difference between max. output and 1 i.e. unit step
Oshoot = y(k) - 1;
fprintf(' The maximum overshoot is: %f \n ',Oshoot)
%to find peak time
%time corresponding to max overshoot is peak time
tp = t(k);
fprintf('The peak time is: %f sec\n', tp)
%to find settling time
%max tolerance for considering output to be in steady state taken as 2%
%to find the value of k when system enters the steady state
%and stays within steady state thereafter
tol = 0.02;
for k = 300 : -1 : 2,           %moving back from steady response at 6 sec.
    if(abs(y(k) - y(300)) >= tol)
%keep moving till difference from steady state is less than tolerance of 2%
```

```
        break,
    end;
end;
stime = t(k);
%store settling time when system enters steady state
fprintf(' The settling time is: %f sec\n', stime)
```

Example 11.24 Obtain the rise time, delay time, maximum overshoot, peak time and settling time of a second-order system:

$$G(s) = \frac{\omega_n^2}{s^2 + 2\xi\omega_n s + \omega_n^2}$$

having following values of damping ratio and natural frequency.

(a) Damping ratio $\xi = 0.5$ and natural frequency, $\omega_n = 2$ rad/sec
(b) Damping ratio $\xi = 0.6$ and natural frequency, $\omega_n = 5$ rad/sec

Solution:

(a) The problem is solved using a function **steptimespec**. On writing the function name `steptimespec` command prompt, and pressing Enter key, the following is displayed and the user will be prompted to enter the values of ξ and ω_n from keyboard.

```
Enter the value of damping ratio     0.5
Enter the value of Natural Frequency     2
```

Once the values are entered, following result will be displayed:

```
The Transfer Function is:
num/den =
      4
   ------------
s^2 + 2 s + 4
The rise time is: 1.080000 sec
The delay time is: 0.660000 sec
The maximum overshoot is: 0.160135
The peak time is: 1.840000 sec
The settling time is: 4.120000 sec
```

The response obtained is as shown in Figure 11.11

(b) Similarly, for Damping ratio $\xi = 0.6$ and natural frequency, $\omega_n = 5$ rad/sec:

```
Enter the value of damping ratio 0.6.
Enter the value of Natural Frequency 5
The Transfer Function is:
num/den =
25
---------------
s^2 + 6 s + 25
The rise time is: 0.480000 sec
The delay time is: 0.280000 sec
The maximum overshoot is: 0.094535
The peak time is: 0.800000 sec
The settling time is: 1.180000 sec
```

The response obtained is shown in Figure 11.12.

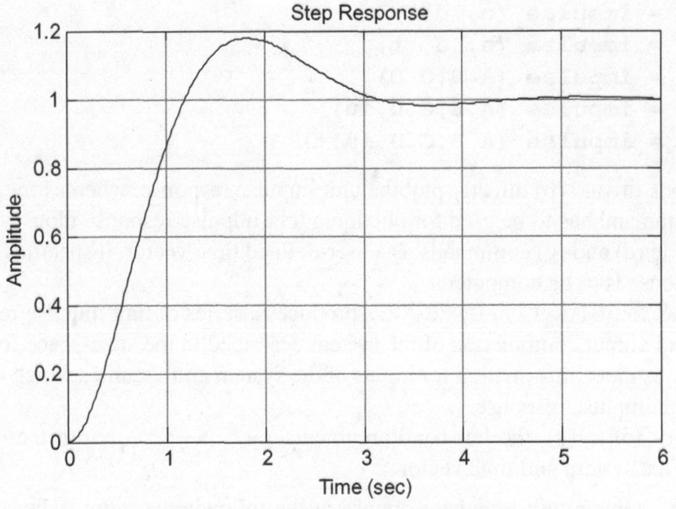

Figure 11.11 Step Response for Example 11.24(a)

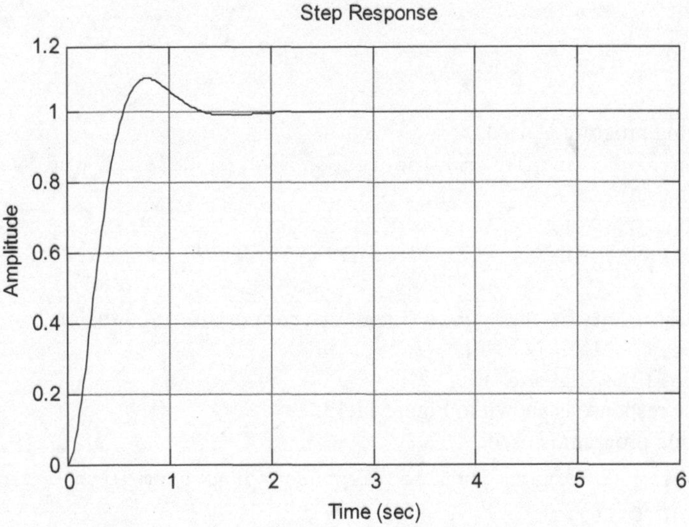

Figure 11.12 Step Response for Example 11.24(b)

11.15 IMPULSE RESPONSE OF CONTROL SYSTEMS

The MATLAB commands used to obtain the impulse response are similar to that used for obtaining step response and are:

```
(a) impulse (n,d)
(b) impulse (A,B,C,D)
```

```
(c)  [y,x,t] = impulse (n, d)
(d)  [y,x,t] = impulse (n, d, t)
(e)  [y,x,t] = impulse (A,B,C,D)
(f)  [y,x,t] = impulse (A,B,C,D,iu)
(g)  [y,x,t] = impulse (A,B,C,D,iu,t)
```

- The commands (a) and (b) directly plot the unit impulse response, whereas for commands (c) to (g), the `plot` command has to be used for obtaining unit impulse response plot.
- The vector `t` in (d) and (g) commands, is a user-defined time vector. It specifies the time at which the impulse response is to be computed.
- The command `impulse(A, B, C, D)` produces a series of unit impulse response plots, one for each input and output combination of the system described in the state-space form.
- The scalar `iu` is index information for inputs of the system and specifies which input is to be used for computing the impulse response.
- For commands (c) to (g), the left hand arguments `[y, x, t]` return the output, state variable responses of the system and time vector `t`.

Example 11.25 Obtain unit impulse response of the following systems, whose closed-loop transfer functions are

(a) $\dfrac{1}{s^2+0.4s+1}$

(b) $\dfrac{16}{s^2+1.6s+16}$

Solution:

(a) The following program is used:

```
%Program to obtain impulse response with default time values.
n = [0 0 1];
d = [1 0.4 1];
impulse(n, d);
grid;
title('Plot of the unit impulse response of G(s)=1/[s^2+0.4s+1]');
xlabel( 'Time');
ylabel('Amplitude');
```

The impulse response is shown in Figure 11.13.

(b) The following program is used:

```
%Program to obtain impulse response for system with default time values.
n = [0 0 16];
d = [1 1.6 16];
impulse(n, d);
grid;
title('Plot of the unit impulse response of G(s)=16/[s^2+1.6s+16]');
xlabel('Time');
ylabel('Amplitude');
```

The response is plotted in Figure 11.14.

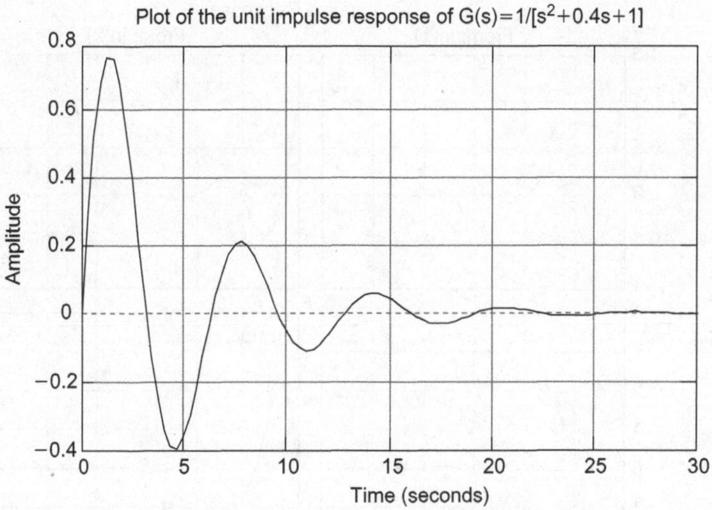

Figure 11.13 Impulse Response for Example 11.25(a)

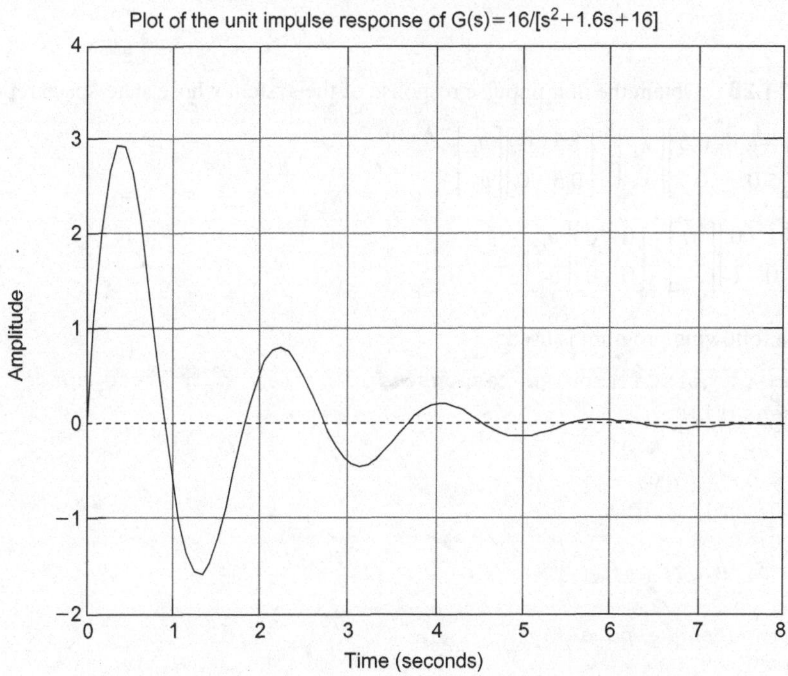

Figure 11.14 Impulse Response for Example 11.25(b)

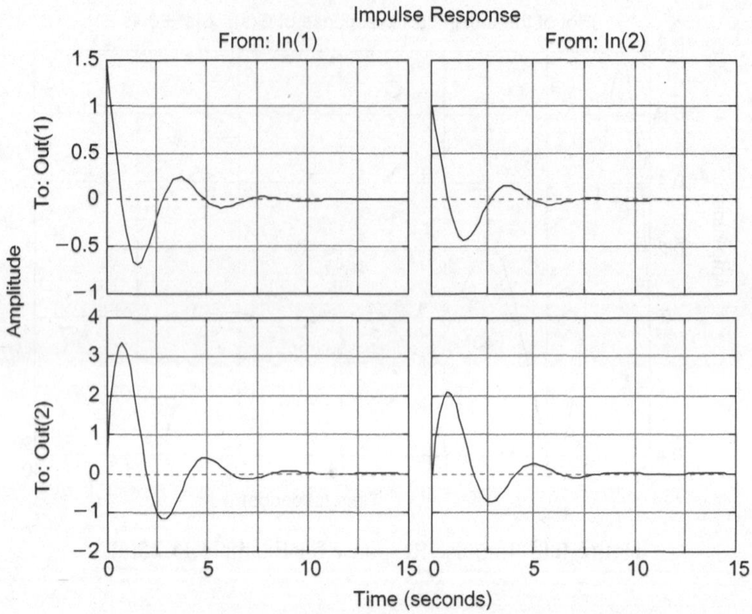

Figure 11.15 Impulse Response for Example 11.26

Example 11.26 Obtain the unit impulse response of the system whose state-space representation is

$$\dot{\underline{x}} = \begin{bmatrix} -1 & -0.5 \\ 5.0 & 0 \end{bmatrix}\begin{bmatrix} x_1 \\ x_2 \end{bmatrix} + \begin{bmatrix} 1.5 & 1 \\ 0.5 & 0 \end{bmatrix}\begin{bmatrix} u_1 \\ u_2 \end{bmatrix}$$

$$\begin{bmatrix} y_1 \\ y_2 \end{bmatrix} = \begin{bmatrix} 1 & 0 \\ 0 & 1 \end{bmatrix}\begin{bmatrix} x_1 \\ x_2 \end{bmatrix} + \begin{bmatrix} 0 & 0 \\ 0 & 0 \end{bmatrix}\begin{bmatrix} u_1 \\ u_2 \end{bmatrix}$$

Solution: The following program is used:

```
%Program to obtain impulse response for system with state space
%representation
A = [-1 -0.5; 5.0 0];
B = [1.5 1; 0.5 0];
C = [1 0; 0 1];
D = [0 0; 0 0];
impulse(A, B, C, D);
grid;
title('Impulse Response');
xlabel('Time');
ylabel('Amplitude');
```

The series of impulse response obtained are shown in Figure 11.15 for different input/output combinations.

11.16 RAMP RESPONSE OF CONTROL SYSTEMS

There is no `ramp` command in MATLAB. However, as the ramp signal is one order higher than step signal, the step input signal can be used to obtain the ramp response by dividing the transfer function by `s` and then evaluating it using the `step` command. If the given transfer function of system is `G(s)`, then the `step` command is used with the modified function `G(s)/s` to obtain the ramp response.

> **Programming Tip 11.6:** Ramp response can be obtained using the `step` command and modified transfer function, `G(s)/s`.

Example 11.27 Obtain the ramp response of the following system transfer functions.

(a) $\dfrac{30}{s^2+5s+30}$

(b) $\dfrac{6}{s^2+5s+6}$

Solution:

(a) The following program is used:

```
%Program to obtain ramp response for system in example 11.27 (a).
n = [0 0 30];
d = [1 5 30];
%The ramp response can be obtained by using step command
%for transfer function divided by 's'
%the transfer function G1(s) = G(s)/s
n1 = [0 0 0 30];
d1 = [1 5 30 0];
%Obtain step response of G1(s) i.e., ramp response of G(s)
[y, x, t] = step(n1, d1);
%to plot output y vs time t and t vs t i.e. ramp signal on
%same graph window
v = [0 6 0 6];
plot(t, y, '*');
axis(v);
hold on;
plot(t, t, '*');
grid on;
title('Plot of unit ramp response of G(s)=[30]/[s^2+5s+30]');
xlabel('Time');
ylabel('Amplitude');
```

The response obtained is shown in Figure 11.16.

(b) The following program is used:

```
%Program to obtain ramp response for system in example 11.27(b).
n=[0 0 6];
d=[1 5 6];
%The ramp response can be obtained by using step command for
%transfer function divided by 's'
```

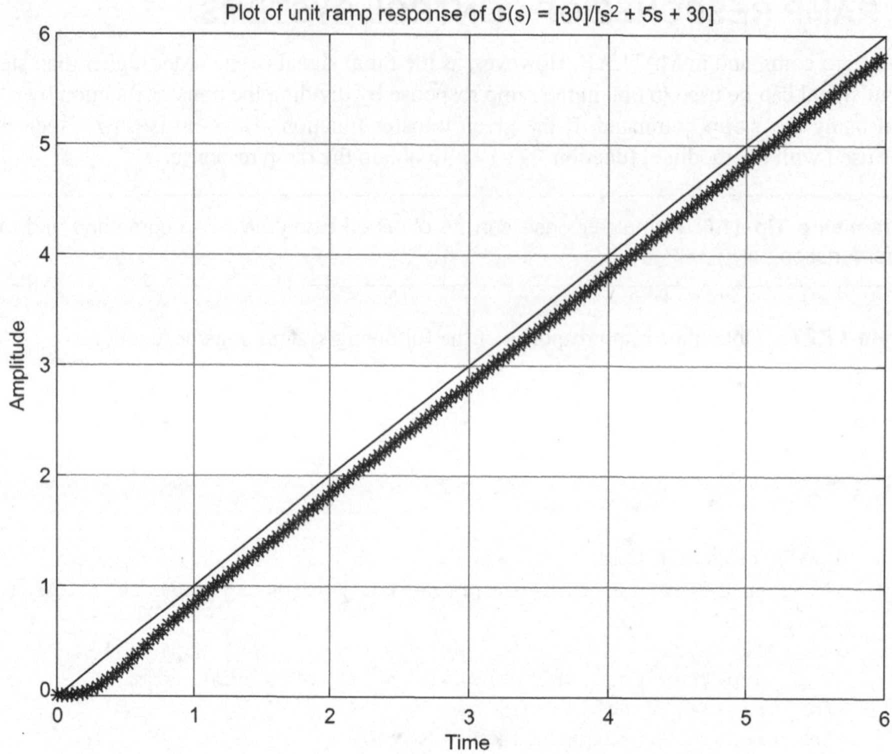

Figure 11.16 Ramp Response for Example 11.27(a)

```
%the transfer function G1(s) = G(s)/s
n1 = [0 0 0 6];
d1 = [1 5 6 0];
%obtain step response of G1(s) or ramp response of G(s)
[y, x, t] = step (n1, d1);
%to plot output y vs time t and t vs t i.e. ramp signal on same
%graph window
v = [0 10 0 10];
plot(t, y, '-+');
axis(v);
hold on;
plot(t, t, '-');
grid;
title('Plot of unit ramp response of G(s)=[6]/[s^2+5s+6]');
xlabel('Time');
ylabel('Amplitude');
```

The response obtained is shown in Figure 11.17.

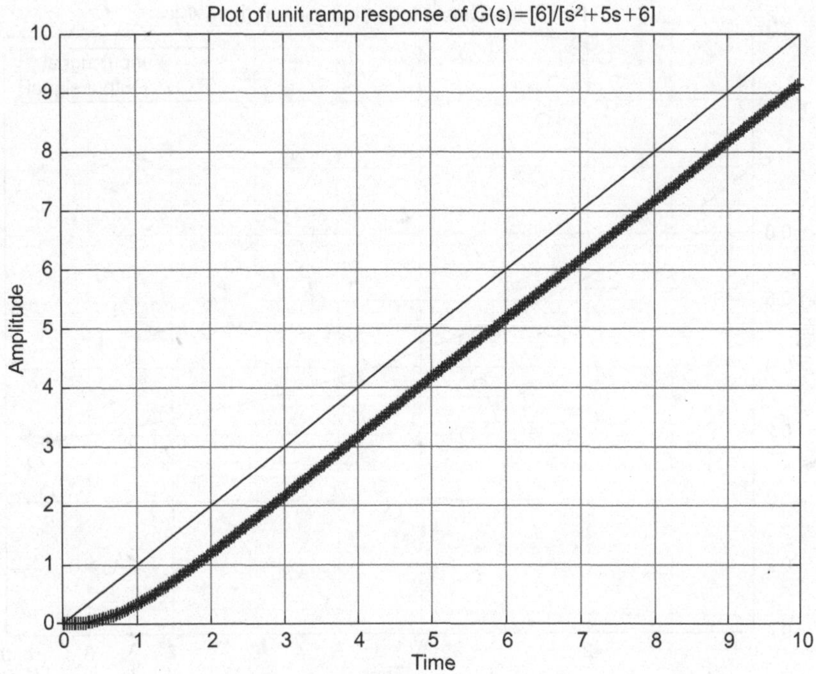

Figure 11.17 Ramp Response for Example 11.27(b)

11.17 RESPONSE TO ARBITRARY INPUT

In case the input signal is not a standard signal, MATLAB command **`lsim`** can be used to obtain the response of the system. The syntax of the command is

```
lsim(n, d, u, t)
```

where `n` and `d` are numerator and denominator polynomials of system transfer function,
`u` is the arbitrary input signal and
`t` defines time for which response of the system is required.

Another form of this command, which gives the output `y` in vector form, without response plot, is

```
[y, t] = lsim(n, d, u, t)
```

In this case, plot of the response is obtained using the `plot` command separately.

Similarly, the commands for state-space representation are

```
lsim(A, B, C, D, u, t)
[y, t] = lsim(A, B, C, D, u, t)
```

Example 11.28 A closed-loop control system has a transfer function, $\frac{C(s)}{R(s)} = \frac{s+5}{s^3+2s^2+3s+5}$.

Obtain the response of this system for an input $r(t) = e^{-0.2t}$, for $t = 0$ to 9 sec, in steps of 0.15 sec.

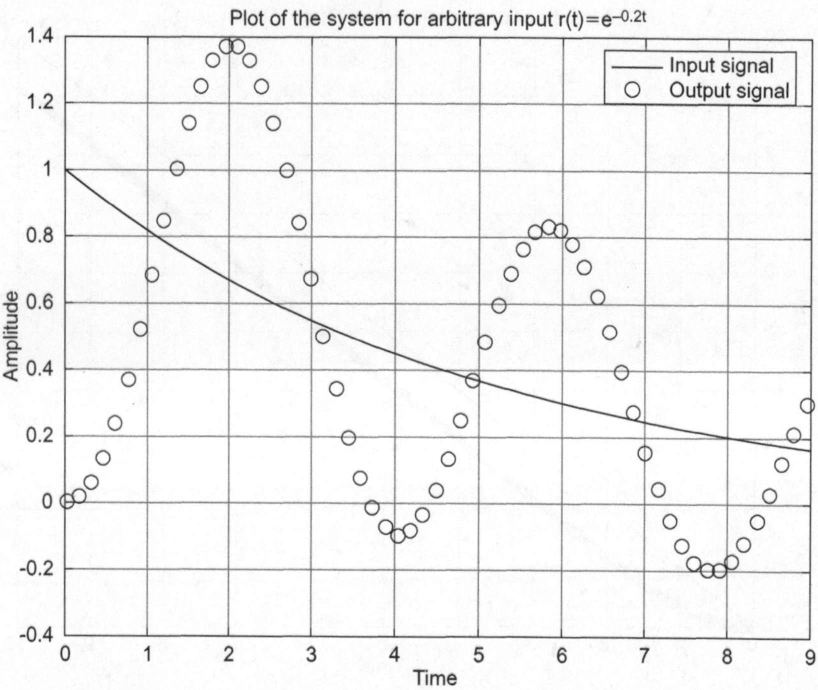

Figure 11.18 Response of the System of Example 11.28, for Input $r(t) = e^{-0.2t}$

Solution: The following program is used:

```
%Program to obtain response for system for the given arbitrary input signal
n = [1 5];
d = [1 2 3 5];
t = 0 : 0.15: 9;
r = exp(-0.2*t);        % input signal r(t)
y = lsim(n, d, r, t);
plot(t, r, '-', t, y, 'o');
grid;
title('Plot of the system for arbitrary input r(t)=e-0.2t');
xlabel('Time');
ylabel('Amplitude');
```

The system response is shown in Figure 11.18.

Example 11.29 Obtain the response for an input $u = 1 + t$, for t varying from 0 to 6 sec, in steps of 0.05 sec, for the system whose state-space representation is given by:

$$\begin{bmatrix} \dot{x}_1 \\ \dot{x}_2 \end{bmatrix} = \begin{bmatrix} -1.5 & 2.0 \\ -0.5 & 0 \end{bmatrix} \begin{bmatrix} x_1 \\ x_2 \end{bmatrix} + \begin{bmatrix} 0 \\ 1 \end{bmatrix} u$$

$$y = \begin{bmatrix} 1 & 0 \end{bmatrix} \begin{bmatrix} x_1 \\ x_2 \end{bmatrix}$$

Solution: The following program is used:

```
%Program to obtain response for system described by state space equations to
%an arbitrary input.
t = 0: 0.05 :6;
A = [-1.5 2.0; -0.5 0];
B = [0; 1];
C = [1 0];
D = [0];
u = 1 + t;              %input signal
z = lsim(A, B, C, D, u, t);
plot(t, u,  '-', t, z, 'o');
grid;
title('Plot of the system for arbitrary input u=1+t');
xlabel('Time');
ylabel('Amplitude');
```

The output response obtained is shown in Figure 11.19.

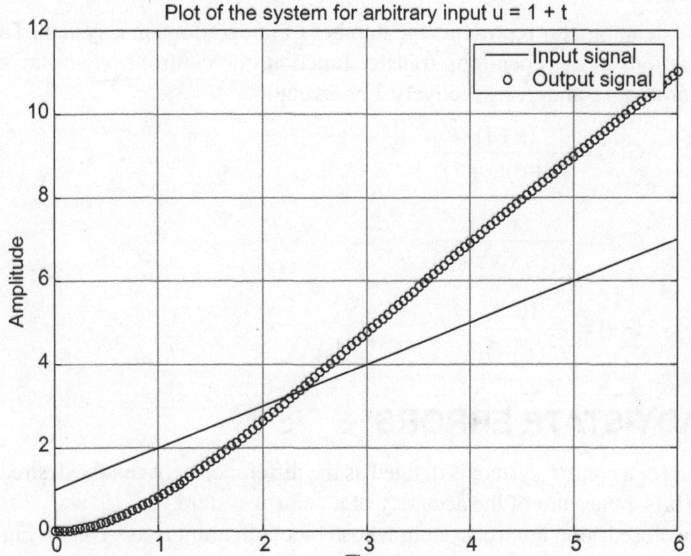

Figure 11.19 Response of the System for a Input `u=1+t` of Example 11.29

11.18 STEADY-STATE ERRORS ANALYSIS

There are several factors which cause errors in a control system and all physical systems have steady-state errors in response to a certain type of input. A system may not have any steady-state error due to one type of input, but may have steady-state errors due to other types of input. The imperfections in the system components, such as static friction, backlash, amplifier drift, are some of the causes of errors in a control system. The good or bad performance of a control system is judged by the steady-state error, in addition to other performance criteria.

11.19 DIFFERENT REPRESENTATIONS OF TRANSFER FUNCTIONS

The open-loop transfer function of a unity feedback control system can be expressed in two forms:

1. Time constant form.
2. Pole–zero form.

For generalized transfer functions, these can be expressed as follows:

1. **Time constant form**

$$G(s)=\frac{k(T_{z1}s+1)(T_{z2}s+1)\ldots(T_{zk}s+1)}{s^n(T_{p1}s+1)(T_{p2}s+1)\ldots(T_{pl}s+1)}$$

where T_{zi} (*i* varies from 1 to *k*) and T_{pj} (*j* varies from 1 to *l*) are the system time constants

2. **Pole–zero form**

$$G(s)=\frac{k(s+z_1)(s+z_2)\ldots(s+z_k)}{s^n(s+p_1)(s+p_2)\ldots(s+p_l)}$$

where z_i ('*i*' varies from 1 to *k*) and p_j (*j* varies from 1 to *l*), represent zeros and poles of the transfer function.

The term s^n in the denominator represents the number of integrations in a system. Thus, depending upon the number of integrations in the open-loop transfer function, the control systems are classified as Type 0, Type 1 and Type 2 for n=0, 1 and 2, respectively. For example:

Type 0: $$G(s)=\frac{(s+1)}{(s+6)(s+7)}$$

Type 1: $$G(s)=\frac{(s+1)}{s(s+6)(s+7)}$$

Type 2: $$G(s)=\frac{10}{s^2(s+1)}$$

11.20 STEADY-STATE ERRORS

The steady-state error for a control system is defined as the difference between the desired output and the final value of the system. It is a measure of the accuracy of a control system.

Consider a simple closed-loop control system whose block diagram is as given in Figure 11.20:

Here,

$$\frac{C(s)}{R(s)}=\frac{G(s)}{1+G(s)H(s)}$$

$$E(s) = R(s) - B(s)$$

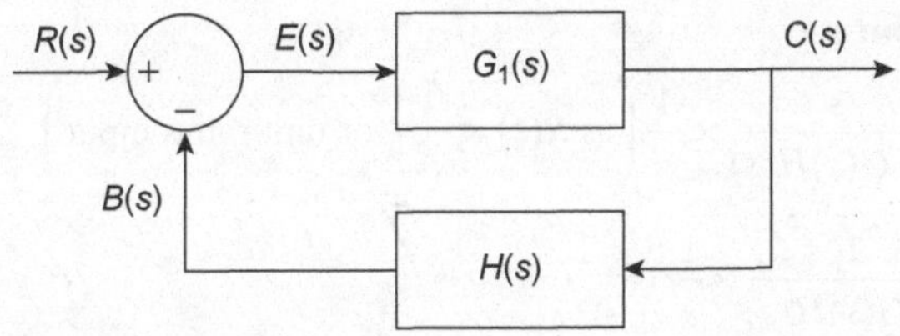

Figure 11.20 Block Diagram for a Closed-Loop System

or

$$E(s) = R(s) - C(s)H(s)$$

$$\frac{E(s)}{R(s)} = 1 - \frac{C(s)H(s)}{R(s)} \quad \text{or} \quad = 1 - \frac{G(s)H(s)}{1+G(s)H(s)}$$

as

$$\frac{C(s)}{R(s)} = \frac{G(s)}{1+G(s)H(s)}$$

$$\therefore \quad \frac{E(s)}{R(s)} = \frac{1}{1+G(s)H(s)}$$

or

$$E(s) = \frac{R(s)}{1+G(s)H(s)}$$

Hence, the steady-state error can be obtained using the final value theorem, i.e.,

$$\lim_{t\to\infty} f(t) = \lim_{s\to 0} sF(s)$$

Hence,

$$e_{ss} = \lim_{t\to\infty} e(t)$$

or Steady-state error,

$$e_{ss} = \lim_{t\to\infty} e(t) = \lim_{s\to 0} sE(s) = \lim_{s\to 0} \frac{sR(s)}{1+G(s)H(s)}$$

That is,

$$e_{ss} = \lim_{s\to 0} \frac{sR(s)}{1+G(s)H(s)}$$

11.21 STEADY-STATE ERRORS FOR DIFFERENT TYPES OF INPUTS

(i) The steady-state error of a system for a **unit step input** is as:

$$e_{ss} = \lim_{s\to 0} \frac{s}{1+G(s)H(s)} \times \frac{1}{s} \left(\text{as } R(s) = \frac{1}{s} \text{ for unit step input} \right)$$

$$= \lim_{s\to 0} \frac{1}{1+G(s)H(s)} = \frac{1}{1+K_p}$$

where $K_p = \lim_{s\to 0} G(s)H(s)$ is called **position error constant.**

(ii) For **unit ramp input**

$$e_{ss} = \lim_{s\to 0}\frac{s}{1+G(s)H(s)}\times\frac{1}{s^2}\left(\text{as } R(s)=\frac{1}{s^2} \text{ for unit ramp input}\right)$$

$$= \lim_{s\to 0}\frac{1}{1+G(s)H(s)}\times\frac{1}{s}$$

$$= \frac{1}{K_v}$$

where $K_v = \lim_{s\to 0} sG(s)H(s)$ is called **velocity error constant.**

(iii) For **unit parabolic input,** the steady-state error is given by

$$e_{ss} = \lim_{s\to 0}\frac{s}{1+G(s)H(s)}\times\frac{1}{s^3}\left(\text{as } R(s)=\frac{1}{s^3} \text{ for unit ramp input}\right)$$

$$= \lim_{s\to 0}\frac{1}{1+G(s)H(s)}\times\frac{1}{s^2}$$

$$= \frac{1}{K_a}$$

where $K_a = \lim_{s\to 0} s^2G(s)H(s)$ is called **acceleration error constant.**

11.22 STEADY-STATE ERRORS FOR DIFFERENT TYPES OF SYSTEMS

The steady-state errors due to different standard input signals and for different types of systems are given in Table 11.2.

Table 11.2 Steady-State Errors for Different Standard Input Signals to Different Types of Systems

System	Unit Step Input	Unit Ramp Input	Unit Parabolic Input
Type0	$\frac{1}{1+K_p}$	∞	∞
Type1	0	$\frac{1}{K_v}$	∞
Type2	0	0	$\frac{1}{K_a}$

where $K_p = \lim_{s\to 0} G(s)H(s)$, $K_v = \lim_{s\to 0} sG(s)H(s)$, $K_a = \lim_{s\to 0} s^2G(s)H(s)$

As can be observed from Table 11.2, the Type 0 system shows steady state errors for all types of input signals. Type 1 system gives steady state errors for two types of inputs and Type 2 gives the steady state error due to one type of input only which is finite.

> **Programming Tip 11.7:** Higher types of systems are better from steady-state error point of view, but are less stable.

There is no built-in function in MATLAB *for finding out steady-state errors. Hence, a user-defined function has been written.*

As the control system can be expressed in pole–zero form or time constant form, separate functions have been written for these different forms:

(a) Function **ssetf** has been written for time constant form.

(b) Function **ssezp** has been written for pole–zero form.

11.22.1 MATLAB Functions for Evaluating the Errors and Error Constants of Different Types of Systems

11.22.1.1 Function ssetf for Time Constant Form of Transfer Function

```
function ssetf(num,den)
%The function 'ssetf' finds the error constants and steady state
%errors for the unit step, ramp and parabolic input signals.
%This function is used when the control system is defined in
%terms of time constant form
%For this function the time constant form is first solved in
%terms of numerator and denominator polynomials.
[z,p,k]=tf2zp(num,den);
%-----------------------Initializing the parameters-----------------------%
p=-p;z=-z;
psys=0; zsys=0;
type=0;
prodz=1;prodp=1;
%------------------Finding the type and Kc of the system------------------%
a=length(p);
b=length(z);
for n=1:b
    if(z(n))==0
    zsys=zsys+1;
    else, end;
  if(z(n)) ~= 0
    if(z(n)) ~=-inf
    prodz=prodz*z(n);
    else, end;
  else, end;
end
for n =1:a
if(p(n))== 0
  psys=psys+1;
  elseif(p(n)) ~=-inf
    prodp=prodp*p(n);
  end
end
```

```
prod=k*prodz/prodp;
type=psys-zsys;
format short
%-----------Defining the error constants and steady-state errors----------%
if (type <1)
    Kp =0; Kv =0;Ka = 0;
    Stepess =inf; Rampess =inf; Parbess =inf;
end
switch type
    case 0
      Kp = prod; Kv = 0; Ka = 0;
      Stepess = 1/(1+Kp); Rampess = inf; Parbess = inf;
    case 1
      Kp = inf; Kv = prod; Ka = 0;
      Stepess = 0; Rampess = 1/Kv; Parbess = inf;
    case 2
      Kp = inf; Kv =inf; Ka =prod;
      Stepess = 0; Rampess = 0; Parbess = 1/Ka;
otherwise
      Kp =inf; Kv =inf;Ka = inf;
      Stepess =0; Rampess =0; Parbess = 0;
end
fprintf('The type of the system is %2.0f \n\n',type);
fprintf('The Error Constants are given as:\n');
fprintf('Kp=%6.2f\nKv=%6.2f\nKa=%6.2f\n\n', Kp,Kv,Ka);
fprintf('The Steady-state Errors for the system are as:\n');
fprintf('Unit Step error\t=\t%6.2f \nUnit Ramp error\t=\t%6.2f\nUnit Para-
bolic ... error\t=\t%6.2f\n',Stepess, Rampess,Parbess);
```

11.22.1.2 Function ssezp for Pole-Zero Form of Transfer Function

```
function ssezp(z,p,k)
%The function 'ssezp' find the error constants and steady state
%errors for the unit step, ramp and parabolic input signals.
%This function is used when the control system is defined in
%terms of pole-zero form
%-----------------------Initializing the parameters-----------------------%
p=-p;z=-z;
psys=0; zsys=0;
type=0;
prodz=1; prodp=1;
%------------------Finding the type and Kc of the system------------------%
a=length(p);
b=length(z);
for n=1:b
      if(z(n))==0
      zsys=zsys+1;
      else, end;
```

```
        if(z(n)) ~= 0
           if(z(n)) ~=-inf
           prodz=prodz*z(n);
           else, end;
        else, end;
  end
  for n = 1:a
  if(p(n))== 0
        psys = psys+1;
        elseif(p(n)) ~=-inf
           prodp = prodp*p(n);
        end
  end
  prod=k*prodz/prodp;
  type=psys-zsys;
  format short
  %----Defining the error constants and steady-state errors----%
  if (type <1)
        Kp =0; Kv =0;Ka = 0;
        Stepess = inf; Rampess =inf; Parbess =inf;
  end
  switch type
        case 0
           Kp = prod; Kv = 0; Ka = 0;
           Stepess = 1/(1+Kp); Rampess = inf; Parbess = inf;
        case 1
           Kp = inf; Kv = prod; Ka = 0;
           Stepess = 0; Rampess = 1/Kv; Parbess = inf;
        case 2
           Kp = inf; Kv =inf; Ka =prod;
           Stepess = 0; Rampess = 0; Parbess = 1/Ka;
        otherwise
           Kp =inf; Kv =inf;Ka = inf;
           Stepess =0;Rampess =0; Parbess = 0;
  end
  fprintf('The type of the system is %2.0f \n\n',type);
  fprintf('The Error Constants are given as:\n');
  fprintf('Kp=%6.2f\nKv=%6.2f\nKa=%6.2f\n\n', Kp,Kv,Ka);
  fprintf('The Steady-state Errors for the system are as:\n');
  fprintf('Unit Step error\t=\t%6.2f \nUnit Ramp error\t=\t%6.2f\nUnit Parabolic
  ... error\t=\t%6.2f\n',Stepess, Rampess,Parbess);
```

Programming Tip 11.8: User-defined functions must be added to current directory before being used in MATLAB.

To use these functions, these have to be included in the current directory of MATLAB. Then, by giving input as parameters for these functions, the errors can be evaluated as illustrated in the following examples.

Example 11.30 For a unity feedback system having open-loop transfer function as

$$G(s)=\frac{10(s+2)}{s^2(s+4)(s+3)}$$

Determine using MATLAB (i) the type of system, (ii) error constants K_p, K_v and K_a, and (iii) steady-state error for step, ramp and parabolic inputs.

Solution: As the given transfer function is in pole–zero form, the MATLAB function to be used is **`ssezp(z,p,k)`**

where *z*— row vector of zeros,

p—row vector of poles and

k—constant.

For this example:

```
z = [-2]
p = [0 0 -4 -3]
k = [10]
```

To evaluate the type of the system and other values, the function used is

```
ssezp(z,p,k)
```

The result obtained is as given below:

```
The type of the system is 2
The Error Constants are given as:
Kp = Inf
Kv = Inf
Ka = 1.67
The Steady-state Errors for the system are as:
Unit Step error = 0.00
Unit Ramp error = 0.00
Unit Parabolic error = 0.60
```

Example 11.31 For a unity feedback system having open-loop transfer function as

$$G(s)=\frac{10(1+4s)(1+6s)}{s^2(s^2+2s+1)}$$

Determine using MATLAB (i) the type of system, (ii) error constants K_p, K_v and K_a, and (iii) steady-state error for step, ramp and parabolic inputs.

Solution: As the given system is in **time constant form,** so function to be used is **`ssetf(num,den)`** and the transfer function is first written in terms of numerator and denominator polynomials as:

$$G(s)=\frac{(240s^2+100s+10)}{(s^4+2s^3+s^2)}$$

The different commands to be used in MATLAB are:

```
num = [240 100 10];
den = [1 2 1 0 0];
```

To determine the type of the system and other values the function used is as follows:

```
ssetf(num,den)
```

The response obtained is give as

```
The type of the system is 2
The Error Constants are given as:
Kp = Inf
Kv = Inf
Ka = 10.00
The Steady-state Errors for the system are as:
Unit Step error = 0.00
Unit Ramp error = 0.00
Unit Parabolic error = 0.10
```

11.23 STABILITY OF CONTROL SYSTEMS

Stability is a very important performance specification of any control system and every control system is designed to be stable. For an LTI system to be stable, it has to satisfy the following conditions:

1. It should produce bounded output for bounded input.
2. Response should approach towards zero for zero input as $t \to \infty$.

The stability investigation is easy up to the second-order system only. For higher order systems, it becomes tedious as handling of system equations is difficult.

11.24 ROUTH-HURWITZ CRITERION

The Routh-Hurwitz criterion determines stability of the system on the basis of the location of roots of a characteristic equation with respect to the imaginary axis of the s-plane without actually solving the equation. This gives just a qualitative result and is the fastest method to know just about the stability of the system. The procedure to be adopted for the application of this criterion is as follows:

1. Determine the characteristic equation of the system.
2. If it has any fractional terms, then multiply the characteristic equation by the denominator so that there is no fractional term.
3. Arrange the resulting equation in descending power of '*s*' with the leftmost term being of the highest power.
4. It must be ensured that all the power terms are present. If some terms are not present, their coefficient should be taken as zero.
5. The last term should be a constant. If it is not there, zero should be taken as the last term.
6. To create the Routh array, consider a characteristic equation given as:

$$a_0 s^n + a_1 s^{n-1} + \cdots + a_{n-1} s + a_n = 0 \tag{11.12}$$

Arrange the coefficients of s terms in the following tabular form:

$$\begin{array}{llll} s^n & a_0 & a_2 & a_4 & \ldots \\ s^{n-1} & a_1 & a_3 & a_3 & \cdots \\ s^{n-2} & b_1 & b_2 & \cdots \\ s^{n-3} & c_1 & c_2 & \cdots \\ s^0 & a_n & \cdots & \cdots \end{array}$$

where $b_1 = \dfrac{a_1 a_3 - a_0 a_3}{a_1}$; $b_2 = \dfrac{a_1 a_4 - a_0 a_5}{a_1}$; $b_3 = \dfrac{a_1 a_6 - a_0 a_7}{a_1}$; and so on

$$c_1 = \frac{b_1a_3 - a_1b_2}{b_1}; \qquad c_2 = \frac{b_1a_5 - a_1b_3}{b_1}; \qquad c_3 = \frac{b_1a_7 - a_1b_4}{b_1}; \quad \text{and so on}$$

$$d_1 = \frac{c_1b_2 - b_1c_2}{c_1}; \qquad d_2 = \frac{c_1b_3 - b_1c_3}{c_1}; \quad \text{and so on}$$

This process is continued until the nth row is completed.

7. Check the number of sign changes in the entries of the first column. This number will give the number of roots of the characteristic equation, which lie in the right half of the s-plane.
8. A system is stable if there is no change in sign in the first column of the Routh array.
9. If there is change in sign in the first column, the system is unstable.

Special cases:

1. If a term in the first column is zero, the remaining terms can be calculated by replacing zero with a small number.
2. If an entire row is zero, create an auxiliary polynomial in `s` and proceed further.

There is no built-in function in MATLAB for checking the stability of the system using a Routh array. So, a user-defined function `routh` has been written and is as follows:

Routh–Hurwitz Stability Criterion Function, `routh`

```
function routh(poly)
%ROUTH(POLY) makes a routh array and checks the stability of
%the system (whose characteristic polynomial is POLY) by finding if
%there are any roots on right half of the s-plane. It also displays
%the routh array and the reports about the stability of the system.
dim = size(poly);
%get size/dimensions of the characteristic polynomial, x
coeff = dim(2);
%find no. of coefficients of the char. Polynomial, x
n = coeff - 1;          %degree of x
if mod(n, 2) == 0,      %If no. of columns in x are even
    ncol = (n/2) + 1; %ncol---no. of columns in routh array
else
    ncol = (n + 1)/2;
end;
a = zeros(n + 1, ncol); %initialize routh array
for i =1:coeff,
    RA(2 - rem(i, 2), ceil(i/2)) = poly(i);
%assemble 1st and 2nd rows of routh array
end;
rows = coeff - 2;              %number of rows that need determinants
index = zeros(rows, 1);        %initialize columns-per-row index vector
for i = 1: rows,
    index(rows -i + 1) = ceil(i/2);
%form index vector from bottom to top
end;
for i = 3:coeff,                          %go from 3rd row to last
    if(all(RA(i - 1, :) == 0)),           %row of zeros
      fprintf('\nSpecial Case: Row of zeros detected.\n\n');
```

```
%-------------Display the Original Routh Array-----------------%
      disp('---------------Routh Hurwitz Array---------------------')
      format short;
      disp(RA);
      fprintf('\n Routh Hurwitz Array is modified and is given as\n\n');
%-------------Check the number of sign changes-----------------%
      a = coeff -i + 2;                              %order of auxiliary equation
      b = ceil(a/2) - rem(a, 2) + 1;
%number of auxiliary coefficients
      temp1 = RA(i - 2, 1 : b);                      %get auxiliary polynomial
      temp2 = a : -2 : 0;                            %auxiliry polynomial powers
      RA(i - 1, 1 : b) = temp1 .* temp2;             %derivative of auxiliary
    elseif(RA(i - 1, 1) == 0),                       %first element in row is zero
      fprintf('\nSpecial Case: First element of row %d is zero and is
      replaced... with 0.0001.\n\n\',i-1);
%-------------Display the Original Routh Array-----------------%
      disp('---------------Routh Hurwitz Array---------------------')
      format short;
      disp(RA);
      fprintf('\n Routh Hurwitz Array is modified and is given as\n\n');
      RA(i - 1, 1) = 0.0001;                         %replace by small value
    end;
%Compute the Routh array elements and display the array
    for j = 1 : index(i - 2),
      RA(i, j) = -det([RA(i - 2, 1) RA(i - 2, j + 1);
      RA(i - 1, 1) RA(i - 1, j + 1)])/RA(i - 1, 1);
    end;
end;
disp('---------------Routh Hurwitz Array---------------------')
format short;
disp(RA);
%-------------Check the number of sign changes-----------------%
k = 0;
c = 0;
for l = 1:coeff
    if RA(l, 1) >= 0,
      if k ==1,
      c = c + 1;
      k = 0;
    end;
    elseif k == 0,
      c = c + 1;
      k = 1;
    end;
end;
%--------------------Display the result----------------------%
```

```
if c == 0,
    fprintf('There is no change of sign in entries of first column.\n');
    fprintf('Therefore no root lie in the right half s-plane. \n');
    fprintf('Hence, system is stable. \n\n');
else
    fprintf('There are %g sign changes in entries of first column.\n',c);
    fprintf('Therefore %g roots lie in the right half s-plane. \n',c);
    fprintf('Hence, system is unstable. \n\n');
end;
```

To use this function, it has to be included in the current directory of MATLAB. Then, by writing input data in the Command Window for this function, the problems are solved as illustrated in the following examples. Data to be fed are the coefficients of the characteristic equation. On execution, routh's array/table is displayed and system stability is checked by checking the sign changes in the first column of this array/table.

Example 11.32 Consider the characteristic equations:

(a) $s^3 + 6s^2 + 11s + 3 = 0$

(b) $s^4 + 10s^3 + 2s^2 + 36s + 20 = 0$

Using MATLAB and Routh–Hurwitz criterion, check whether the systems are stable or not.

Solution:

(a) The MATLAB program is given as

```
%Program to find whether system whose Characteristic
%Equation is s³+6s²+11s+3=0, is stable or not, using routh array
%Define routh polynomial 'p'
p = [1 6 11 3];
%use 'routh' function, to check stablity
routh(p);
```

When executed, the program displays the results as given below:

```
--------------------------Routh Hurwitz Array --------------------------
1.0000e+000  1.1000e+001
6.0000e+000  3.0000e+000
1.0500e+001            0
3.0000e+000            0
There is no change of sign in entries of first column.
Therefore, no root lie in the right half s-plane.
Hence, system is stable.
```

(b) The MATLAB program is given as

```
%Program to find whether system whose Characteristic
%Equation is s^4+10*s^3+2*s^2+36*s+20=0, is stable or not
%using routh array
%Define routh polynomial 'p'
p = [1 10 2 36 20];
%use 'routh' function, to check stablity
routh(p);
```

When executed, the program displays the results as follows:

```
---------------------------Routh Hurwitz Array---------------------------
   1.0000    2.0000   20.0000
  10.0000   36.0000         0
  -1.6000   20.0000         0
 161.0000         0         0
  20.0000         0         0
There are 2 sign changes in entries of first column.
Therefore, 2 roots lie, in the right half s-plane.
Hence, system is unstable.
```

Example 11.33 Consider that the characteristic equations of a system are given by

(a) $s^5 + 2s^4 + 4s^3 + 8s^2 + 3s + 1 = 0$

(b) $s^5 + 2s^4 + 2s^3 + 4s^2 + 4s + 8 = 0$

(c) $s^5 + s^4 + 3s^3 + 3s^2 + 4s + 8 = 0$

Check their stability with Routh–Hurwitz criterion using MATLAB.

Solution:

(a) The following program is used:

```
%Program to find if system whose Characteristic Equation
%is s^5 + 2*s^4 +4*s^3+8*s^2+3*s+1=0 is stable or not,
%using routh array
%Define routh polynomial
p = [1 2 4 8 3 1];
%use routh array, to find stability.
routh(p);
```

When executed, the program displays the results as follows:

```
Special Case: First element of row 3 is zero and is replaced with 0.0001.
---------------------------Routh Hurwitz Array---------------------------
      1.0000     4.0000     3.0000
      2.0000     8.0000     1.0000
           0     2.5000          0
Routh Hurwitz Array is modified and is given as
---------------------------Routh Hurwitz Array---------------------------
1.0e+004 *
      0.0001     0.0004     0.0003
      0.0002     0.0008     0.0001
      0.0000     0.0003          0
     -4.9992     0.0001          0
      0.0003          0          0
      0.0001          0          0
There are 2 sign changes in entries of first column.
Therefore, 2 roots lie in the right half s-plane.
Hence, system is unstable.
```

(b) The following program is used:

```
%Program to find if system whose Charateristic Equation is
%s^5 + 2*s^4 +2*s^3+4*s^2+4*s+8=0 is stable or not, using
%routh array
%Define routh polynomial
p = [1 2 2 4 4 8];
%using routh array, to find stability
routh(p);
```

When executed, the program displays the results as follows:

```
Special Case: Row of zeros detected.
-------------------------Routh Hurwitz Array-------------------------
     1      2      4
     2      4      8
     0      0      0
Routh Hurwitz Array is modified and is given as
-------------------------Routh Hurwitz Array-------------------------
     1      2      4
     2      4      8
     8      8      0
     2      8      0
   -24      0      0
     8      0      0
There are 2 sign changes in entries of first column.
Therefore, 2 roots lie in the right half s-plane.
Hence, system is unstable.
```

(c) The following program is used:

```
%Program to find if system whose Charateristic Equation is
%s^5 + s^4 +3*s^3+3*s^2+4*s+8=0 is stable or not using routh
%array
%Define routh polynomial
p = [1 1 3 3 4 8];
%using routh array, to find stability
routh(p);
```

When executed, the program displays the results as follows:

```
Special Case: First element of row 3 is zero and is replaced with 0.0001.
-------------------------Routh Hurwitz Array-------------------------
     1      3      4
     1      3      8
     0     -4      0
Routh Hurwitz Array is modified and is given as
-------------------------Routh Hurwitz Array-------------------------
1.0e+004 *
       0.0001      0.0003      0.0004
       0.0001      0.0003      0.0008
       0.0000     -0.0004           0
       4.0003      0.0008           0
```

```
-0.0004       0       0
 0.0008       0       0
There are 2 sign changes in entries of first column.
Therefore, 2 roots lie in the right half s-plane.
Hence, system is unstable.
```

11.25 ROUTH STABILITY CRITERION (STATE-SPACE REPRESENTATION)

A single input single output system can be expressed in state variable form as:

$$\dot{\underline{x}} = A\underline{x} + Bu$$
$$y = C\underline{x} \tag{11.13}$$

In such a case, characteristic equation of the system is given by:

$$|\lambda I - A| = 0 \tag{11.14}$$

In MATLAB, the characteristic equation is obtained by using the command:

poly(a);

where

a is matrix A in Eqs. 11.13 and 11.14, and the **routh** function can be used for this characteristic equation to check the stability of the system.

Example 11.34 The dynamics of a system is represented by the vector–matrix differential equation:

$$\dot{\underline{x}} = \begin{bmatrix} 0 & 1 & 0 \\ 0 & 0 & 1 \\ -2 & -4 & -3 \end{bmatrix} \begin{bmatrix} x1 \\ x2 \\ x3 \end{bmatrix} + \begin{bmatrix} 0 \\ 0 \\ 1 \end{bmatrix} u \quad \text{and} \quad [1 \ \ 0 \ \ 0] \begin{bmatrix} x1 \\ x2 \\ x3 \end{bmatrix}$$

Find its characteristic equation and check its stability using the Routh–Hurwitz criterion.

Solution:

The following program is used:

```
%Program to find if system is stable or not using routh array
%define matrix A
A = [0 1 1; 0 0 1; -2 -4 -3];
%obtain characteristic equation i.e. routh polynomial
p = poly(A);
%using routh array, to find stabilty
routh(p);
```

When executed, the program displays the results as follows:

```
-------------------------Routh Hurwitz Array----------------------------
   1.0000     4.0000
   3.0000     2.0000
   3.3333          0
   2.0000          0
There is no change of sign in entries of first column.
Therefore no roots in the right half s-plane.
Hence, system is stable.
```

11.26 LOCATION OF ROOTS OF A CHARACTERISTIC EQUATION IN THE S-PLANE

Since Characteristic Equation of a closed loop system is given by a polynomial in 's', stability of a system can be checked by computing the roots of a polynomial.

If the roots of the characteristic equation of a closed loop system lie in:

(a) Left half of s- plane, system is **stable**.

(b) Right half of s- plane, system is **unstable**.

Following MATLAB command can be used to compute the roots of a polynomial:

r = roots(p), as explained in section 4.4, Chapter 4.

Example 11.35 Consider the systems, whose characteristic equations are given by:

(a) $s^3 + 6s^2 + 11s + 3 = 0$

(b) $s^4 + 10s^3 + 2s^2 + 36s + 20 = 0$

Using MATLAB, check whether the systems are stable or not, by calculating roots of the characteristic equations.

Solution:

(a) Feed the characteristic equation as a polynomial 'p1' in the command window and use the MATLAB command 'roots', as follows:

```
p1 = [1 6 11 3];
roots(p1)
```

Following roots will be displayed:

```
ans =
        -2.8358 + 1.0469i
        -2.8358 - 1.0469i
        -0.3283
```

It can be seen that all the roots lie in the left half s-plane. Hence the system is **stable**.

(b) Feed the characteristic equation as a polynomial 'p2' in the command window and type the MATLAB command 'roots', as follows:

```
p2 = [ 1 10 2 36 20];
roots(p2)
```

Following roots will be displayed:

```
ans =
        -10.1340
          0.3328 + 1.8976i
          0.3328 - 1.8976i
         -0.5317
```

It can be seen that two of the roots lie in the right half s-plane. Hence the system is **unstable**.

11.27 CONVERSION OF CONTINUOUS TIME DYNAMIC SYSTEM TO DISCRETE TIME SYSTEM

Given Continuous time state space equations of a dynamic system:

$$\dot{\underline{x}} = A\,x + B\,u$$

It is desired to convert these equations to the following Discrete time state space equations:

$$x(n+1) = Ad\; x[n] + Bd\; u[n]$$

This can be done by using the following MATLAB command:

```
[Ad,Bd]=c2d(A,B, ts)
```

where 'Ad' is a matrix 'A' in discrete form, 'Bd' is matrix 'B' in discrete form, 'ts' is the desired sampling time.

Example 11.36 Given continuous system matrices A and B:

$$A=\begin{bmatrix}0 & 1\\ -2 & -3\end{bmatrix};\quad B=\begin{bmatrix}0\\ 1\end{bmatrix}$$

Convert these system matrices to discrete time form. Use sampling period, ts = 0.1 seconds.

Solution:

Feed the matrices A and B, in the command window and use the MATLAB command 'c2d', as follows:

```
A=[0 1;-2 -3]; B=[0;1];
[Ad,Bd]=c2d(a,b,0.1)
```

Following discrete time form of matrices will be displayed:

```
Ad =
     0.9909     0.0861
    -0.1722     0.7326
Bd =
     0.0045
     0.0861
```

SUMMARY

In this chapter basic mathematical concepts such as Laplace Transform and partial fractions etc. which are used in control systems have been given before covering the control system concepts. The complete chapter can be summarized as follows:

- The different commands such as laplace, ilaplace used to obtain Laplace Transform and inverse Laplace Transform have been discussed.
- The command residue along with several examples has been discussed to obtain partial fractions.
- The transfer function representation using commands tf, tfdata, ss, printsys, etc, has been illustrated.
- Conversion of transfer function from one form to other form is discussed using commands tf2zp, zp2tf, tf2ss, ss2tf and also pole–zero mapping of transfer function is given by pzmap command.
- The inter connection of transfer functions using series, parallel, feedback connections is illustrated using series, parallel and feedback commands of MATLAB.
- The different forms of step command are elaborated to obtain step response of transfer function.
- A user-defined function steptimespec has been developed and illustrated to calculate time response specifications for step input signal to a second order system.
- The impulse and lsim commands are illustrated to obtain response to impulse and arbitrary input, respectively.
- The use of the step command to obtain ramp response is also discussed.
- User-defined functions ssezp and ssetf are developed and illustrated to compute steady-state errors and constants.
- Routh–Hurwitz criterion for checking the stability of the system is discussed.

- A user-defined function `routh` is developed to obtain the Routh array and to check the stability of a system.
- Conversion of a continuous time system to discrete time system has been discussed.

List of Commands

Command	Description
`laplace`	Gives Laplace Transform of expression
`ilaplace`	Gives Inverse Laplace
`residue`	Finds the residues, poles and direct term of a partial-fraction expansion
`tf`	Creates a continuous-time transfer function
`tfdata`	Returns the numerator(s) and denominator(s) of the transfer function
`tf2zp`	Transfer function to zero–pole conversion
`zp2tf`	Zero–pole to transfer function conversion
`zpk`	Zero–pole to transfer function conversion
`pzmap`	Computes the poles and zeros of the given model and plots them in the complex plane.
`printsys`	Prints transfer functions as a ratio of two polynomials
`ss`	Creates state-space model
`tf2ss`	Transfer function to state-space conversion
`ss2tf`	State-space to transfer function conversion
`series`	Connects two models in series
`parallel`	Connects two models in parallel
`feedback`	Gives feedback connection of two models
`step`	Plots the step response of the given model
`impulse`	Plots the impulse response of the model model sys
`lsim`	Simulates time response of the model to arbitrary inputs
`c2d`	Continuous to discrete form
User-defined functions	
`steptimespec`	Calculates time specifications for step response of second-order system.
`ssezp`	Finds steady-state errors and constants for t.f. in pole–zero form.
`ssetf`	Finds steady-state errors and constants for t.f. in pole–zero form.
`routh`	Gives Routh array and checks the stability of the system.

EXERCISES

11.1 Using MATLAB, find the Laplace Transform of $f(t)$ given by

(a) $f(t) = 1$

(b) $f(t) = \frac{1}{4}e^{-t}$

(c) $f(t) = t^3 \sin 2t$

11.2 Using MATLAB, find the Inverse Laplace Transform of $F(s)$ given by

(a) $F(s) = \dfrac{1}{s+4}$

(b) $F(s) = \dfrac{1}{s^2+2s+17}$

11.3 Using MATLAB `residue` command, compute the partial-fraction expansion of the following transfer functions:

(a) $G(s)=\dfrac{s^2+2s+3}{s^3+2s^2+4s+6}$

(b) $G(s)=\dfrac{s^3+2s^2+4s+6}{s^3+2s+3}$

(c) $G(s)=\dfrac{1}{(s+2)(s^2+4)}$

11.4 Obtain the partial-fraction expansions for the following transfer functions.

(a) $G(s)=\dfrac{2}{s(s^2+2s+2)}$

(b) $G(s)=\dfrac{4(s+1)}{s^2(s+1)(s+5)}$

(c) $G(s)=\dfrac{s^4+3s^3+4s^2+5s+4}{s(s+2)}$

11.5 Given the zeros, poles and gain k, obtain the system transfer function for the following cases:

(a) There is no zero, poles are at -1 and -2 and $k = 5$.

(b) One zero is at '0', poles are at $-1+3j$ and $-1-3j$, $k = 10$.

(c) One zero at -2, poles at -3, -5 and -10, $k = 15$.

11.6 Given the following transfer functions, obtain the locations of poles and zeros.

(a) $G(s)=\dfrac{(s+2)}{s(s+3)(s+4)}$

(b) $G(s)=\dfrac{s}{(s^2+1)}$

11.7 Let the transfer functions of the two systems be given by

$$G_1(s)=\frac{10}{(s+1)(s+2)} \quad \text{and} \quad G_2(s)=\frac{2}{(s^2+4)}$$

Find the overall system transfer function, when these two systems are connected in (a) series, (b) parallel and (c) feedback.

11.8 Plot the unit step responses of the following control systems; whose closed loop transfer functions are given as follows:

(a) $G(s)=\dfrac{2}{(s^2+3s+3)(1+s)}$

(b) $G(s)=\dfrac{15}{(s+1)(s+10)(2s+1)}$

11.9 Plot the impulse response for the transfer functions given in Question 11.8.

11.10 The linearized dynamic model relating changes in the angle of attach of a ship to changes in the angular position of the rudder is given by the transfer function:

$$G(s) = \frac{k(1+2.5s)}{s(1+4s)(1+10s)}$$

Assume that this represents the forward path of a unity feedback system and $k = 2$. Plot the response to a unit step input.

11.11 Obtain the step response of the control systems whose state-space representations are given below:

(a) $$\dot{\underline{x}} = \begin{bmatrix} -1 & 1 & 0 \\ 0 & -4 & 2 \\ 0 & 0 & -10 \end{bmatrix} \underline{x} + \begin{bmatrix} 1 & -1 \\ 0 & 2 \\ -1 & 1 \end{bmatrix} u$$

$$y = \begin{bmatrix} 1 & 0 & 1 \\ 2 & 1 & -3 \end{bmatrix} \underline{x}, \quad D = 0$$

(b) $$\dot{\underline{x}} = \begin{bmatrix} -1.0 & -3 & 0 & 0 \\ -0.002 & 0.8 & 0 & 0 \\ 1 & 0 & 6 & 6 \\ 0 & 1 & 0 & 0 \end{bmatrix} \underline{x} + \begin{bmatrix} 1.0 \\ 0 \\ 0 \\ 0 \end{bmatrix} u$$

$$y = \begin{bmatrix} 1 & 0 & 0 & 0 \end{bmatrix} \underline{x}, \quad D = 0$$

11.12 Obtain the step response of a system described in state-space form and whose system matrices are given below:

$$A = \begin{bmatrix} 1 & 0 & 1 \\ 0 & 2 & 0 \\ 1 & 4 & 5 \end{bmatrix}, \qquad B = \begin{bmatrix} 1 & 2 \\ 0 & -1 \\ 1 & 1 \end{bmatrix}.$$

$$C = \begin{bmatrix} 1 & -2 & 1 \\ 0 & 1 & 1 \end{bmatrix} \quad \text{and} \quad D = 0$$

11.13 The closed-loop transfer function of a second-order system is given by

$$\frac{C(s)}{R(s)} = \frac{4(s+2)}{(s^2+4s+8)}$$

Determine the error constants and steady-sate errors for different inputs.

11.14 Find the error constants and steady-state errors of the control system, whose dynamics is described by the following transfer function:

$$T(s) = \frac{10(s+4)}{s(s+1)(s+2.5+j5)(s+2.5-j5)}$$

11.15 Find the error constants and steady-state error for a unity feedback system having transfer function:

$$G(s) = \frac{10}{s^2(s+1)(s^2+4s+3)}$$

11.16 Repeat the above problem for the following transfer function of the system:

$$G(s) = \frac{100}{s^2(s+4)(s^2+2s+2)}$$

11.17 For the system shown below, determine the steady-state error for a unit ramp input.

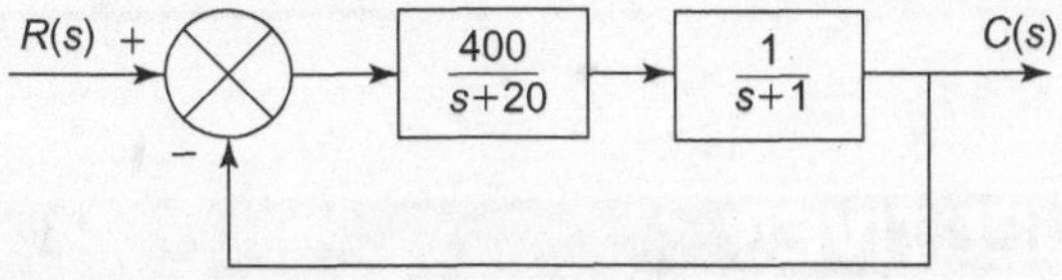

11.18 Using MATLAB commands for the Routh–Hurwitz stability criterion, determine whether or not unity feedback control system having the following open-loop transfer function is stable?

(a) $\frac{100}{s(s^2+8s+24)}$

(b) $\frac{24}{s(s+2)(s+4)}$

(c) $\frac{0.2(s+2)}{s(s+0.5)(s+0.8)(s+3)}$

11.19 Using the Routh–Hurwitz criterion, check the stability of the following system:

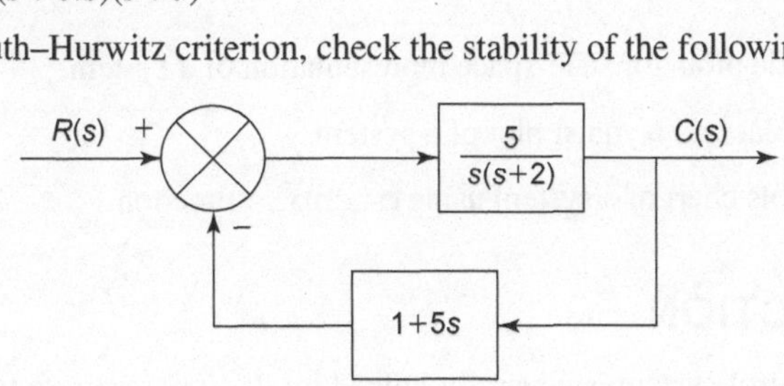

11.20 Using the Routh–Hurwitz criterion in MATLAB, determine whether the following characteristic equations represent stable systems or not?

(a) $s^3+4s^2+8s+16$

(b) $s^4+2s^3+8s^2+15s+50$

(c) $s^5+2s^4+2s^3+4s^2+s+1=0$

11.21 The state equations of a linear systems are

$$\dot{\underline{x}} = \begin{bmatrix} 0 & 1 & -5 \\ 1 & 0 & 4 \\ 0 & -1 & 3 \end{bmatrix} \underline{x} + \begin{bmatrix} 1 \\ 0.5 \\ 0 \end{bmatrix} u \quad \text{and} \quad y = \begin{bmatrix} 0 & 2 & 3 \end{bmatrix} \underline{x}$$

Is this a stable system?

11.22 Determine the number of eigen values with positive real parts using Routh–Hurwitz criterion for each of the matrices given below:

(a) $a = [-12 \quad -5 \quad -20; \quad 10 \quad -8 \quad 0; \quad 0 \quad 1 \quad 0]$

(b) $a = [-1 \quad 2 \quad 0; \quad 0 \quad -5 \quad -3; \quad 2 \quad 1 \quad -6]$

CHAPTER 12

MATLAB Applications in Control Systems-II

LEARNING OBJECTIVES

- To plot root locus diagram of a system using rlocus function.
- To obtain the value of gain at a given point on the root locus using `rlocfind` function.
- To obtain the root locus for state-space representation of systems.
- To obtain frequency response of dynamic systems.
- To plot Bode diagrams and obtain the phase margin, gain margin and associated frequencies using MATLAB functions.
- To compute the frequency response specifications of a system using user defined function `fresp`.
- Draw the Bode plots for state-space representation of a system.
- Obtain the polar and Nyquist plot of a system.
- To plot Nichols chart of a system using `nichols` function.

12.1 INTRODUCTION

The performance of a control system is generally judged by its time response to test signals. The analysis and design of a control system is also carried out based on its frequency response. In the frequency response, response of the system to a sinusoidal input is investigated as the frequency varies. In this chapter, use of the techniques/graphical methods such as Root Locus, Bode diagram, Nyquist plot, Nichols chart, etc. using MATLAB has been described.

12.2 ROOT LOCUS

The location of closed-loop poles in the s-plane gives an idea about stability and transient response of a closed-loop system. With the variation of any system parameter, these poles move from their locations. The knowledge about change in the location of poles is quite useful in the design of a closed-loop system. To find out the location of the poles, the classical techniques of factorizing the characteristic polynomial and determining its roots are used. However, if any system parameter is varied for adjustments, the characteristic equation changes and computations have to be repeated to calculate the roots. The root locus technique, introduced by W.R. Evans, provides a simple graphical method of finding the roots of characteristic equation, with the gain parameter K varying from $-\infty$ to ∞, without solving it.

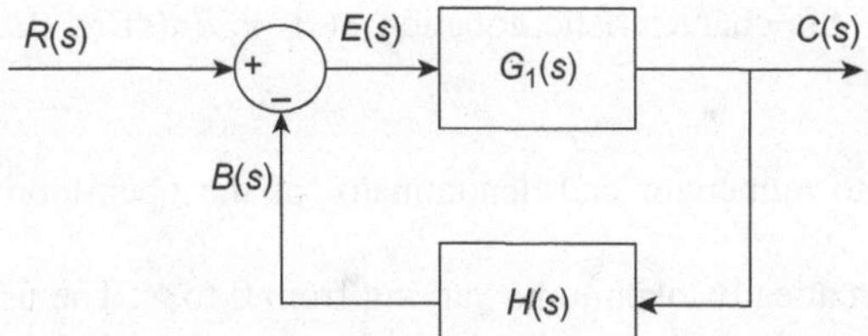

Figure 12.1 A Closed-Loop Feedback System

Consider a closed-loop system as shown in Figure 12.1.

The characteristic equation of this closed-loop system is given by

$$1+G(s)H(s)=0 \tag{12.1}$$

where

$$G(s)=\frac{K(a_n s^n + a_{n-1}s^{n-1} + \cdots + a_1 s^1 + a_0)}{b_m s^m + b_{m-1}s^{m-1} + \cdots + b_1 s^1 + b_0}$$

and `K` is gain of the system and is a variable parameter.

Thus, root locus is defined as the plot of the closed-loop poles as a function of open-loop gain (`K`), when `K` is varied from 0 to ∞.

12.2.1 Angle and Magnitude Criterion

Consider a characteristic equation of a closed-loop system i.e. Eq. 12.1. The roots of the characteristics equation (i.e. closed-loop poles of the system) occur only for those values of `s` which satisfy the following equations:

$$G(s)H(s)=-1 \tag{12.2}$$

As `s` is a complex variable, Eq. 12.2 can be split into two Evan's conditions as follows:

(a) Magnitude Condition $\quad |G(s)H(s)|=1 \qquad (12.3)$

(b) Angle Condition $\quad \angle G(s)H(s)=\pm 180°(2k+1);\quad k=0,1,2,\ldots$

$$= \text{odd multiples of } 180° \tag{12.4}$$

Thus, it is implied that the roots of $1+G(s)H(s)=0$ are those values of `s` at which the magnitude of $G(s)H(s)$ is equal to 1 and angle of $G(s)H(s) = \pm 180°(2k + 1);\quad k = 0,1,2,\ldots$

The first condition i.e. magnitude condition, gives the value of gain corresponding to a point on the root locus, after the root locus has been drawn. The second condition, i.e. angle condition, is used to determine the root locus of the system.

12.3 ROOT LOCUS PLOT USING MATLAB

A number of rules have to be followed for plotting the root locus by conventional method. However, it can be easily plotted by using predefined built-in functions in MATLAB. In general, the open-loop transfer function is given as

$$G(s)H(s)=\frac{Kn(s)}{d(s)} \tag{12.5}$$

where

`n(s)` is the numerator polynomial, and

`d(s)` is the denominator polynomial.

The characteristic equation of the closed-loop transfer function is given by

$$1+G(s)H(s)=0 \quad \text{or} \quad 1+\frac{Kn(s)}{d(s)}=0 \quad \text{or} \quad d(s)+Kn(s)=0 \tag{12.6}$$

To plot the root locus of the characteristic equation $d(s) + Kn(s) = 0$, **rlocus** command is used. The syntax of the command is

```
rlocus (n, d)
```

where n and d correspond to numerator and denominator of the open-loop transfer function, $G(s)H(s)$, respectively.

The gain vector K is automatically taken to be varying from 0 to ∞. The user-defined values of variable parameter K can also be used to obtain the root locus plot by using the following command:

```
rlocus(n, d, K)
```

where vector K contains all the gain values for which closed-loop poles are to be computed.

12.3.1 Test for System Stability

A system is stable, if all the roots of the characteristic equation remain in the LHS of the s-plane i.e. the root locus does not cross into RHS of the s-plane.

> **Programming Tip 12.1:** The relevant information like gain, damping and overshoot at any point on the root locus can be obtained by clicking at the desired point on the plot.

Example 12.1 Plot the root locus for the system whose open-loop transfer function is given as

$$G(s)H(s) = \frac{K(s+2)}{(3s^2+5s+7)}$$

Solution:

```
%Program to plot root-locus of the system
n = [1 2];              %to define the numerator polynomial
d = [3 5 7];            %to define the denominator polynomial
rlocus (n, d);          %to plot the root-locus of the system
```

The root locus plot obtained is as shown in Figure 12.2.

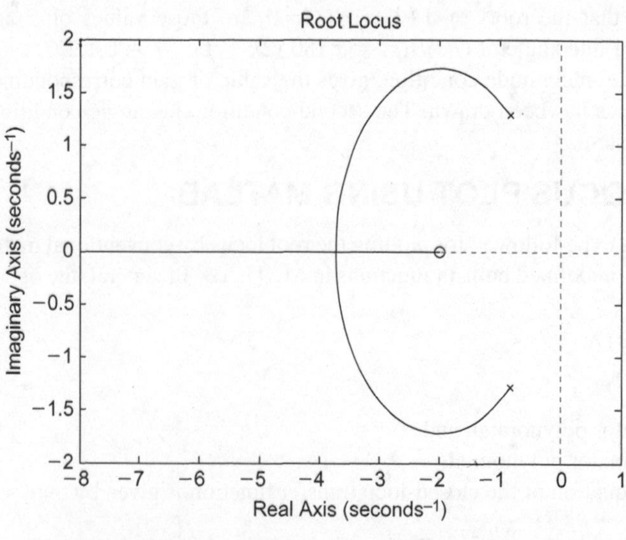

Figure 12.2 Root Locus Plot for Example 12.1

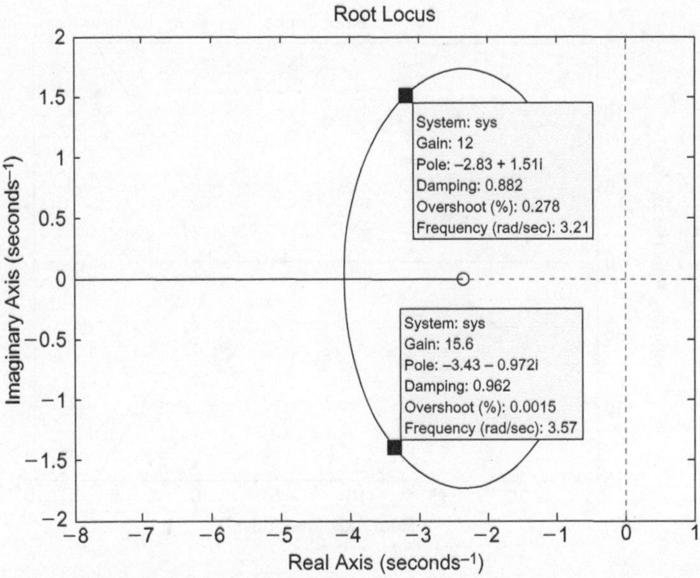

Figure 12.3 Plot to Illustrate the Relevant Information Available

Now, by clicking over any point on the root locus, the relevant information like system gain, damping, overshoot, and natural frequency of oscillation about the locus at that point can be obtained as shown in Figure 12.3.

Example 12.2 Using MATLAB, plot the root loci of the following transfer function:

(a) $\dfrac{K(s+3)}{s(s+2)(s+4)(s+5)}$ (b) $\dfrac{K(s+7)}{s(s+5)(s+15)(s+20)}$

(c) $\dfrac{K(s+15)}{s(s+5)(s+2+j6)(s+2-j6)}$ (d) $\dfrac{K(s+1)}{s^2(s+10)}$

Solution:

(a)
```
%Program to plot root-locus of the system having transfer
    %function, K(s+3)/s(s+2)(s+4)(s+5)
    %Define the numerator polynomial
    n = [1 3];
    %Define the denominator polynomial
    %conv will give the multiplication of two polynomials
    d = conv (conv ([1 0], [1 2]), conv ([1 4], [1 5]));
    %Plot the root-locus of the system
    rlocus(n, d);
```
The root locus plot obtained is shown in Figure 12.4.

(b)
```
%Program to plot root-locus of the system having transfer
    %function K(s+7)/s(s+5)(s+15)(s+20)
    %Define the numerator polynomial
    n = [1 7];
```

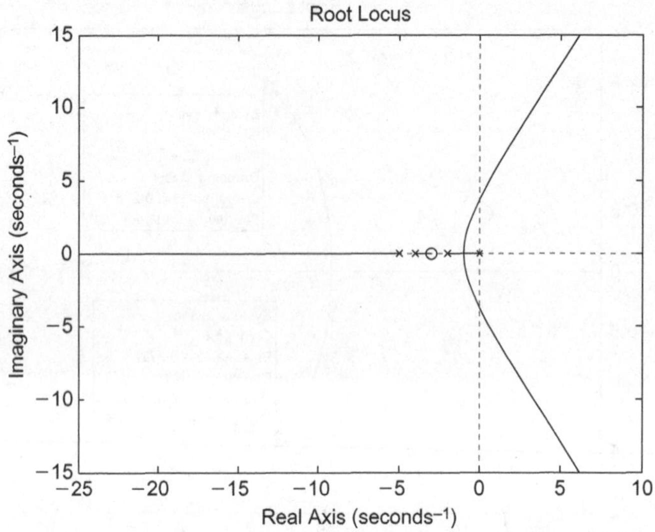

Figure 12.4 Root Locus Plot for Transfer Function $\dfrac{K(s+3)}{s(s+2)(s+4)(s+5)}$

```
%Define the denominator polynomial
d = conv(conv([1 0], [1 5]), conv([1 15], [1 20]));
%Plot the root-locus of the system
rlocus(n, d)    %define the range of x and y axis of the graph
axis([-25 3 - 15 15]).
```

The root locus plot obtained is shown in Figure 12.5.

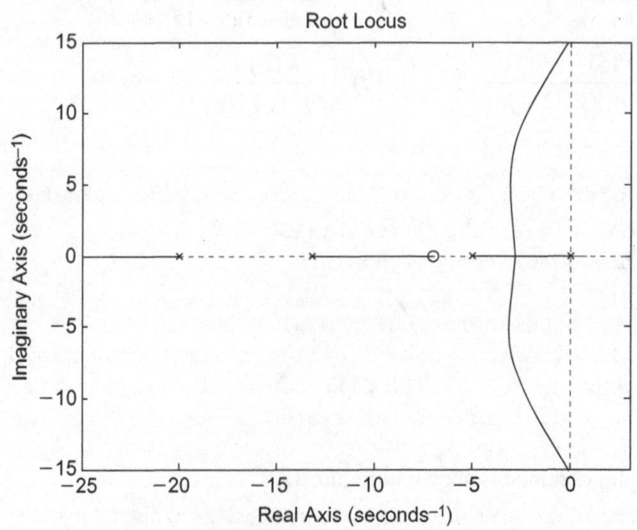

Figure 12.5 Root Locus Plot for Transfer Function $\dfrac{K(s+7)}{s(s+5)(s+15)(s+20)}$

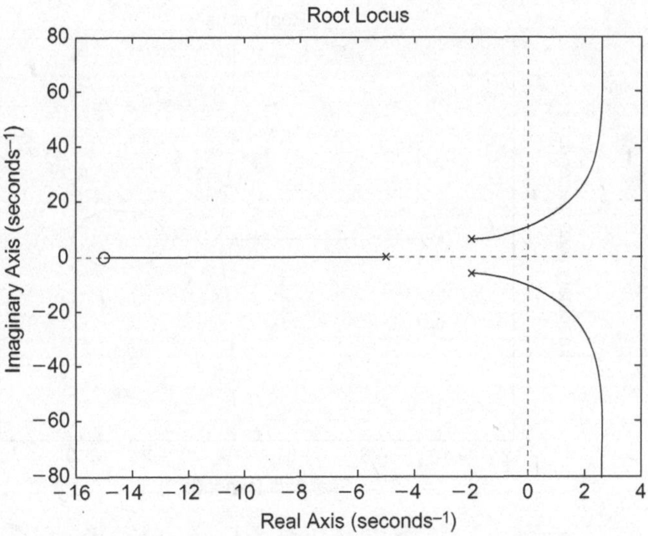

Figure 12.6 Root Locus Plot for Transfer Function $\dfrac{K(s+15)}{(s+5)(s+2+j6)(s+2-j6)}$

(c)

```
%Program to plot root-locus of the system with transfer
%function K(s+15)/(s+5)(s+2+6j)(s+2-6j)
%Define the numerator polynomial
n = [1 15];
d = conv([1 5], conv([1 2+6j ], [1 2-6j]))
%Define the denominator polynomial
rlocus(n, d); %to plot the root-locus of the system
```

The root locus plot is shown in Figure 12.6.

(d)

```
%Program to plot root-locus of the system given in example 12.2d
n = [1 1];          %to define the numerator polynomial
d = [1 10 0 0];     %to define the denominator polynomial
rlocus(n, d);       %to plot the root-locus of the system
```

The root locus plot is shown in Figure 12.7.

Example 12.3 Examine the stability of the unity feedback control system shown in Figure 12.8 for all values of gain, K.

Solution: Closed-loop transfer function of the control system is given by

$$\frac{Ks+3}{s^3+2s^2+s+Ks+3}$$

∴ Characteristic equation for this system is

$$s^3+2s^2+s+Ks+3=0$$

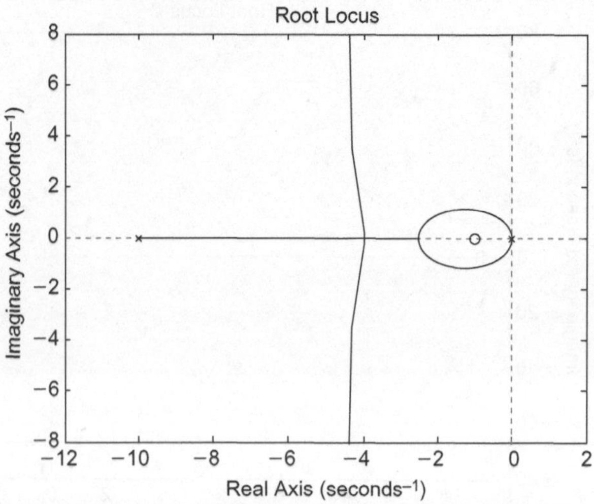

Figure 12.7 Root Locus Plot for Transfer Function $\dfrac{K(s+1)}{s^2(s+10)}$

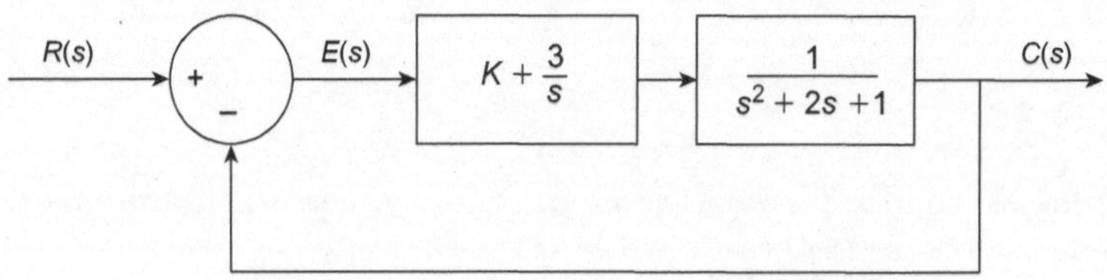

Figure 12.8 Unity Feedback Control System

or

$$(s^3+2s^2+s+3)+Ks=0$$

or

$$1+\frac{Ks}{s^3+2s^2+s+3}=0$$

The MATLAB program for plotting the root locus of the system is as follows:

```
%Program to plot root-locus of the system given in example 12.3
n = [1 0];              %Define the numerator polynomial
d = [1 2 1 3];          %Define the denominator polynomial
rlocus(n, d);           %to plot the root-locus of the system
```

The root locus plot is shown in Figure 12.9.

12.4 ROOT LOCUS USING `plot` COMMAND

To obtain the roots of characteristic equation for values of `K` specified by the user, the following commands can be used:

```
[r, K] = rlocus (n, d)
```

or

```
[r, K] = rlocus (n, d, K)
```

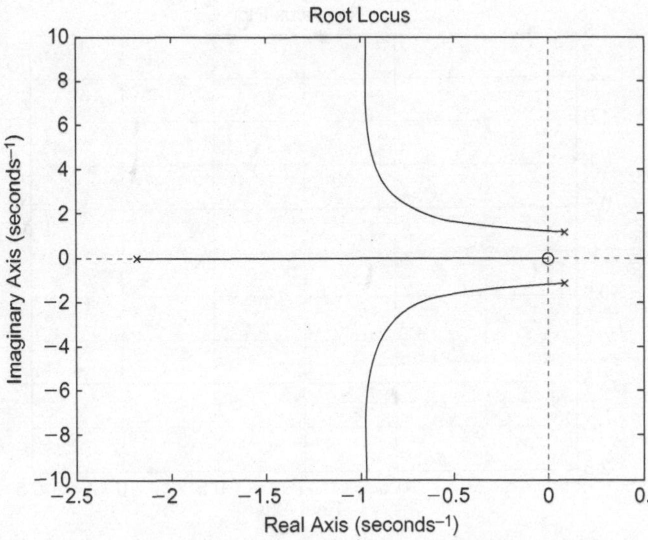

Figure 12.9 Root Locus Plot for Example 12.3

These commands will return matrix `r` containing the values of roots of the characteristic equation for the corresponding values of `K`.

The root locus plot can also be obtained by using `plot` command for matrix `r` obtained as outlined above and is as shown below:

```
r = rlocus (n, d);
plot (r, ' ');
```

The **`plot`** command plots the root locus. Different line styles can be used in these plots. To plot the root loci with marks 'o' or '*x*', the commands `plot (r, 'o')` or `plot (r, 'x')` can be used.

Example 12.4 Plot root locus and examine the stability of the following system:

$$G(s)H(s) = \frac{0.4K}{s^3 + 2s^2 + 4s + 5}$$

if the gain `K` is varied over a range of:

(a) $K = 2, 4, 6, 8$

(b) $K = 2, 4, 6, 8, 10.$

Determine the exact pole locations also in tabular form for part (b).

Solution:

(a)

```
%Program to plot root-locus of the system given in example 12.4
K = 2 : 2 : 8;          %vector K defined for different values of gain
n = [0.4];              %Define the numerator polynomial
d = [1 2 4 5];          %Define the denominator polynomial
[r, k] = rlocus(n, d, K);
%Plot the root-locus of the system for different values of gain K
Plot (r, 'o');
grid;
title ('Root locus Plot');
```

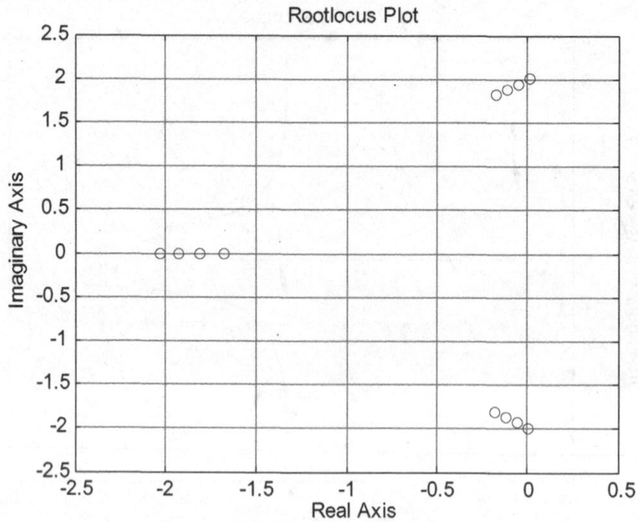

Figure 12.10 Root Locus Plot for Example 12.4 (a)

```
xlabel ('Real Axis');
ylabel ('Imaginary Axis');
```

The roots are plotted in Figure 12.10. It is seen that the roots do not cross the imaginary axis for $K = 2$, 4 and 6. Hence, the system is **stable** for K = 2, 4 and 6 and unstable for k = 8

(b)

```
%Program to plot root-locus of the system given in example
12.4 b
K = 2 :2 :10;
%vector K defined for different values of gain
n = [0.4];              %Define the numerator polynomial
d = [1 2 4 5];          %Define the denominator polynomial
[p, K] = rlocus(n, d, K);
%returns the root-locus points for the system at different
%values of gain K
plot(p, 'o');           %Plot the root-locus points
grid;                   %Show grid
title ('Root locus Plot');
xlabel ('Real Axis');
ylabel ('Imaginary Axis');
```

The roots on the root locus for different values of *K* are given as following:

```
p =
    -0.1615 + 1.8527i   -0.1615 - 1.8527i    -1.6771
    -0.0963 + 1.9085i   -0.0963 - 1.9085i    -1.8073
    -0.0390 + 1.9618i   -0.0390 - 1.9618i    -1.9220
     0.0123 + 2.0124i    0.0123 - 2.0124i    -2.0247
     0.0589 + 2.0606i    0.0589 - 2.0606i    -2.1179

K =
     2     4     6     8    10
```

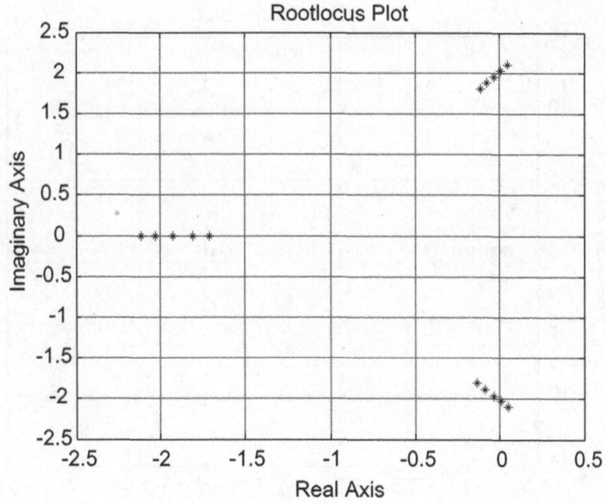

Figure 12.11 Root Locus Plot for Example 12.4 (c)

The roots are plotted in Figure 12.11. It can be seen that the system is **unstable** for $K = 8$ and 10, because the roots cross to right half plane for these values of K.

Example 12.5 Obtain the roots of the characteristic equation for given values of K for the following transfer function:

(a) $\dfrac{(2s+9)K}{s(s^2+6s+13)}$ K= 10:5:50

(b) $\dfrac{K}{s(s^2+7s+20)}$ K= 100:100:1000

Solution:

(a)

```
%Program to plot root-locus of the system given in example 12.5
K = 10 :5 :50;
%vector K defined for different values of gain
n = [2 9];
%Define the numerator polynomial
d = [1 6 13 0];
%Define the denominator polynomial
[p, K] = rlocus(n, d, K);
%Returns the root-locus points for the system at different
%values of gain K
plot(p, 'o');            %Plot the root-locus points
grid;                    %Show grid
title('Root Locus Plot');
xlabel('Real Axis');
ylabel('Imaginary Axis');
```

The response obtained is given in Figure 12.12.

System is **stable** for all values of K, as the root locus does not cross the imaginary axis.

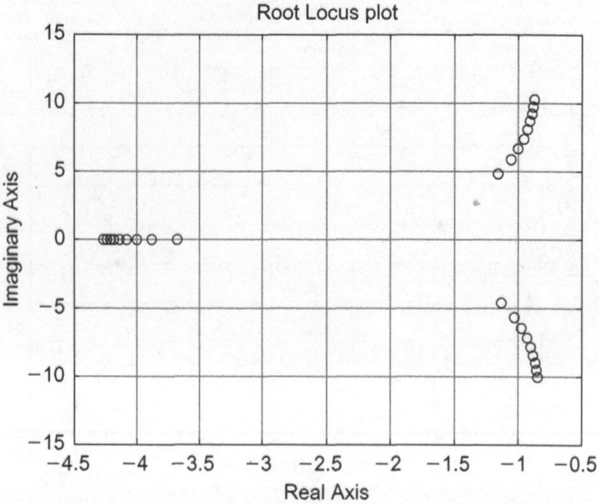

Figure 12.12 Root Locus Plot for Example 12.5 (a)

(b)

```
%Program to plot root-locus of the system given in example 12.5(b)
K = 100 :100 :1000;
%vector K defined for different values of gain
n = [1];
%to define the numerator polynomial
d = [1 7 20 0];
%to define the denominator polynomial
[p, K] = rlocus(n, d, K);
%returns the root-locus points for the system at different
%values of gain K
plot(p, 'o');                       %to plot the root-locus points
grid;                               %to plot the grid
title('Root Locus Plot');
xlabel('Real Axis');
ylabel('Imaginary Axis');
```

The response obtained is given in Figure 12.13.

System is **unstable** for values of $K > 100$, as the root locus crosses the imaginary axis for these values.

Example 12.6 Plot the root locus for the following transfer functions using `plot` command in MATLAB:

(a) $\dfrac{K(s+1)}{s^2(s+2)}$ (b) $\dfrac{K}{(s^2+3s+2)(s^2+2s+5)}$

Solution:

(a)

```
%Program to plot root-locus of the system given in example 12.6.a
n = [1 1];                  %Define the numerator polynomial
```

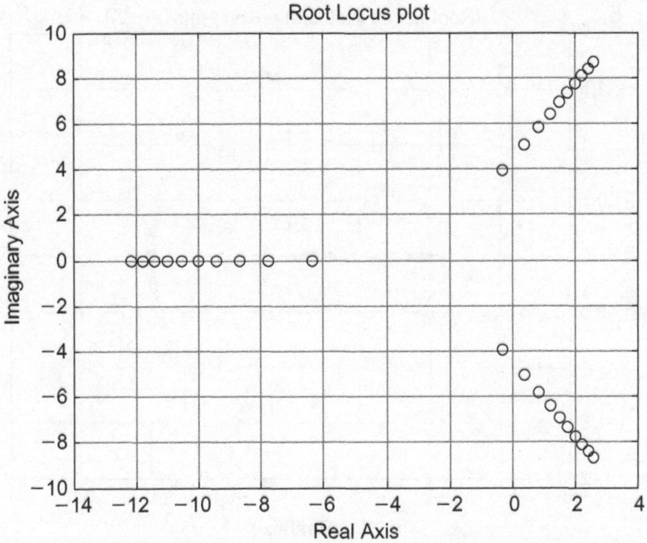

Figure 12.13 Root Locus Plot for Example 12.5 (b)

```
d = [1 2 0 0];           %Define the denominator polynomial
[p] = rlocus(n, d);      %Returns root-locus points for system
plot(p, 'o');            %Plot the root-locus points
v = [ -3 1 -2 2];        %Define vector for axis
axis(v);                 %Define x, y axis
grid;                    %Show grid
title('Root Locus Plot G(s)=K(s+1)/[(s^2)(s+2)]');
xlabel('Real Axis');
ylabel('Imaginary Axis');
```

The response obtained is shown in Figure 12.14.

System is **stable** for all values of K, as the root locus does not cross the imaginary axis.

(b)

```
%Program to plot root-locus of the system given in example 12.6.b
n = [1];                            %Define the numerator polynomial
d = conv([1 3 2], [1 2 5]);         %Define denominator polynomial
[p] = rlocus(n, d);
%returns the root-locus points for the system
plot(p, '-');                       %to plot the root-locus points
v = [ -5 3 -4 4];                   %define vector for axis
axis(v);                            %define x, y axis
grid;                               %to plot the grid
title('Root Locus Plot for G(s)=K/[(s^2+3s+2)(s^2+2s+5)]');
xlabel('Real Axis');
ylabel('Imaginary Axis');
```

The response obtained is shown in Figure 12.15.

System is **unstable** as the root locus crosses the imaginary axis for these values.

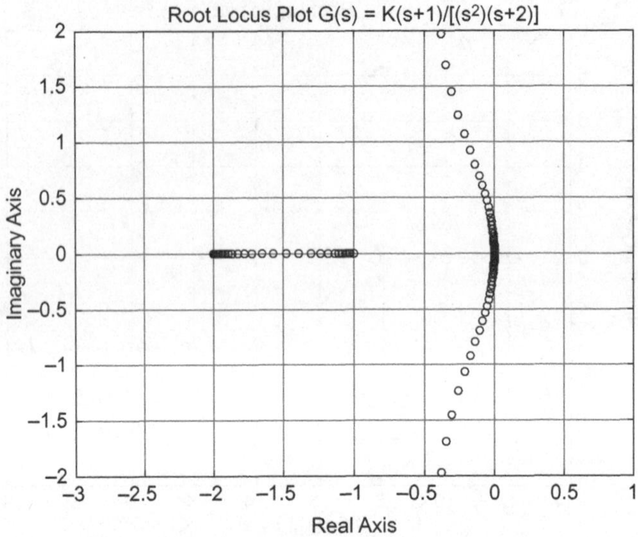

Figure 12.14 Root Locus Plot for Example 12.6 (a)

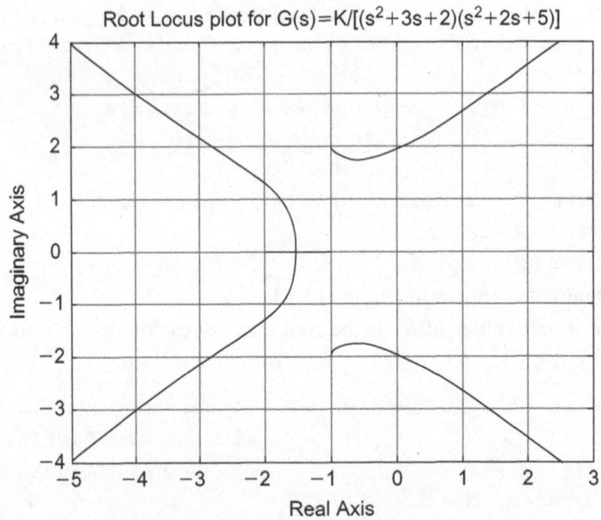

Figure 12.15 Root Locus Plot for Example 12.6 (b)

12.5 POLAR GRID LINES IN ROOT LOCUS DIAGRAM

The damping ratio is used to determine the angular location of the poles while the undamped natural frequency `wn` gives the distance of the pole from origin. Both the damping ratio `z` and natural frequency `wn` can be shown on the root locus diagrams. The damping ratios are indicated by straight lines passing through the origin whereas natural frequencies are indicated by circles for their different values, respectively.

In MATLAB, constant damping ratio and natural frequency grid lines can be drawn in a root locus plot by using the following command(s):

`sgrid` Plots the grid lines of constant damping ratio `z` from 0 to 1 with an increment of 0.1 and circles of constant natural frequency `wn`.

`sgrid(z, wn)` Plots the grid lines for the given values of damping ratio `z` and natural frequency `wn` in row vectors.

If it is desired to omit either the constant `z` lines or constant `wn` circles, empty brackets [ ] can be used in the corresponding arguments of `sgrid` command. For example, `sgrid(0.6, [ ])`, will draw a line for damping ratio `z` = 0.6 only and will not draw any circle.

> **Programming Tip 12.2:** To omit constant `z` lines or `wn` circles, empty brackets [] can be used in corresponding arguments of `sgrid` command.

Example 12.7 Illustrate the use of `sgrid` command.

Solution:

```
%Program to illustrate the use of 'sgrid' command
sgrid ([0.2 0.7], [0.5 1 2] );
%draw grid lines for z = [0.2 0.7] and wn =[0.5 1 2]
axis ([-3 1 -2 2]);            %define x and y axis
title('Illustrate the \zeta lines and \omega_n circles on root locus')
xlabel('Real axis');
ylabel('Imaginary axis');
```

The constant `z` lines or constant `wn` circles obtained are plotted in Figure 12.16.

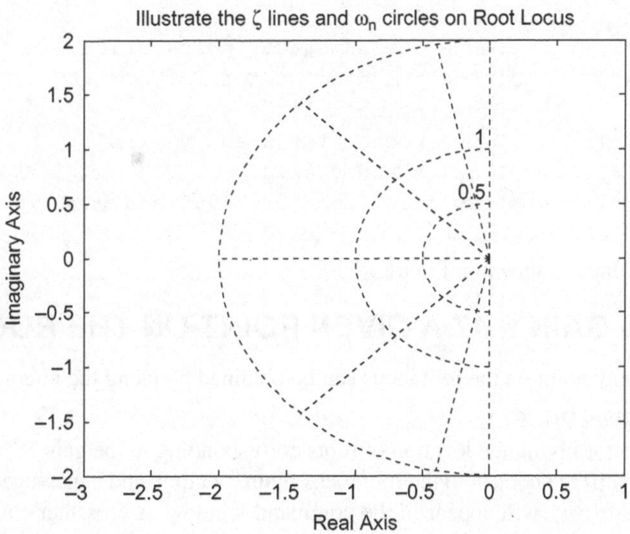

Figure 12.16 Illustration of the Use of `sgrid` Command

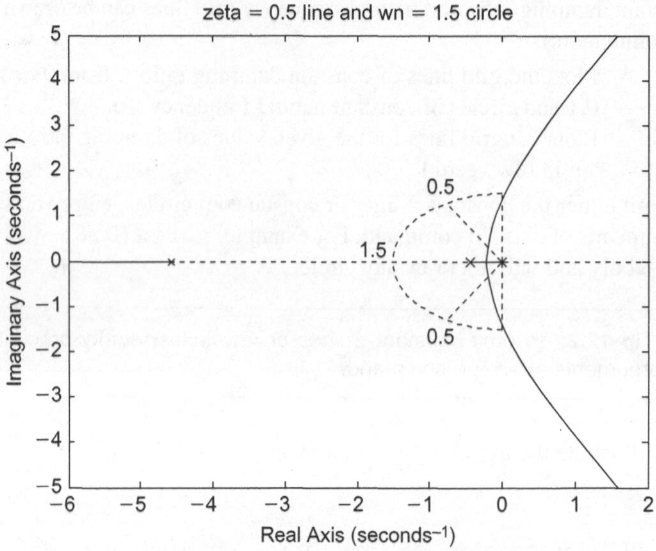

Figure 12.17 Root Locus Plot for Example 12.8

Example 12.8 Plot the root locus and draw grid lines corresponding to (i) $\xi = 0.5$ (ii) $\omega_n = 1.5$, for the system whose open loop transfer function is given as

$$G(s) = \frac{K}{s^3 + 5s^2 + 2s}$$

Solution:

```
%Program to Plot the root locus and draw lines for the
%system given in Example 12.8
n = [0 0 0 1];          %Define the numerator polynomial
d = [1 5 2 0];          %Define the denominator polynomial
rlocus(n, d);           %Draw the root-locus plot
v = [-6 2 -5 5];        %Define vector for x and y axis
axis(v);                %Define x and y axis
sgrid(0.5, 1.5);        %Draw gridlines for z=0.5 and wn=1.5
title('zeta=0.5 line and wn=1.5 circle');
```

The root locus plot obtained is shown in Figure 12.17.

12.6 FINDING GAIN K AT A GIVEN POINT ON THE ROOT LOCUS

The value of gain **K** at any point on the root locus can be obtained by using the interactive command:

```
[K, r] = rlocfind(n, d)
```

where `r` is a column vector giving the location of roots corresponding to the gain `K`.

This command will shift the control to the root locus figure window and a message `'select a point in the figure window'` will appear in the command window. A crosshair cursor will also appear in the figure window, and this cursor can be moved to select the exact point on the root locus using the mouse. At the desired point on the root locus, left button of the mouse is clicked. The values of the selected point, corresponding gain and roots are displayed in the command window.

Programming Tip 12.3: As this command is used to obtain value of gain `K` at any point on the root locus, the command `rlocfind` must follow the `rlocus` command.

Example 12.9 Consider a unity feedback system with the following transfer function:

$$G(s) = \frac{K}{s(s^2 + 2s + 3)}$$

Plot the root locus and draw grid line for damping ratio, `z = 0.5`. Determine closed-loop poles that have the damping ratio `z = 0.5` and find the gain value, `K` at this point, using `rlocfind` command.

```
Solution: %Program to Plot the root locus and find closed loop poles and gain
value K %for damping ratio z=0.5 for the system given in Example 12.9
n = [0 0 0 1];                %Define the numerator polynomial
d = [1 2 3 0];                %Define the denominator polynomial
rlocus(n, d);                 %Draw the root-locus plot
sgrid(0.5, [ ]);              %Draw the grid lines for z= 0.5
[K, r] = rlocfind(n, d)       %Find value of gain K at z=0.5
```

The root locus plot obtained is shown in Figure 12.18. The crosshair cursor appears in the figure window. Select a point on the grid lines drawn corresponding to damping ratio, `z = 0.5` where these intersect the root locus. The selected point, the value of `K` at that point and the roots on the root locus corresponding to that value of `K` are displayed in the command window. The results are as follows:

```
Select a point in the graphics window
selected_point =
   -0.8270 + 1.3168i
K =
  0.8448
```

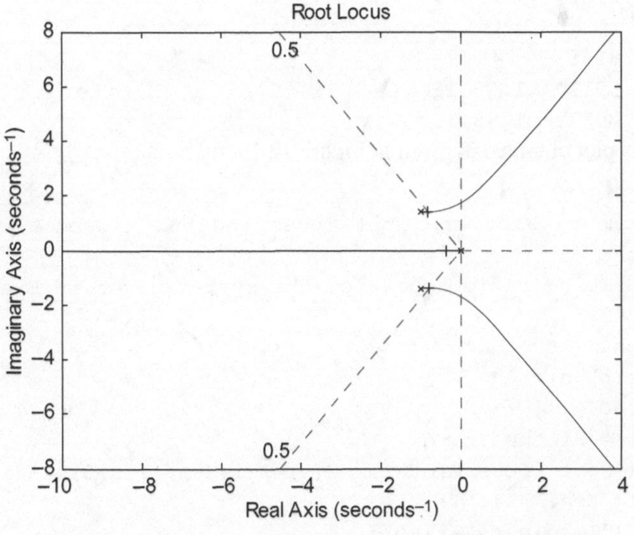

Figure 12.18 Root Locus Plot for Example 12.9

```
r =
     -0.8258 + 1.3201i
     -0.8258 - 1.3201i
     -0.3484
```

Example 12.10 Find the values of K for damping ratios mentioned in the following transfer functions:

(a) $\dfrac{K}{s(s+4)(s+5)}$, for $\xi = 0.5$

(b) $\dfrac{K(2s+2)}{s(s+3)(s+4)}$, for $\xi = 0.4$

Solution:

(a)

```
%Program to Plot the root locus and find closed loop
%poles and gain value K for damping ratio z=0.5 for the
%system given in Example 12.10 (a)
n = [1];
d = conv([1 0], conv([1 4], [ 1 5]));
rlocus(n, d);
sgrid(0.5, [] );
[K, r] = rlocfind(n, d)
title('Root Locus Plot for G(s)=K/[s(s+4)(s+5)]');
xlabel('Real Axis');
ylabel('Imaginary Axis');
```

When executed, the following results are obtained:

```
Select a point in the graphics window
selected_point =
     -1.1552 + 2.0031i
K =
     34.8786
r =
     -6.8166
     -1.0917 + 1.9811i
     -1.0917 - 1.9811i
```

The root locus plot obtained is given in Figure 12.19

(b)

```
%Program to Plot the root locus and find closed loop poles and gain
%value K
%for damping ratio z=0.4 for the system given in Example 12.10(b)
n = [2 2];
d = conv([1 0], conv([1 3], [ 1 4]));
rlocus(n, d);
sgrid(0.4, [] );
[K, r] = rlocfind(n, d)
title('Root Locus Plot for G(s)=2(1+Ks)/[s(s+5)(s+4)]');
xlabel('Real Axis');
ylabel('Imaginary Axis');
```

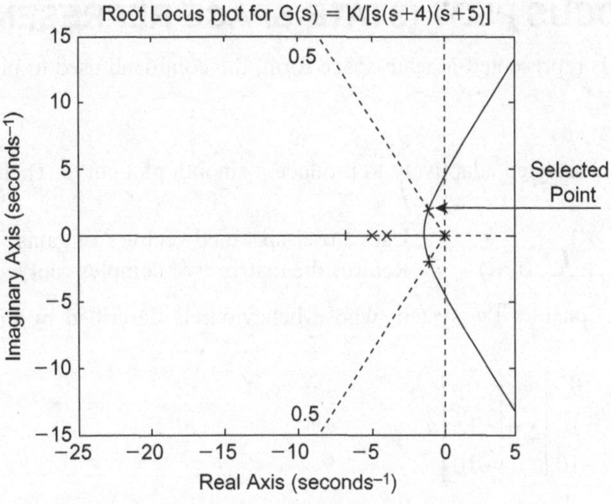

Figure 12.19 Root Locus Plot for Example 12.10 (a)

Similar to the previous case, the following output is obtained:

```
selected_point =
    -3.0604 + 6.9410i
K =
    25.4690
r =
    -3.0572 + 6.9409i
    -3.0572 - 6.9409i
    -0.8855
```

The root locus plot obtained is given in Figure 12.20

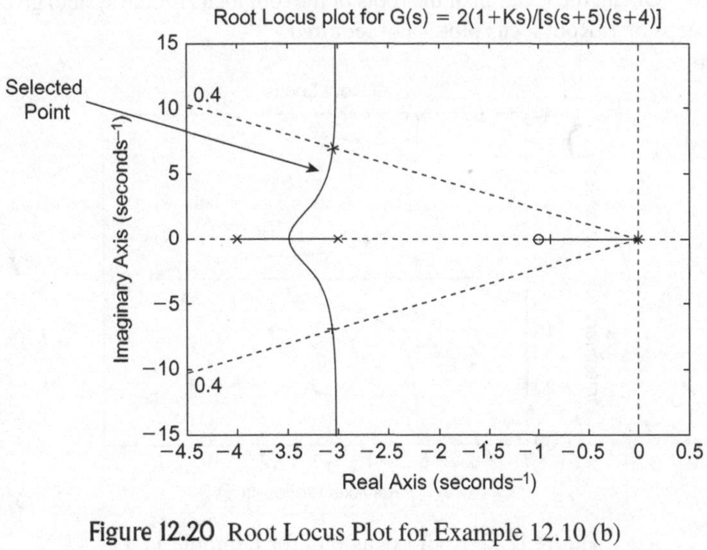

Figure 12.20 Root Locus Plot for Example 12.10 (b)

12.7 ROOT LOCUS PLOT (STATE-SPACE REPRESENTATION)

When a control system is represented in state-space form, the command used to plot the root locus for the system is

```
rlocus(A, B, C, D)
```

The gain vector K is calculated adaptively to produce a smooth plot curve. There are two more types of this **rlocus** command.

rlocus(A,B,C,D,K)	Uses a user-specified vector K of gains.
[r,K]=rlocus(A,B,C,D,K)	Returns the matrix r of complex root locations for the gains K.

Example 12.11 Consider the system whose behaviour is described by the following state-space equations:

$$\dot{\underline{x}} = \begin{bmatrix} 0 & 1 & 0 \\ 0 & 0 & 1 \\ -120 & -40 & -10 \end{bmatrix} \underline{x} + \begin{bmatrix} 0 \\ 1 \\ -10 \end{bmatrix} u$$

$$y = \begin{bmatrix} 1 & 0 & 0 \end{bmatrix} \underline{x} + \begin{bmatrix} 0 \end{bmatrix} u$$

Obtain the root locus plot using MATLAB.

Solution:

```
%Program to Plot the root locus for system described
%in state space form given in Example 12.11
a = [0 1 0; 0 0 1; -120 -40 -10];
b = [0; 1; -10];
c = [1 0 0];
d = [0 ];
rlocus(a, b, c, d);
```

The root locus plot obtained is given in Figure 12.21.

Example 12.12 Obtain the location of the roots of the root locus for the system given in Example 12.11 for K = 1 to 10, in steps of 1. Root locus plot is not required.

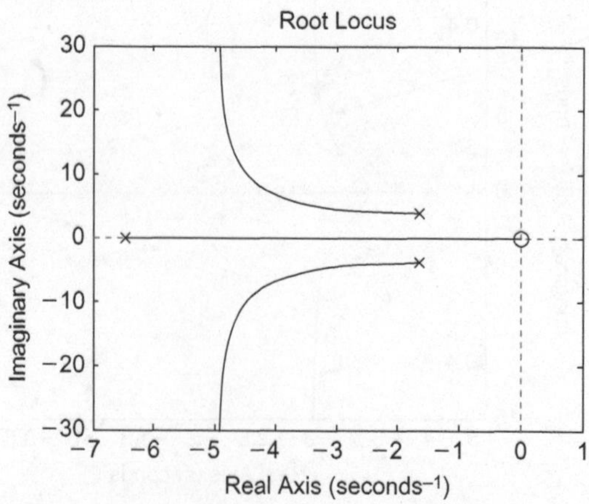

Figure 12.21 Root Locus Plot for Example 12.11

Solution:

```
%Program to Plot the root locus for system described in
%state space form given in example 12.12 for K=1 to 10, in steps of 1
K = 1 : 10;
a = [0 1 0; 0 0 1; -120 -40 -10];
b = [0; 1; -10];
c = [1 0 0];
d = [0];
[r, K] = rlocus(a, b, c, d, K)
```

The roots obtained corresponding to different values of K are as follows and no plot will be shown.

```
r =

   -6.5361            -1.7320 + 3.9192i    -1.7320 - 3.9192i
   -6.3632            -1.8184 + 3.9436i    -1.8184 - 3.9436i
   -6.1846            -1.9077 + 3.9704i    -1.9077 - 3.9704i
   -6.0000            -2.0000 + 4.0000i    -2.0000 - 4.0000i
   -5.8096            -2.0952 + 4.0331i    -2.0952 - 4.0331i
   -5.6136            -2.1932 + 4.0702i    -2.1932 - 4.0702i
   -5.4127            -2.2937 + 4.1121i    -2.2937 - 4.1121i
   -5.2076            -2.3962 + 4.1595i    -2.3962 - 4.1595i
   -5.0000            -2.5000 + 4.2131i    -2.5000 - 4.2131i
   -4.7917            -2.6042 + 4.2734i    -2.6042 - 4.2734i

 K =

    1      2      3      4      5      6      7      8      9      10
```

Example 12.13 Plot the root locus for the control system shown in Figure 12.22.

Solution:

```
%Program to Plot the root locus for system shown in figure 12.22
%calculation of the denominator polynomial
a = [1 4 0];            %a=s(s+4)
b = [1 6];              %b=(s+6)
c = [1 1.4 1];          %c=s^2+1.4s+1
d = conv(a, b);
e = conv(c, d);         %gives e=[1.0 11.4 39.0 43.6 24.0 0]
%The denominator polynomial is thus s^5+11.4s^4+39s^3+43.6s^2+24s
n = [0 0 0 1 2 4];
d = [ 1 11.4 39 43.6 24 0 ];
rlocus (n, d);
v = [-10 10 -10 10];
axis(v);
grid;
title('Root Locus Plot of G(s)=K(s^2+2s+4)/[s(s+4)(s+6)(s^2+1.4 +1)]');
xlabel('Real Axis');
ylabel('Imaginary Axis');
```

The root locus plot obtained is given in Figure 12.23.

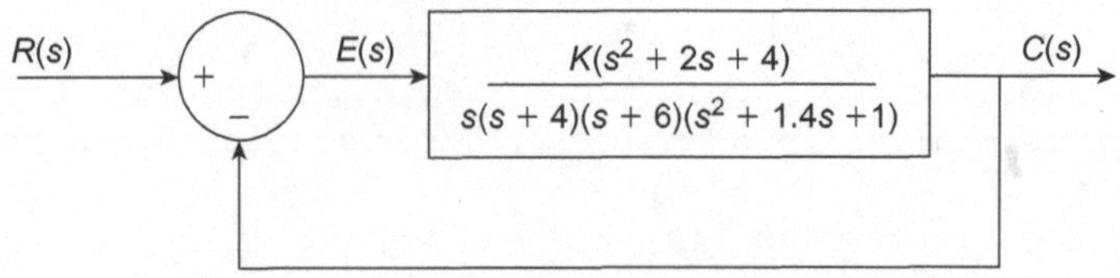

Figure 12.22 Control System for Example 12.13

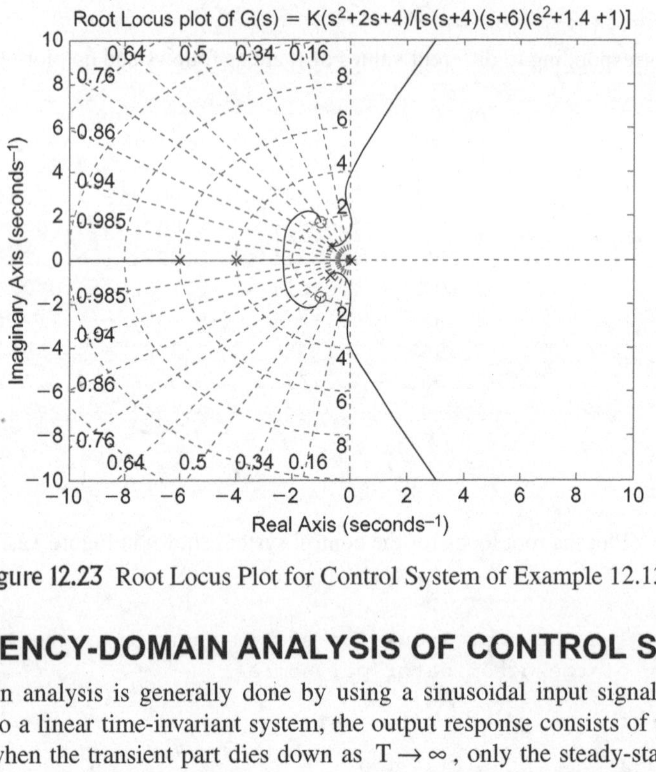

Figure 12.23 Root Locus Plot for Control System of Example 12.13

12.8 FREQUENCY-DOMAIN ANALYSIS OF CONTROL SYSTEMS

The frequency domain analysis is generally done by using a sinusoidal input signal. When a sinusoidal input signal is given to a linear time-invariant system, the output response consists of transient and steady-state parts, whereas when the transient part dies down as $T \to \infty$, only the steady-state part remains. The frequency response is the steady-state response of a system to a sinusoidal input signal. The advantage of frequency response analysis is that stability of a closed-loop system can be determined from the frequency response of an open-loop system, be it Bode plot, Nyquist plot or Log-magnitude versus phase plot.

Consider that a sinusoidal input signal is applied to an LTI system and is given by

`r(t)=Rsin ωt` (12.7)

The output response obtained will be of the same frequency 'ω' but may differ in amplitude and phase angle and is given by

`y(t)=Y sin(ωt ±Φ)` (12.8)

where `Y` and Φ are amplitude and phase angle of the output response, respectively.

12.9 FREQUENCY RESPONSE REPRESENTATION

The frequency response can be represented in any of the following forms:

- Bode or logarithmic plot
- Nyquist or polar plot
- Log-magnitude versus phase plot (Nichols plots)

To plot the frequency response, a vector of frequencies (varying between zero and infinity) is created and the values of system transfer function at those frequencies are computed. If $G(s)$ is the open-loop transfer function of a system and ω is the frequency vector, then a graph of $G(j\omega)$ versus ω is plotted. Since $G(j\omega)$ is a complex number, frequency response plots consist of both its magnitude and phase versus ω (i.e. Bode plot) or its position in the complex plane (i.e. Nyquist Plot). The log-magnitude versus phase angle plot (i.e. Nichols plot) is an extension of Bode plot.

12.10 BODE PLOTS

Bode diagrams (named after Hendrik W. Bode) are logarithmic plots. It has two graphs: one is a plot of logarithm of magnitude of a sinusoidal transfer function and the other is a plot of phase angle, both plotted against the frequency on a logarithmic scale. The basic advantage of logarithmic representation is that multiplication and division operations of the pole–zero representation of a transfer function can be replaced by addition and subtraction operations and greater range of frequencies can be considered.

Octave and Decade. The frequency in logarithmic terms can be represented as

$$u = \log_{10} \omega$$

or

$$\omega = 10^u$$

and $$u_2 - u_1 = \log_{10} \omega_2 - \log_{10} \omega_1 = \log_{10}\left(\frac{\omega_2}{\omega_1}\right)$$

There are two types of frequency intervals:

(i) the octave, for which $\omega_2 = 2\omega_1$ and

(ii) the decade, for which $\omega_2 = 10\omega_1$. Thus, the octave is a frequency band from ω_1 to $2\omega_1$, where ω_1 is any frequency value. A decade is a frequency band from ω_1 to $10\omega_1$.
The slope of straight lines in the Bode plot is expressed in terms of these two frequency intervals i.e. decade or octave. The relation between decade and octave can be obtained as

$$\begin{aligned} 20 \text{ dB/decade} &= 20\log_{10}\left(\frac{\omega_2}{\omega_1}\right) \\ &= 20\times 0.302\log_2\left(\frac{\omega_2}{\omega_1}\right) \\ &= 6\log_2\left(\frac{\omega_2}{\omega_1}\right) \\ &= 6 \text{ dB/octave} \end{aligned}$$

20 dB/decade = 6 dB/octave

12.11 PLOTTING BODE DIAGRAMS

The commands used to plot the Bode diagrams of LTI systems in MATLAB are

```
bode(n,d)
bode(sys)
```

where

`n` and `d` are polynomials representing numerator and denominator of the given transfer function, and `sys` is an LTI model of the system, created with either `tf`, `zpk` or `ss` functions as described earlier in this chapter.

The frequency range and number of points are automatically selected.
Another similar command is

```
bode (n, d, ω)
```

where ω specifies the user-defined frequency range in rad/sec.

When the output response values are to be stored separately in matrices, then the following command with **left-hand arguments** and frequency vector is used:

```
[mag, phase, ω]= bode (n , d, ω)
```

This command will not generate any plot. However, it returns the frequency response of the system in matrices containing magnitude, phase angle and frequency ω.

> **Programming Tip 12.4:** The phase angle in Bode plots is in degrees.

Similarly, the following commands can be used to obtain Bode diagrams:

```
[mag, phase, ω]= bode (n, d)
[mag, phase, ω]= bode (sys)
```

The magnitude `mag` can be converted into decibels with the following command:

```
magdB =20 * log10(mag)
```

12.11.1 Logarithmic Frequency Range

The following command is used to specify the logarithmic frequency range:

```
w =logspace (d1,d2)
```

The above command generates a vector of **50 points**, logarithmically equally spaced between decades 10^{d1} and 10^{d2}.

For example, to generate 50 points between the frequencies 0.1 and 100 rad/sec, the command used is

```
w= logspace(-1, 2)
```

where $d1 = -1$ and $d2 = 2$.

To generate `n` points logarithmically equally spaced between decades 10^{d1} and 10^{d2}, the following command is used:

```
logspace(d1,d2,n)
```

For example, to generate 100 points between 1 and 1,000 rad/sec, enter the following command:

```
w= logspace(0, 3,100)
```

where $d1 = 0$ and $d1 = 3$ and number of points $n = 100$.

Example 12.14 Using MATLAB, obtain the Bode plot of the systems whose open-loop transfer functions are given as following:

(a) $\dfrac{10}{s^2+7s}$

(b) $\dfrac{200(s+3)}{s(s+2)(s^2+4s+100)}$

(c) $\dfrac{10(s^2+s+0.5)}{s(s+1)(s+12)}$

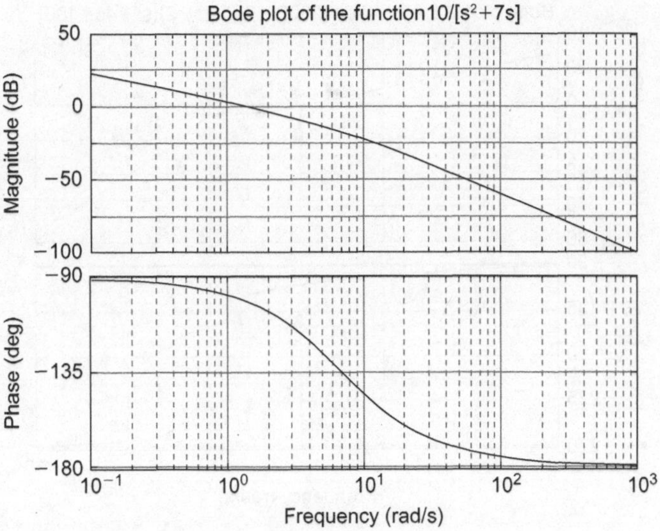

Figure 12.24 Bode Plots for Example 12.14 (a)

Solution:

(a) The following MATLAB commands can be used to plot the Bode diagrams:

```
%Program to plot bode plot of given transfer function
n=[10];
d=[1 7 0];
bode(n,d);
grid;
title(' Bode plot of the function10/[s^2+7s]');
```

The response obtained is as shown in Figure 12.24. It shows two graphs:

1. Magnitude in dB versus frequency in rad/sec on log scale
2. Phase angle in degrees versus frequency in rad/sec on log scale

(b) The MATLAB commands used are as follows:

```
%Program to plot bode plot of given transfer function
n=[200 600];
d=conv([1 2 0], [1 4 100]);
bode(n,d);
grid;
title(' Bode plot of the function [200(s+3)]/[s(s+2)(s^2+4s+100]');
```

The response obtained is as shown in Figure 12.25

(c) The MATLAB commands used are as follows:

```
%Program to plot bode plot of given transfer function
n=[10 10 5];
d=conv([1 1 0], [1 12]);
bode(n,d);
grid;
title(' Bode plot of the function [10(s^2+s+0.5)]/[s(s+1)(s+12)]');
```

The response obtained is as shown in Figure 12.26.

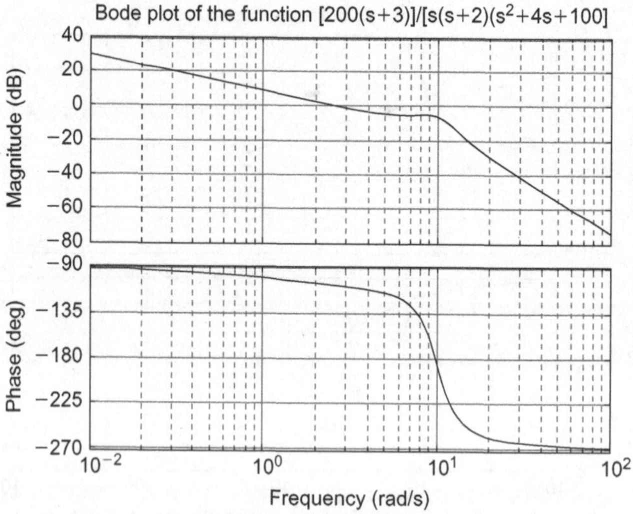

Figure 12.25 Bode Plots for Example 12.14 (b)

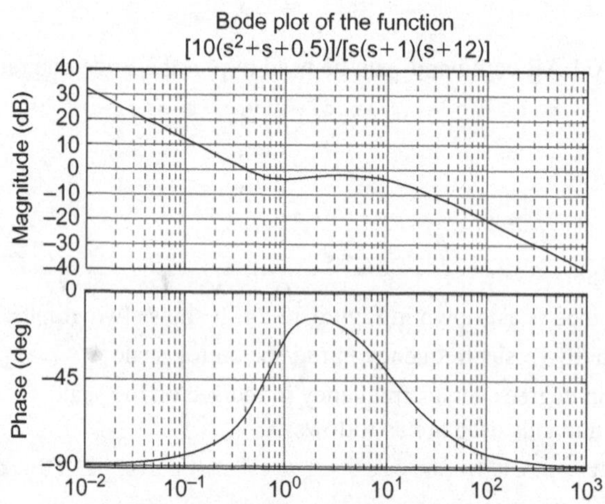

Figure 12.26 Bode Plots for Example 12.14 (c)

Example 12.15 Obtain the Bode diagrams for the following transfer functions in the specified frequency range:

$$\frac{200(s+1)}{s(s^2+10s+100)}, \quad \omega = 0.01 \text{ to } 1{,}000 \text{ rad/sec}$$

Solution:

The following program is used to obtain the desired response:

```
%Program to plot bode plot of given transfer function in given frequency range.
```

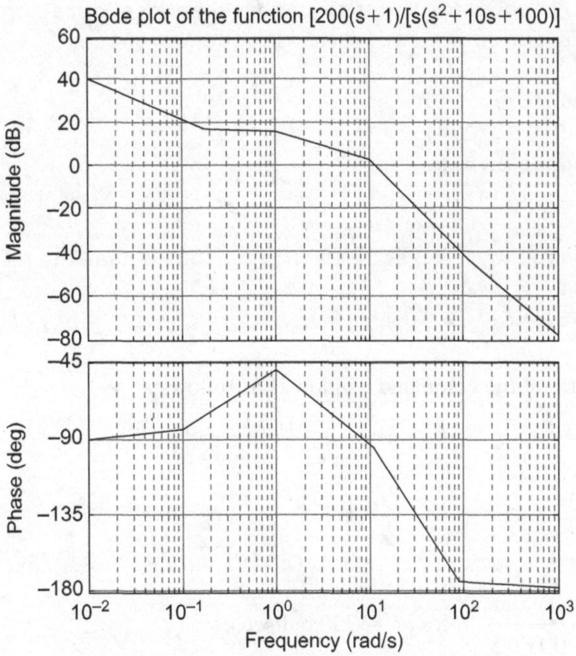

Figure 12.27 Bode Plots for Example 12.15

```
n=[200 200];
d=[1 10 100 0];
w=logspace(-2, 3,6);
bode(n,d,w);
grid;
title(' Bode plot of the function [200(s+1)/[s(s^2+10s+100)]');
```

The response obtained is as shown in Figure 12.27.

Example 12.16 Obtain the frequency response data for the following transfer functions for the specified frequency values:

(a) $\dfrac{50}{s^3+9s^2+30s+40)}$, for ω = 0.1, 1, 10, and 100 rad/sec.

(b) $\dfrac{10}{0.04s^2+0.1s+5}$ for ω = 250 rad/sec.

(c) $\dfrac{5s+12}{6s^2+10s}$ for 10 points in range ω = 0.01 to 100 rad/sec.

Solution:

(a) $G(s) = \dfrac{50}{s^3+9s^2+30s+40}$, for ω = 0.1, 1, 10, 100 rad/sec.

The required program is given as follows:

```
%Program to obtain the frequency response data of the given
%transfer function for given frequency values.
n=[50];
d=[1 9 30 40];
w=logspace(-1, 2,4);
[a,phi]=bode(n,d,w);
mag= 20*log10(a);
x=w';
disp('Frequency(rad/sec) Magnitude(dB) Phase(degrees)');
for i=1:4
        fprintf('%6.3f\t\t  %6.3f\t\t  %5.2f  \n',x(i),mag(i),phi(i));
end
```

The result obtained at the command window is as follows:

```
Frequency(rad/sec)          Magnitude(dB)          Phase(degrees)
  0.100                        1.933                     -4.30
  1.000                        1.422                    -43.09
 10.000                      -26.918                   -219.14
100.000                      -86.030                   -264.84
```

(b) $G(s) = \dfrac{10}{0.04s^2 + 0.1s + 5}$, for $\omega = 250$ rad/sec.

The required program is given as follows:

```
%Program to obtain the frequency response data of the given
%transfer function for given frequency value.
n=[10];
d=[0.04 0.1 5];
w=250;
[a,phi]=bode(n,d,w);
mag= 20*log10(a);
fprintf('The given frequency in rad/sec. is:\t%4.2f\n',w);
fprintf('The magnitude obtained is :\t %g\n',mag);
fprintf('The phase angle in deg is :\t %g\n',phi);
```

The result obtained at the command window is as follows:

```
The given frequency in rad/sec. is:  250.00
The magnitude obtained is : -47.9418
The phase angle in deg is : -179.426
```

(c) $G(s) = \dfrac{5s + 12}{6s^2 + 10s}$, for 10 points in range $\omega = 0.01$–100 rad/sec.

The required program is as follows:

```
%Program to obtain the frequency response data of the given
%transfer function for given frequency values.
n=[5 12];
d=[6 10 0];
w=logspace(-2, 2,10);
```

```
[a,phi]=bode(n,d,w);
mag= 20*log10(a);
x=w';
disp('Frequency(rad/sec)Magnitude(dB)Phase(degrees)');
for i=1:10
    fprintf('%6.3f\t\t  %6.3f\t\t  %5.2f  \n',x(i),mag(i),phi(i));
end
```

The result obtained at the command window is as follows:

Frequency(rad/sec)	Magnitude(dB)	Phase(degrees)
0.010	41.584	-90.11
0.028	32.694	-90.29
0.077	23.801	-90.81
0.215	14.880	-92.24
0.599	5.763	-95.76
1.668	-4.163	-100.22
4.642	-14.415	-97.59
12.915	-23.730	-93.17
35.938	-32.685	-91.17
100.000	-41.582	-90.42

12.12 INDICATING GAIN AND PHASE ANGLES ON THE BODE DIAGRAMS

The Bode diagrams obtained using MATLAB programs can also be used for marking gain and phase angle values corresponding to any frequency graphically. This can be done by clicking the mouse at the desired point on the diagrams. A box indicating values of gain (in dB) and frequency (in rad/sec) or phase (in degrees) and frequency (in rad/sec) appears in the figure window at the desired point.

Example 12.17 Obtain graphically the gain and phase at any desired frequency values on the Bode diagrams for transfer function $\dfrac{s+5}{s(s^2+3s+1)}$.

Solution:

The following program is used to obtain the desired response:

```
%Program to obtain the frequency response data of the given
%transfer function for given frequency values.
n=[1 5];
d=[1 2 3 1];
bode(n,d);
grid
title ('To illustrate obtaining values from plot of the ...
function (s+5)/[s(s^2+3s+1)]')
```

The response obtained is as shown in Figure 12.28.

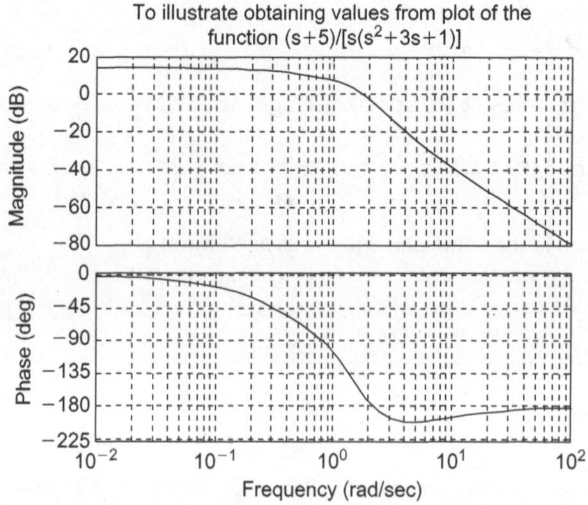

Figure 12.28 Bode Plot of Transfer Function of Example 12.17

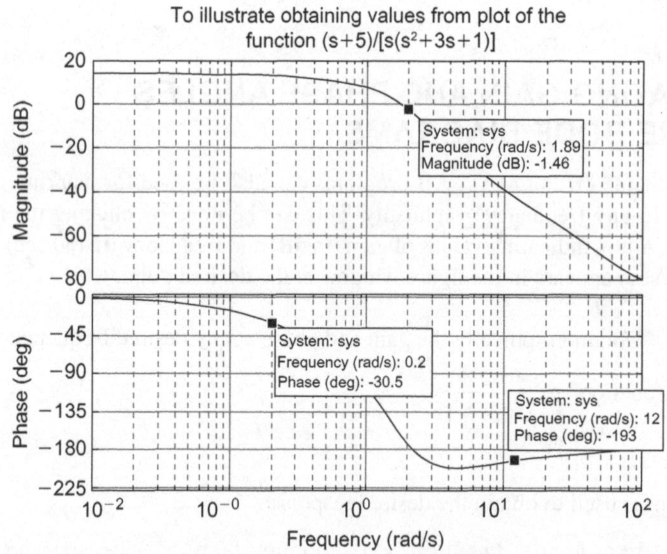

Figure 12.29 Obtaining Gain and Phase Angle Values Graphically for Example 12.17

Now, to obtain the gain and phase values at any desired frequency, click at any point on the plot. Boxes will appear on the figure, showing the values of 'gain and frequency' and 'phase and frequency' respectively as shown in Figure 12.29.

Programming Tip 12.5: The relevant information i.e. gain and phase angle at any frequency can be obtained by clicking at desired points on the Bode plots.

12.13 GAIN MARGIN AND PHASE MARGIN

In the Bode diagrams, there are two plots: one magnitude plot and other phase angle plot against the frequency in radian/sec on log scale. The inferences drawn from Bode diagrams are given as follows:

Gain Crossover Frequency: It is defined as frequency at which magnitude curve of the open-loop transfer function intersects with 0 dB line.

Phase Crossover Frequency: It is defined as frequency at which phase curve of open-loop transfer function intersects with $-180°$ line.

Gain Margin: Gain margin is defined as the difference in the magnitude between magnitude curve and 0 dB line at the phase crossover frequency (i.e. at which phase curve intersects the $-180°$ line).

In other words, Gain margin is the additional gain that can be added before a closed-loop system becomes unstable. Systems with greater gain margins can withstand greater changes in system parameters before becoming unstable in closed loop.

Phase Margin: The phase margin is defined as the difference in phase between the phase curve and $-180°$ at the gain crossover frequency (i.e. at which there is a gain of 0 dB). It can be given as

Phase margin, PM = 180° + phase angle at gain crossover frequency.

In other words, phase margin is defined as the change in open-loop phase shift required to make a closed-loop system unstable.

Thus, from the gain and phase margins of the open-loop transfer function, it can be concluded how much stable the closed-loop system is.

12.14 GAIN MARGIN AND PHASE MARGIN CALCULATIONS USING MATLAB

The gain and phase margins for a system can be obtained using any one of the following MATLAB commands:

`margin (n, d)`

or **`[Gm, Pm, pcf, gcf] = margin(n, d)`**

where

`Gm` and `Pm` are the gain and phase margins, respectively.

`pcf` is the phase crossover frequency.

`gcf` is the gain crossover frequency.

The first command returns the gain and phase margins only whereas the second command returns the gain and phase crossover frequencies in addition to gain and phase margin values.

Example 12.18 Obtain the gain and phase margins, phase crossover and gain crossover frequencies of the following transfer functions:

$$\frac{50}{s^3+9s^2+30s+40)}$$

Solution: The following program is used for obtaining the results:

```
%Program to obtain GM, PM, phase and gain crossover
%frequencies of given transfer function.
n=[50];
d=[1 9 30 40];
fprintf('The given transfer function is:');
printsys(n,d)
[GM,PM,PCF,GCF]= margin(n,d);
mag= 20*log10(GM);
margin(n,d);
```

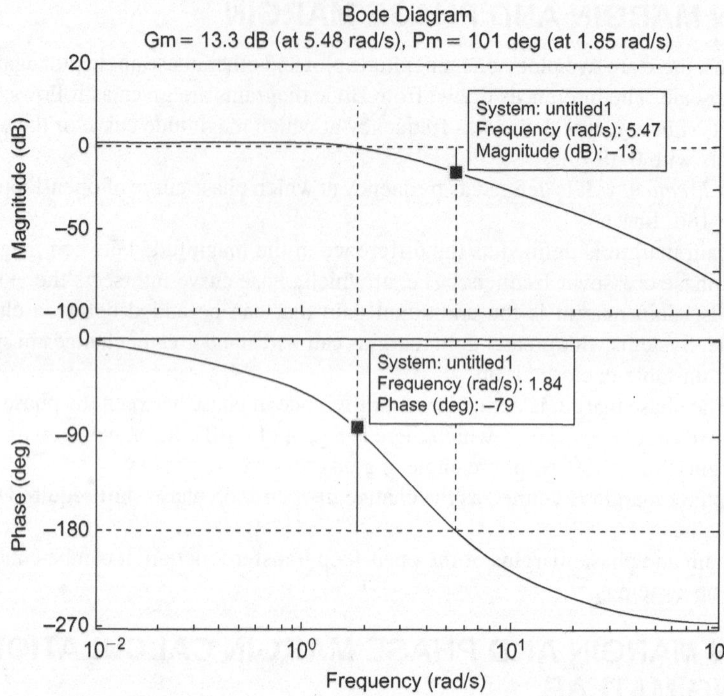

Figure 12.30 Gain Margin and Phase Margin for Example 12.18

```
fprintf('\nThe Gain Margin is:\t%4.2f dB\n',mag);
fprintf('The Phase Margin is :\t %g deg \n',PM);
fprintf('The Phase crossover Frequency is :\t %g rad/sec\n',PCF);
fprintf('The Gain crossover Frequency is :\t %grad/sec\n',GCF);
```

The results obtained in the command window are the following:

```
The given transfer function is:
num/den =
            50
     ----------------------
     s^3 + 9 s^2 + 30 s + 40
The Gain Margin is: 13.26 dB
The Phase Margin is : 100.667 deg
The Phase crossover Frequency is : 5.47817 rad/sec
The Gain crossover Frequency is :  1.84827rad/sec
```

The Bode plot obtained is as shown in Figure 12.30

12.15 FREQUENCY RESPONSE SPECIFICATIONS

Consider a closed-loop system as shown in Figure 12.31.

The transfer function of the system is given as

$$\frac{C(s)}{R(s)} = \frac{G(s)}{1+G(s)H(s)} = M(s)$$

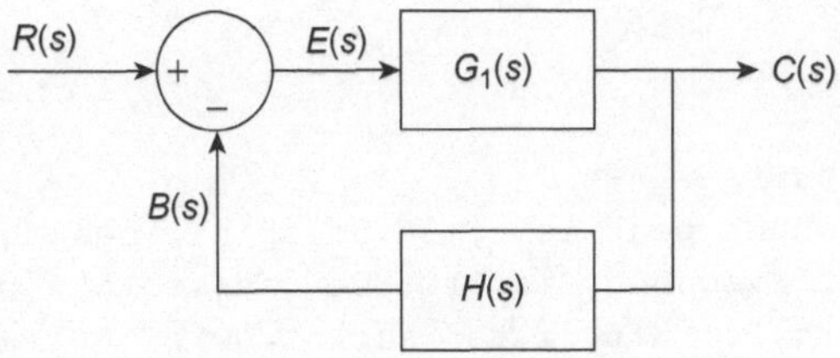

Figure 12.31 Closed-Loop System

or $$M(j\omega)=\frac{G(j\omega)}{1+G(j\omega)H(j\omega)}$$

The frequency response specifications for a system are given as

Resonant Peak (Mr): The maximum value of the magnitude of `M(jω)` is called resonant peak and it is denoted by `Mr`.

Resonant Frequency: The frequency at which peak resonance `Mr` occurs is called resonant frequency. It is denoted as `wr`.

Bandwidth: It is defined as the frequency at which the magnitude of a closed-loop drops to 3 dB below a certain specified level, generally 0 dB level.

Cut-off rate: The slope of log magnitude curve near the cut-off frequency is known as cut-off rate. It indicates about the ability of a system to distinguish the signal from noise.

12.16 CALCULATION OF FREQUENCY RESPONSE SPECIFICATIONS

As there is no built-in function for obtaining the resonant peak, resonant frequency and bandwidth in MATLAB, *so a function* `fresp` *is separately written as shown below and then the same is used to solve the problems.*

12.16.1 Function `fresp`

```
function fresp
%FUNCTION FRESP finds the resonant peak, resonant
%frequency and bandwidth of closed loop transfer function of a system.
%---Obtain values of num. and den.of transfer function---%
n= input('Enter values of coefficients of numerator within square brackets:\n');
d= input('Enter values of coefficients of denominator within square brackets:\ n');
%------- Show the transfer function-------%
fprintf('The transfer function is:');
printsys(n,d)
%---Calculate the bode plot data for the given function---%
w=logspace(-3,4);
[m,ph,w]= bode(n,d,w);
[peak,i]= max(m);                    %Find resonant peak.
peakdb = 20*log10(peak);             %Get the resonant peak in dB.
resfreq =w(i);                       %Get the resonant frequency.
%-----Calculate the bandwidth-----%
x=1;
while 20*log10(m(x))>=-3
```

```
x=x+1;
end;
bw= w(x);
%-----Display the results-----%
fprintf('\n\nThe resonant peak is:\t %6.3f dB\n', peakdb);
fprintf('The resonant frequency is:\t%6.3f rad/sec\n', resfreq);
fprintf('The bandwidth is:\t%6.3f rad/sec\n',bw);
```

Example 12.19 Obtain the value of resonant peak, resonant frequency and bandwidth for the following closed-loop transfer functions:

(a) $\dfrac{7}{s^2+4s+10}$

(b) $\dfrac{10(s+1)}{s(s+3)(s+14)}$

Solution: The aforementioned function **fresp** is used to obtain the desired results.

(a) $G(s)=\dfrac{7}{s^2+4s+10}$

Enter the function name `fresp` in the command window

```
fresp
```

On pressing Enter key, following message will be displayed:

```
Enter values of coefficients of numerator within square brackets:
[7]
Enter values of coefficients of denominator within square brackets:
[1 4 10]
The transfer function is:
num/den =

              7
     --------------
     s^2 + 4 s + 10
```

The following results are obtained in the command window:

```
The resonant peak is: -2.921 dB
The resonant frequency is: 1.389 rad/sec
The bandwidth is: 0.001 rad/sec
```

(b) $G(s) = G(s)=\dfrac{10(s+1)}{s(s+3)(s+14)}$

Enter the function name `fresp` in the command window

```
fresp
```

On pressing Enter key, following message will be displayed:

```
Enter values of coefficients of numerator within square brackets:
[10 10]
Enter values of coefficients of denominator in square brackets:
[conv([1 3 0], [1 14])]
The transfer function is:
num/den =
              10 s + 10
```

```
    --------------------
    s^3 + 17 s^2 + 42 s
```

The following results obtained in the command window:

```
The resonant peak is: 47.535 dB
The resonant frequency is: 0.001 rad/sec
The bandwidth is: 0.373 rad/sec
```

12.17 BODE DIAGRAMS FOR STATE-SPACE REPRESENTATION

If the system is defined in state space, the following commands can be used to obtain the Bode diagrams:

```
bode (A, B, C, D)
bode (A,B,C,D, iu , w)
```

where

w is user-supplied frequency vector.

iu is an index specifying which input is to be used for the response.

Example 12.20 Obtain the Bode diagram for the following system given in state-space form:

$$\begin{bmatrix} \dot{x}_1 \\ \dot{x}_2 \end{bmatrix} = \begin{bmatrix} 0 & 1 \\ -20 & -2 \end{bmatrix} \begin{bmatrix} x_1 \\ x_2 \end{bmatrix} + \begin{bmatrix} 0 \\ 20 \end{bmatrix} u$$

$$y = \begin{bmatrix} 1 & 0 \end{bmatrix} \begin{bmatrix} x_1 \\ x_2 \end{bmatrix}$$

Solution: The following program gives the desired response:

```
%Program to obtain the Bode plot of the given transfer
%function in state space form.
A=[0 1; -20 -2];
B=[0;20];
C=[1 0];
D=[0];
bode(A,B,C,D);
grid;
title('Bode plot for T.F. in state space form');
```

The Bode diagrams obtained are as shown in Figure 12.32.

Example 12.21 Repeat the above example with the user-defined frequency range, w = 0.1 to 1000.

Solution: The following commands can be used:

```
%Program to obtain Bode plot within the specified frequency
%limits for given transfer function in state space form.
A =[0 1 ;-20 -2];
B =[0 ; 20];
C =[1 0];
D =[0];
w = logspace (-1,3);
bode(A,B,C,D,1,w);
grid;
title('Bode plot for T.F. in state space form');
```

The Bode diagrams obtained are as shown in Figure 12.33.

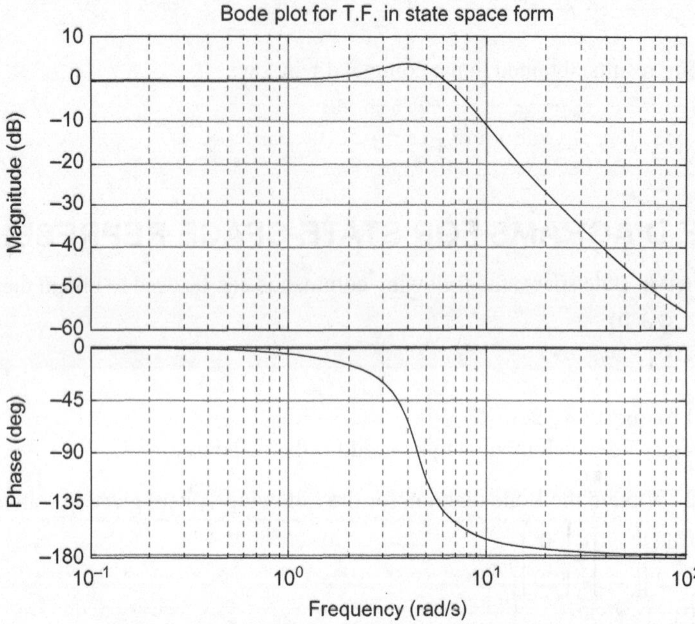

Figure 12.32 Bode Diagram for Example 12.20

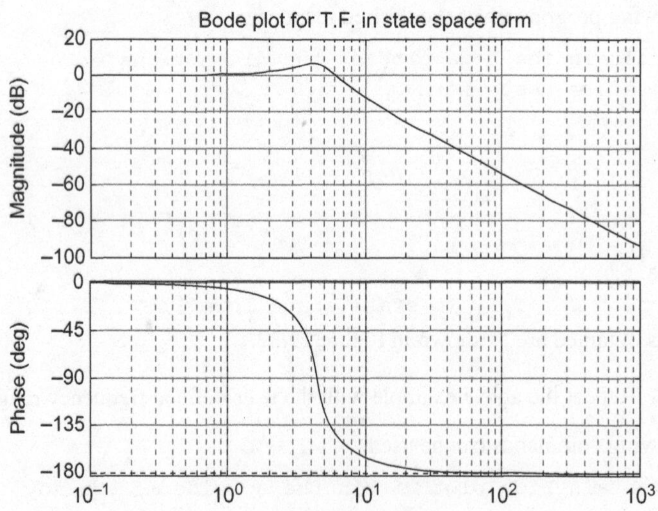

Figure 12.33 Bode Diagrams for Example 12.21

12.18 POLAR PLOTS

The polar plot of a sinusoidal transfer function `G(jω)` is a plot of the magnitude of `G(jω)` versus the phase angle of `G(jω)` on polar co-coordinates as ω is varied from zero to ∞. Thus, the polar plot is the locus of vectors $|G(j\omega)|\angle G(j\omega)$ as ω is varied from 0 to ∞. If the angle is measured from positive x-axis, it is positive in anti-clockwise direction, otherwise it is negative. The polar plot is very useful in determining the stability of a closed-loop system from its open loop frequency response.

> **Programming Tip 12.6:** The polar plot is for the frequency range 0<w<∞ while the Nyquist plot is in the frequency range −∞<w<∞. In general, the polar plot is often called the Nyquist plot.

MATLAB can be used to obtain a polar plot of $G(j\omega)$ or to obtain $|G(j\omega)|$ and $\angle G(j\omega)$ accurately for various value of ω in the frequency range of interest.

12.19 NYQUIST PLOTS

As mentioned earlier, the Nyquist plot is a plot of magnitude $|G(j\omega)|$ versus angle $\angle G(j\omega)$ for the frequency range $-\infty < \omega < \infty$. Nyquist plot and Nyquist stability criterion is useful for determining the stability of the closed-loop system from the open-loop frequency response without determining the closed-loop poles. The stability of a closed-loop system is determined by finding out the number of encirclements of $(-1 + j0)$ point by the Nyquist contour of the open-loop frequency response.

In MATLAB, the commands used to obtain Nyquist plot for a continuous LTI system are:

```
nyquist (n,d)
nyquist (n,d,w)
```

where w is the user-specified frequency vector.

To obtain the real and imaginary values of transfer function at different values of w, the following MATLAB commands are used:

```
[re, im, w] = nyquist (n, d)
[re, im, w] = nyquist (n, d, w)
```

Using these commands, matrices specifying real and imaginary values are obtained but no plot is drawn. To get the plot, the **plot** command has to be used.

Example 12.22 Draw a Nyquist plot using MATLAB for the following open-loop transfer functions:

(a) $\dfrac{1}{s^2+s+1}$

(b) $\dfrac{s+2}{s^2-1}$

Solution:

(a) $\dfrac{1}{s^2+s+1}$

The following program gives the desired Nyquist plot and response is shown in Figure 12.34:

```
%Program to obtain a nyquist plot of the transfer function
n=[0 0 1];
d=[1 1 1];
grid;
nyquist (n,d);
v=[-2 2 -2 2];
axis(v);
title('Nyquist Plot for G(s)=1/[s^2+s+1]');
```

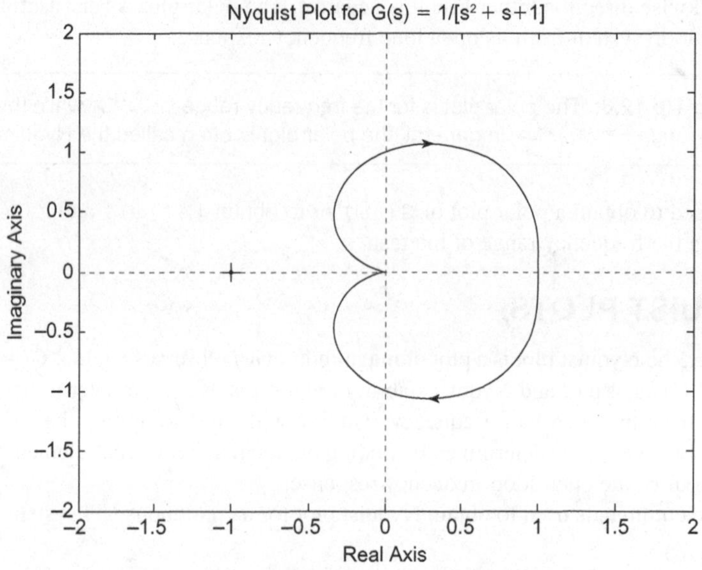

Figure 12.34 Nyquist Plot for Example 12.22 (a)

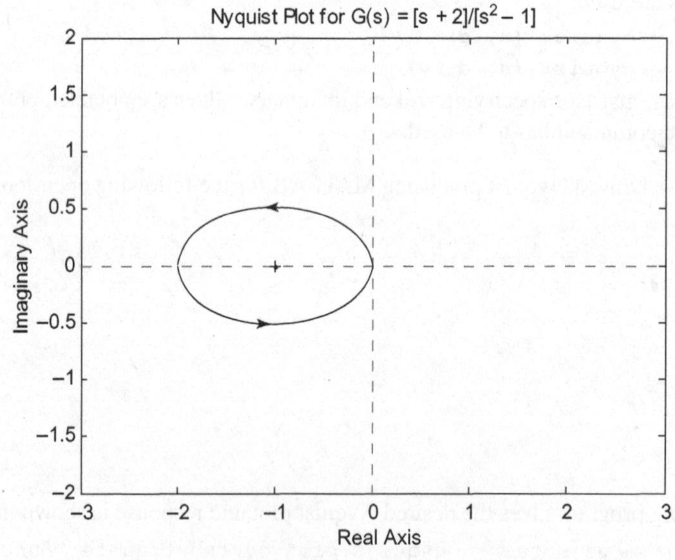

Figure 12.35 Nyquist Plot for Example 12.22 (b)

(b) $\dfrac{s+2}{s^2-1}$

The following program gives the desired Nyquist plot, and the response is shown in Figure 12.35

```
%Program to obtain a nyquist plot of the transfer function
n=[1 2];
```

```
d=[1 0 -1];
grid
nyquist (n,d)
v=[-3 3 -2 2];
axis(v)
title('Nyquist Plot for G(s)=[s+2]/[s^2-1]')
```

12.20 NYQUIST PLOTS FOR STATE-SPACE SYSTEM

If the system is defined in state space, the following commands can be used to obtain the Nyquist plot:

```
nyquist (A,B,C,D)
nyquist (A,B,C,D,iu)
nyquist (A,B,C,D, iu, w)
```

where

`A,B,C,D` are system matrices,

`iu` is an index which specifies which input to use for the frequency response, and

`w` is the user-supplied frequency vector.

This command produces a series of Nyquist plots, one for each input and output combination of the system. The frequency range is automatically determined until and unless it is defined by `w`.

Example 12.23 Consider the system given by

$$\begin{bmatrix} \dot{x}_1 \\ \dot{x}_2 \end{bmatrix} = \begin{bmatrix} 0 & 1 \\ -20 & -4 \end{bmatrix} \begin{bmatrix} x_1 \\ x_2 \end{bmatrix} + \begin{bmatrix} 0 \\ 10 \end{bmatrix} u$$

$$y = \begin{bmatrix} 1 & 0 \end{bmatrix} \begin{bmatrix} x_1 \\ x_2 \end{bmatrix} + [0]u$$

Draw a Nyquist plot. This system has a single input u and a single output y.

Solution: The following program will provide the Nyquist plot shown in Figure 12.36 for the given state-space values of the system:

```
%Program to obtain Nyquist plot of T.F. in state space.
A=[0 1; -20 -4];
B=[0 ; 10];
C=[1 0];
D=[0];
grid;
nyquist (A,B,C,D);
title ('Nyquist Plot for T.F. in State Space Form');
```

12.21 NICHOLS CHART

The constant magnitude loci (M circles) and constant phase angle loci (N circles), when transferred to log-magnitude versus phase plot, are called **Nichols chart**. Thus, Nichols chart is a graph consisting of curves that are maps of M and N circles on a new coordinate system, that is, M and N loci in dB magnitude versus phase plane. The Nichols coordinate system has open-loop gain in decibles on y-axis and phase angle in degrees on x-axis with origin at $|G| = 0$ dB and $\angle G = -180°$.

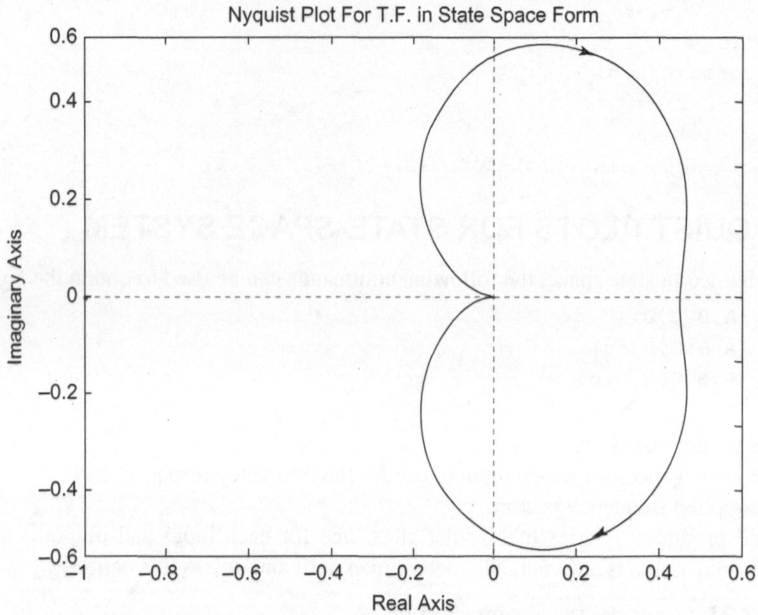

Figure 12.36 Nyquist Plot for Example 12.23

The critical point $(-1 + j0)$ of the polar coordinate plot is mapped to Nichols chart as the point (0 dB, −180°) and becomes the origin of Nichols chart.

In MATLAB, the Nichols chart is obtained by using the following commands:

```
nichols(n, d)
nichols(n, d, w)
```

where w is frequency vector, giving minimum and maximum limits of the frequencies.

The following commands give the response magnitudes and phases in degrees along with the frequency vector w, if specified, however no plot is drawn:

```
[mag, phase]= nichols (n,d,w)
[mag, phase, w]= nichols (n,d)
```

Example 12.24 Obtain the Nichols chart for the following transfer function using MATLAB:

$$G(s) = \frac{10(s+1)}{s^3 + 7s^2 + 10s + 6}$$

Solution: The following MATLAB program can be used:

```
%Program to obtain Nichols frequency response
n=[10 10];
d=[1 7 10 6];
nichols(n,d);
grid;
title('Nichols frequency Response of T.F. 10(s+1)/(s^3+7s^2+10s+6)')
```

The response obtained is shown in Figure 12.37.

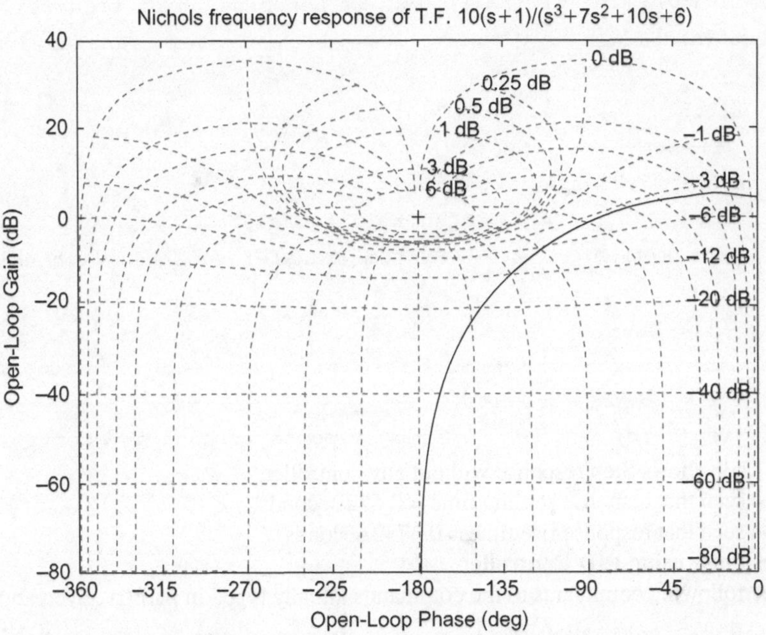

Figure 12.37 Nichols Chart for Example 12.24

12.22 PID CONTROLLER

The transfer function of a PID controller is given by:

$$Gc(s) = K_p + K_d\, s + \frac{K_i}{s}$$

By proper choice of controller parameters i.e. K_p, K_d and K_I ,desired system response can be obtained.

Example 12.25 If armature inductance is neglected, the transfer function of an armature controlled DC servo motor is given by:

$$\frac{\theta(s)}{E(s)} = \frac{(K_t/RJ)}{s^2 + (B/J + K_b K_t/RJ)s}$$

J = 4.0 × 10^{-4} kg m^2/sec^2 B = 5 × 10^{-3} Nm/sec Kt = 0.09 Nm/amp Kb = 0.1 V/rad/sec R = 2.0 ohms

(i) Obtain Step response without any controller

(ii) Obtain Step response using PID controller with the following controller parameters:
$K_p = 8$ $K_d = 0.5$ $K_i = 0.015$

Solution:

(i) **Step response without any controller**

Enter the following commands in the command window:

```
j=4.0*10^-4; b=5*10^-3; kt=0.09; kb=0.1; r=2.0 ;
n=[(kt)/(r*j)];                    % Numerator of transfer function
```

```
    d=[1 (b/j+(kb*kt)/(r*j)) 0];    % Denominator of transfer function
   cl=tf(n,d)                          %  System transfer function
cl =
     112.5
     -------------
     s^2 + 23.75 s
     h=1;                   % unity feedback
clfb=feedback(cl,h)         % System transfer function with unity feedback
clfb =
      112.5
     ----------------------
     s^2 + 23.75 s + 112.5
     step(clfb)             % step response without any controller
```

Figure 12.38 shows Step response without any controller

It can be seen that response settling time = 0.672 seconds

It can be seen that response rise time = 0.3742 seconds

(ii) **Step response using PID Controller**

Add the following commands to the commands already typed in part (i) ,given above.

```
kp=8 ;kd=0.5 ; ki= 0.015 ;
     n1=[ kd  kp  ki] ;
d1=[1 0];
```

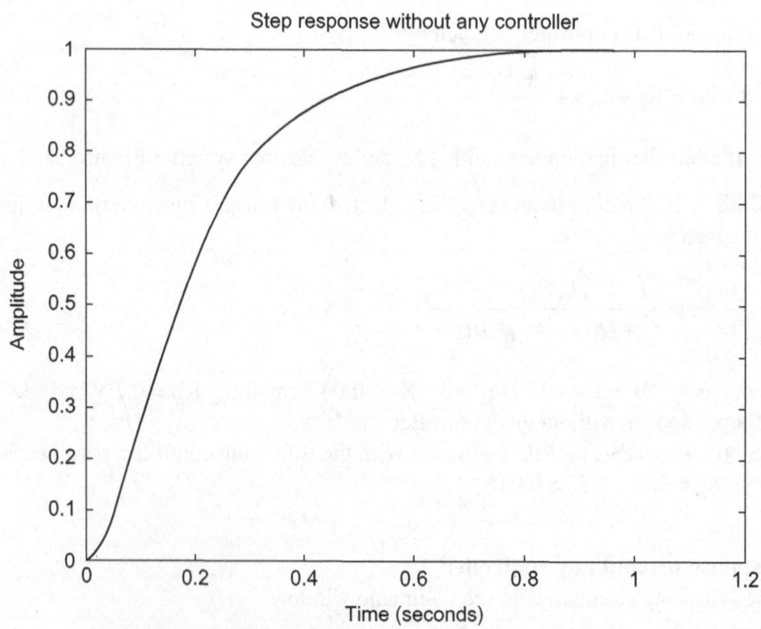

Figure 12.38 Step Response Without any Controller

```
      n2=conv(n1,n)
n2 =
    56.2500   900.0000    1.6875       % Numerator of transfer function
      d2=conv(d1,d)                    % Denominator of transfer function
d2 =
        1.0000   23.7500        0         0
      cl1=tf(n2,d2)
cl1 =
   56.25 s^2 + 900 s + 1.687
   -------------------------
          s^3 + 23.75 s^2
      cl2=feedback(cl1,1)         % Closed loop transfer function using PID
                                    controller
cl2 =
    56.25 s^2 + 900 s + 1.687
   ----------------------------
   s^3 + 80 s^2 + 900 s + 1.687
      step(cl2)                   % Step response using PID Controller
```

Figure 12.39 shows Step response using PID Controller
It can be seen that response settling time = 0.167 seconds, which has reduced with the use of PID controller and rise time = 0.0584 seconds, which has also reduced with the use of PID controller

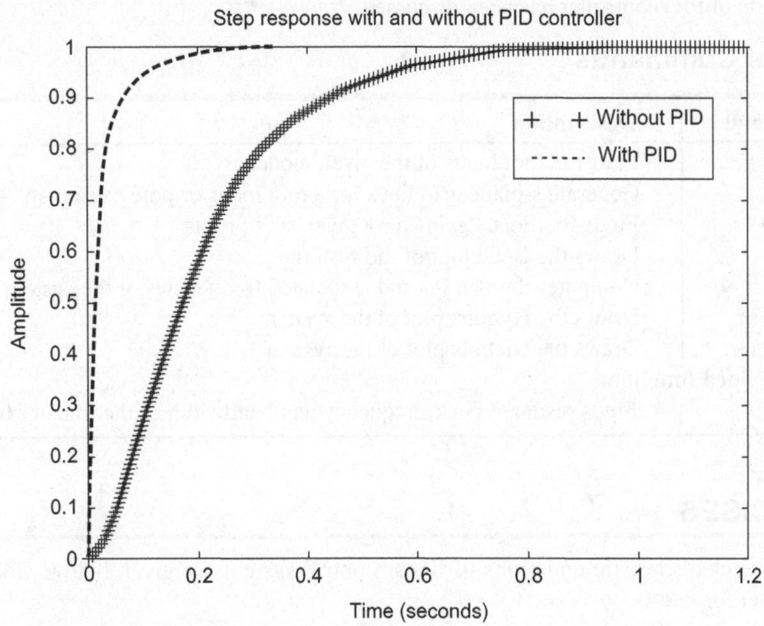

Figure 12.39 Step Response Using PID Controller

SUMMARY

The chapter can be summarized in following points:

- The basic concepts of root locus technique, i.e. magnitude and angle condition are explained.
- The use of MATLAB function `rlocus` to draw root locus is illustrated.
- The plotting of root locus using `plot` command is also described.
- Drawing of polar gridlines in root locus diagram using `sgrid` command is discussed.
- `rlocfind` function, which is used to find gain `K` at a given point on the root locus, is illustrated with suitable examples.
- The plotting of root locus for systems given in state-space representation is also described.
- The basic concepts of frequency domain analysis of control system are discussed.
- The use of `bode` and `logspace` functions to draw bode diagram is illustrated.
- Calculation of gain margin, phase margin, gain crossover and phase crossover frequency, etc. using `margin` function is discussed.
- A user-defined function `fresp` is developed and illustrated to obtain frequency response specifications such as resonant peak, resonant frequency and bandwidth.
- Use of `bode` function to obtain Bode diagram of state-space representation is illustrated.
- Nyquist plots are obtained using `nyquist` function.
- In the last, Nichols chart is discussed using `nichols` function.
- In this chapter, use of MATLAB commands to obtain time and frequency response of dynamic systems has been given. Different commands to plot Root Locus diagram, Bode diagram, Nyquist plots, Nichols chart have been explained and illustrated.
- Simulation of PID controller has been discussed.

List of Commands

Command	Description
`rlocus`	Plots the root locus of the given model
`sgrid`	Generate s-plane grid lines for a root locus or pole–zero map
`rlocfind`	Finds root locus gains for a given set of roots
`bode`	Draws the Bode plot of the system
`margin`	Computes the `Gm`, `Pm` and associated frequencies of the system
`nyquist`	Draws the Nyquist plot of the system
`nichols`	Draws the Nichols plot of the system
User-defined functions	
`fresp`	Finds resonant peak, frequency and bandwidth of the transfer function

EXERCISES

12.1 The characteristic equations of linear control system are given below. Construct the root loci for $k \geq 0$

(a) $s^3 + 3s^2 + (k+2)s + 5k = 0$

(b) $s^4 + 6s^3 + 9s^2 + k(s^2 + 4s + 5) = 0$

12.2 The forward path transfer functions of a unity feedback control system are given below. Construct the root loci for $k \geq 0$.

(a) $G(s) = \dfrac{k(s+4)}{s(s^2+4s+4)(s+5)(s+6)}$

(b) $G(s) = \dfrac{k(s+5)}{s^2(s+3)}$

(c) $G(s) = \dfrac{k(s+2)}{s(s+1)(s+3+j10)(s+3-j10)}$

12.3 Draw the root loci for the unity feedback open-loop systems whose transfer functions are given below:

(a) $G(s) = \dfrac{k(s+1)(s+5)}{s^2(s+2)}$

(b) $G(s) = \dfrac{k(s+2)}{s(s+1)(s+5)(s+8)}$

(c) $G(s) = \dfrac{k}{s(s^2+10s+25)}$

12.4 Draw the root loci for the system shown below:

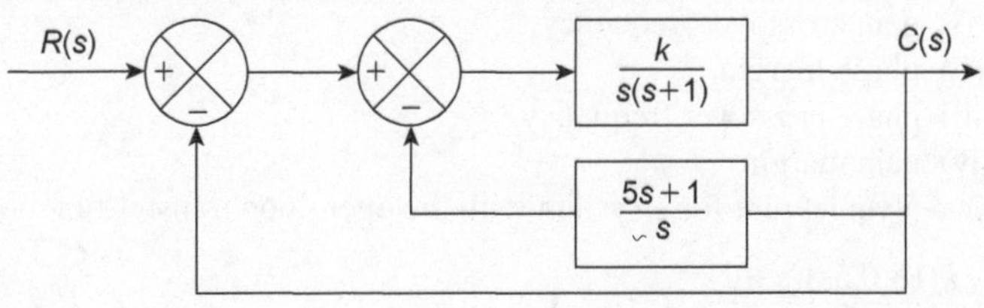

12.5 Find the value of gain at the point on damping ratio line $\xi = 0.4$ for the systems described by following transfer functions $G(s)H(s)$:

(a) $\dfrac{K}{(s+1)(s^2+2s+5)}$

(b) $\dfrac{K(s^2+2s+4)}{s^2(s+2)}$

12.6 Determine the gain, magnitude in dB and phase angle of each of the following transfer functions at the specified frequencies:

(a) $\dfrac{10}{s+2}$ at $\omega = 1$ and 10 rad/sec

(b) $\dfrac{2s+1}{s(s+1)(s+2)}$ at $\omega = 0.1$ and 100 rad/sec

12.7 Calculate and plot the frequency response of the following system over a frequency range of 1.0–1000 rad/sec.

$$\frac{s+2}{s(s+5)}$$

12.8 Draw the frequency response of the following:

(a) $\dfrac{(s^2+2s+10)}{s(s+1)}$

(b) $\dfrac{s(0.1s+1)}{(s+2)(s^2+0.8s+4)}$

12.9 Plot the Bode diagram, and compute the phase and gain margin for the following transfer functions:

(a) $G(s)=\dfrac{0.4(s+2)}{s(1+0.25s)(1+s+0.50s^2)}$

(b) $G(s)=\dfrac{100(s+2)}{s(s^2+10s+100)}$

(c) $G(s)=\dfrac{50}{s(s+2)(1+0.2s^2)}$

12.10 (a) Draw the Bode plot for the following open-loop transfer function:

$$\frac{100(0.02s+1)}{(s+1)(0.1s+1)(0.01s+1)^2}$$

(b) Mark the following on the Bode diagram:

(i) gain crossover frequency
(ii) phase margin
(iii) phase crossover frequency
(iv) gain margin

12.11 Sketch a Nyquist plot for a system with the open-loop transfer function (for $k = 10$):

$$\frac{k(1+0.5s)(s+2)}{(1+5s)(s-2)}$$

12.12 For the unity feedback system having open-loop transfer function:

$$\frac{1000(s+4)(s+32)}{s^3(s+50)(s-10)}$$

Draw the Nyquist plot.

CHAPTER 13

MATLAB Applications in Neural Networks

LEARNING OBJECTIVES

- Salient features of artificial neural networks (ANNs).
- Artificial neuron model, its transfer functions and different architectures.
- MATLAB functions related to creation of multilayer perceptron (`MLP`) (`fitnet`), training (`train`), scaling input–output data (`mapminmax`), checking performance (`perform`)
- Implementation of an example problem using multilayer perceptron (MLP) in graphical user interface (GUI) Tool (`nftool`) available in Neural Networks Toolbox.™
- Solution of the same example using command line functions.
- Basic MATLAB functions related to creation of radial basis function networks (RBF Nets) (`newrb`, `newrbe`) and self-organizing feature maps (SOFMs) (`newsom`, `gridtop`, `hextop`, `randtop`).

13.1 INTRODUCTION

Artificial neural network (ANN) is a computational model inspired by the natural neural system present in a human brain. There are billions of neurons present in one human brain (typically about 10^{11}) and each neuron is connected to about 10,000 other neurons. A natural neuron receives signals through biological element called synapses located on its dendrites or membrane that acts as receiver of signals coming from other neurons. When the signals received are strong enough and surpass a certain threshold, the neuron is activated and transmits the signal though a channel called axon. This signal might be sent to another synapse, and might activate other neurons.

ANNs inspired by biological nervous systems are very smaller in size. Its neurons are composed of simple elements operating in parallel. The complexity of real neurons is highly abstracted when modelling artificial neurons. These basically consist of neurons that receive inputs like synapses, which are multiplied by strength of the interconnection weights, and then computed by a mathematical function which determines the activation of the neuron. ANNs combine artificial neurons in order to process information.

As in nature, the interconnections between elements, i.e., the neurons, largely determine the network function. The neural network can be trained to perform a particular function by adjusting the values of the interconnection weights between its elements. Typically, the weights of the neural networks are adjusted or trained, so that a particular input leads to a specific target output. The network is adjusted, based on the difference of the output from the desired target, until the two matches to an acceptable level known as error tolerance. Typically, many such input/target pairs are required to train a network. ANNs have been trained to perform complex functions in various fields, including pattern recognition, identification, classification, speech recognition, vision, and control systems. The Neural Network Toolbox of MATLAB emphasizes the use of neural network paradigms that can be used to solve various problems and build solutions in engineering, management, financial, and other practical applications.

13.2 SALIENT FEATURES OF ARTIFICIAL NEURAL NETWORKS

The following characteristics and properties of neural networks are significant:

- *Non-linearity*: Neural networks have great promise in diverse fields because of their theoretical ability to approximate arbitrary non-linear mappings. Moreover, in a neural network, the non-linearity is distributed throughout the network.
- *Provide Model Free Environment*: ANN controllers do not require derivation of the mathematical model of the process. Thus, the cumbersome mathematics and the added assumptions which introduce approximations in the model are not needed. Further, the ANN model or controller does not require a priori knowledge of the plant dynamics.
- *Parallel Distributed Processing*: Neural networks have a highly parallel structure, which lends itself immediately to parallel implementation. The basic processing unit in a neural network has a very simple structure. This, along with parallel implementation results in very fast overall processing.
- *Input–Output Mapping*: A popular paradigm of learning called supervised learning involves modification of the synaptic weights of a neural network by applying a set of input–output training samples. The network learns from the examples by constructing an input–output mapping for the problem at hand.
- *Learning with Experience*: Neural networks have a built-in capability to learn and adapt their synaptic weights to changes in the surrounding environment. In particular, a neural network trained to operate in a specific environment can easily adapt to minor changes in the operating environmental conditions.
- *Fault Tolerance*: A neural network, implemented in hardware, has the potential to be inherently fault tolerant, or capable of robust computation, in the sense that its performance degrades gracefully under adverse operating conditions. For example, if a neuron or its connecting links are damaged, recall of a stored pattern is impaired in quality.
- *Data Fusion*: Neural networks can operate simultaneously on both quantitative and qualitative data. The neural network can deal with information that is fuzzy, probabilistic, noisy and inconsistent.
- *Hardware Implementation*: Not only can the networks be implemented in parallel, but also dedicated VLSI implementations are being introduced recently. This brings additional speed and increases the scale of neural networks, which can be implemented.
- *Multivariable Systems*: Neural networks naturally process many inputs and have many outputs. Thus, these are readily applicable to multivariable systems.

13.3 ARTIFICIAL NEURON MODEL

A neuron is an information-processing unit that is fundamental to the operation of a neural network. The block diagram of Figure 13.1 shows the model of a neuron, which form the basis for designing (artificial) neural networks. Three basic elements of neuron model are as follows:

- *Interconnection Weights*: A set of synapses or connecting links, each of which is characterized by a weight or strength of its own. Specifically, a signal x_j at the input of synapse j connected to neuron k is multiplied by synaptic weight w_{kj}. Unlike a synapse in the brain, the synaptic weight of an artificial neuron may lie in a range that includes negative as well as positive values.

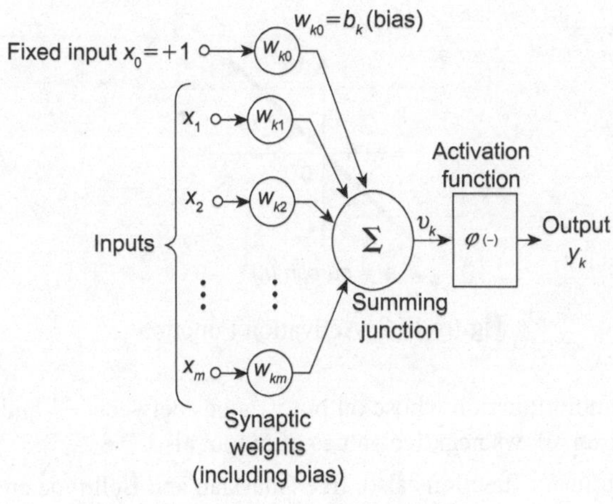

Figure 13.1 Non-linear Model of a Neuron

- *Summing Function*: An adder for summing the input signals, weighted by the respective synapses of the neuron; the operations described here constitutes a linear combiner.
- *Transfer or Activation Function*: An activation or transfer function is the actual processing that is performed in a neuron on the net summed input to the neuron. There are many types of transfer functions depending on the type of network and the application for which the neural net is used.

The neuronal model of Figure 13.1 also includes an externally applied bias, denoted by b_k. The bias b_k has the effect of increasing or decreasing the net input of the activation function, depending on whether it is positive or negative, respectively.

In mathematical terms, we may describe a neuron k by writing the following pair of equations:

$$u_k = \sum_{j=1}^{m} w_{kj} x_j \quad \text{and} \quad y_k = \varphi(u_k + b_k) \tag{13.1}$$

where $x_1, x_2, \ldots, x_m$ are the input signals; $w_{k1}, w_{k2}, \ldots, w_{km}$ are the synaptic weights of neuron k; u_k is the linear combiner output due to the input signals; b_k is the bias; $\varphi(\cdot)$ is the activation function; and y_k is the output signal of the neuron. The use of bias b_k has the effect of applying an affine transformation to the output u_k of the linear combiner in the model as given by the following equation:

$$v_k = u_k + b_k \tag{13.2}$$

13.4 TRANSFER FUNCTIONS

The transfer function of a neuron in a neural network is the only processing function. It is utilized for limiting the amplitude of the output of a neuron. Also known as activation function is referred to as a squashing function as it squashes (limits) the permissible amplitude range of the output signal to some finite values. There are many types of activation functions available in MATLAB Neural Network Toolbox. Some of these functions are as follows:

Purelin: It is purely a linear function ($y = mx + c$). It does not limit the amplitude of the output and the output varies linearly with the amplitude of the input.

Logsig: It is called sigmoid function that resembles a squashed 'S' whose output y ranges between 0 and 1 as input x varies from $-\infty$ to $+\infty$. This function is utilized for networks where output is always positive.

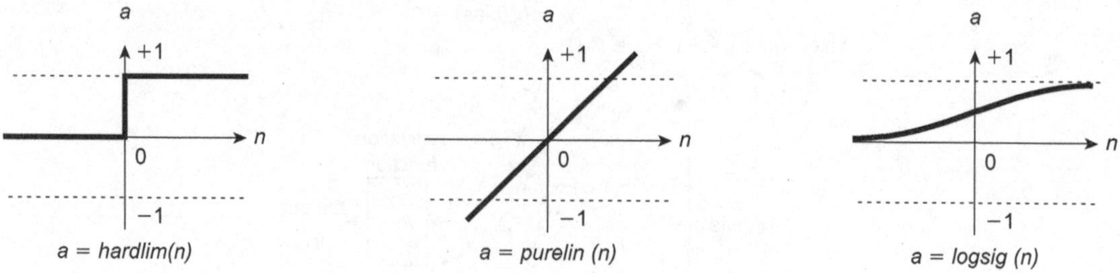

Figure 13.2 Activation Functions

Tansig: It is a tanh sigmoid function whose output *y* ranges between −1 and +1 as input *x* varies from −∞ to +∞. This function allows negative values of output also.

There are other types of transfer functions also, like Gaussian and Bell type and so on. Some of these are illustrated in Figure 13.2.

13.5 ANN ARCHITECTURES

Neural networks can be classified into two main categories based on their connection structures: Feed-forward (Non-recurrent) and Feedback (Recurrent). Feed-forward networks, based on their architectures, are further classified into different categories, that is Multilayer Perceptrons (MLPs), Counter-propagation Networks, Cerebellar Model Articulation Controller and Radial Basis Function Networks (RBF Nets). The discussion in this chapter is restricted to the application of MLPs. A brief introduction of RBF Nets and Self-Organizing Feature Maps (SOFMs) is also given.

13.5.1 Multilayer Perceptron

In ANNs, neurons are arranged into groups called layers. The name Multilayer Perceptron itself indicates that there are multi, i.e., more than one layers of neurons as shown in Figure 13.3. These layers are Input layer, Output layer and Hidden layer.

Input Layer: It consists of set of sensory units that receive inputs form the external environment.

Output Layer: The output layer consists of neurons that communicate the output of the system to the user or external environment.

Hidden Layer: There are usually a number of hidden layers between these two layers.

Figure 13.3(a) shows a simple structure with only one hidden layer while Figure 13.3(b) shows MLP with two hidden layers. When the input layer receives input, its neurons produce output, which becomes input to neurons of the next layer. The process continues until the output layer is invoked and its neurons fire their output to the external environment.

13.5.2 Radial Basis Function Network

RBF Nets are another form of feed-forward neural networks. Their architecture is very similar to the single hidden layer MLP shown in Figure 13.3(a). The difference lies in the way the weight matrices of the hidden layer and output layer are defined and in the transfer functions of the hidden and output layer neurons.

The net input to the hidden neurons of RBF net is the vector distance between its weight vector **w** and the input vector **p**, multiplied by the bias *b*. The transfer function of hidden neurons is Gaussian or Bell shaped function given by the following expression:

$$F(x) = e^{-\text{sqr}(x)} \tag{13.3}$$

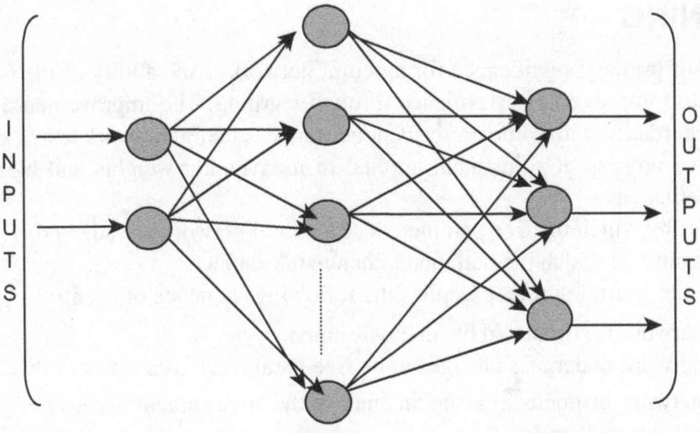

(a)

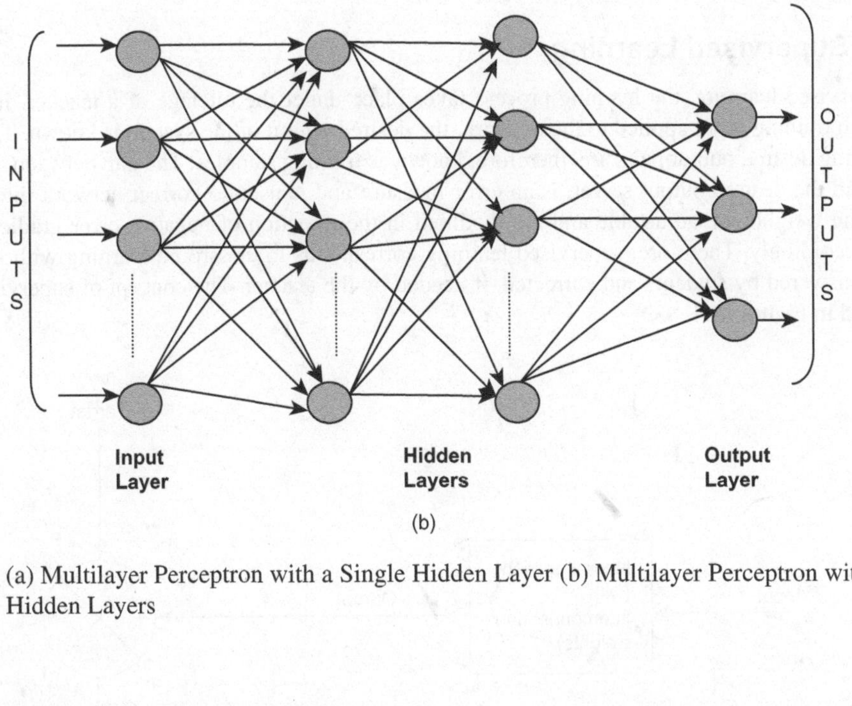

(b)

Figure 13.3 (a) Multilayer Perceptron with a Single Hidden Layer (b) Multilayer Perceptron with Multiple Hidden Layers

where

x is the vector distance between its weight vector **w** and the input vector **p**, multiplied by the bias b and F(x) is the output of the hidden layer neuron.

The output layer neurons operate similar to the output layer neurons in the MLP, except for the difference that their transfer function is `purelin`, (of the form $y = mx + c$), that is the output layer is linear. Therefore, it is seen that the non-linearity in RBF nets is introduced due to the radial basis transfer function of the hidden layer neurons.

13.6 LEARNING

The property that is of primary significance for a neural network is the ability of the network to learn from its environment, and to improve its performance through learning. The improvement in performance takes place over time in accordance with some prescribed measures. A neural network learns about its environment through an interactive process of adjustment applied to its synaptic weights and bias levels. Learning in neural networks is defined as

'Learning is a process by which the free parameters of a neural network are adapted. The type of learning is determined by the manner in which the parameter change takes place.'

This definition of the learning process implies the following sequence of events:

1. The neural network is stimulated by an environment.
2. The neural network undergoes changes in its free parameters as a result of this stimulation.
3. The neural network responds in a new manner to the environment because of the changes that have occurred in its internal structure.

Learning can be defined as a process of forcing a network to yield a particular response to a specific input; a particular response may or may not be specified to provide external correction. Learning is necessary when the information about input–output is unknown in prior. Learning is classified in two different types: supervised learning and unsupervised learning.

13.6.1 Supervised Learning

In the supervised learning, the learning process takes place under the tutelage of a teacher. It is assumed that for each training input applied to the network, the desired output of the system is known. The input and corresponding desired output pairs are, therefore, known as training samples. The gap between actual output obtained and the desired output serves as an error measure and is used to correct network interconnection weights. The weights are adjustable and are modified in the direction of negative error gradient to reduce the error accordingly. Therefore, supervised learning corresponds to classroom learning with the teacher's questions answered by students and corrected, if needed by the teacher. The concept of supervised learning is illustrated in Figure 13.4.

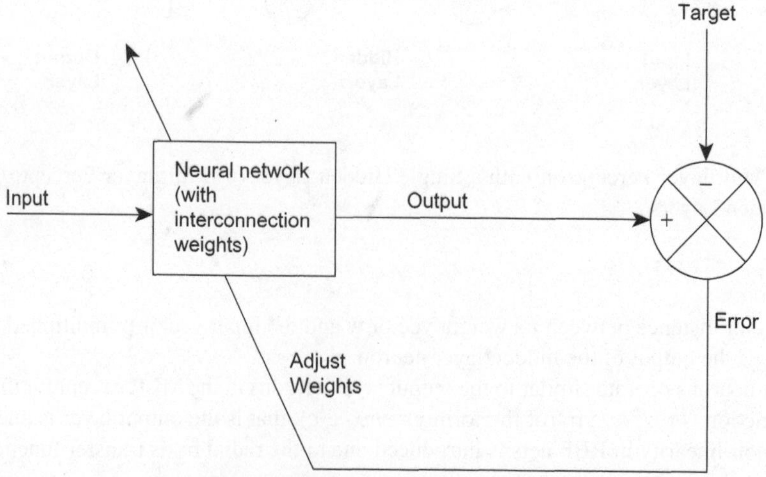

Figure 13.4 Supervised Learning

13.6.2 Unsupervised Learning

In the unsupervised learning there is no external teacher or critic to oversee the learning process. Here, the desired response is not known; thus explicit error information cannot be used to improve network behaviour. Since no information is available as to correctness or incorrectness of responses, learning must somehow be affected through a process of stimulation by the environment in which the network is embedded. It is similar to what human beings learn through their own experience without the help of any supervisor or teacher.

13.7 APPLICATIONS USING MULTILAYER PERCEPTRON

MLPs have been applied successfully to solve some difficult and diverse problems by training them in a supervised manner with a highly popular algorithm known as Error Backpropagation Algorithm (EBP). EBP has been found to be very slow and may not actually converge and achieve desired error tolerance. Therefore, many variants or improved training algorithms have been developed and implemented. Neural Network Toolbox also provides functions to implement many such training algorithms.

Let us learn to apply neural networks with the help of a simple example.

Example 13.1 Create and train an MLP to learn to evaluate the following function:

$$y = \frac{x^2 - 6.5}{x^2 + 6.5} \quad \text{for} -10 < x < 10$$

Solution: The function given above may be changed to

$$\frac{(x^2 - 6.5)*10}{\left(x^2 + 6.5\right)}$$

In order to implement the aforementioned problem on a neural network, the following steps are required:

1. Generate input–output training data.
2. Create an MLP network.
3. Train the MLP.
4. Generate test data.
5. Simulate network.

13.7.1 Generation of Input–Output Training Data

In order to train the neural network using supervised learning algorithm, input–output training pairs or training data is required. This data can be easily generated by varying the input within the range for which the training is required and obtaining the corresponding outputs by solving the system equation. In the aforementioned example the system is described by a simple mathematical expression.

To generate training samples, with input varying in the range $-10 < x < 10$, the following MATLAB commands are used:

```
i = 1;
for x = -10:0.5:10                    %creates input x varying from
                                      %10 to 10 in steps of 0.5
   y = (x^2-6.5)/(x^2+6.5);           %stores the corresponding output values of y.
   i = i + 1;                         %increment the count
end;
```

Or

```
x = -10 : 0.5 : 10;
y = (x .^ 2 - 6.5) ./ (x .^ 2 + 6.5);
```

The variables `x` and `y` are arrays with corresponding values of input–output pairs in corresponding index positions, that is output of `x(2)` is stored in `y(2)` and output of `x(31)` is stored in `y(31)` and so on. The aforementioned commands generate 41 input–output training sample pairs. It must be noted that the data must exist as column vectors.

13.8 USING GRAPHICAL USER INTERFACE

The Neural Network Toolbox also contains a simple and user-friendly Graphical User Interface (GUI). The GUI Neural Network Fitting Tool is initiated using the command `nftool`. This generates its own workspace, separate from the command line workspace. Therefore, the user needs to import or export data/network from one workspace to another depending on the need of the application.

The user can create a network, view it, train it, simulate it and export the final results to the workspace using the GUI Neural Network Fitting Tool. Similarly, data/network can be imported from the normal workspace into the GUI.

Let us illustrate the features of the GUI tool by solving the same example taken in Section 13.7. To start the GUI type the following command in the Command Window:

```
nftool
```

The Neural Network Fitting Tool window is created and is shown in Figure 13.5. The figure contains introduction to the data sets available in the GUI tool and the neural network. Click ***Next*** to proceed ahead.

13.8.1 Generation of Input–Output Data

To generate the input or output data, there are two methods. First, the data can be created in the MATLAB workspace and imported into the GUI workspace by specifying them as inputs and targets, respectively. The second way is to import them from the data files present in the current directory.

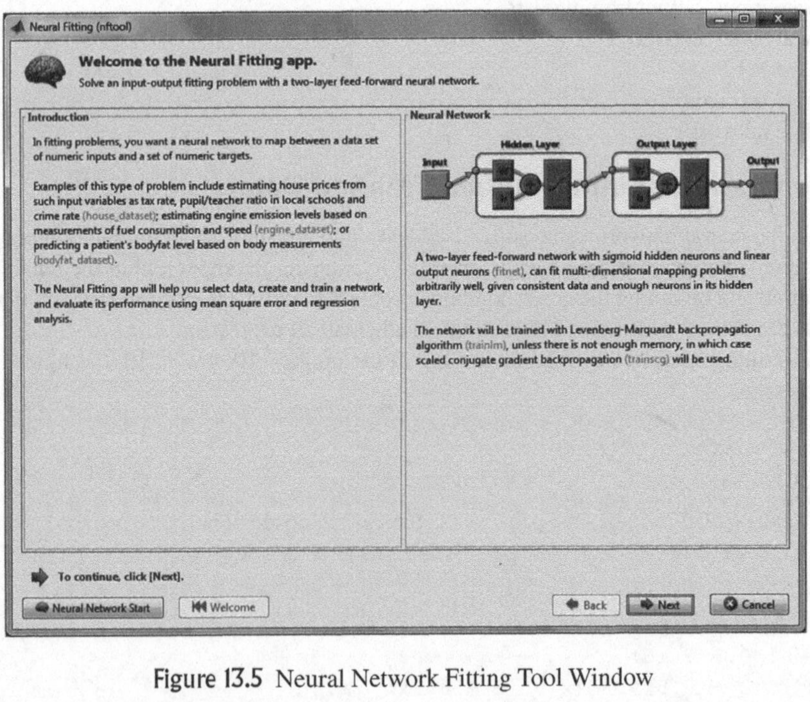

Figure 13.5 Neural Network Fitting Tool Window

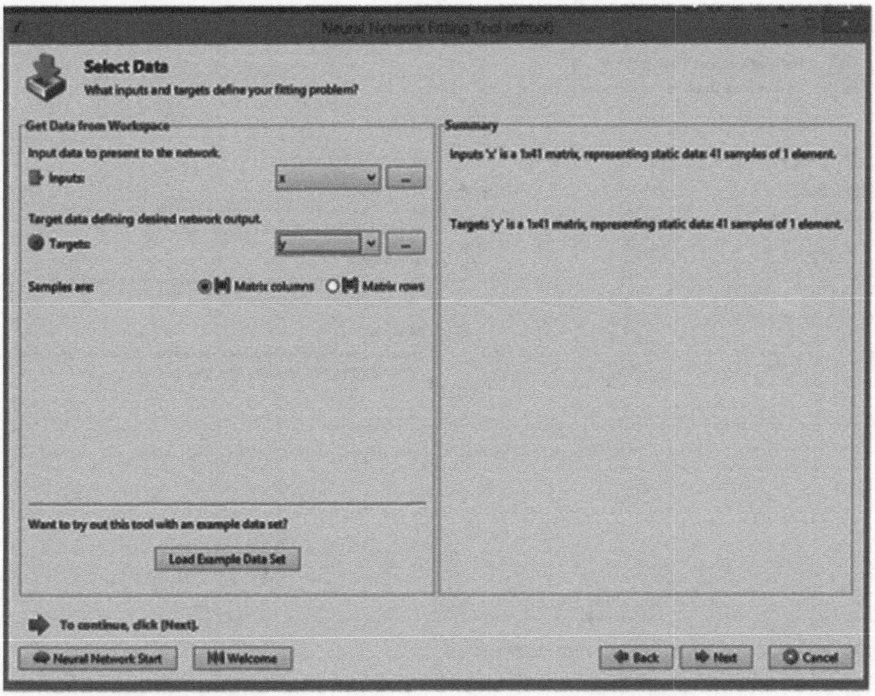

Figure 13.6 The `nftool` Showing Selected Data

To import input and output data for Example 13.1, the variable x is chosen as input and y as the output from the MATLAB workspace by using the Inputs and Targets options in the Select Data window shown in Figure 13.6. The details about the number of data samples, etc. is also given in the window. Click ***Next*** to proceed further.

13.8.2 Divide the Input–Output Data for Training, Validation and Testing

Proceeding further the next window is displayed for dividing the input–output data into three sets: training data, validation data and test data. With these settings, the input vectors and target vectors will be randomly divided into three sets as follows:

- 70% will be used for training.
- 15% will be used to validate that the network is generalizing and to stop training before overfitting.
- The last 15% will be used as a completely independent test of network generalization.

This default proportion can be varied by the user as desired or required by the application. The window is shown in Figure 13.7. The `nftool` also gives a small explanation of the three types of input–output data. Click ***Next*** to proceed further.

13.8.3 Creating Network Architecture

The next task is to create the network architecture. The standard network that is used for function fitting is a two-layer feed-forward network, i.e., having one hidden layer and one output layer. It has a sigmoid transfer

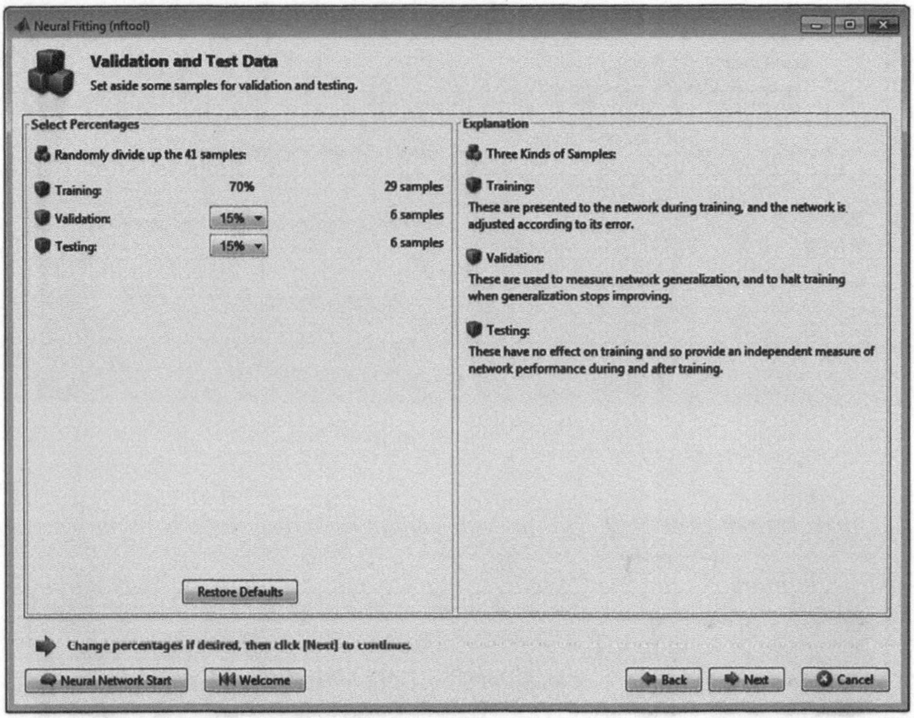

Figure 13.7 Data Division Window

function for the neurons in the hidden layer and a linear transfer function for the output layer neurons. The number of input and output neurons is not required to be defined. The `nftool` automatically fixes their number depending on the dimensions of the input and output data taken for the problem. The default number of hidden neurons is set to 10. The user can vary the number of hidden neurons by specifying them in the window. In Example 13.1, the number of neurons in the hidden layer is taken as 5. The network architecture window is shown in Figure 13.8. It also shows the schematic diagram of the network architecture with the number of neurons in the hidden layer. Click ***Next*** to proceed further.

13.8.4 Training the Network

The next step is to train the network created above. The 'Train network window' is shown in Figure 13.9. It gives the detail of number of input–output data samples for the training, validation and test data. It also tells the user that the error function used for training is MSE, i.e., mean sum squared error and the meaning of regression. The default training algorithm taken is Levenberg–Marquardt (trainlm) as it is a second-order learning algorithm and converges very fast. The default parameters of the learning algorithm are given as follows:

Maximum Epochs	epochs: 1000
Maximum Training Time	time: Inf
Performance Goal	goal: 0
Minimum Gradient	min_grad: 1e-07

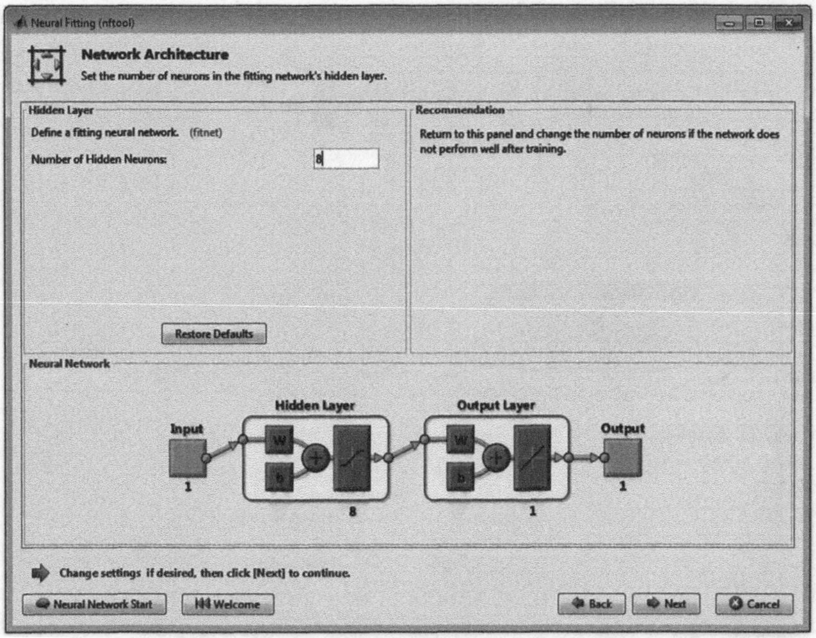

Figure 13.8 The Network Architecture Window

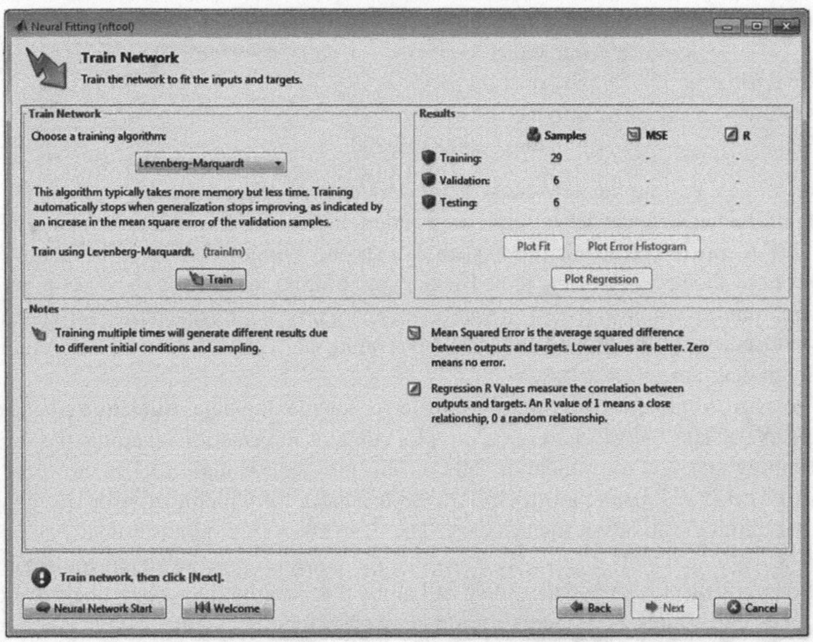

Figure 13.9 The Train Network Window

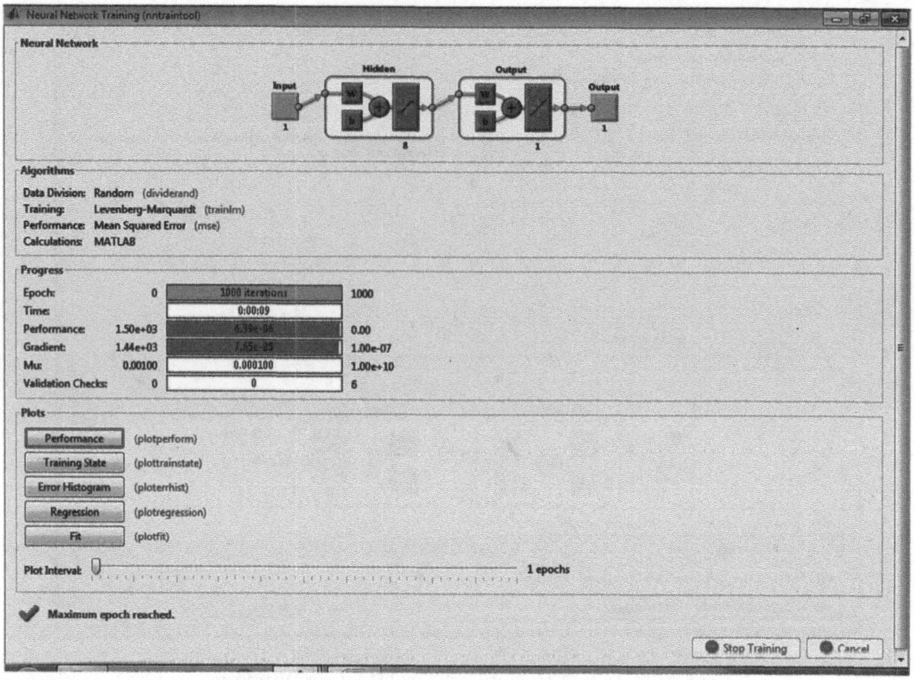

Figure 13.10 The Network Training Window

Maximum Validation Checks max_fail: 6
Mu mu: 0.001
Mu Decrease Ratio mu_dec: 0.1
Mu Increase Ratio mu_inc: 10
Maximum mu mu_max: 10000000000

Click the button `Train` to train the network with the parameters outlined above.

The training of the network carries on until the validation error fails to decrease for six iterations or the maximum number of epochs is reached. It also generates another window that gives the details of the network training completed by the network fitting tool. The network training window is shown in Figure 13.10.

In the network training window, there is a section named '`plots`'. It has buttons for generating plots for checking the performance of the trained network, the training state plot, the error histogram, the regression plot and the plot fit diagram.

The '`Performance`' plot gives the details of the error for training data, validation data and the test data for each training cycle. The '`Training State`' plot contains information regarding the variation of error gradient, the learning rate, and the validation failure. This plot for Example 13.1 is shown in Figure 13.11. The '`Error Histogram`' gives plot of error vs the instances for which that error was generated for the three sets of data: training, validation and test data. The '`Regression`' plot is used to validate the network performance. The regression plots display the network outputs with respect to targets for training, validation, and test sets. For a perfect '`fit`', the data should fall along a 45 degree line, where the network outputs are equal to the targets. In Example 13.1, the fit is reasonably good for all data sets, with *R* values in each case of 0.99 or above. The regression plot is shown in Figure 13.12. The error histogram for Example 13.1 is shown in Figure 13.13.

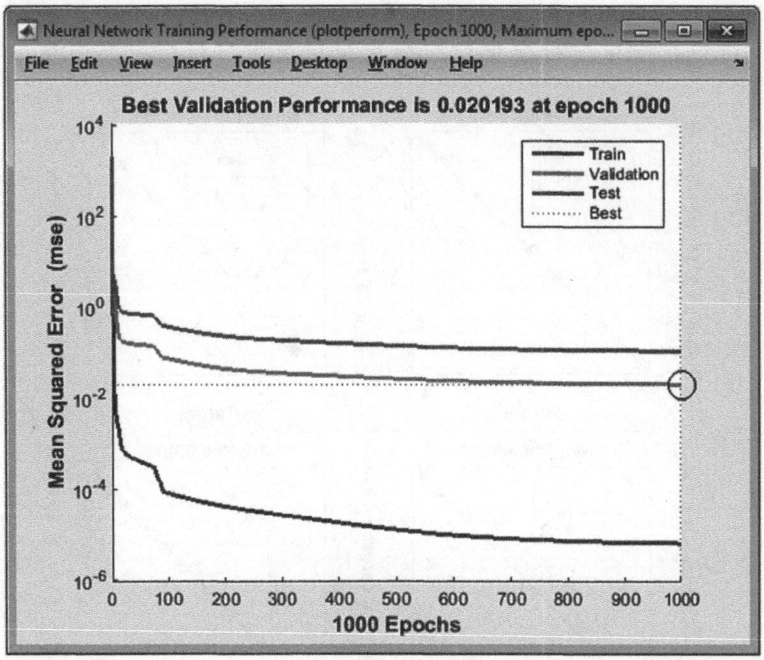

Figure 13.11 The Training State Plot for Example 13.1

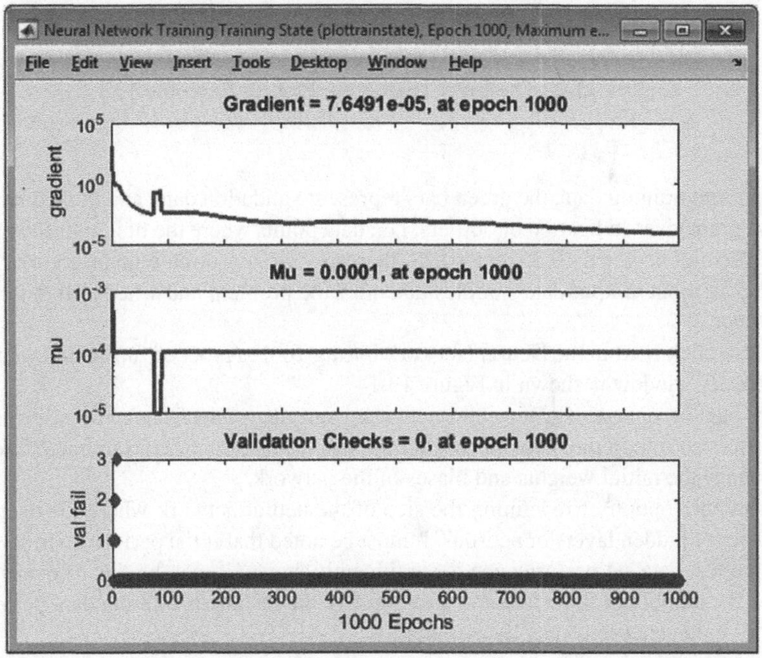

Figure 13.12 Regression Plot for Example 13.1

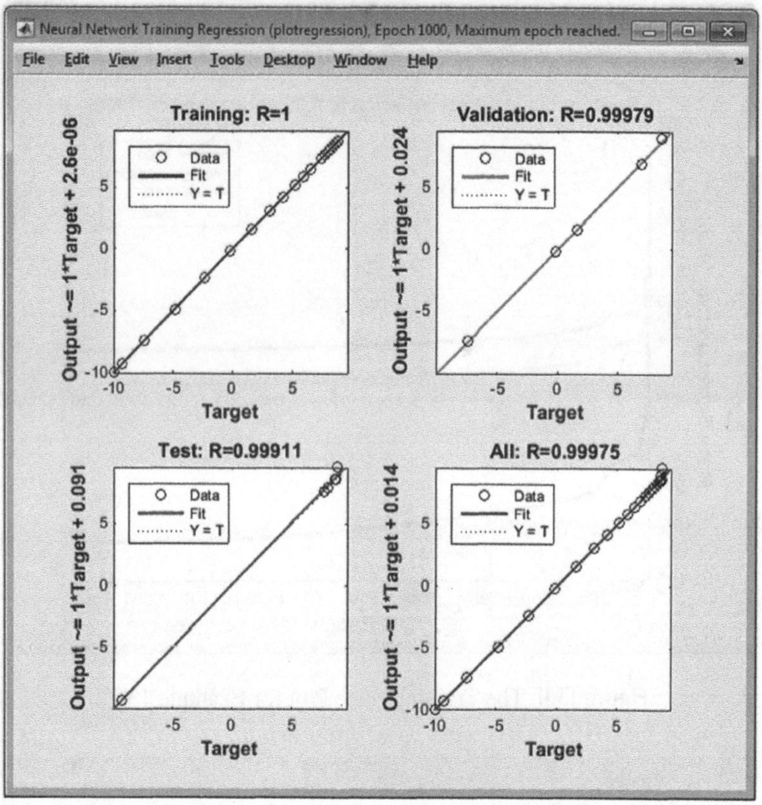

Figure 13.13 The Error Histogram Plot for Example 13.1

The blue bars represent training data, the green bars represent validation data, and the red bars represent testing data. The histogram gives indication of outliers, i.e., data points where the fit is significantly worse. In this example, most errors fall between –0.25 and +0.28, there are two test point with an error >0.34. It gives fair idea of the number of input–output data samples taken for the problem and whether the network is required to be retrained or not.

The user needs to click Next in the Neural Network Fitting Tool to proceed further to evaluate the network. The Evaluate Network window is shown in Figure 13.14 .

Here, the user has the option of testing the network using new set of data. In case the results are not satisfactory, the user can retrain the network by clicking the '`Train Again`' button. While re-training, the `nftool` shall change the initial weights and biases of the network.

There is also another option of redefining the size of the neural network where the user can increase or decrease the number of hidden layers or neurons. It must be noted that if the performance on the training data set is good, but the test data set performance is significantly worse, it may be due to overfitting. Then, it is advised to reduce the number of hidden neurons to improve the results. If training data performance is poor, then the number of hidden neurons may be increased.

Click ***Next*** to proceed further. The last window of `nftool` is generated where the results can be saved, the neural network diagrams can be generated and the script file can be created containing MATLAB code

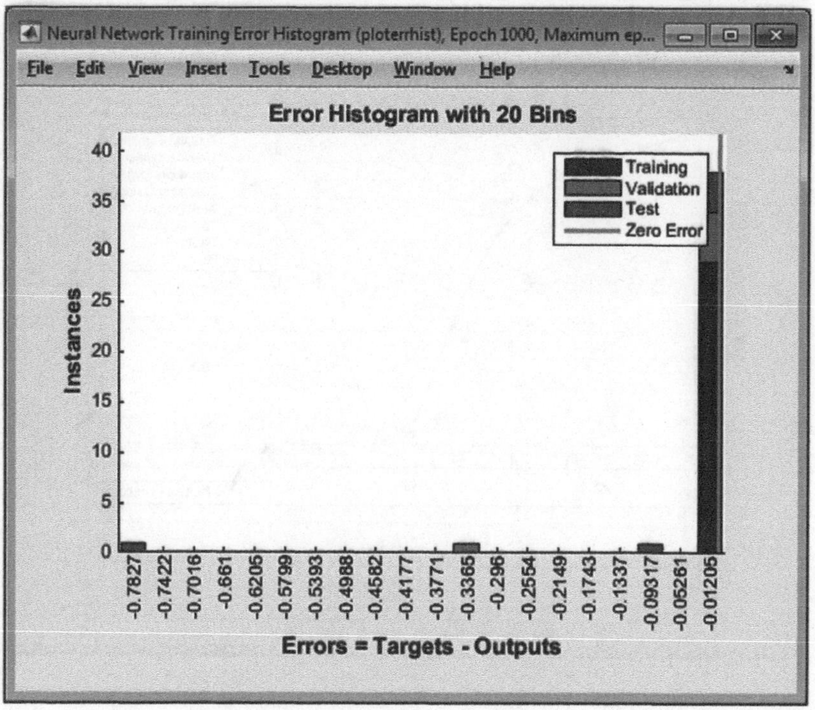

Figure 13.14 The Evaluate Network Window

that can be used to reproduce all of the steps or operations performed using `nftool`, from the command line. The script file can be generated in two forms: 1. Simple script and 2. Advanced script. The simple script contains only the basic commands while the advanced script contains commands where different parameters for the network, its learning algorithm, etc. are also defined. The window also contains an option of generating the Simulink diagram for the network trained for the problem. The Save results window of `nftool` is shown in Figure 13.15 .

13.9 USING COMMAND-LINE FUNCTIONS

Example 13.1 that was approximated using the GUI NFTOOL can also be done through command-line functions. The commands required to be given from the command window for the operations performed using `nftool` are discussed for the reader to understand how similar input-output fitting problems can be solved using command-line functions.

13.9.1 Defining Input and Output Data Variables

In Example 13.1, in Section 13.7.1 input-output data was generated and input samples were stored in variable x and output samples were stored in variable y. It is required to assign the input data to variable '`inputs`' and output data to variable '`targets`'. For that the following commands are used:

```
inputs = x;

targets = y;
```

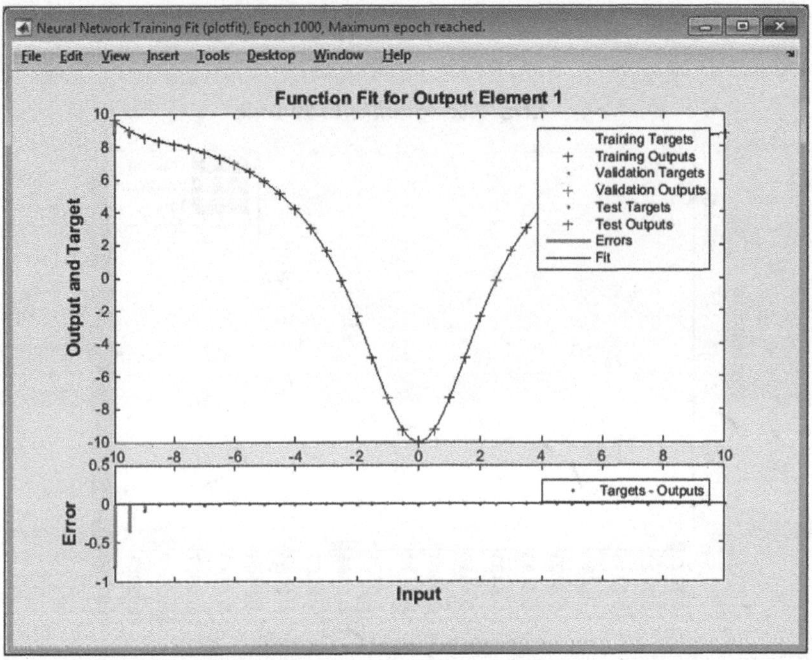

Figure 13.15 The `'Save Results'` Window of NFTOOL

13.9.2 Creating the Neural Network Architecture

The neural network architecture is to be defined. The neural network toolbox reads the input and output data and likewise configures the number of neurons required in the input and output layers. It may be noted that the number of input neurons are equal to the number of inputs, i.e., the dimensions of one input sample. Likewise, the number of output neurons required is equal to the number of outputs, i.e., the dimensions of one output sample. Therefore, it is not required to define the number of input and output neurons. Next, the neural network toolbox by default assumes one hidden layer. The user requires to declare the size of the hidden layer, i.e., the number of neurons in that hidden layer and create the network. The command line statements are as given under:

```
% Create a Fitting Network, i.e., the no. of neurons in hidden layer and
create network

hiddenLayerSize = 5;

net = fitnet(hiddenLayerSize);
```

More the number of layers or neurons, more is the computation required and have a tendency to overfit the data, but they allow the network to solve more complex problems. To use more than one hidden layer, enter the hidden layer sizes as elements of an array in the `fitnet` command.

13.9.3 Pre-processing and Post-processing Inputs and Outputs

Pre- and post-processing training data functions result in faster and efficient training of the network. These functions are assigned automatically by network creation functions. The user can, however, override the default input and output processing functions by adjusting network properties after creating the network. Before training, it is often useful to scale the inputs and targets so that they remain within a specified range. The function `mapminmax` scales inputs and outputs so that they are in the range [–1, 1]. The following MATLAB statements illustrate the use of the function mapminmax:

```
net.inputs{1}.processFcns = {'removeconstantrows', 'mapminmax'};

net.outputs{2}.processFcns = {'removeconstantrows', 'mapminmax'};
```

where inputs and outputs are inputs–outputs associated with the neural network 'net' and `removeconstantrows` and `mapminmax` are the processing functions that are assigned to the network by the function processFcns. The other pre-processing functions available are as given under:

`fixunknowns`	Processes matrix rows with unknown values.
`mapstd`	Map matrix row means and deviations to standard values.
`processpca`	Processes rows of matrix with principal component analysis.
`removerows`	Remove matrix rows with specified indices.

These functions are built into the network class and are processed automatically before and after the data is processed by the network created.

13.9.4 Division of Data into Training, Validation, Testing Data Sets

The input-output data that was created has to be divided into three parts. Major part shall be utilized for training the network and the other two parts Validation and Testing Data sets are required for validation to ensure training is sufficient and also does not result into overfitting. The following commands are utilized for the purpose:

```
net.divideFcn = 'dividerand';  % Divide data randomly

net.divideMode = 'sample';  % Divide up every sample

net.divideParam.trainRatio = 70/100; % for training data set

net.divideParam.valRatio = 15/100;   % for validation Data Set

net.divideParam.testRatio = 15/100;  % for test data set
```

in the above commands 70% of the input-output data is allocated to the training data set, 15% to the validation data set and remaining 15% to the test data set.

The other such divide functions used for the data division available in the neural network toolbox are listed as under:

`divideblock`	Partition indices into three sets using blocks of indices.
`divideind`	Partition indices into three sets using specified indices.
`divideint`	Partition indices into three sets using interleaved indices.
`dividerand`	Partition indices into three sets using random indices.
`dividetrain`	Partition indices into training set only.

13.9.5 Declare Training Algorithm and its Parameters to be Used for Training

By default the neural network uses Levenberg Marquardt (LM) learning algorithm. To declare the learning algorithm the command used is given as under

```
net.trainFcn = 'trainlm';  % Levenberg-Marquardt
```

Other learning algorithms available in Neural network toolbox are given below:

`trainb`	Batch training with weight and bias learning rules.
`trainbfg`	BFGS quasi-Newton backpropagation.
`trainbr`	Bayesian Regulation backpropagation.
`trainbu`	Unsupervised batch training with weight and bias learning rules.
`trainbuwb`	Unsupervised batch training with weight and bias learning rules.
`trainc`	Cyclical order weight/bias training.
`traincgb`	Conjugate gradient backpropagation with Powell–Beale restarts.
`traincgf`	Conjugate gradient backpropagation with Fletcher–Reeves updates.
`traincgp`	Conjugate gradient backpropagation with Polak–Ribiere updates.
`traingd`	Gradient descent backpropagation.
`traingda`	Gradient descent with adaptive lr backpropagation.
`traingdm`	Gradient descent with momentum.
`traingdx`	Gradient descent w/momentum and adaptive lr backpropagation.
`trainoss`	One step secant backpropagation.
`trainr`	Random order weight/bias training.
`trainrp`	RPROP backpropagation.
`trainru`	Unsupervised random order weight/bias training.
`trains`	Sequential order weight/bias training.
`trainscg`	Scaled conjugate gradient backpropagation.

The other parameters of the learning/training the network are also required to be defined. First define the error function to be used in calculating the error in the learning algorithm. It is called performance function of the network and is defined as given below:

```
net.performFcn = 'mse';  % Mean squared error
```

There are other performance functions also available in Neural Network Toolbox and are listed below:

`mae`	Mean absolute error performance function.
`sae`	Sum absolute error performance function.
`sse`	Sum squared error performance function.

There are many plots required to be plotted for checking the success of the training process. The command needed to be given for declaring the plot functions is given below:

```
net.plotFcns = {'plotperform', 'plottrainstate', 'ploterrhist', ...
'plotregression', 'plotfit'};
```

The plot functions for a Feed-forward neural network are listed below:

`ploterrcorr`	Plot autocorrelation of error time series.
`ploterrhist`	Plot error histogram.
`plotfit`	Plot function fit.
`plotperform`	Plot network performance.

`plotregression`	Plot linear regression.
`plotresponse`	Plot dynamic network time-series response.
`plottrainstate`	Plot training state values.
`plotwb`	Plot Hinton diagrams of weight and bias values.

13.9.6 Training the Neural Network

The following command is given for training the network

```
[net, tr] = train(net, inputs, targets);
```

During training, the training window opens and displays the training progress. It allows the user to interrupt training at any point by clicking 'Stop' Training. The training is otherwise stopped when the validation error increases for six iterations or the maximum number of epochs are exceeded. The training errors, validation errors, and test errors can be plotted by clicking the 'Performance' button in the training window.

The output of the 'train' command, i.e., variable 'tr' stores the training record. The record parameters stored in this output are given below:

```
trainFcn: 'trainlm'
trainParam: [1x1 struct]
performFcn: 'mse'
performParam: [1x1 struct]
derivFcn: 'defaultderiv'
divideFcn: 'dividerand'
divideMode: 'sample'
divideParam: [1x1 struct]
trainInd: [1x29 double]
valInd: [2 9 19 26 27 33]
testInd: [1 3 6 7 22 40]
stop: 'Maximum epoch reached.'
num_epochs: 1000
trainMask: {[1x41 double]}
valMask: {[1x41 double]}
testMask: {[1x41 double]}
best_epoch: 1000
goal: 0
states: {1x8 cell}
epoch: [1x1001 double]
time: [1x1001 double]
perf: [1x1001 double]
vperf: [1x1001 double]
```

```
tperf: [1x1001 double]
mu: [1x1001 double]
gradient: [1x1001 double]
val_fail: [1x1001 double]
best_perf: 6.3918e-06
best_vperf: 0.0202
best_tperf: 0.1087
```

13.9.7 Testing the Network

After the network is trained using the 'train' command, the network outputs can be calculated from the trained network. The following commands are used to compute the output, the errors and the performance of the network.

```
outputs = net(inputs);
errors = gsubtract(targets,outputs);
performance = perform(net,targets,outputs)
```

The commands can also be used to calculate output on some other set of data if required. The details of tracking record if seen carefully indicate that the indices of the input–output samples for validation and test data sets are saved in `tr.valInd` and `tr.testInd`, respectively, and can be used to calculate the performance of the network on that data set only. The commands used to calculate network performance on test data set only are given as under:

```
tI = tr.testInd;
tstOutputs = net(inputs(tI));
tstPerform = perform(net, targets(tInd), tstOutputs)
```

13.9.8 View the Network

The neural network formed and trained can be viewed using the command given below:

```
view(net)
```

It generates the schematic diagram of the network.

13.9.9 Plot the Network Parameters

The different plot can be plotted using the commands given below:

```
figure, plotperform(tr)
figure, plottrainstate(tr)
figure, plotfit(net, inputs, targets)
figure, plotregression(targets, outputs)
figure, ploterrhist(errors)
```

Programming Tip 13.1: Output layer size is determined from the target vector size.

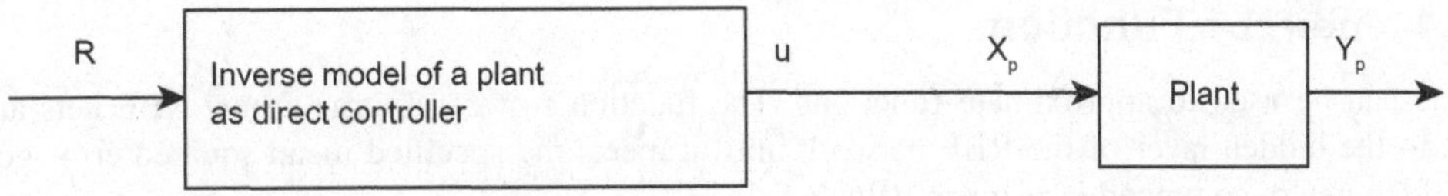

Figure 13.16 Direct Inverse Control

> **Programming Tip 13.2:** `trainlm` is the default training function because it converges very fast, but it requires large memory to run. In case, system is short of RAM, `trainbgf` or `trainrp` algorithms may be used as they require less memory.

13.10 ANN BASED CONTROL

The feedback control has been the basis for the development of simple automatic control systems. Feedback control systems are inherently simple to comprehend and implement but are not very effective in compensating plant parameter variations and changes in the environment. The advent of ANNs and fuzzy logic theory has resulted in possible implementation of better and more efficient control. They do not require a priori mathematical model of the plant and have inherent ability to adapt to the changing environment and the plant dynamics, unlike conventional methods.

Direct Inverse Control is the simplest and most widely used control configuration which makes use of the inverse plant model. The network is required to be trained offline to learn the inverse dynamics of the plant. Once the network is trained to learn the inverse system model, it is placed directly in series with the plant to be controlled. Thus, the overall transfer function of the controller and the plant becomes unity, that is, 1. Therefore, output is equal to the reference input or in other words, output tracks the reference input. The controller configuration is shown in Figure 13.16.

One of the simplest approaches for the implementation of neuro-control is the direct inverse control approach. In this approach, the neural network is first trained offline using EBP algorithm to learn the inverse dynamics of the plant and then configured as direct controller to the plant. It has been shown that delayed plant output signals as input vector elements of neural network model in the training stage have definite effect on the neuro-controller in faster learning of the true inverse plant model. Because the neural network is connected in series with the plant for control purposes the direct inverse control scheme is also called Series Neuro-Control Scheme.

There are generally four steps in controller implementation:

1. Generate input–output training data.
2. Create network object.
3. Train the network.
4. Simulate the network-controlled system.

13.11 CREATING RBF NEURAL NETWORK

Neural Network Toolbox offers two basic functions for designing RBF networks.

1. `newrbe`
2. `newrb`

13.11.1 `newrbe` Function

RBF nets can be used to approximate functions. The function `newrb` returns a new RBF nets and adds neurons to the hidden layer of the RBF network until it meets the specified mean squared error goal. The syntax of the newrb command is as given below:

```
newrb(inputs, targets, goal, spread, maxn, DF)
```

where `inputs` is matrix of input vectors
`targets` is matrix of target vectors.
`goal` is the Mean squared error goal (default value is 0)
`spread` is the spread of RBFs (default value is 1).
`Maxn` is the maximum number of neurons.
`DF` is the number of neurons to add between displays, default = 25.

Larger value of '`spread`' results in smoother function approximation. But, lot of neurons will be required to fit a fast changing function if the spread is too large and too small value may result in requirement of many neurons to fit a smooth function and the network may not generalize well.

13.11.2 `newrb` Function

The function `newrbe` creates an RBF network with zero error on training vectors. The syntax of the function is given below:

```
net = newrb(x, y, error goal, spread)
```

where `x` and `y` are input and output vectors and `spread` determines width of an area in the input space to which each neuron responds. If `spread` is 2.5, then each RBF net hidden layer neuron will respond with 0.5 or more to any input vectors within a vector distance of 2.5 from its weight vector. The maximum response output can be equal to 1.0.

The function `newrbe` creates RBF network with hidden layer neurons equal to the number of input vectors in *x*. Each neuron in hidden layer acts as a detector for a different input vector. The SSE in RBF net created using `newrbe` function is always zero.

> **Programming Tip 13.3:** The value of spread should be large enough so that the hidden layer neurons respond strongly to overlapping regions of the input space. This makes the network function smoother and results in better generalization for new input vectors occurring between input vectors used in the design.

> **Programming Tip 13.4:** As RBF network is created using function `newrbe`. It has hidden neurons equal to number of input vectors. Therefore, the network becomes TOO LARGE when many input vectors are needed to define a network.

> **Programming Tip 13.5:** RBF network can not replace a MLP network. If created using `newrbe` function, these tend to have many times more neurons than a comparable MLP. This is because sigmoidal neurons can have outputs over a large region of the input space, while RBF network neurons respond to relatively small regions of the input space only.

13.12 SELF-ORGANIZING FEATURE MAPS

SOFMs learn to recognize groups of similar input vectors in such a way that neurons physically near each other in the layer respond to similar input vectors. These networks learn to classify input vectors according to how they are grouped in the input space.

SOFMs make use of competitive transfer function that accepts a net input vector and returns neuron outputs of 0 for all neurons except for the winner whose net input is maximum. The winner's output is 1. They differ from competitive layers in which learning function updates neighbouring neurons also based on their distance from the winning neuron. Thus, SOFMs learn both the distribution and topology of the input vectors they are trained on.

The neurons in the layer of an SOFM are arranged originally in physical positions according to a topology function. The different topology functions available in Neural Networks Toolbox are

1. `gridtop`
2. `hextop`
3. `randtop`

These functions arrange the neurons in a grid, hexagonal or random topology respectively.

Likewise, the distances between neurons are calculated from their positions with a distance function. The four distance functions available in Neural Networks Toolbox are

1. `dist`
2. `boxdist`
3. `linkdist`
4. `mandist`

The command `newsom` is used to create a SOFM network. The syntax is as follows:

```
net = newsom(inputs, [m1, m2, …mi],tfcn, dfcn, steps ,in);
```

where `inputs` is matrix of input vectors.

`mi` is the size of *i*th layer dimension
`tfcn` is the topology function, default = 'hextop'.
`dfcn` is the distance function, default = 'linkdist'.
`steps` is steps for neighbourhood to shrink to 1, default = 100.
`in` is the initial neighbourhood size, default = 3.

> **Programming Tip 13.6:** The `hextop` is the default pattern for SOFM networks generated with `newsom`.

The learning in an SOFM occurs for one vector at a time, independent of whether the network is trained directly (`trainr`) or whether it is trained adaptively (`trains`). In either case, `learnsom` is its learning function.

SUMMARY

This chapter first describes the essential theoretical concepts of ANNs so that the reader is able to follow the commands available in The Neural Network Toolbox. The complete chapter can be summarized as follows:

- The basic features of Neural Networks, the different transfer functions and architectures are described.
- The commands in the Neural Network Toolbox are illustrated by implementing a simple example using command line statements.

- Then, the graphic tool for designing Neural Network systems is described by implementing the same example using GUI tool.
- In the end, an introduction to RBF Nets and SOFMs is also given.

List of Commands/Functions

Command/Function	Description
`boxdist`	Calculates distance between neurons in SOFMs using grid topology
`dist`	Calculates Euclidian distance between neurons in SOFMs
`gridtop`	Grid topology of neurons in SOFMs
`hextop`	Hexagonal topology function used in SOFMs
`learsom`	Learning function for SOFMs
`linkdist`	Calculates distance between neurons in SOFMs as no. of links
`logsig`	Sigmoidal transfer function with output range [0 1]
`mandist`	Calculates Manhattan distance between neurons in SOFMs
`mapminmax`	Pre-processes and post-processes the input–output data for better training of ANN
`newff`	To create a new network
`newff`	Create an MLP Neural network
`newrb`	Creates an RBF network one neuron at a time iteratively
`newrbe`	Creates an RBF network with zero error on training vectors
`newsom`	Is used to create a SOFM network
`nntool`	GUI tool to create Neural network based systems
`purelin`	Linear transfer function
`randtop`	Random topology of neurons in SOFMs
`sim`	Simulate a neural network
`tansig`	Tanh sigmoidal transfer function, with output in range [−1 +1]
`train`	To train a neural network
`trainbgf`	Train neural network using BGF training algorithm
`traingd`	Train neural network using gradient descent Backpropagation algorithm
`trainlm`	Train neural network using Levenberg Marquadat Algorithm, is the default training function.
`trainParam.epochs`	Maximum no. of cycles for which network is to trained, a parameter in training algorithm `traingd`
`trainParam.goal`	The error goal, a parameter in training algorithm `traingd`
`trainParam.lr`	learning rate, a parameter in training algorithm `traingd`

(Continued)

(Continued)

`trainParam.show`	Training record display frequency, a parameter in training algorithm `traingd`
`trainr`	To train a neural network directly
`trainrp`	Train neural network using Resilient Backpropagation algorithm
`trains`	To train neural network adaptively

EXERCISES

13.1 Describe the salient features of ANNs. Which features are most important for their application in control systems?

13.2 Discuss various modelling paradigms used for modelling a system using ANN. Also discuss their advantages and disadvantages.

13.3 Describe the steps in implementation of a controller using ANN.

13.4 What is the role played by validation data and testing data in designing effective controller using ANNs?

13.5 What kind of activation functions are used in ANNs? Which activation function is suitable for what kind of application?

13.6 What is the need of scaling the input and output data? Discuss different methods that can be employed for scaling input–output data.

13.7 Describe the different functions available in MATLAB 7 for training an ANN. Which of them is most frequently used and why?

13.8 How does one decide about the number of layers in an ANN? How are the optimum numbers of neurons in the hidden layer determined?

13.9 Discuss the commands used to generate the initial weight matrices for the interconnection weights of the ANN.

13.10 A simple, menu-driven tool named 'NNTOOL' is available in MATLAB 7 for using neural networks for various applications. The reader is advised to go through the tool and implement a neural controller for a simple process defined by $y = 3.5x^2 - 2x + 10$.

13.11 Design a Feedforward Neural Network to simulate a 10 input decimal to binary convertor.

13.12 Using the GUI tool NNTOOL, design a neural network to simulate the function given below:
$y = x_1^3 + 3x_2^2 + 7x_1 x_2 - 6 \qquad -10 < x_1, x_2 < +10.$

CHAPTER 14

MATLAB Applications in Fuzzy Logic Systems

Everything is vague to a degree you do not realize till you have tried to make it precise.

—*Bertrand Russell*

LEARNING OBJECTIVES

- Advantages and concepts of Fuzzy Logic System.
- The linguistic variables, fuzzy sets and their membership functions (MFs) (`trimf, trapmf, guassmf, gbellmf`).
- Comparison of fuzzy and binary operations (`OR, AND NOT`).
- The method of representing knowledge in fuzzy systems through If-Then rules and concept of rule matrix.
- To learn about fuzzy inference system (FIS) components.
  - ❐ Fuzzification of input variables
  - ❐ Application of Fuzzy Operators
  - ❐ Mapping Degree of Matching to Fuzzy Outputs
  - ❐ Aggregation of Outputs
  - ❐ Defuzzification
- Washing Machine Problem Solution using the GUI Fuzzy tool (`fuzzy`).
- Features of FIS Editor, Membership Function (MF) Editor, Rule Editor, Rule Viewer and Surface Viewer.
- The commands available in Fuzzy Logic Toolbox™.
- Solution of Water Bath Temperature Control System using command-line statements like `newfis, addvar, addmf, addrule, evalfis`, etc.

14.1 INTRODUCTION

The concept of Fuzzy Logic was conceived by Lotfi Zadeh, a Professor at the University of California, Berkley. He presented it not as a control methodology, but as a way of processing data by allowing an element to have partial membership of a set. He explained that human reasoning process does not require precise, numerical information input, and yet is capable of performing complex tasks such as natural language understanding and difficult decision-making. Fuzzy Logic provides a simple way to arrive at a definite conclusion based upon vague, ambiguous, imprecise, noisy or missing input information. Fuzzy Logic's approach mimics how a person would make decisions with imprecise and incomplete information.

What is Fuzzy Logic?

'Fuzzy Logic is basically a multi-valued logic that allows intermediate values to be defined between conventional evaluations like yes/no, true/false and black/white. Notions like warm cold or very cold can be formulated mathematically and processed by computers.'

14.1.1 Fuzzy Logic: Advantages

Fuzzy Logic offers several unique features that make it a good choice for many problems.

1. In practice most of the things encountered in life are imprecise. Fuzzy Logic is inherently robust since it does not require precise, noise-free inputs and degrades gradually when system components fail like if a feedback sensor quits or is destroyed.
2. Fuzzy logic is flexible. With any given system, it is easy to manage it and add more functionality on top of it without starting again from scratch. Since the FLC processes user-defined rules governing the system, it can be modified easily to add, improve or alter system performance.
3. Fuzzy Logic is not limited to a few feedback inputs and one or two outputs. Any sensor data that provides some indication of a system's actions and reactions is sufficient. This allows the sensors to be inexpensive and imprecise thus keeping the overall system cost and complexity low.
4. Because of the rule-based operation, system can be easily designed for any reasonable number of inputs and outputs. Defining the rule base becomes complex if number of inputs and outputs becomes large. It would be better to break the system into smaller parts and use several smaller Fuzzy Logic modules distributed on the system, each with more limited responsibilities.
5. Fuzzy logic can model non-linear functions of arbitrary complexity. One can create a fuzzy system to match any set of input–output data. Fuzzy Logic can model or control non-linear systems that would be difficult or impossible to model mathematically. This opens doors for control systems that would normally be deemed unfeasible for automation. This process is made particularly easy by adaptive techniques like Adaptive Neuro-Fuzzy Inference Systems (ANFIS).
6. It can store the knowledge database using the knowledge of experts. In direct contrast to neural networks, which require training data and generate opaque, impenetrable models, fuzzy logic lets one rely on the experience of people who already understand the system.
7. It can be easily combined with conventional and allied control techniques. Fuzzy systems do not necessarily replace conventional methods. In many cases fuzzy systems augment them and simplify their implementation.
8. It is capable of processing linguistic information and, therefore, is conceptually easy to understand.

14.1.2 Fuzzy Logic: An Example

Let us take an example of a common washing machine. The input parameters are the quantity of clothes and their dirtiness. It is desired to find the number of washing cycles or the time needed to wash the clothes. Let us adopt the non-fuzzy approach first. The simplest formula could be that the machine will run for fixed amount of time, say 30 minutes, irrespective of the quantity or dirtiness of clothes. It can be expressed mathematically as

`Washing time` = 30

The above statement when plotted will appear as a horizontal line.

Let us now take the `quantity` of clothes into consideration. Let the time vary from 10 minutes to 50 minutes depending upon the quantity of clothes which may vary from the scale of 0 to 10. It can be expressed mathematically as

`Time` = (40/10)* `quantity` + 10

The above statement when plotted will appear a straight line with slope = 4 and intercept = 10.

If the `dirtiness` of the clothes is also taken into account and `quantity` of clothes is given 75 per cent weightage, then the set of mathematical equations for calculating the `washing time` become lengthy and complicated.

Let us try and express the problem using fuzzy approach and each input/output parameter be assigned linguistic values instead of the numerical values used earlier. Let the `washing time` be allowed to have three linguistic values: `small`, `average` and `large`. Similarly, let the `quantity` of clothes be expressed as `small`, `normal` and `large` and the `dirtiness` of clothes be described as being `low`, `normal` and `high`. Further, let the linguistic values associated with each fuzzy variable be defined using constant values as given in the following code:

```
% set up constants
% WT = washingtime,    QTY =quantity,    DT = dirtiness,
WTsmall = 10;                          % washing time is small
WTavg = 30;                            % washing time is average
WTlarge = 50;                          % washing time is large
WTrange = WTlarge - WTsmall;
QTYsmall= 0;                           % quantity is small
QTYnormal = 3;                         % quantity is normal
QTYmedium = 7;                         % quantity is medium
QTYlarge = 10;                         % quantity is large
QTYrange = QTYlarge - QTYsmall;
DTlow = 0;                             % dirtiness is low
DTnormal = 5;                          % dirtiness is normal
DThigh = 10;                           % dirtiness is high
DTrange = DThigh - DTlow;
ratio = 0.75;                          % 75% weightage
%expressing in linguistic form
%If quantity is small or dirtiness is low, Then washingtime is small
%the code for the above if-then rule is given below
if (quantity < QTYnormal) OR (quality < DTnormal),
  time = [{(WTavg - WTsmall)/(QTYnormal - QTYsmall)}* quantity …
  + WTsmall] * ratio + (1-ratio)*( WTrange/DTrange*quality …
  + WTsmall);
%expressing in linguistic form
%If quantity is medium, Then washingtime is average
%the code for the above if-then rule is given below
elseif quantity < QTYmedium,
   time = WTavg *ratio + (1-ratio)* (WTrange/DTrange * quality …
   + WTsmall);
%expressing in linguistic form
%If quantity is large or dirtiness is high, Then washingtime is %large
%the code for the above if-then rule is given below
else
    time = [{(WTlarge - WTavg)/(QTYlarge - QTYmedium)}*(quantity …
    - QTYmedium) + WTavg] *ratio + (1 - ratio) * (WTrange / DTrange …
    * quality + WTsmall);
end
```

It is noticed that the code has become very lengthy, complex and is difficult to modify it. It is very interesting to note that if we remove the complete code what remains are the comments which are nothing but the fuzzy 'If-Then' rules. These rules are listed below and form the core of the fuzzy system.

```
%If quantity is small or dirtiness is low, Then washingtime is small
%If quantity is medium, Then washingtime is average
%If quantity is large or dirtiness is high, Then washingtime is large
```

In contrast to the code, these fuzzy rules are very simple to understand. Also, it is very easy to add more such 'If-Then' rules or modify the existing ones. Therefore, fuzzy systems that are built using linguistic information are flexible and easy to understand or modify.

14.2 LINGUISTIC VARIABLES AND MEMBERSHIP FUNCTIONS

In 1973, Professor Lotfi Zadeh proposed the concept of linguistic or 'fuzzy' variables, like `temperature`, defined by fuzzy sets and linguistic values such as `hot` and `cold`. A fuzzy set is an extension of a classical set and includes the possibility of partial membership of its elements. The input space is referred to as the universe of discourse (UOD). If X is the UOD and its elements are denoted by x, then a fuzzy set A in X is defined as a set of ordered pairs.

$$A = \{x, \mu_A(x) \mid x \in X\}$$

where $\mu_A(x)$ is called the membership function (or MF) of x in A. The MF associated with a given fuzzy set X, maps each element of X to a membership value between 0 and 1. A MF is a curve that defines how each

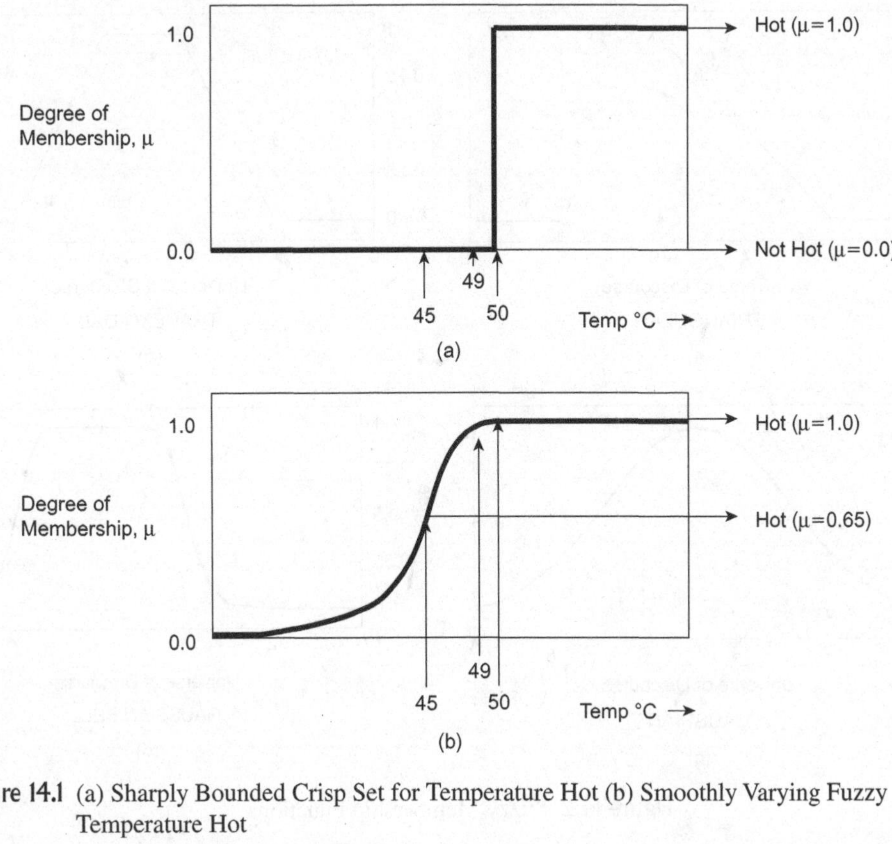

Figure 14.1 (a) Sharply Bounded Crisp Set for Temperature Hot (b) Smoothly Varying Fuzzy Set for Temperature Hot

point in the input space (UOD) is mapped to a membership value (or degree of membership of the fuzzy set) between 0 and 1.

Let us take an example of a fuzzy set of `Hot` temperature. In this case the UOD is temperature values between 10 °C and 100 °C. The linguistic term `Hot` is defined by a curve that gives the degree to which the temperature is hot. For a well-defined (crisp) boundary of a classical set, '`Hot`' may be defined as a temperature that is more than 50 °C. But such a distinction is clearly absurd. It may make sense to consider the set of all real numbers greater than 50 as belonging to set `Hot` but it is unreasonable to reject temperature 49 °C that is just 1 °C short of 50. Then, what is the right way to define the set of `Hot` temperature? Figure 14.1 shows a crisp and a fuzzy set for temperature `Hot`. The output-axis represents the membership value of an element of the fuzzy set that varies between 0 and 1. The curve is known as a MF and is often denoted by μ. Here, all temperature values are considered as `Hot`, 50 °C being 'Hot' to degree = 1.0, 49 °C `Hot` to about 0.9 degree and 45 °C being `Hot` to degree = 0.65.

The simplest MFs are formed using straight lines. Triangular MF (`trimf` in Fuzzy Logic Toolbox™), is the simplest and described by the three points forming a triangle. The trapezoidal MF, (`trapmf`) has a flat top. The two MFs are shown in Figure 14.2(a) and (b), respectively.

Fuzzy Logic Toolbox also provides two MFs built on the Gaussian distribution curve: a simple Gaussian curve `gaussmf` and a two-sided composite of two different Gaussian curves `gauss2mf`. Another MF, the generalized bell function `gbellmf`, is specified by three parameters. Gaussian and bell shaped MFs are very popular because they are smooth, differentiable and non-zero at all points in the UOD. The two MFs are shown in Figure 14.2(c) and (d).

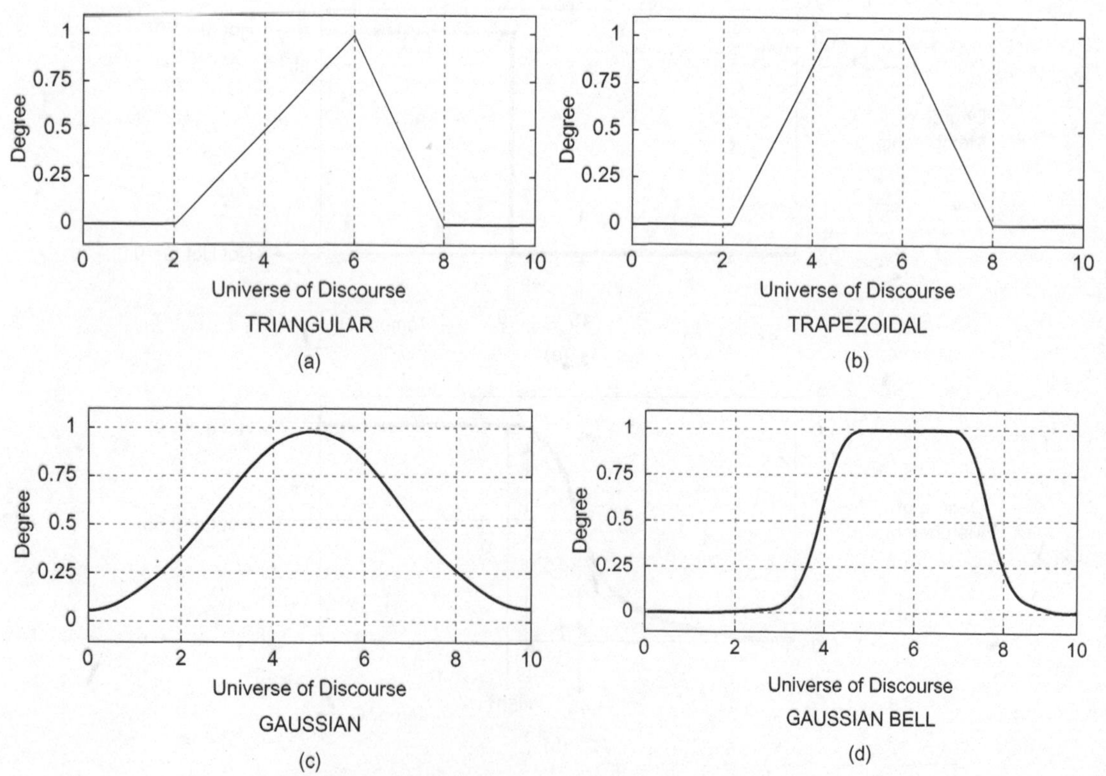

Figure 14.2 Fuzzy Membership Functions

Table 14.1 Binary and Fuzzy Operations on Binary Values

A	B	Min(A, B)	A	B	Max(A, B)	A	(1-A)
0	0	0	0	0	0	0	1
0	1	0	0	1	1	1	0
1	0	0	1	0	1		
1	1	1	1	1	1		
	AND			OR		NOT	

Table 14.2 Fuzzy Operations on Real Values

A	B	Min(A, B)	A	B	Max(A, B)	A	(1-A)
0.50	0.75	0.50	0.50	0.75	0.75	0.76	0.24
0.80	0.51	0.51	0.80	0.51	0.80	0.16	0.84
0.10	0.24	0.10	0.10	0.24	0.24		
1.00	0.95	0.95	1.00	0.95	1.00		
	AND			OR		NOT	

14.3 FUZZY OPERATIONS

Fuzzy logical reasoning is a superset of standard Boolean logic. In other words, if we keep the fuzzy values at their extremes of 1 (completely true), and 0 (completely false), standard logical operations will hold. As an example, consider the standard truth tables given in Table 14.1. The binary AND, OR and NOT operations are implemented by the numeric functions `min` (i.e., minimum), `max` (i.e., maximum) and `complement` (i.e., 1-A), respectively. The three operations also define the fuzzy intersection or conjunction (`AND`), fuzzy union or disjunction (`OR`), and fuzzy complement (`NOT`) operations. It is seen from Table 14.1 that binary and fuzzy operations are identical when the variables A and B are crisp in nature.

But in fuzzy logic the truth of any statement is a matter of degree to which an element is a member of the set and its value can vary between 0 and 1. The fuzzy operations on real (fuzzy) variables are illustrated in Table 14.2. Here, the values of variables in table indicate the degree to which these belong to the fuzzy set. It can be easily seen that the `min`, `max` and `complement` operations used to implement the fuzzy AND, OR and NOT operations for binary values can be used for the real values as well.

> **Programming Tip 14.1:** In fuzzy logic a variety of function pairs can be used to implement the fuzzy intersection or conjunction (`AND`), union or disjunction (`OR`), and complement (`NOT`) operations.

14.4 THE RULE MATRIX

The `If-Then` rule statements illustrated in Section 14.3 are used to formulate the conditional statements that comprise fuzzy logic. A single fuzzy If-Then rule assumes the form

`If` x_1 is 'a_1' AND x_2 is 'a_2' then y_1 is 'b_1'

where a_1, a_2 and b_1 are linguistic values defined by fuzzy sets on the ranges x_1, x_2 and y_1, respectively.

e(t) / c(t)	NL	NM	NS	ZE	PS	PM	PL
NL	–	–	–	NL[25]	–	–	–
NM	–	–	–	NM[24]	–	–	–
NS	–	–	NS[23]	NS[22]	NS[21]	–	–
ZE	NL[20]	NM[19]	NS[18]	ZE[17]	PS[16]	PM[15]	PL[14]
PS			PS[13]	PS[12]	PS[11]	PM[10]	PL[9]
PM	–	–	–	PM[8]	PM[7]	PM[6]	PL[5]
PL	–	–	–	PL[4]	PL[3]	PL[2]	PL[1]

Figure 14.3 An Example Rule Matrix

The If part of the rule 'x_1 is "a_1" AND x_2 is "a_2"' is called the antecedent, while the then part of the rule 'y_1 is "b_1"' is called the consequent. An example of such a rule might be

If temperature is 'hot' AND flow is 'small' then heat is 'zero'

Note that `hot` and `small` are represented by the degree of membership of their respective fuzzy sets. On the other hand, `zero` is represented as a fuzzy set. So, the consequent is an assignment that assigns the entire fuzzy set `zero` to the output variable `heat`. In general, the input to an If-Then rule is the current value for input variable (in example: temperature and flow) and output is an entire fuzzy set (in example: `zero`).

The rule base can also be described as a matrix, where rows are represented by one fuzzy input variable and the columns by the second fuzzy input variable. The elements of the matrix correspond to the output fuzzy variable associated with the inputs indicated by the row–column indices in the matrix. Although not absolutely necessary, rule matrices usually have an odd number of rows and columns to accommodate a `zero` centre row and column region. This may not be needed as long as the functions on either side of the centre overlap somewhat and continuous dithering of the output is acceptable. It is also possible to have a different number of rows than columns. The maximum number of possible rules is simply the product of the number of rows and columns.

> **Programming Tip 14.2:** Definition of all possible rules may not be necessary since some input conditions may never occur in a practical situation.

An example rule matrix is shown in Figure 14.3. The columns represent the fuzzy set of antecedent *e*(*t*), error and the rows represent the antecedent *ce*(*t*), change in error. The entries in the matrix define the '`Then`' side of the rules, that is, the fuzzy set associated with the consequent. The empty entries in the rule matrix indicate that the corresponding input conditions may never occur in practical situations and, therefore, no rules are needed to be defined for them.

14.5 FUZZY INFERENCE SYSTEMS

Fuzzy inference systems (FIS) have been successfully applied in variety of fields such as automatic control, data classification, decision analysis, expert systems etc. Fuzzy inference is the process of mapping a given set of inputs to an output using fuzzy logic defined by the fuzzy 'If-Then' rule database. The mapping provides a basis for computing the decisions. The process of fuzzy inference involves all factors discussed in previous sections, namely MFs, fuzzy logic operators and If-Then rules. There are two types of FIS that can be implemented:

- Mamdani-type
- Sugeno-type

These two types of inference systems vary in the way outputs are determined. Mamdani model was proposed by Ebrahim Mamdani in 1975 and is the most commonly used fuzzy methodology today. It uses fuzzy sets to describe the output variable. To convert the fuzzy output to crisp form, a process called defuzzification is used. In Sugeno-type systems, output variables are described as linear functions or constants and simplifies the computation required. Though, it enhances the efficiency of the defuzzification process, the output cannot be expressed in linguistic terms.

The FIS for Mamdani model can be broadly divided into five major steps:

1. Fuzzification of input variables, i.e., antecedents.
2. Application of fuzzy operator(s) (`AND` or `OR`) to find degree of matching of the antecedents, i.e., the `If` part of the rule base.
3. Mapping degree of matching to fuzzy outputs, i.e., consequents.
4. Aggregation of fuzzy outputs of all rules.
5. Defuzzification of the aggregated fuzzy output.

14.5.1 Fuzzification of Input Variables

The first step is to take the inputs and determine the degree to which they belong to each of the appropriate fuzzy sets with the help of their MFs. In the Fuzzy Logic Toolbox, the input is always a crisp numerical value limited to the UOD of the input variable. The output of its fuzzification is degree of membership corresponding to this numerical value defined by the qualifying linguistic set. Fuzzifying crisp input quantity for one of the fuzzy sets is shown in Figure 14.4. The crisp inputs are fuzzified for all other fuzzy sets defining that variable. For example, variable temperature may be defined by fuzzy sets: `Hot`, `Normal` and `Cold`.

14.5.2 Application of Fuzzy Operators

Normally, there are multiple inputs, that is antecedents, mentioned on the left `If` part of the rule. The fuzzy logic operators that describe the relation between different inputs are then applied in order to combine them

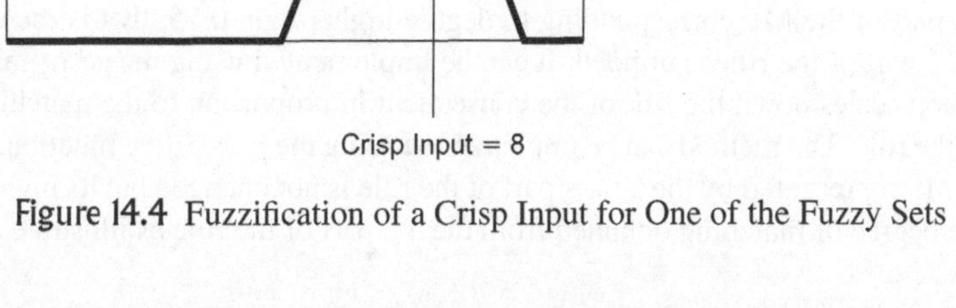

Figure 14.4 Fuzzification of a Crisp Input for One of the Fuzzy Sets

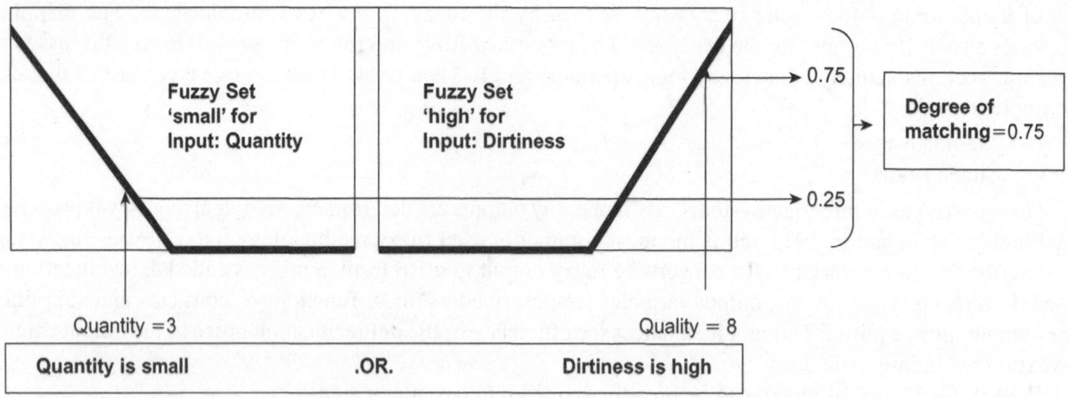

Figure 14.5 Application of Fuzzy Operator to Multiple Part Antecedents

and obtain the result of the left part of the rule. The inputs to a fuzzy operator are two or more membership values (degrees) from the fuzzified input variables. The result is the degree of matching or the degree of support for that rule and its value is between 0 and 1. This degree of matching is determined for each rule describing the system.

In Fuzzy Logic Toolbox, two built-in AND methods: *min* (minimum) and *prod* (product) and two built-in OR methods: *max* (maximum), and the probabilistic OR method, *probor*, are supported. The probabilistic OR method is calculated according to the equation:

```
probor(a, b) = a + b - ab
```

> **Programming Tip 14.3:** In addition to these built-in methods, one can create his own methods for AND and OR by writing any function and setting that to his method of choice.

The application of fuzzy operator OR is illustrated in Figure 14.5. The two inputs `Quantity = 3` and `Dirtiness = 8` are represented by their fuzzified values (i.e., 0.25 and 0.75) in the fuzzy sets `small` and `high`, respectively. The OR fuzzy operator (`max`) is applied on the two inputs to obtain the degree of matching for `If` part of the rule: `If Quantity is small OR Dirtiness is high Then......`

14.5.3 Mapping of Degree of Matching to Fuzzy Outputs

The degree of matching obtained for the left `If` part of each rule by applying the fuzzy operators to the inputs, i.e., antecedents, is used to evaluate the conclusion or inference by mapping it on to the `Then` part of each rule. The mapping can be implemented using two methods: Clipping and Scaling. The two methods map the matching degree of the inputs to obtain the conclusion by modifying the MF of the consequent, i.e., outputs, differently. Both functions are supported by the Fuzzy Logic Toolbox.

The clipping method used in the Mamdani approach cuts or clips off part of the MF of the consequent corresponding to degree higher than that obtained by matching the `If` part of the rule. The method is illustrated in Figure 14.6. The part of the MF corresponding to degree higher than 0.75, that is the degree of matching obtained from the `If` part of the rule is clipped. It can be implemented using the `min` (minimum) function.

The scaling method scales down the MF of the consequent in proportion to the matching degree obtained from the `If` part of the rule. The method can be implemented using the `product` function. In this method, the shape of the output MF represented by the `Then` part of the rule is not changed but its highest degree is scaled by equating it to the degree of matching obtained from the `If` part of the rule as illustrated in Figure 14.7.

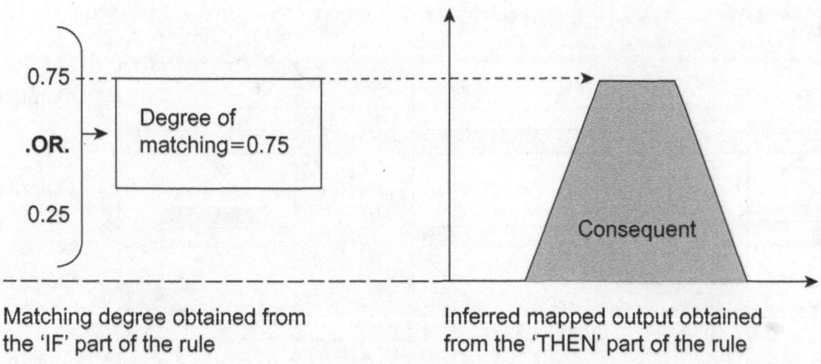

Figure 14.6 Application of Mapping Using Clipping Method

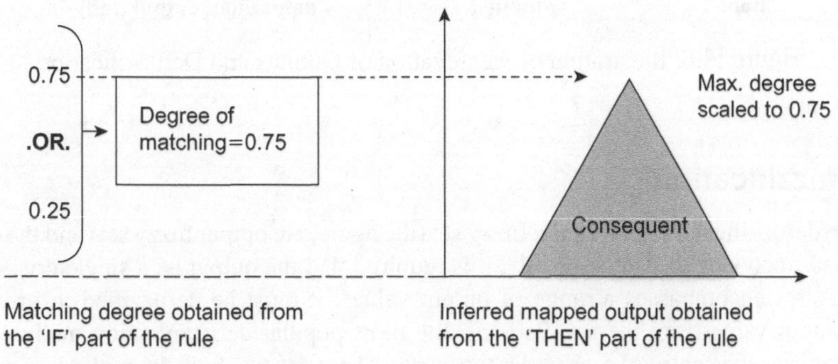

Figure 14.7 Application of Mapping Using Scaling Method

Mapping of degree of matching is implemented for each rule in the rulebase defining the behaviour of the system. Further, every rule has a *weight* (a number between 0 and 1), that is, the importance attached to the rule depending on the problem at hand. This weight value is multiplied to the matching degree obtained from the antecedents.

> **Programming Tip 14.4:** The importance of an `If-Then` rule relative to the others may be varied by changing its weight value.

14.5.4 Aggregation of Outputs

Since decisions are based on all the rules in the rulebase the fuzzy output obtained from each rule must be combined in order to compute the final composite output fuzzy set. This process is called 'Composition' or 'Aggregation'. Aggregation is carried out for each output variable. The output of the aggregation process is one fuzzy set for each output variable. The aggregation method is commutative and the order in which the rules are executed is not important.

Three built-in composition methods are supported in Fuzzy Logic Toolbox: `max` (maximum), `probor` (probabilistic OR), and `sum` (simply the sum of each rule's output set). In Figure 14.8, outputs of three rules defining the washing machine example problem have been placed together to show how they are combined, or aggregated, into a single fuzzy set. The aggregated fuzzy output is also given.

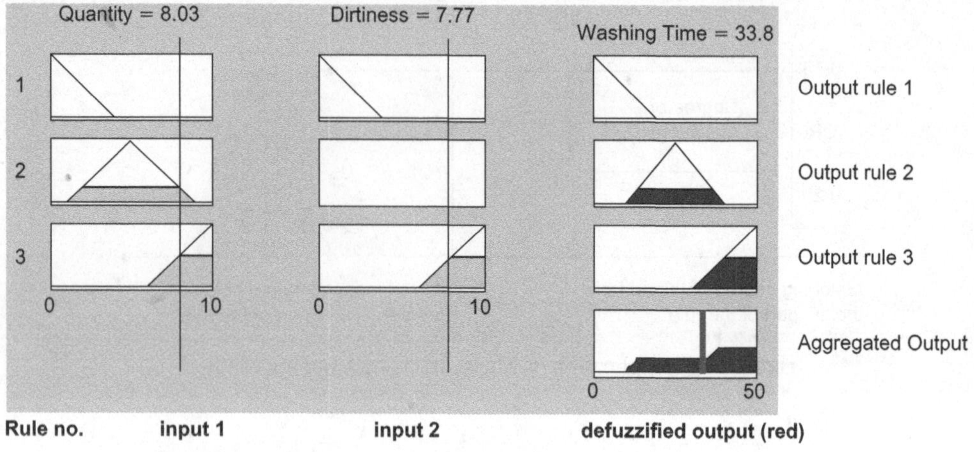

Figure 14.8 Illustration of Aggregation of Outputs and Defuzzification

14.5.5 Defuzzification

The input for the defuzzification process is a fuzzy set (the aggregate output fuzzy set) and the output obtained is also aggregated fuzzy output. But generally, it is required that the output be a single crisp number. As the aggregated fuzzy set encompasses a range of output values, it must be defuzzified in order to resolve to a single crisp output value from the set. Perhaps, the most popular defuzzification method is the centroid method, which returns the centre of area under the curve. There are five built-in methods supported in Fuzzy Logic Toolbox: centroid, bisector, middle of maximum (the average of the maximum value of the output set), largest of maximum and smallest of maximum.

Defuzzification using centroid method is illustrated in Figure 14.8.

14.6 WASHING MACHINE PROBLEM

In the next section we shall build a FLC for the two-input, one-output, three-rule washing machine problem discussed earlier in Section 14.2. The basic structure of FLC is shown in the Figure 14.9.

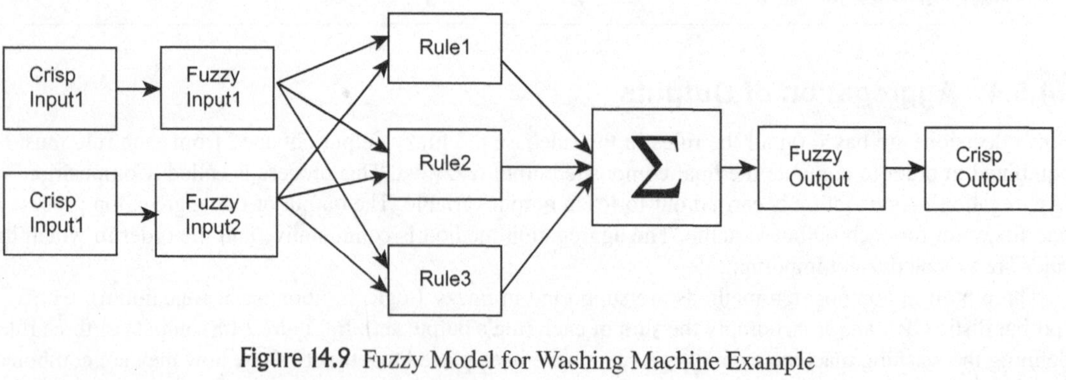

Figure 14.9 Fuzzy Model for Washing Machine Example

The two crisp inputs `Quality` and `Dirtiness` vary from 0 to 10 and are presented as fuzzy sets defined by their respective MFs. Let the output; `washing time` be allowed to have three linguistic values `small`, `average` and `large`. Similarly, let the input variable; `quantity` of clothes be expressed as `small`, `normal` and `large` and `dirtiness` of clothes be described as being `low`, `normal` and `high`. Information flows from left to right, from two inputs to a single output, i.e., `washing time` that varies from 0 to 50 minutes. The inputs are applied in parallel to all the rules, that is, three rules defined in the example. The rules are listed below for the convenience of the reader.

```
%If quantity is small or dirtiness is low, Then washingtime is small
%If quantity is medium, Then washingtime is average
%If quantity is large or dirtiness is high, Then washingtime is large
```

The fuzzy conclusion is derived from each rule and is summed or aggregated to obtain the output. This output is then defuzzified to obtain it in crisp form.

14.7 BUILDING SYSTEMS WITH GRAPHICAL USER INTERFACE

Let us now build a FLC for the example discussed above using GUI tools supported by the Fuzzy Logic Toolbox. It is possible to use the toolbox by working from the command line alone, but it is much easier to build a system graphically using GUI tools. The Fuzzy Inference System is shown in Figure 14.10. There are mainly five primary GUI tools:

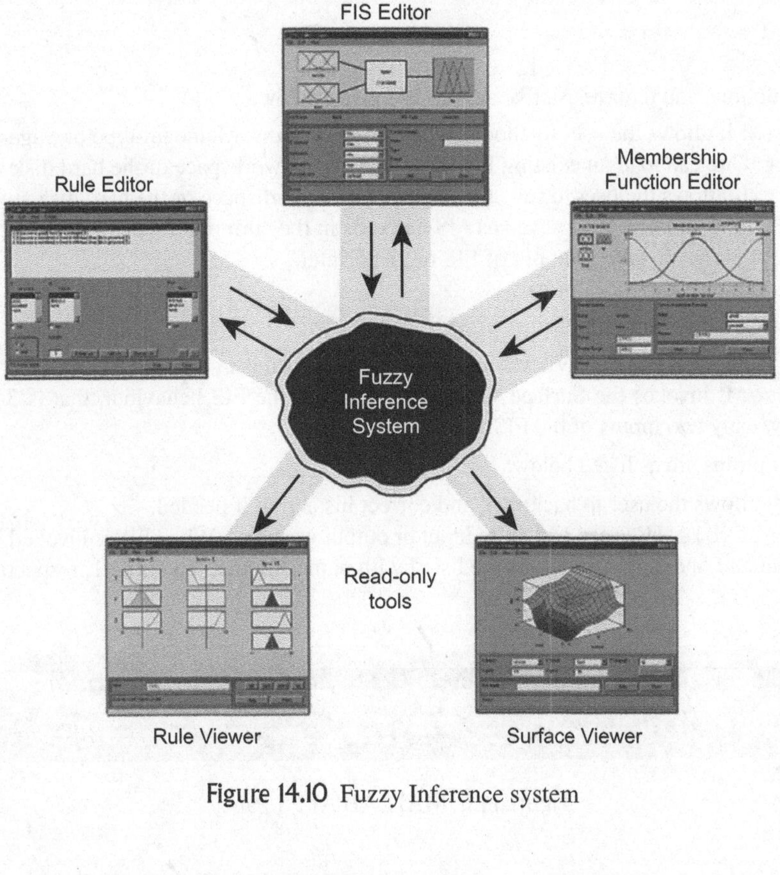

Figure 14.10 Fuzzy Inference system

1. FIS Editor,
2. MF Editor,
3. Rule Editor,
4. Rule Viewer,
5. Surface Viewer.

These GUIs are linked with one another and can all interact and exchange information. Changes made in one GUI are immediately reflected in the other relevant GUI. These can read and write both to from the workspace and the disk. The FIS Editor, the MF Editor, and the Rule Editor can all read and modify the FIS data, but the Rule Viewer and the Surface Viewer are for viewing only and do not modify any FIS data.

In addition to these five primary GUIs, the toolbox includes the graphical ANFIS Editor GUI, which is used for building and analyzing Sugeno-type adaptive neuro-fuzzy systems.

14.7.1 FIS Editor

It is the main GUI that is used to develop FIS graphically. It is used to define the number of inputs and outputs of the fuzzy system. It can be invoked by:

- typing `fuzzy` at the command line.
- Choosing 'APPS' menubar and then clicking 'Fuzzy Logic Designer' icon add icon as shown in Figure 14.11. 

The FIS window is then opened and is shown in Figure 14.12. The main menu in the FIS window carries three items:

(a) File
(b) Edit
(c) View

The File menu options and their respective actions are given below:

- `New FIS`: It allows the user to choose type of FIS systems; Mamdani-type or Sugeno-type.
- `Import`: One can load an existing FIS system from the workspace or the hard disk storage.
- `Export`: It allows the user to save the current FIS in workspace or the hard disk storage. The name of the FIS is given here. It is saved as FIS name.fis in the current directory.
- `Print`: It allows to take print out of FIS on the printer.
- `Close`: It closes the FIS window.

There are only two View menu options:

- `Rules`: It invokes the Rule Viewer and displays all the rules in the FIS.
- `Surface`: It invokes the Surface Viewer and displays the FIS behaviour, that is 3-D graph of the output v/s any two inputs of the FIS.

The Edit menu options are as listed below:

- `Undo`: It allows the user to backtrack and correct his action if needed.
- `Add variable`: User can add more input or output variables. When FIS is invoked, by default only one input and one output variables are listed with names input1 and output1, respectively.

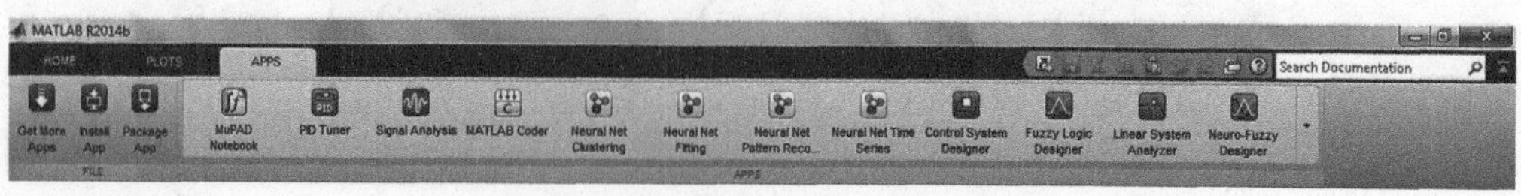

Figure.14.11 MATLAB APPS Panel

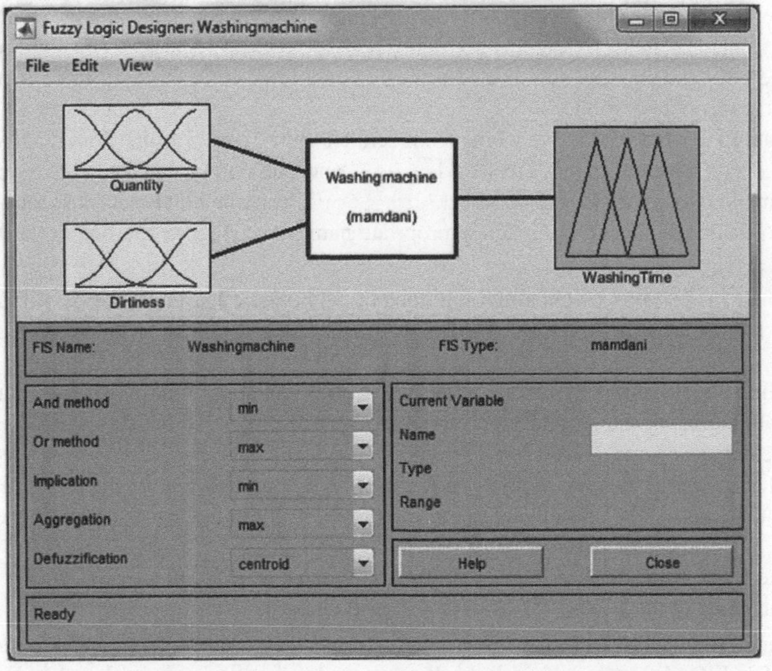

Figure 14.12 The FIS Editor Window for the Washing Machine Fuzzy Inference System

- `Remove variable`: It allows user to remove one or more of the input or output variables from the FIS.
- `Membership Functions`: This option invokes the MF Editor. The editor helps in defining the number and type of MFs of input and output fuzzy variables.
- `Rules`: It invokes the Rule Editor and allows the user to define the If-Then rules defining the knowledge base of the FIS.

The FIS Editor displays general information about a FIS and is shown in Figure 14.12. Below the main menu, the graph field boxes show the names of each input variable (on left), and output variable (on right). The sample MFs shown in the boxes are just icons and do not give the actual shapes of the MFs. The middle box shows the name and the type of FIS, which are also displayed below these boxes in a text field. This part of the FIS window is shown below in Figure 14.13.

Below this text field, there are three more text fields, one on the left and two on the right. The text field on the lower left allows the user to define the fuzzy inference functions, such as `AND` method, `OR` method, `implication` method, `aggregation` method and `defuzzification` method. There are pop-up menus associated with each and help the user to choose from various methods or functions available in the Fuzzy Logic Toolbox.

The text field on the right allow the user to edit the names of the input and output variables. The specific variable needs to be first selected by clicking once on the relevant icon in the graph field before its name can

Figure 14.13 Part of FIS Editor Window Showing the Name and Type of FIS

be changed. The `type` of variable, that is, whether it is input or output variable and its `range` are displayed below its name in the text field. Below this text field there are two `help` and `close` buttons. `Help` button facilitates online help and `close` button closes the FIS window. At the bottom, there is a status line that describes the most recent operation.

To start building FLC for washing machine from scratch, type `fuzzy` at the Command Window prompt. The FIS Editor opens with one input, labelled `input1`, and one output, labelled `output1`. The washing machine problem has two inputs, therefore, select `Add input` from the Edit menu. A second yellow coloured box labelled `input2` will appear. To assign appropriate names to the input and output variables, follow the following steps:

- Select the `input1` box by clicking on it once (a red boundary around the box will appear).
- Change the name of the first input variable to `Quantity` in the text window on the right and press Return.
- Select the `input2` box by clicking on it once (a red boundary around the box will appear).
- Change the name of the second input variable to `Dirtiness` in the text window on the right and press Return.
- Select the `output1` box by clicking on it once (a red boundary around the box will appear).
- Change the name of the output variable to `WashingTime` in the text window on the right and press Return.
- From the `File` menu, select `Export` option and then `To Workspace`.
- Enter the name of the FIS as `WMachineFLC` and click on `OK`.

The functions and methods given in the lower left text field may not be changed and kept in their default positions only. The FIS editor window with the changes updated will appear as shown in Figure 14.12. The name of the FIS will also appear in the workspace. The FIS needs to be exported (saved) to disk as well so that, it may not have to be defined again from scratch.

14.7.2 Membership Function Editor

Membership Function Editor is used to display and edit the types of MFs of the input and output fuzzy variables associated with the FIS. The linguistic names and parameters of each MF can also be defined using this GUI. This GUI shares many features with the FIS Editor. In fact, all five basic GUI tools have similar menu items, status lines, and `Help` and `Close` buttons. The options for menu item `File` and `View` remain the same. The Edit menu options change to take care of new edit functions of the GUI. The Edit options are as listed below:

- `Undo`: It allows the user to backtrack and correct his action if needed.
- `Add MFs`: One can add new MFs to the currently selected input or output variable. When MF Editor is invoked, by default each input or output variable contains three MFs.
- `Add custom MFs`: User defined MFs are added to the currently selected input or output variable.
- `Remove selected MF`: It allows user to remove one or more of MFs from the currently selected input or output variable.
- `Remove All MFs`: It allows user to remove all MFs from the currently selected input or output variable
- `FIS properties`: This option invokes the FIS Editor.
- `Rules`: It invokes the Rule Editor and allows the user to define the If-Then rules defining the knowledge base of the FIS.

Membership Function Editor can be invoked in number of ways:

- From the Edit menu select option: `MFs`
- Double-click on the icon for the input or output variable.
- Type `mfedit` at the command prompt.

The Membership Function Editor Window for the washing machine FIS is shown in Figure 14.14.

The graph field of Membership Function Editor Window displays the FIS input and output variables and all MFs of the variable currently selected. The user can click on a line or curve to select a fuzzy set and can change its shape, parameters, name type etc. The user can make use of mouse to drag, move or change the shape of a selected MF.

The name and type of the current variable are displayed in the text field given on the left side of the window. This field also allows the range and display range of the current variable to be edited. The text field on the right side allows the user to edit the name and numerical parameters of the current MF. The type of current MF can be changed with the help of a pop-up menu.

Let us now follow the steps given below to define the MFs of input and output variables of the washing machine example.

1. Select the first input variable, `Quantity`, by clicking on it.
2. Enter the `Range` and the `Display Range` as [0 10].
3. Using `Edit` menu, select option `Add MFs`.. to add MFs to the current variable and select their type. Select three MFs and type as triangular, i.e., `trimf`.
4. Click on the three MF curves one by one and change their names to `small`, `medium` and `large`. Also use the mouse to change their parameters to [0 0 4], [1 5 9] and [6 10 10], respectively.

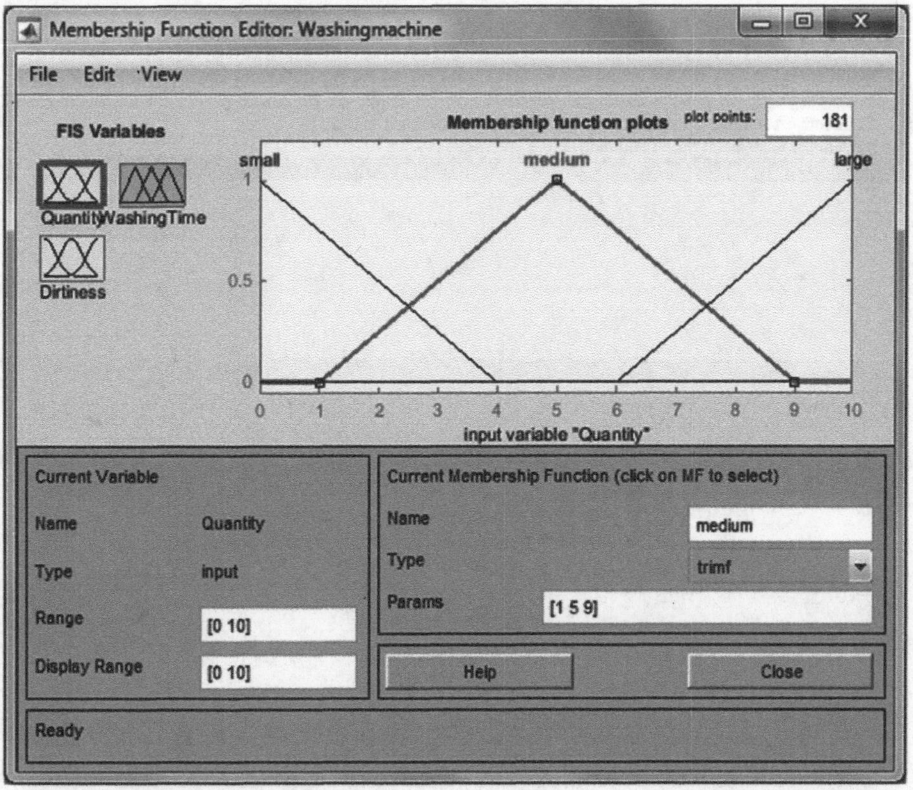

Figure 14.14 The Membership Function Editor Window for the Washing Machine Fuzzy Inference System

5. Select the second input variable, `Dirtiness`, by clicking on it.
6. Enter the ranges and add MFs exactly as done for the first input variable above. The names of the three MFs must be kept as `low`, `normal` and `high`, respectively.
7. Select the output variable, `WashingTime`, by clicking on it.
8. Enter the ranges as [0 50] and add three MFs named `small`, `average` and `large` with parameters [0 0 20], [10 25 40] and [35 50 50], respectively.

The membership Function Editor window will appear as shown in Figure 14.14.

14.7.3 Rule Editor

The Rule Editor is used for defining the rules in the rulebase of the FIS. These rules act as the knowledge store house on the basis of which the system draws the inference.
The Rule Editor can be invoked using two ways:

1. Select `Edit Rules` option from the `View` menu
2. Typing the command `ruleedit` at the command prompt

The Rule Editor window opens and is as shown in Figure 14.15.

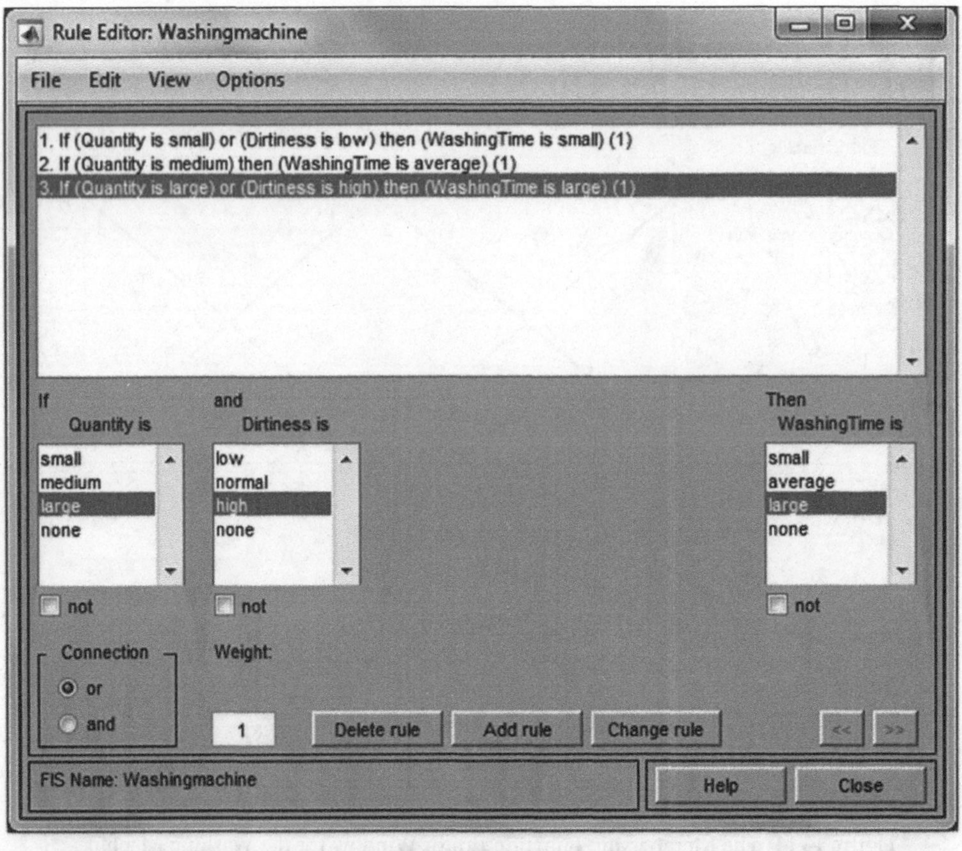

Figure 14.15 Rule Editor Window Showing Rules for the Washing Machine Problem

The main menu has four options, namely `File`, `Edit`, `View` and `Options`. The `File` and `View` menus are same as in FIS editor. The `Edit` menu options are as listed below:

- `Undo`: It allows the user to backtrack and correct his action if needed.
- `FIS properties`: This option invokes the FIS Editor.
- `Membership Functions`: This option invokes the Membership Function Editor.

The Options menu contains the following items:

- From the `Edit` menu select option: `Membership Functions`
- `Language`: This allows the user to select the language for writing the rules. Three languages: English, Dutch and French are available.
- `Format`: There are three formats for displaying the rules in the rulebase, namely `Verbose`, `Symbolic` and `Indexed`.

There is no graph field in the Rule Editor Window. The text field in the top half of the editor window displays the rules defined by the user in the format selected from the `options` menu. The bottom half of the window is again divided into two parts. The left part pertains to the `If` part of the rule and is used to select the inputs and their fuzzy connections or operators. The inputs are included in the order in which they have been defined in the FIS editor automatically. The current input variable appear in a box as shown the Figure 14.15. The appropriate MF to be included in the rule is selected from the box. If any input variable is not to be included in the rule then the `none` option is selected. Selecting `not` for any input will negate the corresponding MF. The inputs are connected by clicking on one of the two fuzzy connection operators `OR` or `AND` given at left bottom corner of the editor window.

The right hand part of the bottom half contains the menu box for constructing the `Then` part of the rule by choosing the appropriate MF of the output. Another edit field at the bottom of the window is `weight`. The user can assign any value between 0 and 1 as per the importance given to that rule in the rulebase.

Three more buttons at the bottom of the window are `Delete` rule, `Add rule` and `Change rule`, respectively, and are used to delete, add or change existing rules. The status line, `Help` and `Close` buttons have their usual functions as described for other GUIs.

To define the three rules that were declared for the washing machine problem: The first rule to be inserted is as follows:

If Quantity is small or Dirtiness is low, Then WashingTime is small.

To insert the rule, follow the steps given below:

- For the first input `Quantity` select the MF `small`.
- For the second input `Dirtiness` select the MF `low`.
- Click on the `or` connection button to connect the two inputs.
- Choose the MF `small` for the output variable `WashingTime`.
- Let the `weight` be equal to 1.

The second rule to be inserted is

If Quantity is medium, Then WashingTime is average.

To insert the rule, follow the steps given below:

- For the first input `Quantity` select the MF `medium`.
- For the second input `Dirtiness` select the MF `none`. Please note that `none` has been chosen as this input is not included in the rule.
- Choose the MF `average` for the output variable `WashingTime`.
- Let the `weight` be equal to 1.

Similarly, insert the third rule given below:

If Quantity is large or Dirtiness is high, Then WashingTime is large

The rules can be displayed in different formats using the `Options` menu. The form of rules mentioned so far is the `Verbose` format which explicitly mentions the `If` and `Then` clause of the rules. The second format available is the `Symbolic` format. Here, the `If` and `Then` words are missing. The `is` connective is replaced by = =, that is `equal to` relational operator for the antecedents and =, the assignment operator for the consequents. The three rules considered in our example, if displayed in `Symbolic` format will appear as shown below:

```
1.   (Quantity = = small) or (Dirtiness = = low) => (WashingTime = small) (1)
2.   (Quantity = = medium) => (WashingTime = average) (1)
3.   (Quantity = = large) or (Dirtiness = = high) => (WashingTime = large) (1)
```

The third format is `indexed` format. In this format the rules appear as a set of numbers. The number in the first column indicates the index number of the MF of the first input variable. Likewise, the number in the second column indicates the index number of the MF of the second input variable. If there are no more input variables, (like in our example of washing machine), the next column indicates the index number of the MF of the output variable. The next column displays the weight applied to that rule. The last column indicates the type of connection used to combine the inputs, that is 2 used for `OR` and 1 used for `AND`.
For first rule, the indexed form will appear as

1, 1, 1(1): 1

It can be read as *If input1 is MF1 (the first MF of input1) or input2 is MF2 (the first MF of input2), then output1 is MF1 (the first MF of output1) with weight* = 1.

The Rule Editor window with rules defined for the washing machine problem in Verbose format is shown in Figure 14.15.

14.7.4 Rule Viewer

The Rule Viewer is used for viewing the FIS. It enables the user to understand how each rule contributes towards the output or the role played by each rule. It also aids the user to find out if the fuzzy system components are behaving in the right manner or not. It shows which rules are active and how each MF influences the results. To invoke the Rule Viewer, select `View rules...` from the `View` menu.

Each row of plots represents one rule. The three small plots across the top of the Rule Viewer window represent the antecedent and consequent of the first rule. Each rule is a row of plots, and each column is a variable. The first two columns of plots show the MFs representing the antecedent, or the If part of each rule. The third column of plots shows the MFs representing the consequent, or the then part of each rule. If you click once on a rule number, the corresponding rule will be displayed at the bottom of the figure. The fourth plot in the third column of plots represents the aggregated fuzzy output of the fuzzy system.

The Rule Viewer window for the Washing Machine problem is shown in Figure 14.16. The crisp inputs to the FIS can be entered in the text field given on the lower right of the window. Upon clicking anywhere on any of the plots, the toolbox immediately evaluates the fuzzy inference and modifies the plots. The crisp inputs can also be changed by dragging the red index lines on the antecedent plots with the help of a mouse.

> **Programming Tip 14.5:** The Rule Viewer can become unwieldy for large multi-input–multi-output systems, but, for a relatively small number of inputs and outputs, it performs well.

14.7.5 Surface Viewer

The Surface Viewer generates and plots an output surface map for the system for one or two of the inputs and the output. It is strictly a read-only tool. The surface view for the washing machine problem is given in Figure 14.17.

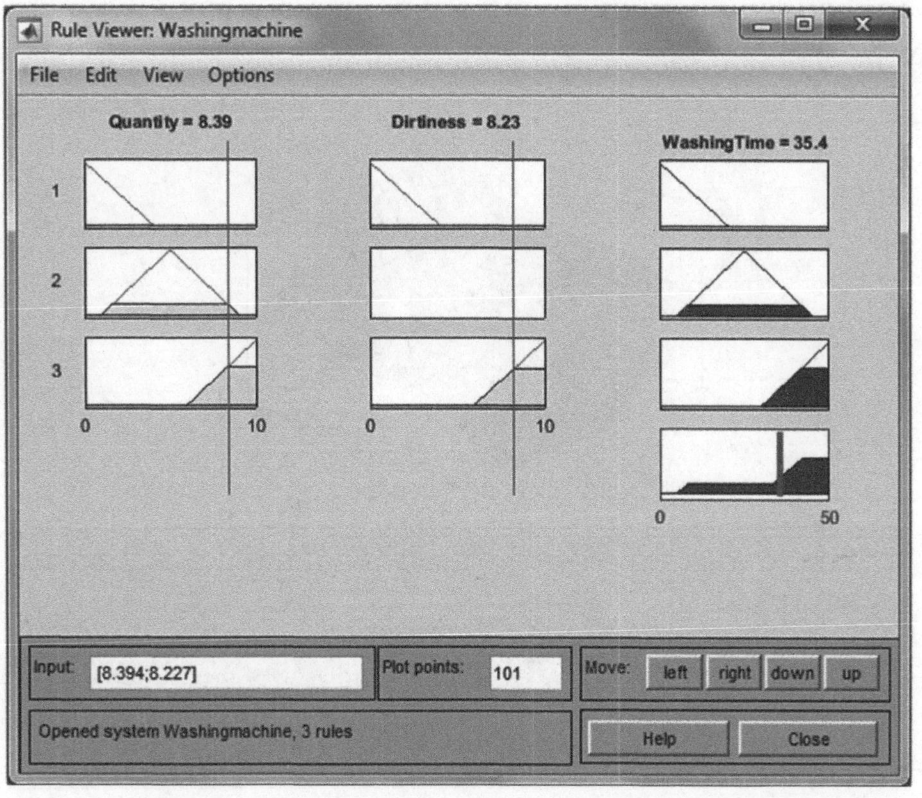

Figure 14.16 Rule Viewer Window for the Washing Machine Problem

For fuzzy systems having more than two inputs and one output, any two inputs and any one output can be selected from the pop-up menu for the plot. The two text input fields allow the user to define the number of x and y-axis grid lines. The surface view for different angles can be generated simply by grabbing the axis with the help of mouse and rotating the figure. Another view of the surface generated in Figure 14.17 is shown in Figure 14.18.

14.7.6 Importing and Exporting FIS System

The fuzzy system designed using fuzzy tools can be saved to disk. MATLAB creates an ASCII text FIS file representing that system with the file suffix `.fis`. The fuzzy system created for Washing Machine problem is saved on disk with the filename `WMachineFLC.fis`. This text file can be edited and modified and is simple to understand. When the fuzzy system is exported or saved to the MATLAB workspace, a variable is created that acts as a MATLAB structure for the FIS system representing the fuzzy system.

> **Programming Tip 14.6:** If the `FIS` is not saved on the disk, but only to the MATLAB `workspace`, it cannot be recovered for later use in a new MATLAB session.

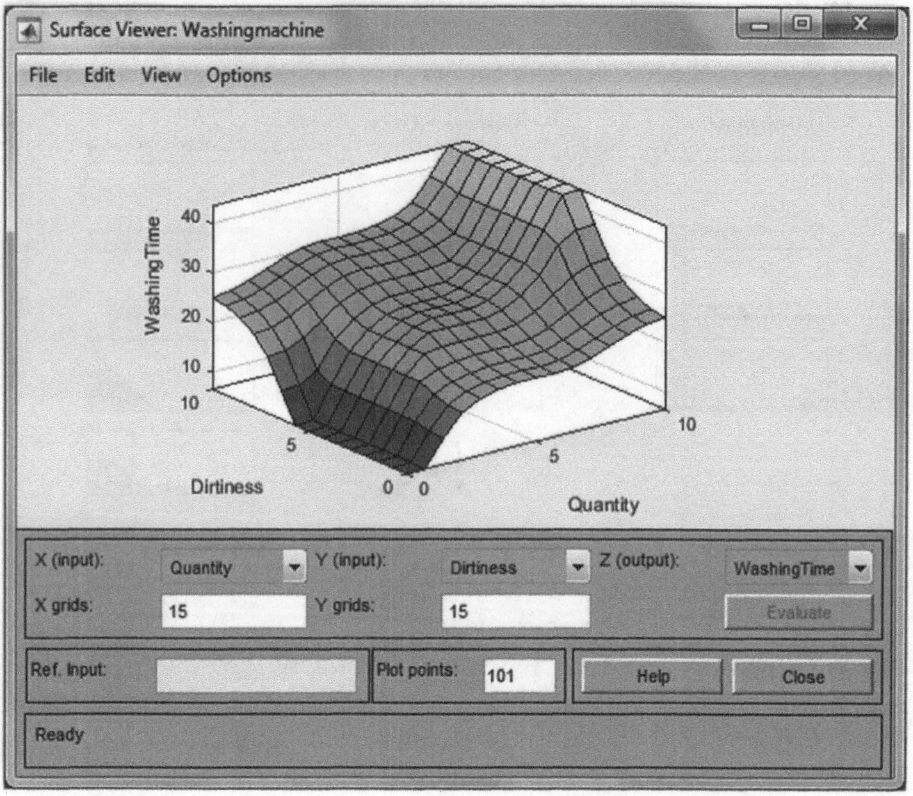

Figure 14.17 The Surface Viewer Window for the Washing Machine Problem

14.8 WORKING FROM THE COMMAND LINE

It is possible to use the Fuzzy Logic Toolbox without using the GUI tools. The command-line functions associated with FIS construction are described in brief hereafter:

1. **newfis**

   The `newfis` command is used to define the name of the new variable that identifies the FIS being created. The syntax of the command is given as under:

   ```
   abc = newfis('WMachineFLC');
   ```

   `abc` is the identifier that is associated with the FIS `WMachineFLC`.

2. **addvar**

   The command `addvar` adds the variable, input or output to the FIS. The syntax is given as under:

   ```
   abc = addvar(abc, 'input', 1, 'Quantity', [0 10]);
   ```

   The statement above adds the input variable `Quantity` having range 0 to 10 to the FIS identified by `abc`.

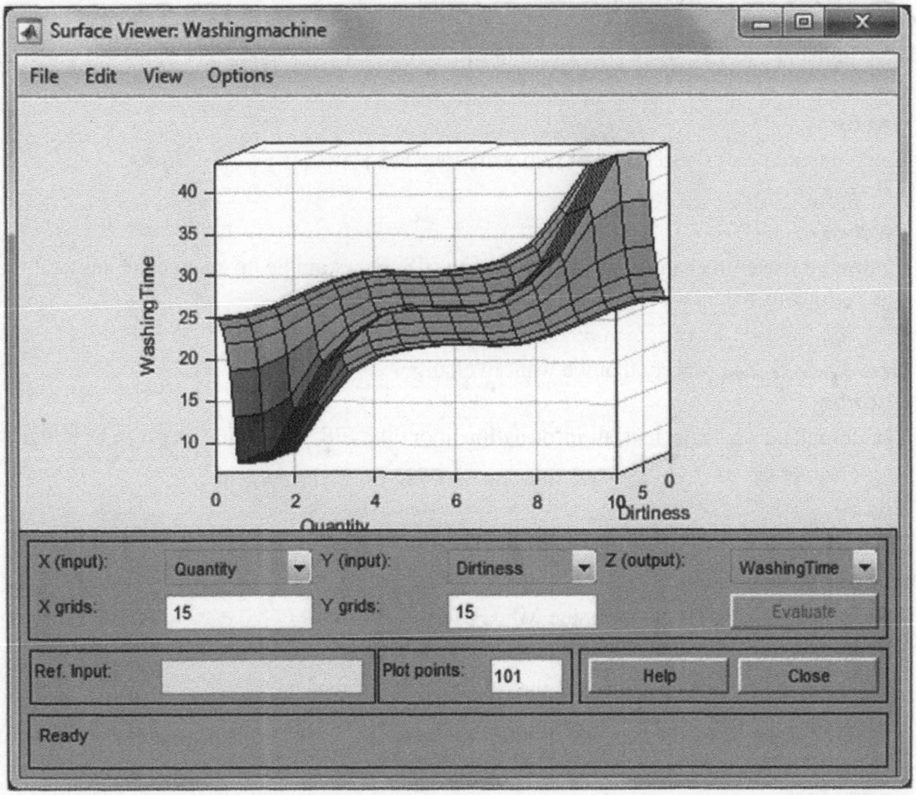

Figure 14.18 The Surface Viewer Window Showing Surface from Different Angle for the Washing Machine Problem

3. **addmf**

The command addmf adds the MF to the variable, input or output to the FIS. The syntax is given as under:

```
abc = addmf(abc,'input',1,'small','trimf',[0 0 1.5]);
```

The statement above adds the MF small to the first input variable, that is Quantity to the FIS identified by abc. The type of MF is triangular with 0, 0 and 1.5 as values on the universe of discourse corresponding to its 3 vertices.

4. **addrule**

The command addrule adds an If-Then rule to the FIS. The syntax is given as under:

```
rulelist = [ ….; 7 7 7 1 1; 1 6 3 1 1; 2 6 4 1 1 ];
abc = addrule(abc, rulelist);
```

or

```
abc = addrule(abc,[..; 7 7 7 1 1; 1 6 3 1 1; 2 6 4 1 1 ] );
```

5. **readfis**

   The command `readfis` reads the FIS into the MATLAB workspace. The syntax is given as under:

```
abc = readfis('WMachineFLC.fis')
```

6. **getfis**

   The command `getfis` gets the FIS information. The syntax is given as under:

```
getfis (abc)
```

7. **setfis**

   It allows the user to change any property of an FIS. For example, to change the name of the system. The following statement is given:

```
abc = setfis(abc, 'name', 'WMflc');
```

   Here `name` is the property that we want to change.

8. **showfis**

   The command `showfis` lists all information about the FIS. The syntax is given as under:

```
showfis(abc)
```

9. **fuzzy**

   The command `fuzzy` invokes the fuzzy GUI tool.

10. **mfedit**

    The command `mfedit` invokes the MF GUI tool.

11. **ruleedit**

    The command `ruleedit` invokes the rule editor GUI tool.

12. **ruleview**

    The command `ruleview` displays the Rule Viewer.

13. **surfview**

    The command `surfview` displays the Surface Viewer.

14. **plotfis**

    The `plotfis` displays the whole FIS system as a block diagram.

15. **plotmf**

    The command `plotmf` plots all the MFs associated with a given variable. The syntax is as given below:

```
plotmf(abc, 'input', 1)
```

16. **gensurf**

    The command `gensurf` generates a plot of two inputs versus any one output of a given system.

17. **evalfis**

    The command `evalfis` is used to evaluate the output of a FIS for a given input. The syntax is as given below:

```
abc = readfis('WMachineFLC');
evalfis([1 2], abc)
ans =
        7.6388
```

`evalfis` command can also be used with multiple inputs. The syntax is shown below:

```
evalfis([1 4; 2 3], abc)
```

```
ans =
        8.1234
        3.6543
```

18. **writefis**

    The command `writefis` is used to save the FIS to disk.

19. **showrule**

    The `showrule` command displays all rules in Verbose format for the FIS associated with the matrix abc.

    ```
    showrule(abc);
    ```

14.9 FUZZY CONTROLLER EXAMPLE

The Water Bath Temperature Control System example taken to describe the building of a neural network controller in Chapter 13 is taken for illustrating the MATLAB commands used in developing the FLC.

14.9.1 Description of Water Bath Temperature Control System

The objective is to implement an ANN controller for a temperature control system. The process considered here is one of the most widely used processes in the process industry, a Water Bath Temperature Control System. The schematic diagram of Water Bath System is shown in Figure 14.19.

The Water Bath System consists of water tank in which cold water is entering from one side and hot water is leaving from other. The water tank used is of capacity of 12 litres. The flow of water is maintained constant with flow rate 1 litre/min. A 2,500 W base heater heats the tank and to ensure even temperature distribution, a stirrer is used which rotates at 120 rpm. As the water is flowing at constant rate so a transport delay 30 sec has been incorporated into the mathematical model of the system. The temperature of water at the inlet is considered to be at room temperature, that is 25 °C. It is required to control the temperature of water in a tank.

The assumptions made for the system are

- The volume of water is constant with constant density and heat capacity.
- The inlet flow rate is equal to outlet flow rate.
- There is no change of state and uniform temperature is maintained in the tank.

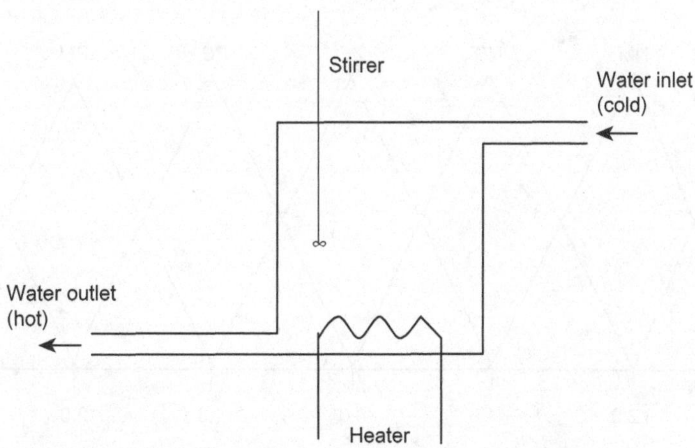

Figure 14.19 Schematic Diagram of Water Bath System

14.9.2 Fuzzy Controller for Water Bath System

The fuzzy controller is designed to obtain the desired output water temperature. The difference of output water temperature from that of the desired, that is the error in output and the change of error, form the two inputs of the fuzzy controller. The change in the heat input to be applied to the water bath is the output of the fuzzy controller. The two inputs and one output parameters of the fuzzy controller are defined over seven fuzzy sets, that is `NL` → negative large, `NM` → negative medium, `NS` → negative small, `ZE` → zero, `PL` → positive large, `PM` → positive medium, `PS` → positive small. Triangular MFs have been chosen for each fuzzy set and are shown in Figure 14.20. The Universe of discourse for the three fuzzy variables is taken to be [−3 3]. The 7 MFs for each of the two input variables make a maximum of 49 combinations. Therefore, 49 `If-Then` rules are defined for the fuzzy controller. In the example, the system is simulated using the differential equation describing the system, which is solved using ODE solver in MATLAB.

The program for defining the FLC for the water bath system is as given below:

```
%Program 14.1
%Fuzzy controller FLC Water Bath Temperature Control System
%function name fcbw
%the inputs to the FLC are Error, ER and Change in error, CE
%the function output, DQ is the change in heat input to be applied
%to the water bath
function [DQ] = fcwb(ER, CE)
%initialize Fuzzy Inference System (FIS) matrix obtained from
%newfis named fcwb
FLCWB = newfis('fcwb');
%define 1st input variable error, called ER in Universe of
%Discourse -3 to +3
%and add to FIS matrix FLCWB using the function addvar().
FLCWB =addvar(FLCWB,'input','ER',[-3 3]);
%define seven membership functions for the first input error, ER
```

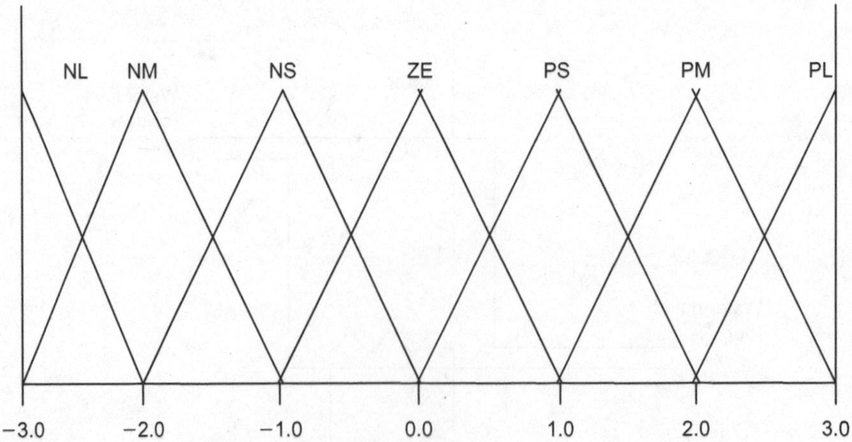

Figure 14.20 Membership Functions for the Three Input–output Variables of Fuzzy Logic Controller for a Simulated Water Bath System

```
%NL→negative large, NM→negative medium, NS→negative small
%ZE→zero, PL→positive large, PM→positive medium, PS→positive %small
%the three values in brackets specify the three vertices of the
%triangular membership functions
%1 indicates 1st input, trimf means triangular membership functions
%and add to FIS matrix FLCWB using the function addmf().
FLCWB = addmf(FLCWB, 'input', 1, 'NL', 'trimf', [-3 -3 -2] );
FLCWB = addmf(FLCWB, 'input', 1, 'NM', 'trimf', [-3 -2 -1] );
FLCWB = addmf(FLCWB, 'input', 1, 'NS', 'trimf', [-2 -1 0] );
FLCWB = addmf(FLCWB, 'input', 1, 'ZE', 'trimf', [-1 0 1] );
FLCWB = addmf(FLCWB, 'input', 1, 'PS', 'trimf', [0 1 2] );
FLCWB = addmf(FLCWB, 'input', 1, 'PM', 'trimf', [1 2 3] );
FLCWB = addmf(FLCWB, 'input', 1, 'PL', 'trimf', [2 3 3] );
%define 2nd input variable change in error, CE and add to FIS
%matrix
%FLCWB using the function addvar()
FLCWB = addvar(FLCWB, 'input', 'CE', [-3 3] );
%define seven membership functions for the second input CE
%and add to FIS matrix FLCWB using the function addmf()
%2 indicates second input
FLCWB = addmf(FLCWB, 'input', 2, 'NL', 'trimf', [-3 -3 -2] );
FLCWB = addmf(FLCWB, 'input', 2, 'NM', 'trimf', [-3 -2 -1] );
FLCWB = addmf(FLCWB, 'input', 2, 'NS', 'trimf', [-2 -1 0] );
FLCWB = addmf(FLCWB, 'input', 2, 'ZE', 'trimf', [-1 0 1] );
FLCWB = addmf(FLCWB, 'input', 2, 'PS', 'trimf', [0 1 2] );
FLCWB = addmf(FLCWB, 'input', 2, 'PM', 'trimf', [1 2 3] );
FLCWB = addmf(FLCWB, 'input', 2, 'PL', 'trimf', [2 3 3] );
%define 1st output variable change in heat, DQ, in Universe of
%Discourse -3 to +3 and add to FIS matrix FLCWB using the function addvar()
FLCWB = addvar(FLCWB, 'output', 'DQ', [-3 3] );
%define seven membership functions for the 1st output variable change
%in heat, DQ and add to FIS matrix FLCWB using the function addmf()
FLCWB = addmf(FLCWB, 'output', 1, 'NL', 'trimf', [-3 -3 -2] );
FLCWB = addmf(FLCWB, 'output', 1, 'NM', 'trimf', [-3 -2 -1] );
FLCWB = addmf(FLCWB, 'output', 1, 'NS', 'trimf', [-2 -1 0] );
FLCWB = addmf(FLCWB, 'output', 1, 'ZE', 'trimf', [-1 0 1] );
FLCWB = addmf(FLCWB, 'output', 1, 'PS', 'trimf', [0 1 2] );
FLCWB = addmf(FLCWB, 'output', 1, 'PM', 'trimf', [1 2 3] );
FLCWB = addmf(FLCWB, 'output', 1, 'PL', 'trimf', [2 3 3] );
%define variable rulelist and store all rules in it, each row
%represents a rule
%1st and 2nd column are indices of membership functions of the two
%input variables
%3rd column is index of membership functions of the output variable
%4th column is weight associated with the rule. The weight must be
%a number between zero and one
```

```
%5th column is 1 if the fuzzy operator for the premise part of the
%rule is AND and is defined as 2 if the fuzzy operator is OR.
%all 49 rules that are possible using 7 membership functions for
%the two inputs are defined.

ruleList = [1 7 4 1 1;
            2 7 5 1 1;
            3 7 5 1 1;
            4 7 6 1 1;
            5 7 6 1 1;
            6 7 7 1 1;
            7 7 7 1 1;
            1 6 3 1 1;
            2 6 4 1 1;
            3 6 5 1 1;
            4 6 5 1 1;
            5 6 6 1 1;
            6 6 7 1 1;
            7 6 7 1 1;
            1 5 2 1 1;
            2 5 3 1 1;
            3 5 4 1 1;
            4 5 5 1 1;
            5 5 5 1 1;
            6 5 7 1 1;
            7 5 7 1 1;
            1 4 1 1 1;
            2 4 2 1 1;
            3 4 3 1 1;
            4 4 4 1 1;
            5 4 5 1 1;
            6 4 6 1 1;
            7 4 7 1 1;
            1 3 1 1 1;
            2 3 1 1 1;
            3 3 3 1 1;
            4 3 3 1 1;
            5 3 4 1 1;
            6 3 5 1 1;
            7 3 6 1 1;
            1 2 1 1 1;
            2 2 1 1 1;
            3 2 2 1 1;
            4 2 3 1 1;
            5 2 3 1 1;
            6 2 4 1 1;
            7 2 5 1 1;
            1 1 1 1 1;
```

```
        2 1 1 1 1;
        3 1 2 1 1;
        4 1 2 1 1;
        5 1 3 1 1;
        6 1 3 1 1;
        7 1 4 1 1 ];
%addrule command adds the rules given by the
%variable ruleList to the fuzzy inference system (FIS) matrix FLCWB
%using the function addrule()
FLCWB = addrule(FLCWB, ruleList);
%showrule command displays all rules in verbose format for the
%fuzzy inference system associated with the matrix FLCWB showrule(FLCWB);
%assign ER and CE to a variable called input
input = [ER CE];
%evalfis command computes the defuzzified output of a fuzzy
%inference system defined by FIS matrix FLCWB for given input.
DQ = evalfis(input, FLCWB);
```

The fuzzy controller has been defined in the Program 14.1 given above. The function also computes the defuzzified output of the controller for the given value of error, ER and change in error, CE, passed as inputs to the function.

The actual crisp values of the input variables and the output variables in practice do not fall in the range defined by the UOD of the fuzzy variables. Therefore, it is desired that these values be scaled so that they fall with in the range prescribed by the UOD. In case the values fall with in a small part of the UOD, then they are scaled up so that they may cover the complete range of UOD. Further, the output response of the controlled systems is characterized by mainly two states: Transient and steady state. The range of `er` and `ce` in the two states vary tremendously. Therefore, different scaling factors are taken for the two states. The program for scaling the input–output values and invoking the fuzzy controller defined in Program 14.2 is given below:

```
%Program 14.2
%To scale the input output variables and obtain crisp value
%of control input from the fuzzy controller defined in program 14.1
%er, ce are real crisp values of the two inputs.
%ER and CE are the scaled values of the two inputs
%Q in heat input of water bath system, DQ is change in heat.
function [Q, ER, CE, DQ] = cal_cinput(er, ce, Q)
%for coarse tuning in the transient state i.e., if error > 2,
%values of scaling parameters are defined
if abs(er) > 2,
    kp = 0.08;            %Kp is scaling parameter for ce
    ki = 0.03;            %Ki is scaling parameter for er
    k = 6.0;              %K is scaling parameter for DQ
%else for fine tuning in the steady state i.e., if error <= 2,
%values of scaling parameters are defined as
else
    kp = 4.0;
    ki  = 0.6;
    k = 0.085;
```

```
end;
%er is actual error, ER is scaled error, obtained as
er(S)*Ki ER = er * ki;
%To ensure that scaled values of ER do not exceed the limits of the
%UOD, Univ. of Discourse i.e., -3 to +3
if ER > 3, ER = 3; end;
if ER < -3, ER = -3; end;
%ce is actual change in error, CE is scaled change in error
CE = ce * kp;
%To ensure that scaled values of CE do not exceed the limits of the
%UOD, Univ. of Discourse i.e., -3 to +3
if CE > 3, CE = 3; end;
if CE < -3, CE = -3; end;
%fuzzy inference system, FIS, defined in program 14.1, is called to
%determine output of fuzzy logic controller i.e., change in heat, DQ
[DQ] = fcwb2(ER, CE);
%output of controller, DQ is scaled using scaling gain factor K
dq = k * DQ;
%change in heat is added to the previous value of the heat to find
%the value of the heat to be given to the water bath system
Q = Q + dq;
%Total heat supplied is restricted between 0 & 0.6 Kcal as heater
%is not designed to provide more than 0.6 Kcal heat.
%if Q > 0.6, make it 0.6, the maximum limit
if  Q > 0.6,
    Q = 0.6;
end;
%if Q < 0, make it 0, as heat cannot be negative
if Q < 0,
    Q = 0;
end;
```

14.9.3 Output Response of Fuzzy Controller

This example has been omitted in last chapter. The conventional controllers fail to perform well for varying set point. Keeping the above in mind, a multi-step reference was used to test the ability of the FLC with respect to set-point regulation for the Water Bath Temperature Control System. The test was conducted over 120 samples using a sampling period of 30 sec, which resulted in 60 minutes duration. The set points followed are:

(a) For first 40 samples, that is from sample 0 to sample 40 the set point is 30 °C.
(b) For sample 41 to sample 80, the set point is 40 °C.
(c) For sample 81 to sample 120, the set point is 50 °C.

The program for fuzzy controller implementation for multi-step tracking response for Water Bath Temperature Control System is given below:

```
%Program 14.3
%To implement fuzzy logic controller for water bath temperature
%control system designed in Program 14.1 for multi-step point
```

```
%tracking ability test
clear all; %To clear all variables in MATLAB workspace
%initialize the different Water Bath System variables
F = 1 / 60;           %tank fluid flow rate in liter/sec
Ti = 25;              %tank inlet temperature of water
Tp = 25;              %initial value of output tank temperature
Q = 0;                %heat input to the water bath heater
DQ = 0;               %change in heat input to the water bath system
Tr = 30;              %initial value of the desired output temperature
%store initial conditions in the array
n = 1;
T(n) = Tp;            %store output tank temp. in an array
q(n) = Q;             %store heat input to water bath system in array
dq(n) = DQ;           %store change in heat in an array
er = Tr - T(1);       %error, er, is set point minus output tank temp.
erp = 0;              %previous value of error
ce = 0;               %initial value of change in error, ce, is zero
%for loop to calculate er and ce at every sample and call the fuzzy
%controller defined in program 14.1 and 14.2 given above to calculate Q
%to repeat the loop for 120 samples, sampling period is 30 seconds
for s = 1:1:120,
    if s <   40,    %for the 1st 40 samples
       Tr = 30;     %1st Set-point temperature
    end;
    if and(s >= 40, s < 80),    %for next 40 samples i.e., 40-80
       Tr = 40;                 %2nd Set-point temperature
    end;
    if s >= 80,                 %for the next 40 samples i.e., 80-120
       Tr = 50;                 %3rd Set-point temperature
    end;
    Trr(s) = Tr;
%call Program 14.2: To scale the input output variables and obtain
%crisp value of the control input from the fuzzy controller defined
%in program 14.1
    [Q, ER, CE, DQ] = cal_cinput1(er, ce, Q);
    tspan = [0 10 30];      %to set the time interval = 30 sec. for
                            %ODE solver
    x0 = [Tp];              %store output temp. in x0
    options = [];           %options for ODE solver are default
    %determine output of Water Bath System using ODE solver
    %t = time, x = tank temperature
    [t, x] = ode45('heater', tspan, x0, options, Ti, Q, F);
    %store output temperature of Water Bath System obtained using
    %ODE solver in the variable Tp
    Tp = x(3, :);
    %store the values of the output temperature of Water Bath and
    %the heat supplied Q to it in an array q
```

```
        n = n + 1;
        T(n)  = Tp;
        q(n)  = Q;
        %equate the present value of error as previous error erp and
        %calculate the new value of error and change in error.
        erp = er;
        er = Tr - Tp;        %error is set point - output tank temp.
        ce = er - erp;       %calculate ce as present error minus
                             %previous error
    end;
    %to plot the response
    subplot(2, 1, 1);
    plot(T, 'r');
    hold on;
    plot(Trr, 'k:');
    legend('FLC', 'setpoint', 0);
    ylabel('tank temp (°C)');
    subplot(2, 1 ,2);
    plot(q, 'r');
    xlabel('sample number');
    ylabel('control input Q');

    %Program 14.4
    %to solve differential equations of Water Bath System
    %using 4th/5th order Runge-Kutta method.
    function xdot = heaterWB(t, x, o, Ti, Q, F)
    %tank fluid is assumed to be water
    %define variables
    %t           time vector
    %x           T, temp in tank
    %o           options, here taken as nil
    %Q           Heat input, in kcal/sec
    %Ti          Tank inlet temp in degrees C
    %xdot        output variable of the function heater1, tank temp
    %define constants
    T    = x;
    V    = 12;      %V, tank volume in litres
    rhocp  = 1;     %rhocp, density * heat capacity of tank fluid
    %differential equations of stirred tank heater (ODES)
    dTdt = (F / V) * (Ti - T) + Q / (V * rhocp);
    %to obtain a column vector, take transpose
    xdot = dTd
```

The response obtained for the multi-set point signal is shown in Figure 14.21. The control input is plotted. It is clearly seen that the fuzzy controller tracks the set points perfectly. The important point to be observed is that the change from the transient to the steady state is quite smooth. The change in control signal also varies smoothly.

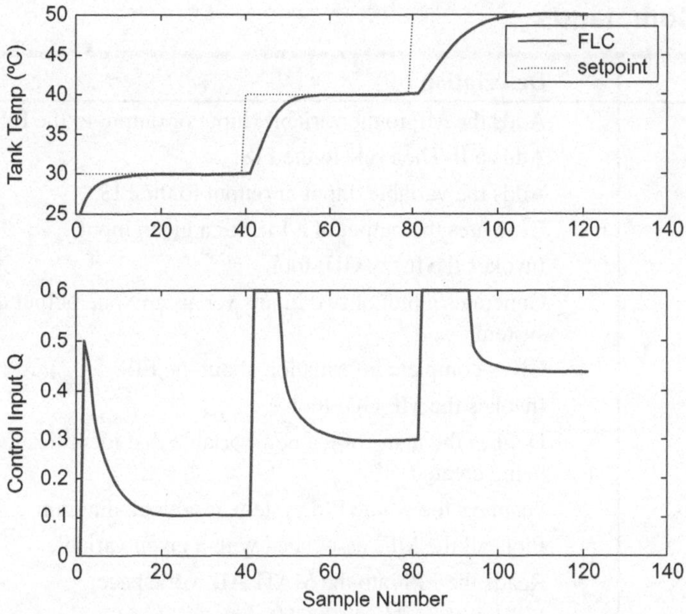

Figure 14.21 Response of a Simulated Water Bath Temperature Control System Using Fuzzy Logic Controller for Variable Set-point Tracking Ability Test

SUMMARY

This chapter does not only introduce the Fuzzy Logic Toolbox of MATLAB and the commands therein but also describes the essential theoretical concepts of Fuzzy Logic Systems. The chapter is summarized as follows:

- First, the advantages of Fuzzy Logic are discussed and then the fuzzy concepts are clarified using an example of a washing machine.
- The basics of fuzzy theory, linguistic variables, fuzzy sets and their MFs are described.
- The fuzzy and binary operations are compared.
- The manner in which knowledge is represented in fuzzy systems through If-Then rulebase is described using well-illustrated examples. The concept of rule matrix is also given.
- Complete FIS components, including fuzzification of input variables, application of fuzzy operators, mapping degree of matching to fuzzy outputs, aggregation of outputs and defuzzification are discussed.
- The washing machine problem is solved using the GUI fuzzy tool.
- All features of FIS Editor, Membership Function Editor, Rule Editor, Rule Viewer and Surface Viewer are described in detail.
- At the end of the chapter, the commands available in Fuzzy Toolbox are introduced.
- Finally, example problem of Water Bath Temperature Control System is solved using command-line statements. Different programs written to design the fuzzy controller for the Water Bath Temperature Controller are given with detailed comments for easy understanding of the reader.

List of Commands

Command	Description
addmf	Adds the MF to the variable, input or output to the FIS.
addrule	Adds a If-Then rule to the FIS.
addvar	Adds the variable, input or output to the FIS.
evalfis	Evaluates the output of a FIS for a given input.
fuzzy	Invokes the fuzzy GUI tool.
gensurf	Generates a plot of two inputs versus any one output of a given system.
getfis	Gives complete information about the FIS.
mfedit	Invokes the MF GUI tool.
newfis	Defines the name of the new variable that identifies the FIS being created.
plotfis	Displays the whole FIS system as a block diagram.
plotmf	Plots all the MFs associated with a given variable.
readfis	Reads the FIS into the MATLAB workspace.
ruleedit	Invokes the rule editor GUI tool.
ruleview	Displays the Rule Viewer.
setfis	Changes any property of an FIS.
showfis	Lists all information about the FIS.
showrule	Displays all rules in Verbose format for the FIS associated with the rule matrix.
surfview	Displays the Surface Viewer.
writefix	Saves the FIS to disk.

EXERCISES

14.1. Discuss the advantages of fuzzy logic compared to discrete logic.

14.2. Why Fuzzy systems become difficult to design for systems with large number of inputs and outputs?

14.3. What is the advantage of the fuzzy GUI tool given in the Fuzzy Logic Toolbox?

14.4. What is the usefulness of the Rule and Surface Viewer? Discuss.

14.5. Design a fuzzy logic system for the common home geyser to maintain uniform temperature of water during bath.

14.6. Design a fuzzy controller for the common water tank used in a small town to maintain constant water level in the tank.

14.7. Compare the advantage of a fuzzy controller compared to a common PID controller used in industries.

14.8. Is it possible to train the fuzzy controllers like the Neural Network systems? Discuss.

14.9. How fuzzy systems allow partial memberships of fuzzy sets? What is their advantage?

14.10. How can the user attach different importance to different rules in the fuzzy rulebase? Give the different commands associated with it.

14.11. Design a Fuzzy model for giving grade to the student. The grades are evaluated using the following inputs: marks, behaviour, punctuality. The grades are A, B, C, D and E, with A being the best and E the poorest. The reader is advised to choose the fuzzy sets for the inputs and outputs as per his design. The Rulebase may be restricted to less than 10 rules.

14.12. Design a fuzzy controller for the Water Bath System described in the Book using the fuzzy tool 'FUZZY'. The design specifications be changed as given below:

- The number of MFs for the input/output variables = 5 each
- Type = Guassian.
- Number of rules: 15.
- Range = no change.

CHAPTER 15

MATLAB Applications in Digital Signal Processing

LEARNING OBJECTIVES

- Study of basic discrete-time signals such as unit impulse, step, ramp, real and complex exponential and their representation using MATLAB functions.
- Study of different types of discrete-time systems.
- Mathematical operations on discrete-time signals such are addition, multiplication, scaling, folding and shifting using user-defined MATLAB functions.
- Use of MATLAB functions such as `decimate`, `interp`, `downsample`, `upsample` and `resample`.
- Use of MATLAB functions to obtain convolution of discrete-time signal.
- Brief introduction to z-Transform, Discrete Time Fourier Transform (DTFT), Discrete Fourier Transform (DFT) and Fast Fourier Transform (FFT).
- Use of `fft` and `ifft` functions to obtain DFT and FFT.
- Digital filter design using MATLAB functions as `buttord`, `cheby1ord`, `cheby2ord`, `ellipord` and `butter`, `cheby1`, `cheby2` etc.
- Use of `freqz` function to obtain response of the filter.
- FIR digital filter design using functions such as `kaiserord`, `firpmord`, `fir1`, `fir2`, `firls` and `fircls`.
- Study of functions for design of FIR filters using `windows` such as `blackman`, `hamming`, `hann` and `kaiser`.
- Use of Window Visualization Tool (WV Tool) to visualize window.
- Study of Filter Design and Analysis Tool (FDA Tool) and Filter Visualization Tool (FV Tool) for designing and visualization of digital filters.
- Design of IIR and FIR filters using FDA Tool.

15.1 INTRODUCTION

Signals are of numerous forms and are used in variety of applications in Science and Engineering such as communications, image processing, bio-medical instrumentation, control systems, weather forecasting, etc. Most of these signals carry raw information and need to be processed in order to extract meaningful information.

Thus, signal processing is a method of extracting information from the signal which in turn depends on the type of signal and the nature of information it carries. The signal processing can be implemented in two different ways:

(a) Analog or continuous-time approach
(b) Digital or discrete-time approach

Analog signal processing relies on the use of analog circuit elements such as resistors, capacitors, inductors, transistor, amplifiers and diodes. Digital Signal Processing (DSP), on the other hand, is based on three basic digital elements i.e., adders, multipliers and memory. With advances in digital computer technology and IC fabrication in last few decades, the applications of DSP have evolved as major scientific area. The availability of cheaper and relatively fast digital circuits has made it possible to develop digital systems capable of performing complex DSP functions and tasks, which were otherwise difficult to perform using analog signal processing systems.

There are many advantages of DSP over analog signal processing which can be summarised as follows:

1. *Storage*: The storage of digital signals is very easy as these can be stored in various storage media such as magnetic tapes, disks, etc.
2. *Accuracy*: In analog system, tolerance of analog circuit components makes it difficult to control accuracy, but in digital systems accuracy can easily be increased or decreased by varying bits in binary words.
3. *Sensitivity*: Digital circuits are less sensitive to changes in component values as well as to variations in temperature, aging and other external parameters.
4. *Cheaper implementation*: Since digital hardware is cheaper as compared to analog components digital systems can be implemented at far less cost.
5. *Multirate processing*: In digital implementation, multirate processing is possible in which digital circuits can be connected in cascade without any loading problems. This is quite difficult in analog circuits.

The MATLAB has emerged as a powerful environment to promote experimental study of signals and systems. The different concepts used in DSP are applied in MATLAB for testing. MATLAB provides efficient computational platform for exploration and analysis of different DSP concepts. In this chapter, different functions in the Signal Processing Toolbox are illustrated.

15.2 SIGNALS AND SYSTEMS CLASSIFICATION

15.2.1 Classification of Signals

Signals are broadly classified into two types: (1) Continuous-time signals (analog signals) and (2) Discrete-time signals (digital signals).

1. **Continuous-time signals (analog signals)**: These signals are defined for every instant of time and take on values in the continuous interval (x, y), where x and y can be ∞. For example,

   $$x(t) = \sin wt \quad \text{where } -\pi \leq wt \leq \pi$$

   Here, wt can assume infinite number of values in the time interval indicated.
   The plot is shown in Figure 15.1.
2. **Discrete-time signals (digital signals)**: The discrete-time signals are defined only at specific instants of time. These instants need not to be equidistant but generally are taken at equally spaced intervals. The discrete-time signal is not defined at instants between two successive instants.

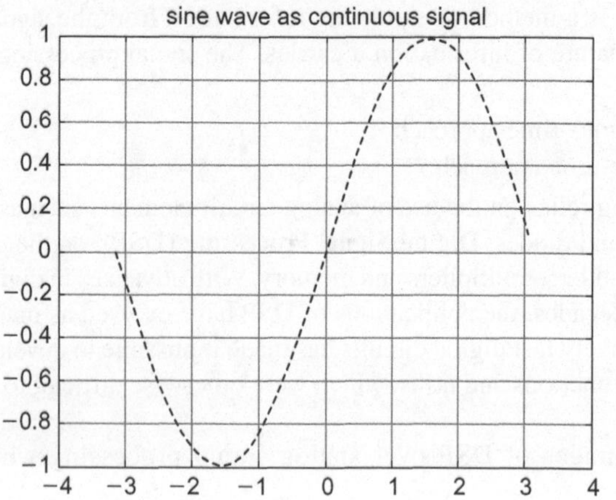

Figure 15.1 'sine' Wave as Continuous Signal

15.2.2 Representation of Discrete Signals

A discrete signal *x*(*n*) is function of an independent variable, *n*, which is an integer. It can be represented in different forms:

(a) Graphical representation
(b) Functional representation
(c) Tabular representation
(d) Sequential representation

(a) **Graphical representation**: A signal can be graphically represented using MATLAB command `stem`. This command shows the data in the form of lines (stems) starting from the baseline along *x*-axis and terminates each stem in a circle (default) or other marker corresponding to data value. The syntax is given as:

```
stem(x)
stem(t,x)
stem(t,x, 'fill')
stem (t,x, 'fill', '- - -')
```

`stem(x)` plots given data sequence *x* as stems along the *x*-axis at equally spaced and automatically generated values.

`stem(t,x)` plots values of `t` versus the columns of `x`.

`t` and `x` must be vector or matrices of same size.

`stem(t,x,'fill')` gives plot similar to above with ending circles filled.

`stem(t,x,'fill', '-')` gives plot similar to above with ending circles filled and lines dashed '- - -'.

Example 15.1 Illustrate the use of `stem` command. Plot the sine wave in discrete signal form.

Solution: The following commands are used:

```
t = linspace(-pi, pi, 10) ;
%Ten equidistant instants between -pi and pi
y = sin(t);              %Evaluate y
stem(t,y)                %Plot the discrete time signal y = sin(t)
```

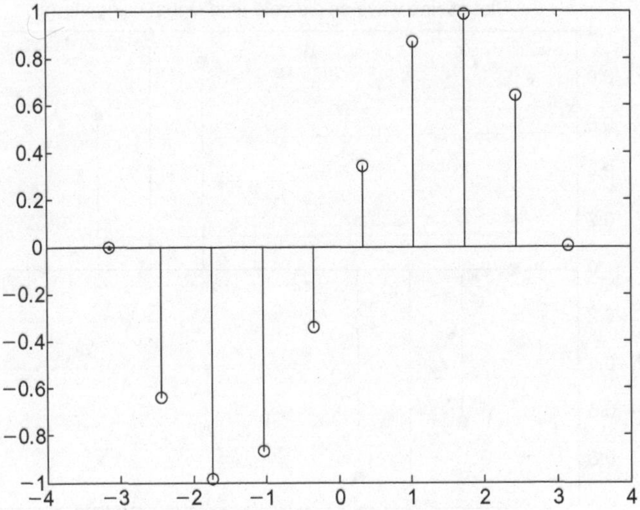

Figure 15.2 `stem` Plot for Example 15.1

The plot obtained is shown in Figure 15.2.

`stem` plot with dashed lines can be plotted using following commands:

```
t = linspace(-pi, pi, 10) ;
%Ten equidistant instants between -pi and pi
y = sin(t);                       %Evaluate y
stem(t,y,'fill','--')             %Plot the discrete time sine signal
title('Plot of sine wave as discrete time signal using stem');
xlabel('Discrete Time Instants');
ylabel('Sine Wave Amplitude');
```

The plot obtained is shown in Figure 15.3. It shows dashed lines terminated with filled circles.

(b) **Functional representation**: In the functional representation, a typical discrete-time signal is represented as a function and is shown as follows:

$$x(n) = \begin{matrix} 1 & \text{for } n = 2, 4, 6 \\ 2 & \text{for } n = 1, 3, 5 \\ 0 & \text{otherwise} \end{matrix}$$

(c) **Tabular representation**: The tabular representation is as shown below:

2	=	−3	−2	−1	0	1	2	3
$x(n)$		0	−1	2	−3	0	−1	−2

(d) **Sequence representation**: A discrete-time signal can be represented as a sequence with origin ($n = 0$) indicated by symbol 'as' shown below:

$$x(n) = \{\ldots\ldots 3 \quad \underset{\uparrow}{8} \quad 3 \quad 4 \quad 5 \quad 2 \quad 9 \ldots\ldots\}$$

Let the same sequence have $x(n) = 0$ for $n < 0$, then it is written as:

$$x(n) = \{\underset{\uparrow}{8} \quad 3 \quad 4 \quad 5 \quad 2 \quad 9 \ldots\ldots\}$$

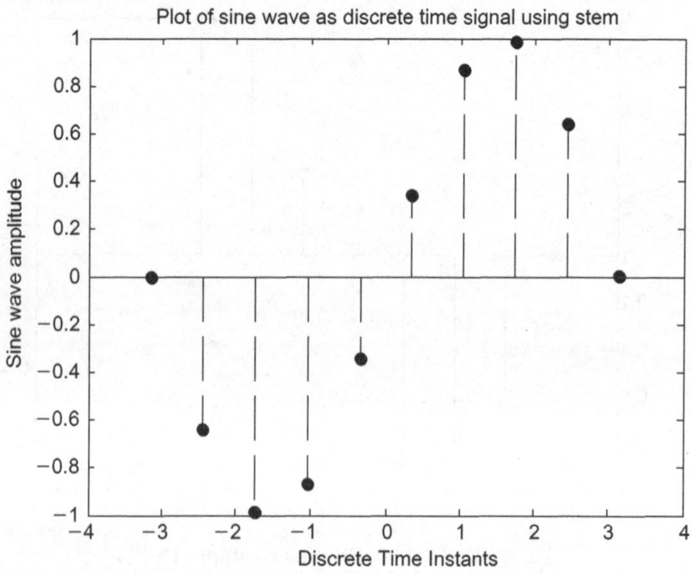

Figure 15.3 `stem` Plot with Dashed Lines for Example 15.1

If the sequence is defined for **finite instants**, then it is written as:

$$x(n) = \{\underset{\uparrow}{8} \quad 3 \quad 4 \quad 5 \quad 2 \quad 9\}$$

This is a six-point sequence with $x(n) = 0$ for $n < 0$.

15.2.3 Basic Discrete-Time Signals

The basic discrete-time signals are given as follows:

1. Unit impulse signal or unit sample signal $\delta(n)$
2. Unit step discrete-time signal $u(n)$
3. Unit ramp discrete-time signal $u_r(n)$
4. Real-valued exponential discrete-time signal $x(n) = a^n$
5. Complex-valued exponential discrete time signal $x(n) = e^{(\sigma + j\omega)n}$

In MATLAB, *there is no built-in function to represent the discrete-time signals. So, functions are developed for representation of basic discrete signals and are given below:*

1. **Unit impulse signal or unit sample signal $\delta(n)$:** The functional (mathematical) representation of unit impulse sequence is given as

$$\delta(n) = \begin{cases} 1\,; & \text{if } n = 0 \\ 0\,; & \text{if } n \neq 0 \end{cases}$$

For impulse value at some other instant say $n = n_0$, the expression is given as

$$\delta(n - n_0) = \begin{cases} 1\,; & \text{if } n = n_0 \\ 0\,; & \text{if } n \neq 0 \end{cases}$$

In MATLAB to represent unit impulse sequence, a new function **`impulseseq`** is developed as

```
function [y,n] =impulseseq(a,b,c)
%This function represent given impulse sequence in graphical form.
```

```
% a and b are the lower and upper limits of given range of the sequence
%respectively
%c is the instant at which impulse signal exits.
%y and n are outputs representing amplitude and instants respectively.
n = [a:b];                              % Range of the given sequence
a1 = abs(a);
y = [zeros(1,a1+c),1,zeros(1,b-c)]; % Generate impulse signal
```

Example 15.2 Plot the following signals using `impulseseq` function.

(a) $\delta(n)$ for $-5 \leq n \leq 5$
(b) $\delta(n+3)$ for $-8 \leq n \leq 8$
(c) $\delta(n-1)$ for $-4 \leq n \leq 4$

Solution:

(a) $\delta(n)$ for $-5 \leq n \leq 5$

In this case, c = 0 and range is [−5 5] i.e., a = −5, b = 5, hence the commands are as follows:

```
[y,n]=impulseseq(-5,5,0);
stem(n,y);
title('Discrete unit impulse sequence at instant n=0');
xlabel('Sample number');
ylabel('Output');
```

The plot obtained is shown in Figure 15.4.

(b) $\delta(n+3)$ for $-8 \leq n \leq 8$

In this case, $c = -3$ and range is [−8 8] i.e., a = −8, b = 8, hence the commands are as follows:

```
[y,n]=impulseseq(-8,8,-3);
stem(n,y);
title('Discrete unit impulse sequence at instant n = -3');
xlabel('Sample number');
ylabel('Output');
```

The plot obtained is shown in Figure 15.5.

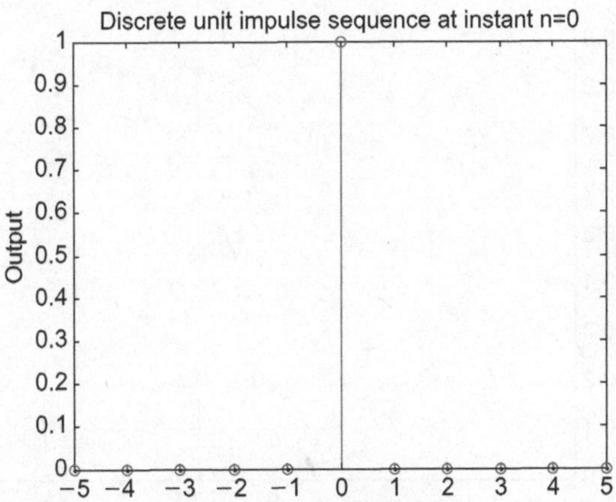

Figure 15.4 Impulse Sequence Plot for Example 15.2(a)

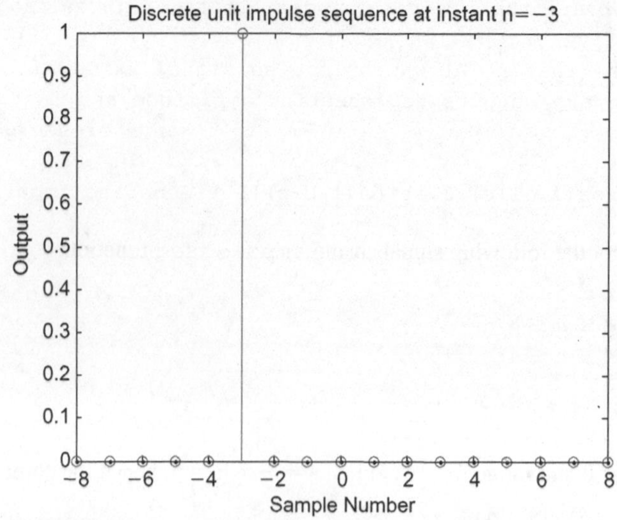

Figure 15.5 Impulse Sequence Plot for Example 15.2(b)

(c) $\delta(n-1)$ for $-4 \leq n \leq 4$

In this case, $c = 1$ and range is $[-4 \quad 4]$ i.e., a = −4, b = 4, hence the commands are as follows:

```
[y,n] = impulseseq(-4,4,1);
stem(n,y);
title('Discrete unit impulse sequence at instant n = 1');
xlabel('Sample number');
ylabel('Output');
```

The plot obtained is shown in Figure 15.6.

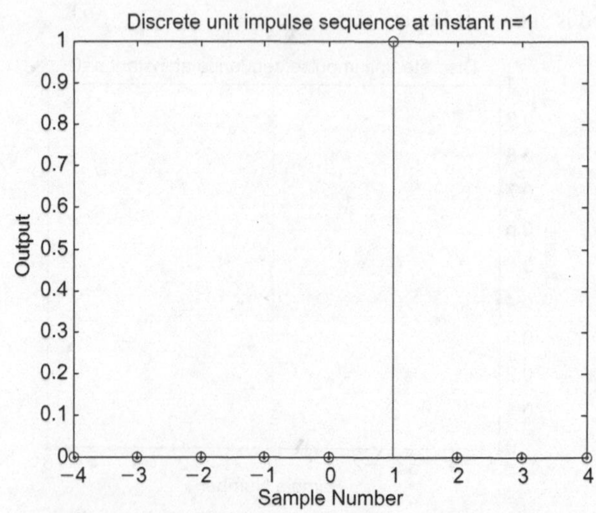

Figure 15.6 Impulse Sequence Plot for Example 15.2(c)

2. **Unit step discrete-time signal:** The functional representation of unit step sequence is given as

$$u(n)=\begin{cases}1; & \text{if } n\ge 0\\ 0; & \text{if } n<0\end{cases}$$

For unit step at any other instant say n_0, the expression is given as

$$u(n-n_0)=\begin{cases}1; & \text{if } n\ge 0\\ 0; & \text{if } n<n_0\end{cases}$$

The function **stepseq** developed to represent unit step sequence is given below:

```
function [y,n] =stepseq(a,b,c)
%'stepseq' function represent the given unit step sequence in graphical
%form.
% a and b are the lower and upper limits of range of sequence
%respectively
% c is the instant at which unit step sequence starts
% y and n are outputs representing amplitude and instants.
n = [a:b];                              % Range of the given sequence
a1 = abs(a);
y = [zeros(1,a1+c),ones(1,b-c+1)];  % Generate step signal
```

Example 15.3 Plot the following signals using `stepseq` function:

(a) $u(n)$ for $-10 \le n \le 10$
(b) $u(n-2)$ for $-5 \le n \le 5$
(c) $u(n+1)$ for $-4 \le n \le 4$

Solution:

(a) $u(n)$ for $-10 \le n \le 10$

In this case $c = 0$ and range is $[-10 \quad 10]$, i.e., $a = -10$ and $b = 10$, hence the commands are as given below:

```
[y,n] = stepseq(-10,10,0);
stem(n,y);
title('Discrete unit step sequence at instant n = 0');
xlabel('Sample number');
ylabel('Output');
```

The plot obtained is shown in Figure 15.7.

(b) $u(n-2)$ for $-5 \le n \le 5$

In this case, $c = 2$ and range is $[-5 \quad 5]$, i.e., $a = -5$ and $b = 5$, hence the commands are as follows:

```
[y,n] = stepseq(-5,5,2);
stem(n,y);
title('Discrete unit step sequence at instant n = 2');
xlabel('Sample number');
ylabel('Output');
```

The plot obtained is shown in Figure 15.8.

(c) $u(n+1)$ for $-4 \le n \le 4$

In this case, $c = -1$ and range is $[-4 \quad 4]$, i.e., $a = -4$ and $b = 4$, hence the commands are as follows:

```
[y,n] = stepseq(-4,4,-1);
stem(n,y);
```

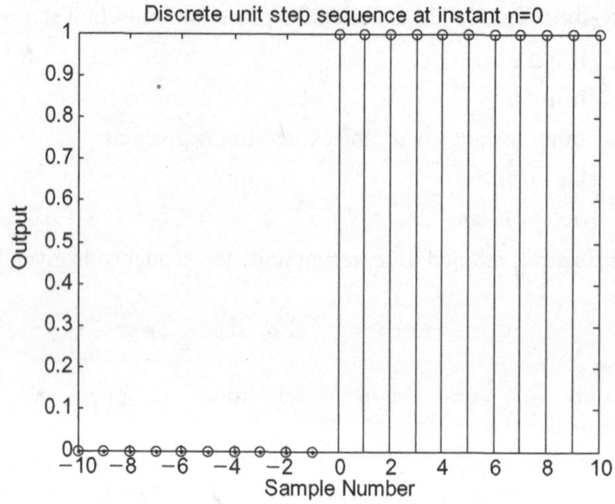

Figure 15.7 Unit Step Sequence Plot for Example 15.3(a)

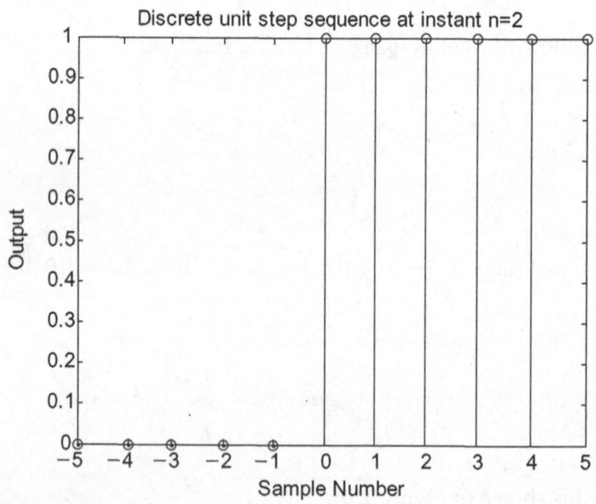

Figure 15.8 Unit Step Sequence Plot for Example 15.3(b)

```
title('Discrete unit step sequence at instant n=-1');
xlabel('Sample number');
ylabel('Output');
```

The plot obtained is as shown in Figure 15.9.

3. **Unit ramp discrete-time signal $u_r(n)$:** The functional representation of ramp sequence is given as

$$u_r(n) = \begin{cases} n; & \text{if } n \geq 0 \\ 0; & \text{if } n < 0 \end{cases}$$

The function **rampseq** developed to represent unit step sequence is given below:

```
function [x,n] = rampseq(n1,n2)
% 'rampseq' function represents given ramp sequence
```

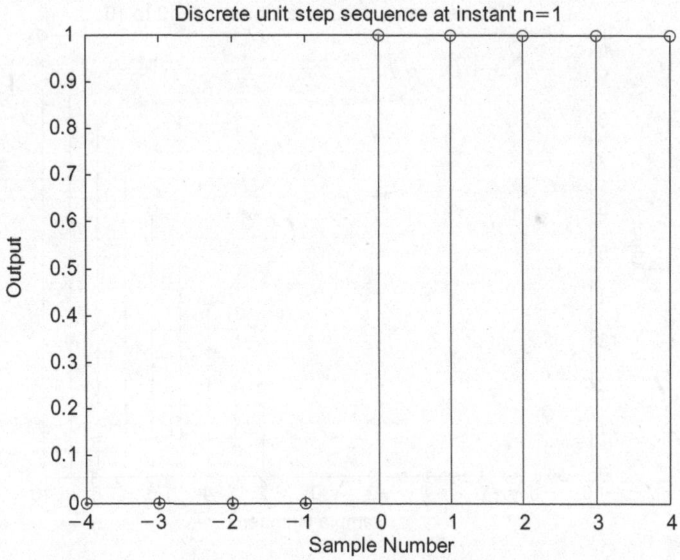

Figure 15.9 Unit Step Sequence Plot for Example 15.3(c)

```
%x(n)= n for n>=0 and x(n)=0 for n<0 in graphic form in the
%range of n1 to n2.
%n1 and n2 are the minimum and maximum limits of given
%range respectively
%x and n are outputs.
n = [n1:n2];      %Specifies the given range
k = n2-n1+1;      %calculate the total instants.
m = n1;
for i = 1:k       %Loop to find values of x at all instants.
    if(m<0)
       x(i) = 0;
    else
       x(i) = m;
    end
    m = m + 1;
end
```

Example 15.4 Plot ramp sequence for the interval −10 to 10 using `rampseq` function.

Solution: In this example, $n1 = -10$ and $n2 = 10$, hence the commands are as follows:

```
[x,n]=rampseq(-10,10);     %Call the function
stem(n,x);                 %Plot as stem
title('Discrete ramp sequence for range -10 to 10');
xlabel('Sample number');
ylabel('Output');
```

The plot obtained is as shown in Figure 15.10.

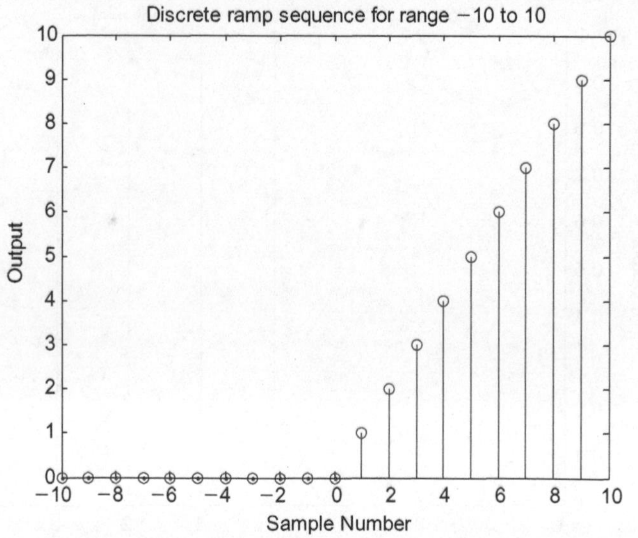

Figure 15.10 Ramp Sequence Plot for Example 15.4

4. **Real-valued exponential sequence:** The functional or mathematical representation is given as

$$x(n) = (k)^n$$

where

k is a real number and
n is the instant value.

The sequence can be obtained by using simple mathematical expression.

Example 15.5 Obtain and plot discrete-time sequence for following expression:

$x(n) = (1.5)^n$, n varies from -8 to 8.

Solution: The commands used are as follows:

```
n = [-8:8];
x = (1.5).^n;
stem(n,x);          %Plot as stem
title('Plot to show real-values exponential sequence');
xlabel('Sample number');
ylabel('Output');
```

The plot obtained is as shown in Figure 15.11.

5. **Complex-valued exponential sequence:** The functional or mathematical representation is given as

$$x(n) = e^{(a+jb)n}$$

where

a and b are real values and
n is the instant value.

This sequence can be obtained in the same manner as used for real-valued exponential sequence.

Example 15.6 Obtain and plot discrete-time sequence for following expression:

$x(n) = e^{(i+j0.3)n}$ for n varies from -3 to 3.

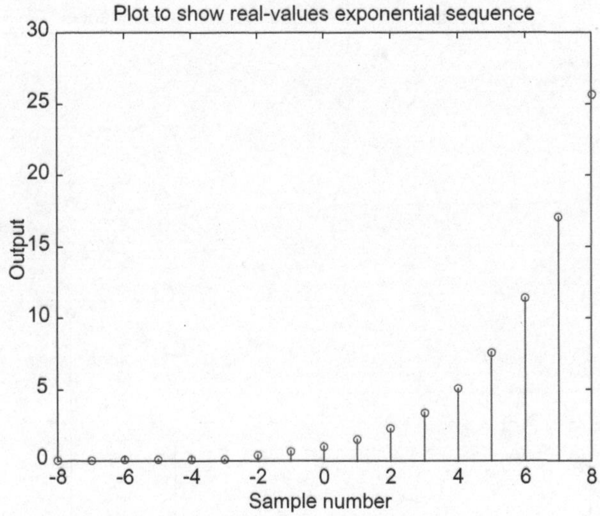

Figure 15.11 Exponential Response for Example 15.5

Solution: The commands used are as follows:

```
n = [-3:3];
x = exp((1+j*0.3)*n);
stem(n,x);                          %Plot as stem
title('Plot to show complex-valued exponential sequence');
xlabel('Sample number');
ylabel('Output');
```

The plot obtained is as shown in Figure 15.12.

15.2.4 Classification of Discrete-Time Signals

The discrete-time signals can be further classified as

1. Deterministic and Non-Deterministic signals
2. Periodic and Aperiodic signals
3. Even and Odd signals
4. Energy and Power signals

1. **Deterministic and Non-Deterministic signals:** The signals which are completely specified in time are called deterministic signals. The nature and amplitude of such a signal can be predicted at any instant of time. For example, unit step sequence. These signals can be predicted in advance.

   The signals which are random and whose pattern is irregular are called non-deterministic signals. These can not be predicted in advance. These are also called random signals.

2. **Periodic and Aperiodic signals:** A signal which repeats over and over periodically, with a fixed repetition interval of time is called periodic signal. A periodic signal satisfies the following condition:

   $$x(n + N) = x(n)$$

   where N is sampling period measured as number sample spacing.

   If a signal does not satisfy the above condition, it is called aperiodic signal.

3. **Even and Odd signals (Symmetric and Anti-Symmetric signals):** A discrete-time signal is called even signal if

   $$x(-n) = x(n)$$

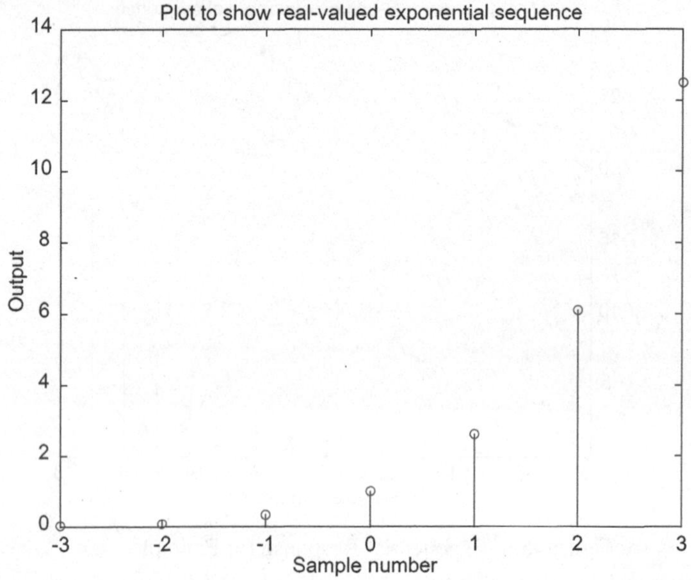

Figure 15.12 Complex-Valued Exponential Sequence Plot for Example 15.6

It is called odd (anti-symmetric) signal if

$$x(-n) = -x(n)$$

For example,

$$x(n) = [8\ 3\ 6\ 4\ 0\ 4\ 6\ 3\ 8]$$

is an even signal.
whereas

$$x(n) = [-8\ -3\ -6\ -4\ 0\ 4\ 6\ 3\ 8]$$

is an odd signal.
The even and odd signals are shown in Figures 15.13 and 15.14, respectively.

4. **Energy and Power signals:** If a signal has finite energy, it is called Energy signal and if a signal has infinite energy but finite power, it is called Power signal.

   As power is time average of energy. As average is over a large time interval, a signal with finite energy has zero power and signal with finite power has infinite energy. Therefore, signal cannot be both an energy signal and power signal simultaneously. If it is one, it cannot be the other. However, there are signals that are neither energy signals nor power signals.

15.2.5 Classification of Discrete-Time Systems

The discrete-time systems can be classified as follows:

1. Static and Dynamic systems
2. Linear and Non-Linear systems
3. Time-variant and Time-Invariant systems
4. Causal and Non-Causal systems
5. Stable and Unstable systems

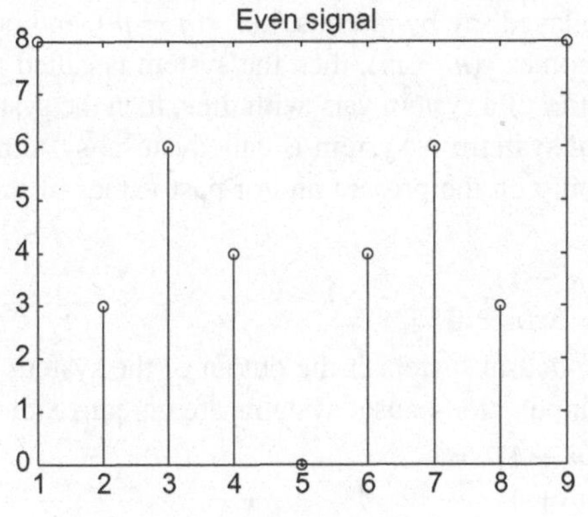

Figure 15.13 Even Signal

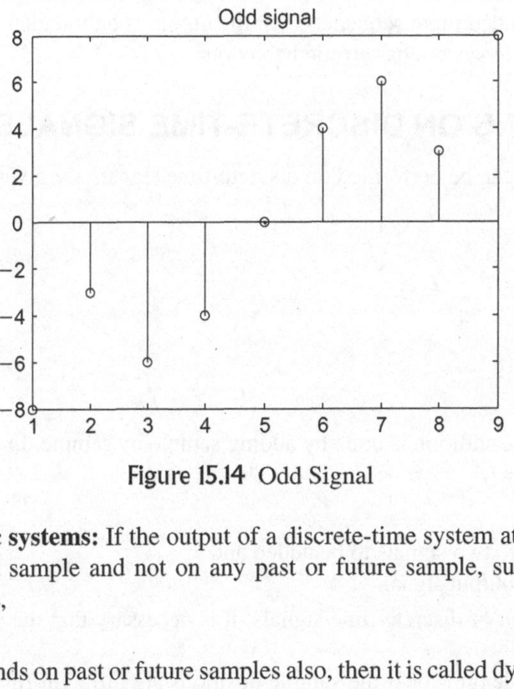

Figure 15.14 Odd Signal

1. **Static and Dynamic systems:** If the output of a discrete-time system at any instant n depends only on the present input sample and not on any past or future sample, such a system is called static system. For example,

   $$y(n) = 5x(n)$$

   If the output depends on past or future samples also, then it is called dynamic system. For example,

   $$y(n - 1) + 5y(n - 1) = 2x(n + 1) - 3x(n)$$

   Static systems do not require any memory whereas it is essential for dynamic systems.
2. **Linear and Non-Linear systems:** A system which follows the principle of superposition is called a linear system. The principle of superposition is given as

   $$K[a1\ x1(n) + a2\ x2\ (n)] = a1\ K\ [x1(n)] + a2\ K\ [x2\ (n)]$$

   In other words, it is defined as a system whose response to sum of weighted inputs is same as the sum of weighted responses. If a system does not satisfy principle of superposition, it is known as non-linear system.
3. **Time-variant and Time-Invariant systems:** A system is called time invariant if its input–output characteristics do not change with time. Suppose, an input signal $x(n)$ is given to a system and output $y(n)$

is obtained. If input is delayed say by m units, i.e., $x(n - m)$, and output obtained is also delayed by same m units, i.e., it becomes $y(n - m)$, then the system is called time-invariant system. In case, if input–output characteristics of a system vary with time, then the system is called time-variant system.

4. **Causal and Non-Causal system:** A system is called causal system if the output of the system $y(n)$ at any instant depends only on the present and/or past values of input and is independent of future values. For example,

$$y(n) = 2x(n) + x(n - 1)$$
$$y(n) = x(n - 2) + 3x(n - 3)$$

A system is called a non-causal system if the output of the system $y(n)$ at any instant n depends on the future values of the input. Non-causal systems are unrealizeable. For example,

$$y(n) = x(n) + 3x(n + 1)$$
$$y(n) = x(n) + 2x(n + 1)$$

5. **Stable and Unstable systems:** A system is said to be stable if and only if the bounded input produces a bounded output (BIBO). A bounded signal has an amplitude that remains finite.

If, for some bounded input sequence $x(n)$, the output is unbounded (infinite), the system is called unstable. An unstable system has erratic behaviour.

15.3 OPERATIONS ON DISCRETE-TIME SIGNALS

The various operations that can be performed on discrete-time signals are given as

1. Addition
2. Multiplication
3. Scaling
4. Folding
5. Shifting

15.3.1 Addition

For discrete-time signals, the addition is done by adding sample by sample. In general form, it is given as

```
z(n) = x1(n) + x2(n)
```

where

`x1(n)` and `x2(n)` are two signals to be added and

`z(n)` is the resultant output signal.

In MATLAB, for addition of discrete-time signals, it is necessary that the sequences should be of equal lengths.

If signals are of unequal lengths or if the sample positions are different for equal length sequences, then simple addition using '+' operator is not possible. Hence, signals $x1(n)$ and $x2(n)$ need to be modified so that they have same length position vector. A function `addsig` is developed as follows:

15.3.1.1 `addsig` *Function*

```
function [z,n] = addsig(x1,a,x2,b)
%'addsig' function add the two discrete time signals x1 and x2 with the
%ranges a = [n11:n12] and b=[n21:n22] where 'a' may be different from 'b'.
%It makes the two given signals equal in length and have same position
%vector before adding them.
%z is the final output signal obtained and n is the range of final output signal.
```

```
%Plot the given sequences
n11 = min(a);
n12 = max(a);
subplot(2,2,1)
stem(a,x1)
title('First sequence')
n21 = min(b);
n22 = max(b);
subplot(2,2,2)
stem(b,x2)
title('Second sequence')
%Make two signals' lower limits equal by prefixing zeros to requisite
%signal
k = abs(n11)-abs(n21);
o = abs(k);
if (k>0)
  x2 = [zeros(1,o),x2];       %Prefix zeros to x2 signal
elseif(k<0)
  x1 = [zeros(1,o),x1];       %Prefix zeros to x1 signal
end
%Make two signals' upper limits equal by suffixing zeros to requisite
%signal
m = abs(n12)-abs(n22);
p = abs(m);
if (m>0)
  x2 = [x2,zeros(1,p)];       %Suffix zeros to x2 signal
elseif(m<0)
  x1 = [x1,zeros(1,p)];       %suffix zeros to x1 signal
end
%Calculate the sum of two sequences x1 and x2
z = x1+x2;
%Find the limits n1 and n2 for the output sequence
%Find the lower limit
if(abs(n11)>abs(n21))
  n1 = n11;
else
  n1 = n21;
end;
%Find the upper limit
if(abs(n12)>abs(n22))
  n2 = n12;
else
  n2 = n22
end;
n = n1:n2;
%Plot the resultant output sequence
```

```
subplot(2,2,3)
stem(n,z)
title('Resultant added sequence')
```

Hence, the syntax for function **`addsig`** is

```
[z,n]= addsig(x1,a,x2,b)
```

where

`x1` and `x2` are given discrete-time signals,
`a = [n11:n12]` and `b = [n21:n22]` are respective intervals and
`z` is resultant output sequence.
`n` is interval of output sequence.

Note: User defined function `addsig` must be saved in current directory before using it.

Example 15.7 Obtain the sum of following discrete-time sequences and plot the responses:

(a) $x1 = \{3 \;\; \underset{\uparrow}{4} \;\; 2 \;\; 1 \;\; 3\}$

$x2 = \{1 \;\; 5 \;\; \underset{\uparrow}{3} \;\; 6 \;\; 4 \;\; 7\}$

(b) $x1 = \{6 \;\; \underset{\uparrow}{0} \;\; -1 \;\; 3 \;\; 5\}$

$x2 = \{4 \;\; \underset{\uparrow}{1} \;\; 6 \;\; 2\}$

(c) $x1 = \{5 \;\; -4 \;\; \underset{\uparrow}{2} \;\; 3\}$

$x2 = \{4 \;\; \underset{\uparrow}{6} \;\; 1 \;\; 9 \;\; 7\}$

Solution:

(a) $x1 = \{3 \;\; \underset{\uparrow}{4} \;\; 2 \;\; 1 \;\; 3\}$

$x2 = \{1 \;\; 5 \;\; \underset{\uparrow}{3} \;\; 6 \;\; 4 \;\; 7\}$

The commands used are as follows:

```
x1 = [3 4 2 1 3];               %First sequence
x2 = [1 5 3 6 4 7];             %Second sequence
a = [-1:3];                     %Range of samples of first sequence
b = [-2:3];                     %Range of samples of second sequence
[z,n] = addsig(x1,a,x2,b)       %Calling of 'addsig' function
```

The response obtained is as follows:

```
z =

     1     8     7     8     5    10

n =

    -2    -1     0     1     2     3
```

The plot obtained is shown in Figure 15.15.

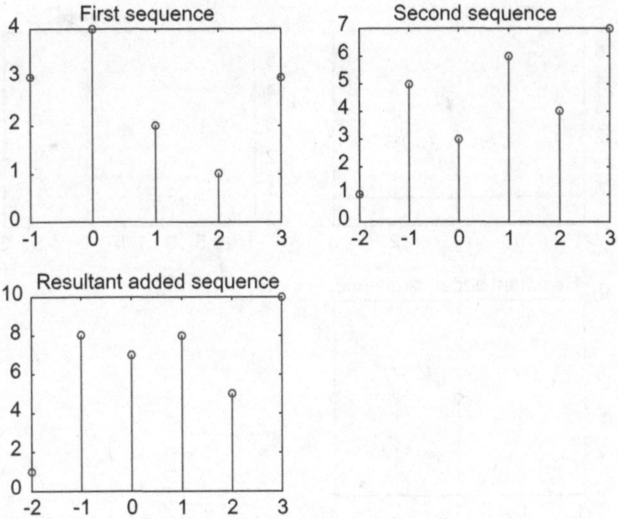

Figure 15.15 Plot Showing Sum of Discrete-time Signals of Example 15.7(a)

(b)
$$x1 = \left\{6 \quad \underset{\uparrow}{0} \quad -1 \quad 3 \quad 5\right\}$$
$$x2 = \left\{4 \quad \underset{\uparrow}{1} \quad 6 \quad 2\right\}$$

The commands used are as given below:

```
x1 = [6 0 -1 3 5];              %First sequence
x2 = [4 1 6 2];                 %Second sequence
a = [-1:3];                     %Range of samples of first sequence
b = [-1:2];                     %Range of samples of second sequence
[z,n] = addsig(x1,a,x2,b)       %Calling of 'addsig' function
```

The response obtained is as follows:

```
z =
    10      1     5     5     5
n =
    -1      0     1     2     3
```

The plot obtained is shown in Figure 15.16.

(c)
$$x1 = \left\{5 \quad -4 \quad \underset{\uparrow}{2} \quad 3\right\}$$
$$x2 = \left\{4 \quad \underset{\uparrow}{6} \quad 1 \quad 9 \quad 7\right\}$$

The commands used are as given below:

```
x1 = [5 -4 2 3];                %First sequence
x2 = [4 6 1 9 7];               %Second sequence
a = [-2:1];                     %Range of samples of first sequence
b = [-1:3];                     %Range of samples of second sequence
[z,n] = addsig(x1,a,x2,b)       %Calling of 'addsig' function
```

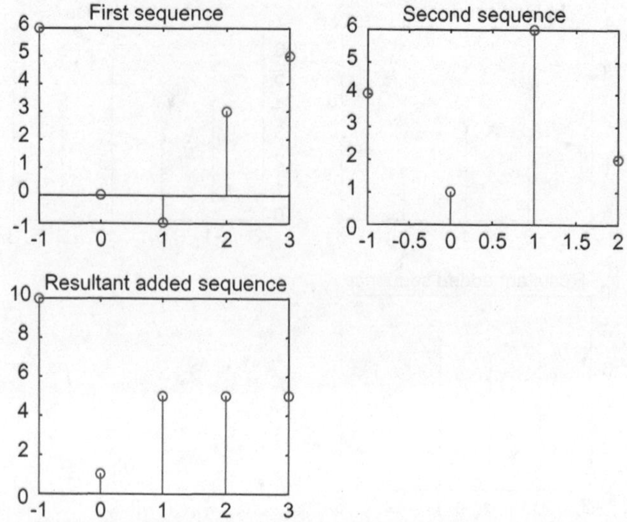

Figure 15.16 Plot Showing Sum of Discrete-time Signals of Example 15.7(b)

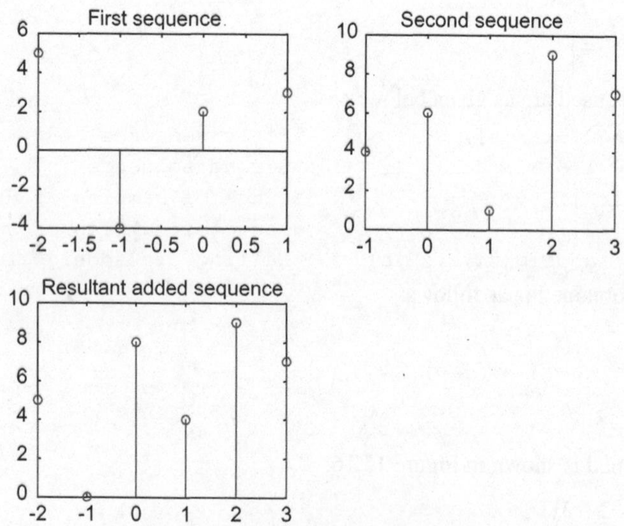

Figure 15.17 Plot Showing Sum of Discrete-time Signals of Example 15.7(c)

The response obtained is as follows:

```
z =
     5     0     8     4     9     7
n =
     2    -1     0     1     2     3
```

The plot obtained is shown in Figure 15.17.

15.3.2 Multiplication

Similar to addition, multiplication is also done by multiplying a sample by the corresponding sample. In general, it is given as

```
x(n) = x1(n).* x2(n)
```

where

`x1(n)` and `x2(n)` are two signals to be multiplied and
`x(n)` is the resultant output signal.

As in the case of addition, multiplication also requires position vectors of two signals to be of equal length before multiplication. The signals are made to have equal lengths by prefixing or suffixing zeros to requisite signal. Hence, a function `prodsig` is developed for this purpose.

15.3.2.1 `prodsig` Function

```
function [x,n] = prodsig(x1,a,x2,b)
% 'prodsig' function multiply the two discrete time signals x1 and x2 with
% the ranges a=[n11:n12] and b=[n21:n22] where a may be different from b.
% It makes the two given signals equal in length and have same position
% vector before multiplying them.
% z is the final output signal obtained and n is the range of final
% output signal.
% Plot the given sequences
n11 = min(a);
n12 = max(a);
subplot(2,2,1);
stem(a,x1);
title('First sequence');
n21 = min(b);
n22 = max(b);
subplot(2,2,2);
stem(b,x2);
title('Second sequence');
% Make two signals' lower limits equal by prefixing zeros to requisite
% signal
k = abs(n11)-abs(n21);
o = abs(k);
if (k>0)
  x2 = [zeros(1,o),x2];     %Prefix zeros to x2 signal
elseif(k<0)
  x1 = [zeros(1,o), x1];    %Prefix zeros to x1 signal
end
% Make two signals' upper limits equal by suffixing zeros to requisite
% signal
m = abs(n12)-abs(n22);
p = abs(m);
if (m>0)
  x2 = [x2,zeros(1,p)];     %Suffix zeros to x2 signal
elseif(m<0)
  x1 = [x1,zeros(1,p)];     %Suffix zeros to x1 signal
```

```
end
% Calculate the product of two sequences x1 and x2 x=x1.*x2;
% Find the limits n1 and n2 for the output sequence
% Find the lower limit
if (abs(n11)>abs(n21))
  n1 = n11;
else
  n1 = n21;
end;
% Find the upper limit
if(abs(n12)>abs(n22))
  n2 = n12;
else
  n2 = n22;
end;
n = n1:n2;
% Plot the resultant output sequence
subplot(2,2,3)
stem(n,x)
title('Resultant multiplied sequence');
```

The syntax for function **prodsig** is as follows:

```
[x,n]= prodsig(x1,a,x2,b)
```

where

x1 and x2 are given discrete-time signals,
a = [n11:n12] and b = [n21:n22] are respective time intervals and
x is resultant output sequence.
n is interval of output sequence.

Note: User-defined function `prodsig` must be saved in current directory before using it.

Example 15.8 Obtain the product of following discrete-time sequences, and plot the responses.

(a) $x1=\{1 \quad 4 \quad \underset{\uparrow}{6} \quad 3\}$

$x2=\{3 \quad \underset{\uparrow}{4} \quad 1\}$

(b) $x1=\{3 \quad 2 \quad \underset{\uparrow}{4}\}$

$x2=\{5 \quad 4 \quad \underset{\uparrow}{-3} \quad 1\}$

(c) $x1=\{8 \quad 1 \quad \underset{\uparrow}{7} \quad 2\}$

$x2=\{-1 \quad 3 \quad \underset{\uparrow}{1}\}$

Solution:

(a) $x1=\{1 \quad 4 \quad \underset{\uparrow}{6} \quad 3\}$

$x2=\{3 \quad \underset{\uparrow}{4} \quad 1\}$

The commands used are as follows:

```
x1 = [1 4 6 3];                         %First sequence
x2 = [3 4 1];                           %Second sequence
a = [-2:1];                             %Range of samples of first sequence
b = [-1:1];                             %Range of samples of second sequence
[x,n] = prodsig(x1,a,x2,b)              %Call the 'prodsig' function
```

The response obtained is as follows:

```
x =
      0      12      24      3
n =
     -2      -1       0      1
```

The plot obtained is shown in Figure 15.18.

(b) $x1 = \{3 \quad 2 \quad \underset{\uparrow}{4}\}$

$x2 = \{5 \quad 4 \quad \underset{\uparrow}{-3} \quad 1\}$

The commands used are as follows:

```
x1 = [3 2 4];                           %First sequence
x2 = [5 4 -3 1];                        %Second sequence
a = [-2:0];                             %Range of samples of first sequence
b = [-2:1];                             %Range of samples of second sequence
[x,n] = prodsig(x1,a,x2,b)              %Call the 'prodsig' function
```

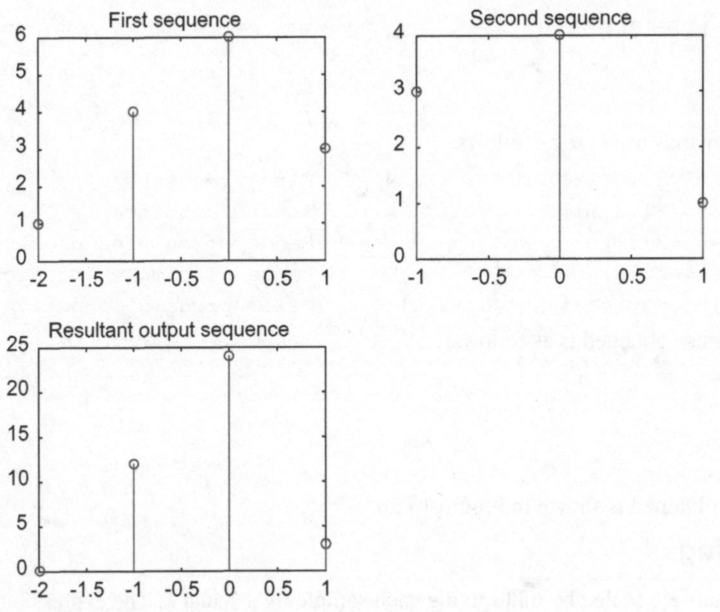

Figure 15.18 Plot Showing Product of Discrete-time Signals of Example 15.8(a)

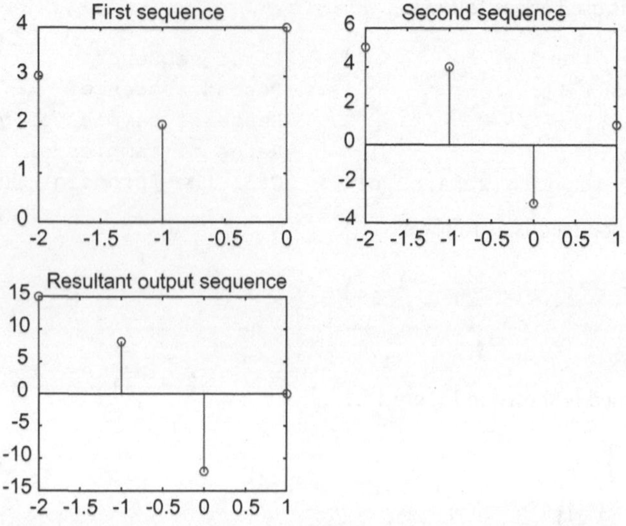

Figure 15.19 Plot Showing Product of Discrete-time Signals of Example 15.8(b)

The response obtained is as follows:

```
x =
     15     8   -12     0
n =
     -2    -1     0     1
```

The plot obtained is shown in Figure 15.19.

(c) $x1 = \{8 \quad 1 \quad \underset{\uparrow}{7} \quad 2\}$

$x2 = \{-1 \quad 3 \quad \underset{\uparrow}{1}\}$

The commands used are as follows:

```
x1 = [8 1 7 2];                  %First sequence
x2 = [-1 3 1];                   %Second sequence
a = [-2:1];                      %Range of samples of first sequence
b = [-2:0];                      %Range of samples of second sequence
[x,n] = prodsig(x1,a,x2,b)       %Call 'prodsig' function
```

The response obtained is as follows:

```
x =
     -8     3     7     0
n =
     -2    -1     0     1
```

The plot obtained is shown in Figure 15.20.

15.3.3 Scaling

Discrete-time signals are scaled by multiplying each sample by a scalar *k*. The expression is given below:

$$a(n) = k\,x(n)$$

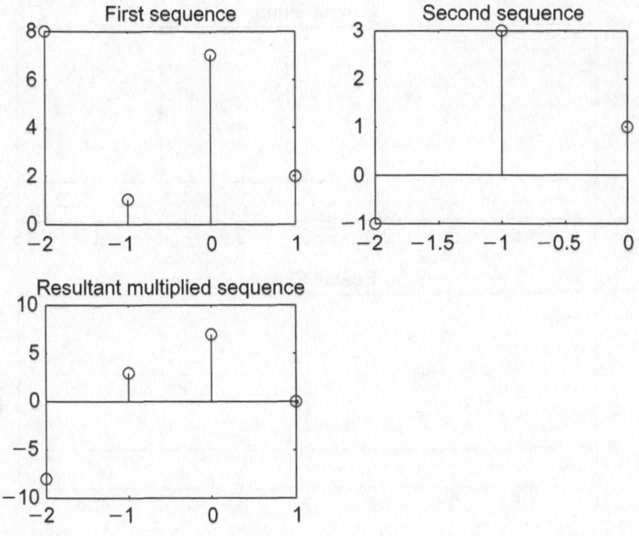

Figure 15.20 Plot Showing Product of Discrete-time Signals of Example 15.8(c)

where

$x(n)$ is discrete-time signal,
k is scalar and
$a(n)$ is output signal.

Example 15.9 Increase the magnitude of the following signal by a factor of 2.

```
x = [2 -1 4 3 1]
```

Solution: The MATLAB program to scale and plot the discrete signal is given below:

```
%Program to illustrate the scaling of a discrete signal
x = [2 -1 4 3 1];
z = 2*x;
subplot(2,1,1);
stem(x,'fill');
title('Simple Signal');
subplot(2,1,2);
stem(z,'fill');
title('Scaled Signal');
```

The response obtained is given as in Figure 15.21.

15.3.4 Folding

When for a given signal $x(n)$, the independent variable n is replaced by $-n$, it results in folding of the signal about the origin, i.e., $n = 0$. The expression for folding signal is given below:

$$a(n) = x(-n)$$

In MATLAB, folding is obtained by using function **fliplr**. The syntax is given as

```
fliplr(x)
```

where x is the input sequence.

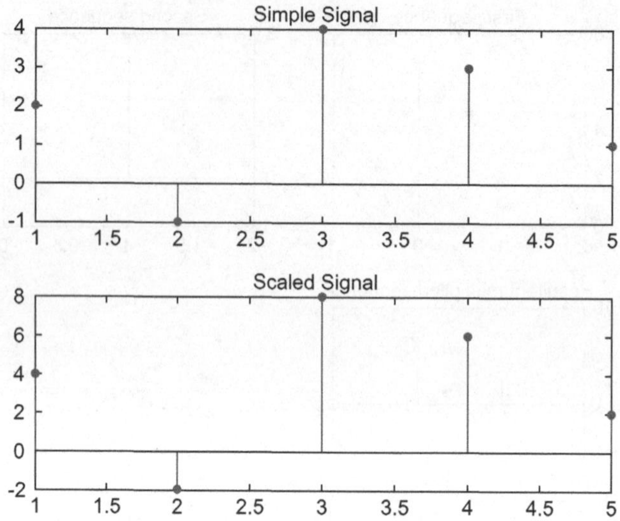

Figure 15.21 Illustration of Scaling for Example 15.9

The function `fliplr` returns a vector of same length with the order reversed, i.e., flipped over the vertical axis. *However, in case a sequence has unequal number of instants around its origin then correct result cannot be obtained. For such cases, function* `fold` *is developed.*

A user-defined function **`fold`** is developed and is given as follows:

```
function fold
%fold Function is used for folding a given sequence
%It diplays the response of input as well as folded sequence.
x = input('Enter the given sequence within square brackets: ');
n1 = input('Enter the lower limit of range of sequence: ');
n2 = input('Enter the upper limit of range of sequence: ');
n = [n1:n2];
m = -fliplr(n);
z = fliplr(x);
disp('The instants of the sequence are: ');
disp(n);
disp('The given sequence is as: ');
disp(x);
disp('The instants for folded sequence are as:');
disp(m);
disp('The resultant folded sequence is as: ');
disp(z);
subplot(2,1,1);
stem(n,x, 'fill');
title('Given Signal');
subplot(2,1,2);
stem(m,z, 'fill');
title('Folded Signal');
```

Note: User defined function `fold` must be saved in current directory before using it.

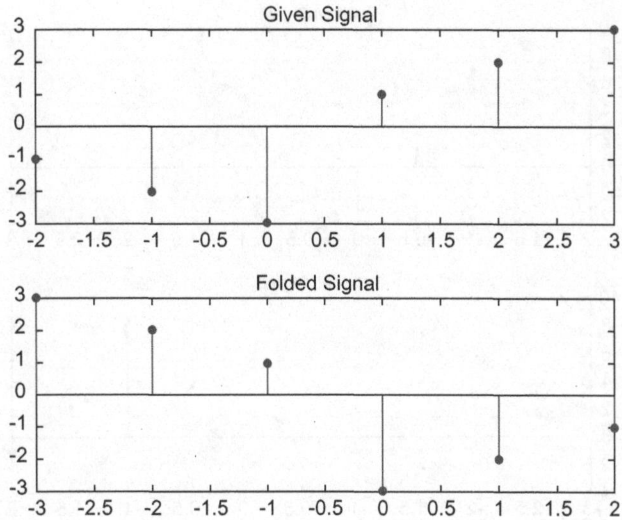

Figure 15.22 Plot Folding Sequence Obtained for Example 15.10

Example 15.10 Obtain the folding of the sequence given below:

$$x(n)=\{-1 \quad -2 \quad \underset{\uparrow}{-3} \quad 1 \quad 2 \quad 3\}$$

Solution: The user-defined function `fold` is used to obtain the folded sequence.

The MATLAB response is given below:

```
fold
Enter the given sequence within square brackets: [-1 -2 -3 1 2 3]
Enter the lower limit of range of sequence: -2
Enter the upper limit of range of sequence: 3
The instants of given sequence are:
    -2      -1       0       1       2       3
The given sequence is as:
    -1      -2      -3       1       2       3
The instants for folded sequence are as:
    -3      -2      -1       0       1       2
The resultant folded sequence is as:
     3       2       1      -3      -2      -1
```

The response is plotted and shown in Figure 15.22.

Example 15.11 Obtain the folding of the following sequence:

$$x(n)=\{-1 \quad 7 \quad \underset{\uparrow}{-4} \quad 5 \quad 3 \quad 9\}$$

Solution: The user-defined function `fold` is used to obtain the folded sequence. The response obtained is as follows:

```
fold
Enter the given sequence in square brackets: [-1 7 -4 5 3 9]
```

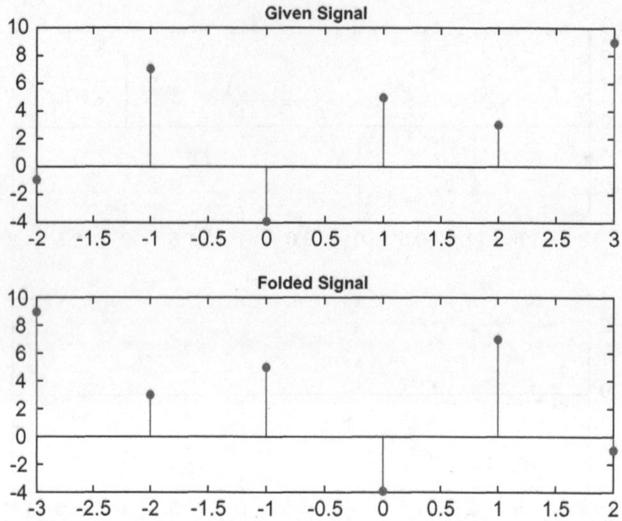

Figure 15.23 Plot of Folding Sequence Obtained for Example 15.11

```
Enter the lower limit of range of sequence: -2
Enter the upper limit of range of sequence: 3
The instants of given sequence are:
    -2        -1         0         1         2         3
The given sequence is as:
    -1         7        -4         5         3         9
The instants for folded sequence are as:
    -3        -2        -1         0         1         2
The resultant folded sequence is as:
     9         3         5        -4         7        -1
```

The response is plotted and shown in Figure 15.23.

15.3.5 Shifting

In discrete-time signals, the independent variable n may be shifted, i.e., the signal can be either advanced or delayed in time axis. If given signal $x(n)$ is shifted by k, then the resultant shifted signal is given by the expression:

$$a(n) = x(n - k)$$

if k is positive, the signal is delayed by k units and if k is negative the signal is advanced.

15.4 MULTIRATE SIGNAL PROCESSING FUNCTIONS

Some of the MATLAB functions used in signal processing are discussed as follows:

1. `decimate`
2. `interp`
3. `downsample`
4. `upsample`
5. `resample`

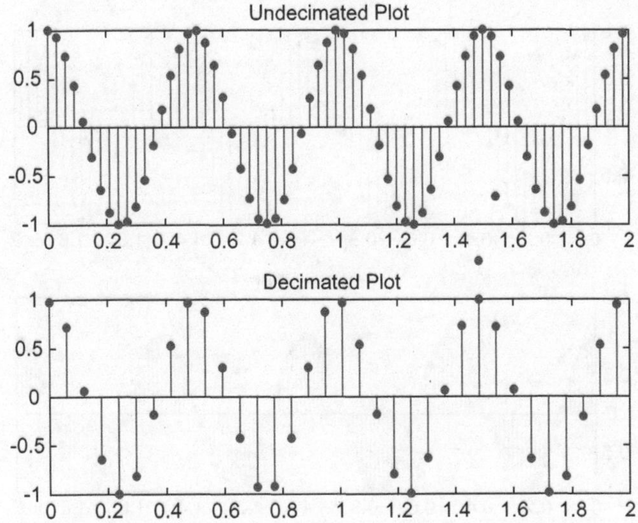

Figure 15.24 Illustration of Decimate Function

15.4.1 `decimate`

This function is used to decrease the sampling rate of a sequence. The syntax is given as

```
a = decimate(h,k)
```

It reduces the sampling rate of a given sequence `h` by a factor `k`. The resultant sequence `a` is `k` times shorter in length than the original given sequence `h`.

Example 15.12 Plot, the given expression $x = \cos(4\pi t)$ for $0 \le t \le 2$ in steps of 0.03 and illustrate the use of `decimate` function to reduce the sampling rate by 2.

Solution: The MATLAB program is given below:

```
%Program to illustrate the use of decimate function
t = 0:0.03:2;
x = cos(4*pi*t);
y = decimate(x,2);
t1 = decimate(t,2);
subplot(2,1,1);
stem(t,x,'fill');
title('Undecimated Plot');
subplot(2,1,2);
stem(t1,y,'fill');
title('Decimated Plot');
```

The response is shown in Figure 15.24.

15.4.2 `interp`

This function is used to increase the sampling rate by an integer factor. It is just opposite to that of `decimate` function. The syntax is given as

```
a = interp(h,k)
```

This increases the sampling rate of sequence h by a factor of k. The resultant vector 'a' is k times longer than the original input vector h.

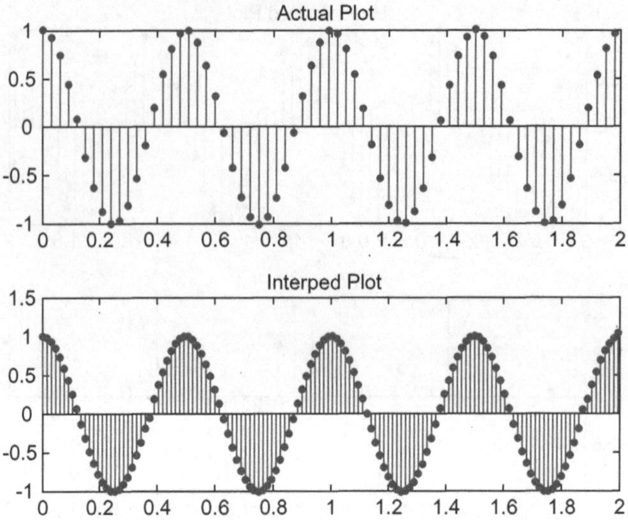

Figure 15.25 Illustration of `interp` Function

Example 15.13 Use the expression in Example 15.2 to illustrate the use of `interp` function to increase the sampling rate by 2.

Solution: The MATLAB program is given below:

```
%Program to illustrate the use of interp function
t = 0:0.03:2;
x = cos(4*pi*t);
y = interp(x,2);
t1 = interp(t,2);
subplot(2,1,1);
stem(t,x,'fill');
title('Actual Plot');
subplot(2,1,2);
stem(t1,y,'fill');
title('Interped Plot');
```

The response is shown in Figure 15.25.

15.4.3 `downsample`

This function decreases the sampling rate of input signal. The syntax is given as

```
a = downsample(x,n)
a = downsample(x,n,phase)
```

where

x is a given sequence
n is an integer indicating the number of times the sampling rate is to be decreased
a is a resultant sequence

`a = downscale(x,n)` decreases the sampling rate of sequence x by keeping every *n*th sample starting with first sample.

a = downscale(x,n,phase) specifies the number of samples by which to offset the downsampled sequence.
phase must be an integer from 0 to $(n-1)$

Example 15.14 Decrease the sampling rate of the following sequence by 2:

```
x = [2 4 7 1 4 3]
```

Solution: The commands used are as following:

```
x= [2 4 7 1 4 3]
a = downsample(x,2)
```

The result obtained is as follows:

```
x =
     2     4     7     1     4     3
a =
     2     7     4
```

It is seen that the first, third and fifth samples are retained i.e., every 2nd sample starting with first sample is retained.

Example 15.15 Decrease the sampling rate of the following sequence by 2 and add a phase offset of 1:

```
x = [2 3 5 7; 1 3 8 9; 9 3 5 0; 1 3 6 2]
```

Solution: The commands used are as

```
x = [2 3 5 7; 1 3 8 9; 9 3 5 0; 1 3 6 2]
a = downsample(x,2,1)
```

The result obtained is as

```
x =
     2     3     5     7
     1     3     8     9
     9     3     5     0
     1     3     6     2
a =
     1     3     8     9
     1     3     6     2
```

Here, each column of matrix x is considered as a separate sequence and as offset is one thus, first sample is skipped and starting from second sample every second sample is retained.

15.4.4 upsample

This function is used to increase the sampling rate of the sequence by inserting zeros between the samples. The syntax is given as

a = upsample(x,n)

where

x is a given sequence
n is an integer indicating the number of times the sampling rate is to be increased.
a is a resultant sequence.

This function increases the sampling rate of x by inserting n-1 zeros between samples

x can be a vector or a matrix.

> **Programming Tip 15.1:** In case x is a matrix, each column is considered as a separate sequence in `downsample` and `upsample` functions.

The other form of this function is given as

```
a = upsample(x,n,phase)
```

where `phase` specifies the number of samples by which to offset the upsampled sequence. It must be an integer.

Example 15.16 Increase the sampling rate of the given sequence by 2

$x = [3 \quad 9 \quad 5 \quad 4 \quad 7]$

Solution: The commands used are as given below:

```
x = [3  9  5  4  7]
a = upsample(x, 2)
```

The result obtained is as follows:

```
x =
       3    9    5    4    7
a =
       3    0    9    0    5    0    4    0    7    0
```

Example 15.17 Increase the sampling rate of the given sequence by 3 and add phase offset by 2

$x = [8 \quad 6 \quad 2 \quad 5]$

Solution: The commands used are as given below:

```
x = [8  6  2  5]
a = upsample(x, 3, 2)
```

The result obtained is as follows:

```
x =
       8    6    2    5
a =
       0    0    8    0    0    6    0    0    2    0    0    5
```

15.4.5 resample

This function changes the sampling rate of the sequence by rational factor. The syntax is given as:

```
a= resample (x, n, m)
```

This function resamples the sequence x at m/n times the original sampling rate. m and n must be positive integers.

The length of a will be equal to `ceil(length(x)*m/n)`

If x is matrix, each column is considered as a separate sequence.

Example 15.18 Change the sampling rate of the following sequence to 3/2 of original sampling rate.

$x = [4 \quad 1 \quad 5 \quad 8 \quad 3]$

Solution: The commands used are as below:

```
x = [4  1  5  8  3]
a = resample(x, 3, 2)
```

The result obtained is as follows:

```
x =
    4   1   5   8   3
a =
    4.0000  2.1126  1.0981  5.0000  8.2471  6.6824  3.0000  0.5114
```

15.5 CONVOLUTION

In linear and time-variant systems, the response of the system to any arbitrary input signal can be expressed in terms of unit sample response of the system. The general form of expression that relates the unit sample response of the system and the arbitrary input signal to the output signal, called the convolution sum or convolution formula. Thus, it determines the out of any linear, time-variant system to any arbitrary input. Convolution is of two types: linear and circular

Methods to Compute Linear Convolution

1. Convolution sum method
2. With the help of circular convolution
3. Using Fast Fourier Transform (FFT)

15.5.1 Linear Convolution (Convolution Sum Method)

If `y(n)` is a sequence whose values are a function of the two sequences `h(n)` and `x(n)` as given in equation (15.1), then `y(n)` is called **convolution** of `x(n)` with `h(n)`:

$$y(n) = \sum_{k=-\infty}^{\infty} x(n) * h(n-k) \tag{15.1}$$

The convolution is represented as:

```
y(n) = x(n)*h(n)
```

The operation of discrete-time convolution takes two sequences `x(n)` and `h(n)` as input and produces a third sequence *y*(*n*).

In MATLAB, convolution of any two causal signals (that depends only on present and future samples) can be done by using `conv` command as shown below:

```
conv(x, h)
```

where `x` and `h` represent discrete-time causal sequences `x(n)` and `h(n)`.

Example 15.19 Compute the convolution for the following sequences:

(i)	$x(n) = [2 \quad 1 \quad 0 \quad 0.5]$	$h(n) = [2 \quad 2 \quad 1 \quad 1]$
(ii)	$x(n) = [1 \quad 2 \quad 3 \quad 6 \quad -2]$	$h(n) = [1 \quad 1 \quad 1]$
(iii)	$x(n) = [2 \quad 5 \quad 9 \quad 3 \quad 4]$	$h(n) = [3 \quad 1 \quad 6]$

Solution: These are the causal sequences, hence built-in function `conv` can be used for calculating the convolution.

(i) The commands used are as

```
x = [2 1 0 0.5];
h = [2 2 1 1];
y = conv(x,h)
```

The result obtained is as follows:

```
y =
      4.0000    6.0000    4.0000    4.0000    2.0000    0.5000    0.5000
```

(ii) The commands used are as

```
x = [1 2 3 6 -2];
h = [1 1 1];
y = conv(x,h)
```

The result obtained is as follows:

```
y =
    1    3    6    11    7    4    -2
```

(iii) The commands used are as

```
x = [2 5 9 3 4];
h = [3 1 6];
y = conv(x,h)
```

The result obtained is as follows:

```
y =
    6    17    44    48    69    22    24
```

However, for discrete-time non-causal signals (i.e., which depends upon past, present and future sample values), the built-in function conv cannot be used. As in causal signals, the time instants start from instant 0 onwards, thus resultant output starts from zero instant onwards. But in non-causal signals the samples are starting from some past instant value, thus to get proper output past instants have to be determined which are not possible in built-in conv function. So, a new modified convolution function **dsconv** is developed and is given as under:

```
function dsconv
%dsconv computes the convolution for discrete time sequences.
%This function is used for non-causal as well as causal
%sequences.
a = input('Enter the first sequence in square bracket: ');
b = input('Enter the second sequence in square bracket: ');
m1 = input('Enter the lower limit of range of first sequence: ');
m2 = input('Enter the upper limit of range of first sequence: ');
p1 = input('Enter the lower limit of range of second sequence: ');
p2 = input('Enter the upper limit of range of first sequence: ');
m = [m1:m2];
p = [p1:p2];
%Calculate the range for resultant sequence
n1 = m1+p1;
n2 = m2+p2;
%Calculate the resultant sequence
fprintf('The resultant convolution sequence is:\n\t');
c = conv(a,b)
fprintf('The corresponding sampling instants are:\n\t');
n = [n1:n2]
```

Note: User-defined function `dsconv` must be saved in current directory before using it.

Example 15.20 Compute the convolution for the following non-causal sequences:

(i) $x(n) = \{-1 \;\; 3 \;\; \underset{\uparrow}{2} \;\; 0 \;\; 1\}, \quad h(n)\{-3 \;\; \underset{\uparrow}{5} \;\; 0 \;\; 1\}$

(ii) $x(n) = \{3 \;\; \underset{\uparrow}{2} \;\; -1 \;\; 0 \;\; 4 \;\; 3\}, \quad h(n)\{-2 \;\; 1 \;\; \underset{\uparrow}{0} \;\; 1\}$

(iii) $x(n) = \{-5 \;\; 4 \;\; \underset{\uparrow}{1} \;\; 3 \;\; 0\}, \quad h(n)\{1 \;\; 3 \;\; \underset{\uparrow}{0} \;\; 6 \;\; 7\}$

Solution: Here the built-in MATLAB function `conv` cannot be used as such. For calculating the convolution of these sequences, user-defined function `dsconv` is used. The function is called by writing the function name `dsconv` on the command prompt and the response obtained is as given below:

(i)
```
dsconv
Enter the first sequence in square bracket: [-1 3 2 0 1]
Enter the second sequence in square bracket: [-3 5 0 1]
Enter the lower limit of range of first sequence: -2
Enter the upper limit of range of first sequence: 2
Enter the lower limit of range of second sequence: -1
Enter the upper limit of range of first sequence: 2
The resultant convolution sequence is:
c =
    3   -14    9    9    0    7    0    1
The corresponding sampling instants are:
n =
   -3    -2   -1    0    1    2    3    4
```

(ii)
```
dsconv
Enter the first sequence in square bracket: [3 2 -1 0 4 3]
Enter the second sequence in square bracket: [-2 1 0 1]
Enter the lower limit of range of first sequence: -1
Enter the upper limit of range of first sequence: 4
Enter the lower limit of range of second sequence: -2
Enter the upper limit of range of first sequence: 1
The resultant convolution sequence is:
c =
   -6    -1    4    2   -6   -3    3    4    3
The corresponding sampling instants are:
n =
   -3    -2   -1    0    1    2    3    4    5
```

(iii)
```
dsconv
Enter the first sequence in square bracket: [-5 4 1 3 0]
Enter the second sequence in square bracket: [1 3 0 6 7]
Enter the lower limit of range of first sequence: -2
Enter the upper limit of range of first sequence: 2
Enter the lower limit of range of second sequence: -2
Enter the upper limit of range of first sequence: 2
```

```
The resultant convolution sequence is:
c =
    -5    -11    13    -24    -2    34    25    21    0
The corresponding sampling instants are:
n =
    -4    -3    -2    -1    0    1    2    3    4
```

15.5.2 Circular Convolution

Circular convolution is used to convolve two discrete Fourier transform (DFT) sequences. For very long sequences, circular convolution may be faster than linear convolution.

The MATLAB function to perform circular convolution is **cconv** and general syntax for cconv is given below:

```
c = cconv(a,b,n)
```

Circularly convolves vectors ***a*** and ***b***. ***n*** is the length of the resulting vector. If you omit ***n***, it defaults to length(a) + length(B) – 1. When ***n*** = length(a) + length(B) – 1, the circular convolution is equivalent to the linear convolution computed with conv.

Example 15.21 Compute the circular convolution for the following sequences:

(i) $x(n) = [2\ \ 1\ \ 0\ \ 0.5]$, $h(n) = [2\ \ 2\ \ 1\ \ 1]$

(ii) $x(n) = [1\ \ 2\ \ 3\ \ 6\ \ -2]$, $h(n) = [1\ \ 1\ \ 1]$

(iii) $x(n) = [2\ \ 5\ \ 9\ \ 3\ \ 4]$, $h(n) = [3\ \ 1\ \ 6]$

Solution: For these sequences, build-in function `cconv` can be used for calculating circular convolution.

(i) The commands used are as

```
a = [2 1 0 0.5];
b = [2 2 1 1];
% n is maximum length of input vector.
n = 4;
y = cconv(a,b,n)
```

The result obtained is as follows:

```
y =
        6.0000        6.5000        4.5000        4.0000
```

(ii) The commands used are as

```
a = [1 2 3 6 -2];
b = [1 1 1];
% n is maximum length of input vector.
n = 5;
y = cconv(a,b,n)
```

The result obtained is as follows:

```
y =
        5     1     6    11     7
```

(iii) The commands used are as

```
a = [2 5 9 3 4];
b = [3 1 6];
```

```
%n is maximum length of input vector.
n = 5;
y = cconv(a,b,n)
```

The result obtained is as follows:

```
y =
        28.0000    41.0000    44.0000    48.0000    69.0000
```

Maximum length of input vector and to enter any arbitrary sequence, a new modified circular convolution function dscconv is developed and is given as follows:

```
function dscconv
a =input('Enter the first sequence in square bracket:');
b =input('Enter the second sequence in square bracket:');
if length(a)> length(b)
   n =length(a)
else
   n = length(b)
end
y =cconv(a,b,n)
fprintf('The resultant circular convolution sequence is: \n\t')
```

Note: User-defined function `dscconv` must be saved in current directory before using it.

15.5.2.1 Linear Convolution using Circular Convolution

To perform linear convolution with the help of circular convolution, replace the conv command with syntax cconv(u,v).

Example 15.22 Compute the linear convolution using circular convolution for the following sequences:

(i) $x(n) = [2\ \ 1\ \ 0\ \ 0.5]$, $h(n) = [2\ \ 2\ \ 1\ \ 1]$

(ii) $x(n) = [1\ \ 2\ \ 3\ \ 6\ \ -2]$, $h(n) = [1\ \ 1\ \ 1]$

(iii) $x(n) = [2\ \ 5\ \ 9\ \ 3\ \ 4]$, $h(n) = [3\ \ 1\ \ 6]$

Solution: To compute linear convolution using circular convolution, build-in function cconv is used.

(i) The commands used are as

```
a = [2 1 0 0.5];
b = [2 2 1 1];
y = cconv(a,b)
```

The result obtained is as follows:

```
y =
4.0000    6.0000    4.0000    4.0000    2.0000    0.5000    0.5000
```

(ii) The commands used are as

```
a = [1 2 3 6 -2];
b = [1 1 1];
y = cconv(a,b)
```

The result obtained is as follows:

```
y =
        1.0000   3.0000    6.0000   11.0000    7.0000    4.0000    -2.0000
```

(iii) The Commands used are as follows

```
a = [2 5 9 3 4];
b = [3 1 6];
y = cconv(a,b)
```

The result obtained is as follows:

```
y =
        6.0000   17.0000   44.0000   48.0000   69.0000   22.0000   24.0000
```

Note: For discrete-time non-causal signals, replace `conv` with `cconv` in user-defined function `dsconv`.

15.5.3 Linear Convolution using FFT

Convolution in time domain is equal to multiplication in frequency domain. To perform linear convolution using FFT, make length of both sequence equal by appending zeros, then take FFT of individual sequence, then multiply it and perform inverse of multiplied sequence. The user-defined MATLAB function confft is used for causal and non-causal discrete-time sequences given as follows:

```
function confft
a =input('Enter the first sequence in square bracket: ');
b =input('Enter the second sequence in square bracket: ');
m1 =input('Enter the lower limit of range of first sequence: ');
m2 =input('Enter the upper limit of range of first sequence: ');
p1 =input('Enter the lower limit of range of second sequence: ');
p2 =input('Enter the upper limit of range of first sequence: ');
m = [m1:m2];
p = [p1:p2];
%Calculate the range for resultant sequence
n1 = m1+p1;
n2 = m2+p2;
%Calculate the resultant sequence
fprintf('The resultant convolution sequence is:\n\t');
x = [a zeros(1, length(b)-1)];
y = [b zeros(1, length(a)-1)];
A =fft(x);
B =fft(y);
C =A.*B;
fprintf('The resultant linear convolution using FFT is: \n\t')
D =ifft(C)
fprintf('The corresponding sampling instants are:\n\t');
n = [n1:n2]
```

Example 15.23 Compute the linear convolution for the following sequences:

(i) $x(n)=\{-1\ 3\ \underset{\uparrow}{2}\ 0\ 1\},\ h(n)=\{-3\ \underset{\uparrow}{5}\ 0\ 1\}$

(ii) $x(n)=[1\ 2\ 3\ 6\ -2],\ h(n)=[1\ 1\ 1]$

Solution: For calculating the convolution of these sequences, user-defined function confft is used. The function is called by writing the function name confft on command prompt and the response obtained is as given below:

(i)
```
confft
Enter the first sequence in square bracket: [-1 3 2 0 1]
Enter the second sequence in square bracket: [-3 5 0 1]
Enter the lower limit of range of first sequence: -2
Enter the upper limit of range of first sequence: 2
Enter the lower limit of range of second sequence: -1
Enter the upper limit of range of first sequence: 2
The resultant convolution sequence is:
The resultant linear convolution using FFT is:
D =
Columns 1 through 7
3.0000   -14.0000    9.0000    9.0000    0.0000    7.0000   -0.0000
  Column 8
1.0000
The corresponding sampling instants are:
n =
    -3    -2    -1    0    1    2    3    4
```

(ii)
```
confft
Enter the first sequence in square bracket: [1 2 3 6 -2]
Enter the second sequence in square bracket: [1 1 1]
Enter the lower limit of range of first sequence: 0
Enter the upper limit of range of first sequence: 4
Enter the lower limit of range of second sequence: 0
Enter the upper limit of range of first sequence: 2
The resultant convolution sequence is:
The resultant linear convolution using FFT is:
D =
1.0000    3.0000    6.0000    11.0000    7.0000    4.0000   -2.0000
The corresponding sampling instants are:
n =
    0    1    2    3    4    5    6
```

15.5.4 Correlation

Correlation gives a measure of similarity between two data sequences. In this process, two sequences are compared and the degree to which the two signals are similar is computed.

The cross-correlation between pair of sequence $x(n)$ and $y(n)$ is given by

$$R_{xy} = \sum_{k=-\infty}^{\infty} x(k)y(k-n)$$

$$= \sum_{k=-\infty}^{\infty} x(k+n)y(k) \qquad n = 0, \pm 1, \pm 2, \ldots\ldots$$

The index n is shifting (lag) parameter. The order of subscripts xy indicates that $x(n)$ is the reference sequence that remains fixed, i.e., unshifted in time, whereas the sequence $y(n)$ is shifted n units in time w.r.t. $x(n)$.

Note: $R_{xy} \neq R_{yx}$

The expression for $R_{xy}(n)$ can be written as

$$R_{xy} = \sum_{k=-\infty}^{\infty} x(k)y[-(n)-k]$$

$$= x(n) * y(-n)$$

Above equation shows that the correlation of two sequences is same as the convolution of two sequences in which one sequence has been reversed, i.e., correlation is the convolution of one signal with a folded version of the second sequence.

The MATLAB command for correlation is xcorr and general syntax for command xcorr is:

```
c = xcorr(x,y)
```

It returns the cross-correlation sequence in a length $2*N - 1$ vector, where x and y are length N vectors ($N > 1$). If x and y are not the same length, the shorter vector is zero-padded to the length of the longer vector.

Example 15.24 Compute the cross-correlation for following sequences:

(i) $x(n) = [1\ \ 0\ \ 0\ \ 1]$, $h(n) = [4\ \ 3\ \ 2\ \ 1]$

(ii) $x(n) = [1\ \ 2\ \ 3\ \ 4]$, $h(n) = [1\ \ 1\ \ 1]$

Solution: To calculate correlation build in function xcorr is used.

(i) The commands used are

```
a = [1 0 0 1];
b = [4 3 2 1];
D =xcorr(a,b)
```

The result obtained is as follows:

```
D =
1.0000    2.0000    3.0000    5.0000    2.0000    3.0000    4.0000
```

(ii) The commands used are

```
a = [1 2 3 4];
b = [1 1 1];
D = xcorr(a,b)
```

The result obtained is as follows:

```
D =
0    1.0000    3.0000    6.0000    9.0000    7.0000    4.0000
```

15.5.4.1 Cross-Correlation using Convolution

The user-defined MATLAB function circon is used to compute cross-correlation with the help of circular convolution is given as follows:

```
function circon
a = input('Enter the first sequence in square bracket:');
b = input('Enter the second sequence in square bracket:');
fprintf('The resultant cross-correlation sequence using circular convolution
is: \n\t')
c = cconv(a,(fliplr(b)))
```

Example 15.25 Compute cross-correlation with the help of circular convolution of following sequences:

(i) $x(n) = [1\ 0\ 0\ 1]$, $h(n) = [4\ 3\ 2\ 1]$

(ii) $x(n) = [1\ 2\ 3\ 4]$, $h(n) = [1\ 1\ 1]$

Solution: For calculating cross-correlation with the help of circular convolution of these sequences, user-defined function circon is used. The function is called by writing the function name circon on command prompt and the response obtained is as given below:

(i)
```
circon
Enter the first sequence in square bracket: [1 0 0 1]
Enter the second sequence in square bracket: [4 3 2 1]
The resultant cross-correlation sequence using circular convolution
is:
c =
1.0000    2.0000    3.0000    5.0000    2.0000    3.0000    4.0000
```

(ii)
```
circon
Enter the first sequence in square bracket: [1 2 3 4]
Enter the second sequence in square bracket: [1 1 1]
The resultant cross-correlation sequence using circular convolu-
tion is:
c =
    1.0000    3.0000    6.0000    9.0000    7.0000    4.0000
```

15.5.4.2 Autocorrelation

The autocorrelation of a sequence is correlation of a sequence with itself. It gives a measure of similarity between a sequence and its shifted version. The autocorrelation of sequence is defined as:

$$R_{xx} = \sum_{k=-\infty}^{\infty} x(k)x(k-n)$$

Or autocorrelation can be given as

$$R_{xx}(n) = x(k)*x(-k)$$

Autocorrelation is the special case of cross-correlation. The MATLAB command used to perform autocorrelation is `c = xcorr(x)` is the autocorrelation sequence for the vector $\boldsymbol{x}$. If $\boldsymbol{x}$ is an N-by-P matrix, **c** is a matrix with $2N - 1$ rows whose P^2 columns contain the cross-correlation sequences for all combinations of the columns of $\boldsymbol{x}$.

15.6 Z-TRANSFORM

Similar to Laplace Transform which used for analysis of continuous-time signals and LTI systems, z-transform is used for analysis of discrete-time signals and LTI systems.

The discrete-time Fourier Transform of discrete-time signals and LTI systems results in frequency domain representation. However, in many cases, convergence of discrete-time Fourier Transform does not exist thus frequency-domain characterization of such cases cannot be made. Hence, the complex sinusoidal representation provided by discrete-time Fourier Transform is generalized and is represented in terms of complex exponential signals, called **z-transform**.

Basically, z-transform is used to study the system characteristics and derivation of computational structures for implementing discrete-time systems on computers. As many algebraic manipulations using z-transform are possible, it has become an important tool in the analysis and design of digital filters.

Mathematically, z-transform of an arbitrary signal $x(n)$ is given as

$$X(z) = \sum_{n=-\infty}^{\infty} x(n) z^{-n} \tag{15.2}$$

where z is a complex variable

Substituting $z = re^{jw}$, we get:

$$X(z)\big|_{z=re^{jw}} = X\left(re^{jw}\right) = \sum_{n=-\infty}^{n=\infty} x(n) r^{-n} e^{-jwn} \tag{15.3}$$

This expression is same as discrete-time Fourier Transform of modified discrete-time signal $x(n)\ r^{-n}$

If $r = 1$, then $|z| = 1$, $X(z)$ reduces to its Fourier Transform as given by

$$X(z) = \sum_{n=-\infty}^{n=\infty} x(n) e^{-jwn} = \text{Fourier Transform of } x(n) \tag{15.4}$$

The expression of $X(z)$ [Eq. (15.2)] will converge if $[x(n)z^{-n}]$ is absolutely summable, that is if

$$\sum_{n=-\infty}^{n=\infty} \left|x(n) z^{-n}\right| < \infty \tag{15.5}$$

Hence, for $x(n)$ to be finite, the magnitude of its z-transform $X(z)$ must also be finite.

The range of z for which this condition is satisfied is termed as the Region of Convergence (ROC).

The process of finding the time domain signal $x(n)$ from its Z-transform $X(z)$ is called inverse Z-transform, where $x(n)$ is

$$= \frac{1}{2\pi j} \oint X(z) z^{n-1} \mathrm{d}z$$

Or $\quad x(n) = Z^{-1}[X(z)]$

The MATLAB command used for Z-transform is `ztrans` and general syntax is given as

```
ztrans(f,trans_index,eval_point)
```

computes the Z-transform of '*f*' with respect to the transformation index `trans_index` at the point `eval_point`.

15.6.1 Input Arguments

F	Symbolic expression, symbolic function, or vector or matrix of symbolic expressions or functions.
trans_index	Symbolic variable representing the transformation index. This variable is often called the 'discrete time variable'. **Default:** The variable *n*. If f does not contain *n*, then the default variable is determined by symvar.
eval_point	Symbolic variable or expression representing the evaluation point. This variable is often called the 'complex frequency variable'. **Default:** The variable *z*. If *z* is the transformation index of *f*, then the default evaluation point is the variable *w*.

15.6.2 Inverse Z-Transform

To compute the inverse Z-transform, MATLAB function iztrans is used. The syntax is given below:

```
iztrans(F,trans_index,eval_point)
```

computes the inverse Z-transform of *f* with respect to the transformation index trans_index at the point eval_point.

The notations used are similar to those for Z-transform.

Example 15.26 Compute Z-transform and inverse Z-transform for following sequences:

(i) na^n

(ii) $e^{jn(\Pi/4)}$

(iii) $\cos(\omega n)$

Solution:

(i) The commands used are as

```
syms a n z
f = n*(a^n);
fprintf('Z-transform of given sequence is: \n\t')
X = ztrans(f)
fprintf('Inverse Z-transform of  sequence is: \n\t')
Y = iztrans(X)
```

The result obtained is as follows:

```
Z-transform of given sequence is:
X =
(a*z)/(a - z)^2
Inverse Z-transform of  sequence is:
Y =
piecewise([a == 0, 0], [a ~= 0, a*(a^n/a - kroneckerDelta(n, 0)/a)
+ a^2*(kroneckerDelta(n, 0)/a^2 + (a^n*(n - 1))/a^2)])
```

(ii) The commands used are as

```
syms j n pi z
```

```
f = exp(j*n*(pi/4));
fprintf('Z-transform of given sequence is: \n\t')
X = ztrans(f)
fprintf('Inverse Z-transform of  sequence is: \n\t')
Y = iztrans(X)
```

The result obtained is as follows:

```
Z-transform of given sequence is:
X =

    z/(z - exp((pi*j)/4))
Inverse Z-transform of sequence is:
Y =
exp((pi*j)/4)*(exp(-(pi*j)/4)*exp((pi*j)/4)^n-exp(-(pi*-
j)/4)*kroneckerDelta(n, 0)) + kroneckerDelta(n, 0)
```

(iii) The commands used are as

```
syms w n z
f = cos(w*n);
fprintf('Z-transform of given sequence is: \n\t')
X = ztrans(f)
fprintf('Inverse Z-transform of  sequence is: \n\t')
Y = iztrans(X)
```

The result obtained is

```
Z-transform of given sequence is:
X =
(z*(z - cos(w)))/(z^2 - 2*cos(w)*z + 1)
Inverse Z-transform of  sequence is:
Y =

    cos(n*w)
```

> **Programming Tip 15.2:** If you call ztrans with two arguments, it assumes that the second argument is the evaluation point eval_point.

If f is a matrix, ztrans applies the *Z*-transform to all components of the matrix.
To compute the inverse *Z*-transform, use iztrans.

15.6.3 Pole-Zero Plot of Transfer Function

The MATLAB Command to create transfer function is `tf` and syntax for `tf` is given below:

`sys = (num,den) sys = tf(num,den,Ts)`

`sys = tf(num,den)` creates a continuous-time transfer function with numerator(s) and denominator(s) specified by num and den. The output sys is a TF object storing the transfer function data.

`sys = tf(num,den,Ts)` creates a discrete-time transfer function with sample time T_s (in seconds). Set $T_s = -1$ to leave the sample time unspecified. The input arguments num and den are as in the continuous-time case and must list the numerator and denominator coefficients in *descending* powers of *z*.

`tf` switches convention based on the choice of variable (value of the 'Variable' property).

Variable	Convention
'z' (default), 'q'	Use the row vector `[ak ... a1 a0]` to specify the polynomial $a_k z^k + \cdots + a_1 z + a_0$ (coefficients ordered in *descending* powers of z or q).
'z^-1'	Use the row vector `[b0 b1 ... bk]` to specify the polynomial $b_0 + b_1 z^{-1} + \cdots + b_k z^{-k}$ (coefficients in ascending powers of z^{-1}).

To plot poles and zeros of transfer function in z-plane. The MATLAB function z-plane is used. The syntax is given below:

```
zplane(b,a)
```

where ***b*** and ***a*** are row vectors, the zeros and poles of the transfer function represented by numerator coefficients ***b*** and denominator coefficients ***a***. The transfer function is defined in terms of z^{-1}:

$$H(z) = \frac{B(z)}{A(z)} = \frac{b(1) + b(2)z^{-1} + \cdots + b(n+1)z^{-n}}{a(1) + a(2)z^{-1} + \cdots + a(m+1)z^{-m}}$$

Example 15.27 Compute pole-zero plot for following equations:

(i) $H(z) = \dfrac{z^2 - z + 1}{z^2 - z + 1/2}$

(ii) $H(z) = \dfrac{3 + z^{-1}}{1 + z^{-1} - (4/9)z^{-2}}$

Solution:

(i) The commands used are:

```
b = [1 -1 1];
a = [1 -1 1/2];
h = tf(b,a,1)
zplane(b,a)
The result obtained is given as
h =
   z^2 - z + 1
  -------------
z^2 - z + 0.5
Sample time: 1 seconds
Discrete-time transfer function.
```

(ii) The commands used are:

```
b = [3 1];
a = [1 1 -4/9];
h = tf(b,a,1, 'variable', 'z^-1')
z-plane(b,a)
```

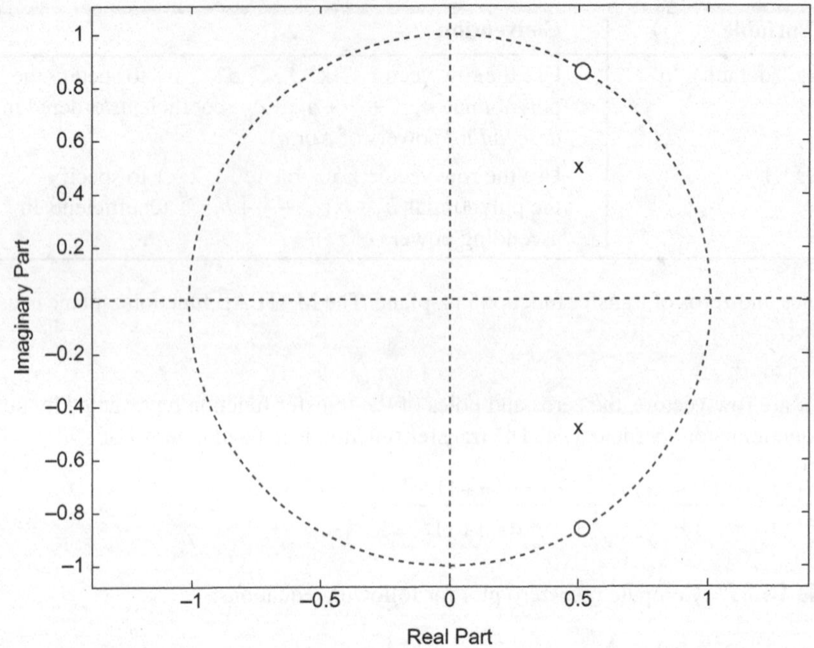

(a)

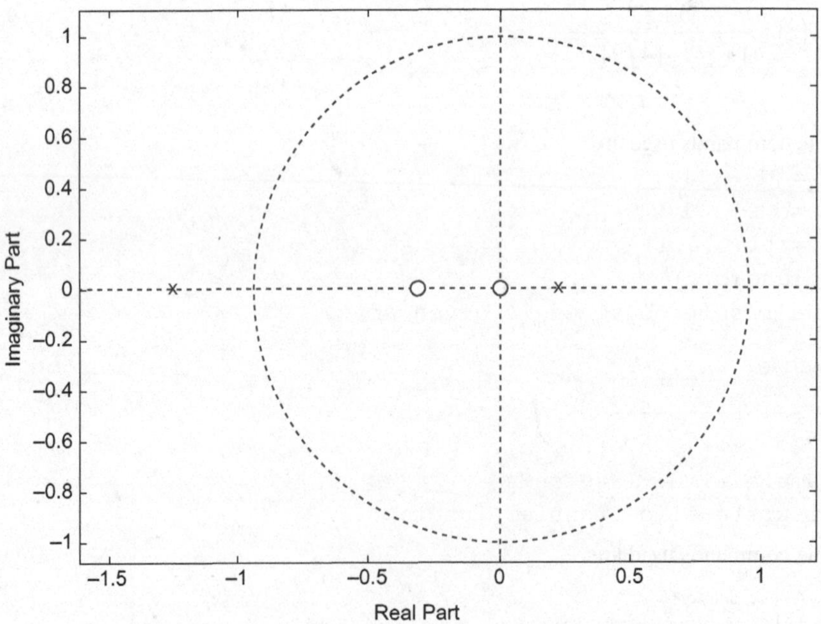

(b)

Illustration of z-plane function

The result obtained is as follows:

```
h =

        3 + z^-1
        ----------------------
        1 + z^-1 - 0.4444 z^-2

Sample time: 1 second
Discrete-time transfer function
```

15.7 DISCRETE-TIME FOURIER TRANSFORM

Discrete-Time Fourier Transform (DTFT) is Fourier Transform of discrete-time sequence. It represents the discrete-time sequence $x(n)$ in terms of complex exponential sequence (e^{jw}) where w is the real frequency variable. Mathematically, DTFT $X(e^{jw})$ of a sequence $x(n)$ is given as

$$X\left(e^{jw}\right) = \sum_{n=-\infty}^{n=\infty} x(n)e^{-jwn} \tag{15.6}$$

Also $x(n)$ can be represented vice versa, that is

$$x(n) = \frac{1}{2\pi}\int_{-\pi}^{\pi} X\left(e^{jw}\right)e^{jwn}dw$$

$$\Rightarrow \text{IDFT } X\left(e^{jw}\right) = x(n) \tag{15.7}$$

Symbolically,

$$x(n) \xleftrightarrow{\text{DTFT}} X\left(e^{jw}\right)$$

In MATLAB, user-defined function can be developed to evaluate DTFT of a given sequence.

15.8 DISCRETE FOURIER TRANSFORM

It is observed that DTFT is defined for any infinite sequence. In case of finite-length sequence $x(n)$, $0 \le n \le N-1$, there exists a relation between sequence and its DTFT $X(e^{jw})$. Thus, for length N sequence, N values of $X(e^{jw})$ at different frequency points are sufficient to determine $x(n)$ and hence $X(e^{jw})$. This evaluation of finite length sequence leads to Discrete Fourier Transform (DFT).

> **Programming Tip 15.3:** DTFT is applicable to any arbitrary sequence whereas DFT is used for finite length sequence only.

Mathematically, DFT of discrete-time sequence $x(n)$ is given as

$$X(k) = \sum_{n=0}^{N-1} x(n)e^{-j2\pi nk/N}, k = 0, 1, 2, \ldots, N-1 \tag{15.8}$$

or $\quad W_N = e^{-j2\pi/N}$

we have,

$$X(k) = \sum_{n=0}^{N-1} x(n) W_N^{kn}, \quad k = 0, 1, 2, \ldots, N-1$$

The Inverse Discrete Fourier Transform (IDFT) is given by

$$x(n) = \frac{1}{N} \sum_{k=0}^{N-1} X(k) W_N^{-kn}, \quad n = 0, 1, 2, \ldots, N-1 \tag{15.9}$$

15.9 FAST FOURIER TRANSFORM (FFT)

From the mathematical expressions of DTFT, it is clear that for all the values of k, approximately N^2 complex multiplications and $N(N - 1)$ complex additions are required to be done. To reduce this computational complexity to about $N(\log_2 N)$ computations, efficient algorithm is used called Fast Fourier Transform (FFT) algorithm. This algorithm uses the periodicity and symmetry properties of complex number W_N^{kn} and thus reduces the computational complexity. The two main categories of FFT algorithms are as follows:

- Decimation in time FFT algorithm
- Decimation in frequency FFT algorithm

In MATLAB, for calculating DFT with FFT algorithm of a given sequence, **fft** function is used. The syntax is given below:

```
a = fft(x)
```

where

x is given discrete sequence

a is the resultant FFT of sequence x.

If x is a matrix, it returns Fourier transform of each column of matrix and if x is a multidimensional array, it operates on first non-singleton dimension.

Another form of fft function is:

```
a = fft(x, N)
```

This returns N-point DFT of the sequence x. If the length of x is less than N, x is padded with trailing zeros.

If length of x is greater than N, the sequence x is truncated.

When x is a matrix, the length of columns are adjusted in the same manner.

Third form of fft function is:

```
a = fft(x,N,dim)
```

This applies FFT operation across the dimension dim.

15.9.1 Inverse Fast Fourier Transform

To compute the Inverse Fast Fourier Transform, MATLAB function **ifft** is used. The syntax is given below:

```
b = ifft(x)
b = ifft(x,N)
b = ifft(x,N,dim)
```

The notations used are similar to those for fft function.

Example 15.28 Obtain DFT of the following sequences:

(a) $x(n) = \{0 \quad 2 \quad 4 \quad 1 \quad 5\}$
(b) $x(n) = 3^n$, for $N = 4$
(c) $x(n) = n + 1$, for $N = 8$
(d) $x(n) = [4 \quad 5 \quad 8; 2 \quad 5 \quad 4; 1 \quad 9 \quad 6]$

Solution:

(a) The commands used are:

```
x = [0 2 4 1 5];
a = fft(x)
```

The result obtained is given as

```
a =
    12.0000    -1.8820 + 1.0898i    -4.1180 + 4.6165i    -4.1180 - 4.6165i
    -1.8820 - 1.0898i
```

(b) The given sequence is:

$x(n) = \{1 \quad 3 \quad 9 \quad 27\}$ for $N = 4$

The commands to obtain FFT are:

```
x = [1 3 9 27];
a = fft(x,4)
```

The result obtained is:

```
a =
    40.0    -8.0000+24.0000i    -20.0000    -8.0000-24.0000i
```

(c) The given sequence is:

$x(n) = \{0 \quad 1 \quad 2 \quad 3 \quad 4 \quad 5 \quad 6 \quad 7\}$ for $N = 8$

The commands used are:

```
x = [0 1 2 3 4 5 6 7];
a = fft(x,8)
a =
Columns 1 through 6
28.0000                         -4.0000 + 9.6569i    -4.0000 + 4.0000i
-4.0000 + 1.6569i    -4.0000                         -4.0000 - 1.6569i
Columns 7 through 8
-4.0000 - 4.0000i    -4.0000 - 9.6569i
```

(d) The commands used are:

```
x = [4 5 8; 2 5 4 ; 1 9 6]
a = fft(x)
```

The result obtained is:

```
x =
      4     5     8
      2     5     4
      1     9     6

a =
    7.0000              19.0000              18.0000
```

```
2.5000 - 0.8660i    -2.0000 + 3.4641i    3.0000 + 1.7321i
2.5000 + 0.8660i    -2.0000 - 3.4641i    3.0000 - 1.7321i
```

15.10 DIGITAL FILTER DESIGN

The process of deriving a realizable transfer function of a digital filter by considering given frequency response specifications is known as digital filter design. The digital filters can be classified as:

- Finite-duration impulse response (FIR) filter
- Infinite-duration impulse response (IIR) filter

In MATLAB, there are built-in functions which can be used to design digital filters like IIR and FIR.

15.10.1 IIR Digital Filter Design

The different types of IIR digital filters are:

- Butterworth filter
- Chebyshev Type I filter
- Chebyshev Type II filter
- Elliptic filter

Before designing a filter, it is necessary to obtain the order of the filter. The syntax of different MATLAB functions used to obtain the **order of a filter** is given below:

```
[N, Wn] = buttord(Wp, Ws, Rp, Rs)
[N, Wp] = cheb1ord(Wp, Ws, Rp, Rs)
[N, Ws] = cheb2ord(Wp, Ws, Rp, Rs)
[N, Wp] = ellipord(Wp, Ws, Rp, Rs)
```

where

`Wp` and `Ws` are edge frequencies for passband and stopband, respectively, normalized from 0 to 1,
`Rp` is passband ripple in dB,
`Rs` is stopband attenuation in dB and
`N` is order of the filter.

In case edge frequencies `Wp` and `Ws` are not given in data, then these have to be calculated from given frequencies. The formulas used for calculating `Wp` and `Ws` are:

```
Wp = 2*fp/Fs
Ws = 2*fs/Fs
```

where

`Fs` is sampling frequency, and
`fp` and `fs` are passband and stopband frequencies.

In case of lowpass and highpass filters, the frequency scaling factor `Wn` is having only one value whereas for passband and stopband filters `Wn` is length-2 vector and N is half the order of the filter to be designed.

Example 15.29 Find the order of lowpass Butterworth IIR digital filter having following specifications:

Passband frequency	1,500 Hz
Stopband frequency	1,800 Hz
Sampling frequency	5,000 Hz
Passband ripple	2 dB
Stopband attenuation	40 dB

Solution: The commands used are:

```
%Given specifications
fp = 1500;
fs = 1800;
Fs = 5000;
Rp = 2;
Rs = 40;
%Calculate edge frequencies
Wp = 2*fp/Fs;
Ws = 2*fs/Fs;
%Calculate order of the filter
[N, Wn] = buttord(Wp, Ws, Rp, Rs);
fprintf('Order of the filter is:   %f \n',N);
```

The result obtained is:

```
Order of the filter is: 12.000000
```

15.10.1.1 MATLAB *Functions for Designing IIR Filters*

After obtaining the order of the filter, the different built-in functions of MATLAB are used to design IIR digital filters. The general syntax for MATLAB functions is given below:

```
[b,a] = butter(N,Wn)
[b,a] = cheby1(N,Rp,Wp)
[b,a] = cheby2(N,Rs,Ws)
[b,a] = ellip(N,Rp,Rs,Wp)
```

where

N	gives filter order,
Wn	edge frequency,
Rp	passband peak to peak ripples in dB,
Rs	stopband peak to peak ripples in dB and
b,a	filter coefficients of length $N + 1$, vector b gives numerator and vector a gives denominator values in descending powers of z.

These functions give the filter coefficients *b* and *a*. After obtaining the filter coefficients, filter response can be obtained using **freqz** function.

In case where the zeros and poles of a transfer function are required, following functions are used:

```
[z,p,k] = butter(N,Wn)
[z,p,k] = cheby1(N,Rp,Wp)
[z,p,k] = cheby2(N,Rs,Ws)
[z,p,k] = ellip(N,Rp,Rs,Wp)
```

where

z	vector of length *N* columns giving zeros,
p	vector of length *N* columns giving poles and
k	gain.

In case where, state space matrices are needed, the functions used are:

```
[A,B,C,D] = butter(N,Wn)
[A,B,C,D] = cheby1(N,Rp,Wp)
[A,B,C,D] = cheby2(N,Rs,Ws)
```

```
[A,B,C,D] = ellip(N,Rp,Rs,Wp)
```

where A, B, C, D are state space matrices.

Example 15.30 Obtain the frequency response of Butterworth IIR filter for specifications given in Example 15.29.

Solution: The program is given below:

```
%Program to find the response of lowpass IIR Butterworth filter
%Given specifications:
fp=1500;
fs=1800;
Fs=5000;
Rp= 2;
Rs=40;
%Calculate edge frequencies
Wp = 2*fp/Fs;
Ws = 2*fs/Fs;
%Calculate order of the filter
[N, Wn] = buttord(Wp, Ws, Rp, Rs);
fprintf('Order of the filter is: %f \n',N);
%response of the filter
[b,a]=butter(N,Wn);
freqz(b);
```

The result obtained is given as

```
Order of the filter is:   12.000000
b =
    Columns 1 through 12
0.0064    0.0772    0.4248    1.4158    3.1856    5.0970
5.9465    5.0970    3.1856    1.4158    0.4248    0.0772
Column 13
0.0064
a =
    Columns 1 through 12
1.0000    2.7575    4.9313    5.8618    5.2618    3.5782
1.8938    0.7714    0.2398    0.0550    0.0088    0.0009
Column 13
0.0000
```

The response obtained is shown in Figure 15.26.

15.10.2 FIR Digital Filter Design

The different types of FIR filters are listed as follows:

- Window techniques based FIR filters
    - Rectangular window
    - Hamming window
    - Hanning window
    - Blackman window

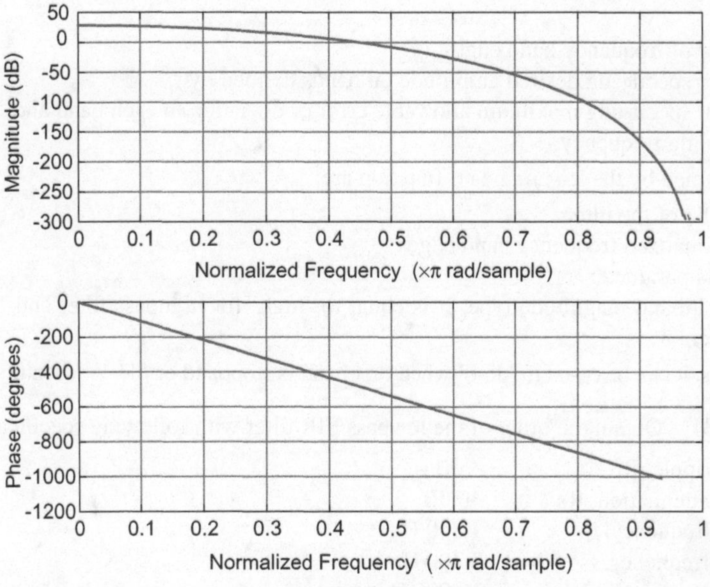

Figure 15.26 Response of Lowpass Butterworth IIR Filter of Example 15.23

- ○ Barlett window
- ○ Kaiser window
- Equiripple linear phase FIR filters
- Least-squares error FIR filters

15.10.2.1 FIR Filter Order

Before designing FIR digital filters, it is necessary to obtain the order of the filter. It can be obtained by using MATLAB function **firpmord**. The syntax for this function is given as:

```
[n,fo,ao,w]= firpmord(f,a,dev)
[n,fo,ao,w]= firpmord(f,a,dev,fs)
```

where

`f`	vector of frequency band edges,
`a`	vector specifying desired amplitude on bands defined by *f*,
`dev`	vector specifying maximum allowable error or deviation in each band and
`fs`	sampling frequency.

Output arguments:

`n`	order of the filter
`fo`	vector representing normalized frequency band edges
`ao`	frequency band amplitudes
`w`	weights

The order of a filter using Kaiser window technique is obtained by using MATLAB function **kaiserord**. The syntax for this function is given as:

```
[n,Wn,beta,ftype]= kaiserord(f,a,dev)
[n,Wn,beta,ftype]= kaiserord(f,a,dev,fs)
```

where

`f`	vector of frequency band edges,
`a`	vector specifying desired amplitude on bands defined by *f*,
`dev`	vector specifying maximum allowable error or deviation in each band and
`fs`	sampling frequency.

The arguments returned by the `kaiserord` function are:

`n`	order of the filter
`Wn`	normalized frequency band edges
`beta`	beta parameter
`ftype`	multiband magnitude type. It is equal to 'high' for highpass filter and 'stop' for bandstop filter.

For multiband filters, it can be equal to 'dc-0' when first band is stopband or 'dc-1' when first band is passband.

Example 15.31 Obtain the order of the lowpass FIR filter with following specifications:

Passband ripple, Rp	3 dB
Stopband attenuation, Rs	40 dB
Passband frequency, fp	1,800 Hz
Stopband frequency, fs	2,400 Hz
Sampling frequency, Fs	10,000 Hz

Solution: The order of the filter can be obtained by using `firpmord` function.

In this problem, passband and stopband ripples are calculated first using following formulas:

$$\delta_p = 1-10^{-Rp/20}$$

$$\delta_s = 10^{-Rs/20}$$

where Rp is passband ripple in dB, and
Rs is stopband attenuation in dB.

The program is given below:

```
%Given specifications
fs = 10000;
f = [1800 2400];            %specify frequency band edges
a = [1 0];                  %specify desired amplitude on bands
Rp = 3;
Rs = 40;
%Calculate allowable deviation or ripples
dp = 1-10^(-Rp/20);
ds = 10^(-Rs/20);
dev = [dp ds];
%Calculate order of the filter
[n,fo,ao,w] = firpmord(f,a, dev,fs);
fprintf('The order of the filter is : %f \n',n);
```

The result obtained is:

```
The order of the filter is: 15.000000
```

15.10.2.2 FIR Filter Design

Once the order of the filter is known, the FIR filter can be designed using following functions:

1. **firpm:** This function designs a linear phase FIR filter using the Parks-McClellan algorithm. The syntax for **firpm** function is given as

```
b=firpm(n,f,a)
b=firpm(n,f,a,w)
b=firpm(n,f,a,ftype)
b=firpm(n,f,a,w,ftype)
```

where input arguments are as

`n`	order of the filter,
`f`	vector of pairs of normalized frequency points,
`a`	vector containing the desired amplitudes at the points specified in `f` and
`ftype`	specifies filter type. It can be 'hilbert' and 'differentiator'.

Output argument is given as

`b` row vector containing $n + 1$ coefficients of the filter.

The response of the filter is obtained using **`freqz`** function.

> **Programming Tip 15.4:** Vector `f` containing normalized frequency points and vector `a` containing desired amplitudes must be of same length. The length must be an even number.

2. **`fir1`:** This function is used to design windowed linear phase FIR digital filter. It designs filter in standard lowpass, highpass, bandpass and bandstop configurations. The syntax for this function is as

```
b=fir1(n,Wn)
b=fir1(n,Wn,'ftype')
b=fir1(n,Wn,window)
b=fir1(n,Wn,'ftype', window)
```

where

`n`	is order of the filter,
`Wn`	normalized cutoff frequency, In case `Wn` is two-element vector, `Wn=[w1 w2]`, then `fir1` returns a bandpass filter with passband w1 < w < w2,
`ftype`	specifies filter type, that is 'high' for a highpass filter with cut-off frequency `Wn`. 'stop' for a bandstop filter, if `Wn = [w1 w2]`. 'DC-1' to make the first band of a multiband filter a passband. 'DC-0' to make the first band of a multiband filter a stopband.
`window`	species the window be used for the design and
`b`	row vector containing $n + 1$ coefficients of the filter.

The response of the filter is obtained using `freqz` function.

3. **fir2:** The syntax for **fir2** function is given as

```
b = fir2(n,f,m)
b = fir2(n,f,m,window)
b = fir2(n,f,m,npt)
b = fir2(n,f,m,npt,window)
```

where

`n` is order of the filter,

`f` is a vector of frequency points in the range from 0 to 1, where 1 corresponds to the Nyquist frequency. The first point of `f` must be 0 and the last point 1. The frequency points must be in increasing order,
`m` is a vector containing the desired magnitude response at the points specified in `f`,
`window` species the window be used for the design and
`npt` specifies number of points for the grid onto which `fir2` interpolates the frequency response, with or without a window specification.

> **Programming Tip 15.5:** `fir1` and `fir2` functions designs hamming window as default window.

4. **firls:** This function is used to design any type of multiband linear phase FIR filter based on least-squares method. The syntax for **firls** function is given as

```
b = firls(n,f,a)
b = firls(n,f,a,w)
b = firls(n,f,a, 'ftype')
b = firls(n,f,a,w, 'ftype')
```

where input arguments are as

`n` order of the filter,
`f` vector of pairs of normalized frequency points,
`a` vector containing the desired amplitudes at the points specified in `f`,
`w` vector containing weights to weight the fit in each frequency band. The length of `w` is half the length of `f` and a, so there is exactly one weight per band and
`ftype` specifies filter type. It can be `'hilbert'` and `'differentiator'`.

5. **fircls:** This function is used for designing linear phase FIR filter using constrained least-squares method. The syntax is given as

```
b = fircls(n,f,amp,up,lo)
```

where

`n` is order of the filter,
`f` is a vector of transition frequencies in the range from 0 to 1. The frequency points must be in increasing order,
`amp` is a vector describing the piecewise constant desired amplitude of the frequency response, and
`up, lo` define upper and lower bounds for the frequency response in each band.

6. Using Windows

In MATLAB, the different functions used to generate the windows are:

```
k = blackman(m)
k = hamming(m)
k = hann(m)
k = flattopwin(m)
k = kaiser(m,beta)
```

These functions return `m`-point respective window in column vector `k`.
`m` must be positive integer.

`beta` is the Kaiser window β parameter that affects the side lobe attenuation of the Fourier transform of the window. The default value for `beta` is 0.5.

The respective window is viewed by using command

```
wvtool(k)
```

where **wvtool** is Window Visualization Tool.

Example 15.32 Obtain the frequency response of lowpass FIR filter for specifications given in Example 15.31.

Solution: The program is given as:

```
%Program to obtain the response of lowpass FIR filter
%Given specifications
fs = 10000;
f = [1800 2400];        %specify frequency band edges
a = [1 0];              %specify desired amplitude on bands
Rp = 3;
Rs = 40;
%Calculate allowable deviation or ripples
dp = 1-10^(-Rp/20);
ds = 10^(-Rs/20);
dev = [dp ds];
%Calculate order of the filter
[n,fo,ao,w]=firpmord(f,a, dev,fs);
fprintf('The order of the filter is : %f \n',n);
fprintf('The filter coefficients are given as: \n');
b = firpm(n,fo,ao)
freqz(b)
```

The result obtained is as

```
The order of the filter is : 15.000000
The filter coefficients are given as:
b =
    Columns 1 through 12
      -0.0207    0.0527    0.0479    -0.0183    -0.0831    -0.0193    0.1920
    0.3899    0.3899    0.1920    -0.0193    -0.0831
Columns 13 through 16
  -0.0183    0.0479    0.0527    -0.0207
```

The response obtained is shown in Figure 15.27.

15.11 FILTER DESIGN AND ANALYSIS TOOL

Filter Design and Analysis Tool (FDA Tool) is Graphic User Interface for designing and analysing filters. It is used to design FIR and IIR filters by entering the desired filter specifications, or by importing filter from MATLAB workspace or by adding, moving or deleting poles and zeros. After designing a filter, the response can be viewed and analysed in other Graphic User Interface tool named **Filter Visualization Tool (FV Tool)** linked with FDA Tool. The different types of responses that can be viewed are listed below:

- Magnitude response
- Phase response
- Group delay

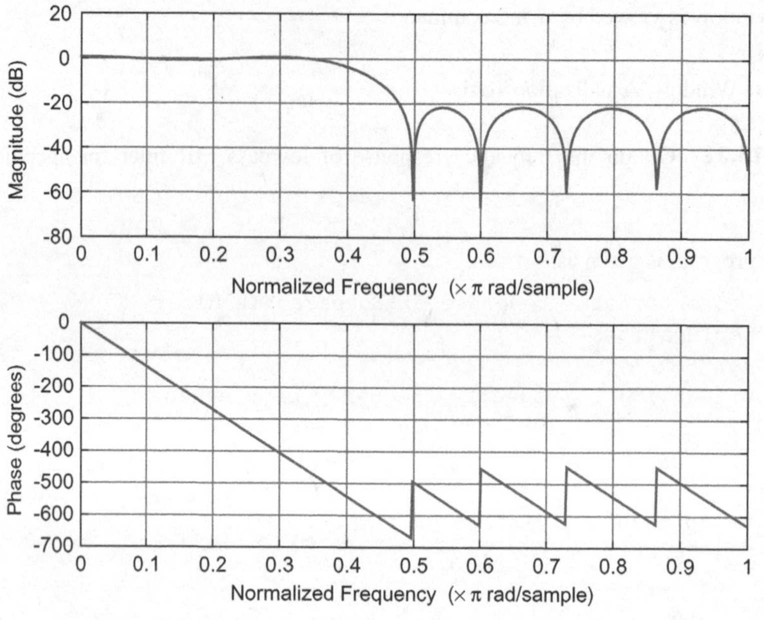

Figure 15.27 Response of Lowpass FIR Filter of Example 15.32

- Phase delay
- Impulse response
- Step response
- Pole-zero plot
- Zero-phase plot

15.11.1 Opening FDA Tool Window

FDA Tool can be opened using command:

```
fdatool
```

The FDA Tool window will open and is shown in Figure 15.28.

The different steps involved in designing a filter using FDA Tool can be listed as:

1. Selection of type of response required
2. Selection of type of filter design
3. Specifying the filter order
4. Entering the filter specifications
5. Entering the magnitude specifications

After providing the information listed above, filter can be designed and its response can be viewed and analysed.

The complete description of the FDA Tool window and different steps required to design a filter are elaborated below:

1. **Selecting response type:** The desired response type is selected from the list of available options, i.e., lowpass, highpass, bandpass, bandstop, differentiation, multiband, peaking etc.
2. **Type of design method:** The design can be of FIR or IIR filter. Depending upon whether FIR or IIR filter design is selected, further options are available in the dropdown menu. In IIR filter design, the different options available in dropdown menu are as given below:

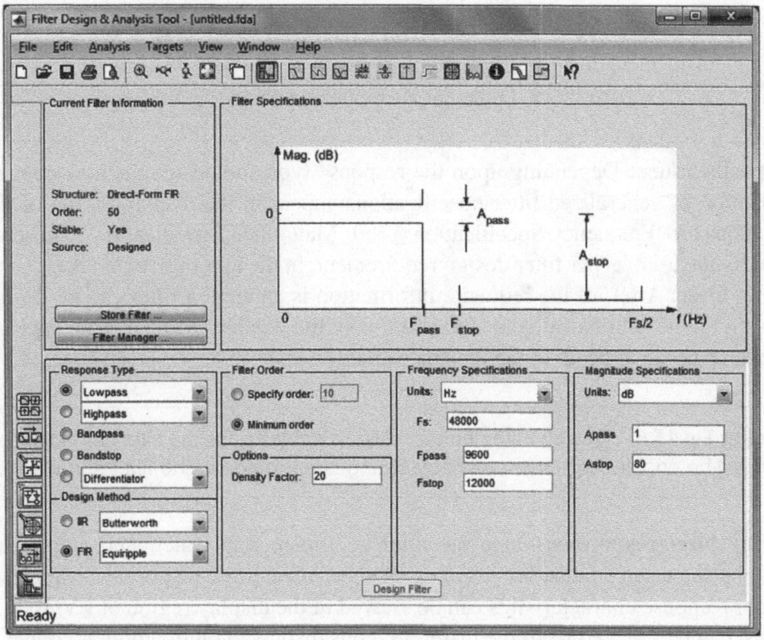

Figure 15.28 Filter Design and Analysis Tool (FDA Tool) Window

- Butterworth
- Chebyshev type I
- Chebyshev type II
- Elliptic
- Maximally flat
- Least Pth-norm
- Const least Pth-norm

In FIR filter design the options available are listed as follows:

- Equirriple
- Least square
- Window
- Const least squares
- Complex equiripple
- Least Pth norm
- Constrained equiripple
- Generalized equiripple
- Constrained band equirriple
- Interpolated FIR

The options available depend upon the selection of response type.

3. **Filter order:** Under this, two options available are as
   - User-defined order: Under this option user has to enter the order of the filter.
   - Minimum order: The other option available for selecting the filter order is minimum order. It is calculated by system itself.

Figure 15.29 Different Response Icons on the Toolbar

4. **Filter specifications:** Depending upon the response type and design method selected, the graphical representation of generalized filter specifications appear in the display region of FDA Tool. These specifications are 'Frequency Specifications' and 'Magnitude Specification'. These specifications are provided by the user, as per filter design requirement, in the appropriate blocks.
5. **Designing filter:** After all the requisite information is entered, a filter can be designed by clicking the 'Design Filter' button available at the bottom of the window. Filter coefficients are calculated and magnitude response appears in the display region.

> **Programming Tip 15.6:** 'Design Filter' button will be disabled once the filter coefficients are computed. This button will be enabled again in case any changes are made in the filter specifications.

6. **Displaying filter responses:** Once the filter coefficients are calculated as per the specifications provided by the user, the display region will show magnitude response of the designed filter. The other filter response characteristics can be viewed in the display region or FV Tool. The response to be viewed can be selected from the different icons displayed on the toolbar shown in Figure 15.29. The purpose of different icons is illustrated in Table 15.1.

> **Programming Tip 15.7:** The different responses for display can also be selected from the 'Analysis' menu on menu bar.

Table 15.1 Response Icon Buttons on Toolbar and their Purpose

Icons	Purpose
	Magnitude response
	Phase response
	Magnitude and phase response
	Group delay response
	Phase delay
	Impulse response
	Step responses
	Pole/zero plot
	Filter coefficients
	Filter information
	Magnitude response estimate
	Round off noise power spectrum

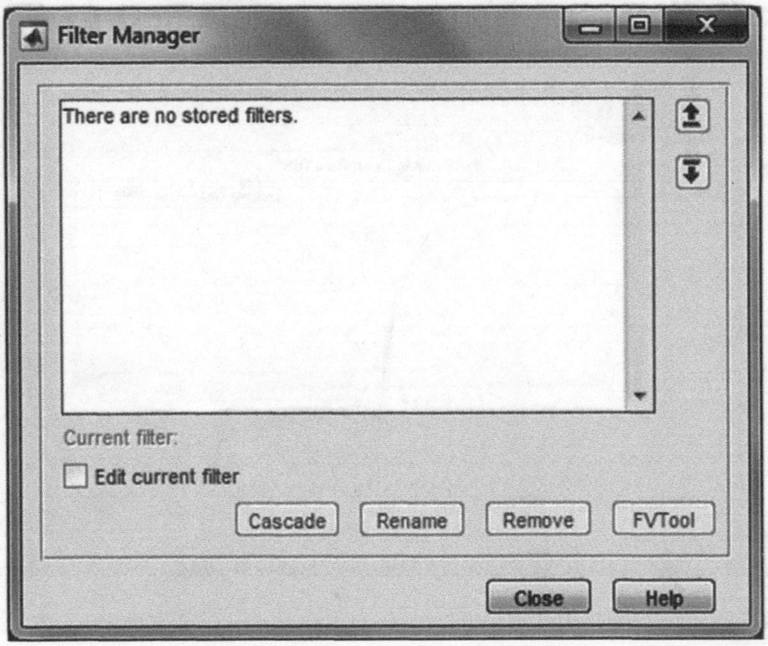

Figure 15.30 Filter Manager Window

7. **Current filter information:** The information about the designed filter is given in the 'Current Filter Information' region of FDA Tool window as shown in Figure 15.28. The information provided is about the 'structure', 'order', 'stability' and 'source'.
   - **Storing a filter**

   The designed filter is stored by clicking 'Store Filter' button in the 'Current Filter Information' region.
   - **Filter manager**

     The 'Filter Manager' button opens up a new Filter Manager window (Figure 15.30) showing the list of filters stored. This window also has options as: Edit current filter, Cascade, Rename, Remove and FV Tool.

   To cascade two or more filters, highlight the designed filters and press 'Cascade' button. A new cascaded filter is added to the 'Filter Manager'.
8. **Saving and opening filter design session:** The filter design session is saved as MAT-file and can be used later on. It can be saved by clicking save icon or selecting save session option in File menu and giving desired session name. Similarly, the saved session can be opened by clicking open icon or by selecting open option in file menu and selecting the previously saved filter design session.

15.12 FILTER VISUALIZATION TOOL

The response characteristics can be viewed in a separate window by selecting the 'Filter Visualization Tool' (FV Tool) from 'view' menu or clicking the 'Full View Analysis' button on the toolbar. The FV Tool window is shown in Figure 15.31.

FV Tool has most of the menus on the menu bar and icons on the toolbar similar to that FDA Tool with some additional icons which are mainly used to work with representation of the responses.

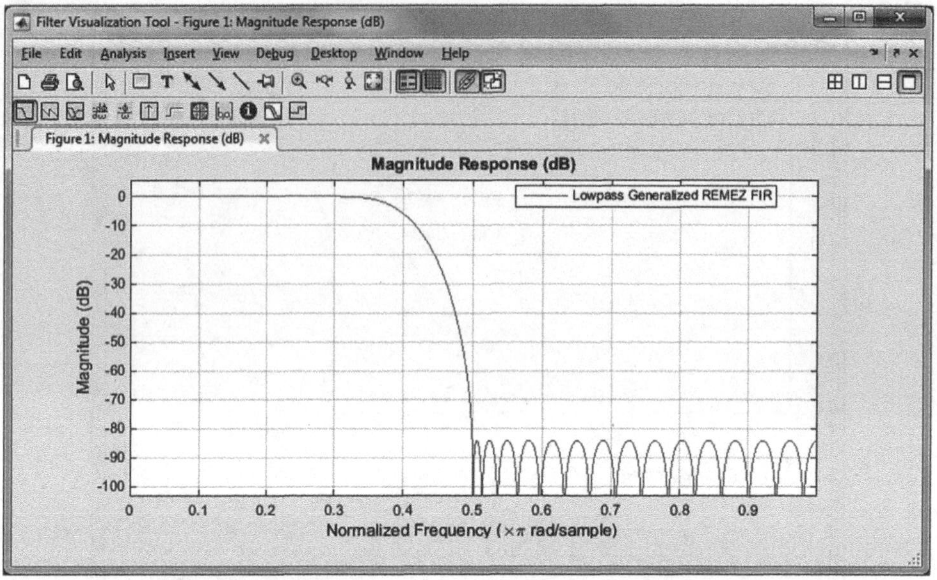

Figure 15.31 Filter Visualization Tool (FV Tool) Window

15.13 IIR FILTER DESIGN USING FDA TOOL

Example 15.33 Design an IIR Butterworth bandpass filter with the following specifications:

Normalized passband edges at 0.40 and 0.65	
Normalized stopband edges at 0.3 and 0.75	
Passband ripple	1 dB
Minimum stopband attenuation	40 dB

Show (i) Magnitude response (ii) Phase response (iii) Group delay (iv) Phase delay response.

Solution: As per the given specifications, the requisite data is entered in new FDA Tool window as shown in Figure 15.32.

The filter is designed for minimum order so as to reduce the complexity of the design. In case, it has to be designed for user defined order, then the order of the filter has to be calculated first by user using appropriate formulas or MATLAB function.

The other responses can be viewed by clicking on the appropriate icon on the toolbar and responses obtained are shown in Figures 15.33 to 15.36.

These responses can also be viewed in FV Tool.

Example 15.34 Design a Type II Chebyshev IIR lowpass filter with the following specifications:

Passband ripple	0.50 dB
Stopband attenuation	50 dB
Passband frequency	1,200 Hz
Stopband frequency	1,700 Hz
Sampling frequency	6,000 Hz

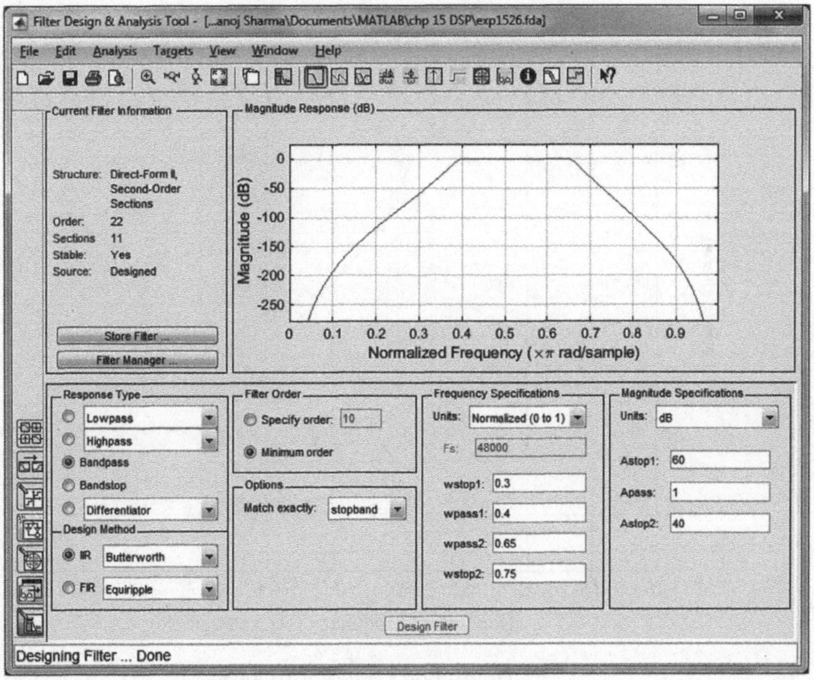

Figure 15.32 FDA Tool Window Showing Specification Entered and Magnitude Response for Example15.33

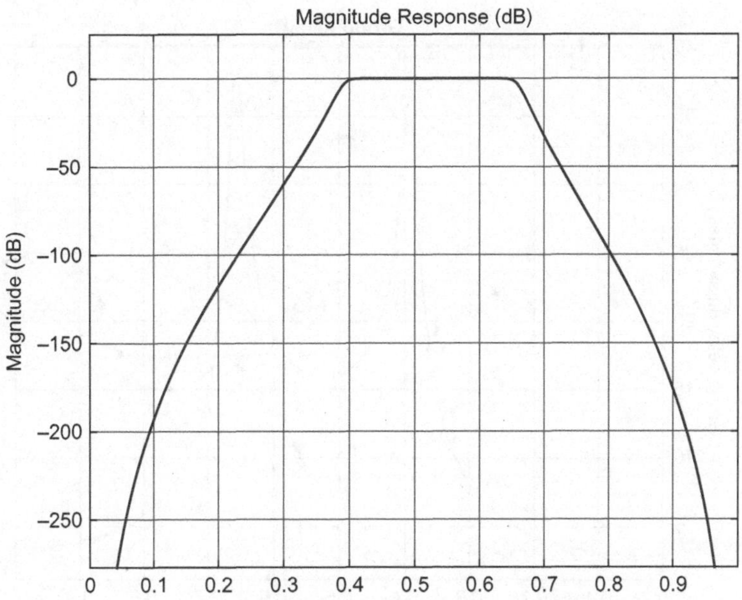

Figure 15.33 Magnitude Response in dB

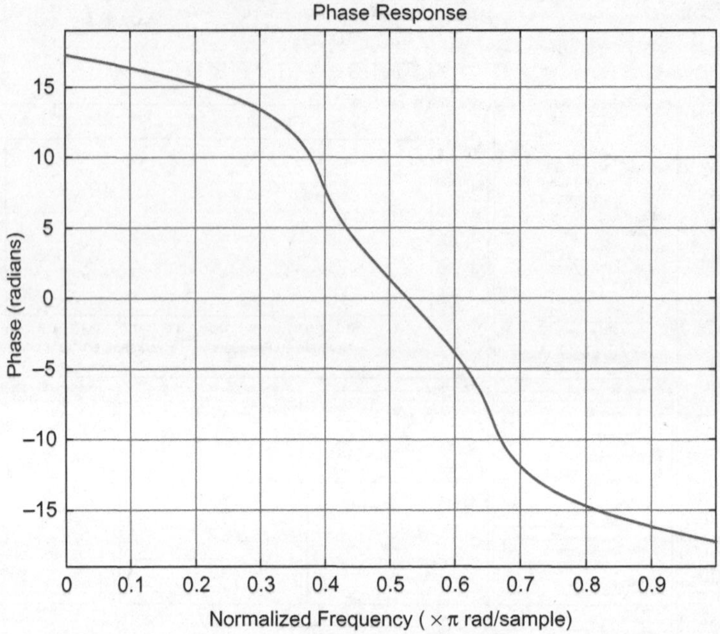

Figure 15.34 Phase Response

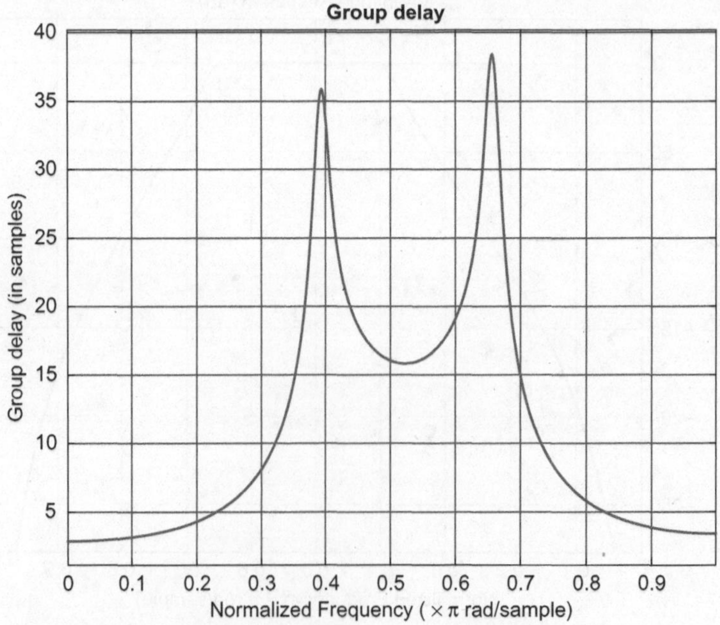

Figure 15.35 Group Delay Response

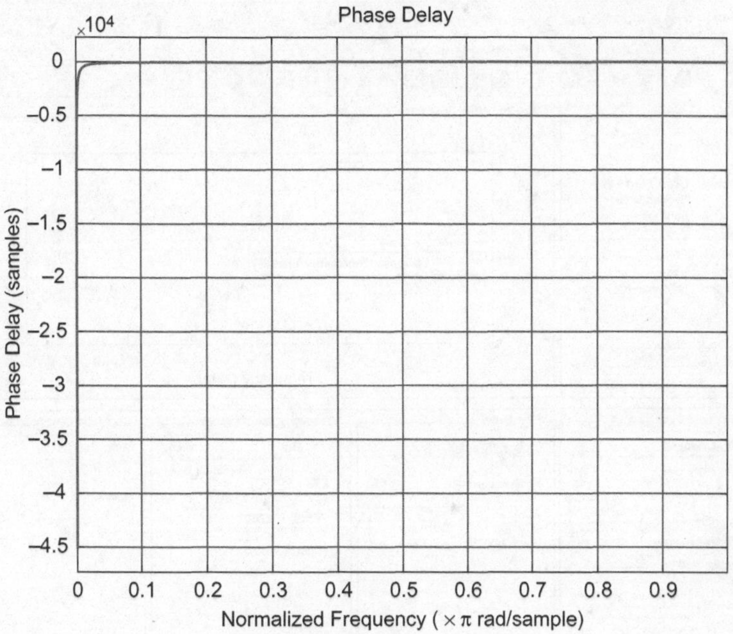

Figure 15.36 Phase Delay

(i) Show magnitude response.

(ii) Show pole/zero plot.

Solution: FDA Tool Window showing given specifications duly entered and magnitude response in response display region is shown in Figure 15.37.

By using the FV Tool, the magnitude response and pole/zero plot is obtained as separate figures and is shown in Figures 15.38 and 15.39, respectively.

Example 15.35 Design an elliptic IIR lowpass filter with following specifications:

Passband ripple	0.5 dB
Stopband attenuation	40 dB
Passband frequency	800 Hz
Stopband frequency	1,000 Hz
Sampling frequency	4,000 Hz

(a) Show magnitude and phase response in the same window.

(b) Obtain filter information.

Solution: As per given specifications, the requisite data is entered in FDA Tool window. By clicking appropriate icon on toolbar, the magnitude and phase responses are obtained in the same window.

(a) These magnitude and phase responses obtained are viewed in FV Tool window also and are shown in Figure 15.40.

(b) To obtain the information about the filter 'Filter Information' icon on Toolbar of FDA Tool Window is clicked or 'Filter Information' option is selected from 'Analysis' menu. The detailed filter information appears in the display region as shown in Figure 15.41.

The filter information is obtained by scrolling down the text in the window shown in Figure 15.41.

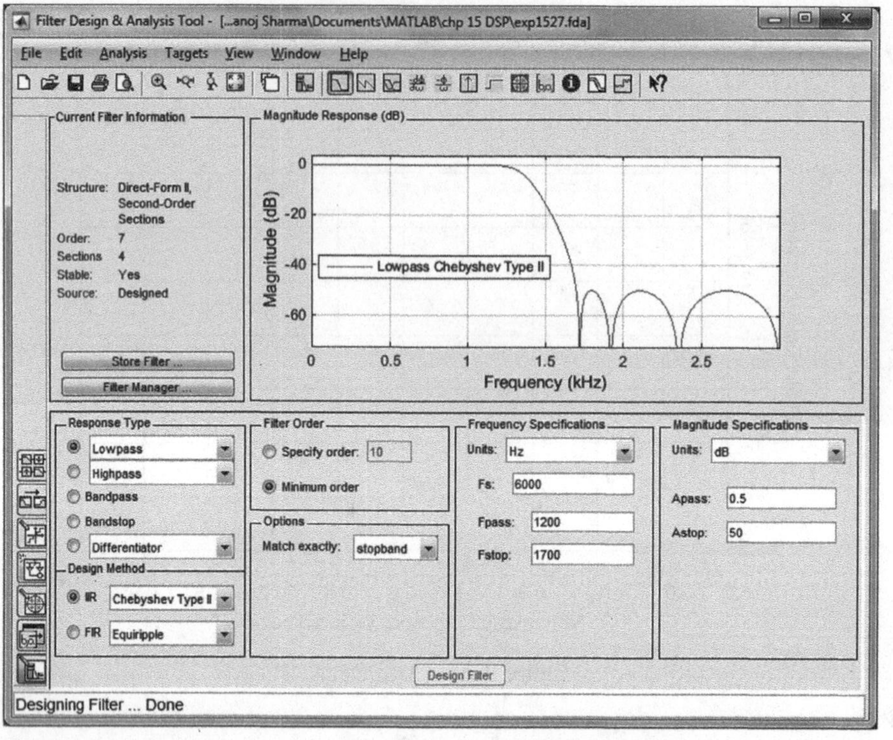

Figure 15.37 FDA Tool Window for Example 15.37

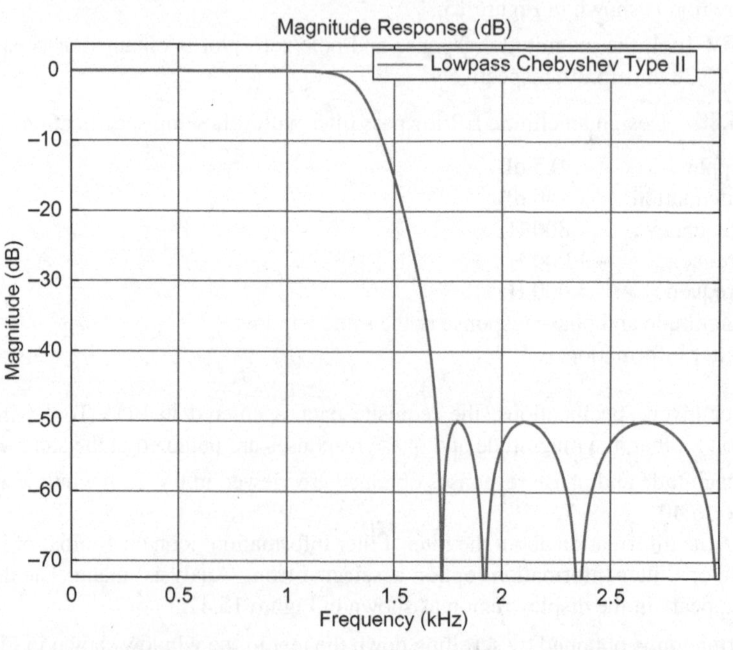

Figure 15.38 Magnitude Response for Example 15.37

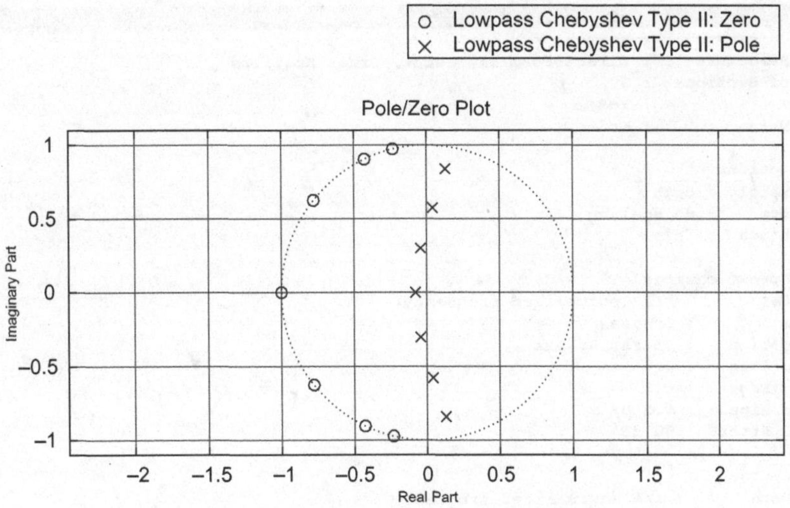

Figure 15.39 Pole/zero Plot for Example 15.34

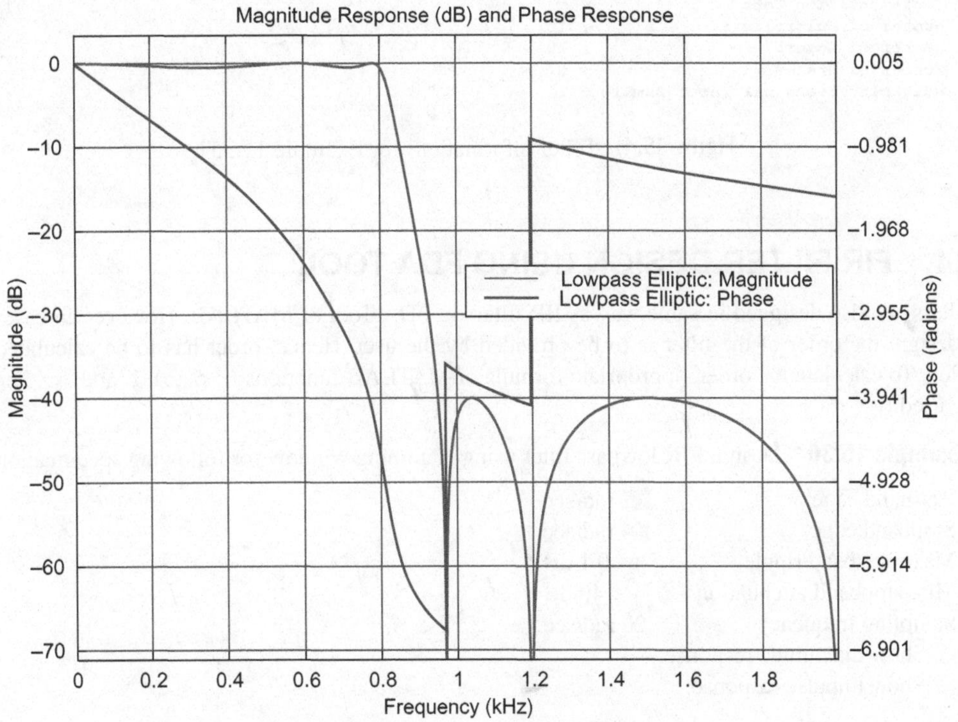

Figure 15.40 Magnitude and Phase Response for Example 15.35

```
Discrete-Time IIR Filter (real)
-------------------------------
Filter Structure    : Direct-Form II, Second-Order Sections
Number of Sections  : 3
Stable              : Yes
Linear Phase        : No

Design Options
Match Exactly : both
Scale Norm    : no scaling
SystemObject  : false

Design Specifications
Sample Rate      : N/A (normalized frequency)
Response         : Lowpass
Specification    : Fp,Fst,Ap,Ast
Passband Edge    : 0.4
Stopband Edge    : 0.5
Passband Ripple : 0.5 dB
Stopband Atten. : 40 dB

Measurements
Sample Rate       : N/A (normalized frequency)
Passband Edge     : 0.4
3-dB Point        : 0.41021
6-dB Point        : 0.41752
Stopband Edge     : 0.5
Passband Ripple   : 0.5 dB
Stopband Atten.   : 40 dB
Transition Width : 0.1

Implementation Cost
Number of Multipliers            : 10
Number of Adders                 : 10
Number of States                 : 5
Multiplications per Input Sample : 10
```

Figure 15.41 'Filter information' for Example 15.35

15.14 FIR FILTER DESIGN USING FDA TOOL

FIR filters are also designed in same way as IIR filters in FDA Tool of MATLAB. However, in case of FIR filter design, the order of the filter is to be provided by the user. Hence, order has to be calculated if not specified. To calculate the order, appropriate formula or MATLAB functions `firpmord` and `kaiserord` can be used.

Example 15.36 Design FIR lowpass filter using Hamming window for following specifications:

Passband edge	2 rad/sec
Stopband edge	4 rad/sec
Max. passband ripple	0.1 dB
Min. stopband attenuation	40 dB
Sampling frequency	20 rad/sec

(a) Show magnitude response.
(b) Show impulse response.

Solution: As order of the filter is not given hence it has to be calculated using `firpmord` function as given below:

Filter Order Calculation

The syntax for MATLAB function `firpmord` (see section 15.10.2.1) for calculating order is given below:

```
[n,fo,ao,w] = firpmord(f,a,dev,Fs)
```

The specifications given are as

Passband edge, fp	2 rad/sec
Stopband edge, fs	4 rad/sec
Max. passband ripple, Rp	0.1 dB
Min. stopband attenuation, Rs	40 dB
Sampling frequency, Fs	20 rad/sec

In this problem, passband and stopband ripples are calculated first using following formulae:

$$\delta_p = 1 - 10^{-Rp/20}$$

$$\delta_s = 10^{-Rs/20}$$

where

Rp is passband ripple in dB and
Rs is stopband attenuation in dB.

The program is given below:

```
%Given specifications
fs = 20;
f = [2 4];        %specify frequency band edges
a = [1 0];        %specify desired amplitude on bands
Rp = 0.1;
Rs = 40;
%Calculate allowable deviation or ripples
dp = 1-10^(-Rp/20);
ds = 10^(-Rs/20);
dev = [dp ds];
%Calculate order of the filter
[n,fo,ao,w] = firpmord(f,a, dev,fs)
```

The result obtained is as

```
n =
    18
fo =
         0
    0.2000
    0.4000
    1.0000
ao =
    1
    1
    0
    0
w =
    1.0000
    1.1447
```

Using above obtained results, filter is designed in FDA Tool Window and desired responses are obtained.

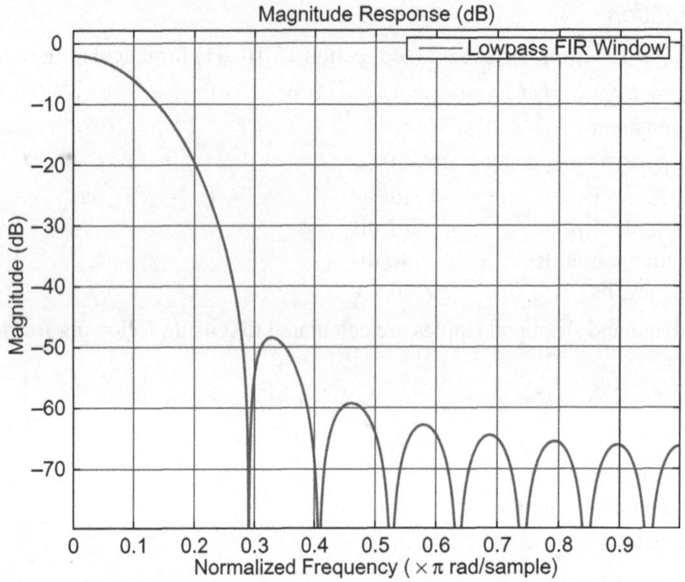

Figure 15.42 Magnitude Response for Example 15.36

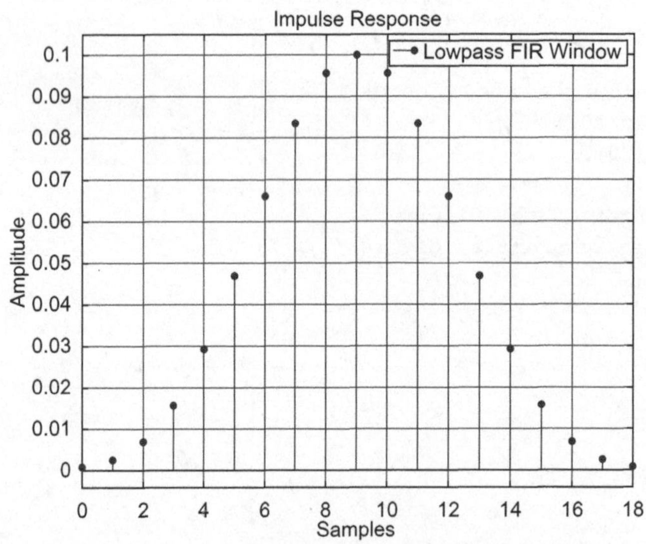

Figure 15.43 Impulse Response for Example 15.36

The magnitude response and impulse response of the filter are given in Figures 15.42 and 15.43, respectively.

Example 15.37 Design FIR filter using Kaiser window for specifications given in Example 15.36. Show the magnitude response.

Solution: The FIR filter design using Kaiser window requires 'order' of the filter to be provided by the user. Hence, this is calculated using MATLAB function `kaiserord` as shown below:

The program is given below:

```
%Given specifications
fs = 20;
f = [2 4];        %specify frequency band edges
a = [1 0];        %specify desired amplitude on bands
Rp = 0.1;
Rs = 40;
%Calculate allowable deviation or ripples
dp = 1-10^(-Rp/20);
ds = 10^(-Rs/20);
dev = [dp ds];
%Calculate order of the filter
[n,Wn,beta,ftype] = kaiserord(f,a, dev,fs)
```

The result obtained is given as

```
n =
    23
Wn =
     0.3000
beta =
       3.3953
ftype =
        low
```

Now, using above result obtained, the filter is designed in FDA Tool Window and its magnitude response is shown in Figure 15.44.

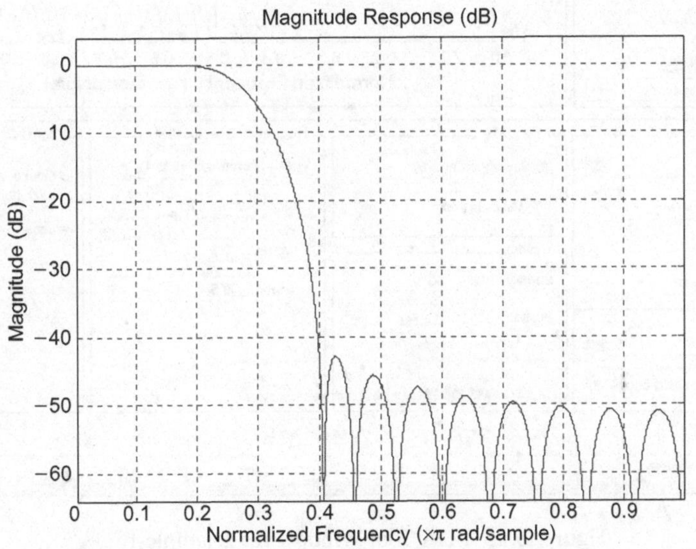

Figure 15.44 Magnitude Response for FIR Filter Design Using Kaiser Window for Example 15.37

Example 15.38 Design a linear phase bandpass FIR filter of order 50 with passband edges as wp1 = 0.3π and wp2 = 0.5π. Show impulse and magnitude response.

Solution: The FDA Tool window showing the magnitude response for the given specifications is shown in Figure 15.45.

The impulse response is shown in Figure 15.46.

Example 15.39 Design a bandpass equiripple FIR filter of order 60 with passband from 0.3 to 0.5 and stopbands from 0 to 0.25 and 0.6 to 1. Show phase and magnitude response.

Solution: The FDA Tool window showing the phase response for the given specifications is shown in Figure 15.47.

The magnitude response is shown in Figure 15.48.

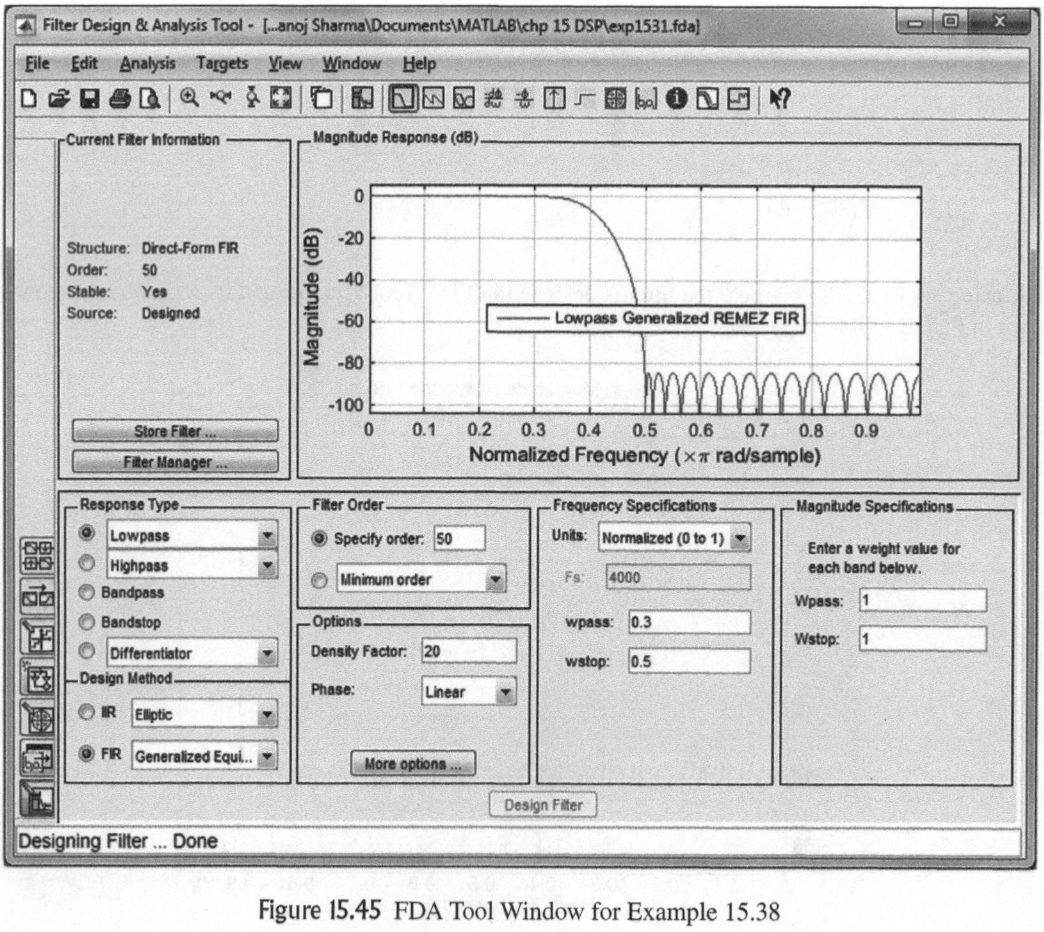

Figure 15.45 FDA Tool Window for Example 15.38

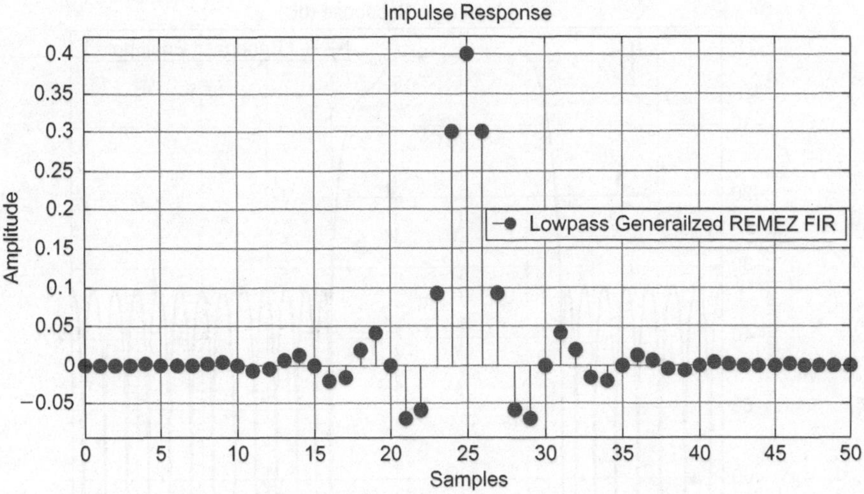

Figure 15.46 Impulse Response for Example 15.38

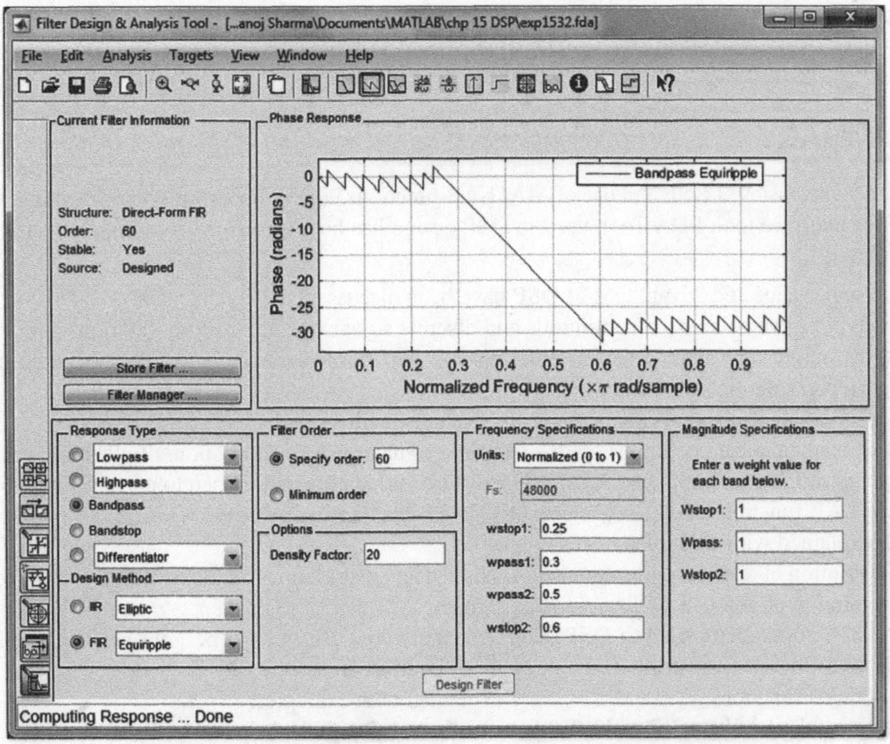

Figure 15.47 FDA Tool Window for Example 15.39

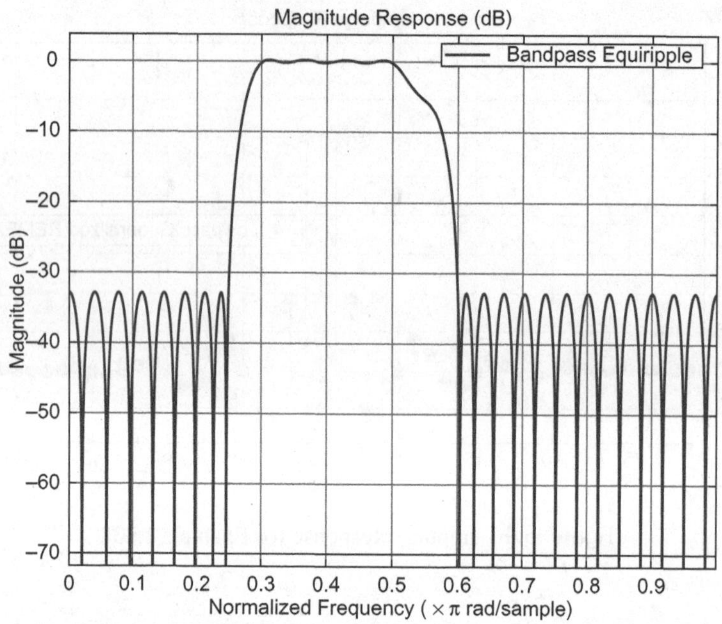

Figure 15.48 Magnitude Response for Example 15.39

SUMMARY

In this chapter, the basics of DSP and use of MATLAB functions in DSP operations have been discussed. The Graphic User Interface tool, FDA Tool, used in DSP design has been described. The chapter can be summarized as follows:

- The importance and advantages of DSP have been discussed.
- The types of signals i.e., is continuous and discrete signals and their representations, are detailed.
- Basic discrete-time signals such as unit impulse, step, ramp and exponential discrete-time signals and their representations are described.
- Classification of discrete-time signals and systems is illustrated.
- Basic mathematical operations on discrete-time signals such as addition, multiplication, scaling, folding and shifting are explained. User-defined functions are also developed to perform these operations.
- MATLAB functions such as `decimate, interp, downsample, upsample` and `resample` are explained with examples.
- Convolution of discrete-time signals is explained and user-defined function `dsconv` is developed for convolution of non-causal discrete-time signals.
- The basic operations used in DSP such as z-transform, Discrete-Time Fourier Transform (DTFT), Discrete Fourier Transform (DFT) and Fast Fourier Transform (FFT) are discussed in brief and MATLAB functions `fft` and `ifft` are explained with examples.
- Design of digital filters, IIR and FIR filters, is illustrated with the help of MATLAB functions.
- Filter Design and Analysis Tool (FDA Tool) and Filter Visualization Tool (FV Tool) available in Signal Processing Toolbox are explained.
- The digital filter design using FDA Tool and FV Tool is illustrated with examples.

List of Commands/Functions

Command/Function	Purpose
stem	Plots the discrete-time sequence
decimate	Resamples data at a lower rate after lowpass filtering
interp	Resamples data at a higher rate using lowpass interpolation
downsample	Downsamples input signal
upsample	Upsamples input signal
resample	Changes the sampling rate of a signal
conv	Convolution and polynomial multiplication
cconv	Modulo-N Circular convolution
xcorr	Cross-correlation
fft	Computes discrete Fourier transform
ifft	Computes inverse discrete Fourier transform
buttord	Computes Butterworth filter order
cheb1ord	Computes Chebyshev Type I filter order
cheb2ord	Computes Chebyshev Type II filter order
ellipord	Computes elliptic filter order
butter	Designs Butterworth filter
cheby1	Designs Chebyshev Type I filter
cheby2	Designs Chebyshev Type II filter
ellip	Designs elliptic filter
freqz	Gives frequency response of digital filter
zp2tf	Zero-pole to transfer function conversion
kaiserord	Estimates FIR filter order
firmord	Estimates equiripple FIR filter order
blackman	Generates Blackman window
hamming	Generates Hamming window
hanning	Generates Hanning window
chebwin	Generates Chebyshev window
kaiser	Generates Kaiser window
firpm	Designs equiripple FIR filter
fir1	Designs FIR filter
fir2	Designs arbitrary shape FIR filter
firls	Designs linear phase FIR filter using least-squares error minimization
fircls	Designs linear phase FIR filter using constrained least squares

User-Defined Functions

Function	Purpose
`impulseseq`	Represents impulse sequence in graphic form
`stepseq`	Represents step sequence in graphic form
`rampseq`	Represents ramp sequence in graphic form
`addsig`	Adds two discrete-time signals
`prodsig`	Multiplies two discrete-time signals
`fold`	Folds the given sequence
`dsconv`	Gives the convolution of discrete-time signals
`Dscconv`	Gives circular convolution of discrete time signal
`Confft`	Linear convolution using FFT
`Circon`	Cross-correlation using circular convolution

EXERCISES

15.1 Show properly labelled graphical representation of the following sequences using `stem` function:

(a) $x(n)=\{1 \quad -3 \quad 4 \quad \underset{\uparrow}{2} \quad -8 \quad 5\}$

(b) $x(n)=\{4 \quad -3 \quad 3 \quad 6 \quad -1\}$

(c) $x(n)=\{3 \quad 7 \quad \underset{\uparrow}{5} \quad 4 \quad -2\}$

15.2 Obtain the response for the following impulse signals using `impulseseq` function:

(a) $\delta(n)$ for $-3 \le n \le 3$
(b) $\delta(n + 1)$ for $-4 \le n \le 4$
(c) $\delta(n - 2)$ for $-5 \le n \le 5$

15.3 Plot the following step signals using `stepseq` functions:

(a) $u(n)$ for $-5 \le n \le 5$
(b) $u(n - 1)$ for $-3 \le n \le 3$
(c) $u(n + 3)$ for $-8 \le n \le 8$

15.4 Plot the ramp sequence for interval -8 to 8 using `rampseq` function

15.5 Plot discrete-time sequences for the following expressions:

(a) $x(n) = 2^n$ for $-4 \le n \le 4$
(b) $x(n) = 3^{n+1}$ for $-3 \le n \le 2$
(c) $x(n) = e^{(-1+j0.3)n}$ for $-2 \le n \le 3$
(d) $x(n) = e^{-j0.2n}$ for $0 \le n \le 10$

15.6 Obtain sum of the following discrete-time signals using `addsig` function and plot all the responses:

(a) $x1 = \{\underset{\uparrow}{3} \quad 12 \quad 6 \quad 8 \quad 9\}$

$x2 = \{\underset{\uparrow}{4} \quad 5 \quad 3\}$

(b) $x1 = \{4 \quad \underset{\uparrow}{3} \quad -1 \quad 2 \quad -5\}$

$x2 = \{5 \quad 6 \quad \underset{\uparrow}{11} \quad 3 \quad 7 \quad 8\}$

(c) $x1 = \{4 \quad \underset{\uparrow}{3} \quad -1 \quad 2 \quad -5\}$

$x2 = \{5 \quad 6 \quad \underset{\uparrow}{11} \quad 3 \quad 7 \quad 8\}$

15.7 Obtain product of the following discrete-time signals using `prodsig` function and plot all the responses:

(a) $x1 = \{3 \quad \underset{\uparrow}{2} \quad 6 \quad 1\}$

$x2 = \{1 \quad \underset{\uparrow}{4} \quad 6 \quad 8 \quad 7\}$

(b) $x1 = \{\underset{\uparrow}{4} \quad -6 \quad 0 \quad 3\}$

$x2 = \{\underset{\uparrow}{5} \quad 0 \quad 7 \quad 1\}$

15.8 Obtain the folding of the following sequences using `fold` function:

(a) $x(n) = \{-2 \quad 3 \quad \underset{\uparrow}{4} \quad 6 \quad -3\}$

(b) $x(n) = \{4 \quad -3 \quad 5 \quad 1 \quad \underset{\uparrow}{2} \quad -6 \quad 1\}$

(c) $x(n) = \{-5 \quad 3 \quad \underset{\uparrow}{2} \quad 4 \quad 8 \quad 0 \quad 3\}$

15.9 Obtain the delayed response delayed by a factor of 2 for the following signals:

(a) $x(n) = \{3 \quad \underset{\uparrow}{4} \quad 6 \quad 1\}$

(b) $x(n) = \{8 \quad -3 \quad \underset{\uparrow}{4} \quad 6 \quad 2\}$

(c) $x(n) = \{\underset{\uparrow}{3} \quad 6 \quad 11 \quad -3\}$

15.10 Decrease the sampling rate of the following sequence by a factor of 2:

(a) $x(n) = 4^{*}\,\text{rands}(1, 25)$ for $0 \le n \le 24$

(b) $x(n) = \cos(2\pi n)$ for $-1 \le n \le 1$

15.11 Increase the sampling rate of the following sequence by a factor of 3:

(a) $x(n) = \{21 \quad 34 \quad 5 \quad 2 \quad 65 \quad 23 \quad 53 \quad 43 \quad 12\}$

(b) $x(n) = \{-2 \quad -3 \quad 2 \quad 5 \quad -1 \quad 8 \quad 9 \quad 4 \quad 6\}$

15.12 Decrease the sampling rate of the following sequences by a factor of 2 and add phase offset of 1:

(a) $x(n) = \{7 \quad 3 \quad 4 \quad 6 \quad 5 \quad 3\}$

(b) $x(n) = \{3 \quad 4 \quad 6 \quad 1; \quad 9 \quad 16 \quad 3 \quad 4; \quad 8 \quad 3 \quad 5 \quad 6\}$

(c) $x(n) = \{8 \quad 4 \quad -5 \quad 3; \quad 6 \quad -11 \quad 4 \quad 9; \quad 2 \quad -12 \quad 4 \quad 6\}$

15.13 Increase the sampling rate of the following sequences by a factor of 2 and add phase offset of 1:

(a) $x(n) = \{23 \quad 4 \quad 51 \quad -6 \quad -4 \quad 32 \quad 2 \quad 15\}$

(b) $x(n) = \{13 \quad -24 \quad 16 \quad 8 \quad 4\}$

(c) $x(n) = \{4 \quad 13 \quad 8; \quad 9 \quad 5 \quad -12; \quad 1 \quad 17 \quad 24\}$

15.14 Change the sampling rate of the following sequences to 3/2 of original sampling rate:

(a) $x(n) = \{27 \quad 13 \quad 16 \quad 24 \quad 9 \quad 32\}$

(b) $x(n) = \{14 \quad 21 \quad 23 \quad 9 \quad 11 \quad 7\}$

15.15 Compute the convolution of the following sequences:

(a) $a(n) = \{3 \quad 4 \quad 6\}$; $b(n) = \{5 \quad 9 \quad 13 \quad 14\}$

(b) $a(n) = \{15 \quad -2 \quad 4 \quad 9 \quad 6\}$; $b(n) = \{-2 \quad 16 \quad 5 \quad 3\}$

(c) $a(n) = \{7 \quad 14 \quad 8 \quad 5\}$; $b(n) = \{6 \quad 9 \quad 15 \quad 3\}$

15.16 Compute the convolution of the following sequences using `dsconv` function:

(a) $a(n) = \left\{3 \quad \underset{\uparrow}{4} \quad 6\right\}$

$b(n) = \left\{\underset{\uparrow}{4} \quad 6 \quad 8 \quad 7\right\}$

(b) $a(n) = \left\{-5 \quad \underset{\uparrow}{3} \quad 2 \quad -1 \quad 6\right\}$

$b(n) = \left\{-10 \quad 4 \quad \underset{\uparrow}{9} \quad 1\right\}$

(c) $a(n) = \left\{4 \quad 3 \quad \underset{\uparrow}{1} \quad 5 \quad 6\right\}$

$b(n) = \left\{3 \quad 11 \quad \underset{\uparrow}{8} \quad 13 \quad 9\right\}$

15.17 Find linear convolution of following signals by all methods:

(a) $x(n) = [1, 0, 2, 0]$, $h(n) = [-1, -1, 2, 4]$

(b) $x(n) = [4, -3.1, -2]$, $h(n) = [2, -1, 3]$

(c) $x(n) = [2, 3, 4]$, $h(n) = [2, 2]$

15.18 Find cross-correlation of below sequences:

(a) $x(n) = [2, 5, -7, 9]$, $h(n) = [1, 0, 2, 0]$

(b) $x(n) = [4, 3, 2]$, $h(n) = [1, 1]$

(c) $x(n) = [1, -2, 3, 4]$, $h(n) = [1, 1, 2, -2]$

15.19 Find autocorrelation of below sequences:

(a) $x(n) = [4, -8, 2, 1]$

(b) $x(n) = [3, 2, 1]$

(c) $x(n) = [-1, 1, -1]$

15.20 Find Z-transform and inverse Z-transform of sequences:

(1) $x(n) = \sin(wn)$

(2) $x(n) = n2^n$

(3) $x(n) = (1/2)^n \cos(n\pi/2)$

15.21 Obtain the Discrete Fourier Transform of the following sequences:

(a) $x(n) = \{12 \quad 9 \quad 6 \quad 4 \quad 5\}$

(b) $x(n) = 2^{3n-1}$ for $N = 4$

(c) $x(n) = \{3 \quad 9 \quad 6 \quad 12; \quad 5 \quad 4 \quad 8 \quad 10; \quad 9 \quad 2 \quad 34 \quad 12; \quad 6 \quad 11 \quad 2 \quad 16\}$

15.22 Find the order of highpass Type II Chebyshev IIR digital filter with following specifications:

Passband frequency	1,300 Hz
Stopband frequency	1,000 Hz
Sampling frequency	4,000 Hz
Passband ripple	1 dB
Stopband attenuation	40 dB

15.23 Obtain the frequency response of Butterworth IIR filter with specifications given in Problem 15.18.

15.24 Obtain the zeros and poles IIR filter with specifications given in Problem 15.18.

15.25 Using FDA Tool, design a Butterworth IIR stopband filter with the following specifications:

Normalized passband edges at 0.30 and 0.75

Normalized stopband edges at 0.4 and 0.6

Passband ripple	3 dB
Minimum stopband attenuation	40 dB

Show (i) Magnitude response (ii) Phase response (iii) Impulse response.

15.26 Using FDA Tool, design a elliptic IIR highpass filter with the following specifications:

Passband ripple	1 dB
Stopband attenuation	30 dB
Passband frequency	500 Hz
Stopband frequency	300 Hz
Sampling frequency	2,000 Hz

(a) Show magnitude response.

(b) Show Pole/zero plot.

15.27 Using FDA Tool, Design a Type II Chebyshev IIR lowpass filter with the following specifications:

Passband ripple	0.50 dB
Stopband attenuation	30 dB
Passband frequency	1,000 Hz
Stopband frequency	1,200 Hz
Sampling frequency	5,000 Hz

(a) Show group delay response.

(b) Phase response.

15.28 Using FDA Tool, Design a Butterworth IIR highpass digital filter with the following specifications:

Passband ripple	1 dB
Stopband attenuation	50 dB
Passband frequency	2.400 Hz
Stopband frequency	2.000 Hz
Sampling frequency	6.000 Hz

(a) Show group delay response.

(b) Phase response.

CHAPTER 16

MATLAB Applications in Computational Mathematics

Learning Objectives

- Solution of various numerical analysis problems such as solution of simultaneous linear algebraic equations
- Finding Eigen values and Eigen vectors of a matrix
- Factorization of matrices
- Optimization techniques such as linear programming, minimization of functions of a single variable, non-linear optimization
- Statistical analysis, regression analysis, correlation analysis
- Solution of non-linear algebraic equations
- Numerical integration and interpolation
- Curve fitting

16.1 INTRODUCTION

In this chapter, solution methods of various numerical analysis problems such as solution of simultaneous linear algebraic equations, finding Eigen values and Eigen vectors of a matrix, factorization of matrices, optimization techniques such as linear programming, minimization of functions of a single variable, non-linear optimization, statistical analysis, regression analysis, correlation analysis, solution of non-linear algebraic equations, numerical integration, interpolation, etc., using MATLAB have been explained.

16.2 SOLUTION OF SIMULTANEOUS LINEAR ALGEBRAIC EQUATIONS

A set of simultaneous linear algebraic equations can be written as:

$$\begin{aligned} a_{11}x_1 + a_{12}x_2 + \text{--------------} + a_{1n}x_n &= b_1 \\ a_{21}x_1 + a_{22}x_2 + \text{--------------} + a_{2n}x_n &= b_2 \\ \text{--------------------------------} & \\ a_{n1}x_1 + a_{n2}x_2 + \text{--------------} + a_{nn}x_n &= b_n \end{aligned} \tag{16.1}$$

These equations can be written in matrix form as:

$$[A][x] = [b] \tag{16.2}$$

where 'A' is a matrix of constant coefficients, 'x' is a vector of unknowns or variables, whose values are to be determined, 'b' is a column vector consisting of a set of constants on the right-hand side of these equations.

Solution of matrix equation (16.2) can be obtained as follows:

$$[x] = [A]^{-1}[b] \tag{16.3}$$

where $[A]^{-1}$ is the inverse of matrix 'A'.

In MATLAB, this solution can be obtained by using the following MATLAB commands:

```
x = inv(A)*b
```

or

```
x = A\b
```

Example 16.1 Solve the following set of linear algebraic equations using MATLAB.

$$5x_1 - 2x_2 - 3x_3 = 10$$
$$-2x_1 + 8x_2 + 2x_3 = 15$$
$$3x_1 + 6x_2 + 9x_3 = 12$$

Solution: These equations can be written in matrix form as follows:

$$\begin{bmatrix} 5 & -2 & -3 \\ -2 & 8 & 2 \\ 3 & 6 & 9 \end{bmatrix} \begin{bmatrix} x_1 \\ x_2 \\ x_3 \end{bmatrix} = \begin{bmatrix} 10 \\ 15 \\ 12 \end{bmatrix}$$

This matrix equation can be solved by using the following MATLAB commands:

Feed the coefficients of matrix 'A' and of vector 'b' as follows:

```
A= [5 -2 -3; -2 8 2; 3 6 9];
b = [10; 15; 12];
x = inv (A) *b
```

On pressing the enter key, the following solution will be obtained

```
x =
        2.3333
        2.7833
       -1.3000
```

Alternatively, we can write the following MATLAB command in the command window:

```
x = A\b          % (left division)
```

Same result will be obtained, on pressing the enter key.

i.e.

$x_1 = 2.333$ $\quad x_2 = 2.7833$ $\quad x_3 = -1.3$

This command is faster than matrix inversion command.

16.3 FINDING EIGEN VALUES AND EIGEN VECTORS OF A MATRIX

Following MATLAB command can be used to obtain the required Eigen values and Eigen vectors:

```
[V,D] = eig (A)
```

Columns of the matrix 'V' contain the **Eigen vectors** of matrix A.

Diagonal values of matrix 'D' give the **Eigen values** of 'A' matrix.

Example 16.2 Find the Eigen values and Eigen vectors of the matrix 'A', given below:

$$A = \begin{bmatrix} 5 & 2 & 3 \\ 2 & 8 & 2 \\ 3 & 6 & 9 \end{bmatrix}$$

Eigen values and Eigen vectors of this matrix can be obtained by using the following MATLAB commands:

```
A = [5     2     3; 2   8   2   ; 3   6   9];

[V,D] = eig (A)
```

On pressing the enter key, the following solution will be obtained:

```
V =

     0.3856     0.8944     0.7921

     0.4305    -0.4472    -0.5676

     0.8161     0.0000     0.2246
```

Columns of this matrix 'V' contain the Eigen vectors of matrix **A**.

Diagonal matrix 'D' is given by:

```
D =   13.5826              0          0

           0          4.0000          0

           0               0     4.4174
```

where diagonal values of matrix 'D', give the Eigen values of 'A' matrix.

i.e. Eigen values are: 13.582 4.0 4.4174

16.4 FACTORIZATION OF MATRICES

Matrices can be factorized by different methods described below:

16.4.1 LU Factorization

Any Matrix 'A' can be factorized into **Lower triangular matrix, 'L'** and **Upper triangular matrix 'U'**, such that

```
[L] *[U] = [A]
```

by using the following MATLAB command.

```
[L,U] = lu(A)
```

16.4.2 QR Factorization

Any matrix 'A' can be factorized into an **Orthogonal matrix Q** and **Upper triangular matrix R**, such that

```
[Q]*[R] = [A],
```

by using the following MATLAB command:

```
[Q,R] = qr(A)
```

16.4.3 Singular Value Decomposition

Any matrix 'A' can be factorized into matrices **U**, **V** and **D**, where matrices 'U' and 'V' are **orthogonal matrices** and 'D' is a **diagonal matrix**, by using the following MATLAB command:

```
[U,D,V] = svd(A)
```

Diagonal matrix 'D' contain the Eigen values of matrix 'A'.

Example 16.3 Factorize the following matrix 'A'.

$$A = \begin{bmatrix} 5 & 2 & 3 \\ 2 & 8 & 2 \\ 3 & 6 & 9 \end{bmatrix}$$

using (i) LU factorization (ii) QR Factorization (iii) Singular value decomposition.

Solution:

(i) **LU factorization**

Following MATLAB commands can be used:

```
A = [5  2  3; 2  8  2; 3  6  9];

[L,U] = lu (A)
```

On pressing **enter** key, following results will be obtained:

```
L =

1.0000         0         0

0.4000    1.0000         0

0.6000    0.6667    1.0000

U =

5.0000    2.0000    3.0000

     0    7.2000    0.8000

     0         0    6.6667
```

where 'L' is lower triangular matrix, and 'U' upper triangular matrix.

(ii) **QR Factorization**

```
[Q,R] = qr(A)
```

On pressing **enter** key, following results will be obtained:

```
Q =

0.8111   -0.5203   -0.2673

0.3244    0.7804   -0.5345

0.4867    0.3468    0.8018

R =

6.1644    7.1377    7.4622

     0    7.2837    3.1216

     0         0    5.3452
```

(iii) Singular Value Decomposition

```
[U,D,V] = svd (A)
```

On pressing **enter** key, following results will be obtained:

```
U =
    -0.3605     0.3549    -0.8626
    -0.5238    -0.8422    -0.1276
    -0.7718     0.4059     0.4896
D =
    14.1456          0              0
          0     4.8803              0
          0          0         3.4765
V =
    -0.3652     0.2680    -0.8915
    -0.6746    -0.7361     0.0550
    -0.6415     0.6215     0.4496
```

16.5 OPTIMIZATION TECHNIQUES

There are a large number of techniques for the solution of non-linear and linear optimization problems. **Linear programming** is one of these techniques.

16.5.1 Linear Programming

Linear programming problem can be stated as follows:

Find the value of 'x', which minimizes the linear objective function $f(x) = c^{T}x$ subject to the **inequality constraints:**

$Ax \leq b$, and $x_{lb} \leq x \leq x_{ub}$,

and

Equality constraints: $A_{eq}\, x = b_{eq}$

where **A** and $\mathbf{A}_{eq}$ are $(m \times n)$ coefficient matrices of the constants in the inequality and equality constraints respectively, n is the number of variables and m is the number of constraints.

'b' and 'b_{eq}' are the R.H.S. 'm' element column vectors of the inequality and equality constraints, respectively.

x_{lb} is the **lower bound** on variable 'x'

x_{ub} is the **upper bound** on variable 'x'

This problem can be solved by using any one of the following MATLAB commands, depending upon the type of problem:

```
x = linprog (c,A,b)                      % If there are no equality constraints
or
x = linprog (c,A,b,xlb,xub,lb)           % If there are no equality constraints
or
[x, fval]= linprog (c, A, b, xlb, xub, lb)   % If there are no equality con-
                                               straints
[x, fval]= linprog (c, A, b, Aeq, beq, xlb, xub, lb)  % If equality con-
                                                        straints are present
```

where,

lb is the lower bound on the variables.

fval = minimum value of function at the solution point.

Set A_{eq} = [] and b_{eq} = [], if there are no equality constraints.

Example 16.4 Minimize the function:

$$f(x) = -2x_1 + x_2$$

subject to the constraints:

$$-3x_1 + 2x_2 \le 2$$

$$2x_1 - 4x_2 \le 3$$

$$x_1 + x_2 \le 6$$

Solution: Feed the coefficients of the objective function, constants on the right-hand side of inequality constraints and the MATLAB command for linear programming as follows:

```
c = [-2; 1];
a = [-3  2; 2  -4;  1  1];
b = [2; 3; 6]
x = linprog (c,a,b)
```

Following answer will be displayed.

Optimization terminated.

```
x =      4.5000      1.5000
```

i.e. $\mathbf{x_1 = 4.5}$ **and** $\mathbf{x_2 = 1.5}$ will minimize the function and these values satisfy all the constraints.

Example 16.5 Minimize the function

$$f(x) = 5x_1 + 6x_2$$

subject to the constraints:

$$-11x_1 - 9x_2 \le -99$$

$$-7x_1 - 12x_2 \le -84$$

$$-6x_1 - 16x_2 \le -96$$

and

$$x_1, x_2 \ge 0$$

Solution: Feed the different coefficients and the MATLAB command for linear programming as follows:

```
c = [5; 6];
a = [-11 -9; -7 -12; -6 -16];
b = [-99; -84; -96];
lb = [0;0];
[x,fval]= linprog (c,a,b,[],[],lb)
```

Following answer will be displayed:

Optimization terminated.

```
x = 5.9016          3.7869
fval = 52.2295
```

i.e. $x_1 = 5.9016$ and $x_2 = 3.78$ will minimize the function and these values satisfy all the constraints.

Example 16.6 Minimize the function

$$z = 4x_1 + 5x_2$$

subject to the constraints:

$$2x_1 + x_2 \le 6$$
$$x_1 + 2x_2 \le 5$$
$$x_1 + 2x_2 \le 2$$
$$-x_1 + x_2 \le 2$$
$$-x_1 - x_2 \le -1$$

and $x_1, x_2 \ge 0$

Solution: Feed the coefficients of the objective function, inequality constraints and the MATLAB command for linear programming as follows:

```
f = [4;5]
A = [2 1;1 2;1 -2;-1 1;-1 -1]
b = [6;5;2;2;-1]
lb = [0;0]
[x,fval] = linprog (f,A,b,[ ],[ ],lb)
```

On pressing the **enter** key, following results will be obtained:

Optimization terminated.

```
x =    1.0000    0.0000
fval =    4.0000
```

Example 16.7 Minimize the function

$$f(x) = 6000x_1 + 4000x_2$$

subject to the constraints:

$$-3x_1 - x_2 \le -40$$
$$-x_1 - 2.5x_2 \le -22$$

and $x_1, x_2 \ge 0$

Solution: Feed the coefficients of the objective function and the MATLAB command for linear programming as follows:

```
c = [6000    4000]
a = [-3 -1;-1 -2.5]
b = [-40; -22]
lb = [0;0]
[x,fval]=linprog(c,a,b,[],[],lb)
```

On pressing **enter** key, following results will be obtained:
Optimization terminated.

```
x =    12.0000            4.0000

fval = 8.8000e+04    i.e. minimum value of function=88000
```

Example 16.8 Minimize the function

$$f(x) = -3x_1 - 4x_2$$

subject to the constraints:

$$4x_1 + 2x_2 \le 80$$
$$2x_1 + 5x_2 \le 180$$

and $x_1, x_2 \ge 0$

Solution: Feed the coefficients of the objective function and the MATLAB command for linear programming as follows:

```
c=[-3 -4]
a=[4 2;2 5]
b=[80;180]
lb=[0;0]
[x,fval]=linprog(c,a,b,[],[],lb)
```

On pressing **enter** key, following results will be obtained:
Optimization terminated.

```
x =     2.5000            35.0000

fval = -147.5000
```

16.6 FUNCTION MINIMIZATION

16.6.1 Minimization of a Function of a Single Variable

This problem can be stated as follows:

Find 'x' which minimizes function $f(x)$, subject to the constraints:

$$x_1 \le x \le x_2$$

where x, x_1, x_2 are scalars and $f(x)$ is a function of x.

To solve this problem, following MATLAB commands can be used:

x=fminbnd(fun,x_1,x_2) or

[x,fvalue]=fminband(fun,x_1,x_2)

where 'fun' is a function handle for an m-file function

This function finds the minimum of a function of one variable in a fixed given interval x_1, x_2.

Example 16.9 Find the minimum of the function:

$$f(x) = (x - 4)^2 - 2$$

such that $0 \le x \le 4$.

Solution: At first, create and save a function 'testfun' in the edit window, as follows:

```
function f = testfun(x)
f = (x-4)^2 -2
end
```

Save this function as testfun.m

Type the MATLAB optimization function **fminbnd** in the command window as follows:

```
[x,fvalue] = fminbnd(@testfun,0,4)
```

Press enter key.

Following answer will be displayed:

```
x = 3.9999

fvalue = -2.0000
```

16.6.2 Nonlinear Unconstrained Optimization

This problem can be stated as follows:

Find the minimum of an unconstrained multivariable function, $f(\boldsymbol{x})$, when there are no constraints on the variable, $\boldsymbol{x}$.

This problem can be solved using the following MATLAB command:

```
x = fminsearch (fun,xo)
```

Or

```
[x,fvalue] = fminsearch (fun, xo)
```

where 'x_o' is the initial starting value of 'x' and **'fun'** is a function that accepts a vector 'x' and returns a scalar 'f', evaluated at 'x'

'fun' can also be a function handle for an anonymous function.

Example 16.10 Minimize the function:

$$f(x) = x_1^{\,2} + x_2^{\,2} + 4x_1 + 6x_2 + 5$$

Choose initial values as: $x_1 = 1.0$, $x_2 = 0.5$

Solution: Following MATLAB commands can be used, using an **anonymous function, f:**

```
f = @ (x) x(1)*x(1) +x(2)* x(2) +4*x(1)+6*x(2)+5;
x0= [1.0 0.5];
[x,fvalue]=fminsearch (f,x0)
```

Following result will be displayed:

```
x = -2.0000 -3.0000

fvalue = -8.0000
```

16.6.3 Constrained Non-linear Optimization

In such problems, a given non-linear objective function is optimized (maximized or minimized), subject to the inequality constraints.

For the solution of such problems, following MATLAB command can be used:

```
[x, fvalue] = fmincon (@testfun2,x0,a,b)
```

where 'x_0' is a vector consisting of initial guess,
'a' is a constant matrix consisting of the coefficients of inequality constraints,
'b' is the RHS column vector of the constraints.
'testfun2' is the function to be minimized.

Example 16.11 Find the values of 'x' which minimizes the objective function

$$f(x) = -x_1x_2x_3,$$

subject to the constraints:

$$-x_1 - 2x_2 - 2x_3 \le 0$$
$$x_1 + 2x_2 + 2x_3 \le 72$$

Assume initial guess of the variables as $x_0 = \begin{bmatrix} 5 \\ 5 \\ 5 \end{bmatrix}$

Solution Following MATLAB commands can be used, using a function subprogram:
Write an m-file which returns a scalar value 'f' of the function evaluated at 'x'.

```
function f = testfun2(x)
f = -x(1) * x (2) *x (3);
```

Save this function with file name **testfun2.m**
Enter the following data in the command window:

```
a= [-1   -2   -2;   1   2   2]
b=[0;   72]
x0 = [5; 5;   5]
[x, fvalue] = fmincon (@testfun2,x0,a,b)
```

Following answers will be obtained:

$x_1 = 24$ $x_2 = 12$ $x_3 = 12$

and fvalue = $- 3.456 \times 10^3$

16.7 STATISTICAL ANALYSIS OF DATA

Statistical analysis of data generally involves calculation of its mean, median, max, min, sum, product, standard deviation and coefficient of variation, variance, etc.

The MATLAB command:

`mean(x)` is used to obtain arithmetic mean of data 'x'.

`median(x)` is used to obtain middle value of data 'x'.

`max(x)` is used to obtain largest value of data set 'x'.

`min(x)` is used to obtain smallest value of data 'x'.

`sum(x)` is used to obtain sum of all the elements of data 'x'.

`prod(x)` is used to obtain product of all the elements of data 'x'

`sort(x)` is used to sort the data in the ascending order.

`std (x)` is used to obtain standard deviation of 'x', based on $(n - 1)$ samples.

`std (x,1)` is used to obtain standard deviation of 'x', based on (n) samples.

`Var = std (x) ^ 2` is used to obtain **variance.**

16.7.1 Statistical Analysis Using MATLAB Commands

Example 16.12 Calculate the mean, median, max, min, sum, product, standard deviation, coefficient of standard deviation, coefficient of variation and variance, etc. for the following data using MATLAB.

x	1	2	3	4	5	6	7	8	9	10
y	10	12	18	22	26	30	32	45	50	55

Solution: Let us calculate all these statistical values for variable 'y'

Feed the values of 'y' as a row vector:

```
y = [10   12   18   22   26   30   32   45   50   55];
```

Type MATLAB functions one by one and the corresponding results obtained are given below:

```
(i) mean (y)
    ans = 30
(ii) median (y)
    ans = 28
(iii) max(y)  = 55
(iv) min(y)  = 10
(v) sum(y)  = 300
(vi) prod(y)  = 1.4678e+014
(vii) sigma1 = std (y) =15.6418      % standard deviation, (n-1) samples
(viii) sigma2= std (y,1)=14.8391     % standard deviation, (n) samples
(ix). Variance = sigma1 ^2
    Variance = 244.66
```

16.7.2 Data Analysis using Graphics Interface

Data can be also analysed using Graphical user Interface of MATLAB.

Many calculations of data analysis and statistics such as finding mean, median, standard deviation, max, min, etc. can be done by following simple steps in the **figure window** of MATLAB:

Step 1: Plot the given data in the figure window of MATLAB, using appropriate MATLAB commands for plotting.

Step 2: Go to **tools** menu of the **figure window (Figure 16.1).**

Step3: Select **data statistics** from the **tools menu.**

Data statistics window will be displayed automatically, as shown in Figure16.2.

Step 4: Select the appropriate box as per requirement to analyse the data, e.g. min, max, mean, median, mode; standard deviation, etc.

Step 5: The numerical value of the corresponding required result can be seen in the **data statistics–I** window.

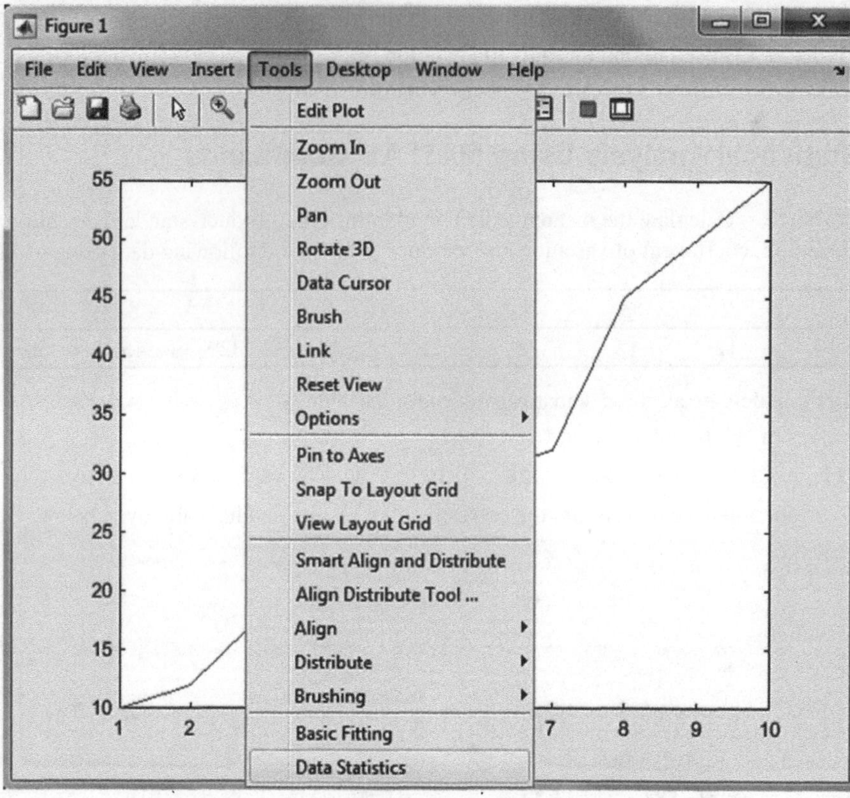

Figure 16.1 Figure Window Showing 'Tools' Menu

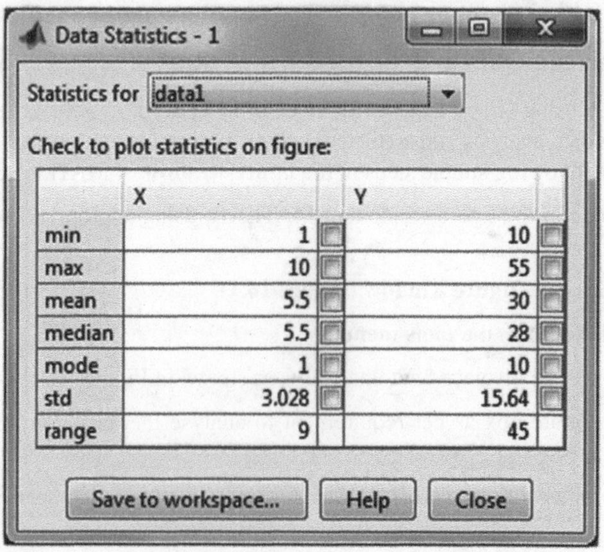

Figure 16.2 Data Statistics Window

Example 16.13 Calculate the minimum, maximum, mean, standard deviation, for the following data; using graphical interface of MATLAB.

x	1	2	3	4	5	6	7	8	9	10
y	10	12	18	22	26	30	32	45	50	55

Solution:

Step 1: Plot the given data in the figure window of MATLAB using the following commands:

```
>> x = [1     2     3     4     5     6     7     8     9     10];
>> y = [10    12    18    22    26    30    32    45    50    55];
>> plot(x,y)
```

Graph as shown in Figure16.1 will be obtained.

Step 2: Go to **tools** menu of the **figure window.**

Step 3: Select **data statistics** from the **tools menu.**

Step 4: The numerical values of the corresponding statistical result will be shown in the **data statistics–I** window, as shown in Figure 16.2.

16.7.3 Regression Analysis

Regression analysis is a technique which refers to the functional relationship between two variables and estimates the value of dependent variables, ‘y’ for given values of the independent variable, ‘x’.

The regression equation ‘y’ on ‘x’ ascertains the value of ‘y’ at a given value of ‘x’ and is given by the following relation:

$$y = a + bx$$

where ‘x’ and ‘y’ are variables and ‘a’ and ‘b’ are constants.

‘polyfit’, command of MATLAB can be used to obtain these constants ‘a’ and ‘b’ for given values of variables ‘x’ and ‘y’.

The command

```
p = polyfit (x,y,n)
```

returns the coefficients of polynomial $p(x)$ of degree ‘n’.

‘p’ is a row vector, which contains the coefficients of the polynomial ‘p’ in descending powers.

i.e. $p_1x^n + p_2x^{n-1}$ _ _ _ _ _ _ _ $p_nx + p_{n+1}$

For linear regression, $n = 1$, and polynomial $p(x)$ can be written as:

$$p(x) = p_1x + p_2$$

which can be written as $y = bx + a$, where $b = p_1$ and $a = p_2$

Example 16.14 From the following information, obtain the regression equation ‘y’ on ‘x’.

x	5	7	8	9	6
y	2	3	6	5	4

Estimate ‘y’ when ‘x’ is 10.

Solution:

(i) If polynomial of degree 1 is to be fitted, type the following MATLAB commands:

```
x = [5      7      8      9      6]
y = [2      3      6      5      4]
p = polyfit (x, y, 1)
```

On pressing enter key, following result will be obtained:

```
p =      0.8000        -1.6000
```

i.e. $b = 0.8$ and $a = -1.6$

or $y = -1.6 + 0.8x$ is the regression equation of 'y' on 'x'.

When $x = 10$, value of 'y' can be calculated by substituting the value of 'x' in the above equation.

$y = -1.6 + (0.8)(10) = -1.6 + 8.0 = 6.4$

(ii) If a polynomial of degree 2 ($n = 2$) is to be fitted to the data, type the following command:

```
polyfit (x, y, 2)
```

On pressing enter key, following answer will be displayed:

```
ans =
          -0.1429      2.8000      -8.3143
```

These are the coefficients of a second-degree polynomial, which means:

$\mathbf{y = -0.1429x^2 + 2.8x - 8.314}$

and

at $x = 10$, value of $y = 5.4$

16.7.4 Multiple Regression

Multiple regression allows us to identify a set of independent variables, x, which together provide a useful estimate of a dependent variable 'y'.

For two independent variables x_1 and x_2, and dependent variable 'y', the regression equation can be expressed as:

$$y = a + b_1x_1 + b_2x_2$$

This equation is called the **regression equation** for **multiple linear regression.**

To obtain the coefficients a, b_1, b_2 of this equation, following MATLAB command can be used:

regress (y,x)

such that matrix 'x' includes an additional **column having all elements equal to one.**

The output of this MATLAB command will give the values of constants a, b_1, b_2.

Example 16.15 Find the multiple regression equation, which can be used for evaluating sales with given **'advertising expenditure' and 'numbers of selling agents'**. The data for different **sales territories** are given below:

Sales Territories	Sales, y	Advertising Expenditure, x_1	Numbers of Selling Agents, x_2
1	100	40	10
2	80	30	10

(Continued)

(Continued)

Sales Territories	Sales, y	Advertising Expenditure, x_1	Numbers of Selling Agents, x_2
3	60	20	7
4	120	50	15
5	150	60	20
6	90	40	12
7	70	20	8
8	130	60	14

Solution: Adding a **column of 'ones'** in the 'x' matrix consisting of column vectors x_1 and x_2,the data of matrix 'x' and vector 'y' can be written in matrix form as follows:

$$\mathbf{x} = \begin{bmatrix} 40 & 10 & 1 \\ 30 & 10 & 1 \\ 20 & 7 & 1 \\ 50 & 15 & 1 \\ 60 & 20 & 1 \\ 40 & 12 & 1 \\ 20 & 8 & 1 \\ 60 & 14 & 1 \end{bmatrix}, \quad \mathbf{y} = \begin{bmatrix} 100 \\ 80 \\ 60 \\ 120 \\ 150 \\ 90 \\ 70 \\ 130 \end{bmatrix}$$

Following 'MATLAB' commands can be used:

```
x = [40  10  1;   30  10  1;   20  7  1;   50  15  1;   60  20  1;
    40  12  1;  20  8  1;   60  14  1];
y = [100   ;  80    ;  60  ;   120   ; 150   ;  90   ; 70    ;   130];
regress (y, x)
```

On pressing enter key, following answer will be obtained:

```
ans =      1.1933              2.9117              17.3270
```

i.e. $a = 17.327$, $b_1 = 1.193$, $b_2 = 2.9117$

i.e. the required multiple regression equation is:

$$y = 17.327 + 1.193x_1 + 2.9117x_2$$

Alternative Method: Use the following MATLAB command to obtain the coefficients a, b_1 and b_2.

```
fit([x1,x2],y,'poly11')
```

where x_1,x_2 and y are column vectors and 'poly11' indicates linear polynomial surface.

For the example given above, following MATLAB commands can be given:

```
x1 = [40;30;20;50;60;40;20;60]
x2 = [10;10;7;1.5;20;12;8;14]
y= [100;80;60;120;150;90;70;130]
fit([x1,x2],y,'poly11')
```

on pressing enter key, following result will be displayed:

```
Linear model Poly11:
Coefficients (with 95% confidence bounds):
p00 =        23.17
p10 =        1.833
p01 =       0.3381
```

i.e. The required multiple regression equation is:

$$y = 23.17 + 1.833x_1 + 0.3381x_2$$

16.7.5 Correlation

In the case of multivariate population, we wish to know the relation of variables with one another. Hence, we have to know whether there exists any correlation between the two variables.

Correlation can be studied through the **Karl Pearson's Method.**

Karl Pearson's Method

It measures the linear relationship between the two variables 'x' and 'y'.

Following MATLAB command can be used to obtain the **coefficient of correlation, 'r':**

```
corr (x, y)
```

Example 16.16 Find the coefficient of correlation 'r' between 'x' and 'y' for the following data:

x	5	3	2	1	4
y	6	4	5	6	4

Solution: Enter the values of 'x' and 'y' as **column vectors.**

```
x = [5 ; 3 ; 2 ; 1 ; 4]
y = [6 ; 4 ; 5 ; 6 ; 4]
corr(x, y)
```

On pressing enter key, following coefficient of correlation 'r' will be obtained:

```
Ans, r = -0.1581
```

16.8 SOLUTION OF NON-LINEAR ALGEBRAIC EQUATIONS

16.8.1 Solution of Non-linear Algebraic Equations Involving Only One Variable

Non-linear algebraic equations, such as $f(x) = 0$, involving only one variable, can be solved using the following MATLAB function:

```
fzero ('Name of the function containing the equation', initial guess)
```

This function can be used by adopting the following procedure:

1. Write the non-linear equation in the standard form
   $f(x) = 0$.

2. Write a function subprogram to compute the value of $f(x)$.

   Save this function as an M-file, with file name as f.m.

3. Write the MATLAB function **'fzero'**, in the command window to find the solution of the give non-linear equation.

Example 16.17 Solve the following nonlinear equation:

$$f(x) = x^2 - x - 6 = 0$$

Assume initial value of x, i.e. $x(0) = 1$.

Solution:

1. Put the non-linear equation in the standard form i.e.

   $$f(x) = x^2 - x - 6 = 0$$

2. Write the function subprogram $f_1(x)$, which computes the value of function $f(x)$, as follows:

```
function f=f1(x)
f=x*x-x-6
end
```

   Save this function as an m-file and name it as: f1.m

3. Call this function in the command window as follows:

```
x=fzero('f1',1)
```

   On pressing the enter key, following final answer will be displayed:

   x = 3.0, f = $4.4*10^{-15}$

This problem can also be solved by treating the given non-linear equation as a polynomial, and using the MATLAB command **'roots'** to obtain the roots of a polynomial.

i.e. Enter the coefficients of the polynomial in the command window:

```
p=[1  -1   -6]
roots(p)
```

On pressing the enter key, following roots of the polynomial will be displayed:

```
x = 3, -2
```

Example 16.18 Solve the following non-linear equation:

$$x = e^{-x}$$

Assume initial value of $x = 1$.

Solution

Put the equation in the standard form i.e.

$$f(x) = xe^x - 1 = 0$$

1. Write the function $f_z(x)$, which computes the value of function as follows:

```
function f=fz(x)
f = x* exp(x) -1
end
```

   Save this function as an m-file and name it as: fz.m

   Call this function in the command window as follows:

```
x = fzero('fz',1)
```

   On pressing the enter key, following final answer will be displayed:

```
x = 0.5671,
```

2. Alternatively,
   Following MATLAB commands can be used, using **'inline'** function:

```
f=inline('x*exp(x)-1')
x=fzero(f,1)
```

   On pressing the enter key, following answer will be displayed:

```
x=0.5671
```

16.8.2 Solution of a System of Non-linear Algebraic Equations of Several Variables

Non-linear algebraic equations of the form: $f(\mathrm{x}) = 0$, involving several variables can be solved using the following MATLAB command:

```
[x, fval]=fsolve('funnl', x(0))
```

where `'funnl'` is the name of the function, which contains the Non-linear equation to be solved.

It returns the value of function, `'fval'` at the solution point, x.

Example 16.19 Solve the equation $2x_1 - x_2 - e^{-x_1} - x_1 + 2x_2 - e^{-x_2} = 0$

Choose initial guess as: $x_1(0) = -4$, $x_2(0) = -4$

Solution: Write the function subprogram as follows:

```
function f=funnl(x)
f=[2*x(1)-x(2)-exp(-x(1))-x(1)+2*x(2)- exp(-x(2))]
end
```

Save this function as an m-file with the name **funnl.m**

```
[x, fval]=fsolve('funnl',[-4;-4])
```

On pressing the enter key, following answer will be displayed:

```
x =
    0.5671
    0.5671
fval = -1.54 × 10-8
```

16.8.2.1 Newton–Raphson Method

Newton–Raphson Method is a technique for finding successively better approximations to the roots of a non-linear algebraic equation.

In this method, we start with an initial guess x_0 which is reasonably close to the true root. The following algorithm can be used for solving a problem by this method.

Algorithm

Consider a function $f(x)$ of single variable 'x' and evaluate its derivative $f'(x)$, analytically.

1. Take an initial guess x_0. Set iteration count = 1. Specify maximum number of iterations.
2. Evaluate $f(x)$ and the first derivative of the function $f'(x)$ with respect to x at x_0.
3. Calculate the next estimate of the root, i.e.

   $x_{i+1} = x_i - \{ f(x_i)/f'(x_i) \}$

4. Increase the iteration count by 1 and check whether specified number of iterations have been completed.
5. If not, go to Step 2, else stop the algorithm and print the answer.

Example 16.20 Consider a function, $f(x) = 4x^2 - 2x - 2$. Find the roots of this function using Newton–Raphson method. Choose initial guess as $x(0) = 0.5$ and number of iterations =10

Solution: Following MATLAB commands can be used to find the roots:

```
x0=0.5;
x =x0;
n =10;                          % number of iterations
for iter=1:n
f=4*x^2-2*x-2                   % Evaluation of function, f
dfdx=8*x-2                      % dfdx is a derivative of 'f' w.r.t 'x'
x=x-f/dfdx;                     % updated value of 'x'
end
f, x, iter
```

Following final answer will be displayed:

```
f = 0, x = 1, iter = 10
```

16.8.2.2 Newton–Raphson Method for n-variables

A set of non-linear algebraic equations in matrix form can be written as:

$$\mathrm{f(x)} = \begin{bmatrix} f_1(\mathrm{x}) \\ f_2(\mathrm{x}) \\ --- \\ f_n(\mathrm{x}) \end{bmatrix} = 0$$

where x and f(x) are n-vectors.

Taylor series expansion of f(x), neglecting higher-order terms can be written as:

$$f_1(x+\Delta x) = f_1(x) + \frac{\partial f_1(x)}{\partial x_1}\Delta x_1 + \ldots\ldots + \frac{\partial f_1(x)}{\partial x_n}\Delta x_n$$

$$f_2(x+\Delta x) = f_2(x) + \frac{\partial f_2(x)}{\partial x_1}\Delta x_1 + \ldots\ldots + \frac{\partial f_2(x)}{\partial x_n}\Delta x_n$$

$$f_n(x+\Delta x) = f_n(x) + \frac{\partial f_n(x)}{\partial x_1}\Delta x_1 + \ldots\ldots + \frac{\partial f_n(x)}{\partial x_n}\Delta x_n$$

where $\frac{\partial f_i(x)}{\partial x_j}$ means the partial derivatives of f_i with respect to x_j.

Using matrix notation, we can write:

$$\mathrm{f}(\mathrm{x}+\Delta\mathrm{x}) = \mathrm{f}(\mathrm{x}) + \mathrm{J}(\mathrm{x})\Delta\mathrm{x}, \text{ where}$$

$$J(x) \triangleq \begin{bmatrix} \frac{\partial f_1(x)}{\partial x_1} & \cdots & \frac{\partial f_1(x)}{\partial x_n} \\ \vdots & & \vdots \\ \frac{\partial f_n(x)}{\partial x_1} & \cdots & \frac{\partial f_n(x)}{\partial x_n} \end{bmatrix}, \quad \Delta \mathrm{x} \triangleq \begin{bmatrix} \Delta x_1 \\ \vdots \\ \Delta x_n \end{bmatrix}$$

J(x) is called the **Jacobian Matrix** of 'f' evaluated at **x**.

Step-by-step procedure of Newton–Raphson method for *n*-variables

1. Choose initial guess, $x(0)$, Number of maximum iterations and set iteration count = 1.
2. Calculate $\mathbf{f}(\mathbf{x}_0)$
3. Calculate the elements of Jacobian matrix, $\mathbf{J}(\mathbf{x}_0)$.
4. Calculate increment $\Delta x(i)$ in the value of x, i.e. $\mathbf{\Delta x(i) = -J^{-1} f(x)}$.
5. Calculate updated value of **x,** i.e.

   $\mathbf{x(i+1) = x(i) + \Delta\, x(i)}$
6. Increase the iteration count by 1.
7. Continue the procedure until the specified number of iterations is completed.

Example 16.21 Obtain the solution of following two non-linear algebraic equations:

$$f_1 = x_1^{\,2} - x_2^{\,2} - 10 = 0$$

$$f_2 = x_1 x_2 + x_2^{\,2} - 4 = 0$$

Choose initial guess: $x_1(0) = 1$, $x_2(0) = 1$,
Maximum number of iterations = 10.

Solution: Jacobian matrix **J** for this problem is given by:

$$\mathbf{J} = \begin{bmatrix} \frac{\partial f_1}{\partial x_1} & \frac{\partial f_1}{\partial x_2} \\ \frac{\partial f_2}{\partial x_1} & \frac{\partial f_2}{\partial x_2} \end{bmatrix} = \begin{bmatrix} 2x_1 & -2x_2 \\ x_2 & x_1 + 2x_2 \end{bmatrix}$$

MATLAB Program

Following MATLAB commands can be used:

```
x=[1;1];
iteration=0;
for i=1:10
f=[x(1)*x(1)-x(2)^2-10;x(1)*x(2)+x(2)^2-4];
J=[2*x(1) -2*x(2) ;x(2) x(1)+2*x(2)];          % Jacobian matrix
inicx=-inv(J)*f;                               % increment in x
x=x+inicx        ;                             % updated value of x
```

```
iteration=iteration+1
end
```

Following answer will be displayed:

```
x = 3.2998
    0.9428
Iteration = 10
```

16.9 INTERPOLATION

A general function can be approximated by a class of simple functions. There are two reasons for approximation of functions.

(i) The first is to replace complicated functions by some simpler functions.
(ii) The second is for interpolating in tables for evaluating a function at some unknown point when values of the function are known at a set of tabular points.

16.9.1 1-D Interpolation

Following MATLAB commands can be used for 1-D interpolation:

y_i = interp1 (x, y, x_i) or

y_i = interp1 (x, y, x_i, 'method')

where 'method' is the name of any one of the following methods of interpolation:

(i) Nearest (ii) linear (iii) cubic (iv) spline

Any one of these four names has to be written in the place of **'method'** and has to be enclosed within the single quotes.

These commands interpolate to find y_i, the values of the function y at the points in the array x_i.

Here, table is given by the elements [x,y] and the MATLAB command **interp1**, 'looks up' the elements of x_1 in x and, returns element y_i interpolated within the elements of y.

Interpolation is similar to the table look-up operation.

Example 16.22 Generate a coarse cosine wave and interpolate over a finer abscissa.

Solution: Following MATLAB commands can be used:

```
x = 0:10;
y = cos (x);                              % cosine wave generation
xi = 0:0.5:10;
yi = interp1(x, y, xi)
```

Following interpolated values of y_i at intervals of 0.5 will be displayed:

```
yi=
1.0    .77   .54   .06   -.41   -.7   -.99   -.82   -.65   -.18
0.28   .62   .96   .85   .75    .30   -.14   -.52   -.91   -.87
```

It can be seen that the values of y_i have been interpolated at the intermediate values of x_i.

Example 16.23 A table containing values of x and y is given as follows:

x	5	10	15	20
y	15	32	40	60

Find y_i at $x_i = 7, 12, 25$

Solution: Enter the following MATLAB commands to obtain the values of y_i at specified values of x_i:

```
x = [5    10    15    20];
y = [15   32    40    60];
xi = [7    12    25    ];
yi = interp1 (x, y, xi, 'cubic')                    % Using cubic method.
```

Following values of 'y_i' will be displayed:

```
23.0355    35.2856    86.8571
yi = interp1 (x, y, xi, 'spline')                    % Using spline method.
```

Following values of 'y_i' will be displayed:

```
24.2            35.10          113.0
```

16.10 NUMERICAL INTEGRATION

Numerical integration or numerical quadrature is a technique for estimating the value of following definite integral:

$$I(f) = \int_a^b f(x)\,dx$$

Such problems occur when the integration cannot be carried out exactly or when $f(x)$ is known only at a finite number of points.

There are several rules or functions for numerical integration. Some of these are:

1. Trapezoidal rule
2. Simpson's rule

16.10.1 Trapezoidal Rule

In MATLAB, this rule can be applied by using the following MATLAB command.

```
z =trapz(x,y)
```

It computes the integral 'z' of 'y' with respect to 'x' using **trapezoidal integration.**

Example 16.24 Find the value of following integral, using **TRAPEZOIDAL rule.**

$$z = \int_0^1 e^{-x^2}\,dx$$

Solution Let $y = e^{-x^2}$

Following MATLAB commands can be used to obtain the integral:

```
x = 0:0.01:1
y = exp(-x.*x)
z = trapz(x,y)
```

On pressing the enter key, following value of the desired definite integral, z, will be displayed:

```
z = 0.7468
```

Example 16.25 Evaluate the following integral

$$z = \int_0^{\pi} \sin x \, dx$$

Solution: Following MATLAB commands can be used to obtain the integral:

```
x=0:pi/100:pi
y=sin(x)
z=trapz(x,y)
```

On pressing the enter key, following answer will be displayed:

```
z=1.9998
```

Example 16.26 Evaluate the following integral:

$$z = \int_1^2 (x+1) dx$$

Solution Following MATLAB commands can be used to obtain the integral:

```
x=1:0.01:2
y=(x+1)
z=trapz(x,y)
```

On pressing the enter key, following value of the desired definite integral, z, will be displayed:

```
z = 2.5000
```

16.10.2 Simpson's Rule of Integration

Define the integrand of the integral as a function subprogram. The command:

```
q=quad(fun,a,b)
```

evaluates the integral of scalar valued function 'fun' from a to b, within an error of 1×10^{-6}, using **Simpson's Rule of Integration.**

Example 16.27 Find the value of following integral, using Simpson's rule:

$$q = \int_0^1 e^{-x^2} dx$$

Solution: Following MATLAB commands can be used to obtain the integral:

```
f = inline('exp(-x.*x)')        % define 'f' as inline function
q =quad(f,0,1)
```

On pressing the enter key, following value of the desired definite integral, q, will be displayed:

```
q = 0.7468
```

Example 16.28 Evaluate the following integral

$$q = \int_{1}^{2} (x+1)\,dx$$

Solution: Create an m-file function, **tfun.m** as follows:

```
function y=tfun(x)
y=(x+1)
end
```

Save this function file as **tfun.m**
Type the following command in the command window

```
q =quad('tfun',1,2)
```

On pressing the enter key, following value of the desired definite integral, q, will be displayed:

```
q = 2.5000
```

Example 16.29 Evaluate the following integral

$$I = \int_{2}^{3} \log(x)\,dx$$

Solution: Following MATLAB commands can be used to obtain the integral:

```
f=inline('log(x)')              % inline function 'f'
i=quad(f,2,3)
```

On pressing the enter key, following value of the desired definite integral, i, will be displayed:

```
i = 0.9095
```

16.10.3 Numerical Double Integration

Following command can be used to evaluate double integration of a function numerically.

```
i=dblquad(user defined function, xmin,xmax,ymin,ymax)
```

where xmin, xmax, ymin, ymax are the limits of integration.

Example 16.30 Evaluate the following integral:

$$I = \int_{0}^{1}\int_{0}^{1} e^{(x+y)}\,dx\,dy$$

Solution Following MATLAB commands can be used to obtain the integral:

```
f =inline('exp(x+y)')                    % inline function 'f'
I =dblquad(f,0,1,0,1)
```

On pressing the enter key, following value of the desired definite integral, I, will be displayed:

```
I = 2.9525
```

Example 16.31 Evaluate the following integral

$$\text{defi} = \int_{-1}^{-2}\int_{-1}^{-2} (1-6x^2 y)\mathrm{d}x\mathrm{d}y$$

Solution: Following MATLAB commands can be used to obtain the integral:

```
intg = inline('1-6.*x.*x.*y')            % inline function 'intgf'
defi =dblquad(intg,-1,-2,-1,-2)
```

On pressing the enter key, following value of the desired definite integral, **defi,** will be displayed:

```
defi = 22
```

Example 16.32 Evaluate the following integral:

$$I = \int_{3}^{4}\int_{1}^{2} \sin(x)\cos(y)\mathrm{d}x\mathrm{d}y$$

Solution: Following MATLAB commands can be used to obtain the integral:

```
f = inline('sin(x)*cos(y)')
i =dblquad(f,1,2, 3,4)
```

On pressing the enter key, following value of the desired definite integral, *I*, will be displayed:

```
i = -0.8588
```

16.11 CURVE FITTING

Suppose we are given a set of values for two variables x and y in a tabular form and it is desired to find an algebraic relationship between these two variables. The technique of finding this mathematical relationship is known as **'curve fitting'**.

This mathematical relationship can be linear or non-linear. If the relationship is linear, it is called **'linear curve fitting'** and if the relationship is non-linear, it is called **non-linear curve fitting** or **'polynomial curve fitting'**.

Curve fitting in MATLAB can be done by any one of the following two methods:

1. Using MATLAB commands in the command window.
2. Using Graphic User Interface.

16.11.1 Linear Curve Fitting

Suppose we are given two vectors 'x and y', the MATLAB command:

```
p = polyfit (x, y, 1)
```

will fit a polynomial of degree '1' to the given data. This command has been already explained in Section 16.7.3.

16.11.2 Curve fitting Using Graphics User Interface

In the figure window of MATLAB, **Tools menu** helps us to fit a polynomial curve (up to tenth order) to the given data. To illustrate this procedure, let us take an example.

Example 16.33 Given the values of vectors ***x*** and ***y*** as follows, fit the linear curve to this data:

x	1	2	3	4	5
y	5	7	9	11	13

Solution:

Step 1: Plot the given *data*, using '**plot**' command as follows:

```
x = [1   2   3   4   5];

y = [5   7   9   11   13];

plot (x, y, '_')

% graph will be plotted in the figure window, Figure 16.3.
```

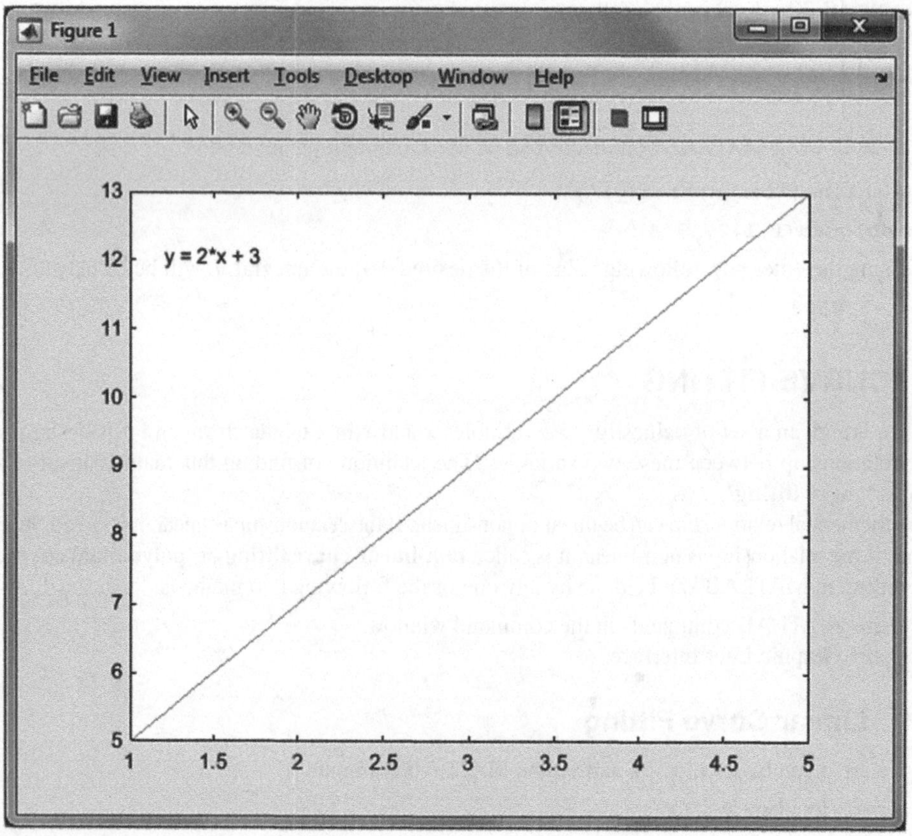

Figure 16.3 Plot of Graph

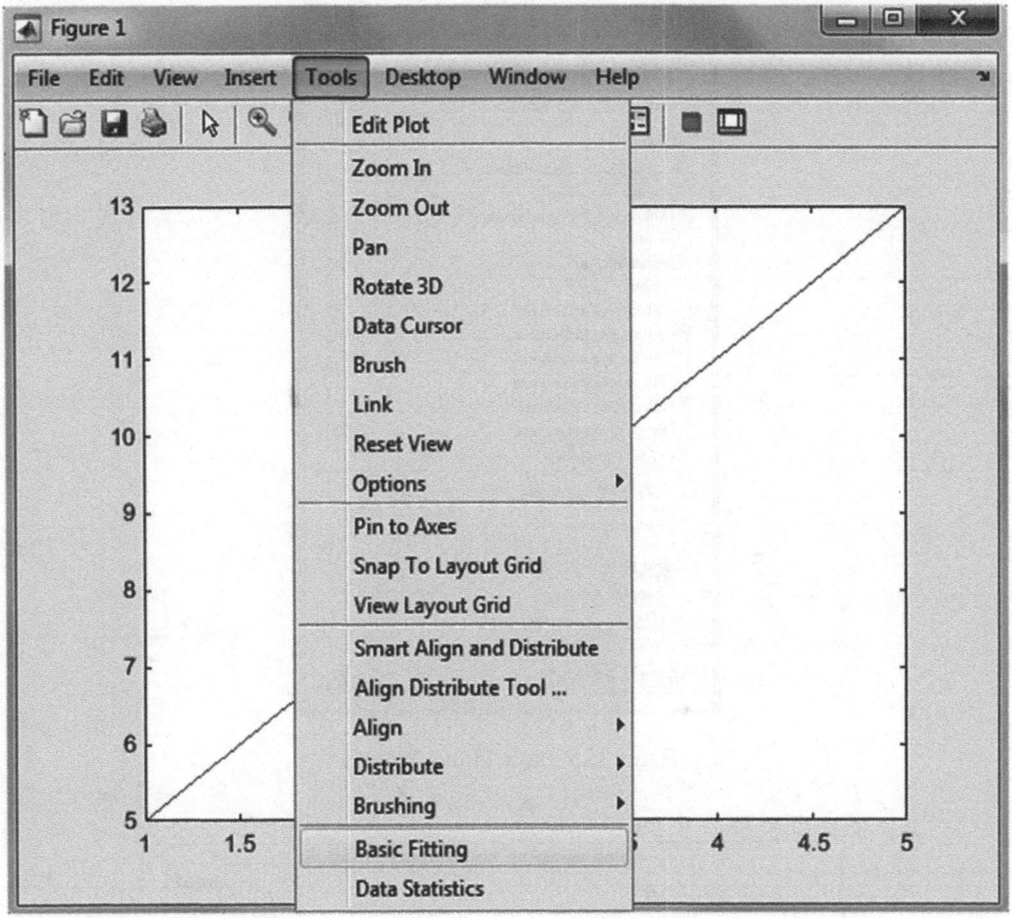

Figure 16.4 Figure Window Showing **Basic Fitting** in Tools Menu

Step 2: Click on **tools menu**, in the figure window and select **Basic fitting** from the pull-down menu (as shown in Figure 16.4). A basic fitting window will appear (Figure 16.5).

Step 3: Tick /check the appropriate box to display fits, from different available options, i.e. linear or a polynomial of proper degree.

In this example, tick the following boxes:

Linear and **show equations.**

Best fitted line along with its equation will be displayed in the figure window, as shown in Figure 16.6.

i.e. $y = 2x + 3$ is displayed.

16.11.3 Alternative Method for Curve Fitting

Curve fitting can also be done by using the following MATLAB command:

```
fit(x,y,'poly1')
```

where x and y are **column vectors** and **'poly1'** is the linear polynomial curve to be fitted.

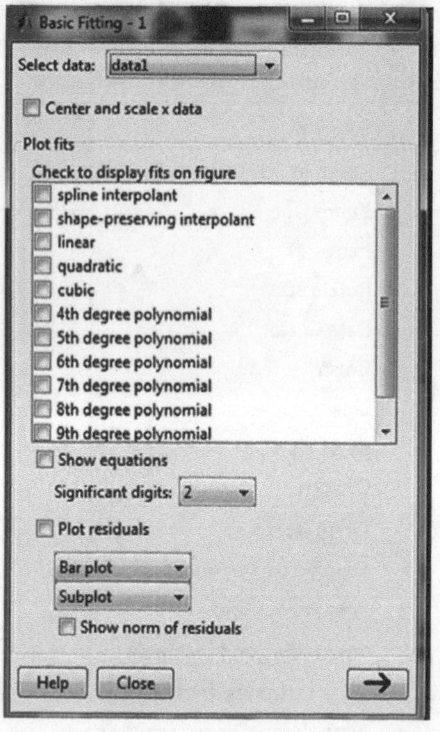

Figure 16.5 Basic Fitting Window

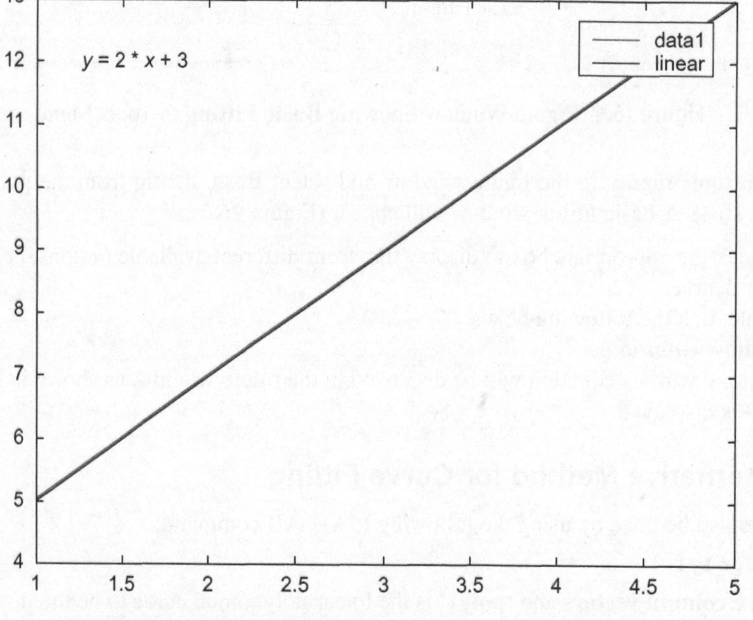

Figure 16.6 Best Fitted Line Along with Its Equation

For the example given above, following MATLAB commands can be given:

```
x = [1 ;  2 ;  3 ;  4 ;  5];
y = [5 ;  7 ;  9  ; 11 ; 13];
fit(x,y,'poly1')
```

On pressing enter key, following answer will be displayed:

```
ans =
Linear model Poly1:
ans(x) = p1*x + p2
Coefficients (with 95% confidence bounds):
        p1 = 2
        p2 = 3
```

i.e. The required equation is:

y = 2x +3

which is the same, as obtained by the earlier method.

SUMMARY

In this chapter, MATLAB commands for the solution of simultaneous linear and non-linear algebraic equation; finding Eigen values and Eigen vectors of a matrix; factorization of matrices, linear programming, non-linear programming, statistical analysis of data, interpolation, numerical integration and curve fitting etc. have been explained through solved examples.

List of Commands/Functions

Commands	Description
eig (A)	To obtain the desired Eigen values and Eigen vectors:
lu(A)	LU Factorization
qr(A)	QR Factorization
svd(A)	Singular value decomposition
linprog (c,A,b)	Linear programming
fminbnd(fun,x1,x2)	Minimization of a function
fminsearch	Non-linear unconstrained optimization
fmincon	Constrained non-linear optimization
fit	Curve fitting
mean (x)	Used to obtain arithmetic mean of data 'x'
median(x)	Used to obtain middle value of data 'x'
max(x)	Used to obtain largest value of data 'x'
min(x)	Used to obtain smallest value of data 'x'
sum(x)	Used to obtain sum of all the elements of data 'x'
prod(x)	Used to obtain product of all the elements of data 'x'

(Continued)

(*Continued*)

`sort(x)`	Used to sort the data in the ascending order.
`std (x)`	Used to obtain standard deviation of 'x', based on $(n - 1)$ samples
`std (x,1)`	Used to obtain standard deviation of 'x', based on (n) samples
`polyfit`	Curve fitting of degree 'n'
`regress`	Multiple regression
`corr`	Coefficient of correlation.
`fzero`	To find the solution of a non-linear algebraic equation
`fsolve`	For the solution of non-linear algebraic equation involving several variables.
`interp1`	One-dimensional interpolation.
`trapz`	Numerical integration (trapezoidal rule)
`quad`	Simpson's rule of integration
`dblquad`	Numerical double integration

EXERCISES

16.1 Find the Eigen values and Eigen vectors of the matrix, A:

$$\mathbf{A} = \begin{bmatrix} 2 & 4 & 6 \\ 3 & 5 & 7 \\ 4 & 6 & 9 \end{bmatrix}$$

16.2 Obtain (I) LU factorization (II) QR factorization (III) Singular value decomposition of the following matrix, **P**:

$$\mathbf{P} = \begin{bmatrix} 1 & 2 & 3 \\ 7 & 8 & 9 \\ 6 & 5 & 4 \end{bmatrix}$$

16.3 Minimize the function:

$$z = 4x_1 + 5x_2$$

Subject to the constraints:

$$2x_1 + x_2 \le 6$$
$$x_1 + 2x_2 \le 5$$
$$-x_1 + x_2 \le 2$$

and

$$x_1, x_2 \ge 0$$

16.4 Find the minimum of the function:

$f(x) = x^2 - 6x + 10$

Such that $0 \le x \le 3$

16.5 Minimize the function:

$f(x) = x_1^2 + 2x_2^2 + 3x_1 + 5x_2 + 6$

Choose initial values: $x_1(0) = 0.5, x_2(0) = 0.6$

16.6 Calculate the mean, median, maximum, minimum, sum, product, standard deviation for the following data:

$x = [5 \quad 10 \quad 15 \quad -4 \quad 6 \quad 8]$

16.7 From the following information, obtain the regression equation 'y' on 'x'.

x	0	1	2	3	4	5
y	4	6	8	10	12	14

16.8 Find the multiple regression equation to evaluate sales. The data for different sales territories, advertising expenditure and number of selling agents are as follows:

Sales Territories	**Sales, y**	**Advertising Expenditure, x_1**	**Numbers of Selling Agents, x_2**
1	90	35	5
2	75	25	8
3	50	15	6
4	100	40	10
5	120	50	12
6	130	60	14
7	140	70	16

16.9 Find the coefficient of correlation 'r' between x and y for the following data:

x	2	6	18	54
y	4	12	36	108

16.10 Solve the following non-linear equation:

$x^2 + 4x + 4 = 0$

Assume initial value $x(0) = 0.5$

16.11 Obtain the solution of following three, simultaneous non-linear algebraic equations:

$x_1^2 - x_2^2 + x_3^2 - 10 = 0$

$x_1x_2 + x_2^2 - 4x_3 - 4 = 0$

$x_1 - x_1x_3 + x_2x_3 - 5 = 0$

Assume initial guess as $x(0) = [\,1 \quad 2 \quad 3]$

16.12 A table containing values of x and y is given as follows:

x	5	10	15	20	25
y	15	30	45	60	75

Find y at $x = 12$

16.13 Obtain the following integrals.

(i) $I = \int_0^2 e^{-x} dx$

(ii) $I = \int_1^2 (x^2 + 2) dx$

16.14 Evaluate the following integral:

$$I = \int_3^4 \int_1^2 \sin(x)\cos(y) dx dy$$

Appendix 1

Graphical User Interface

A graphical user interface (GUI) enables a user to interact with the system through graphic components like menus, toolbars, push buttons, radio buttons, list boxes and sliders. Each component in the GUI is associated with one or more user-written routines known as callbacks. The execution of each callback is activated by a user action such as a button push, mouse click, selection of a menu item etc. This kind of programming is called event-driven programming. GUI can be created using MATLAB® programs or with GUIDE, an interactive GUI builder tool.

GUIDE, the MATLAB GUI development environment, provides a set of tools for creating GUIs. These tools simplify the process of laying out the graphic components and programming the GUI. The GUI components can be placed into the layout area by simply clicking and dragging them into the layout area. It also allows the user to create menus, resize the GUI, align components, set tab order and view a hierarchical list of component objects.

When the GUI layout is saved, GUIDE automatically generates an M-file that controls the operations in the GUI. This M-file contains code for initializing the GUI and a framework for the GUI callback functions associated with each component that is included in the particular GUI generated by the user. The user needs to write these callback functions as per the requirement of the GUI function associated with the components.

A1.1 BUILDING A NEW GUI

To build a new GUI, type `guide` at the MATLAB prompt. The GUIDE Quick Start window is opened as shown in Figure A1.1.

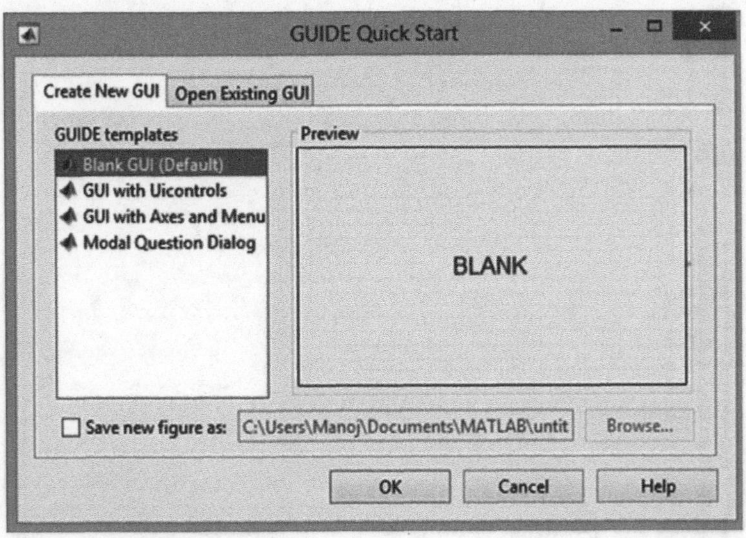

Figure A1.1 The GUIDE Quick Start Window

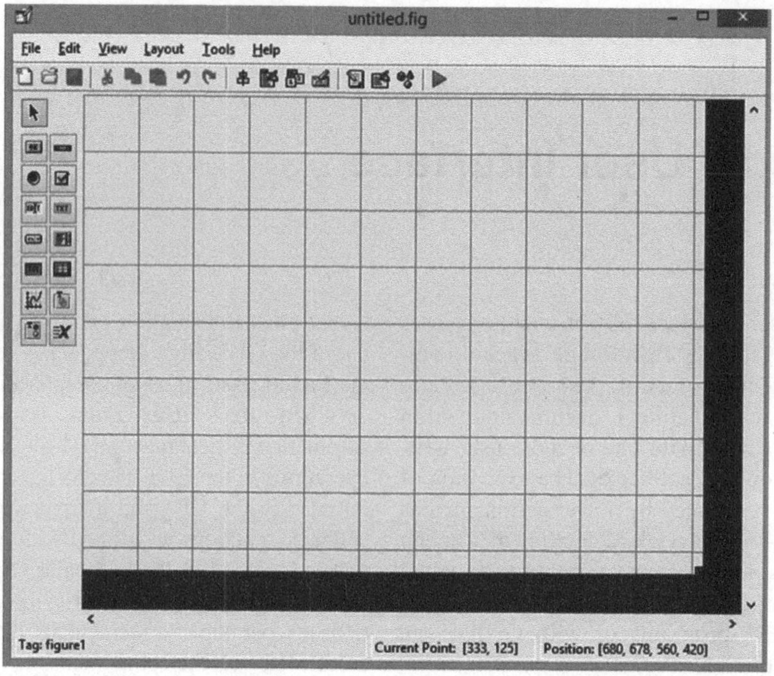

Figure A1.2 GUIDE Quick Start Layout Editor with Blank GUI Template

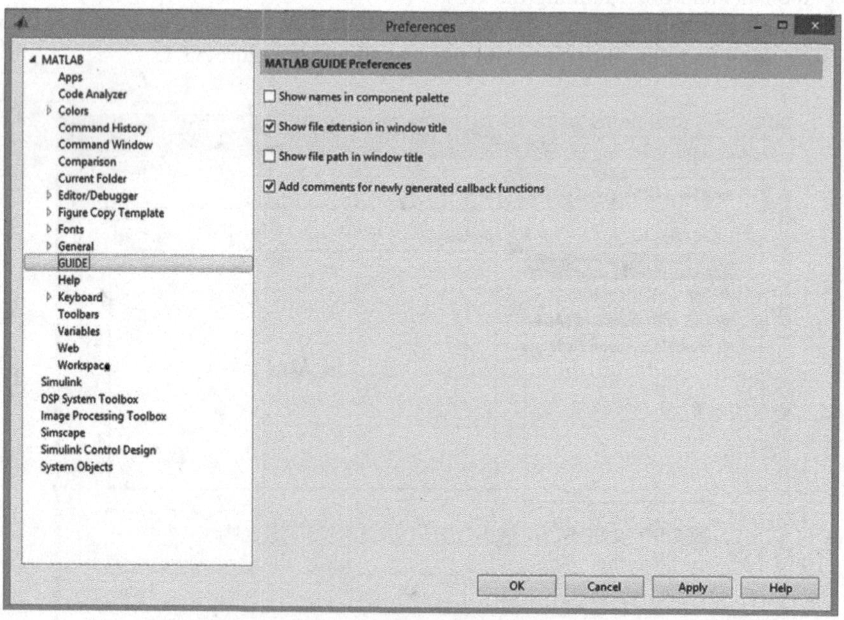

Figure A1.3 GUIDE Preferences Window

Select the 'Create New GUI' tab and further select the 'Blank GUI (Default)' template. Click 'OK'. The Layout Editor window will be opened with a blank GUI as shown in Figure A1.2.

The components palette on the extreme left of the Layout Editor is difficult to comprehend. To display the names of the GUI components in the component palette, select 'Preferences' from the MATLAB desktop window 'File' menu. Then, select 'GUIDE' option mentioned in the left part of the window. Further, select 'Show names in component palette' in the right part of the window and click OK as shown in Figure A1.3.

The Layout Editor with component names in the component palette will be displayed as shown in Figure A1.4.

Programming Tip A1.1: Just as any other window, the size of the GUI can be changed by resizing the grid area in the Layout Editor.

Example A1.1

Create a GUI for plotting a bar graph, a pie chart or a histogram. The user should also have choice of choosing single row array, two row array and three row array as data to be plotted.

Solution:

Start from the GUIDE Quick Start Layout Editor shown in Figure A1.4.

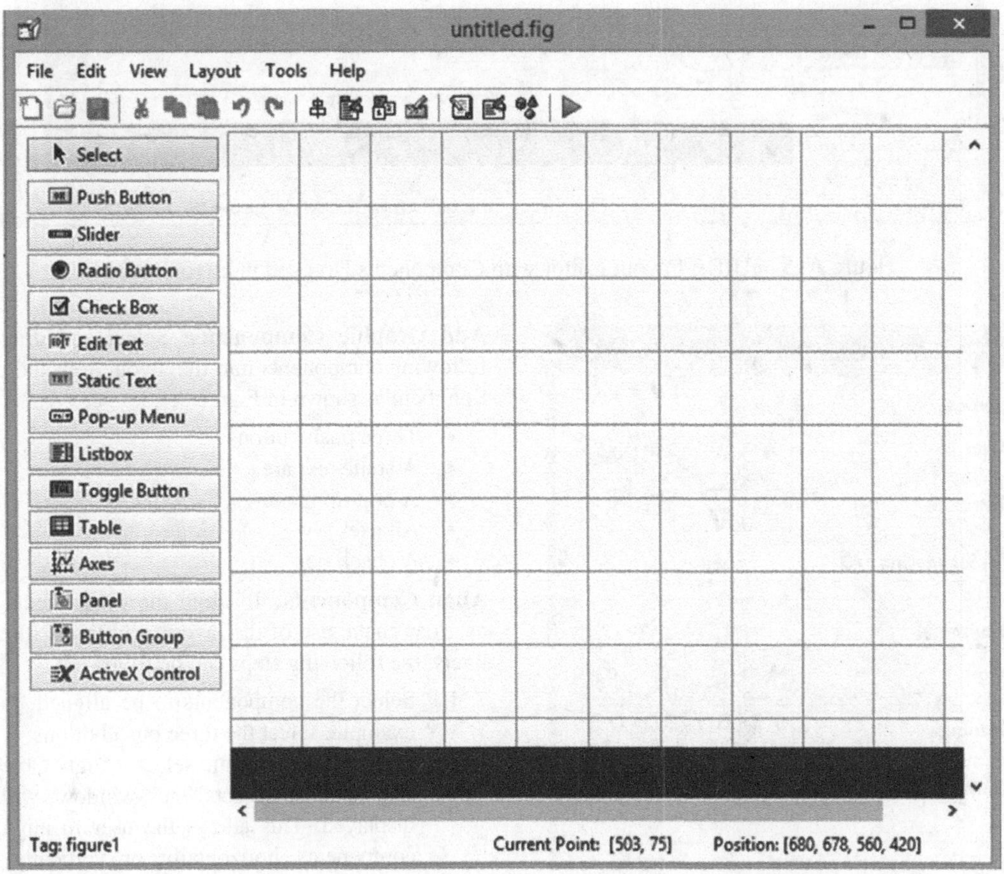

Figure A1.4 GUIDE Quick Start Layout Editor with Component Names in Palette

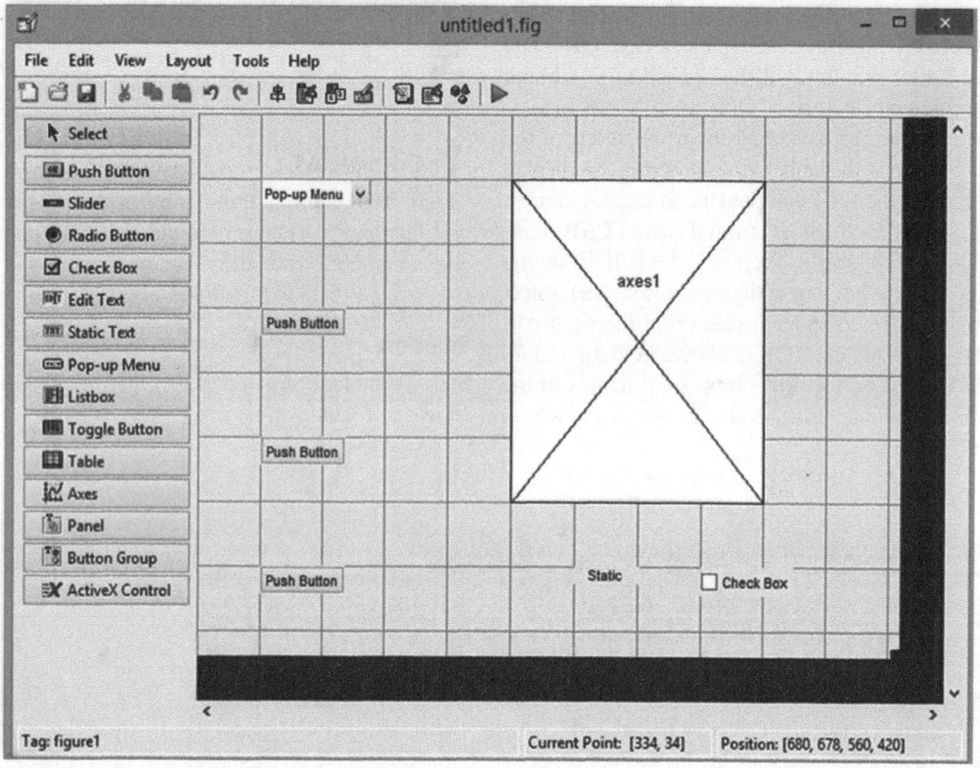

Figure A1.5 GUIDE Layout Editor with Components Dragged in Layout Area

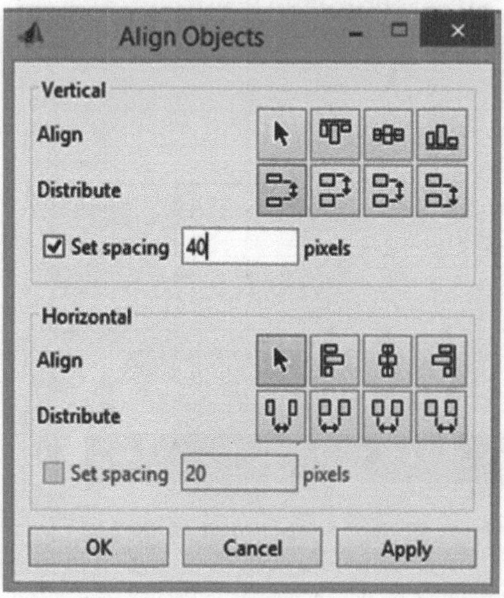

Figure A1.6 Physical Alignment of Components

Add Graphic Components: Select and drag the following components into the layout area and position them as shown in Figure A1.5:

- Three push buttons
- A static text area
- A pop-up menu
- An axes
- A check box

Align Components: To align the components, the user can make use of the layout grid lines. Alternatively, the following steps can be followed:

1. Select the components to be aligned. In the example, select the three push buttons.
2. From 'Tools' menu, select 'Align Objects'. The 'Align Objects' sub-window will be displayed. This allows the user to align the components horizontally or vertically and also define the space between them and so on. The 'Align Objects' sub-window is shown in Figure A1.6.

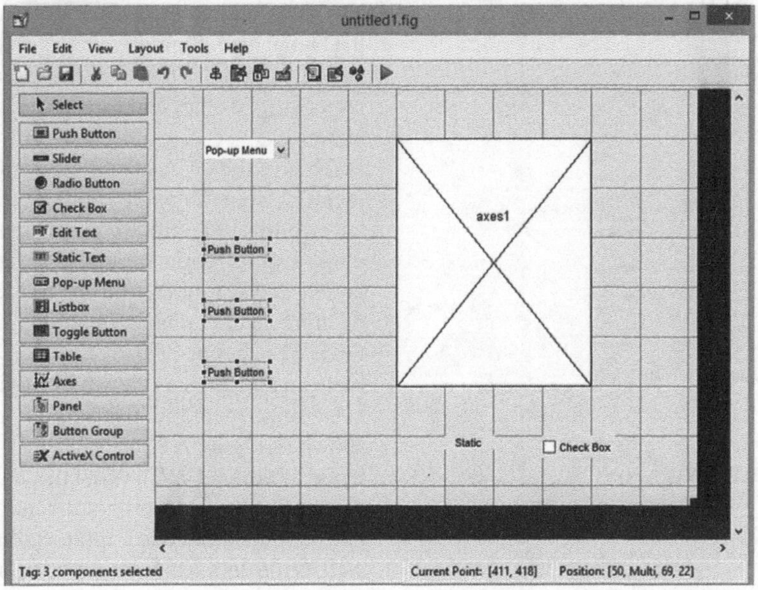

Figure A1.7 Layout Editor Window with Aligned Components

3. Select 'left aligned' in vertical direction with 40 pixels spacing between the push buttons.
4. Click 'OK' to align the objects.

The GUI layout with components aligned with above specifications is shown in Figure A1.7.

Label and Add Text to Components: The push buttons, pop-up menu etc. should be given proper names, menu option names, so that the user is able to infer what operation will be performed when a particular button is clicked.

Enter Pop-up Menu Items: The 'Pop-up' menu is to provide choice of three data sets: single array, two arrays and three arrays. To add the list of these three choices in the Pop-up menu, follow these steps:

1. In the layout area, select the Pop-up menu component.
2. From the 'View' menu, select 'Property Inspector'.
3. The 'Property Inspector' window is opened as shown in Figure A1.8. Click the button next to 'String' option. The String dialog box is displayed.
4. Replace the existing text with the names of the three data sets: one array, two arrays and three arrays (as in Figure A1.9) and press 'OK'.

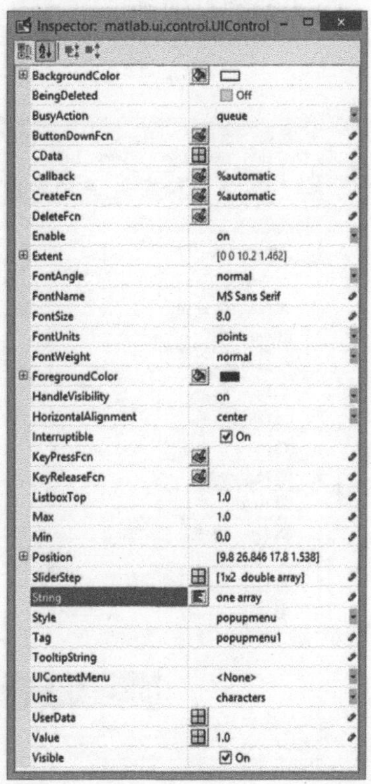

Figure A1.8 Property Inspector Window

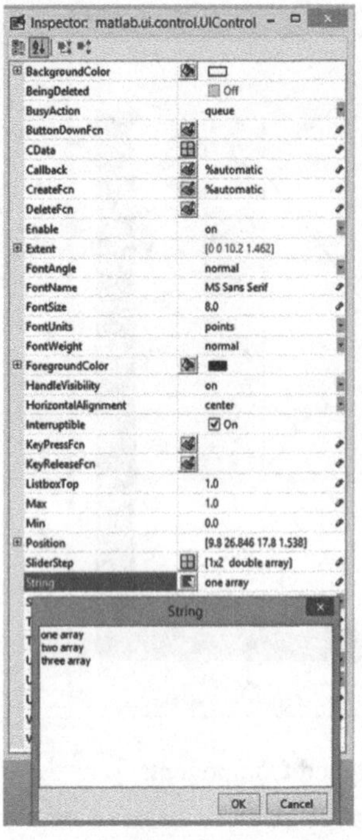

Figure A1.9 String Dialog box

The three data items appear in the Pop-up menu in the layout area. Similarly, text is entered for the push buttons and static text. For this example, enter text: bar chart, pie chart and histogram for the three push buttons.

To save the GUI, select 'Save As' from the 'File' menu. Assign the name 'gui001'. GUIDE will create two files: (1) gui001.fig, a binary file that contains a description of the GUI graphic interface layout and (2) gui001.m, an M-file containing the opening and callback functions that control the GUI. The layout of the example problem is complete and appears as shown in Figure A1.10. MATLAB Editor window with gui001.m file opened is shown in Figure A1.11.

Program the GUI: The GUI that has been just saved cannot be run as its program control file, gui001.m does not contain code for the callback functions as well as the data sets have not been created. To create the code, follow the procedure mentioned hereafter.

Generate Data Sets: The data sets are generated in the 'opening function'. The opening function is the first callback subroutine in every GUIDE-generated

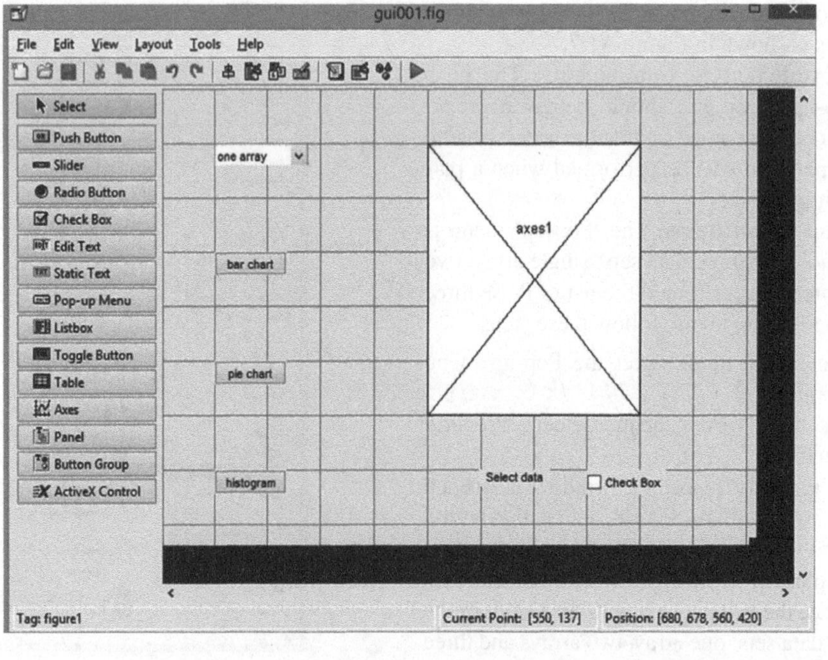

Figure A1.10 GUI Figure Window with Labelled Components

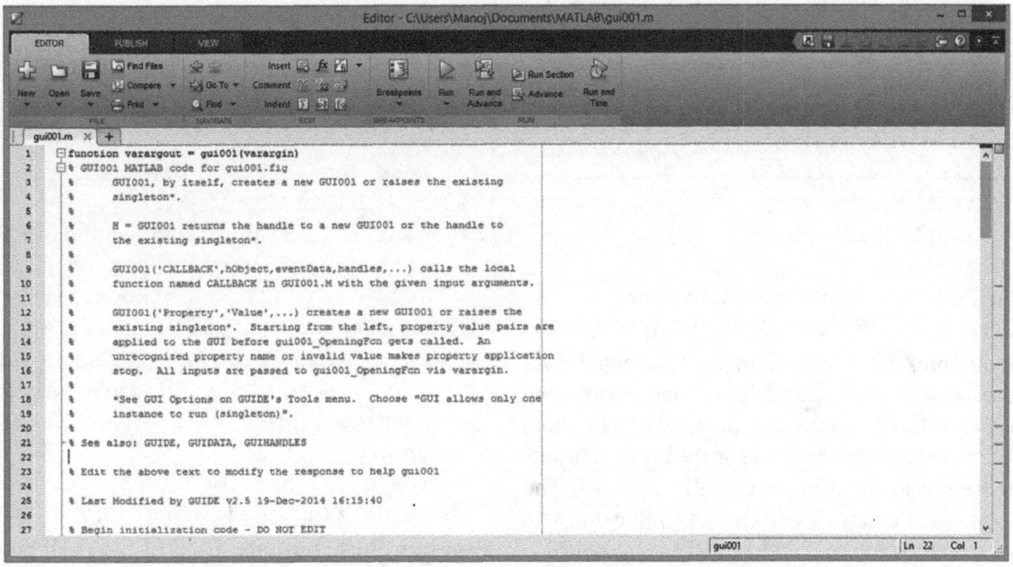

Figure A1.11 MATLAB Editor Window with GUI M-file

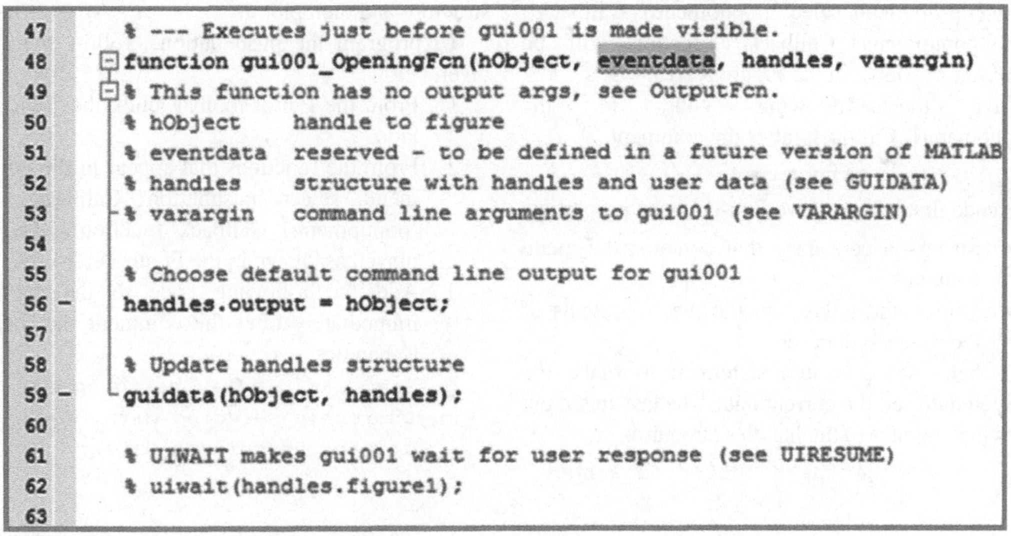

Figure A1.12 GUI Opening Function in M-file

GUI M-file. It is used to perform tasks at the time of opening of the GUI.

To create the three data sets, one array, two arrays and three arrays, open the gui001.m file in the MATLAB Editor. In the Editor window, click the function icon on the toolbar. The different functions contained in the file gui001.m will appear in a Pop-up menu. Select 'gui001_OpeningFcn'. The opening function will be displayed as shown in the Figure A1.12.

Create data for the GUI to plot by adding the following code to the opening function immediately after the comment: `%varargin command line arguments` ...

```
%Create the data to plot.
x1 = rand(1, 8);
x2 = rand(1, 8);
x3 = rand(1, 8);
x12 = [x1; x2];
x123 = [x1;x2;x3];
handles.x1 = x1;
handles.x12 = x12;
handles.x123 = x123;
%Set the current data value.
handles.current_data = handles.x1;
```

The variables x1, x12 and x123 created contain data sets corresponding to one array, two array and three arrays, respectively. The data handle structures are created for the three data sets to be passed as an argument to all callbacks. The last statement creates a current data value and sets it to variable x1.

Program Pop-up Menu: The Pop-up menu enables the user to select the data set. From the Editor toolbar, click the function icon. From the functions that appear in the Pop-up menu, select 'popupmenu1_Callback'. The 'popupmenu1_Callback' function will be displayed as shown in the Figure A1.13.

Add the following code to the 'popupmenu1_Callback' after the comment:

```
%handles structure …
```

This code first retrieves two Pop-up menu properties:

- String—a cell array that contains the menu contents
- Value—the index into the menu contents of the selected data set

It then uses a switch statement to make the selected data set, the current data. The last statement saves the changes to the handles structure.

```
%Determine the selected data set.
str = get(hObject, 'String');
val = get(hObject, 'Value');
%Set current data to the selected
%data set.
switch str{val}
case 'one array'  %User selects one
                  %array.
handles.current_data = handles.x1;
case 'two arrays'  %User selects
                   %two arrays.
handles.current_data = handles.x12;
case 'three arrays'  %User selects
                     %three arrays.
handles.current_data = handles.x123;
end;
%Save the handles structure.
guidata(hObject, handles);
```

Program Push Buttons: Each of the push buttons creates a different type of plot using the data specified by the current selection in the Pop-up menu. The push button callbacks get data from the handles structure and then plot it.

To program the push buttons, follow the steps given below:

1. From the Editor toolbar, click the 'function' icon.
2. From the functions that appear in the Pop-up menu, select 'pushbutton1_Callback'. The 'popupmenu1_Callback' function will be displayed as shown in the Figure A1.14.
3. Add the following code to the callback immediately after the comment that begins % handles:

```
%Draw and display bar graph of the
%currently selected data.
bar(handles.current_data);
```

```
% --- Executes on selection change in popupmenu1.
function popupmenu1_Callback(hObject, eventdata, handles)
% hObject    handle to popupmenu1 (see GCBO)
% eventdata  reserved - to be defined in a future version of MATLAB
% handles    structure with handles and user data (see GUIDATA)

% Hints: contents = cellstr(get(hObject,'String')) returns popupmenu1 contents as cell array
%        contents{get(hObject,'Value')} returns selected item from popupmenu1

```

Figure A1.13 GUI Pop-up Menu Callback Function in M-file

```
% --- Executes on button press in pushbutton1.
function pushbutton1_Callback(hObject, eventdata, handles)
% hObject    handle to pushbutton1 (see GCBO)
% eventdata  reserved - to be defined in a future version of MATLAB
% handles    structure with handles and user data (see GUIDATA)
```

Figure A1.14 GUI Pushbutton Callback Function in M-file

Repeat Steps 1 to 3 for the other two push buttons with the difference that instead of bar chart, the two buttons are for pie chart and histogram, respectively.

Add the following code for plotting pie chart:

```
%Draw and display pie chart of the
%currently selected data.
pie(handles.current_data);
```

Add the following code for plotting histogram:

```
%Draw and display histogram of the
%currently selected data.
hist(handles.current_data);
```

Save and Execute GUI: The M-file is saved by selecting 'Save' from the 'File' menu. The GUI is ready to run.

To run the GUI from the Layout Editor, select 'Run' from the 'Tools' menu.

In the Pop-up menu, select 'one array', then click the 'pie chart' button. The GUI displays a pie chart of the data selected. The GUI window showing the pie chart is shown in Figure A1.15.

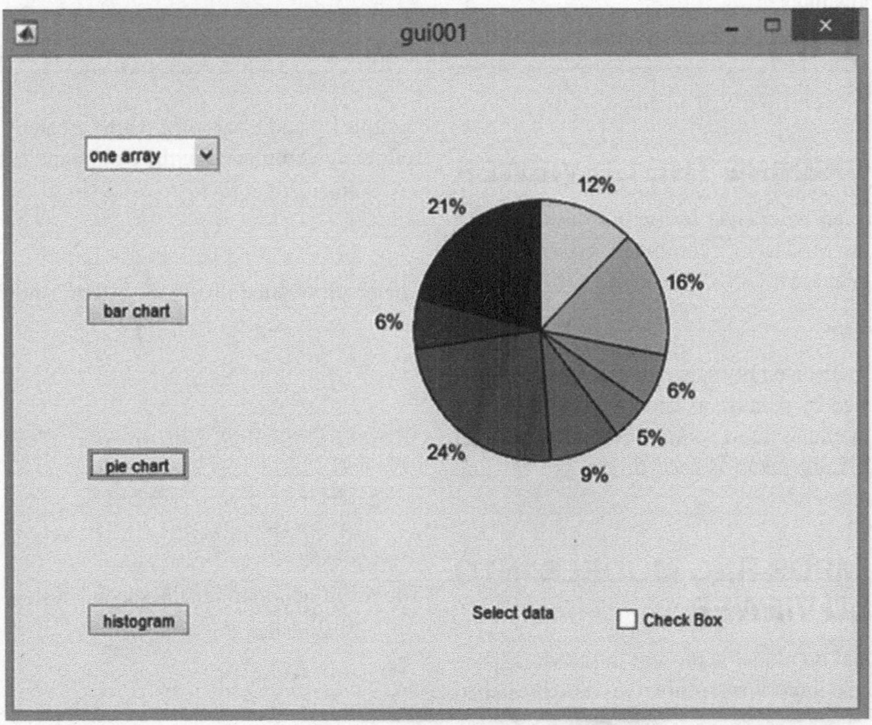

Figure A1.15 GUI with Labelled Components Executed and Pie Chart Drawn

Appendix 2

Control System Analysis Using LTI Viewer

A2.1 INTRODUCTION

Linear Time Invariant (LTI) viewer is a GUI which simplifies the analysis of linear, time invariant control systems and is used for viewing and manipulating the response plots of linear models. The LTI Viewer displays up to six different types of plot types simultaneously.

Following plot types for linear models can be displayed, using the LTI Viewer:

- Step response
- Impulse response
- Bode plots
- Nyquist plots
- Nichols plots
- Singular values of the frequency response
- Pole/Zero plots
- I/O Pole plots Zero

A2.2 OPENING THE LTI VIEWER

LTI Viewer can be opened by typing the following command on MATLAB® command prompt in the Command Window:

```
ltiview
```

LTI Viewer with an empty step response plot window will be opened by default, as shown in Figure A2.1. The 'File' menu is used to import models in LTI Viewer and 'Edit' menu is used to edit the existing models.

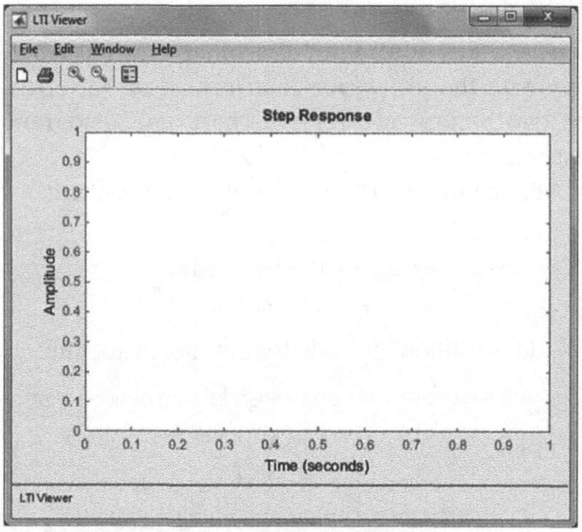

Figure A2.1 LTI Viewer

A2.3 IMPORTING MODELS INTO LTI VIEWER

Assuming that no model is present in the workspace to illustrate the import procedure, two models named 'sample1' and 'sample2' are created by typing following commands in the Command Window:

```
num1=[0 1 3];
den1=[2 4 1];
sample1=tf(num1,den1);
```

The result obtained for first system 'sample1' is:

```
Transfer function:
      s + 3
-------------------
2 s^2 + 4 s + 1
```

To create second system 'sample2', the commands used are:

```
num2=[3 2];
den2=[6 4 5];
sample2=tf(num2,den2);
```

The result obtained for the second system is

```
Transfer function:
     3 s + 2
-----------------
6 s^2 + 4 s + 5
```

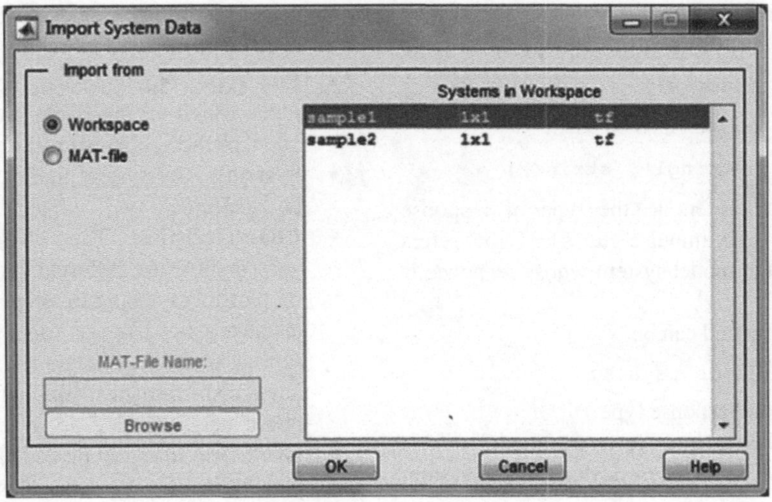

Figure A2.2 Window for Importing Data to LTI Viewer

To import a model, `Import` option from `File` menu of LTI viewer is selected. This will open the 'Import System Data' window, which gives the list of all the models that are available in the MATLAB workspace as shown in Figure A2.2. The two models created earlier are available in workspace, therefore, the window shows their names. Select the name of the system (say sample1) for which step response is to be obtained from the list of available models shown and click 'OK' button to close the window. The desired system model will be imported to the LTI Viewer and step response of the system i.e. sample1, will be shown as given in Figure A2.3.

Alternatively, LTI Viewer can be opened and the desired system model can be imported directly from the MATLAB prompt by typing the following command in the command window:

```
ltiview(string)
```

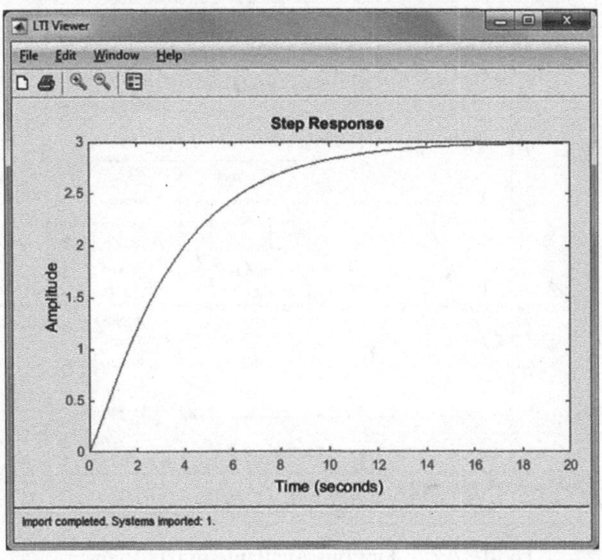

Figure A2.3 Step Response for Selected System 'sample1'

where `string` represents the name of the system under study. In this case it is:

```
ltiview (sample1)
```

Following command can also be used:

```
ltiview('string1', string2)
```

where `string1` refers to the type of response desired such as step, impulse etc. `string2` refers to the name of the model/system whose response is to be obtained.

A typical command can be

```
ltiview('bode',sys1);
```

where `bode` is the response type

`sys1` is the name of the system model

This command will plot the Bode diagrams of system 'sys1'.

A2.4 CONTROLS AND OPTIONS IN LTI VIEWER

Once the system model to be analysed has been imported and selected into the LTI Viewer, a set of controls and options can be accessed on the LTI Viewer by right clicking the mouse in the blank space of window. The following options (Figure A2.4) are made available:

- **Plot type**: Plot type can be changed. Plot types which are available are step, impulse, bode, Nichols, Nyquist plots etc.
- **Systems**: Any system model can be selected or deselected.
- **Characteristics**: The characteristics that are available are different for different types of plots. For example, step responses have characteristics like rise time, peak overshoot, settling time, steady state etc.; bode diagrams have characteristics like gain margin and phase margin etc.
- **Grid:** Grid lines can be added to plots.
- **Normalize**: This option scales the response to fit the view.
- **Full View**: It makes the complete response visible in the window by automatically adjusting the limits.
- **Properties**: Property Editor can be used to customize various attributes of the plot like labels, limits, style etc. Property Editor as shown in Figure A2.5 can also be opened by double clicking in an empty region of the response plot.

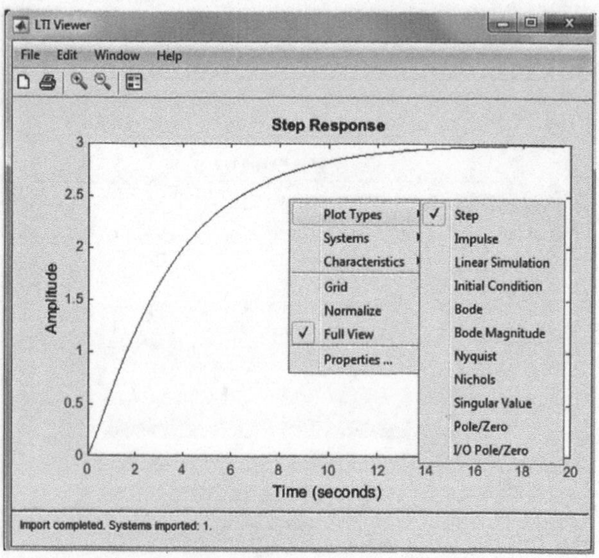

Figure A2.4 Options Available in LTI Viewer

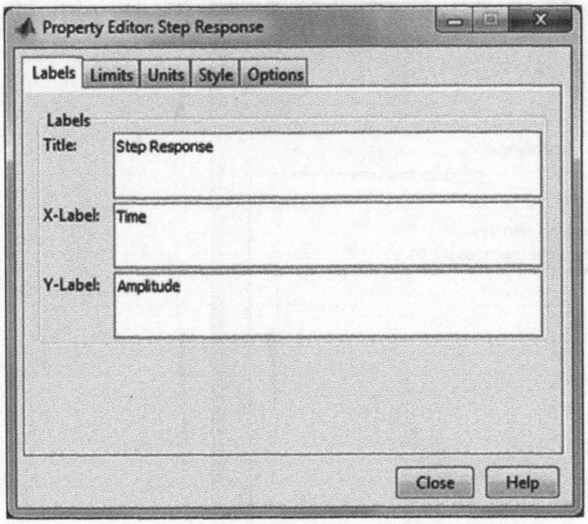

Figure A2.5 Property Editor

A2.5 DISPLAYING RESPONSE CHARACTERISTICS ON A PLOT

The characteristics for different types of plots, like rise time, peak overshoot, settling time, steady state etc. for step responses and gain margin and phase margin for bode diagrams can be obtained and displayed. The procedure for obtaining rise time for a step response is as follows:

1. Right click the mouse in the LTI Viewer window.
2. From the 'Characteristics' option, select 'Rise Time' as shown in the Figure A2.6, a dotted line showing the rise time will appear.
3. To display the value, click on the 'blue dot' which appears on the plot. The value of rise time will be displayed as shown in Figure A2.7.
4. By left-clicking anywhere on a particular point on a plot line, the response values of that plot at that point i.e. time and amplitude values can be seen.

A2.6 CHANGING PLOT TYPE

Plot type is another option available in LTI Viewer. Other types of system response plots can be viewed by right-clicking the mouse in the blank space in the LTI Viewer. The different types of plots available are Step, Impulse, Linear Simulation, Initial Condition, Bode, Bode Magnitude, Nyquist, Nichols, Singular Value, Pole/Zero and I/O Pole/Zero as shown in Figure A2.8. For example, if impulse plot is to be seen, select 'plot type' and then select 'impulse' from the menu. Impulse response will be displayed automatically as shown in Figure A2.9

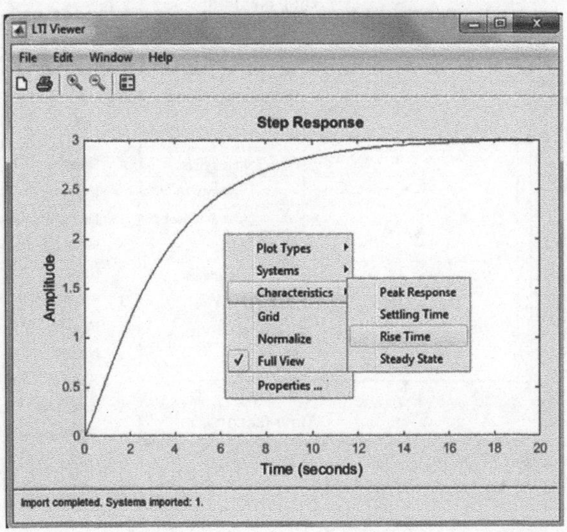

Figure A2.6 Characteristic Options Available for Step Response

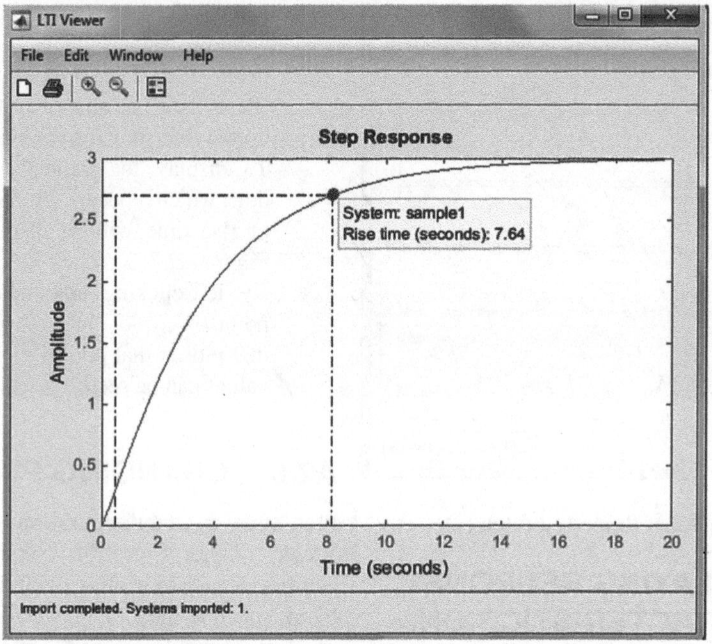

Figure A2.7 Response Values of the Plot

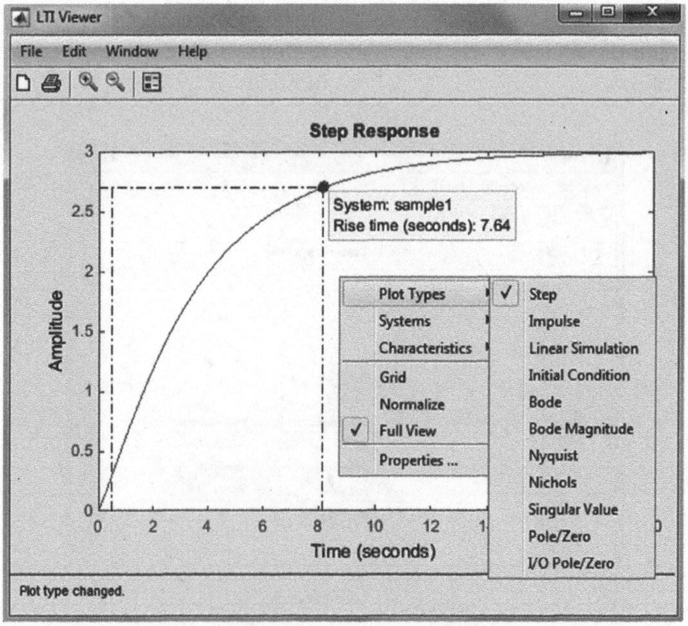

Figure A2.8 Plot Type Options

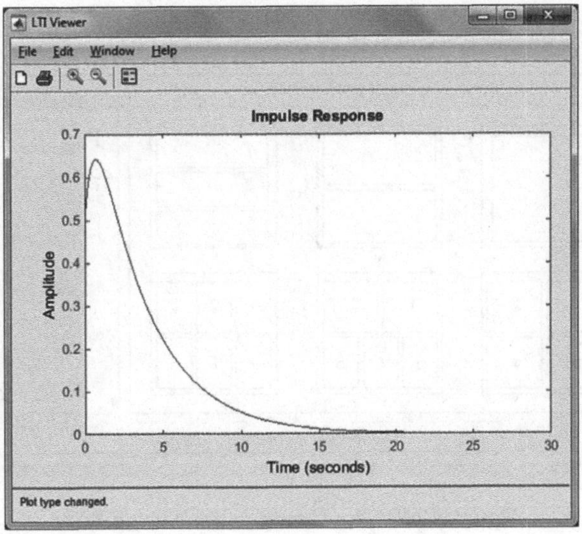

Figure A2.9 Impulse Response

A2.7 SHOWING MULTIPLE RESPONSE TYPES

If multiple responses, for example, a step response, a bode plot and a Nyquist plot are to be seen simultaneously, then the LTI Viewer should be reconfigured. To view more than one response types in a single LTI Viewer, open the 'Edit' menu of the LTI Viewer and select 'Plot Configurations' from the drop down menu. This will open the 'Plot Configurations' dialog box as shown in Figure A2.10.

In one LTI Viewer, up to six plots can be selected. A response plot configuration can be selected from the six options available by clicking inside the appropriate circle option.

Example A2.1

Obtain the step response, Bode diagrams and six different plots for the following control system:

$$G(s) = \frac{2}{s^2 + 15s + 45}$$

Solution: To generate a given system in the workspace, the following MATLAB commands are used:

```
%To define the numerator
n = 2;
%To define the denominator
d = [1 15 45];
%To generate the transfer function
%and assign it to variable sys1
sys1 = tf(n,d);
```

The result obtained is the transfer function:

```
Transfer function:
      2
-----------
s^2+15s+45
```

To launch LTI Viewer for the system 'sys1': type the following commands in the command window:

```
ltiview(sys1)
```

LTI viewer will be launched.

Right click on the blank space, select 'Characteristics' option and then select the desired options, that is Settling Time, Rise Time etc. (Figure A2.11). The different values can be seen by clicking on the dots as shown in the Figure A2.12.

To draw Bode plot: Select 'Bode' plot from the 'Plot Types' option. Bode diagrams will be displayed as shown in Figure A2.13.

Right click in the blank space of the plot and select properties and select limits in the dialog box as follows:

x-limits = 0.01 to 10^3
y-limits = −80 to −20

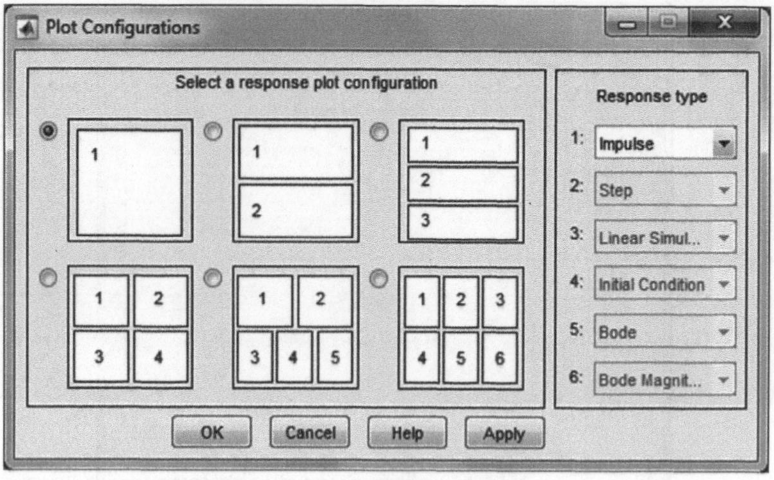

Figure A2.10 Plot Configuration Dialog Box

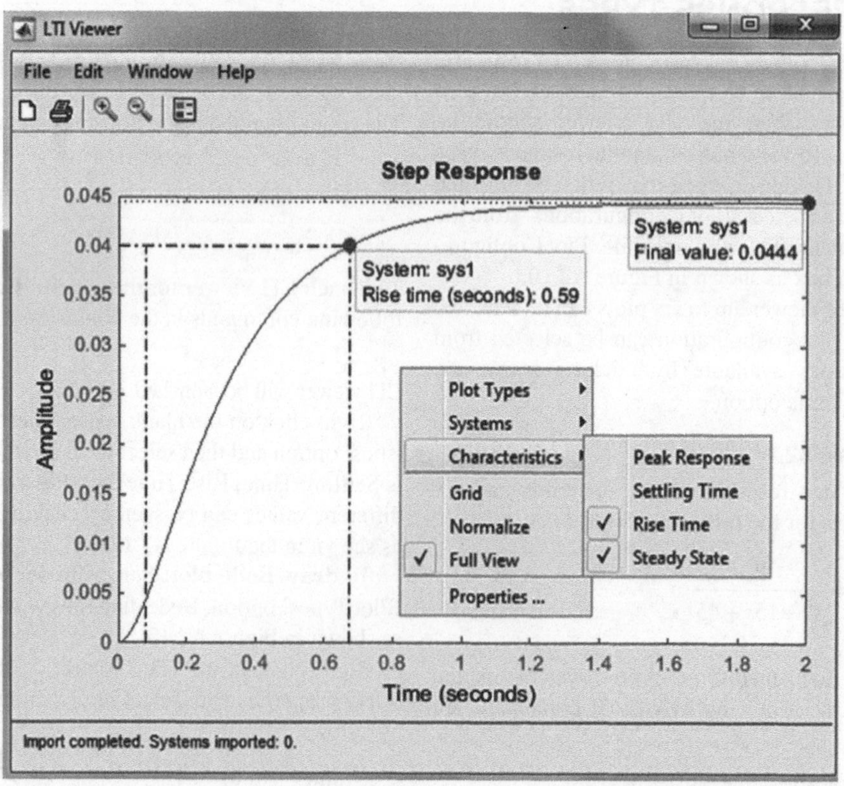

Figure A2.11 Selection of Different Characteristic Options for Example A2.1

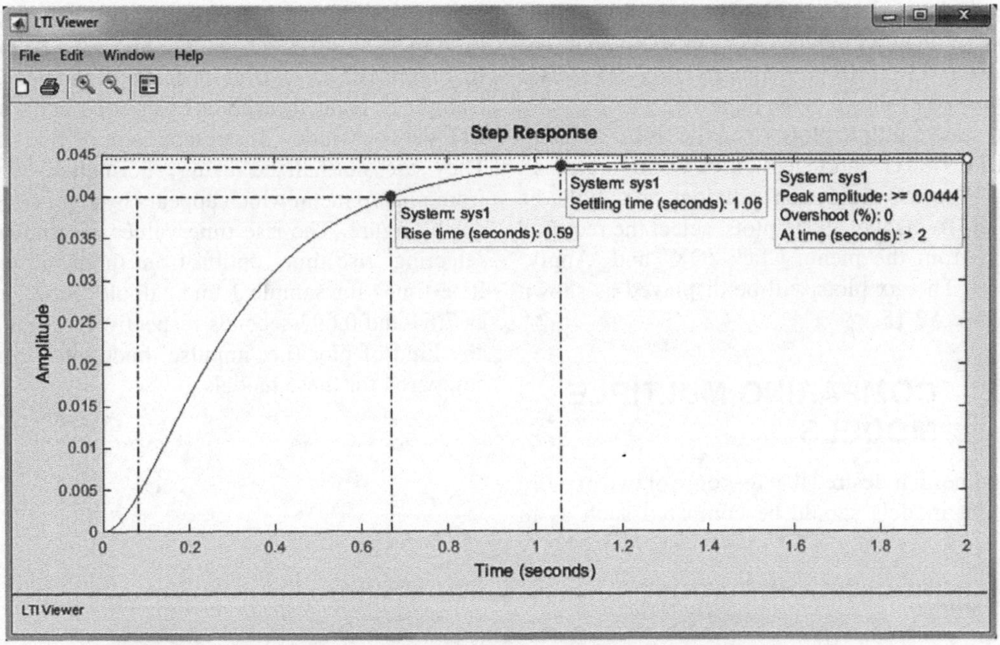

Figure A2.12 Display of the Values for the Different Characteristics

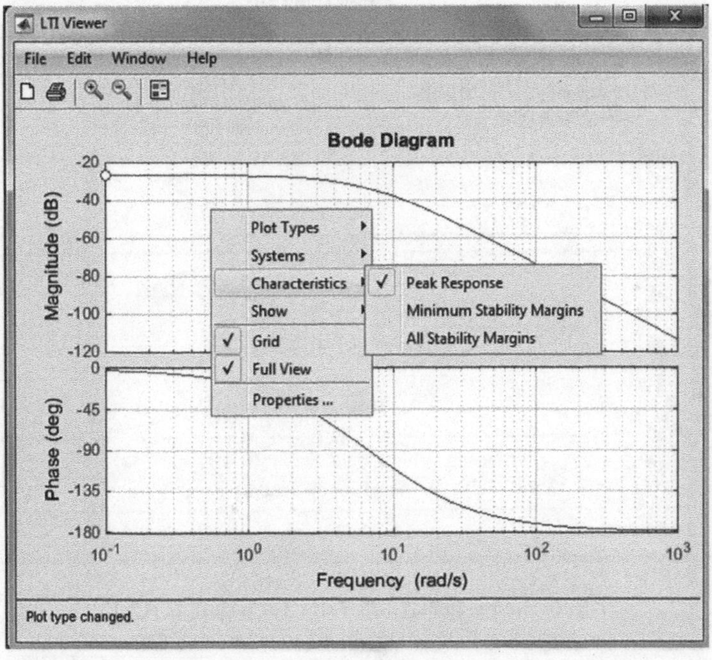

Figure A2.13 Bode Plot for Example A2.1

To display peak gain and the frequency, select 'Peak Response' option from the characteristics menu. The peak gain = −27 dB at frequency = 0.0105 rad/sec is displayed as shown in the Figure A2.14.

To draw multiple plots, open the 'Edit' menu of the LTI Viewer and select 'Plot Configurations'. The 'Plot Configuration' dialog box will be opened. To display all six plots, select the required option from the menu. Click 'OK' and 'Apply' buttons. The six plots will be displayed as shown in Figure A2.15.

A2.8 COMPARING MULTIPLE MODELS

Sometimes it is desired that response of two or more different models should be compared such as in case of designing a compensator. This can be done by importing different models in the LTI Viewer. In Figure A2.16, two models, i.e. 'sample1' and 'sample2', created earlier are imported in the same LTI Viewer window for comparison of rise times. They are normalized using 'normalize' option from pop up menu which appears by right clicking on the figure. The rise time values are shown by selecting 'rise time' option from the same menu. Rise times for sample 1 and sample 2 are shown as 7.64 and 0.697 seconds respectively. Similarly, any kind of plot (i.e. impulse, bode, etc.) can be compared for these models.

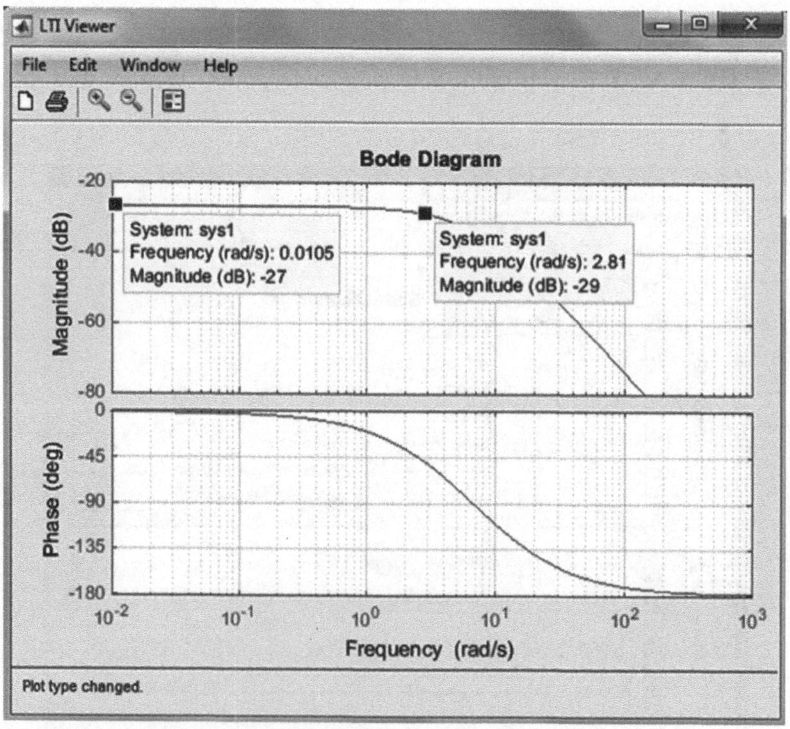

Figure A2.14 Peak Gain Value for Example A2.1

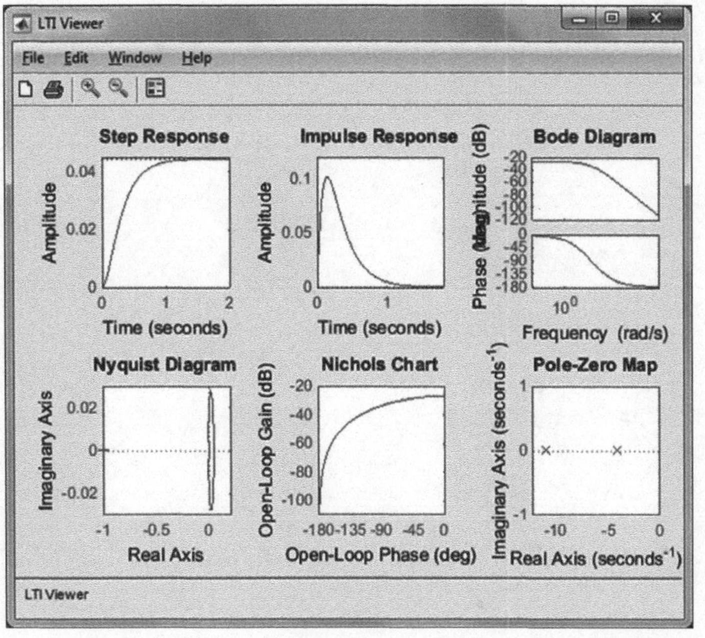

Figure A2.15 Multiple Responses for Example A2.1

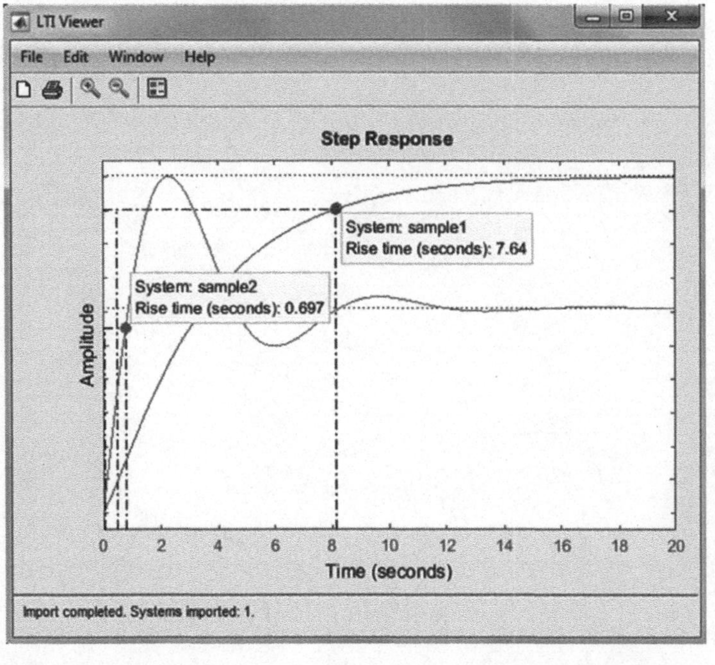

Figure A2.16 Step Response of Two Models in the Same LTI Viewer

Colour Illustrations

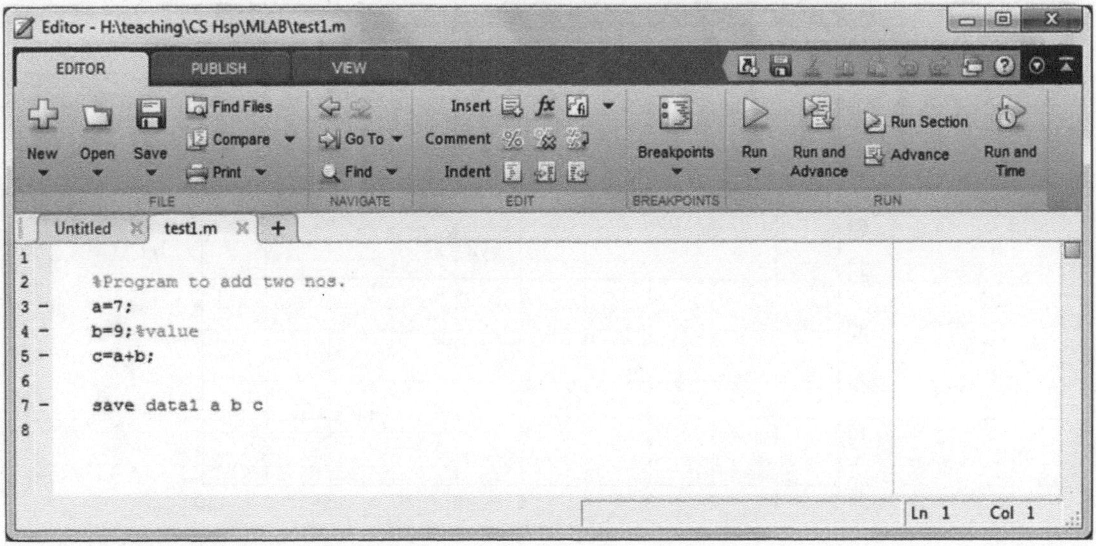

Plate 1 Editor Window (See Page 17)

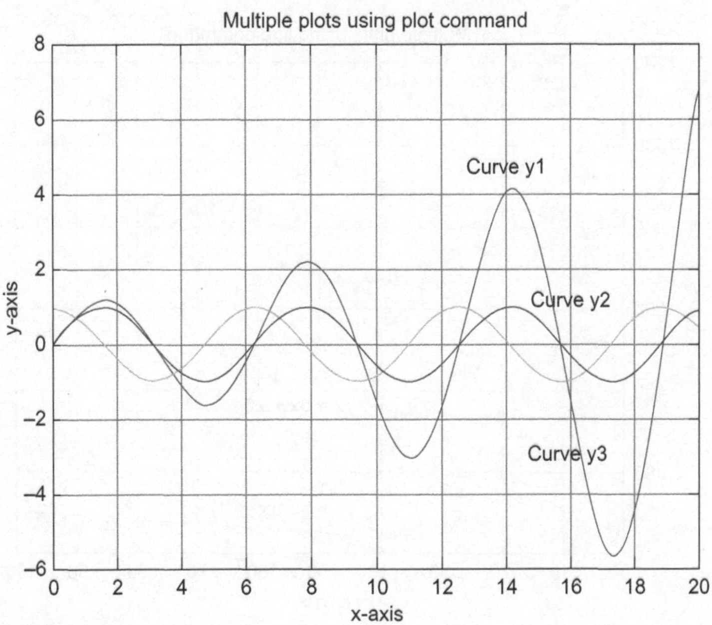

Plate 2 Plot to Illustrate `plot` Command for Multiple Plots (See Page 140)

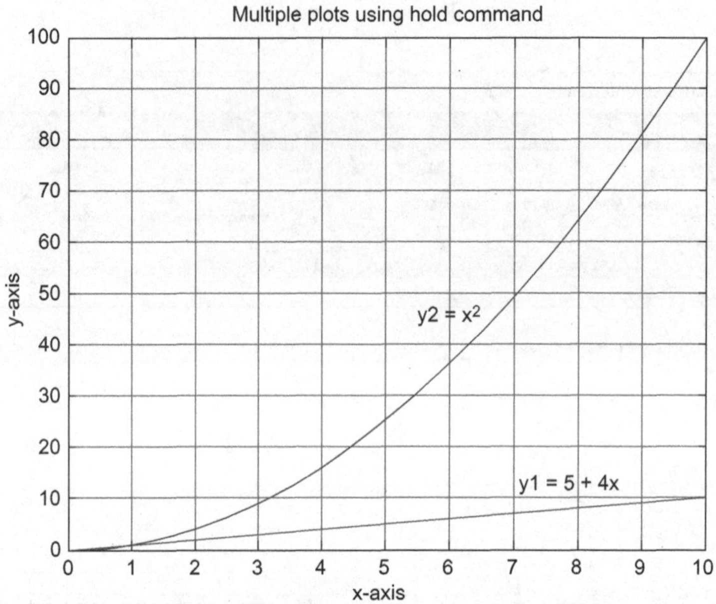

Plate 3 Plot to Illustrate use of `'hold'` Command (See Page 141)

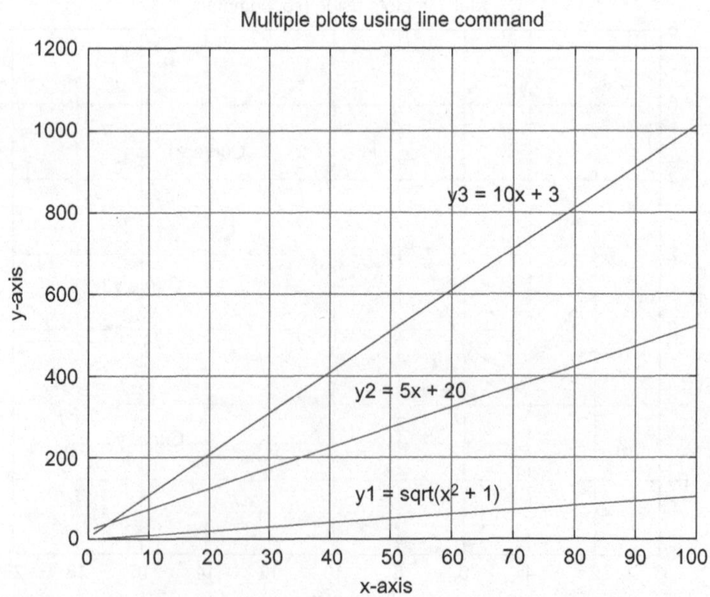

Plate 4 Multiple Plots Using `'line'` Command (See Page 142)

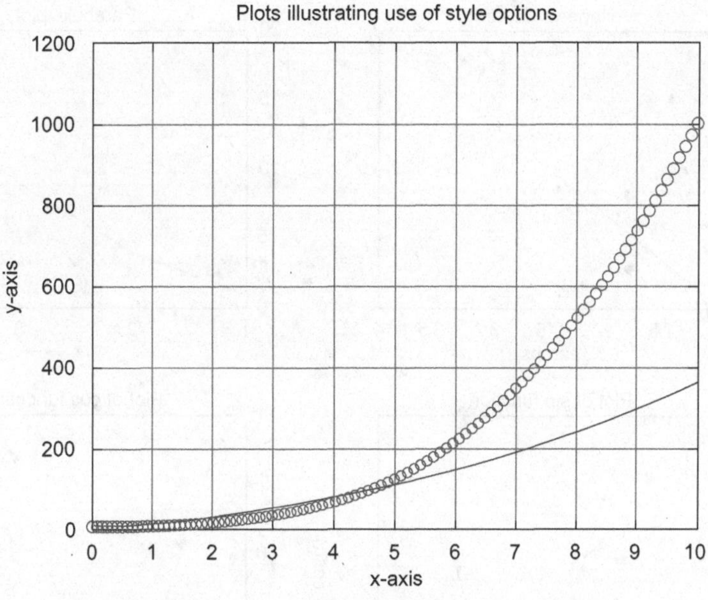

Plate 5 Plot Showing Use of Style Options (See Page 144)

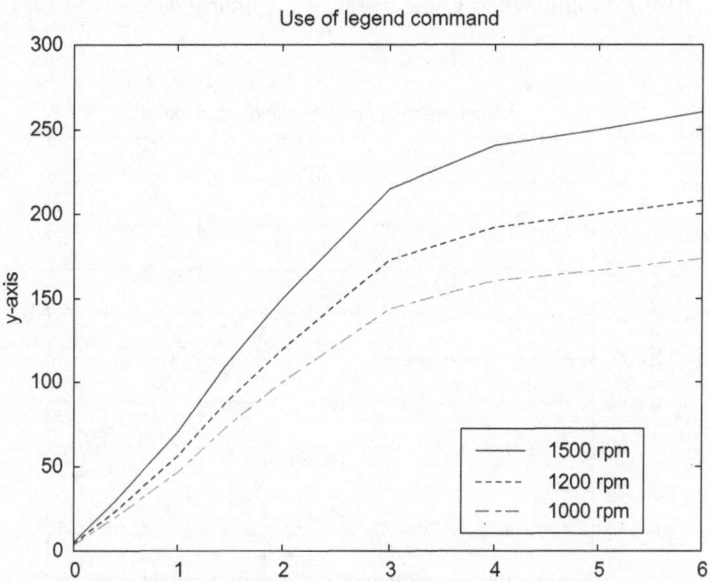

Plate 6 Plot Showing Use of 'legend' Command (See Page 146)

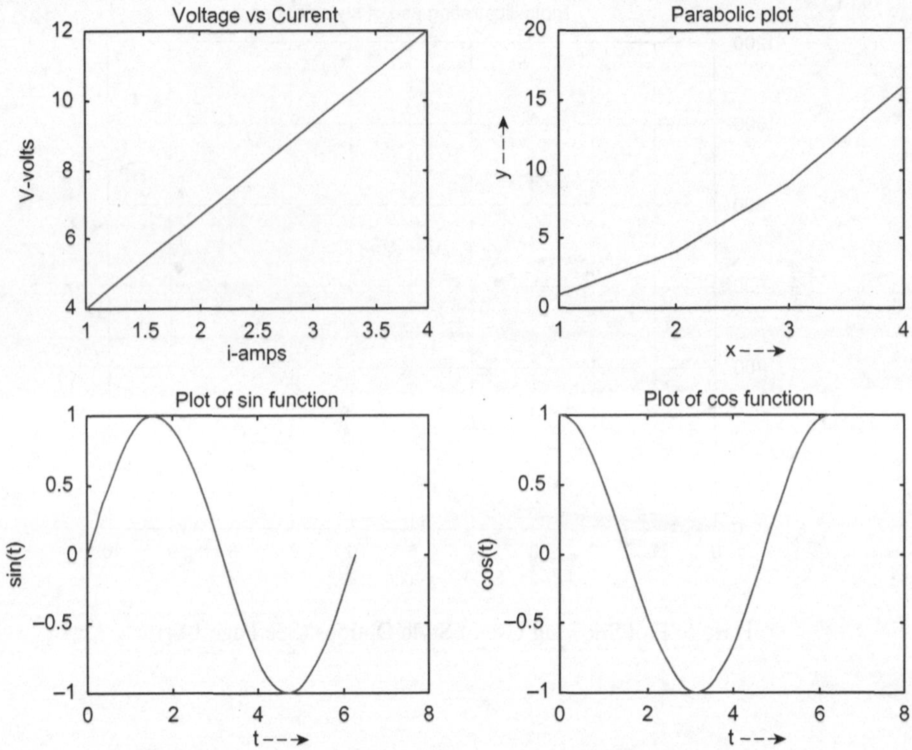

Plate 7 Multiple Plots Using `subplot` Command (See Page 148)

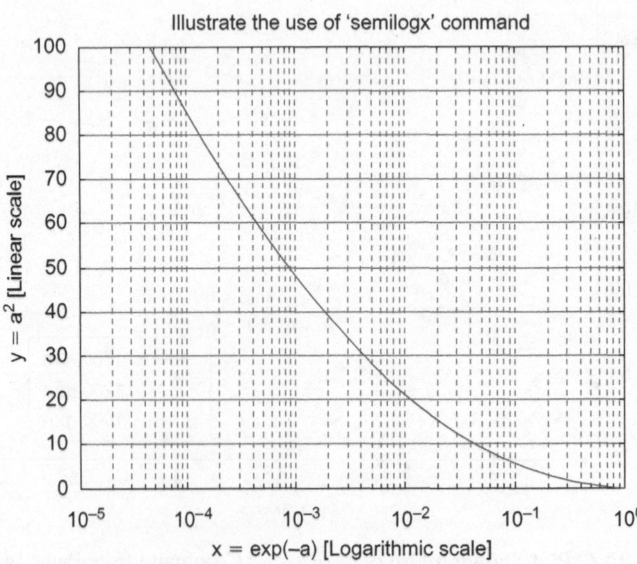

Plate 8 `semilogx` Plot (See Page 149)

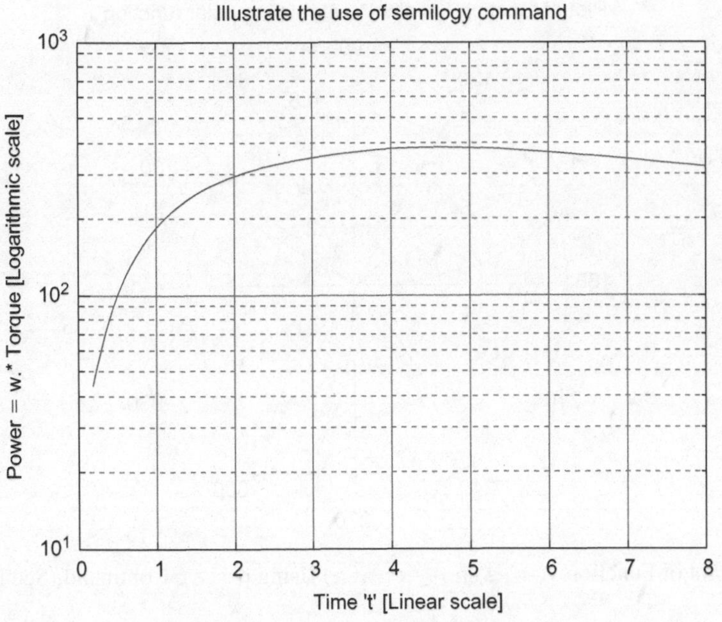

Plate 9 `semilogy` Plot (See Page 150)

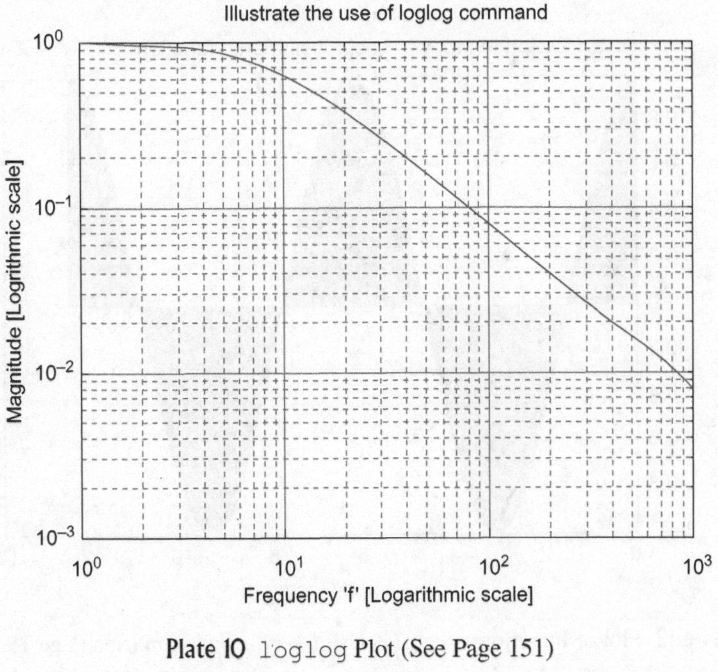

Plate 10 `loglog` Plot (See Page 151)

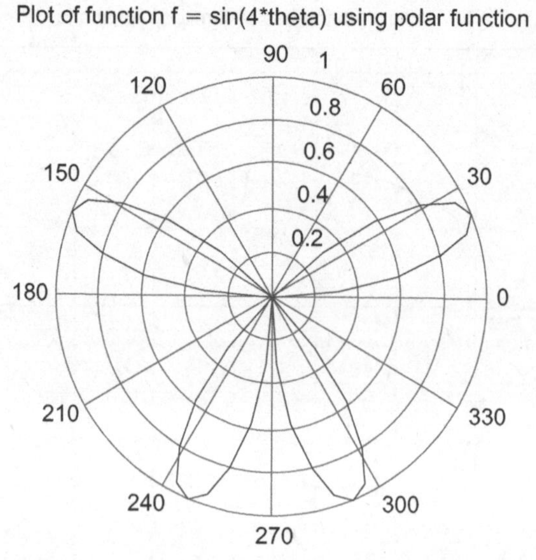

Plate 11 Plot of Function `f = sin(4*theta)` Using `polar` Command (See Page 152)

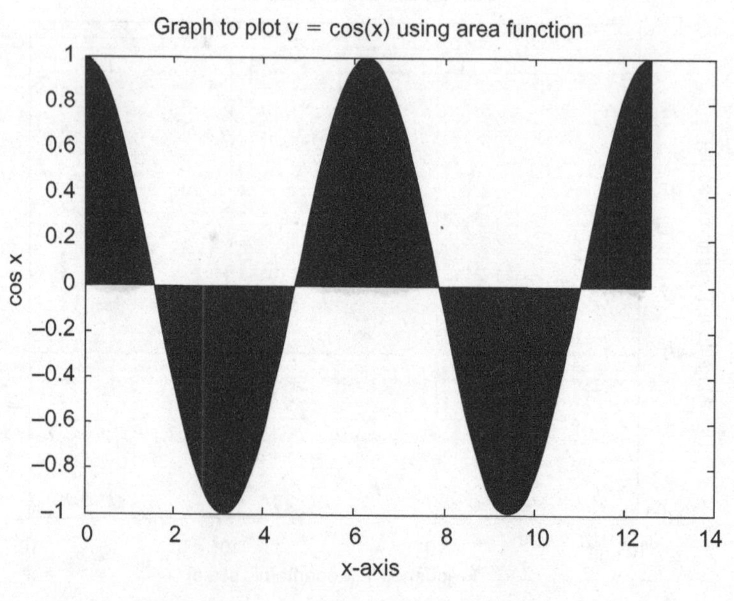

Plate 12 Plot of Function $y = \cos(x)$ Using `area` Function (See Page 153)

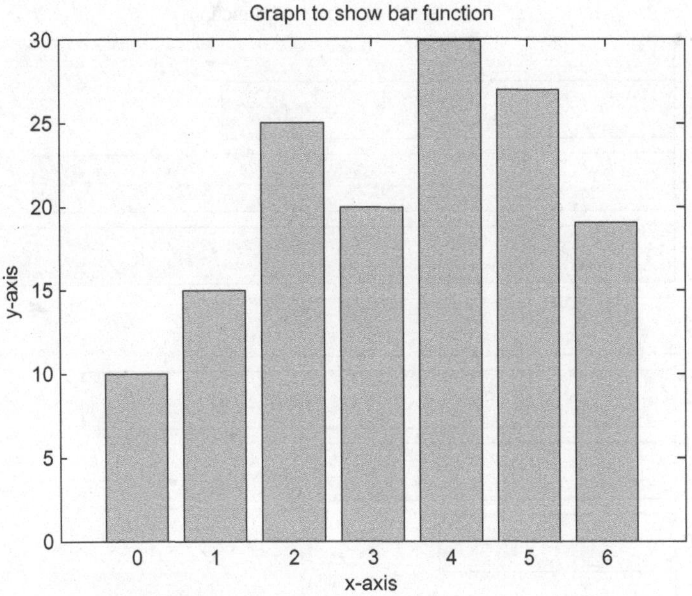

Plate 13 Bar Graph to Plot the given Data (See Page 154)

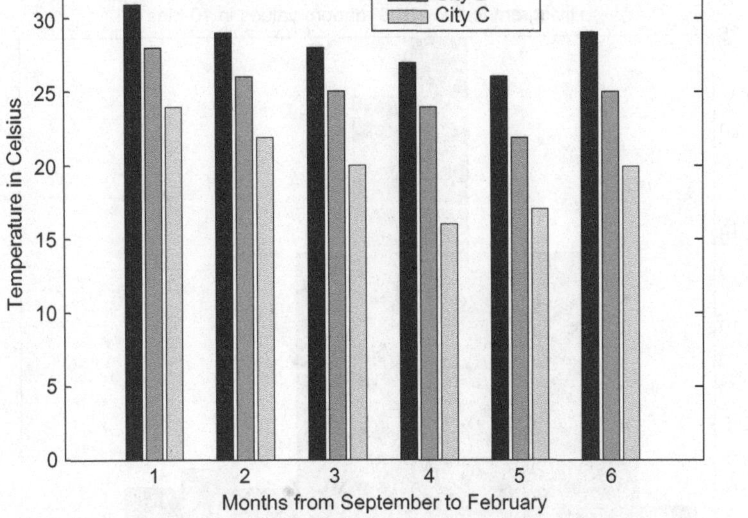

Plate 14 Bar Graph to Show the Comparison of Temperature in City A, City B and City C for the Months from September to February (See Page 155)

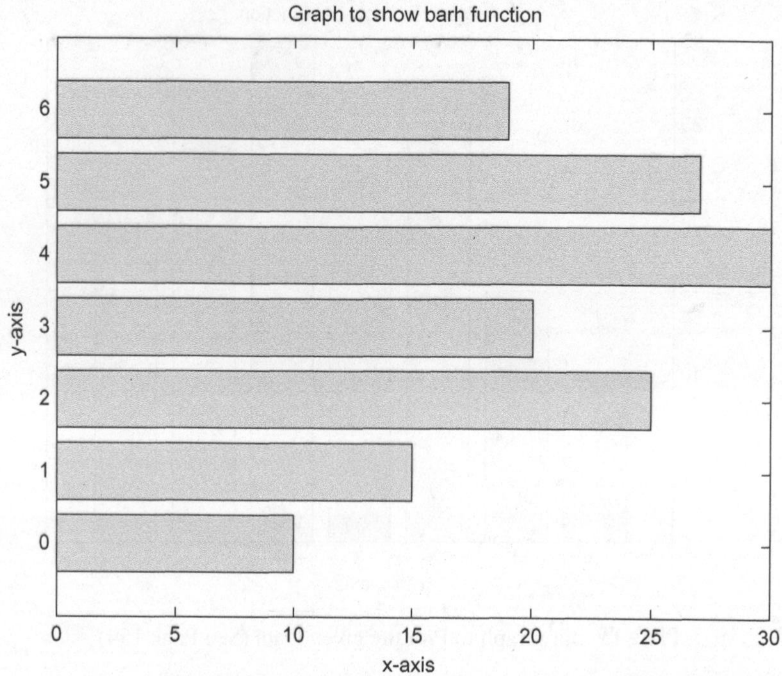

Plate 15 Horizontal Bar Graph Using `barh` Command (See Page 156)

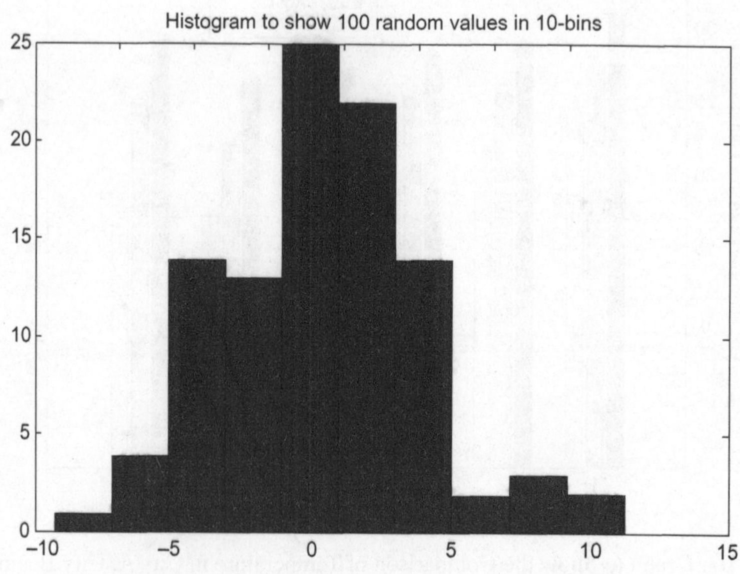

Plate 16 Histogram Plot (For 100 Random Values) (See Page 157)

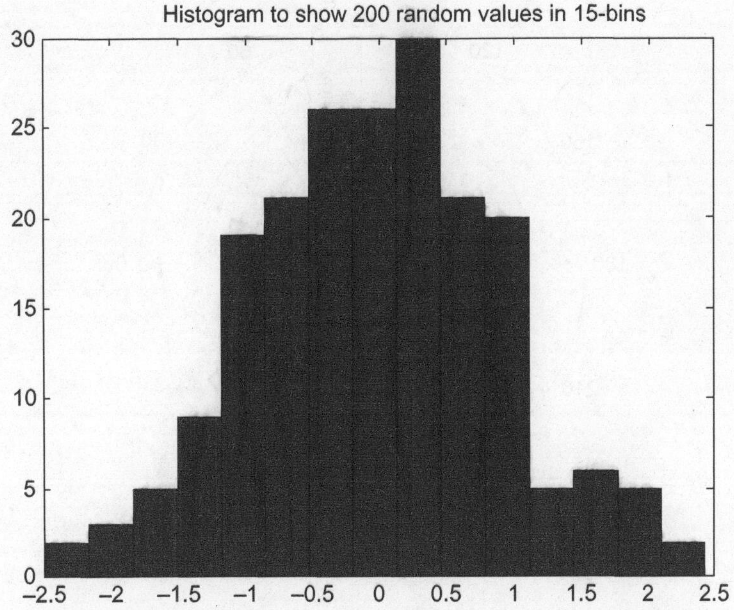

Plate 17 Histogram Plot (For 200 Random Values) (See Page 158)

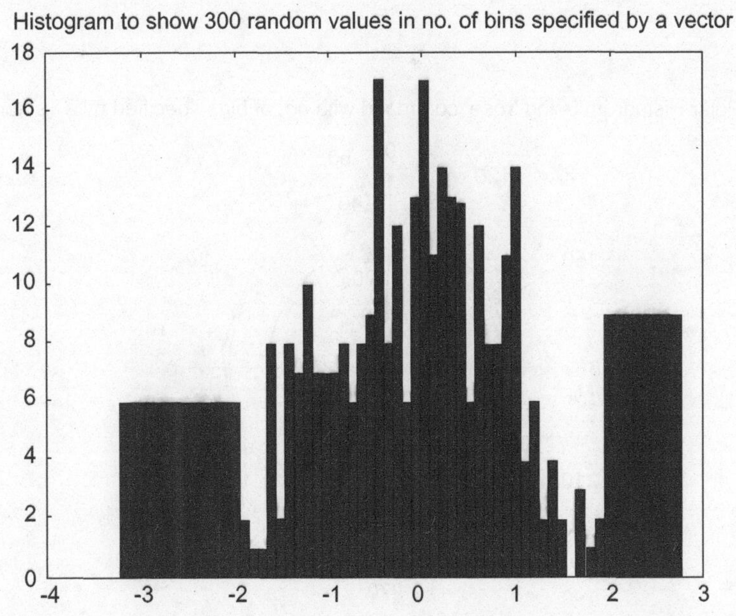

Plate 18 Histogram Plot (For 300 Random Values) (See Page 158)

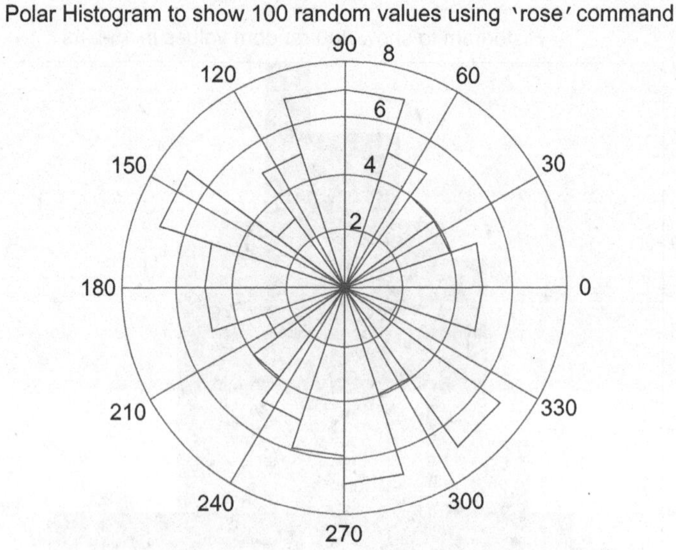

Plate 19 `'rose'` Plot (See Page 159)

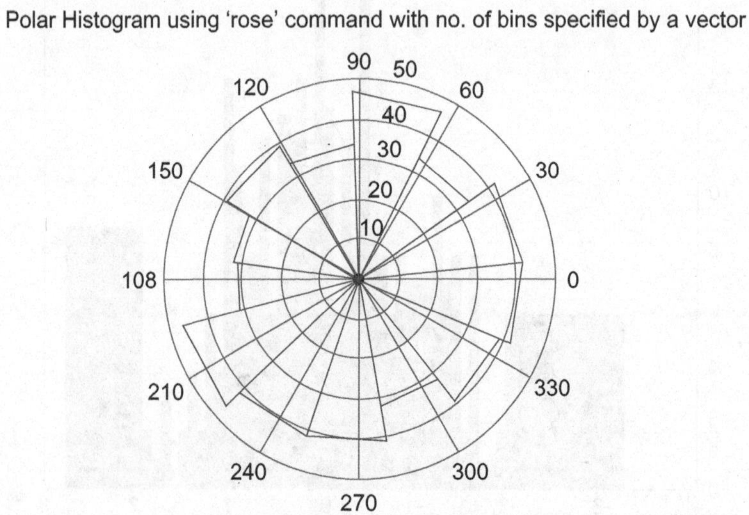

Plate 20 `'rose'` Plot Using Vector to Specify no. of Bins (See Page 160) .

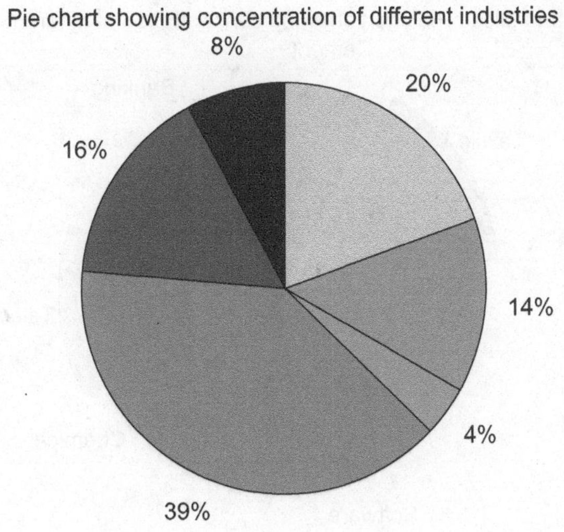

Plate 21 Pie Chart Showing the Concentration of Industries in a Region (See Page 161)

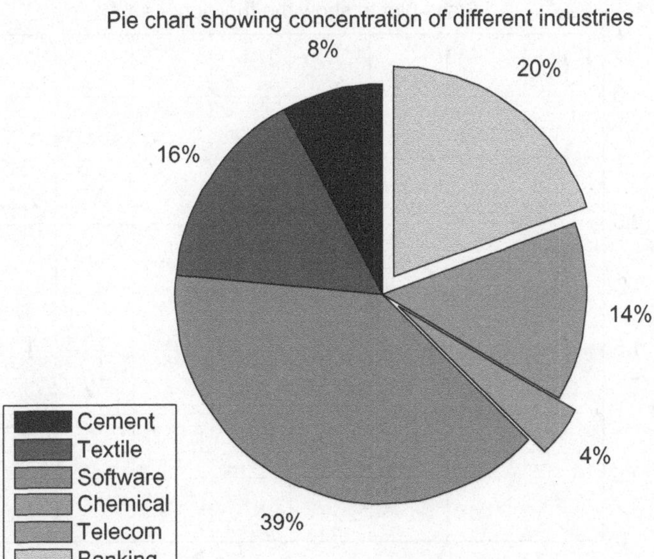

Plate 22 Sliced Pie Chart (See Page 162)

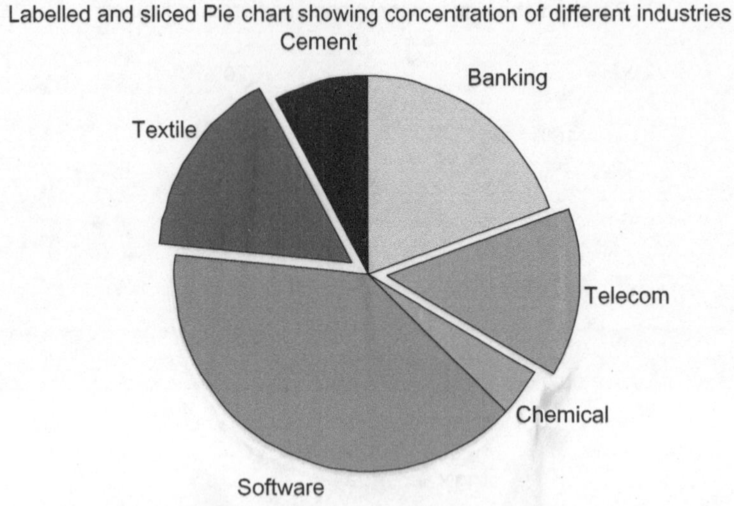

Plate 23 Labelled and Sliced-out Pie Chart (See Page 163)

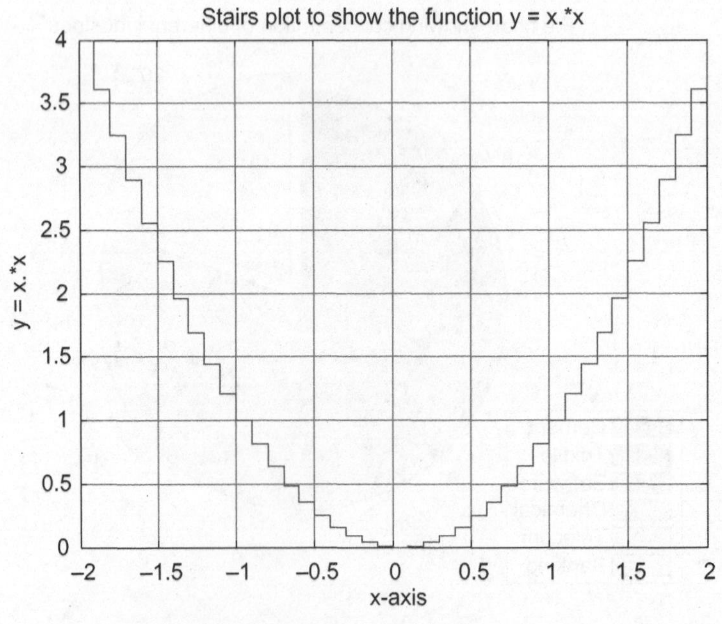

Plate 24 Stairs Plot to Show the Function $y = x.*x$ (See Page 164)

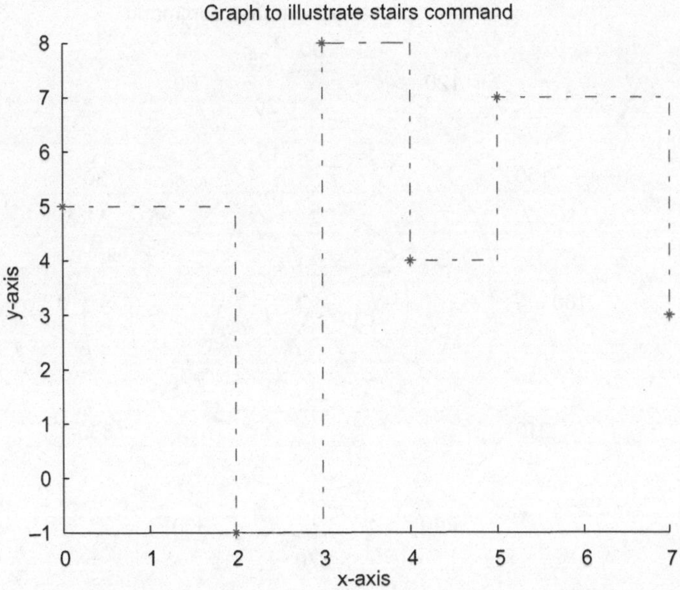

Plate 25 Stairs Plot for Given Data (See Page 165)

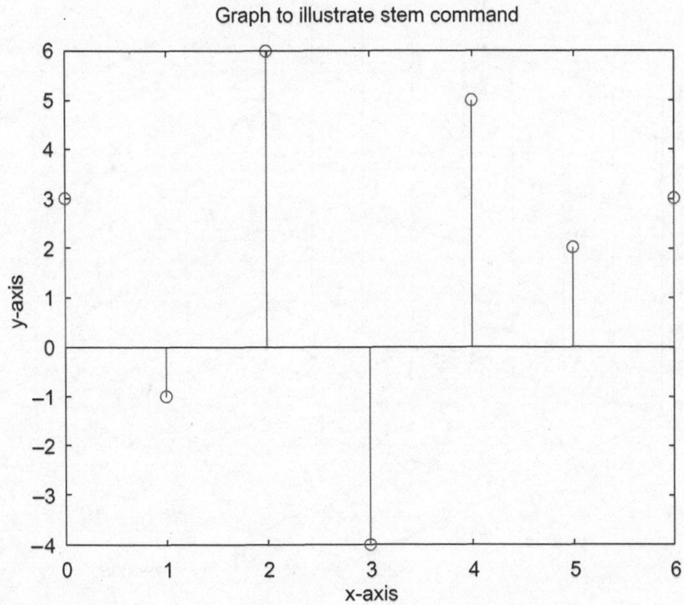

Plate 26 Plot to Illustrate the `stem` Command (See Page 166)

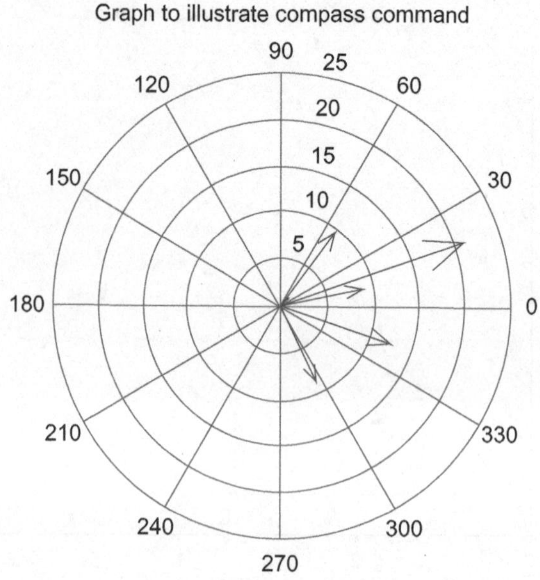

Plate 27 Plot to Illustrate the `compass` Command (See Page 167)

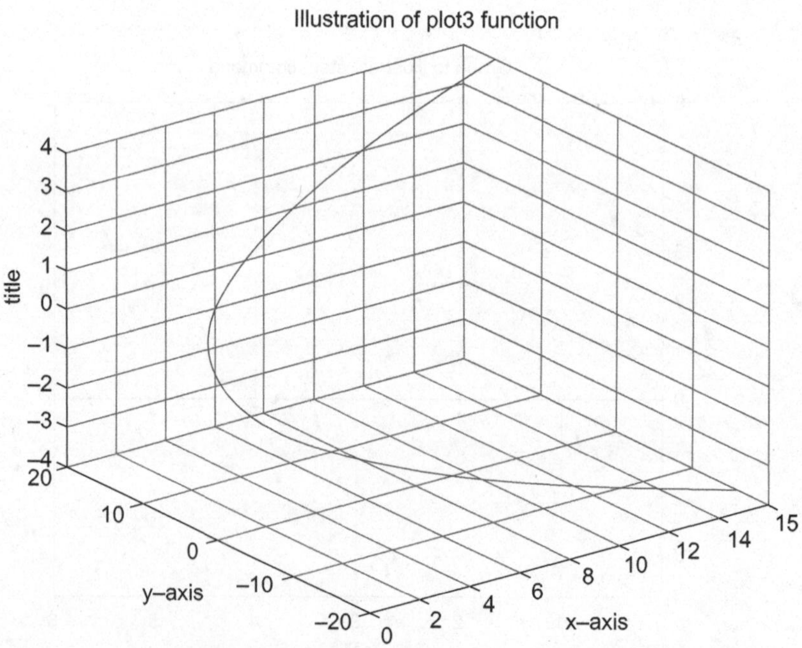

Plate 28 Three-dimensional Line Plot Using `plot3` Function (See Page 168)

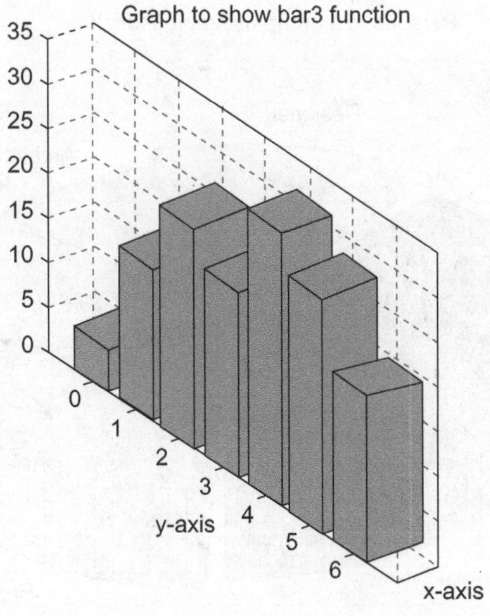

Plate 29 Plot to Show 3D Bar Graph of the Given Data (See Page 169)

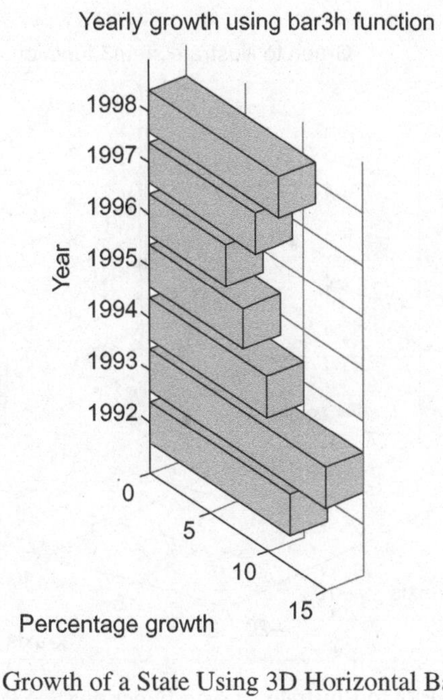

Plate 30 Plot to Show Growth of a State Using 3D Horizontal Bar Graph (See Page 170)

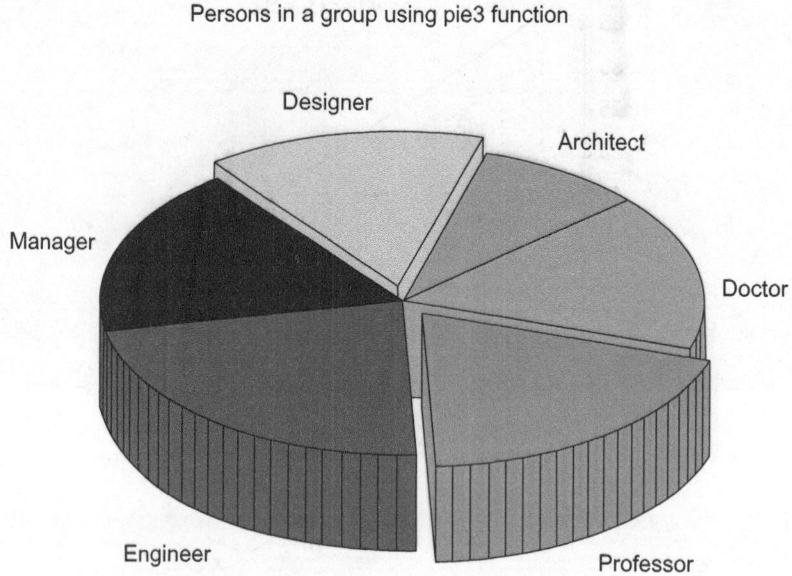

Plate 31 Plot to Illustrate `pie3` Function (See Page 171)

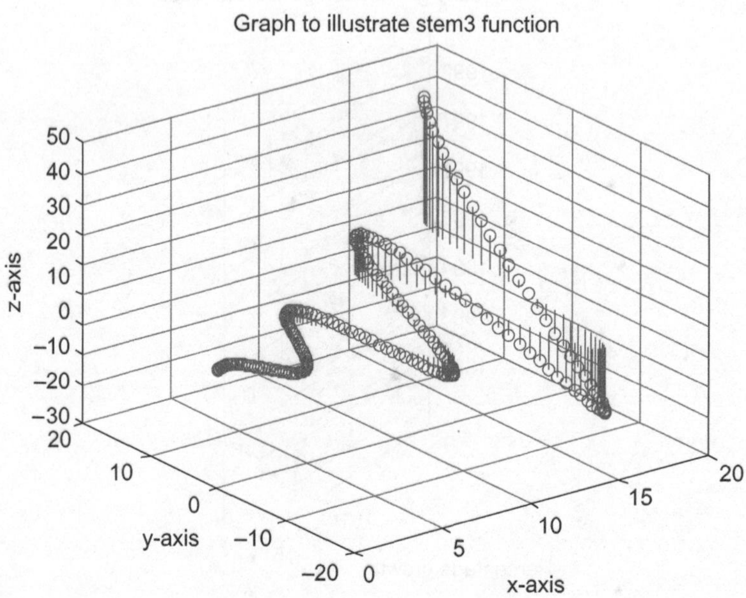

Plate 32 Plot to Illustrate `stem3` Function (See Page 172)

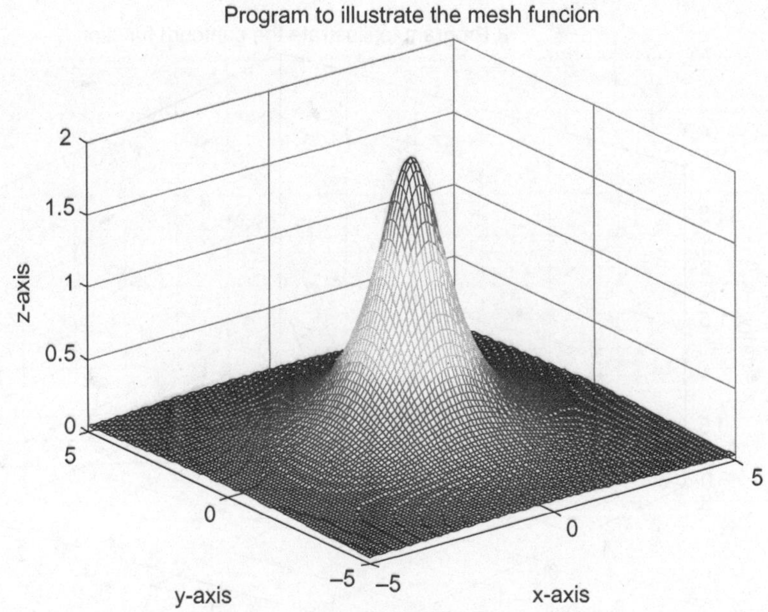

Plate 33 `mesh` Plot (See Page 174)

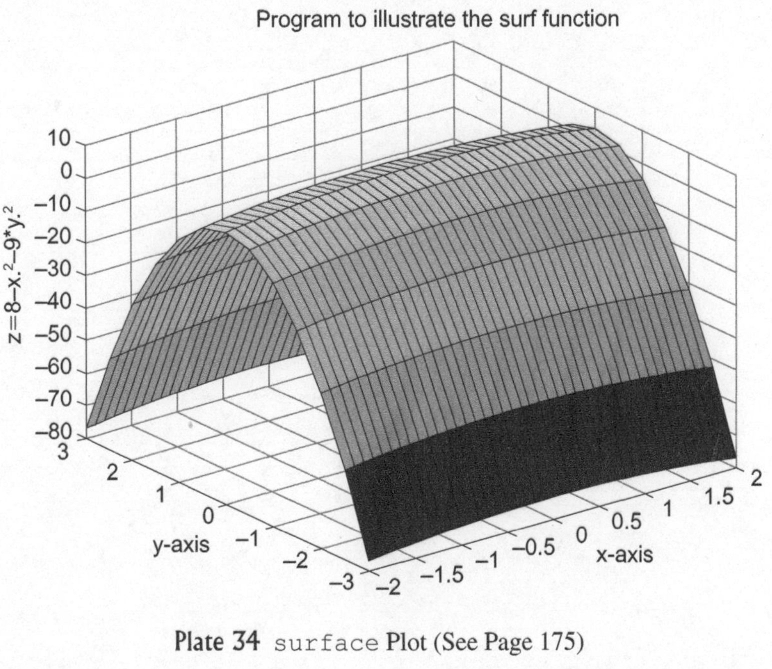

Plate 34 `surface` Plot (See Page 175)

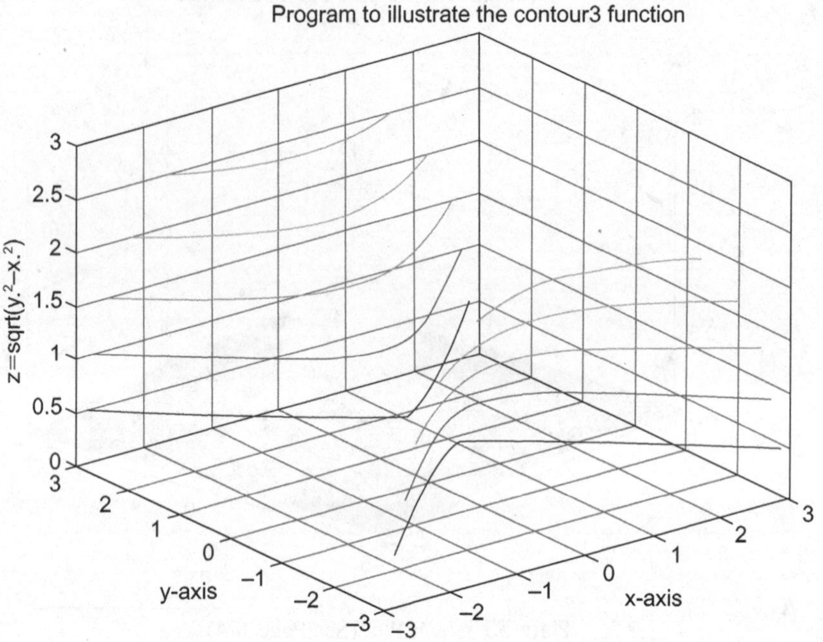

Plate 35 `contour3` Plot (See Page 176)

Bibliography

Alan V. Oppenheim, Ronald W. Schafer, and John R. Buck, *Discrete-Time Signal Processing* (New Delhi: Pearson Education, 2003).

Bart Kosko, *Neural Networks and Fuzzy Systems* (PHI Publication).

Benjamin C. Kuo, *Automatic Control Systems* (Englewood Cliffs, NJ: Prentice-Hall).

Delous Metter, David C. Kuncicky, and Doug Hall, *Mastering MATLAB 6* (New Delhi: Pearson Education, 2004).

Duane Hanselman and Bruce Littlefield, *Mastering MATLAB 7* (New Delhi: Pearson Education, 2005).

Gordon S G Beveridge, *Optimization Theory and Practice*, (Tokyo: McGraw Hill).

I. J. Nagrath and M. Gopal, *Control System Engineering*, 3rd edn. (New Age International Pvt. Ltd. Publishers, 2004).

Jacek M. Zurada, *Introduction to Artificial Neural Systems* (Jaico Publishing House, 1997).

Jay B. Brockman, *Introduction to Engineering: Modelling and Problem Solving* (John Wiley & Sons, 2009).

John Yen and Reza Langari, *Fuzzy Logic: Intelligence Control and Information* (Pearson Education, 2003).

Junhong Nie and Derek A. Linkens, *Fuzzy-Neural Control: Principles, Algorithms and Applications* (New Delhi: PHI Publication, 1998).

K. V. Krishnamurthy and S. K. Sen, *Programming in MATLAB* (New Delhi: East-West Press, 2003).

Katsuhiko Ogata, *Modern Control Engineering*, 4th edn. (New Delhi: Pearson Education, 2004).

M. Gopal, *Modern Control System Theory* (Delhi: Wiley Eastern).

Marc E. Herniter, *Programming in MATLAB* (Thomson Brooks/Cole, 2003), Second reprint.

Michael A. Gray, *Introduction to the Simulation of Dynamics Using Simulink* (CRC Press, 2011).

Mohammad H. Hassoun, *Fundamentals of Artificial Neural Networks* (New Delhi: PHI Publication, 1995).

Norman S. Nise, *Control System Engineering* (India: Wiley).

Rudra Partap, *Getting Started with MATLAB 7: A quick Introduction for Scientists and Engineers* (Oxford University Press, 2006).

S. Salivahanan, A. Vallavaraj, and C. Gnanapriya, *Digital Signal Processing* (New Delhi: Tata McGraw-Hill, 2006), Twentieth reprint.

Samuel D. Conte *Elementary Numerical Analysis – An Algorithmic Approach* (Tokyo: McGraw Hill).

Stephen J. Chapman, *MATLAB Programming for Engineers* (Asia: Cengage Learning, 2007).

Sanjit K. Mitra, *Digital Signal Processing: A Computer Based Approach* (New Delhi: Tata McGraw-Hill, 2001).

Satish Kumar, *Neural Networks* (New Delhi: Tata McGraw-Hill, 2004).

Simon Haykin, *Neural Networks: A Comprehensive Foundation*, 2nd edn. (Pearson Education, 1999).

Simon Haykin and Barry Van Veen, *Signal and Systems* (John Wiley & Sons Inc., 2002).

Smarajit Ghosh, *Control System Theory and Applications*, 1st edn. (New Delhi: Pearson Education, 2004).

Sriman Kumar Bhattacharya, *Control System Engineering*, 1st Indian edn. (New Delhi: Pearson Education, 2005).

Stephen J. Chapman, *MATLAB Programming for Engineers* (Australia: Thomson learning, 2005).

Valluru Rao and Hayagriva Rao, *Neural Networks and Fuzzy Logic*, 2nd edn. (New Delhi: BPB Publication, 1996).

Vinay K. Ingle and John G. Proakis, *Digital Signal Processing using MATLAB* (Thomson Brooks/Cole, 2003), Fourth reprint.

W. Thomas Miller III, Richard S. Sutton, and Paul J. Werbos, *Neural Networks for Control* (London: The MIT Press, 1995).

Index